# CCIE Routing and Switching Practice Labs

Martin Duggan, CCIE No. 7942
Maurilio Gorito, CCIE No. 3807

**Cisco Press**

800 East 96th Street
Indianapolis, IN 46240  USA

# CCIE Routing and Switching Practice Labs

Martin Duggan and Maurilio Gorito

Copyright© 2004 Cisco Systems, Inc.

Published by:
Cisco Press
800 East 96th Street
Indianapolis, IN 46240 USA

Printed in the United States of America 1 2 3 4 5 6 7 8 9 0

First Printing   June 2004

Library of Congress Cataloging-in-Publication Number: 2003105055

ISBN: 1-58705-147-8

## Warning and Disclaimer

This book is designed to provide information to help you prepare for the CCIE Routing and Switching exam. Every effort has been made to make this book as complete and as accurate as possible, but no warranty or fitness is implied.

The information is provided on an "as is" basis. The authors, Cisco Press, and Cisco Systems, Inc. shall have neither liability nor responsibility to any person or entity with respect to any loss or damages arising from the information contained in this book or from the use of the discs or programs that may accompany it.

The opinions expressed in this book belong to the author and are not necessarily those of Cisco Systems, Inc.

## Feedback Information

At Cisco Press, our goal is to create in-depth technical books of the highest quality and value. Each book is crafted with care and precision, undergoing rigorous development that involves the unique expertise of members from the professional technical community.

Readers' feedback is a natural continuation of this process. If you have any comments regarding how we could improve the quality of this book, or otherwise alter it to better suit your needs, you can contact us through email at feedback@ciscopress.com. Please make sure to include the book title and ISBN in your message.

We greatly appreciate your assistance.

## Trademark Acknowledgments

All terms mentioned in this book that are known to be trademarks or service marks have been appropriately capitalized. Cisco Press or Cisco Systems, Inc. cannot attest to the accuracy of this information. Use of a term in this book should not be regarded as affecting the validity of any trademark or service mark.

## Corporate and Government Sales

Cisco Press offers excellent discounts on this book when ordered in quantity for bulk purchases or special sales. For more information, please contact:

**U.S. Corporate and Government Sales** 1-800-382-3419 corpsales@pearsontechgroup.com

For sales outside of the U.S. please contact:

**International Sales** international@pearsontechgroup.com

| | |
|---|---|
| Publisher | John Wait |
| Editor-in-Chief | John Kane |
| Executive Editor | Brett Bartow |
| Cisco Representative | Anthony Wolfenden |
| Cisco Press Program Manager | Nannette M. Noble |
| Production Manager | Patrick Kanouse |
| Development Editor | Christopher Cleveland |
| Technical Editors | William R. Parkhurst, Elaine Bonotto Lopes, Leah Lynch |
| Team Coordinator | Tammi Barnett |
| Cover Designer | Louisa Adair |
| Composition | Mark Shirar |
| Proofreader | Katherin Bidwell |

**CISCO SYSTEMS**

**Corporate Headquarters**
Cisco Systems, Inc.
170 West Tasman Drive
San Jose, CA 95134-1706
USA
www.cisco.com
Tel: 408 526-4000
 800 553-NETS (6387)
Fax: 408 526-4100

**European Headquarters**
Cisco Systems International BV
Haarlerbergpark
Haarlerbergweg 13-19
1101 CH Amsterdam
The Netherlands
www-europe.cisco.com
Tel: 31 0 20 357 1000
Fax: 31 0 20 357 1100

**Americas Headquarters**
Cisco Systems, Inc.
170 West Tasman Drive
San Jose, CA 95134-1706
USA
www.cisco.com
Tel: 408 526-7660
Fax: 408 527-0883

**Asia Pacific Headquarters**
Cisco Systems, Inc.
Capital Tower
168 Robinson Road
#22-01 to #29-01
Singapore 068912
www.cisco.com
Tel: +65 6317 7777
Fax: +65 6317 7799

Cisco Systems has more than 200 offices in the following countries and regions. Addresses, phone numbers, and fax numbers are listed on the
**Cisco.com Web site at www.cisco.com/go/offices.**

Argentina • Australia • Austria • Belgium • Brazil • Bulgaria • Canada • Chile • China PRC • Colombia • Costa Rica • Croatia • Czech Republic
Denmark • Dubai, UAE • Finland • France • Germany • Greece • Hong Kong SAR • Hungary • India • Indonesia • Ireland • Israel • Italy
Japan • Korea • Luxembourg • Malaysia • Mexico • The Netherlands • New Zealand • Norway • Peru • Philippines • Poland • Portugal
Puerto Rico • Romania • Russia • Saudi Arabia • Scotland • Singapore • Slovakia • Slovenia • South Africa • Spain • Sweden
Switzerland • Taiwan • Thailand • Turkey • Ukraine • United Kingdom • United States • Venezuela • Vietnam • Zimbabwe

Printed in the USA

## About the Authors

**Martin James Duggan**, CCIE No. 7942, is a network architect for IBM. He designs network solutions for customers globally and specializes in Campus LAN, ATM WAN, and network integration. Martin mentors colleagues through their Cisco qualifications and holds regular internal training classes. Previous to this, Martin was a senior network consultant for ntl, performing IP network designs and large-scale integrations on its corporate network. Martin has been in the industry for 14 years focusing on Cisco solutions for the previous 7 years.

**Maurilio de Paula Gorito,** CCIE No. 3807, is a triple CCIE, having been certified in Routing and Switching in 1998, WAN Switching in 2001, and Security in 2003. Maurilio has more than 18 years of experience in networking including Cisco networks and IBM/SNA environments. Maurilio's experience includes the planning, designing, implementation, and troubleshooting of large IP networks running RIP, IGRP, EIGRP, BGP, OSPF, QoS, and SNA worldwide, including Brazil and the United States. He also has more than seven years of experience in teaching technical classes at schools and companies. Maurilio currently works for Cisco Systems as part of the CCIE Team. As a content lead, Maurilio is responsible for managing the content development process for the CCIE Routing and Switching Lab and Written Exams, being in touch with candidates as part of the CCIE Customer Service, and proctoring CCIE Routing and Switching and CCIE Security Lab Exams at the CCIE Lab in San Jose, California. Maurilio has also presented Power Sessions at Cisco Seminars. He holds degrees in mathematics and pedagogy.

## About the Technical Reviewers

**William R. Parkhurst**, Ph.D., CCIE No. 2969, is on the CCIE team at Cisco Systems. During his tenure on the CCIE team, Bill has been responsible for the Service Provider and Voice CCIE Tracks. Prior to joining the CCIE team, Bill was a consulting systems engineer supporting Sprint. In a former life, Bill was an associate professor of electrical and computer engineering at Wichita State University. Bill is the author of the Cisco Press books *OSPF Configuration Handbook* and *BGP-4 Command and Configuration Handbook*.

**Elaine Bonotto Lopes**, CCIE No. 4478, has more than 12 years of experience in networking, 6 of them with Cisco networks. She was certified in Routing and Switching in 1999 and in Service Provider (formerly known as Communications and Services) in 2003. She is a content engineer for Cisco Systems in Sao Paulo, Brazil. Working for the CCIE Program, she was responsible for the standard configuration and implementation of the network used in the CCIE Labs worldwide and has developed most of the Routing and Switching lab exams. Currently, she proctors the Routing and Switching and Service Provider CCIE Lab in Sao Paulo, Brazil, and is involved with content development for both tracks' lab exams. She is also certified as Novell Master CNI and Master CNE, and prior to joining Cisco, she used to teach all the official NetWare curriculum.

**Leah Lynch**, CCIE No. 7220 (Routing and Switching), is a network engineer with a large financial institution. Leah has more than seven years of experience in the IT industry with four years focused on heterogeneous internetwork environments, including banking, retail, medical, government, manufacturing, corporate, sales, network service provider, telecommunications, and 2.5/3G wireless networks. Leah also holds several other Cisco certifications and is currently working on her Service Provider CCIE. Leah is coauthor of the Cisco Press title, *CCIE Practical Studies*, Volume II.

## Dedications

**Martin Duggan:** I would like to dedicate this book to my family. Mum and Dad, thanks for your love and support and always being there. Adela, you are my inspiration; I love you dearly. Anna, you amaze me with your aptitude and ability for someone of six years. James, your fooling around lightens my day. I am blessed to have children as wonderful and as perfect as you. Y a mi familia Española, gracias por hacerme sentir parte de la familia y por vuestro apoyo.

Rebecca, we miss you.

**Maurilio Gorito:** I would like to dedicate this book to my lovely and wonderful family for their support and understanding during many late nights, weekends, and holidays I spent working on it. My wife Aurea and my sons Mario Henrique and Leonardo are my inspiration and encouragement. They have been the support for everything that happened in my life, and my life has been wonderful. Without them I could not go anywhere. I love you so much.

To my parents Maurilio and Delicia for their love, dedication, and encouragement. I love you.

# Acknowledgments

**Martin Duggan:** This is my first book for Cisco Press, and it has been an absolute honor to complete this project. I express gratitude to the whole team at Cisco Press for taking this idea from conception to completion so professionally. It has been very hard to keep to the deadlines working on this project in the evenings and weekends. If those who know me see a few more grey hairs, this book is the reason why.

I would like to thank Brett Bartow for keeping us on track and structuring the book so well. I am also very grateful to Christopher Cleveland for the effort he has put into this project; in fact, his name should be up there with mine and Maurilio's on the front cover. The sheer professionalism of everybody I have dealt with in Cisco Press has amazed me. I hope they stay in publishing and do not enter the networking profession as there will be no work for the likes of Maurilio and me.

To the technical reviewers, William Parkhurst, Elaine Bonotto Lopes, and Leah Lynch, you have shaped this book, and we are indebted to your hard work and commitment to detail. We were extremely fortunate to have you as part of the team, and your expertise in this subject is second to none.

I would like to thank my coauthor and friend Maurilio; he has been an absolute joy to work with. His knowledge and experience have really made this book. Maurilio was always happy to help out with any problem I encountered, and I am envious of his ability to write this book in his second language. Cisco is lucky to have him.

To all the guys from my previous role in IBM working on the ntl account—Martin Harper, Steve Goddard, Hanik Kang, George Smith, Graham Hemmings, Dean Hassan, and Steve Gowers—you guys helped me more than you realize and you made work fun.

Most of all I want to thank my family for their loving support. I could not have completed this project or my CCIE without your help.

**Maurilio Gorito**: Thank God for guiding me throughout my life and giving me through Jesus the strength to overcome all my challenges.

Working with Cisco Press has been a wonderful and pleasant experience. They are an extraordinary and talented group of people who made this book possible. Thank you for giving me the opportunity to work with you. A special thanks to Brett Bartow, the executive editor, for his guidance and for always being available to answer all my questions. Many thanks to Chris Cleveland, the development editor, whose great job and extreme competence helped to polish our work and added great value to this book.

To the technical reviewers, William Parkhurst, Elaine Bonotto Lopes, and Leah Lynch—thank you for the deep and great feedback that made the book richer. It was a pleasure to have this team of experts working with us. Thank you for your dedication, hard work, and commitment.

It is difficult to find words to express all the gratitude to have worked with Martin. We started this project as coauthors, then we built a task force, and finally we became good friends. Along with the Cisco Press team we had a real valuable teamwork experience. Martin's knowledge and experience added quality to our project, and all the discussions we had were to improve the quality of the book. Being always available and kind, and keeping things on track, I can just say I am grateful to have worked with Martin. Thank you my friend.

Thank you to all the CCIE team. It has been a pleasure to work with such extremely qualified people from whom I am still learning. Thank you all for the support, help, and the opportunities you gave me. A special thanks to my colleagues and friends Tom Eggers and Ben Ng, who everyday at the CCIE Lab in San Jose, California, allow me to explain my thoughts, share their knowledge, and even listen to my jokes.

It has been a long time since I started in networking and I have made a lot of good friends that will be impossible to list here, but each one of you knows how important you are in my life. A special thank you to all of you.

To my family, who without their support and understanding I would not have been able to complete this book.

# Contents at a Glance

# Contents

# Icons Used in This Book

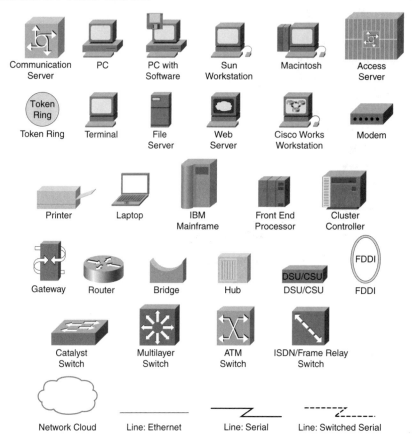

# Command Syntax Conventions

The conventions used to present command syntax in this book are the same conventions used in the IOS Command Reference. The Command Reference describes these conventions as follows:

- **Boldface** indicates commands and keywords that are entered literally as shown. In actual configuration examples and output (not general command syntax), boldface indicates commands that are manually input by the user (such as a **show** command).

- *Italics* indicate arguments for which you supply actual values.

- Vertical bars (l) separate alternative, mutually exclusive elements.

- Square brackets [ ] indicate optional elements.

- Braces { } indicate a required choice.

- Braces within brackets [{ }] indicate a required choice within an optional element.

# Foreword

The most frequently asked questions in CCIE certification forums have always been "What does it take to become a CCIE? Is there a magic formula?" Anyone who has ever felt the special ambience that exists in the actual lab environment knows that there's a considerable amount of sweat and tears lingering in the air at any given time. I remember running my hand across the desk of the candidate who had just left and brushing the all too familiar sediment of erasure shavings, pencil points, and skin cells into the wastebasket. I always felt great empathy, as I clearly know the heat of the stress of this battle. Many candidates compare sitting the exam to sitting on the edge of a cliff between heaven and hell. All the months of study seems to create a sort of inertia of nervous anticipation that keeps a body rigid and bent and motionless in front of that exam in those final eight hours. Will this day's efforts put an end to all the pain?

It would be great if a magic formula could be conjured up that would take one soaring to the winning peak, but unfortunately this writer does not believe that one exists. There are plenty of websites out there that boast that they can guarantee a win, and there are even those sites willing to stand in for you and hand success to you on a very tarnished silver platter. But the fact is the true reward of CCIE certification is that gratification that one gets from having pushed themselves hard enough to earn it, through hard work and sacrifice. One could argue what the rewards really are or what is the value of a CCIE certification. Some say it's that raise in pay or the confidence of the customer, but the best will admit the real rewards are the realization that they actually had an incredible learning experience.

Every person approaches exam certification study from his or her own unique position and with his or her own theories on how to study. The qualities that make an expert lie in that person who understands that they have to go far beyond the surface of any topic and meet the challenge of the exam head on. After all, one has just enough time to get it right the first time. Countless hours of practice are a huge part of this type of study. The person with the persistence to revisit concepts in different scenarios as the core of their practice knows that it takes great persistence, intelligent use of resources, and ultimately countless hours of rack time. The hunger for different scenarios to bring back to one's gear to chew up as they hammer away at the keyboard for hours is the nature of the CCIE candidate facing his or her lab.

The Routing and Switching exam is the core of the CCIE program. The popularity of this exam is proof of the fact that every network deployment rests on a routing and switching infrastructure. Therefore it makes absolute sense that regardless of what one's personal pursuit is in the networking industry, that a CCIE Routing and Switching certified professional will always have a fundamental role in any project. This book possesses solid and practical guidance for anyone pounding away at the keyboard whether it is in pursuit of the CCIE or of the source of a real problem. This is a resource that was written by folks who have not only shared the experience of the exam but have also shared in the experiences of many who have sat before them as candidates. There are few that can offer advice with the empathy and experience of a lab proctor. Therefore, in the spirit of an old proctor and fellow CCIE, I say, "Take this book and go forth with keyboard and pound away."

--Kathe Saccenti, fellow CCIE No. 2099 and CCIE Product Manager, Cisco Systems, Inc.

# Introduction

We have been exactly where you are now. We read countless theory books and worked through the few practical ones available that generally tackled subjects in isolation, but there was something key missing in our study plan—this book. We wrote this book to fill the study void and show you what it is like to actually take the CCIE exam. While we cannot offer you exactly what you will find in your own exam, we can take you as close as possible without breaking strict Cisco NDA policy.

The CCIE program has been running for 10 years and only 3 percent of certified individuals go on to attempt the CCIE, let alone pass it. The majority of candidates that take the exam fail at the first attempt because they are not fully prepared. They generally find to their own cost that their study plan did not match what was expected of them in the exam. By the time you complete this book, you will know if you have what it takes to become CCIE qualified. You might find that you have some additional work to do, but do not be disheartened as you will be far better prepared in the long run.

## Objectives

The purpose of this book is twofold—the primary reason being to evaluate your technical ability to demonstrate if you are ready to take the CCIE Lab examination. The secondary purpose is to show you what you can expect in terms of format from the examination by taking away the mystery of the exam. This book will help prepare you for your big day by coaching you. It will improve your technical knowledge, speed, and your ability to analyze questions successfully. You will be guided through six full-blown labs that are as close as you can get to the real thing, and you will be using the same equipment running the same IOS level as found in the lab. You will need to be strict with yourself to get the maximum benefit from these practice labs. You will have to treat them as if you were taking the real exam.

## Audience

This book is primarily aimed at CCIE Routing and Switching candidates who have previously passed the CCIE written examination and are about to schedule their practical exam. The common format and content ensure that other CCIE track candidates will also benefit from these practice exams. This book can also be used by network engineers looking for a challenge and testing the waters to see if they feel capable of taking the CCIE exam for real in the future. CCIEs who are due for recertification will also benefit from this book by using it as a practical revision tool to reinforce the theory with which they are already conversant.

All readers of this book are assumed to have attained a solid understanding of networking theory. Cisco Press offers the following titles, which should be considered if readers require detailed theory or further information:

- *Routing TCP/IP,* Volumes I and II, Jeff Doyle and Jennifer DeHaven Carroll—Cisco Press

- *Internet Routing Architectures*, Second Edition, Sam Halibi—Cisco Press

- *IP Quality of Service*, Srinivas Vegesna—Cisco Press

- *Cisco LAN Switching*, Kennedy Clark, Kevin Hamilton—Cisco Press

- *CCIE Practical Studies*, Volumes I and II, Karl Solie and Leah Lynch—Cisco Press

## Organization

This book has six full-blown lab exercises and is split into two main parts:

- **Part 1:** Chapters 1–3, covering Lab Exercises 1 through 3, have been created using one distinct equipment topology with one switch.

- **Part 2:** Chapters 4–6, covering Lab Exercises 4 through 6, have been created using a different topology and introducing an additional switch.

Each chapter consists of the following components:

- **Pre-lab tasks**—You will be guided through the requirements for each lab including physical cabling, Frame Relay, ATM, and ISDN instructions and finally IP address details, which should be entered before the lab commences.

- **General Guidelines**—Here you will find the specific instructions and rules for each lab exercise.

- **Practice Lab**—The timed examination with the questions and points rating for each topic.

- **Ask the Proctor**—You will find clues to the questions should you require them.

- **Lab Debrief**—Each question will be analyzed detailing the required answers along with point ratings to gain an overall score for your lab.

- **How did you do?**—A post-lab evaluation with further reading references.

In addition, the three appendixes provide details on the following topics:

- Appendix A, "Frame Relay Switch Configuration"

- Appendix B, "LS1010 ATM Switch Configuration"

- Appendix C, "Troubleshooting Tips"

Finally, the book is accompanied by a CD-ROM, which contains initial configurations on a per chapter basis for loading onto your routers and switches and the final configurations you can load onto your equipment for testing and verification purposes.

You should work through these lab exercises sequentially, paying particular attention to the instructions and lab guidelines. Like the real exam, each lab has an eight-hour time constraint. Do not run over the time limit on the initial run through but do use all eight hours. Then see how you have done with the aid of the supplied debrief section that will walk you through the questions and supply you with the required configuration and points score. You should use the "Ask the Proctor" section for clues if you are having difficulties but try not to use this too often. Plot your progress throughout the book and see how you improve. After you have completed a lab under exam conditions, go through the questions in your own time and experiment. Look at the clues, take the time to research any topics with which you are not familiar, and get to a point where you are comfortable with each lab before moving on. Each chapter concludes with a "How Did You Do?" section where you will find a post-lab evaluation and further reading details for the topics that may require attention.

As you will find in the "Are You Ready Section?" do not be afraid to change your lab date if you have already booked it and you find you have more work to do. It is better to take the exam one or two months later after you have discovered your weaknesses and turned them into your strengths. This is ultimately how you will pass the hardest examination this industry has ever known.

## Are You Ready?

This became a well-known Cisco Systems slogan that identified the Internet revolution. By the end of this book you should know if you are ready. Will you feel confident working through the labs or will it be a complete shock to the system? Are you more used to being spoon fed solitary scenarios than actually having to analyze questions and piece together parts of a complex network jigsaw puzzle?

Life is full of challenges. During your education and career, the CCIE Certification is as tough as it gets. The exam is designed to test your technical skills, your understanding and analysis of complex topologies, and your capacity to build a network with IP routing protocols and features. Problems might occur during the exam that you will need to rectify, and you only have eight hours to achieve a minimum score of 80 percent to pass. You will be well prepared to take the real exam when you have achieved 90 percent in eight hours for each one of the six labs. It pays to ensure you are ready to take this challenge.

## Preparing for the Exam

The preparation for the Routing and Switching Lab Exam involves immense training and study, including at least two years' experience in designing, implementing, and troubleshooting medium to large networks, mostly containing Cisco hardware and software. The years of experience along with the theory and concepts you gained from training will give you the building blocks required to take the exam. This book is the icing on the cake and the final stage of your study program. Follow our tips to ensure you are fully prepared for your big day.

- Look at http://www.cisco.com/go/ccie for the latest information regarding the CCIE Certification, including suggested training and reading

- Keep your schedule flexible during your preparation. Include time for breaks and relaxation, you will often find that five minutes away from the keyboard can help you consider possible solutions. Most importantly do not forget the people you care for and make time for them also.

- Build your study plan based on a balance between theory and practice. You need to understand the concepts through the theory and then consolidate this during your rack time.

- Begin with simple topics in isolation and then work up to complex lab scenarios. Spend as much time repeating your configurations as possible to improve your speed and ability to perform basic configurations with your eyes shut. This will save you time for when you need it during the exam.

- Explore the Cisco CD documentation or the URL http://www.cisco.com/univercd/home/home.htm. This will be your research lifeline during the exam where you can find information, concepts, and samples regarding all technologies involved in the exam.

- Start to plan for your exam at least six months before the lab date. This will ensure you have sufficient time to come up with a sound plan, which will help alleviate stress.

- If you find this book has highlighted weak areas, do not be afraid to postpone your lab date. Cisco is very accommodating with dates since the change to the one-day format.

We believe if you keep these tips in mind, you will be ready to take the Routing and Switching Lab Exam with confidence.

## What Else Do You Need to Do?

We tried to fit within the six labs the greatest variety of topics to guide you to all possible content that can be found within the real Routing and Switching Lab Exam. We have included all possible sections that you will find on the real exam, but unfortunately we could not cover all features and subjects of the program because of the size of the content and the strict NDA. In addition to taking and passing all six labs found in the book, you should consider exploring in further detail the following subjects:

- Frame Relay configuration
- 3550 switch configuration
- ATM PVC and SVC configuration
- IP Routing Protocol: RIP V2, EIGRP, OSPF, IS-IS
- IBGP and EBGP
- IP multicast
- Security
- IP and IOS features
- DLSw over Ethernet
- Voice over IP

Practice all these subjects exploring different scenarios and features.

## How Can I Schedule My CCIE Lab Exam?

As stated previously, go to http://www.cisco.com/go/ccie, and you will find all information on how to schedule your exam including locations, start times, and more. You must have a CCO user ID, your CCIE written exam date, and score to be able to view your profile and schedule your exam.

## The Day Before...

If you are traveling to take your exam, try to arrive the day before to familiarize yourself with the area. Take a tour to the lab location, so you will not be late on the day; the last thing you need is to arrive flustered. The day before is a day to relax and not stress with last minute studies. Have a light dinner, go to bed early, and try to have a good night's sleep. Most importantly, save the beer until after the exam, pass or fail you will feel like one or two for sure. If you are taking the exam in Brussels, you will be spoiled for choice!

## What Actually Happens During the Exam?

On the day of the exam, you should plan to arrive at least 15 minutes before the exam begins for registration. The proctor will walk you to the lab and will give you a briefing before the exam starts telling you about the lab environment, on which rack or station you will be working, and the general guidelines for the day.

The proctor will not discuss solutions or possible solutions for a given question with you. The proctor will be available to help you understand the wording or meaning of the questions; make sure the backbone routers, ISDN switches, and Frame Relay switches are working properly; and the hardware and software on your rack are working perfectly so your exam runs smoothly. Ask the proctor for any assistance or verification, the worst he or she can say is, "Sorry everything looks okay from my side, please check your configuration." Read the entire exam before you start to see the bigger picture ensuring you fully understand each question and its requirements. Begin by performing easier tasks, leaving the most difficult to later. Take some small breaks during the morning and the afternoon to refresh yourself and to relieve the stress.

## What If I Fail?

Do not worry and do not take it personally—most people fail the first time around. You will have to chalk it up to experience and get back on your kit as soon as you can to work out what went wrong. You will more than likely be successful next time around and will ultimately become a better engineer for your extra rack time.

We hope the book and these tips will be helpful and guide you to take your exam with success. Good luck and, if you do pass, we know you will be looking in the CCIE store. Just please think twice before buying that leather jacket.

# Topology 1, the Single Switch Labs

# CHAPTER 1

# Practice Lab 1

Each lab has a time constraint of eight hours and a point scale weighting of 100; you will need to score at least 80 marks to pass. The lab has been designed to challenge you in areas that you will find in the real exam with each lab having a distinct theme to enhance your study plan; Routing Information Protocol (RIP V2 is the theme of Lab 1).

You will, of course, find the old favorites such as BGP, DLSw+, and Voice but a complete understanding of RIP V2 will earn you extra points in this lab.

Aim to adhere to the time limit on this lab on the initial run through and then either score yourself at this point or continue until you feel you have met all the objectives. Keep a note of your score to plot your progress throughout the book and remember you are aiming to improve your technical knowledge, speed, and examination technique.

If you find that you complete all the configuration tasks within the time limit, congratulations, you are a quick on the keyboard but will you achieve the desired results? If time allows, get into the habit of going back through the questions and ensuring that you have answered them down to the letter. If you are unsure, turn to the Lab 1 "Ask the Proctor" section but try not to use this too often as you will find that real-life proctors do not like to give anything away. However, throughout this book, it can be used as a handy tool to provide assistance and clues to ensure you are working on the correct solution for the question. Unfortunately you won't have this luxury in your real exam.

You might find the questions misleading or vague but if you re-read the information given and analyze the scenario, you will find that you have been given sufficient information to successfully solve the problem.

To assist you, initial and final solutions are provided for the entire lab including configurations and common show command outputs from all the devices in the topology on the accompanying CD. The aforementioned "Ask the Proctor" section is included at the end of the lab, which gives you clues, if required, followed by the lab debrief that analyzes each question showing you what was required and how to achieve the desired results. Finally, you will find handy references should you require additional study information.

You will now be guided through the equipment requirements and pre-lab tasks in preparation for taking Practice Lab 1.

# Equipment List

You need the following hardware and software components to begin Lab 1.

- Eight routers are required loaded with Cisco IOS Software Release 12.2-16
- Enterprise image and the minimum interface configuration as documented in Table 1-1:

**Table 1-1**   *Interfaces Required per Router*

| Router | Ethernet Interface | Serial Interface | BRI Interface | Voice | ATM Interface |
|--------|--------------------|------------------|---------------|-------|---------------|
| R1 | 1 | 2 | 1 | 1 X FXS | - |
| R2 | 1 | 1 | - | - | - |
| R3 | 1 | - | - | - | - |
| R4 | 1 | 1 | 1 | 1 X FXS | - |
| R5 | 1 | 3 | - | - | 1 |
| R6 | 2 | 1 | - | - | 1 |
| R7 | 1 | - | - | - | - |
| R8 | 1 | - | - | - | - |

**NOTE**   Lab 1 was produced with Routers R1, R2, R3, R4, R7, and R8 using 2600s and R5 and R6 using 7200s.

- One Switch 3550 with Cisco IOS Software Release 12.1(12c) enterprise: c3550-i5q3l2-mz.121-12c.EA1.bin

# Setting Up the Lab

Feel free to use any combination of routers as long as you fulfill the topology diagram as shown in Figure 1-1. It is not compulsory to use the same model of routers, but this will make life easier should you want to load configurations directly from the CD-ROM into your own devices.

**NOTE**   For each lab in the book you will have a set of initial configuration files that can be different from each other. Notice that some interfaces will not have the P address preconfigured, because you will either not be using that interface on that specific lab or because you will need to work on this interface through the exercise. The initial configurations can be found on the CD-ROM and should be used to preconfigure your routers and switch before the lab starts.

If you use the same equipment as used to produce the lab, you can simply paste the
configurations into your own equipment; if not, just configure your own equipment
accordingly using the information supplied within the initial configurations.

Labs 1 through 3 in this book have been completed using 100-Mbps Fast Ethernet interfaces
so if you have a mix of 10- and 100-Mbps Ethernet interfaces, adjust the bandwidth
statements on the relevant interfaces to keep all interface speeds common. This will ensure
that you do not get unwanted behavior because of differing IGP metrics.

## Lab Topology

Practice Lab 1 uses the topology as outlined in Figure 1-1, which you need to create using
the switch, Frame Relay, ATM, and ISDN information that follows.

**Figure 1-1**    *Lab 1 Topology Diagram*

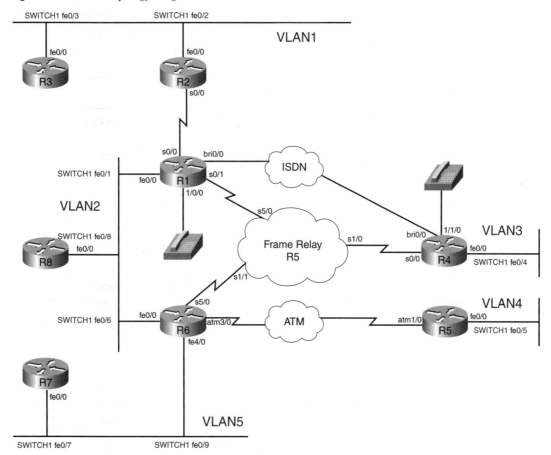

## Cabling Instructions

Follow the cabling requirements as outlined in Figure 1-2 and Table 1-2 to connect your routers to the switch.

**Figure 1-2**   *3550 Cabling Diagram*

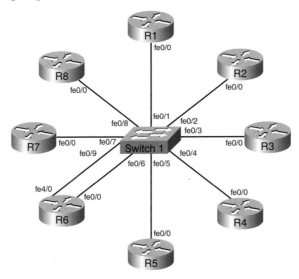

**Table 1-2**   *3550 Cabling Guide*

| Ethernet Cabling | Switch1 Port Number |
|---|---|
| R1-Fast Ethernet0/0 | Port 0/1 |
| R2-Fast Ethernet0/0 | Port 0/2 |
| R3-Fast Ethernet0/0 | Port 0/3 |
| R4-Fast Ethernet0/0 | Port 0/4 |
| R5-Fast Ethernet0/0 | Port 0/5 |
| R6-Fast Ethernet0/0 | Port 0/6 |
| R7-Fast Ethernet0/0 | Port 0/7 |
| R8-Fast Ethernet0/0 | Port 0/8 |
| R6-Fast Ethernet4/0 | Port 0/9 |

## Frame Relay Switch Instructions

The Frame Relay portion of the lab is achieved by following the physical connectivity using R5 as a Frame Relay switch as shown in Figure 1-3.

**Figure 1-3**    *Frame Relay Switch Physical Connectivity*

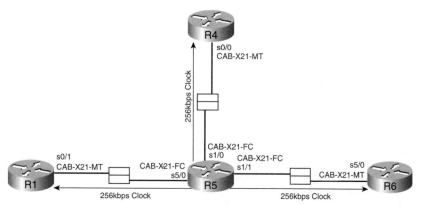

The physical Frame Relay connectivity (after configuration) will represent the logical Frame Relay network as shown in Figure 1-4.

**Figure 1-4**    *Frame Relay Switch Logical Connectivity*

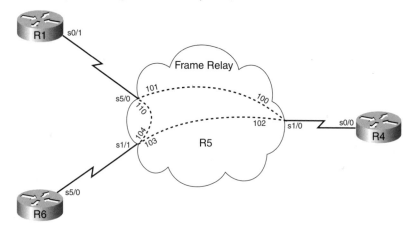

Configure one of your routers as a Frame Relay switch or have a dedicated router purely for this task. The first three lab scenarios use R5 to form the Frame Relay switch and a fully meshed environment is configured between R1-R4-R6, so pay attention in the lab to which PVCs are actually required. Keep the encapsulation and Local Management Interface (LMI) settings to default for this exercise, but experiment with the settings outside the labs.

Keep your DCE cables at the Frame Relay switch end for simplicity and provide a clock rate of 256 kbps to all links. Should you require detailed information on how to configure one of your routers as a Frame Relay switch, this information can be found in Appendix A, "Frame Relay Switch Configuration."

| | |
|---|---|
| **NOTE** | The Frame Relay switch configuration for R5 is supplied on the CD-ROM, if required. |

## ATM Switch Instructions

The ATM portion of the lab is achieved by following the physical connectivity between R5 and R6 as shown in Figure 1-5.

**Figure 1-5**   *ATM Physical Connectivity*

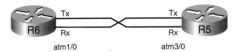

The physical ATM connectivity will, after configuration, represent the logical ATM network as shown in Figure 1-6.

**Figure 1-6**   *ATM Logical Connectivity*

The ATM connectivity in Labs 1-5 will be provided by back-to-back connections between R6 and R5 over E3 ATM interfaces (you could also use a LightStream or whichever back-to-back flavor of ATM you have available). Configure the PVCs as requested during the Lab exercise. If you are using a LightStream to provide your ATM connectivity and require information on how to set this up, this information can be found in Appendix B, "LS1010 ATM Switch Configuration."

## Serial Back-to-Back Instructions

R1 and R2 are connected back-to-back with serial cables as shown in Figure 1-7. Ensure that the DCE cable is connected to R1 and generate a 2 Mbps clock from this point if using X21 cables as shown or reduce this to suit your own serial interfaces such as 1.5 Mbps for T1 connectivity.

**Figure 1-7**    *Serial Connectivity*

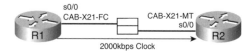

## ISDN Instructions

Connect R1 and R4 into either ISDN lines or an ISDN simulator. It is preferable that the ISDN supports CLI. Reconfigure the numbers as required if you are using live ISDN lines.

The lab has been produced using BRI S/T interfaces on R1 and R4 as shown in Figure 1-8.

**Figure 1-8**    *ISDN Connectivity*

## IP Address Instructions

Configure the IP addresses as shown in Figure 1-9 or load the initial router configurations for Lab 1 that can be found on the CD-ROM. If manually configuring, ensure you include the following loopback addresses:

R1 lo0 10.1.1.1/28
R4 lo0 10.4.4.4/29
R5 lo0 10.5.5.5/30
R6 lo0 10.6.6.6/29
R7 lo0 10.7.7.7/28
R8 lo0 10.8.8.8/32

**Figure 1-9** *IP Addressing Diagram*

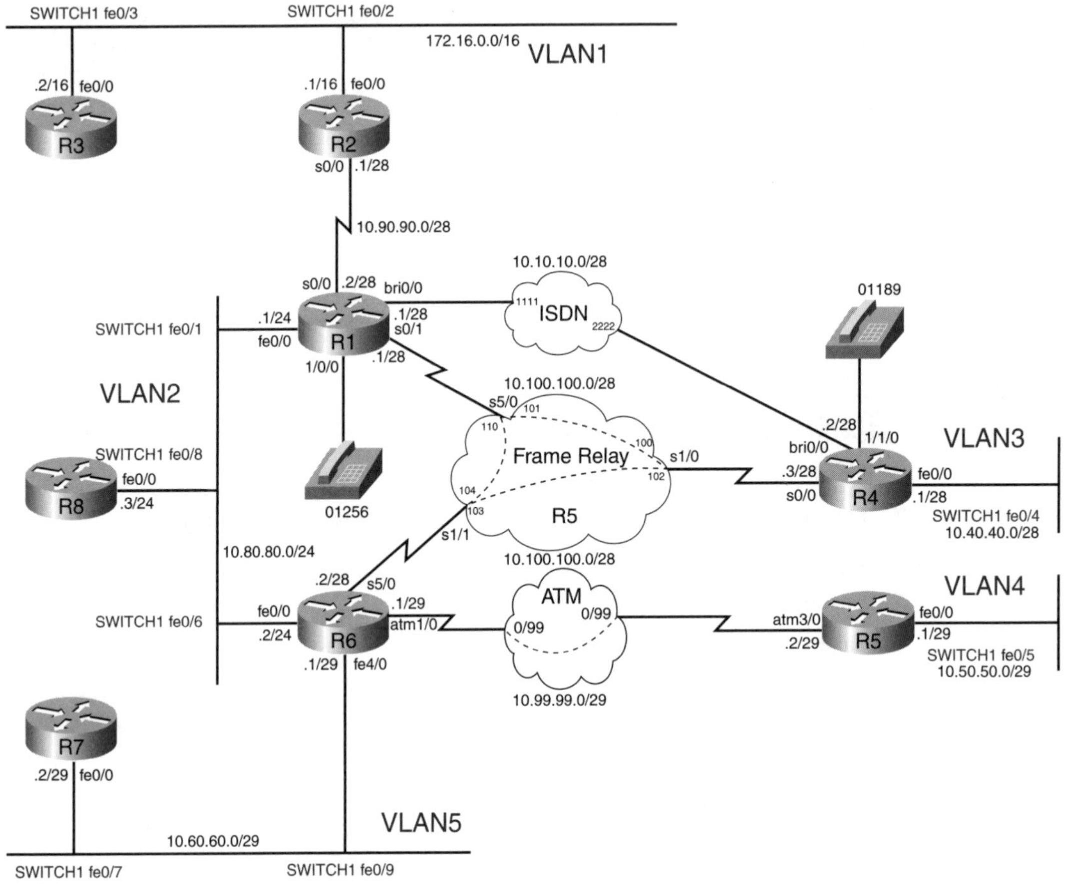

# Pre-Lab Tasks

- Build the lab topology as per Figure 1-1 and Figure 1-2.

- Configure your chosen Frame Relay switch router to provide the necessary data-link control identifiers (DLCIs) as per Figure 1-4 or load the Frame Relay switch configuration from the CD-ROM.

- Configure the IP addresses on each router as shown in Figure 1-9 and add the loopback addresses (do not configure the Frame Relay or ATM IP addresses yet as you will need to select interface types within the lab beforehand); alternatively, you can load the initial configuration files from the CD-ROM.
- Configure passwords on all devices for console and vty access to "cisco" if not loading the initial configuration files.
- If you find yourself running out of time, choose questions that you are confident you can answer correctly. Another approach would be to choose questions with a higher point rating to maximize your potential score.
- Get into a comfortable and quiet environment where you can focus for the next eight hours.

# General Guidelines

- Please read the whole lab before you start.
- Do not configure any static/default routes unless otherwise specified.
- Use only the DLCIs and ATM PVCs provided in the appropriate figures.
- Ensure full IP visibility between routers for ping testing/telnet access to your devices.
- Take a 30-minute break midway through the exercise.
- Have available a Cisco Documentation CD-ROM or access online the latest documentation from the following URL:

  http://www.cisco.com/univercd/home/home.htm

---

**NOTE**    Consider accessing only the preceding URL, not the entire Cisco.com website. If you will be allowed to use online documentation during your CCIE lab exam, it will be restricted.

---

# Practice Lab 1

You will now be answering questions in relation to the network topology as shown in Figure 1-10.

**Figure 1-10**    *Lab 1 Topology Diagram*

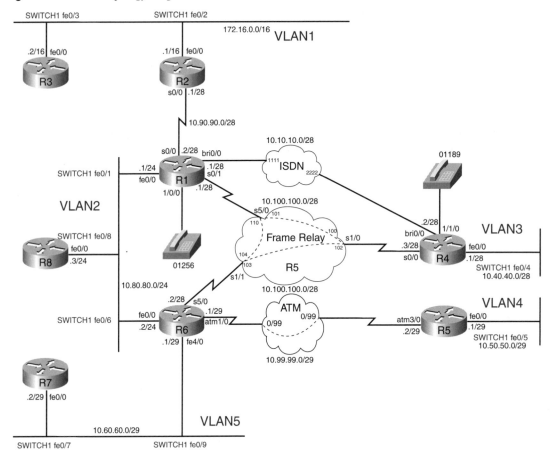

# Section 1: Bridging and Switching (15 Points)

## Section 1.1: Frame Relay Configuration (6 points)

- Configure the Frame Relay portion of the network as shown in Figure 1-11; ensure that DLCIs 110 and 104 between R1-R6 are not used.

- The routers are to be on the same subnet and should be configured with subinterfaces.

**Figure 1-11**  *Frame Relay Diagram*

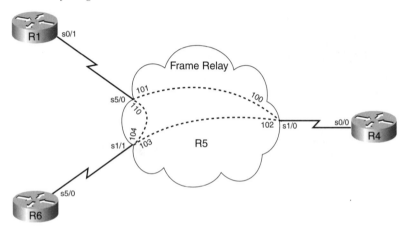

## Section 1.2: 3550 LAN Switch Configuration (6 Points)

- Configure VLAN numbers, VLAN names, and port assignment as per the topology diagram as shown in Figure 1-10.

- There is to be a host connected on interface 0/16 in the future; the network administrator requires that this host is authenticated by a radius server before access to the switch is granted. The radius server is to be located on the IP address 172.16.100.100 with the key **radius14.**

- Ensure the switch is reachable via Telnet to the IP address of 10.80.80.8/24.

## Section 1.3: ATM Configuration (3 Points)

- Configure the ATM network as shown in Figure 1-12.

- Use a subinterface on R6 for the ATM matching the VCI number and ensure the latest method of PVC configuration is used on this router. For R5 ATM, use the physical interface and legacy PVC configuration; after you have configured your Layer 2 information, you may then add the Layer 3 addresses.

- Do not rely on inverse Address Resolution Protocol (ARP).

**Figure 1-12**  *ATM Diagram*

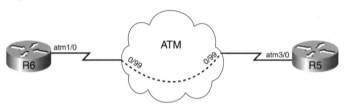

# Section 2: IP IGP Protocols (28 Points)

Configure the IP routing as in Figure 1-13 and redistribute protocols to ensure full IP visibility between routers. Advertise all router networks within the appropriate routing protocol.

## Section 2.1: RIP (16 Points)

- On all RIP routers, ensure that **version 2** is used under the process.

- Ensure that VLSM is supported on advertisements between all RIP routers.

- Add a loopback interface with the address of 60.60.60.1/24 onto R3 and advertise this out to R2 but ensure that it is not seen by the rest of your network; do not perform any configuration on R2 or R1.

- Configure R3 to unicast its RIP routing updates to R2. Do not use the **neighbor** command to achieve this but consider using other IP features to aid you.

- Ensure that VLAN2 is advertised to the RIP domain as a /28 network. Do not use either RIP or EIGRP features to accomplish this. You can, however, configure R6.

## Section 2.2: EIGRP (5 Points)

- R8 is very low on memory and CPU resource; accommodate this information within the configuration on R8.

- Configure R8 to have an EIGRP hello interval of 25 seconds on its FastEthernet0/0 interface.

**Figure 1-13**   *IP IGP Diagram*

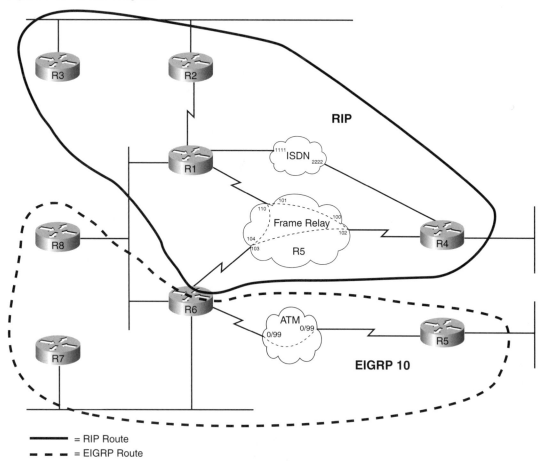

——— = RIP Route
- - - = EIGRP Route

## Section 2.3: Redistribution (7 Points)

- Redistribute IGP protocols to ensure full IP visibility between all routers.
- As a safety precaution, ensure that R6 can not learn the EIGRP routes it previously advertised into the RIP domain back from R4.

# Section 3: ISDN (8 Points)

- Ensure that VLAN3 and R4 Lo0 are accessible from R1 and beyond should the Frame Relay network fail either physically or logically. If VLAN3 and R4 Lo0 networks are restored while the ISDN line is active, ensure that traffic is routed over the Frame Relay network to these destinations immediately.

- Configure R1 so that if half of the ISDN traffic to R4 is of an unacceptable quality, the line is automatically disconnected.

- Allow only R1 to dial into R4. Do not use any PPP feature in your solution.

- Do not allow the ISDN to flap if the Frame Relay network goes up and down; only allow the line to be dropped if the Frame Relay connectivity is deemed to be reliable for 90 seconds.

# Section 4: EGP Protocols (17 Points)

- Configure BGP, as shown in Figure 1-14, with the following peering: R3–R2, R8–R2, R6–R2, R6–R8, R7–R8, R6–R5. Ensure the most suitable interfaces are used to maintain resilience for BGP peering (except for R2 and R3, use 172.16.0.0/16 addresses for all peering to and from these routers).

- Ensure minimal configuration on R8.

- Inject the following networks into BGP via new loopback interfaces:

  R3: 20.200.200.1/24 and 20.20.20.1/24

  R5: 20.20.20.1/24 and 200.20.20.1/24

  R7: 30.30.30.30/29

- Ensure that R6 BGP routing table prefers to use AS1000 for network 20.20.20.0/24; do not use BGP weight, BGP local preference, MED, neighbor metric related statements, metric manipulation, summarization, or pre-pending to achieve this. Perform configuration on R6 only.

- All BGP speakers are to be able to communicate with all advertised BGP networks.

**Figure 1-14**  *IP EGP Diagram*

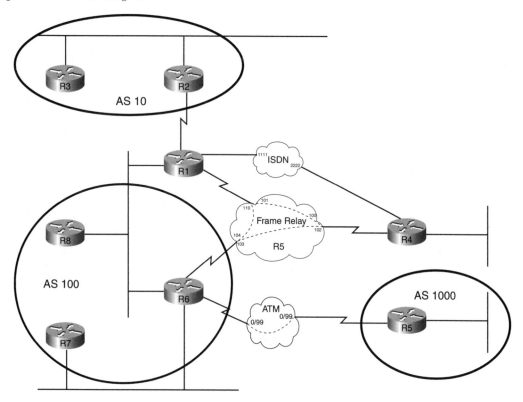

# Section 5: Voice (6 Points)

- Both phones should be able to ring each other using the numbers supplied. Use the most efficient method of transporting the voice from R1 to R4.

- Ensure that voice is still available if the main connection between R1 and R4 fails.

- Make the phone on R1 also answer calls if 01962 is dialed on the R4 connected handsets; do not use number expansion to achieve this.

# Section 6: DLSw+ (4 Points)

- Configure DLSw+ between VLAN2 and VLAN4; use routers R8 and R5. Peer from Lo0 on R8 and the VLAN4 interface on R5; ensure that R8 can accept DLSw+ connections from only unknown TCP peers.

- Set up a one-line filter, which only allows common SNA traffic to egress from R5 VLAN4 into the DLSw+ network.

# Section 7: IOS and IP Features (10 Points)

- R2 is sited in a shared data center; make the serial link back into R1 as secure as possible at Layer 2.

- Ensure traffic from VLAN4, including any attached router interfaces to VLAN4, is hidden behind R5 lo0 address when directed toward all external router networks.

- A router is to be installed onto VLAN4 in the future. This router will have a default configuration, so allow R6 to assist dynamically to aid the configuration process. The router will require an IP address of 10.50.50.6 and should load a configuration file called R9-config from a fictitious TFTP server on 172.16.0.59.

# Section 8: QoS (8 Points)

- Achieve maximum quality of voice calls by ensuring the real-time packet interval of 10 ms is not exceeded. Do not use RSVP in your solution.

- To reduce the packet fragmentation in your network, allow R5 to determine appropriate fragmentation requirements when TCP sessions are originated from it to any part of the network.

# Section 9: Multicast (4 Points)

- Enable your network to allow hosts on VLAN4 to receive and send multicast traffic from and to VLAN2; only perform configuration on R5 and R6 using PIM sparse dense mode.

- Configure R6 to respond to pings from R5 to the multicast address of 224.4.4.4.

- Do not allow R5 to fully participate in the PIM process by not allowing it to become a neighbor, but do allow any IGMP messages generated by hosts on VLAN4 to be received by R6.

# Practice Lab 1: "Ask the Proctor"

This section should be used only if you require clues to complete the questions. In the real CCIE Lab, the Proctor will not enter into any discussion regarding the questions or the answers. He or she will only be present to ensure you do not have problems with the lab environment and to maintain the timing element of the exam.

## Section 1.1: Frame Relay Configuration

Q: If I don't configure the PVC between R1-R6, surely it won't be used?
A: You have to make sure that the PVC is not used.

Q: But if it's not configured, surely it won't be used?
A: Use the command **show frame relay pvc**; if the PVC shows any input packets or output packets, you have not answered the question. You can also use the command **show frame map.**

Q: It says the routers must use subinterfaces. Can I use point-to-point everywhere?
A: This does not address the question.

Q: Can I use two separate point-to-point subinterfaces from R4 out to individual point-to-point subinterfaces on R1 and R6?
A: If the routers were not on a common subnet you could, but this is not the case.

Q: Can I put a point to multi-point interface on R4 and point-to-point interfaces on R1 and R6?
A: Yes.

Q: Do you want me to configure "**broadcast**" under my Frame Relay interfaces?
A: You need to determine what type of traffic/protocols will use the Frame Relay network.

## Section 1.2: 3550 LAN Switch Configuration

Q: Do I have to configure the switch as a VTP server?
A: The questions do not ask you to do this and there is only one switch in the network.

Q: Why can't I rename VLAN1?
A: You can't so don't waste time on this.

Q: Can I leave my switch ports in auto mode?
A: The questions do not specifically ask you to configure speed and duplex, but you should do this to avoid any mismatches that could cause you problems.

Q: For the future port 0/16, can I leave it in VLAN1?
A: There is no specific VLAN stated in the question, so yes.

# Section 1.3: ATM Configuration

Q: What kind of subinterface do you want on R6?
A: There are only two routers connected over ATM; choose a suitable subinterface type to reflect this.

Q: When you say latest method of configuration, do you mean using the **pvc** command?
A: Yes.

Q: When you say legacy configuration, do you mean using the **map-list** command?
A: Yes.

Q: What ATM encapsulation should I use?
A: This is a back-to-back configuration so use a suitable type of your choice.

Q: Do you want me to configure "**broadcast**" under my ATM interfaces?
A: You need to determine what type of traffic/protocols will use the ATM network.

# Section 2.1: RIP

Q: Can I use a **distribute-list** to stop the advertisement of network 60.60.60.0/24?
A: You cannot configure R2 or R1; R2 must see the network so you cannot configure a distribute-list on R3 either.

Q: Surely the only way to make RIP unicast routing updates is to use the **neighbor** command and **passive-interface**?
A: There is another way of forcing this; try to use other IP features if you find that you can not accomplish this using RIP features.

Q: Is it acceptable to use a NAT list to convert my RIP multicast into a unicast?
A: If you answer the question effectively, this is acceptable.

Q: I used NAT and now my connectivity is lost between R2 and R3. Is this supposed to happen?
A: You need to maintain full IP connectivity between all routers as well as answering specific questions.

Q: Can I use summarization to advertise VLAN2 into the /28 RIP V2 domain?
A: The question clearly states no RIP or EIGRP features may be used.

Q: Can I run ospf on my router and redistribute this into RIP with an ospf summary of VLAN2?

A: The question states that no RIP feature may be used; redistribution is a feature of RIP.

Q: Am I permitted to add a secondary address to my configuration?

A: If this achieves the desired result, yes.

Q: I am having problems connecting to VLAN2 from R1 after answering the VLAN2 question. Is this expected?

A: If you experience any connectivity issues, you should investigate and rectify them.

# Section 2.2: EIGRP

Q: Can I just use passive interfaces to reduce the CPU processing?

A: Passive interfaces with no requirements for adjacencies will reduce CPU processes, but a superior way to enable this within EIGRP exists.

Q: If I use the **neighbor** command, won't that be sufficient as I will no longer be multicasting my EIGRP "hellos"?

A: This will not be sufficient.

Q: I have modified my hello timer on R8 and now my routes are flapping. Is this acceptable?

A: No, you need to remember that R8 will have formed a neighbor relationship on VLAN2; you should ensure that all routers are configured in the same manner.

Q: I have configured R6 and R8 with identical hello intervals but I find that my routes are still flapping. Is this acceptable?

A: No, you should maintain a reliable neighbor relationship with R4; consider adjusting other EIGRP parameters.

# Section 2.3: Redistribution

Q: I believe I can complete my redistribution without any filtering. Is this acceptable?

A: To avoid suboptimal routing and potential routing loops, it is always good practice to filter when redistributing.

Q: But no way exists that I could create suboptimal routes in this scenario?

A: Correct. Use this question as practice.

# Section 3: ISDN

Q: Can I use **backup interface** on R1 to protect the Frame Relay network?

A: The question specifically asks you for visibility of VLAN3 and R4 lo0 networks, Further networks would be available if you were to use the backup interface. This command would also only work if there was a physical Layer 1 problem with the Frame Relay connection.

Q: Can I use floating static routes for VLAN3 and R4 lo0 networks?

A: You are not permitted to use any static routes in any part of the lab.

Q: I have managed to get the ISDN to dial out if I loose visibility of VLAN3 and Lo0 but the line will not stay down. Is this acceptable?

A: If the Frame Relay network is restored, your ISDN line should eventually be disconnected.

Q: Do you want CHAP or PAP configured over the ISDN so only R1 dials into R4?

A: The question does not specifically ask for CHAP or PAP or give sufficient information to configure either.

Q: Can I use my **dialer idle-timeout** set to 90 seconds to ensure the ISDN does not flap?

A: Adjusting the **dialer idle-timeout** is not sufficient.

# Section 4: EGP Protocols

Q: Is it sufficient if I peer from connected interfaces as default?

A: Where possible, you should peer using the most resilient method as instructed.

Q: I have just configured my routers to peer from their loopback interfaces and now not all of my BGP neighbors are showing up. Is this acceptable?

A: No, you need to remember the rules for EBGP peering.

Q: To minimize the configuration on R8, can I leave out statements such as **update-source**?

A: No, find a way to maintain the required features but cut down on the size of your configuration.

Q: Can I advertise my new loopback interfaces as I see fit.

A: Use the most appropriate method of advertising your new networks.

Q: Can I change router IDs to manipulate the path selection on R6?

A: You can try anything not listed in the question if it achieves the desired results.

Q: If I have the BGP routes in my BGP tables, surely this is sufficient to prove my BGP is functioning correctly and I have full IP visibility?

A: Potentially yes, however, it would be prudent to perform extended pings or by using **traceroute** to be 100-percent certain.

# Section 5: Voice

Q: Because voice should be available over the Frame Relay and ISDN, is it acceptable to run just Voice over IP?

A: A more efficient means of transportation of Voice over the Frame Relay network exists.

Q: If I can't use **num-exp**, surely I can't get the other phone to ring?

A: A method is available.

# Section 6: DLSw+

Q: Can I set up multiple **remote-peer** statements on R8 from other loopback interfaces within the network for future peering?

A: You need to allow for any unknown future peering.

Q: With my filter, I can't allow for every form of SNA SAP?

A: Allow for the most common SAPs but keep your list to one line.

# Section 7: IOS and IP Features

Q: Do you require IPsec configured between R1 and R2?

A: The question refers to Layer 2; IPsec is a Layer 3 protocol.

Q: Can I use access lists to just allow R2 to communicate with R1?

A: This is again Layer 3.

Q: Do you want me to authenticate my routing updates to ensure security?

A: You need a Layer 2 solution.

Q: Do you want me to use a single NAT instance to hide behind my loopback interface?

A: You may find that you require multiple instances to answer the question effectively.

Q: Surely the new router will have at least been configured to pick up a DHCP address?

A: The new router is out of the box with a factory configuration only.

Q: Do you actually want the configuration of R9 to be stored on R6?

A: No, the configuration is to be held on a fictitious TFTP server.

# Section 8: QoS

Q: Do you just want me to configure custom queuing for voice?

A: No, you must ensure that voice is transmitted within 10 ms intervals so the quality is not impaired.

Q: Do you want the QoS for the voice when it is transmitted over Frame Relay or ISDN?

A: It is your decision how and where you activate QoS, sufficient information is available in the paper for you to make an informed decision.

Q: For R5 packet fragmentation, is it acceptable to work out the smallest MTU in the network and configure this on all interfaces on R5?

A: Although this might reduce fragmentation at other points within the network, it does not allow R5 to determine the fragmentation itself.

# Section 9: Multicast

Q: Do you want me to configure any multicast parameters on my switch?

A: The question states only R5 and R6 should be configured.

Q: Can I create a standard access-list blocking PIM from R5 and R6?

A: A more elegant PIM filtering method of achieving this exists.

# Practice Lab 1 Debrief

The lab debrief section will now analyze each question showing you what was required and how to achieve the desired results. You should use this section to produce an overall score for your test.

# Section 1: Bridging and Switching (15 Points)

## Section 1.1: Frame Relay Configuration (6 points)

- *Configure the Frame Relay portion of the network as shown in Figure 1-8; ensure that DLCIs 110 and 104 between R1-R6 are not used.*

The question clearly states that DLCIs 110 and 104 are not to be used; you must, therefore, disable **inverse-arp** on the routers. It is good practice to ensure that all routers do not rely on **inverse-arp** so if you have configured **no frame-relay inverse-arp** under routers R1,R4 and R6 serial interfaces 0/0, you have scored 2 points.

If you experience difficulties and can not clear any dynamic map entries, reload your routers to remove these, a drastic measure but every point counts.

- *The routers are to be on the same subnet and should be configured with subinterfaces.*

R4 will need to be a multipoint subinterface to accommodate both R1 and R6 on the same subnet; R1 and R6 only have PVCs to R4, hence, they will require point-to-point subinterfaces. R4 will require manual **frame-relay map** statements pointing to both R1 and R6 as inverse arp is disabled. The maps require the **broadcast** keyword as RIP will multicast the routing updates over the PVCs. It should be apparent that when RIP is run over a multipoint interface, split horizon will be enabled by default and routing updates from R6 into R1 will never be propagated by the hub router R4 because of the rule of not advertising a network that was received on the same interface; R4 will, therefore, require **no ip split-horizon** configured under its Frame Relay interface. If you have configured all items correctly as in Example 1-1 through Example 1-3, you have scored 4 points, unfortunately no marks if you have omitted anything.

| NOTE | For clarity only, the required configuration details will be listed to answer the specific questions instead of full final configurations. |
|------|------|

**Example 1-1**  *R4 Initial Frame Relay Solution Configuration*

```
interface Serial0/0
 no ip address
 encapsulation frame-relay
 no frame-relay inverse-arp
!
interface Serial0/0.1 multipoint
 ip address 10.100.100.3 255.255.255.240
 no ip split-horizon
 frame-relay map ip 10.100.100.1 100 broadcast
 frame-relay map ip 10.100.100.2 102 broadcast
```

**Example 1-2**  *R1 Initial Frame Relay Solution Configuration*

```
interface Serial0/1
 no ip address
 encapsulation frame-relay
 no frame-relay inverse-arp
!
interface Serial0/1.101 point-to-point
 ip address 10.100.100.1 255.255.255.240 frame-relay interface-dlci 101
```

**Example 1-3**  *R6 Initial Frame Relay Solution Configuration*

```
interface Serial5/0
 no ip address
 encapsulation frame-relay
 no frame-relay inverse-arp
!
interface Serial5/0.103 point-to-point
 ip address 10.100.100.2 255.255.255.240
 frame-relay interface-dlci 103
```

# Section 1.2: 3550 LAN Switch Configuration (6 Points)

- *Configure VLAN numbers, VLAN names, and port assignment as per the topology diagram as shown in Figure 1-10.*

The switch in this instance is isolated but you can still use the default mode of VTP Server. From the VLAN database, add the required VLANs and name them accordingly; you should note that you can not change the VLAN name of VLAN1. You must ensure that the port speed and duplex is fixed to 100 Mbps and full duplex, if your routers support this; leaving your ports in auto mode could cause connectivity problems. If you have configured these items correctly as in Example 1-4, you have scored 2 points.

**Example 1-4**    *3550 Switch1 Initial Configuration*

```
Switch1#vlan database
Switch1(vlan)#vlan 2 name VLAN2
VLAN 2 modified:
    Name: VLAN2
Switch1(vlan)#vlan 3 name VLAN3
VLAN 3 modified:
    Name: VLAN3
Switch1(vlan)#vlan 4 name VLAN4
VLAN 4 modified:
    Name: VLAN4
Switch1(vlan)#vlan 5 name VLAN5
VLAN 5 modified:
    Name: VLAN5
Switch1(vlan)#exit
APPLY completed.
Exiting....
interface FastEthernet0/1
 switchport access vlan 2
 switchport mode access
 no ip address
 duplex full
 speed 100
!
interface FastEthernet0/2
 switchport mode access
 no ip address
 duplex full
 speed 100
!
interface FastEthernet0/3
 switchport mode access
 no ip address
 duplex full
 speed 100
!
interface FastEthernet0/4
 switchport access vlan 3
 switchport mode access
 no ip address
 duplex full
 speed 100
!
interface FastEthernet0/5
 switchport access vlan 4
 switchport mode access
 no ip address
```

*continues*

**Example 1-4** *3550 Switch1 Initial Configuration (Continued)*

```
 duplex full
 speed 100
!
interface FastEthernet0/6
 switchport access vlan 2
 switchport mode access
 no ip address
 duplex full
 speed 100
!
interface FastEthernet0/7
 switchport access vlan 5
 switchport mode access
 no ip address
 duplex full
 speed 100
!
interface FastEthernet0/8
 switchport access vlan 2
 switchport mode access
 no ip address
 duplex full
 speed 100
!
interface FastEthernet0/9
 switchport access vlan 5
 switchport mode access
 no ip address
 duplex full
 speed 100
```

**NOTE**   The VLAN configuration is completed under **vlan database.**

- *There is to be a host connected on interface 0/16 in the future; the network
  administrator requires that this host is authenticated by a radius server before access
  to the switch is granted. The radius server is to be located on the IP address
  172.16.100.100 with the key* **radius14.**

This question calls for 802.1X Authentication before a port is granted access to the switch
and network. If configured correctly as in Example 1-5, you have scored 3 points.

**Example 1-5** *802.1X Switch Configuration*

```
aaa new-model
aaa authentication dot1x default group radius
!
interface FastEthernet0/16
```

**Example 1-5**    *802.1X Switch Configuration (Continued)*

```
switchport mode access
no ip address
dot1x port-control auto
!
radius-server host 172.16.100.100 auth-port 1812 key radius14
```

- *Ensure the switch is reachable via Telnet to the IP address of 10.80.80.8/24.*

Configure VLAN2 with the IP address of 10.80.80.8 255.255.255.0. The switch will also need a **default-gateway** configured; you could use 10.80.80.2 or 10.80.80.1 here. The previous question requires that you enable AAA. Enabling AAA prompts you for a username when you telnet to the switch from one of your routers. To ensure typical access to the preconfigured line and to ensure that the enable password is used for telnet access to the switch, you should add the **aaa authentication login default enable** authentication configuration onto the switch.

**Example 1-6**    *Switch1 Management IP Configuration*

```
aaa authentication login default enable
enable password cisco
!
interface Vlan2
 ip address 10.80.80.8 255.255.255.0
!
ip default-gateway 10.80.80.2
!
line con 0
 password cisco
line vty 0 15
 password cisco
```

# Section 1.3: ATM Configuration (3 Points)

- *Configure the ATM network as shown in Figure 1-12.*

- *Use a subinterface on R6 for the ATM matching the VCI number and ensure the latest method of PVC configuration is used on this router. For R5 ATM, use the physical interface and legacy PVC configuration; after you have configured your Layer 2 information, you may then add the Layer 3 addresses.*

- *Do not rely on inverse ARP.*

R6 requires a point-to-point subinterface named ATM1/0.99 with the PVC details configured under the separate PVC; R5 requires the legacy style with the **map-list** to achieve the PVC connectivity in this back-to-back configuration. The **map-list, ip 10.99.99.1 atm-vc 1 broadcast**, and **protocol ip 10.99.99.2** commands ensure that **inverse-arp** is not relied upon.

You can use whichever encapsulation suits the three tasks in Section 1.3 as it has not been defined which type must be used.

If you have successfully configured all items as in Example 1-7 and Example 1-8, you have scored 3 points.

**Example 1-7** *R6 ATM Configuration and Map Verification*

```
interface ATM1/0
 no ip address
 no atm ilmi-keepalive
!
interface ATM1/0.99 point-to-point
 ip address 10.99.99.1 255.255.255.248
pvc 0/99
  protocol ip 10.99.99.2  broadcast
  encapsulation aal5snap
R6#show atm map
Map list ATM1/0.99pvc1 : PERMANENT
ip 10.99.99.2 maps to VC 1, VPI 0, VCI 99, ATM1/0.99
        , broadcast
```

**Example 1-8** *R6 ATM Configuration and Map Verification*

```
interface ATM3/0
 ip address 10.99.99.2 255.255.255.248
 map-group atm
 atm pvc 1 0 99 aal5snap
 no atm ilmi-keepalive
!
map-list atm
 ip 10.99.99.1 atm-vc 1 broadcast

R5#show atm map
Map list atm : PERMANENT
ip 10.99.99.1 maps to VC 1
         , broadcast
```

# Section 2: IP IGP Protocols (28 Points)

## Section 2.1: RIP (16 Points)

- *On all RIP router, ensure that **version 2** is used under the process.*

Add **version 2** under the RIP process. You receive no points here; this just ensures your routers behave correctly during the lab.

You should have at this point also enabled RIP for your networks using the **network** command and as a matter of good practice configured router interfaces that are not part of the RIP domain as passive using the command **passive-interface** under the RIP process of each router.

- *Ensure that VLSM is supported on advertisements between all RIP routers.*

This is just a case of manually configuring the RIP routers to disable auto summarization mainly for the benefit of R3, which would otherwise receive a classfull network 10.0.0.0/8 route from R2. If you have configured this correctly as shown in Example 1-9 on all RIP routers with the resulting routing table shown for R3 in Example 1-10, you have scored 2 points.

**Example 1-9**   *RIP VLSM Configuration on R1, R2, R3, R4, and R6*

```
router rip
 no auto-summary
```

**Example 1-10**  *R3 RIP Routing Table Output*

```
R3#sh ip route

C    172.16.0.0/16 is directly connected, FastEthernet0/0
     10.0.0.0/8 is variably subnetted, 9 subnets, 3 masks
R        10.100.100.0/28 [120/2] via 172.16.0.1, 00:00:24, FastEthernet0/0
R        10.99.99.0/29 [120/4] via 172.16.0.1, 00:00:24, FastEthernet0/0
R        10.90.90.0/28 [120/1] via 172.16.0.1, 00:00:24, FastEthernet0/0
R        10.80.80.0/24 [120/2] via 172.16.0.1, 00:00:24, FastEthernet0/0
R        10.60.60.0/29 [120/4] via 172.16.0.1, 00:00:26, FastEthernet0/0
R        10.40.40.0/28 [120/3] via 172.16.0.1, 00:00:26, FastEthernet0/0
R        10.6.6.0/29 [120/4] via 172.16.0.1, 00:00:26, FastEthernet0/0
R        10.4.4.0/29 [120/3] via 172.16.0.1, 00:00:26, FastEthernet0/0
R        10.1.1.0/28 [120/2] via 172.16.0.1, 00:00:26, FastEthernet0/0
```

- *Add a loopback interface with the address of 60.60.60.1/24 onto R3 and advertise this out to R2 but ensure that it is not seen by the rest of your network; do not perform any configuration on R2 or R1.*

Add the loopback as Lo0 on R3 and enable the 60.60.60.0/24 network under RIP; this automatically advertises network 60.60.60.0/24 out to R2 and the rest of your RIP network over the 172.16.0.0/16 network, which you should have already configured according to the IGP diagram. The usual method to stop the propagation of this network would be via distribute lists, but the question states that R2 must see the network so you can not put a distribute list out on R3; the question also states that you can not configure R2 or R1 so you will have to configure R3. You need to get back to basics here and recall that RIP has a maximum hop count of 15 with 16 hops marked as unreachable so you will need to ensure that when network 60.60.60.0/24 egresses R3 the hop count is already set at 14. This way when R2 sees the route it knows that it has a hop count of 15 to reach it; it, in turn, will then advertise network 60.60.60.0/24 with a hop count of 16, which is, of course, unreachable and, hence, it will not be included in the routing table of R1 and beyond. To achieve the artificial hop count, an **offset-list** is required for network 60.60.60.0/24 on R3. If you have configured this correctly as in Example 1-11 with validation shown in Example 1-12 and Example 1-13, you have scored 4 points.

You could have also gained full marks for advertising the loopback interface on R3 within RIP as a connected interface and assigned a metric of 15 to this route, which provides exactly the same result.

**Example 1-11** *R3 Hop Count Configuration*

```
interface Loopback0
 ip address 60.60.60.1 255.255.255.0
!
router rip
 version 2
 offset-list 1 out 14 FastEthernet0/0
 network 60.0.0.0
 network 172.16.0.0
!
access-list 1 permit 60.60.60.0
```

**Example 1-12** *R2 Routing Entry for 60.60.60.0/24*

```
R2#show ip route 60.60.60.0
Routing entry for 60.60.60.0/24
  Known via "rip", distance 120, metric 15
  Redistributing via rip
  Last update from 172.16.0.2 on FastEthernet0/0, 00:00:15 ago
  Routing Descriptor Blocks:
  * 172.16.0.2, from 172.16.0.2, 00:00:15 ago, via FastEthernet0/0
        Route metric is 15, traffic share count is 1
```

**Example 1-13** *R1 RIP* **debug**

```
R1#debug ip rip
2w1d: RIP: received v2 update from 10.90.90.1 on Serial0/0
2w1d:       60.60.60.0 in 16 hops (inaccessible)
2w1d:      172.16.0.0 in 1 hops
```

- *Configure R3 to unicast its RIP routing updates to R2. Do not use the* **neighbor** *command to achieve this but consider using other IP features to aid you.*

Normally, you would use the **neighbor** command in conjunction with **passive-interface** to ensure that a router unicasts its routing updates instead of multicasting them in the usual manner. To achieve this without the neighbor command, you will need to use NAT to turn a multicast into a unicast; this is your additional IP feature. A simple NAT statement causing any packet with a destination address as a multicast to destination address 224.0.0.9 with the UDP port equal to that of RIP (520) to be converted into a destination address of 172.16.0.1 (R2 FastEthernet0/0) will cause R3 to now unicast its routing updates directly to R3.

If you have configured this correctly as in Example 1-14 and with the resulting output on R2 as shown in Example 1-15, you have scored 6 points.

**Example 1-14**  *R3 NAT Configuration and* **debug**

```
interface FastEthernet0/0
 ip address 172.16.0.2 255.255.0.0
 ip nat outside
!

ip nat outside source static udp 172.16.0.1 520 224.0.0.9 520

R3#debug ip nat det
IP NAT detailed debugging is on
R3#clear ip route *
R3#

00:57:29: NAT: i: udp (172.16.0.2, 520) -> (224.0.0.9, 520) [0]
00:57:29: NAT: s=172.16.0.2, d=224.0.0.9->172.16.0.1 [0]
```

**Example 1-15**  *R2 RIP* **debug**

```
R2#debug ip pack det
IP packet debugging is on (detailed)
R2#
00:54:56: IP: s=172.16.0.2 (FastEthernet0/0), d=172.16.0.1 (FastEthernet0/0), len 5
2, rcvd 3
00:54:56:      UDP src=520, dst=520
```

- *Ensure that VLAN2 is advertised to the RIP domain as a /28 network. Do not use either RIP or EIGRP features to accomplish this. You can, however, configure R6.*

VLAN2 has a subnet mask of /24, and as such, the RIP domain would see this as network 10.80.80.0/24.

You could quite easily summarize network 10.80.80.0/24 within RIP or later within EIGRP to change the network to 10.80.80.0/28, but the question clearly states that no RIP or EIGRP feature must be used. The lab rules are also not static routes; policy routing won't help as the network should be present in all routing tables so the only way to get VLAN2 from a /24 into a /28 is to think laterally and add a secondary address on R6 FastEthernet0/0 within the /28 range (i.e., 10.80.80.14/28). This will then ensure the network 10.80.80.0/28 is advertised into the RIP domain.

| | |
|---|---|
| **NOTE** | The new RIP advertisement of 10.80.80.0/28 will be received by R1, which already has a connected interface into the real 10.80.80.0/24 network. This is a longer match than its own connected interface and, hence, will cause suboptimal routing for R1 to communicate on VLAN2 within the range of the /24 subnet. A **distribute-list** must be used on R1 to filter this network. Remember that the RIP route for this network could arrive on both the Frame Relay interface and the BRI if the Frame Relay network fails later in the lab; as such the **distribute-list** is required in-bound on both interfaces. |

If you have configured this correctly including filtering network 10.80.80.0/28 from entering R1 as in Example 1-16 and Example 1-17, you have scored 4 points. If you have only configured the **distribute-list** on the Frame Relay network, you have only scored 2 points.

**Example 1-16** *R6 Secondary Address Configuration*

```
interface FastEthernet0/0
 ip address 10.80.80.14 255.255.255.240 secondary
 ip address 10.80.80.2 255.255.255.0
```

**Example 1-17** *R1 RIP Distribute-List Configuration*

```
router rip
 distribute-list 1 in Serial0/1.101
  distribute-list 1 in BRI0/0
 !
 access-list 1 deny    10.80.80.0 0.0.0.15
 access-list 1 permit any
```

# Section 2.2: EIGRP (5 Points)

You should have configured EIGRP using AS10 as shown in Figure 1-13 on R5, R6, R7, and R8. R6 has RIP enabled on the Frame Relay network, so you can either use a **network** statement for each EIGRP required interface with an inverse mask or simply use the **passive-interface** command as required. All EIGRP routers should also have auto summarization disabled using the command **no auto-summary**. No extra points here in Lab 1, but you will find in later labs that you will earn points for the correct basic configuration.

| | |
|---|---|
| **NOTE** | The IGP questions do not stipulate if R6 should advertise it's loopback interface via RIP or EIGRP because R6 runs both protocols, in this case it is prudent to do so in both instances. |

- *R8 is very low on memory and CPU resource; accommodate this information within the configuration on R8.*

EIGRP supports stub routing, which improves network stability, reduces resource, and simplifies configuration. R8 does not participate in any summary advertisements so it purely requires **eigrp stub connected** configured under its EIGRP process to ensure that its connected interfaces are successfully advertised out to its neighbors. If you have configured this correctly as in Example 1-18, you have scored 3 points.

**Example 1-18**  *R8 EIGRP Stub-Routing Configuration and R6 EIGRP Neighbor Output*

```
router eigrp 10
 network 10.0.0.0
 no auto-summary
 eigrp stub connected

R6#sh ip eigrp neighbors detail
IP-EIGRP neighbors for process 10
H   Address                 Interface       Hold Uptime    SRTT   RTO  Q  Seq Type
                                            (sec)          (ms)        Cnt Num
2   10.99.99.2              Se0/0            167 05:30:02    4    200  0  2
    Version 12.2/1.2, Retrans: 6, Retries: 0
1   10.60.60.2              Fa0/1             12 05:30:02  340   2040  0  3
    Version 12.1/1.2, Retrans: 0, Retries: 0
0   10.80.80.3              Fa0/0             14 05:30:05    9    200  0  4
    Version 12.1/1.2, Retrans: 2, Retries: 0
    Stub Peer Advertising ( CONNECTED ) Routes
```

- *Configure R8 to have an EIGRP hello interval of 25 seconds on its FastEthernet0/0 interface.*

The EIGRP hello interval is by default set at 5 seconds for FastEthernet. This is not a difficult question but you must ensure if you are changing any EIGRP interval that you should also configure that of your neighbors on the common subnet exactly the same otherwise your neighbor adjacencies will be fluctuating as will your routing table. You should also be aware that the EIGRP hold interval should be three times that of the hello interval otherwise you will experience difficulties in maintaining your neighbor relationship. You should, therefore, configure the **ip hold-time eigrp** interval on R8 under the FastEthernet0/0 as 75 seconds. Configure R6 under its FastEthernet0/0 with the same configuration as R8 as it is a neighbor to R8 on VLAN2. If you have configured this correctly as shown in Example 1-19, you have scored 2 points.

**Example 1-19**  *R8 and R6 EIGRP Hello and Hold Interval Configuration*

```
interface FastEthernet0/0
 ip hello-interval eigrp 10 25
 ip hold-time eigrp 10 75
```

# Section 2.3: Redistribution (7 Points)

- *Redistribute IGP protocols to ensure full IP visibility between all routers.*

You can see via the IGP diagram in Figure 1-13 that there will only be one redistribution point required, this being R6.

Mutual redistribution between RIP and EIGRP is required. Don't forget your default metrics under each process otherwise the different protocols will have no means of

applying relevant metrics to the routes you wish to advertise. If you have configured your
redistribution correctly as shown in Example 1-20 and Example 1-21 and have full IP
visibility of all networks, you have scored 4 points.

**Example 1-20**  *R6 EIGRP Redistribution to RIP Configuration*

```
router rip
 version 2
 redistribute eigrp 10
 passive-interface default
 no passive-interface Serial5/0.103
 network 10.0.0.0
 default-metric 3
 no auto-summary
```

**Example 1-21**  *R6 RIP Redistribution to EIGRP Configuration*

```
router eigrp 10
 redistribute rip
 passive-interface default
 no passive-interface FastEthernet0/0
 no passive-interface ATM1/0.99
 no passive-interface FastEthernet4/0
 network 10.0.0.0
 default-metric 100000 0 255 1 1500
 no auto-summary
```

- *As a safety precaution, ensure that R6 can not learn the EIGRP routes it previously*
  *advertised into the RIP domain back from R4.*

This question is just a straightforward practice of distribute lists and ensuring that the
correct networks are filtered. In this scenario, R6 would ignore any routes back from RIP
to which it had redistributed into RIP originally from EIGRP because of the external
EIGRP route feature (any routes redistributed into EIGRP are subject to an increased
Administritive Distance from 90 to 170). The redistributed RIP routes would simply be
ignored. To answer the question as requested, though, you will need to configure a
**distribute-list** within RIP on R6 Serial5/0.103, which blocks the EIGRP routes that R6
advertises out to the RIP domain. Do not include the connected interfaces on R6 in your
ACL as these would be advertised within the RIP domain anyway and not redistributed into
RIP from EIGRP. If you have configured this correctly as shown in Example 1-22, you have
scored 3 points.

**Example 1-22**  *R6 Distribution List Configuration*

```
router rip
 distribute-list 1 in Serial5/0.103
 !
access-list 1 deny    10.8.8.8
access-list 1 deny    10.5.5.4 0.0.0.3
access-list 1 deny    10.7.7.0 0.0.0.15
access-list 1 deny    10.50.50.0 0.0.0.7
access-list 1 permit any
```

# Section 3: ISDN (8 Points)

- *Ensure that VLAN3 and R4 Lo0 are accessible from R1 and beyond should the Frame Relay network fail either physically or logically. If VLAN3 and R4 Lo0 networks are restored while the ISDN line is active, ensure that traffic is routed over the Frame Relay network to these destinations immediately.*

As no static routes are permitted and backing up the Frame Relay interface will not help as this only works if the Frame Relay interface is physically down, the only option will be to use the **dialer-watch** feature. Both networks must be down before the router dials out so VLAN3 and R4 Lo0 should be added to a **dialer watch-list** and corresponding **dialer watch-group** number under the BRI interface on R1. R1 is used to dial out as the question states that the two networks should be accessible from R1. You are also later advised that only R1 should dial into R4.

You should notice that when you fail the Frame Relay network to test this that after the ISDN is activated and the Frame Relay network is then restored that the routing table on R1 shows identical hop counts for all remote networks via R4 over both the Frame Relay and ISDN line as shown in Example 1-23.

This condition can keep the ISDN line from ever deactivating as the ISDN network can now be used as a valid means to transport data to the RIP advertised remote networks, you should also notice that the question requires that the Frame Relay routes should be used "immediately" when restored and, at this point, routers R1 and R4 can choose between Frame Relay and ISDN.

RIP obviously does not take into account the bandwidth of available routes. You, therefore, need to make the ISDN routes less desirable and add additional hop count to RIP using an **offset-list** on R4 and R1 out over the ISDN line (inbound over both routers will also be acceptable). This ensures when the Frame Relay is restored and for the period where both Frame Relay and ISDN lines are active and receiving RIP routes that the hop count is more favorable over Frame Relay because of the additional hop count incurred over ISDN after the **offset-list** is applied.

The ISDN line can not be used to route traffic while a higher-speed Frame Relay connection is available as shown in Example 1-25. **Dialer-watch** does not require interesting traffic to trigger the dial so the **dialer-list** should be an implicit deny of any IP traffic; otherwise, any traffic will potentially keep the line up after initiated. It is better practice and shows a better understanding of the dialer-watch process to, therefore, have the following **dialer-list** on R1; **dialer-list 10 protocol ip deny**. You will find with this strict policing of the interesting traffic, your ISDN line will stay down when the networks are restored over the Frame Relay. If you have configured this question correctly as in Example 1-24, you have scored 5 points; if you have used a **dialer-list** that denies RIP and the line stays down, you have only scored 3 points. Test your scenario thoroughly if you have first denied RIP then allowed all other IP traffic and also not applied the **offset-list**; you could find that with two routes in the routing table with identical metrics that traffic, such as BGP, will toggle between the two routes and keep the line up constantly. In addition, other IP traffic could be classed as interesting and keep the line up.

**Example 1-23** *R1 Routing Table Pre Offset-List with the ISDN Line Active After the Frame Relay Network Has Been Restored*

```
R1#sh ip route
R    172.16.0.0/16 [120/1] via 10.90.90.1, 00:00:22, Serial0/0
     10.0.0.0/8 is variably subnetted, 16 subnets, 5 masks
R       10.8.8.8/32 [120/4] via 10.10.10.2, 00:00:14, BRI0/0
                    [120/4] via 10.100.100.2, 00:00:14, Serial0/1.101
C       10.10.10.2/32 is directly connected, BRI0/0
C       10.100.100.0/28 is directly connected, Serial0/1.101
R       10.99.99.0/29 [120/2] via 10.10.10.2, 00:00:14, BRI0/0
                      [120/2] via 10.100.100.2, 00:00:14, Serial0/1.101
R       10.60.60.0/29 [120/2] via 10.10.10.2, 00:00:14, BRI0/0
                      [120/2] via 10.100.100.2, 00:00:14, Serial0/1.101
R       10.50.50.0/29 [120/4] via 10.10.10.2, 00:00:14, BRI0/0
                      [120/4] via 10.100.100.2, 00:00:14, Serial0/1.101
R       10.40.40.0/28 [120/1] via 10.10.10.2, 00:00:16, BRI0/0
                      [120/1] via 10.100.100.3, 00:00:16, Serial0/1.101
R       10.7.7.0/28 [120/4] via 10.10.10.2, 00:00:16, BRI0/0
                    [120/4] via 10.100.100.2, 00:00:16, Serial0/1.101
R       10.6.6.0/29 [120/2] via 10.10.10.2, 00:00:16, BRI0/0
                    [120/2] via 10.100.100.2, 00:00:16, Serial0/1.101
R       10.4.4.0/29 [120/1] via 10.10.10.2, 00:00:16, BRI0/0
                    [120/1] via 10.100.100.3, 00:00:16, Serial0/1.101
C       10.80.80.0/24 is directly connected, FastEthernet0/0
C       10.90.90.0/28 is directly connected, Serial0/0
C       10.1.1.0/28 is directly connected, Loopback0
C       10.10.10.0/28 is directly connected, BRI0/0
C       10.90.90.1/32 is directly connected, Serial0/0
R       10.5.5.4/30 [120/4] via 10.10.10.2, 00:00:16, BRI0/0
                    [120/4] via 10.100.100.2, 00:00:16, Serial0/1.101
R1#sh isdn history
--------------------------------------------------------------------------------
                         ISDN CALL HISTORY
--------------------------------------------------------------------------------
Call History contains all active calls, and a maximum of 100 inactive calls.
Inactive call data will be retained for a maximum of 15 minutes.
--------------------------------------------------------------------------------
Call   Calling    Called     Remote  Seconds Seconds Seconds Charges
Type   Number     Number     Name    Used    Left    Idle    Units/Currency
--------------------------------------------------------------------------------
Out               2222               82      37      82      0
--------------------------------------------------------------------------------
```

**NOTE**    The routing table output is taken after a Frame Relay failure is restored and the ISDN line is still active. The shading shows you the two available routes with the identical hop count on R1 before the **offset-list** is applied.

**Example 1-24**  *Increasing the Hop Count Out of R4 and R1 ISDN Configuration*

```
R1
router rip
 offset-list 0 out 2 BRI0/0
R4
router rip
 offset-list 0 out 2 Dialer0
```

**NOTE**    **offset-list 0** will apply the chosen additional hop count (2) to all networks being advertised from R4 and R1 out of their interfaces BRI0/0. A similar configuration could be placed on each BRI0/0 but inbound.

**Example 1-25**  *R1 Routing Table Post Offset-List with the ISDN Line Active After the Frame Relay Network Has Been Restored*

```
R1#sh ip route
R    172.16.0.0/16 [120/1] via 10.90.90.1, 00:00:09, Serial0/0
     10.0.0.0/8 is variably subnetted, 16 subnets, 5 masks
R       10.8.8.8/32 [120/4] via 10.100.100.2, 00:00:28, Serial0/1.101
C       10.10.10.2/32 is directly connected, BRI0/0
C       10.100.100.0/28 is directly connected, Serial0/1.101
R       10.99.99.0/29 [120/2] via 10.100.100.2, 00:00:28, Serial0/1.101
R       10.60.60.0/29 [120/2] via 10.100.100.2, 00:00:28, Serial0/1.101
R       10.50.50.0/29 [120/4] via 10.100.100.2, 00:00:28, Serial0/1.101
R       10.40.40.0/28 [120/1] via 10.100.100.3, 00:00:28, Serial0/1.101
R       10.7.7.0/28 [120/4] via 10.100.100.2, 00:00:28, Serial0/1.101
R       10.6.6.0/29 [120/2] via 10.100.100.2, 00:00:28, Serial0/1.101
R       10.4.4.0/29 [120/1] via 10.100.100.3, 00:00:28, Serial0/1.101
C       10.80.80.0/24 is directly connected, FastEthernet0/0
C       10.90.90.0/28 is directly connected, Serial0/0
C       10.1.1.0/28 is directly connected, Loopback0
C       10.10.10.0/28 is directly connected, BRI0/0
C       10.90.90.1/32 is directly connected, Serial0/0
R       10.5.5.4/30 [120/4] via 10.100.100.2, 00:00:00, Serial0/1.101

R1#sh isdn hist
--------------------------------------------------------------------------
                          ISDN CALL HISTORY
--------------------------------------------------------------------------
Call History contains all active calls, and a maximum of 100 inactive calls.
```

*continues*

**Example 1-25** *R1 Routing Table Post Offset-List with the ISDN Line Active After the Frame Relay Network Has Been Restored (Continued)*

```
Inactive call data will be retained for a maximum of 15 minutes.
- - - - - - - - - - - - - - - - - - - - - - - - - - - - - - - - - - - - - - - - - - - - - - - - - - - - -
Call    Calling    Called    Remote  Seconds Seconds Seconds Charges
Type    Number     Number    Name    Used    Left    Idle    Units/Currency
- - - - - - - - - - - - - - - - - - - - - - - - - - - - - - - - - - - - - - - - - - - - - - - - - - - - -
Out                2222              92      27      92      0
- - - - - - - - - - - - - - - - - - - - - - - - - - - - - - - - - - - - - - - - - - - - - - - - - - - - -
```

**NOTE**   The routing table output is taken after a Frame Relay failure is restored and the ISDN line is still active. This shows that the ISDN routes are no longer entered into the routing table on R1 because of the increased hop count over this environment. The routing table on R4 will act in exactly the same manner.

- *Configure R1 so that if half of the ISDN traffic to R4 is of an unacceptable quality, the line is automatically disconnected.*

Configure **ppp quality 50** under both R1 and R4 BRI0/0 interfaces, the figure (percentage) is for both incoming and outgoing directions on the interface, PPP will drop the line if the quality falls below 50 percent and initiate a timer before re-establishing the link. If you have configured this correctly, you have scored 1 point.

- *Allow only R1 to dial into R4. Do not use any PPP feature in your solution.*

The question is not seeking configuration of CHAP on both routers as any router configured with the correct CHAP password could emulate R1 and gain access to R4. It is, therefore, required to configure R4 with **isdn caller 1111** if using legacy DDR or **dialer-caller 1111** if using dialer profiles to ensure that only R1, which is connected to the ISDN number 1111, can actually gain access by having R4 check the CLI before answering. You may have automatically assumed this must require CHAP but there is not sufficient detail in the question to suggest that CHAP or PAP is required. These are both also PPP features so it is disallowed anyway. If you have configured this correctly, you have scored 2 points.

**NOTE**   Your ISDN line or simulator must support CLI to test this feature.

- *Do not allow the ISDN to flap if the Frame Relay network goes up and down; only allow the line to be dropped if the Frame Relay connectivity is deemed to be reliable for 90 seconds.*

By default, the ISDN line will be dropped when dialer-watch again has visibility if the networks listed in the dialer watch-list. To ensure the line remains active for 90 seconds the command **dialer watch-disable 90** should be added to the BRI0/0 interface of R1. If you have configured this correctly, you have scored 1 point.

Example 1-26 and Example1-27 show the full final ISDN and relevant RIP configuration required for the ISDN backup on R1 and R4, using a mix of legacy and dialer profile commands.

**Example 1-26**  *R1 Final ISDN and Relevant RIP Configuration*

```
interface BRI0/0
 ip address 10.10.10.1 255.255.255.240
 encapsulation ppp
 dialer watch-disable 90
 dialer string 2222
 dialer watch-group 5
 dialer-group 10
 isdn switch-type basic-net3
 no peer neighbor-route
 ppp quality 50
!
router rip
 version 2
 passive-interface default
 no passive-interface BRI0/0
 offset-list 0 out 2 BRI0/0
 network 10.0.0.0
!
dialer watch-list 5 ip 10.4.4.0 255.255.255.240
dialer watch-list 5 ip 10.40.40.0 255.255.255.240
dialer-list 10 protocol ip deny
```

**Example 1-27**  *R4 Final ISDN and Relevant RIP Configuration*

```
interface BRI0/0
 encapsulation ppp
 isdn switch-type basic-net3
 dialer pool-member 1

!
interface Dialer0
 ip address 10.10.10.2 255.255.255.240
 encapsulation ppp
 dialer pool 1
 dialer-group 10
 ppp quality 50
 dialer-caller 1111
!
router rip
 version 2
 passive-interface default
 no passive-interface Serial0/0.1
 no passive-interface Dialer0
 offset-list 0 out 2 D0
 dialer-list 10 protocol ip permit
```

# Section 4: EGP Protocols (17 Points)

- *Configure BGP as shown in Figure 1-14 with the following peering: R3–R2, R8–R2, R6–R2, R6–R8, R7–R8, R6–R5. Ensure that most suitable interfaces are used to maintain resilience for BGP peering (except for R2 and R3 that use 172.16.0.0/16 addresses for all peering to and from these routers).*

You are required to configure the peering between the BGP autonomous systems as described. You should ensure that **no synchronization** is configured on all IBGP routers (R2, R3, R6, R7, and R8) as BGP in this scenario is not synchronized with the underlying IGP and, hence, it would not be able to advertise transit routes to external autonomous sytems. As requested, you should peer from your loopback interfaces where present to maintain resiliency except for R2 and R3. This requires BGP Multihop on all external BGP connections sourced from the loopbacks because, by default, a BGP speaker drops any UPDATE message from its EBGP peer, unless it is on the same connected network. By adding a number of hops to the command, you can ensure that the peering is achieved regardless of the traffic path taken (**ebgp-multihop 5**). Multihop should be used in conjunction with the **update-source** command to ensure that peering is maintained correctly by making the source IP address used for the BGP session the same as the remote BGP speakers neighbor statement address and not that of the connected interface. If you have configured this correctly as in Example 1-28 through Example 1-32, you have scored 3 points.

**Example 1-28**  *R2 Initial BGP Peering Configuration*

```
router bgp 10
 no synchronization
 neighbor 10.6.6.6 remote-as 100
 neighbor 10.6.6.6 ebgp-multihop 5
 neighbor 10.6.6.6 update-source FastEthernet0/0
 neighbor 10.8.8.8 remote-as 100
 neighbor 10.8.8.8 ebgp-multihop 5
 neighbor 10.8.8.8 update-source FastEthernet0/0
 neighbor 172.16.0.2 remote-as 10
```

**Example 1-29**  *R3 Initial BGP Peering Configuration*

```
router bgp 10
 no synchronization
 neighbor 172.16.0.1 remote-as 10
```

**Example 1-30**  *R5 Initial BGP Peering Configuration*

```
router bgp 1000
 neighbor 10.6.6.6 remote-as 100
 neighbor 10.6.6.6 ebgp-multihop 5
 neighbor 10.6.6.6 update-source Loopback0
```

**Example 1-31**  *R6 Initial BGP Peering Configuration*

```
router bgp 100
 no synchronization
 neighbor 10.8.8.8 remote-as 100
 neighbor 10.8.8.8 update-source Loopback0
 neighbor 10.5.5.5 remote-as 1000
 neighbor 10.5.5.5 update-source Loopback0
 neighbor 10.5.5.5 ebg-multihop 5
 neighbor 172.16.0.1 remote-as 10
 neighbor 172.16.0.1 ebgp-multihop 5
 neighbor 172.16.0.1 update-source Loopback0
```

**NOTE**  There is no **ebg-multihop** required to peer to 10.8.8.8 in AS100 as this is internal BGP (IBGP) and not external BGP (EBGP).

**Example 1-32**  *R7 Initial BGP Peering Configuration*

```
router bgp 100
 no synchronization
 neighbor 10.8.8.8 remote-as 100
 neighbor 10.8.8.8 update-source Loopback0
```

**NOTE**  R8 initial BGP peering configuration is covered in the following question.

 - *Ensure minimal configuration on R8.*

R8 peers to three other routers, two of which belong to the same AS. You can, therefore, take advantage of BGP peer groups to reduce the required configuration for the policies to R6 and R7. You should be aware that full IBGP peering between R8-R7-R6 does not exist. Both R7 and R6 peer to R8 so, as well as running peer-groups, R8 should also be a route-reflector to overcome the IBGP peering problem. If you have configured this correctly as in Example 1-33, you have scored 1 point.

**Example 1-33**  *R8 Initial BGP Peering Configuration*

```
router bgp 100
 no synchronization
 neighbor cisco peer-group
 neighbor cisco remote-as 100
 neighbor cisco update-source Loopback0
 neighbor cisco route-reflector-client
 neighbor 10.6.6.6 peer-group cisco
 neighbor 10.7.7.7 peer-group cisco
```

*continues*

**Example 1-33** *R8 Initial BGP Peering Configuration (Continued)*

```
 neighbor 172.16.0.1 remote-as 10
 neighbor 172.16.0.1 ebgp-multihop 5
 neighbor 172.16.0.1 update-source Loopback0
```

- *Inject the following networks into BGP via new loopback interfaces:*

  *R3: 20.200.200.1/24 and 20.20.20.1/24*

  *R5: 20.20.20.1/24 and 200.20.20.1/24*

  *R7: 30.30.30.30/29*

You should add the loopback interface and address as requested. The loopbacks are advertised into BGP simply with the network command. You should notice that both R3 and R5
will be advertising the same network (more of this later). If you have configured this
correctly as in Example 1-34 through Example 1-36, you have scored 1 point.

**Example 1-34** *R3 Loopback and BGP Advertisement Configuration*

```
interface Loopback1
 ip address 20.20.20.1 255.255.255.0
!
interface Loopback2
 ip address 20.200.200.1 255.255.255.0
!
router bgp 10
 network 20.20.20.0 mask 255.255.255.0
 network 20.200.200.0 mask 255.255.255.0
```

**Example 1-35** *R5 Loopback and BGP Advertisement Configuration*

```
interface Loopback1
 ip address 20.20.20.1 255.255.255.0
!
interface Loopback2
 ip address 200.20.20.1 255.255.255.0
!
router bgp 1000
 network 20.20.20.0 mask 255.255.255.0
 network 200.20.20.0
```

**NOTE**    Network 200.20.20.0 on R5 does not require an explicit **mask** because of being a class C
network. As such, it will automatically summarize on the classfull network boundary if the
**mask** command is omitted.

**Example 1-36**  *R7 Loopback and BGP Advertisement Configuration*

```
interface Loopback1
 ip address 30.30.30.30 255.255.255.248
!
 router bgp 100
  network 30.30.30.24 mask 255.255.255.248
```

Example 1-37 shows a snapshot of the BGP routing tables for all BGP routers at this point in time. You can use this as a quick check to ensure you see the advertised networks correctly on all routers and specifically on R6 before the complex BGP scenarios begin.

**Example 1-37**  **show ip bgp** *Output from Each BGP Router*

```
R2#sh ip bgp
BGP table version is 24, local router ID is 172.16.0.1
Status codes: s suppressed, d damped, h history, * valid, > best, i - internal
Origin codes: i - IGP, e - EGP, ? - incomplete

   Network          Next Hop          Metric LocPrf Weight Path
*>i20.20.20.0/24    172.16.0.2             0    100      0 i
*>i20.200.200.0/24  172.16.0.2             0    100      0 i
*> 30.30.30.24/29   10.6.6.6                              0 100 i
*                   10.8.8.8                              0 100 i
*  200.20.20.0      10.8.8.8                              0 100 1000 i
*>                  10.6.6.6                              0 100 1000 i
R3#sh ip bgp
BGP table version is 20, local router ID is 20.200.200.1
Status codes: s suppressed, d damped, h history, * valid, > best, i - internal
Origin codes: i - IGP, e - EGP, ? - incomplete

   Network          Next Hop          Metric LocPrf Weight Path
*> 20.20.20.0/24    0.0.0.0                0          32768 i
*> 20.200.200.0/24  0.0.0.0                0          32768 i
*>i30.30.30.24/29   10.6.6.6                   100        0 100 i
*>i200.20.20.0      10.6.6.6                   100        0 100 1000 i
R5#sh ip bgp
BGP table version is 13, local router ID is 200.20.20.1
Status codes: s suppressed, d damped, h history, * valid, > best, i - internal
Origin codes: i - IGP, e - EGP, ? - incomplete

   Network          Next Hop          Metric LocPrf Weight Path
*  20.20.20.0/24    10.6.6.6                              0 100 10 i
*>                  0.0.0.0                0          32768 i
*> 20.200.200.0/24  10.6.6.6                              0 100 10 i
*> 30.30.30.24/29   10.6.6.6                              0 100 i
*> 200.20.20.0      0.0.0.0                0          32768 i
R6#sh ip bgp
BGP table version is 5, local router ID is 10.6.6.6
Status codes: s suppressed, d damped, h history, * valid, > best, i - internal
Origin codes: i - IGP, e - EGP, ? - incomplete
```

*continues*

**Example 1-37** show ip bgp *Output from Each BGP Router (Continued)*

```
   Network          Next Hop        Metric LocPrf Weight Path
*> 20.20.20.0/24    172.16.0.1                        0 10 i
*                   10.5.5.5             0            0 1000 i
* i                 172.16.0.1                 100    0 10 i
*> 20.200.200.0/24  172.16.0.1                        0 10 i
* i                 172.16.0.1                 100    0 10 i
*>i30.30.30.24/29   10.7.7.7             0     100    0 i
*> 200.20.20.0      10.5.5.5             0            0 1000 i
R7#sh ip bgp
BGP table version is 18, local router ID is 30.30.30.30
Status codes: s suppressed, d damped, h history, * valid, > best, i - internal
Origin codes: i - IGP, e - EGP, ? - incomplete

   Network          Next Hop        Metric LocPrf Weight Path
*>i20.20.20.0/24    172.16.0.1                 100    0 10 i
*>i20.200.200.0/24  172.16.0.1                 100    0 10 i
*> 30.30.30.24/29   0.0.0.0              0         32768 i
*>i200.20.20.0      10.5.5.5             0     100    0 1000 i
R8#sh ip bgp
BGP table version is 18, local router ID is 10.8.8.8
Status codes: s suppressed, d damped, h history, * valid, > best, i - internal
Origin codes: i - IGP, e - EGP, ? - incomplete

   Network          Next Hop        Metric LocPrf Weight Path
* i20.20.20.0/24    172.16.0.1                 100    0 10 i
*>                  172.16.0.1                        0 10 i
* i20.200.200.0/24  172.16.0.1                 100    0 10 i
*>                  172.16.0.1                        0 10 i
*>i30.30.30.24/29   10.7.7.7             0     100    0 i
*>i200.20.20.0      10.5.5.5             0     100    0 1000 i
```

- *Ensure that R6 BGP routing table prefers to use AS1000 for network 20.20.20.0/24; do not use BGP weight, BGP local preference, MED, neighbor metric related statements, metric manipulation, summarization, or prepending to achieve this. Perform configuration on R6 only.*

When you look at the BGP routing table on R6 as in Example 1-37, you can see that it has a best path to 20.20.20.0/24 from AS10 next hop 172.16.0.1 (R2 propagating the route from R3). It would be very straightforward to manipulate weight or local preference to ensure R6 prefers the same route received from AS1000 (R5), but the question is very strict. You can tell that both routes are EBGP and, hence, the distance to both routes is an Administrative Distance of 20, so why is the route to 172.16.0.1 preferred?

Example 1-37 also shows the routing table on R6. You can see that the IGP metric to neighbor (R2) 172.16.0.1 is 3 compared to that of 208384 to neighbor (R5) 10.5.5.5 and this is why the next hop to network 20.20.20.0/24 on R6 is 172.16.0.1. This is in accordance to Step 8 (prefer the path with the lowest IGP metric to the BGP next hop) in the 13 steps of Best Path Algorithm according to Cisco. You could reduce the IGP metric to R5 down to 0 on R6 by peering directly to the connected ATM interface (10.99.99.2) on R5 from R6 instead of the loopback on R5 from R6. This would ensure that R6 then prefers the route to network 20.20.20.0/24 from R5, but this would infringe how you have been asked to peer in the original BGP setup question. As you can not manipulate favored attributes such as weight, local preference, AS-Path, summarization, or metrics, you are only left with Step 5 (prefer the path with the lowest origin type: IGP is lower than EGP, and EGP is lower than INCOMPLETE). As can be seen in Example 1-38, all routes for network 20.20.20.0/24 have an origin of IGP. As you may only configure R6, you can place an inbound **route-map** for neighbor 172.16.0.1 and change the origin of the received route for network 20.20.20.0/24 on R6. The solution as shown in Example 1-39 changes the origin to "incomplete" but if you have configured it to "external," this is also acceptable. If you have configured this correctly with the resulting BGP routing table on R6 as shown in Example 1-40 and BGP show output for network 20.20.20.0/24 as shown in Example 1-41, you have scored 7 points.

**Example 1-38**  **show ip route** *and* **show ip bgp** *Output*

```
R6#sh ip route
B     200.20.20.0/24 [20/0] via 10.5.5.5, 00:00:38
      20.0.0.0/24 is subnetted, 2 subnets
B        20.200.200.0 [20/0] via 172.16.0.1, 00:00:38
B        20.20.20.0 [20/0] via 172.16.0.1, 00:00:38
R     172.16.0.0/16 [120/3] via 10.100.100.1, 00:00:02, Serial5/0.103
      10.0.0.0/8 is variably subnetted, 16 subnets, 5 masks
D        10.8.8.8/32 [90/156160] via 10.80.80.3, 00:20:29, FastEthernet0/0
R        10.90.90.0/28 [120/2] via 10.100.100.1, 00:00:02, Serial5/0.103
R        10.1.1.0/28 [120/2] via 10.100.100.1, 00:00:03, Serial5/0.103
D        10.7.7.0/28 [90/156160] via 10.60.60.2, 00:20:30, FastEthernet4/0
R        10.40.40.0/28 [120/1] via 10.100.100.3, 00:00:03, Serial5/0.103
R        10.10.10.0/28 [120/1] via 10.100.100.3, 00:00:03, Serial5/0.103
R        10.4.4.0/29 [120/1] via 10.100.100.3, 00:00:03, Serial5/0.103
C        10.100.100.0/28 is directly connected, Serial5/0.103
D        10.50.50.0/29 [90/82944] via 10.99.99.2, 00:21:08, ATM1/0.99
C        10.99.99.0/29 is directly connected, ATM1/0.99
C        10.6.6.0/29 is directly connected, Loopback0
C        10.60.60.0/29 is directly connected, FastEthernet4/0
C        10.80.80.0/28 is directly connected, FastEthernet0/0
C        10.80.80.0/24 is directly connected, FastEthernet0/0
R        10.90.90.1/32 [120/2] via 10.100.100.1, 00:00:04, Serial5/0.103
D        10.5.5.4/30 [90/208384] via 10.99.99.2, 00:21:08, ATM1/0.99
      30.0.0.0/29 is subnetted, 1 subnets
B        30.30.30.24 [200/0] via 10.7.7.7, 00:00:40

R6#sh ip bgp
BGP table version is 7, local router ID is 10.6.6.6
Status codes: s suppressed, d damped, h history, * valid, > best, i - internal
Origin codes: i - IGP, e - EGP, ? - incomplete

   Network          Next Hop            Metric LocPrf Weight Path
*> 20.20.20.0/24    172.16.0.1                          0 10 i
*                   10.5.5.5                 0          0 1000 i
* i                 172.16.0.1                    100   0 10 i
*> 20.200.200.0/24  172.16.0.1                          0 10 i
* i                 172.16.0.1                    100   0 10 i
*>i30.30.30.24/29   10.7.7.7                 0    100   0 i
*> 200.20.20.0      10.5.5.5                 0          0 1000 i
```

**Example 1-39** *R6* **show ip bgp 20.20.20.0** *Output*

```
R6#sh ip bgp 20.20.20.0
BGP routing table entry for 20.20.20.0/24, version 6
Paths: (3 available, best #1, table Default-IP-Routing-Table)
  Advertised to non peer-group peers:
  10.5.5.5 10.8.8.8
  10
    172.16.0.1 (metric 3) from 172.16.0.1 (172.16.0.1)
      Origin IGP, localpref 100, valid, external, best
  1000
    10.5.5.5 (metric 208384) from 10.5.5.5 (200.20.20.1)
      Origin IGP, metric 0, localpref 100, valid, external
  10
    172.16.0.1 (metric 3) from 10.8.8.8 (10.8.8.8)
      Origin IGP, localpref 100, valid, internal
```

**Example 1-40** *R6 Origin Configuration*

```
router bgp 100
neighbor 172.16.0.1 route-map 20.20.20.0 in
!
access-list 2 permit 20.20.20.0
route-map 20.20.20.0 permit 10
 match ip address 2
 set origin incomplete
!
route-map 20.20.20.0 permit 10
```

**Example 1-41** *R6* **show ip bgp** *Output*

```
R6#sh ip bgp
BGP table version is 5, local router ID is 10.6.6.6
Status codes: s suppressed, d damped, h history, * valid, > best, i - internal
Origin codes: i - IGP, e - EGP, ? - incomplete

   Network          Next Hop        Metric LocPrf Weight Path
*> 20.20.20.0/24    10.5.5.5             0             0 1000 i
*                   172.16.0.1                         0 10 ?
* i                 172.16.0.1                  100    0 10 i
*> 20.200.200.0/24  172.16.0.1                         0 10 i
* i                 172.16.0.1                  100    0 10 i
*>i30.30.30.24/29   10.7.7.7             0      100    0 i
*> 200.20.20.0      10.5.5.5             0             0 1000 i
```

**Example 1-42** *R6* **show ip bgp 20.20.20.0** *Output*

```
R6#sh ip bgp 20.20.20.0
BGP routing table entry for 20.20.20.0/24, version 2
Paths: (3 available, best #1, table Default-IP-Routing-Table)
  Advertised to non peer-group peers:
  10.8.8.8 172.16.0.1
  1000
    10.5.5.5 (metric 208384) from 10.5.5.5 (10.5.5.5)
```

**Example 1-42** *R6* **show ip bgp 20.20.20.0** *Output (Continued)*

```
        Origin IGP, metric 0, localpref 100, valid, external, best
   10
     172.16.0.1 (metric 3) from 172.16.0.1 (172.16.0.1)
       Origin incomplete, localpref 100, valid, external
   10
     172.16.0.1 (metric 3) from 10.8.8.8 (10.8.8.8)
       Origin IGP, localpref 100, valid, internal
```

- *All BGP speakers are to be able to communicate with all advertised BGP networks.*

The BGP routes are in the BGP speakers routing tables so you should be able to ping the BGP networks, but can you? Without further configuration the answer is no. It should be painfully obvious that not all your routers are running BGP. You have not been requested to redistribute BGP into your IGP, so R1 and R4 will have no knowledge of any BGP networks. Example 1-43 shows what happens if you attempt to ping 30.30.30.30 from R2.

**Example 1-43** *R2 Show IP Route Output and Connectivity Testing*

```
R2#sh ip route 30.30.30.30
 Routing entry for 30.30.30.24/29
   Known via "bgp 10", distance 20, metric 0
   Tag 100, type external
   Last update from 10.6.6.6 00:28:44 ago
   Routing Descriptor Blocks:
   * 10.6.6.6, from 10.6.6.6, 00:28:44 ago
       Route metric is 0, traffic share count is 1
       AS Hops 1
R2#ping 30.30.30.30
Type escape sequence to abort.
Sending 5, 100-byte ICMP Echos to 30.30.30.30, timeout is 2 seconds:
U.U.U
Success rate is 0 percent (0/5)
```

As you can see in Example 1-43, R2 obviously has a route to the destination address 30.30.30.30 but R2 is receiving ICMP unreachable messages from R1 as R1 does not have visibility of network 30.30.30.24/29 and, hence, is dropping the packets and informing R2. Example 1-44 shows R1 and R4 have no visibility of the BGP networks.

**Example 1-44** *R1 and R4 IGP out of Sync* **show output** *and R2 Traceroute*

```
R1#sh ip route 30.30.30.30
% Network not in table
R4#sh ip route 30.30.30.30
% Network not in table
R2#traceroute 30.30.30.30

Type escape sequence to abort.
Tracing the route to 30.30.30.30

  1 10.90.90.2 4 msec 4 msec 4 msec
  2 10.90.90.2 !H  *   !H
```

You, therefore, need to policy route at R1 and R4 for the specific BGP routes at these routers as shown in Example 1-45 and Example 1-46.

**Example 1-45** *R1 Required Policy-Routing Configuration*

```
interface Serial0/0
 ip policy route-map as100-1000
 !
interface Serial0/1.101 point-to-point
ip policy route-map as10
 !
route-map as100-1000 permit 10
 match ip address 102
 set ip next-hop 10.100.100.2
 !
route-map as10 permit 10
 match ip address 101
 set ip next-hop 10.90.90.1
 !
access-list 101 permit ip any 20.200.200.0 0.0.0.255
access-list 102 permit ip any 30.30.30.24 0.0.0.7
access-list 102 permit ip any 200.20.20.0 0.0.0.255
```

**NOTE**   Two separate route-maps are shown in Example 1-45 for traffic flowing towards network 20.200.200.0, which should be forwarded onto R2 and traffic flowing toward 30.30.30.0 and 200.20.20.0, which should be forwarded onto R6. No requirement exists to policy route traffic across the BRI on R1 or R4 as ISDN should only be used for the requirements stated in the questions.

No requirement exists to policy route traffic destined for network 20.20.20.0/24 on R1 as traffic will stay local to AS10 between R2 and R3 and never attempt to flow through R1. Similarly, R1 will never receive traffic destined for network 20.20.20.0/24 from AS100 as the preferred route will be to AS1000 R5 via R6.

**Example 1-46** *R4 Required Policy-Routing Configuration*

```
interface Serial0/0.1 multipoint
ip policy route-map as10
 !
route-map as10 permit 10
 match ip address 101
 set ip next-hop 10.100.100.1
 !
route-map as10 permit 20
 match ip address 102
 set ip next-hop 10.100.100.2
 !
access-list 101 permit ip any 20.200.200.0 0.0.0.255
access-list 102 permit ip any 200.20.20.0 0.0.0.255
access-list 102 permit ip any 30.30.30.24 0.0.0.7
```

**NOTE**

Example 1-46 shows two separate route-map sequences for traffic flowing toward network 20.200.200.0, which should be forwarded onto R2, and traffic flowing toward 30.30.30.0 and 200.20.20.0, which should be forwarded onto R6.

No requirement exists to policy route traffic destined for network 20.20.20.0/24 on R4 as R6 will never send traffic to R4 destined for this network as it has a more preferable route to R5.

You should notice that both R7 and R8 show the next hop to 20.20.20.0/24 as 172.16.0.1. Traffic would egress R7 and R8 toward R2 172.16.0.1 and flow through R6 en route to R2, R6 would then send this to R5 as it is its own preferred route to 20.20.20.0/24. You therefore could consider policy routing at R6 for traffic sourced from R7 and R8 toward network 20.20.20.0/24. If you have configured this, it was a prudent action but the question did not ask you to accomplish this so no extra points or more, importantly, none deducted. You should seek advice from the proctor if an issue like this arises in your real exam, though. If you have configured this correctly as in Example 1-45 and Example 1-46, you have scored 5 points.

# Section 5: Voice (6 Points)

- *Both phones should be able to ring each other using the numbers supplied. Use the most efficient method of transporting the voice from R1 to R4.*

Did you jump straight in with Voice over IP (VoIP)? VoIP is not the most efficient means of transporting voice between R1 and R4 as they have a dedicated Frame Relay connection between them. If you were to use VoIP, the voice would have to be encapsulated into IP and then into Frame Relay before it is even transmitted. The most efficient method is therefore to encapsulate directly into Frame Relay using Voice over Frame Relay (VoFR). VoFR requires a **map-class** on the Frame Relay DLCI. Otherwise, it will break the existing data connectivity between R1 and R4, so pay particular attention to the commands, which must include **frame-relay fragment** and under the physical Frame Relay interface, you must configure the command **frame-relay traffic shaping**. The **dial-peers** for the remote site numbers simply point to the DLCIs between R1 and R4. Ensure you configure the command **frame-relay voice bandwidth** under the Frame Relay **map-class** on routers R1 and R4; otherwise, your voice will not work. This value could be calculated exactly using the standard voice codec g729r8 with associated overhead and the number of required calls but the question does not request this. If you configured this correctly as in Example 1-47 and Example 1-48, you have scored 3 points. If you succeeded in the VoFR but have broken the data connectivity, you have scored no points.

**Example 1-47** *R1 Voice and VoFR Configuration*

```
interface Serial0/1
 frame-relay traffic-shaping
 !
interface Serial0/1.101 point-to-point
 frame-relay  interface-dlci 101
  class ccie
  vofr cisco
 !
map-class frame-relay ccie
 frame-relay fair-queue
 frame-relay voice bandwidth 64000
 frame-relay fragment
 !
dial-peer voice 1 pots
 destination-pattern 01256
 port 1/0/0
 !
dial-peer voice 2 vofr
 destination-pattern 01189
 session target Serial0/1 101
```

**Example 1-48** *R4 Voice and VoFR Configuration*

```
interface Serial0/0
   frame-relay traffic-shaping
 !
interface Serial0/0.1 multipoint
frame-relay interface-dlci 100
   class ccie
   vofr cisco
 no frame-relay inverse-arp
 !
map-class frame-relay ccie
frame-relay fair-queue
 frame-relay voice bandwidth 64000
frame-relay fragment
 !
dial-peer voice 1 pots
 destination-pattern 01189
 port 1/1/0
 !
dial-peer voice 2 vofr
 destination-pattern 01256
 session target Serial0/0 100
```

- *Ensure that voice is still available if the main connection between R1 and R4 fails.*

It is now time to configure VoIP, because if the Frame Relay network fails, you will need to run voice over the ISDN network between R1 and R4. The only method available to you is VoIP. Additional dial-peers are required each end pointing to the loopback IP addresses of each remote router. You must ensure that the VoFR is used before the VoIP so you will need to allocate a preference to the dial-peers. The lowest number dial-peers will have preference so it is advised that the VoFR dial-peers should be configured before the VoIP. Alternatively the VoIP dial-peers can have a priority manually configured higher than the default 0, which ensures if your dial-peer numbering is out of sync, the router still chooses VoFR before VoIP. Both methods of priority have been shown in the configuration for clarity. If you have configured this correctly as in Example 1-49 and Example 1-50, you have scored 2 points.

**Example 1-49**  *R1 VoIP Configuration*

```
dial-peer voice 3 voip
 preference 5
 destination-pattern 01189
 session target ipv4:10.4.4.4
```

**Example 1-50**  *R4 VoIP Configuration*

```
dial-peer voice 3 voip
 preference 5
 destination-pattern 01256
 session target ipv4:10.1.1.1
```

- *Make the phone on R1 also answer calls if 01962 is dialed on the R4 connected handsets; do not use number expansion to achieve this.*

You are required to simply add additional dial-peers for 01962 on R4 (both VoFR and VoIP) pointing to R1, and then configure R1 with an additional dial-peer POTS pointing to the original FXS phone port, which currently contains 01256. If you have configured this correctly as in Example 1-51 and Example 1-52, you have scored 1 point.

**Example 1-51**  *R1 01962 Configuration*

```
dial-peer voice 6 pots
 destination-pattern 01962
 port 1/0/0
```

**Example 1-52**  *R4 01962 Configuration*

```
dial-peer voice 4 VoFR
 destination-pattern 01962
 session target Serial0/0 100
!
dial-peer voice 5 voip
 preference 5
 destination-pattern 01962
 session target ipv4:10.1.1.1
```

# Section 6: DLSw+ (4 Points)

- *Configure DLSw+ between VLAN2 and VLAN4; use routers R8 and R5. Peer from Lo0 on R8 and the VLAN4 interface on R5; ensure that R8 can accept DLSw+ connections from only unknown TCP peers.*

Peer as requested from Lo0 on R8 and configure this peer as promiscuous with TCP for the future connections. Configure R5 as requested and configure your bridging parameters to ensure the required connectivity. You should be concerned about this question; it is too easy and this should be ringing alarm bells. If you have configured this correctly as in Example 1-53 and Example 1-54, you have scored 2 points.

**Example 1-53** *R5 Iinitial DLSw+ Configuration and* **show output**

```
dlsw local-peer peer-id 10.50.50.1
dlsw remote-peer 0 tcp 10.8.8.8
dlsw bridge-group 1
!
interface FastEthernet0/0
bridge-group 1
!
bridge 1 protocol ieee

R5#sh dlsw peer
Peers:              state      pkts_rx   pkts_tx  type  drops ckts TCP   uptime
  TCP 10.8.8.8      CONNECT    11914     11344    conf    0    0    0    3d22h
Total number of connected peers: 1
Total number of connections:    1
```

**Example 1-54** *R8 DLSw+ Connectivity and* **show output**

```
dlsw local-peer peer-id 10.8.8.8 promiscuous
dlsw bridge-group 1
!
interface FastEthernet0/0
bridge-group 1
!
bridge 1 protocol ieee

R8#sh dlsw peer
Peers:              state      pkts_rx   pkts_tx  type  drops ckts TCP   uptime
  TCP 10.50.50.1    CONNECT    11346     11916    prom    0    0    0    3d23h
Total number of connected peers: 1
Total number of connections:    1
```

- *Set up a one-line filter, which only allows common SNA traffic to egress from R5 VLAN4 into the DLSw+ network.*

You are required to configure **lsap-output-list**, which allows only the SNA common traffic listed under access-list 200 to egress the DLSw+ connection to R8 on R5. If you have configured this correctly as in Example 1-55, you have scored 2 points.

**Example 1-55** *R5 LSAP Filter Configuration*

```
dlsw remote-peer 0 tcp 10.8.8.8 lsap-output-list 200
!
access-list 200 permit 0x0000 0x0D0D
```

# Section 7: IOS and IP Features (10 Points)

- *R2 is sited in a shared data center; make the serial link back into R1 as secure as possible at Layer 2.*

Did you think about IP Security (IPsec)? Well that is Layer 3; as is any form of access-list, you should realize that PPP is Layer 2 and this protocol has the capability to run CHAP over it, which makes the serial link very secure. PPP with CHAP over a serial link is just as happy as PPP over ISDN; the configuration is exactly the same. If you have configured this correctly as in Example 1-56 and Example 1-57, you have scored 2 points. Example 1-58 shows CHAP in action over the serial link.

**Example 1-56** *R1 Serial Line PPP CHAP Configuration*

```
username disco password 0 cisco
!
interface Serial0/0
 ip address 10.90.90.2 255.255.255.240
 encapsulation ppp
 clockrate 2000000
 ppp authentication chap
 ppp chap hostname misco
```

**Example 1-57** *R2 Serial Line PPP CHAP Configuration*

```
username misco password 0 cisco
!
interface Serial0/0
 ip address 10.90.90.1 255.255.255.240
 encapsulation ppp
 ppp authentication chap
 ppp chap hostname disco
```

**Example 1-58** **R1 debug ppp authentication** *Output*

```
R1#debug ppp authentication
PPP authentication debugging is on
3d23h: Se0/0 PPP: Treating connection as a dedicated line
3d23h: %LINK-3-UPDOWN: Interface Serial0/0, changed state to up
3d23h: Se0/0 CHAP: Using alternate hostname misco
3d23h: Se0/0 CHAP: O CHALLENGE id 2 len 26 from "misco"
```

*continues*

**Example 1-58**  *R1* **debug ppp authentication** *Output (Continued)*

```
3d23h: Se0/0 CHAP: I CHALLENGE id 5 len 26 from "disco"
3d23h: Se0/0 CHAP: Using alternate hostname misco
3d23h: Se0/0 CHAP: O RESPONSE id 5 len 26 from "misco"
3d23h: Se0/0 CHAP: I RESPONSE id 2 len 26 from "disco"
3d23h: Se0/0 CHAP: O SUCCESS id 2 len 4
3d23h: Se0/0 CHAP: I SUCCESS id 5 len 4
3d23h: %LINEPROTO-5-UPDOWN: Line protocol on Interface Serial0/0, changed state to
up
```

- *Ensure traffic from VLAN4, including any attached router interfaces to VLAN4, is hidden behind R5 Lo0 address when directed toward all external router networks.*

The question requires NAT configuration from VLAN4 R5 FastEthernet0/0 to all external networks egressing from R5 ATM3/0. The configuration is not complex so this should start the alarm bells ringing again. Where else did you hear them? The DLSw+ was not difficult so it may be worth checking as this does not break any previous connectivity. In fact, you should get into the habit of frequently checking your work to ensure your points are still safe.

With NAT enabled, R5's VLAN4 interface will NAT from the original source address 10.50.50.1 into source address 10.5.5.5; this will affect the DLSw+ peering that has been configured. When DLSW+ initiates, two connections are set up between the routers; after a capabilities exchange, the router with the lowest peer IP address has its connection dropped with the other maintained. Originally R5 (10.50.50.1) had a higher peer IP address than R8 (10.8.8.8), so it dropped the connection to R8. Now R5 has been NAT'd into source address 10.5.5.5; however, R5 still uses the source address 10.50.50.1 for its peering and drops the connection to R8 believing it is lower than its own source address. R8, as it is promiscuous, sees a connection coming in from 10.5.5.5 and then drops the connection, which is lower than its own peer address of 10.8.8.8. You can imagine that the DLSW+ will never peer correctly now with both peers dropping their connections as shown in Example 1-59. The only way to overcome this is by excluding the actual DLSw+ process from the NAT. To do this you will have to know that DLSw+ over TCP uses ports 2065 and 2067 for read and write; these should, therefore, not be NAT'd. You could gain the port information from an appropriate debug but ideally you should know this. If you have configured this correctly as in Example 1-60, you have scored 3 points.

**Example 1-59**  *R5* **debug dlsw** *Output*

```
R5#debug dlsw
4w0d: DLSw: START-TPFSM (peer 10.8.8.8(2065)): event:DLX-KEEPALIVE REQ
state:CONNECT
4w0d: DLSw: dtp_action_q() keepalive request from peer 10.8.8.8(2065)
4w0d: DLSw: Keepalive Response sent to peer 10.8.8.8(2065))
4w0d: DLSw: END-TPFSM (peer 10.8.8.8(2065)): state:CONNECT->CONNECT
4w0d: DLSw: dlsw_tcpd_fini() for peer 10.8.8.8(2065)
4w0d: DLSw: tcp fini closing connection for peer 10.8.8.8(2065)
```

**Example 1-59** *R5* **debug dlsw** *Output (Continued)*

```
4w0d: DLSw: START-TPFSM (peer 10.8.8.8(2065)): event:ADMIN-CLOSE CONNECTION
  state:CONNECT
4w0d: DLSw: dtp_action_b() close connection for peer 10.8.8.8(2065)
4w0d: DLSw: END-TPFSM (peer 10.8.8.8(2065)): state:CONNECT->DISCONN
```

**Example 1-60** *R5 Required NAT Modification Configuration*

```
interface FastEthernet0/0
 ip address 10.50.50.1 255.255.255.248
 ip nat inside
interface ATM3/0
 ip address 10.99.99.2 255.255.255.248
 ip nat outside
!
ip nat inside source list 100 interface Loopback0 overload
!
access-list 100 deny   tcp host 10.50.50.1 eq 2065 host 10.8.8.8
access-list 100 deny   tcp host 10.50.50.1 eq 2067 host 10.8.8.8
access-list 100 deny   tcp host 10.50.50.1 host 10.8.8.8 eq 2065
access-list 100 deny   tcp host 10.50.50.1 host 10.8.8.8 eq 2067
access-list 100 permit ip 10.50.50.0 0.0.0.255 any
```

- *A router is to be installed onto VLAN4 in the future. This router will have a default configuration, so allow R6 to assist dynamically to aid the configuration process. The router will require an IP address of 10.50.50.6 and should load a configuration file called R9-config from a fictitious TFTP server on 172.16.0.59.*

The question requires that AutoInstall is used. This is a recent feature, which allows you to place a router with a default configuration onto a network, and it can be configured dynamically by receiving a DHCP address and TFTP server location for its own valid configuration. R6 is required to issue the DHCP address, TFTP server details, and **default-router** of R5 (10.50.50.1) that the router requires to contact the TFTP server on 172.16.0.59. The DHCP pool configuration on R6 excludes the majority of host addresses for network 10.50.50.0/29; this ensures that the only address offered to DHCP request is 10.50.50.6. You should notice that R6 is not connected to VLAN4 and AutoInstall works by DHCP request; for this reason, you must configure a **helper-address** on R5 to forward the request to R6. If you have configured this correctly as shown in Example 1-61 and Example 1-62, you have scored 5 points.

**Example 1-61** *R6 Required Configuration for AutoInstall*

```
service dhcp
!
ip dhcp excluded-address 10.50.50.1 10.50.50.5
!
ip dhcp pool 1
   network 10.50.50.0 255.255.255.248
   bootfile R9-config
   option 150 ip 172.16.0.59
   default-router 10.50.50.1
!
```

**Example 1-62**  *R5 VLAN4 DHCP Relay Configuration*

```
interface FastEthernet0/0
 ip address 10.50.50.1 255.255.255.248
 ip helper-address 10.6.6.6
```

# Section 8: QoS (8 Points)

- *Achieve maximum quality of voice calls by ensuring the real-time packet interval of 10 ms is not exceeded. Do not use RSVP in your solution.*

This question requires that fragmentation is used over the Frame Relay and ISDN networks that will transport voice traffic. You should remember that voice is still required should the Frame Relay network fail. By fragmenting the data, you can tailor the packet interval and ensure that voice quality is not compromised over low bandwidth links. Some basic math is required to calculate the current real-time packet interval over the Frame Relay and ISDN network to begin as detailed in Table 1-3. Note the Frame Relay speed is 256 kbps and the ISDN is 64 kbps using only one B channel.

**Table 1-3**  *MTU Values According to Bandwidth*

|  | Frame Relay (256 kbps) | ISDN (64 kbps) |
|---|---|---|
| No. Bytes TX'd per second | 32,000 | 8,000 |
| No. of bytes TX'd in 10ms | **320** | **80** |

As Table 1-3 shows, 32,000 are bytes transmitted every second over the Frame Relay circuit (256,000 divided by 8) if the real-time delay or serialization delay is to be 10 ms; 320 bytes can be transmitted in this period (32,000 * 10 ms). Similarly, 80 bytes can be transmitted for the ISDN with the circuit speed of 64 kbps.

After you have calculated that 320 bytes will be transmitted over the Frame Relay network and 80 bytes over the ISDN in the 10 ms interval, you can adjust the interface MTU to reflect this for the ISDN and then change the **frame-relay fragmentation** to **320** under the VoFR map-class on both R1 and R4. If you have configured this correctly as shown in Example 1-63 and Example 1-64, you have scored 4 points.

**Example 1-63**  *R1 QOS MTU Configuration*

```
interface BRI0/0
 ip mtu 80
!
map-class frame-relay ccie
 frame-relay fragment 320
```

**Example 1-64**  *R4 QOS MTU Configuration*

```
interface BRI0/0
 ip mtu 80
!
map-class frame-relay ccie
 frame-relay fragment 320
```

- *To reduce the packet fragmentation in your network, allow R5 to determine appropriate fragmentation requirements when TCP sessions are originated from it to any part of the network.*

R5 should be configured with the global command **ip tcp path-mtu-discovery**. If you have configured this correctly, you have scored 2 points.

# Section 9: Multicast (4 Points)

- *Enable your network to allow hosts on VLAN4 to receive and send multicast traffic from and to VLAN2; only perform configuration on R5 and R6 using PIM sparse dense mode.*

This question simply requires basic multicast setup between R5 and R6 using PIM **sparse-dense-mode**. If you have configured this correctly as shown in Example 1-65 and Example 1-66, you have scored 1 point.

**Example 1-65**  *R5 Multicast Configuration*

```
ip multicast-routing
!
interface FastEthernet0/0
 ip pim sparse-dense-mode
!
interface ATM3/0
 ip pim sparse-dense-mode
```

**Example 1-66**  *R6 Multicast Configuration*

```
ip multicast-routing
!
interface FastEthernet0/0
 ip pim sparse-dense-mode
!
interface ATM1/0.99 point-to-point
 ip pim sparse-dense-mode
```

- *Configure R6 to respond to pings from R5 to the multicast address of 224.4.4.4.*

Configure **ip igmp join-group 224.4.4.4** under R6 fastEthernet0/0. If you have configured this correctly, you have scored 1 point.

- *Do not allow R5 to fully participate in the PIM process by not allowing it to become a neighbor but do allow any IGMP messages generated by hosts on VLAN4 to be received by R6.*

This question requires Stub Multicast Routing. This allows you to configure remote/stub routers as IGMP proxy agents. The stub router does not fully participating in PIM and, hence, is not seen as a PIM neighbor; access-list 11 blocks the neighbor. If you have configured this correctly as in Example 1-67, you have scored 2 points.

**Example 1-67** *R6 Stub Multicast Configuration*

```
interface ATM1/0.99 point-to-point
 ip pim neighbor-filter 11
!
access-list 11 deny    10.99.99.2
```

# How Did You Do?

With the aid of the answers section, full configurations, and routing tables on the CD, you should now have an accurate evaluation of your lab. If you scored more than 80 points within the time frame, you should congratulate yourself; you are well on the way to becoming a CCIE, you have demonstrated the ability to think laterally and shown an impressive knowledge of your subject. If you scored less than 80 don't worry, this will improve as you progress throughout the book and learn how to analyze each question and improve your core skills.

Did you spot the landmines in the lab? The classics in Lab 1 where EIGRP neighbor issues, the ISDN line staying up, the BGP requiring policy routing, and the NAT breaking DLSw+, ideally you should be able to spot these before configuration and factor them in; if not, it shows you how important it is to read the paper thoroughly and ensure everything works over and over again after configuration.

This is not to say that in the real exam there will be any items that could catch you out, but by being on your guard, you will ensure that your quality of work is far higher.

You might feel that the questions were too vague or you did not have sufficient time to complete the lab but this is what you will be met with when you open your folder containing your real exam at the test center; your ability to spot landmines (if present), ask the right questions, and configuration speed will improve as you tackle each practice lab.

For each question that you did not answer correctly, take the time to research the subject thoroughly and turn your weaknesses into your strengths. This with plenty of practice is how ultimately you will gain your number.

# Further Reading/URLs

To better prepare yourself and follow up on the topics covered in this lab, you should consult the http://www.cisco.com/public/pubsearch.html website for more information on the following topics:

- 3550 802.1X
- EIGRP Stub Routing
- Dialer-Watch
- PPP Link Quality
- DLSW Filtering SNA
- DLSw and NAT
- AutoInstall
- PIM Neighbor Filtering

# CHAPTER 2

# Practice Lab 2

Each lab has a time constraint of eight hours and a point scale weighting of 100; you will need to score at least 80 marks to pass. The lab has been designed to challenge you in areas that you will find in the real exam with each lab having a distinct theme to enhance your study plan with Lab 2's being Open Shortest Path First (OSPF).

You will, of course, find the old favorites such as BGP, DLSw+, and voice; however, a complete understanding of OSPF will earn you extra points in this lab.

Aim to adhere to the eight-hour time limit on this lab on the initial run through and then either score yourself at this point or continue until you feel you have met all the objectives. Keep a note of your score to plot your progress throughout the book and remember you are aiming to improve your technical knowledge, speed, and examination technique. The sections that follow guide you through the equipment requirements and pre-lab tasks in preparation for taking practice Lab 2.

## Equipment List

You will need the following hardware and software components to commence Lab 2.

- Eight routers are required loaded with Cisco IOS Software Release 12.2-16 Enterprise image and the minimum interface configuration as documented in Table 2-1. Routers R1 and R4 must be either 1700, 2600, 3600, or 3700 variants to complete the voice section in this lab.

**Table 2-1**    *Interfaces Required per Router*

| Router | Ethernet Interface | Serial Interface | BRI Interface | Voice | ATM Interface |
|--------|--------------------|------------------|---------------|-------|---------------|
| R1 | 1 | 2 | 1 | 1 X FXS | - |
| R2 | 1 | 1 | - | - | - |
| R3 | 1 | - | - | - | - |
| R4 | 1 | 1 | 1 | 1 X FXS | - |
| R5 | 1 | 3 | - | - | 1 |

*continues*

**Table 2-1** *Interfaces Required per Router (Continued)*

| Router | Ethernet Interface | Serial Interface | BRI Interface | Voice | ATM Interface |
|--------|--------------------|------------------|---------------|-------|---------------|
| R6 | 2 | 1 | - | - | 1 |
| R7 | 1 | - | - | - | - |
| R8 | 1 | - | - | - | - |

**NOTE**    Lab 2 was produced with Routers R1, R2, R3, R4, R7, and R8 using 2600s and R5 and R6 using 7200s.

- One Switch 3550 with Cisco IOS Software Release 12.1(12c) enterprise: c3550-i5q3l2-mz.121-12c.EA1.bin

# Setting Up the Lab

Feel free to use any combination of routers as long as you fulfill the topology diagram as shown in Figure 2-1. It is not compulsory to use the same model of routers but this will make life easier should you like to load configurations directly from the CD-ROM into your own devices.

**NOTE**    For each lab in the book, you will have a set of initial configuration files that can be different from each other. Notice that some interfaces will not have the IP address preconfigured because you will either not be using that interface on that specific lab or because you will need to work on this interface through the exercise. The initial configurations can be found on the CD-ROM and should be used to preconfigure your routers and switch before the lab starts.

If you use the same equipment as used to produce the lab, you can simply paste the configurations into your own equipment. If not, just configure your own equipment accordingly using the information supplied within the initial configurations.

Labs 1 through 3 in this book have been completed using 100-Mbps Fast Ethernet interfaces; so if you have a mix of 10- and 100-Mbps Ethernet interfaces, adjust the bandwidth statements on the relevant interfaces to keep all interface speeds common. This will ensure that you do not get unwanted behavior because of differing IGP metrics.

## Lab Topology

Practice Lab 2 uses the topology as outlined in Figure 2-1, which you need to create using the switch, Frame Relay, ATM, and ISDN information that follows.

**Figure 2-1**    *Lab 2 Topology Diagram*

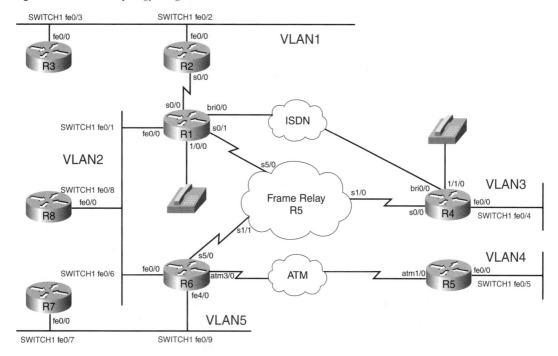

## Cabling Instructions

Follow the cabling requirements as outlined in Figure 2-2 and Table 2-2 to connect your routers to the switch.

**Figure 2-2**    *3550 Cabling Diagram*

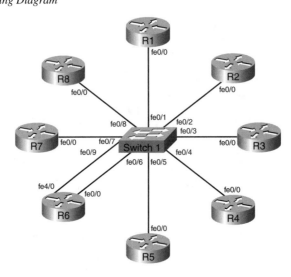

**Table 2-2**    *3550 Cabling Guide*

| Ethernet Cabling | Switch1 Port Number |
| --- | --- |
| R1-Fast Ethernet0/0 | Port 0/1 |
| R2-Fast Ethernet0/0 | Port 0/2 |
| R3-Fast Ethernet0/0 | Port 0/3 |
| R4-Fast Ethernet0/0 | Port 0/4 |
| R5-Fast Ethernet0/0 | Port 0/5 |
| R6-Fast Ethernet0/0 | Port 0/6 |
| R7-Fast Ethernet0/0 | Port 0/7 |
| R8-Fast Ethernet0/0 | Port 0/8 |
| R6-Fast Ethernet4/0 | Port 0/9 |

# Frame Relay Switch Instructions

The Frame Relay portion of the lab is achieved by following the physical connectivity using R5 as a Frame Relay switch as shown in Figure 2-3.

**Figure 2-3**    *Frame Relay Switch Physical Connectivity*

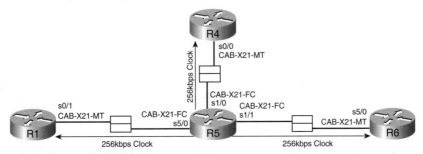

The physical Frame Relay connectivity (after configuration) will represent the logical Frame Relay network as shown in Figure 2-4.

**Figure 2-4**    *Frame Relay Switch Logical Connectivity*

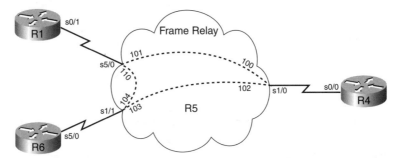

Configure one of your routers as a Frame Relay switch or have a dedicated router purely for this task. The first three lab scenarios use R5 to form the Frame Relay switch, and a fully meshed environment is configured between R1-R4-R6, so pay attention in the lab to which permanent vitual circuits (PVCs) are actually required. Keep the encapsulation and Local Management Interface (LMI) settings to default for this exercise but experiment with the settings outside the labs.

Keep your data communications equipment (DCE) cables at the Frame Relay switch end for simplicity and provide a clock rate of 256 kbps to all links. Should you require detailed information on how to configure one of your routers as a Frame Relay switch, this information can be found in Appendix A, "Frame Relay Switch Configuration."

**NOTE**    The Frame Relay switch configuration for R5 is supplied on the CD-ROM if required.

## ATM Switch Instructions

The ATM portion of the lab is achieved by following the physical connectivity between R5 and R6 as shown in Figure 2-5.

**Figure 2-5** *ATM Physical Connectivity*

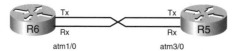

The physical ATM connectivity will, after configuration, represent the logical ATM network as shown in Figure 2-6.

**Figure 2-6** *ATM Logical Connectivity*

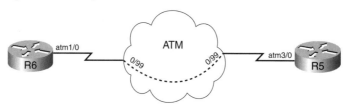

The ATM connectivity in Labs 1-3 will be provided by back-to-back connections between R6 and R5 over E3 ATM interfaces; you could also use a LightStream if available. Configure the PVCs as requested during the lab exercise. If you are using a LightStream to provide your ATM connectivity and require information on how to set this up, this information can be found in Appendix B, "LS1010 ATM Switch Configuration."

## Serial Back-to-Back Instructions

R1 and R2 are connected back-to-back with serial cables as shown in Figure 2-7. Ensure that the DCE cable is connected to R1 and generate a 2 Mbps clock from this point if using X21 cables as shown or reduce this to suit your own serial interfaces such as 1.5 Mbps for T1 connectivity.

**Figure 2-7** *Serial Connectivity*

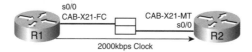

## ISDN Instructions

Connect R1 and R4 into either ISDN lines or an ISDN simulator. It is preferable that the ISDN supports CLI. Reconfigure the numbers as required if you are using live ISDN lines.

The lab has been produced using BRI S/T interfaces on R1 and R4 as shown in Figure 2-8.

**Figure 2-8** *ISDN Connectivity*

## IP Address Instructions

Configure the IP addresses as shown in Figure 2-9 or load the initial router configurations for Lab 2 that can be found on the CD-ROM. If manually configuring, ensure you include the following loopback addresses:

R1 Lo0 10.1.1.1/28
R4 Lo0 10.4.4.4/29
R5 Lo0 10.5.5.5/30
R6 Lo0 10.6.6.6/29
R8 Lo0 10.8.8.8/32

---

**NOTE**      R7 FastEthernet 0/0 has been assigned an IP address of 10.50.50.2/29 in the initial configuration and is physically connected into VLAN5, which is network 10.60.60.0/29; this is the required configuration for the lab.

---

# Pre-Lab Tasks

- Build the lab topology as per Figure 2-1 and Figure 2-2.

- Configure your chosen Frame Relay switch router to provide the necessary Data Link Control Identifiers (DLCIs) as per Figure 2-4 or load the Frame Relay switch configuration from the CD-ROM.

- Configure the IP addresses on each router as shown in Figure 2-9 and add the loopback addresses (do not configure the Frame Relay or ATM IP addresses yet as you will need to select interface types within the lab beforehand); alternatively, you can load the initial configuration files from the CD-ROM.

**Figure 2-9**    *IP Addressing Diagram*

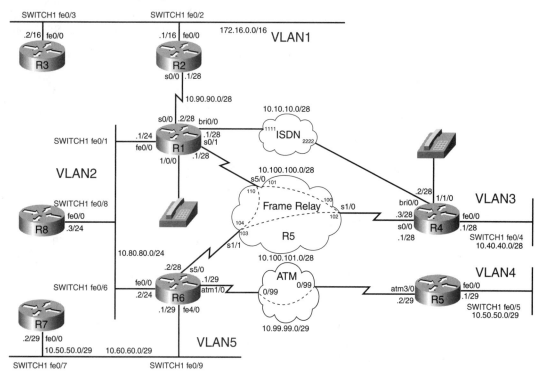

- Configure passwords on all devices for console and vty access to "cisco" if not loading the initial configuration files.

- If you find yourself running out of time, choose questions that you are confident you can answer correctly. Failing this approach, choose questions with a higher point rating to maximize your potential score.

- Get into a comfortable and quiet environment where you can focus for the next eight hours.

# General Guidelines

- Please read the whole lab before you start.
- Do not configure any static/default or policy routes unless otherwise specified.
- Use only the DLCIs and ATM PVCs provided in the appropriate figures.
- Ensure full IP visibility between routers for ping testing/telnet access to your devices with an exception to VLAN5.
- Take a 30-minute break midway through the exercise.
- Have available a Cisco Documentation CD-ROM or access on-line the latest documentation from the following URL: http://www.cisco.com/univercd/home/home.htm

---

**NOTE**    Consider accessing only the preceding URL, not the whole Cisco.com website. If you are allowed to use online documentation during your CCIE lab exam, it will be restricted.

---

# Practice Lab 2

You will now be answering questions in relation to the network topology as shown in Figure 2-10.

**Figure 2-10** *Lab 2 Topology Diagram*

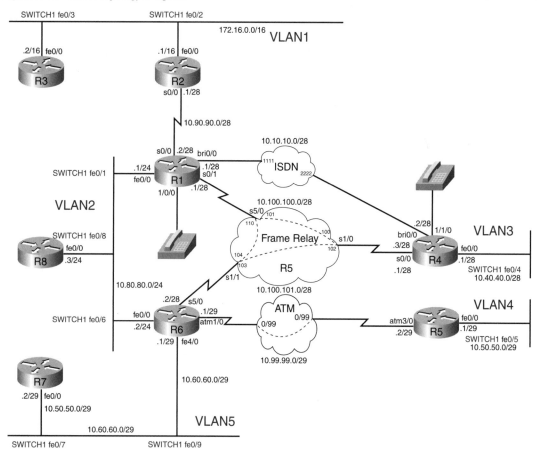

# Section 1: Bridging and Switching (16 Points)

## Section 1.1: Frame Relay Configuration (6 Points)

- Configure the Frame Relay portion of the network as shown in Figure 2-11 and ensure that DLCIs 110 and 104 between R1 and R6 are not used.

- Use point-to-point subinterfaces with a number equal to that of 10 + the listed DLCIs.

- Ensure that the Frame Relay subinterfaces contain purely Layer 2 information, configure virtual Layer 3 addresses elsewhere for the Frame Relay connectivity, and make this connectivity as secure as possible. This configuration does not require any form of bridging.

- For IGP configuration, PVC 103-102 has a CIR of 512 kbps and PVC 101-100 has a CIR of 256 kbps. Use these figures appropriately as an IGP reference for the maximum capacity of the links.

**Figure 2-11**   *Frame Relay Diagram*

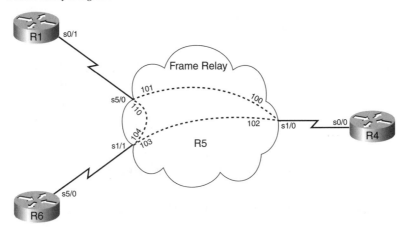

## Section 1.2: 3550 LAN Switch Configuration (9 Points)

- Configure VLAN numbers, VLAN names, and port assignment as per the topology diagram.

- Your customer has decided to test Voice over IP (VoIP) and is trialing Cisco 7960 and 7905 IP phones. The customer wants to take advantage of the auxiliary VLAN feature where possible. The 7960 is to be installed on port 0/16 and the 7905 on port 0/17. Use a separate VLAN for the voice of VLAN50 and assume that the customer will also require data access to VLAN2 for this trial; configure your switch appropriately.

- A server running Cisco CallManager and the associated IP requirements will also be installed with the IP phones and located in VLAN1; it will be reachable via the address of 172.16.0.10. You have been allocated the network 10.70.70.0/24 for the voice VLAN. You are not required to advertise the voice VLAN network but ensure you have configured your switch sufficiently so that if connected, the IP phones within this VLAN would be able to load their configuration files from CallManager.

- The customer also has a requirement to trial a standard OEM IP 10BASE-T telephone alongside the Cisco IP phones on port 0/18; configure your switch appropriately.

- Ensure the switch is reachable via the IP address of 10.80.80.8/24.

## Section 1.3: ATM Configuration (1 Point)

- Configure the ATM PVCs as shown in Figure 2-12. Do not use subinterfaces and use the new format **PVC** *vpi/vci* when configuring the PVCs. Assume aal5snap; do not use the commands **protocol ip** *destination address* or **broadcast** under the PVC configuration mode.

**Figure 2-12** *ATM Diagram*

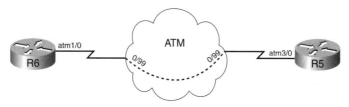

# Section 2: IP IGP Protocols (28 Points)

Configure the IP routing as in Figure 2-13 and redistribute protocols to ensure full IP visibility between routers. Advertise all router networks within the appropriate routing protocol.

**Figure 2-13**  *IP IGP Diagram*

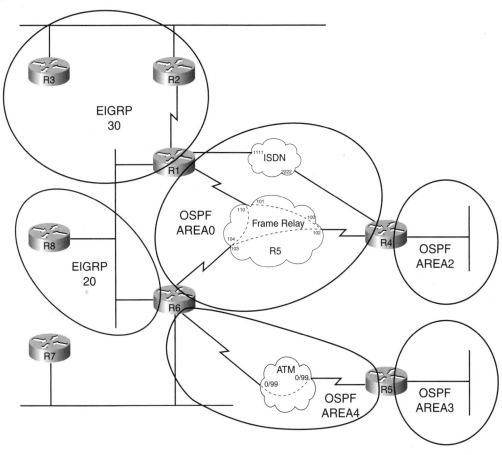

## Section 2.1: EIGRP (8 Points)

- Configure EIGRP AS20 and AS30 as shown in Figure 2-13.

- Ensure that any router running EIGRP has its loopback interface advertised within EIGRP.

- Inject at 10/8 summary route into EIGRP AS30 from R1.

- Make R1 generate a default route into EIGRP AS30 without using static/default routes.

- Ensure that no host routes are propagated throughout the network at this point of the lab.

- Encrypt all EIGRP routing updates using a method that will be difficult to detect the password.

## Section 2.2: OSPF (13 Points)

- Configure OSPF as shown in Figure 2-13 with the process on each router as 30.
- Ensure that OSPF-only routers have their loopback interfaces advertised in the same area as that of the Ethernet interface.
- Do not use the interface command **ip ospf network** over the ATM network.
- Add a loopback address of 10.200.200.1/29 onto R5 and ensure that this network is seen and reachable via the entire network. Do not add this network into existing R5 OSPF areas, redistribute as a connected network, or add further routing protocols on R5. Do not add any static routes pointing to R5 on any other routers. You may policy route in your solution.
- Ensure the only types of LSA propagated within OSPF area 2 are type 1, 2, and 3.
- Encrypt all OSPF routing updates using a method that will be difficult to detect the password.
- Ensure no host routes are propagated throughout the network at this point of the lab.

## Section 2.3: Redistribution (7 Points)

- Redistribute EIGRP AS30 into OSPF, allow all routes found in AS30 into OSPF except for the 0/0 route and do not use any distribute lists.
- Redistribute only the EIGRP AS30 routes into EIGRP AS20; once again do not use any distribute lists and do not selectively redistribute by matching external OSPF routes to achieve this.
- Redistribute EIGRP AS20 into OSPF.

# Section 3: ISDN (4 Points)

- Ensure that the ISDN is used should the Frame Relay network fail; use a Layer 3 method of invoking the line. Make R1 initiate the call. Use CHAP for authentication.

# Section 4: EGP Protocols (16 Points)

- Configure BGP as shown in Figure 2-14 with the following peering: R3–R2, R2–R1, R8–R1, R8–R6, R6–R1, R6–R4, R4–R1, R6–R5. Ensure loopback interfaces are used to peer where possible. Ensure minimal configuration on all BGP routers with multiple peers.

- Inject the following networks into BGP via new loopback interfaces:

  R2: 2.2.2.2/29

  R4: 4.4.4.4/24

  R5: 5.5.5.5/27

  R8: 8.8.8.8/28

- Configure your network so that when network 5.5.5.0/27 is advertised to AS62555 it appears as if the network originated from AS61555; do not perform any configuration on R5.

- Make the route 8.8.8.0/28 from AS63555 into R6 and R1 appear as if the previous autonomous system path was from AS60000. Do not use any autonomous system prepending and make sure that R8 is running router BGP 63555 as its BGP process.

- You will find that R4 prefers the BGP route to network 5.5.5.0/27 via next-hop R1 10.1.1.1. Ensure that R4 prefers this network via the next-hop of R5 10.5.5.5. You are only permitted to perform configuration on R1 within BGP and not by manipulating the underlying IGP. You must also not use any form of route map, autonomous system path manipulation, metric, or filter-related configuration.

- You will find that R4 prefers the BGP route to network 8.8.8.0/28 via next-hop R1 10.1.1.1. Ensure that R4 prefers this network via the next-hop of R6 10.6.6.6. You are only permitted to perform configuration on R1 and should use a Multi Exit Discriminator (MED) technique to ensure that this and only this route from R1 is effectively penalized.

**Figure 2-14** *IP EGP Diagram*

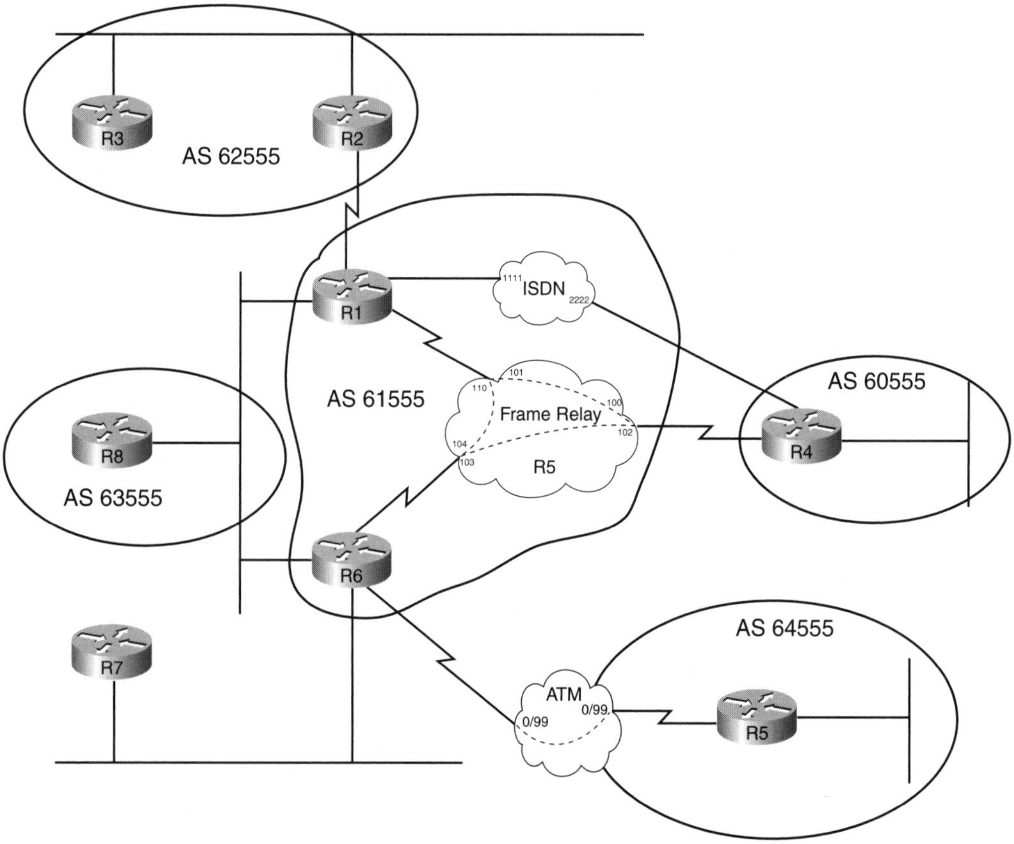

# Section 5: Voice (8 Points)

- Use a Hoot and Holler configuration on your voice network so that you do not have to dial the remote phone numbers to make a connection. Use any numbering plan you wish. Configure VoIP in such a way that numerous further phones can be added into the network and these additional phones can join in the conversation automatically as if on a conference call, but without the need to dial any numbers. If you need to add any further networks to achieve this, use an OSPF area of your choice.

**NOTE**       Ensure you are using a 1700, 2600, 3600, or 3700 voice-enabled router for this question.

# Section 6: DLSw (4 Points)

- The network manager deems the Frame Relay service to be susceptible to packet loss and requires that only TCP is used for DLSw+ features such as address resolution packets and unnumbered information frames. With this in mind, configure DLSw between VLAN3 and VLAN2. Peer from R4-R1 and R4-R6. Use the most appropriate encapsulation and peering method.

- Ensure both Frame Relay PVCs are utilized alternatively for each new circuit from R4.

- Your network administrator complains of unnecessary DLSw traffic being sent over the network; keep the traffic off the network unless valid user traffic exists that is required to be sent between VLAN2 and VLAN3.

# Section 7: IOS and IP Features (14 Points)

- Ensure that when pinging to destination 10.80.80.255 from R3 that R1, R6, R8, and Switch1 reply.

- R7 used to belong to VLAN4 but has been moved to VLAN5 and is now unreachable; configure the network in such a way that communication can still exist between VLAN4 and just the Ethernet address of R7 without modifying the IP address of R7.

- Allow R7 to ping the IP addresses assigned to Loopback0 on R1, R4, R5, R6, and R8 do not assign any static, dynamic, or policy routes to achieve this. Perform configuration only on R7.

- Configure R4 so that if R1 and R6 both advertised VLAN2 within OSPF in the future that R4 would be able to load share to this destination across both Frame Relay PVCs; do not change the bandwidth statements on your PVCs.

# Section 8: QoS (8 Points)

- Configure your switch to trust DSCP QoS from the Cisco IP phones.

- Ensure your switch does not trust QoS from the OEM IP phone.

- You have a requirement to connect a PC that will be used in your office reception in the future. You have not been told the speed requirements or which VLAN this should be assigned to. You have been told that the PC will connect to port 0/15 on your 3550 and that a policy will be required to ensure that an IP precedence of critical is assigned to web traffic to an intranet server on 172.16.0.9; configure your switch appropriately.

- Configure your voice to be of IP precedence flash value.

# Section 9: Multicast (2 Points)

- Ensure that R6 responds to pings from R4 to multicast address of 224.0.0.9; do not use PIM, or any static mappings.

# Practice Lab 2: "Ask the Proctor"

This section should only be used if you require clues to complete the questions. In the real CCIE lab, the proctor will not enter into any discussions regarding the questions or answers. He or she will be present to ensure you do not have problems with the lab environment and to maintain the timing element of the exam.

## Section 1.1: Frame Relay Configuration

Q: Are the PVCs on the same subnet or do you want them on separate subnets?
A: Look at Figure 2-10; this contains all relevant IP address information.

Q: Do you want me to add 10 to my DLCI numbers under my interface configuration?
A: No, you are required to add 10 to your DLCI numbers to gain a number for your sub-interfaces.

Q: If I keep Layer 2 information only on the Frame Relay subinterfaces, how do I gain Layer 3 connectivity.
A: A method exists of providing Layer 3 information elsewhere on the router.

Q: If I put Layer 3 on elsewhere, how do I make this connection secure?
A: After you have discovered how to provide Layer 3 connectivity, it will become apparent how you would then make this secure.

Q: Is it adequate if I make a tunnel and then run IPsec over it?
A: You have not been provided sufficient information to run IPsec.

Q: Can I use a Virtual Template for the Layer 3 portion of the question?
A: Yes.

Q: If I run PPP on the PVC, can I then put CHAP over this; does this make the Frame Relay secure?
A: Yes.

## Section 1.2: 3550 LAN Switch Configuration

Q: Do you want me to configure trunking for the Cisco IP phones?
A: Yes.

Q: Should I configure the data VLAN over and above the Aux VLAN?
A: If this answers the question.

Q: Do both Cisco IP phones support trunking?
A: You need to research this.

Q: For the OEM 10BASE-T phone, is it acceptable to use 10 Mbps and half duplex?
A: Yes.

Q: Do you want me to actually configure an interface VLAN50 on the switch and is this sufficient to ensure the phones could operate with CallManager?
A: Yes, you will need to configure VLAN50 on the switch and assign an address to it within the range supplied for VLAN50. You will find you require further configuration on VLAN50 for the IP phones to contact CallManager.

Q: Will the phones just send unicast traffic directly to the CallManager on 172.16.0.10?
A: Some phones may; however, the Cisco IP telephones are designed to be just plugged into a network without any previous configuration. For this to function correctly, they require the capability to be assigned with a dynamic IP address.

Q: So do you want me to set up DHCP on the switch to assign addresses within network 10.70.70.0/24?
A: No, CallManager incorporates the DHCP scope and tftp functions to download configuration files to Cisco IP telephones.

Q: So just set up a DHCP relay on VLAN50 pointing to CallManager on 172.16.0.10?
A: Yes.

Q: Can I use a default gateway for the switch?
A: Yes.

Q: Can I use R1 or R6 as my default gateway?
A: Yes, use whichever you choose but ensure full visibility from your network.

# Section 1.3: ATM Configuration

Q: What kind of interface type do you want on R1 and R6?
A: The question states that the configuration should be completed under the physical interfaces.

Q: If I do not use **protocol ip** under my ATM interfaces will this stop me from communicating with the remote router?
A: Experiment and you will find out.

Q: If I don't use **broadcast** under my ATM interfaces will this stop my IGPs from working?
A: You might need to address this issue during IGP configuration.

# Section 2.1: EIGRP

Q: Will my loopback interface be advertised out into EIGRP, by default anyway.
A: This depends on how you configure your EIGRP.

Q: If I inject a summary 10/8 into EIGRP will this create a static route into null 0; is this acceptable as the lab states no static routes?

A: The question specifically requests a summary route so in this case, it is acceptable.

Q: If I inject a 0/0 into EIGRP this must be a static route. Is this acceptable?

A: Do not inject a static route; find another way to accomplish this.

Q: The question states that no host routes should be visible in the network, but I have one after configuring my network. Is this acceptable?

A: No, find a way to remove the host route but maintain connectivity to the host.

# Section 2.2: OSPF

Q: I cannot get an adjacency across my ATM as this is NBMA. How can I form a neighbor if I cannot adjust what network it is under OSPF?

A: This is a back-to-basics type question; what mechanisms are available to you for NBMA network types?

Q: Can I advertise the loopback address of 10.200.200.1/29 into another OSPF process and then redistribute this into OSPF 30?

A: The question states that you must not add this subnet into any routing protocol on R5.

Q: If I can't add the subnet onto R5, can I add it onto R6?

A: If, by doing this, R5 responds to pings from another router for the 10.200.200.0/29 subnet then yes.

Q: I've added the subnet onto R6 and my whole network now has reach ability of 10.200.200.0/29 but only to R6; does this count for any partial marks?

A: You need to answer the question exactly to score marks.

Q: Is it acceptable to policy route traffic destined for R5 from R6?

A: Yes, the question does state that you may use policy routing.

Q: If I set up an area range within area 2, will this be sufficient?

A: No, back to basics again; think about the different types of areas that are available to you.

Q: My loopback interfaces have come out as host routes; is this acceptable?

A: No, use an OSPF feature to ensure they are advertised with the correct mask.

Q: Do you want me to summarize the networks to achieve the correct mask?

A: No, there is a much easier method available to you.

Q: Can I modify my router ID as I have noticed that I need to add further loopbacks, which could affect my OSPF?

A: This is your choice.

# Section 2.3: Redistribution

Q: Can I just redistribute EIGRP AS30 into OSPF on R1?

A: You can but you may then have difficulty in answering the following questions.

Q: Can I use a prefix-list to differentiate my networks?

A: This is not the desired method, and you have a number of EIGRP and OSPF subnets with the same mask value.

Q: EIGRP routes coming into OSPF will be shown as external routes; can I use a route-map to redistribute these routes only into EIGRP20?

A: You have been told in the question not to match on external routes.

Q: If I cannot match on external routes, can I deny internal routes on a route map and then allow all other routes in?

A: This still matches external routes via inverse logic, so no.

Q: Can I use the route tagging feature?

A: Yes.

# Section 3: ISDN

Q: Dialer watch is a Layer 3 method of DDR, is this acceptable?

A: You haven't been given sufficient details or networks to back up to perform dialer watch.

Q: Can I use a default floating static route?

A: You are only permitted to use static routes where specifically told that you can.

Q: Can I use a demand circuit as I am running OSPF over my ISDN?

A: Yes.

# Section 4: EGP Protocols

Q: Not all of my routers have loopbacks, is it acceptable to peer from the closest interfaces to my BGP neighbors?

A: Yes, this is fine.

Q: For minimal configuration, are you looking for route reflectors?

A: No, just limit your configuration where possible.

Q: Do you want me to redistribute my loopback interfaces into BGP?

A: You won't lose points by doing this but keep it simple at this point.

Q: Can I use prepending to make it look like network 5.5.5.0/27 came from AS61555?

A: No, if you managed to do this, the original advertised autonomous system would still be present in the autonomous system path.

Q: The question states that I cannot modify the autonomous system in R8; can I modify the autonomous system number that R8's peers communicate with?

A: Yes.

Q: Can I use the local-autonomous system feature on R8?

A: Yes.

Q: I am trying to get R4 to prefer the next-hop to 10.5.5.5 for network 5.5.5.0/27 and have found that I cannot ping the network anyway when the next-hop is 10.1.1.1; is this as expected?

A: Yes, if you investigate you will find that the traffic will bounce between R1 and R4.

Q: Will this issue be cured when the next-hop is updated to 10.5.5.5 on R4?

A: Yes.

Q: Will it be acceptable to use the **next-hop-self** command on R1 for the neighbor statement to R4?

A: No, but you are almost there.

Q: I am trying to get R4 to prefer the next-hop to 10.6.6.6 for network 8.8.8.0/28 and have found that I cannot ping the network anyway when the next-hop is 10.1.1.1; is this as expected?

A: Yes, once again you will find traffic bouncing between R1 and R4. After you answer the question, you will cure this issue.

Q: So can I just set up a MED value for network 8.8.8.0/28 for my neighbor 10.4.4.4 on R1?

A: Yes.

Q: I have verified all my BGP networks in my BGP and routing tables; is this sufficient?

A: Possibly, but you should always test connectivity to ensure your configurations are correct.

# Section 5: Voice

Q: Do you want me to use connection PLAR so I don't dial any numbers?

A: No, you should be able to pick up one of the phones and have a connection through to the other without it ringing first.

Q: So is this a permanent connection?

A: It is a little more complicated than that, but yes.

Q: If other phones can connect to the same conversation, do I need to configure some form of Conference Bridge somewhere in the network?

A: No, configured correctly you should be able to add another router in the network with voice connectivity and have that phone dedicated for the group call.

Q: So these phones are then limited to only conversations between the group and then they lose the option to dial any other numbers?
A: Yes.

Q: I have thought of a way of achieving this, but it is with multicast and this is a voice question; is that acceptable?
A: Yes, this is how Hoot and Holler works.

Q: So if I manage to get the phones to multicast their IP traffic to each other I have answered the question correctly?
A: Yes.

Q: Do you want me to configure a routemap to assign IP precedence matching on my voice traffic and change the precedence as it leaves the router?
A: A much easier method exists of achieving this.

Q: Do you want voice available if the Frame Relay network fails?
A: The ISDN question does not state that voice is required should the network fail.

# Section 6: DLSw

Q: So are you asking me to use TCP encapsulation rather than FST or direct?
A: You need to decide which encapsulation to use; sufficient details are available in the question.

Q: Acceptable I have used TCP encapsulation; can I move onto the next question?
A: You have missed an extra item of configuration.

Q: Do you want me to load share?
A: Yes, choose the most suitable type with the information you have been supplied with.

# Section 7: IOS and IP Features

Q: Can I configure bridging to get R1, R6, R8, and Switch1 to reply to pings?
A: No.

Q: R3 is on a different subnet; will the broadcast get blocked?
A: By default, yes; find a way of allowing it through without bridging.

Q: Can I configure mobile IP for R7?
A: Look for a less complex method of achieving connectivity.

Q: Can I put a secondary address on R6 in the same subnet as R7 and then somehow give connectivity to VLAN4?
A: No.

Q: Can I enable Local Area Mobility (LAM) in my network?
A: Yes.

Q: LAM will produce a host route, is that acceptable at this point in the lab?
A: Yes, the question does not state that there should be no host route at this point; there is an earlier reference to your IGP routes though.

Q: Surely R6 will proxy-ARP for the loopbacks on R4, R5, R6, and R8 if I enable it?
A: Proxy-ARP is enabled by default and it will not initially work.

Q: Can I change the mask on the 10.50.50.0/29 network on R7 so it becomes a /8 to then make R7 send ARP requests for the destination networks?
A: No.

Q: If I add a secondary address as network 10 with a mask of /8, is this acceptable?
A: Yes.

Q: I have added the secondary address, but I still do not have connectivity to the remote networks.
A: You need to add further configuration.

Q: My ARP table is not complete for the destination addresses; is it acceptable to add static entries on R7 for these?
A: Yes.

Q: To load share, can I just put an OSPF cost on my Frame Relay interfaces?
A: Yes.

# Section 8: QoS

Q: Do you want me to configure a route map to allow the Cisco IP Phone QoS settings and disallow the OEM QoS settings?
A: This is not the required solution.

Q: Are you looking for a policy map for the reception PC?
A: Yes.

# Section 9: Multicast

Q: Can I achieve any multicast without PIM?
A: It is possible.

Q: But will my multicast traffic propagate over my interfaces if I do not use PIM?
A: This is another back-to-basics type question; do you recognize the address 224.0.0.9?

Q: Is the address that of the RIP V2 update address?
A: Yes.

Q: But the question does not state that I can use a routing protocol to achieve this?
A: It does not say you cannot.

Q: So I can enable RIP V2 between the routers?
A: If this allows R6 to respond to the pings, then yes.

# Practice Lab 2 Debrief

The lab debrief section will now analyze each question showing you what was required and how to achieve the desired results. You should use this section to produce an overall score for your test.

# Section 1: Bridging and Switching (16 Points)

## Section 1.1: Frame Relay Configuration (6 Points)

- *Configure the Frame Relay portion of the network as shown in Figure 2-11 and ensure that DLCIs 110 and 104 between R1 and R6 are not used.*

The question clearly states that DLCIs 110 and 104 are not to be used; you must, therefore, disable **inverse-arp** on the routers. It is good practice to ensure that all routers do not rely on **inverse-arp** so if you have configured **no frame-relay inverse-arp** under routers R1, R4, and R6 serial interfaces, you have scored 1 point.

If you experience difficulties and can not clear any dynamic map entries, reload your routers to remove these, a drastic measure but every point counts.

- *Use point-to-point subinterfaces with a number equal to that of 10 + the listed DLCIs.*

You will need to configure your Frame Relay interfaces as follows: R1- **interface Serial0/1.111 point-to-point**, R4 - **interface Serial0/0.110 point-to-point** and **interface Serial0/0.112 point-to-point**, and finally R6 - **interface Serial5/0.113 point-to-point**. If you have configured these items correctly, you have scored 1 point.

- *Ensure that the Frame Relay subinterfaces contain purely Layer 2 information, configure virtual Layer 3 addresses elsewhere for the Frame Relay connectivity, and make this connectivity as secure as possible. This configuration does not require any form of bridging.*

Usually, you would keep your Layer 3 information under the subinterface, but it can be configured in another place. The clues to the question are in keeping it at Layer 2, making it secure, and putting the Layer 3 elsewhere on a virtual interface. The only way to achieve this is by using PPP. Frame Relay is capable of running PPP but it requires the **dlci** statement to point to a virtual template, which, by default, is a PPP-encapsulated virtual interface. Once created, the virtual template can then contain the Layer 3 address and CHAP statement required to make the PPP connection secure. You will also need a username and password as

with ISDN CHAP. If you have configured these items correctly as in Example 2-1 through
Example 2-3, you have scored 3 points.

**Example 2-1**   *R1 PPP Frame Relay Solution Configuration*

```
username R4 password 0 cisco
!
interface Serial0/1
 no ip address
 encapsulation frame-relay
 no frame-relay inverse-arp
!
interface Serial0/1.111 point-to-point
 frame-relay interface-dlci 101 ppp Virtual-Template1
!
interface Virtual-Template1
ip address 10.100.100.1 255.255.255.240
 ppp authentication chap
!
```

**Example 2-2**   *R4 PPP Frame Relay Solution Configuration*

```
username R1 password 0 cisco
username R6 password 0 cisco
!
interface Serial0/0
 no ip address
 encapsulation frame-relay
 no frame-relay inverse-arp
!
interface Serial0/0.110 point-to-point
 frame-relay interface-dlci 100 ppp Virtual-Template1
!
interface Serial0/0.112 point-to-point
 frame-relay interface-dlci 102 ppp Virtual-Template2
!
!
interface Virtual-Template1
 ip address 10.100.100.3 255.255.255.240
 ppp authentication chap
!
interface Virtual-Template2
ip address 10.100.101.1 255.255.255.240
 ppp authentication chap
!
```

**Example 2-3**   *R6 PPP Frame Relay Solution Configuration*

```
username R4 password 0 cisco
!
interface Serial5/0
 no ip address
 encapsulation frame-relay
 no frame-relay inverse-arp
```

*continues*

**Example 2-3**  *R6 PPP Frame Relay Solution Configuration (Continued)*

```
!
interface Serial5/0.113 point-to-point
 frame-relay interface-dlci 103 ppp Virtual-Template1
 !
interface Virtual-Template1
 ip address 10.100.101.2 255.255.255.240
 ppp authentication chap
```

- *For IGP metric calculation, PVC 103-102 has a CIR of 512 kbps and PVC 101-100 has a CIR of 256 kbps. Use these figures appropriately as an IGP reference for the maximum capacity of the links.*

Simply configure **bandwidth** statements under your virtual-template interfaces, R1-**bandwidth 256**, R4 - **bandwidth 256 (interface virtual-template 1)** and **bandwidth 512 (interface virtual-template 2),** and R6 - **bandwidth 512**. If you have configured this correctly, you have scored 1 point.

## Section 1.2: 3550 LAN Switch Configuration (9 Points)

- *Configure VLAN numbers, VLAN names, and port assignment as per the topology diagram.*

The switch in this instance is isolated as in Chapter 1, but you can still use the default mode of VTP Server. From the VLAN database, add the required VLANs and name them accordingly. You should note that you cannot change the VLAN name of VLAN1. You must ensure that the port speed and duplex is fixed to 100 Mbps and full duplex if your routers support this; leaving your ports in auto mode could cause connectivity problems. If you have configured these items correctly as in Example 2-4, you have scored 2 points.

**Example 2-4**  *3550 Switch1 Initial Configuration*

```
Switch1#vlan database
Switch1(vlan)#vlan 2 name VLAN2
VLAN 2 modified:
    Name: VLAN2
Switch1(vlan)#vlan 3 name VLAN3
VLAN 3 modified:
    Name: VLAN3
Switch1(vlan)#vlan 4 name VLAN4
VLAN 4 modified:
    Name: VLAN4
Switch1(vlan)#vlan 5 name VLAN5
VLAN 5 modified:
    Name: VLAN5
Switch1(vlan)#exit
APPLY completed.
Exiting....

interface FastEthernet0/1
 switchport access vlan 2
```

**Example 2-4**     *3550 Switch1 Initial Configuration (Continued)*

```
 switchport mode access
 no ip address
 duplex full
 speed 100
!
interface FastEthernet0/2
 switchport mode access
 no ip address
 duplex full
 speed 100
!
interface FastEthernet0/3
 switchport mode access
 no ip address
 duplex full
 speed 100
!
interface FastEthernet0/4
 switchport access vlan 3
 switchport mode access
 no ip address
 duplex full
 speed 100
!
interface FastEthernet0/5
 switchport access vlan 4
 switchport mode access
 no ip address
 duplex full
 speed 100
!
interface FastEthernet0/6
 switchport access vlan 2
 switchport mode access
 no ip address
 duplex full
 speed 100
!
interface FastEthernet0/7
 switchport access vlan 5
 switchport mode access
 no ip address
 duplex full
 speed 100
!
interface FastEthernet0/8
 switchport access vlan 2
 switchport mode access
 no ip address
 duplex full
 speed 100
!
```

*continues*

**Example 2-4**    *3550 Switch1 Initial Configuration (Continued)*

```
interface FastEthernet0/9
 switchport access vlan 5
 switchport mode access
 no ip address
 duplex full
 speed 100
```

**NOTE**    The VLAN configuration is completed under **Vlan database.**

- *Your customer has decided to test Voice over IP (VoIP) and is trialing Cisco 7960 and 7905 IP phones. The customer wants to take advantage of the auxiliary VLAN feature where possible. The 7960 is to be installed on port 0/16 and the 7905 on port 0/17. Use a separate VLAN for the voice of VLAN50 and assume that the customer will also require data access to VLAN2 for this trial; configure your switch appropriately.*

First of all, you should be asking are the two Cisco phones identical, and why does it say "take advantage of the auxiliary VLAN feature where possible"? In fact, the phones are very different indeed. The 7960 has the capability to trunk to the 3550. Because it has an onboard 3 port switch, it can separate the voice and data traffic appropriately using the Auxillary VLAN feature and direct data traffic on a separate VLAN to the user port on the phone. The 7905 is a low-end IP phone, which is only 10BASE-T; it simply connects into the switch as a dedicated device and will require insertion manually into VLAN50. It is not typical to be asked product-specific information in the lab but it could happen. The question provides some big clues, so if you are not familiar with the technology, use your CD or online connection (if provided with one). It will save you valuable time and ensure you score the points you need. Example 2-5 shows the 7960 phone configuration for port 0/16. Ensure that you configure the port as a trunk using dot1q encapsulation and that the native VLAN is 2. The **switchport voice vlan 50** command sets the Auxillary VLAN for voice communication to and from the 7960.

**Example 2-5**    *3550 Configuration for the 7960 IP Phone*

```
vlan 50
 name VOICE-VLAN
!
interface FastEthernet0/16
 switchport access vlan 2
 switchport trunk encapsulation dot1q
 switchport trunk native vlan 2
 switchport mode trunk
 switchport voice vlan 50
 no ip address
 duplex full
 speed 100
 spanning-tree portfast
```

The 7905 phone configuration for port 0/17. You should simply configure the port for access to VLAN50 and ensure the speed is set to 10Mbs as this is a 10BASE-T device. If you have configured these items correctly as in Example 2-5 and Example 2-6, you have scored 4 points.

**Example 2-6**    *3550 Configuration for the 7905 IP Phone*

```
interface FastEthernet0/17
 switchport access vlan 50
 no ip address
 duplex half
 speed 10
```

- *A server running Cisco CallManager and the associated IP requirements will also be installed with the IP phones and located in VLAN1; it will be reachable via the address of 172.16.0.10. You have been allocated the network 10.70.70.0/24 for the voice VLAN. You are not required to advertise the voice VLAN network but ensure you have configured your switch sufficiently so that if connected, the IP phones within this VLAN would be able to load their configuration files from CallManager.*

You should be aware that the majority of Cisco IP phones actually use DHCP to gain an IP address and their configuration files via TFTP from CallManager. From the information supplied, you will just need to configure an IP address and a helper address on VLAN50 in the switch, which will forward the DHCP requests to CallManager.

The specific IP address on VLAN50 of the switch can be any address within the range of 10.70.70.1 to 10.70.70.254/24. This information is required so when Call Manager receives the DHCP request from an IP phone, it can assign an address from the correct subnet. As instructed in the question, you will not be required to advertise network 10.70.70.0/24 as this network is purely required for the hypothetical DHCP operation to function correctly within CallManager.

If you have configured this correctly as shown in Example 2-7, you have scored 1 point.

**Example 2-7**    *3550 Configuration for CallManager Readiness*

```
interface Vlan50
 ip address 10.70.70.1 255.255.255.0
 ip helper-address 172.16.0.10
```

- *The customer also has a requirement to trial a standard OEM IP 10BASE-T telephone alongside the Cisco IP phones on port 0/18; configure your switch appropriately.*

This question should give you a clue in regard to the 7960 and 7905 IP phones earlier. Configure port 0/18 similar to the configuration for the 7905 to provide access to VLAN50 with the speed set at 10Mbs. If you have configured this correctly, as shown in Example 2-8, you have scored 1 point.

**Example 2-8** *3550 Configuration for Port 0/16 OEM IP Phone*

```
interface FastEthernet0/18
 switchport access vlan 50
 no ip address
 duplex half
 speed 10
```

- *Ensure the switch is reachable via the IP address of 10.80.80.8/24.*

You will need to configure an **ip default-gateway 10.80.80.1** onto the 3550; this could also point to 10.80.80.2. If you have configured this correctly, you have scored 1 point.

## Section 1.3: ATM Configuration (1 Point)

- *Configure the ATM PVCs as shown in Figure 2-12. Do not use subinterfaces and use the new format **PVC** vpi/vci when configuring the PVCs. Assume aal5snap; do not use the commands **protocol ip** destination address or **broadcast** under the PVC configuration mode.*

This is a straightforward configuration that relies on inverse ARP to function. The ATM configuration should be performed under the physical interfaces and because broadcasts will not be sent, you will need to adjust the behavior of OSPF later in the lab. The question forces you into making the ATM into an OSPF Non Broadcast Multiple Access (NBMA) network. If you have configured this correctly as shown in Example 2-9 and Example 2-10, you have scored 1 point.

Examples 2-9 and 2-10 also show the dynamic ATM maps created using inverse ARP and a ping test across the ATM for both R5 and R6.

**Example 2-9** *R5 ATM Configuration: ATM Map and Ping Test*

```
interface ATM3/0
 ip address 10.99.99.2 255.255.255.248
 pvc 0/99
  encapsulation aal5snap

R5#sh atm map
Map list ATM3/0_ATM_INARP : DYNAMIC
ip 10.99.99.1 maps to VC 1, VPI 0, VCI 99, ATM3/0

R5#ping 10.99.99.1

Type escape sequence to abort.
Sending 5, 100-byte ICMP Echos to 10.99.99.1, timeout is 2 seconds:
!!!!!
Success rate is 100 percent (5/5), round-trip min/avg/max = 1/3/4 ms
```

**Example 2-10**   *R6 ATM Configuration: ATM Map and Ping Test*

```
interface ATM1/0
 ip address 10.99.99.1 255.255.255.248
 pvc 0/99
  encapsulation aal5snap

R6#sh atm map
Map list ATM1/0_ATM_INARP : DYNAMIC
ip 10.99.99.2 maps to VC 1, VPI 0, VCI 99, ATM1/0

R6#ping 10.99.99.2

Type escape sequence to abort.
Sending 5, 100-byte ICMP Echos to 10.99.99.2, timeout is 2 seconds:
!!!!!
Success rate is 100 percent (5/5), round-trip min/avg/max = 1/2/4 ms
```

# Section 2: IP IGP Protocols (28 Points)

Configure the IP routing as in Figure 2-13, redistribute protocols to ensure full IP visibility between routers. Advertise all router networks within the appropriate routing protocol.

## Section 2.1: EIGRP (8 Points)

- *Configure EIGRP AS20 and AS30 as shown in Figure 2-13.*

- *Ensure that any router running EIGRP has its loopback interface advertised within EIGRP.*

You should configure EIGRP AS30 on R1-R2-R3 and EIGRP AS20 on R6 and R8. You could just enable EIGRP with a **network 10.0.0.0** statement everywhere, but as you can see in Figure 2-13, R6 and R1 do not have all their network 10 interfaces included into EIGRP. You will need to configure an inverse mask for the networks you require advertised and included in EIGRP on these routers. This is more preferable than removing the network with a distribute list later; in fact, you will find that you are not permitted to use any distribute lists in the redistribution section. Do not forget to disable auto summarization on all your routers as a matter of good practice. If you have configured this correctly as shown in Example 2-11 through Example 2-15, you have scored 2 points.

**Example 2-11**   *R1 Initial EIGRP Configuration*

```
router eigrp 30
 passive-interface Loopback0
 network 10.1.1.0 0.0.0.15
 network 10.80.80.0 0.0.0.255
 network 10.90.90.0 0.0.0.15
 no auto-summary
```

**Example 2-12** *R2 Initial EIGRP Configuration*

```
router eigrp 30
 network 10.90.90.0 0.0.0.15
 network 172.16.0.0
 no auto-summary
```

**NOTE**     You could have configured the **network** statement on R2 covering the entire classfull 10.0.0.0/8 network.

**Example 2-13** *R3 Initial EIGRP Configuration*

```
router eigrp 30
 network 172.16.0.0
 no auto-summary
```

**Example 2-14** *R6 Initial EIGRP Configuration*

```
router eigrp 20
 network 10.6.6.0 0.0.0.7
 network 10.80.80.0 0.0.0.255
 no auto-summary
```

**Example 2-15** *R8 Initial EIGRP Configuration*

```
router eigrp 20
 network 10.8.8.8 0.0.0.0
 network 10.80.80.0 0.0.0.255
 no auto-summary
```

**NOTE**     You could have configured the **network** statement on R8 covering the entire classfull 10.0.0.0/8 network.

- *Inject at 10/8 summary route into EIGRP AS30 from R1.*

Add the EIGRP summary statement for network 10/8 on R1 S0/0 as shown in Example 2-16. If you have configured this correctly, you have scored 1 point.

**Example 2-16** *R1 EIGRP Summary 10/8 Configuration*

```
interface Serial0/0
 ip address 10.90.90.2 255.255.255.240
 ip summary-address eigrp 30 10.0.0.0 255.0.0.0
```

- *Make R1 generate a default route into EIGRP AS30 without using static/default routes.*

You are not permitted to configure a default route so no statics can be redistributed. Hopefully, the previous question may have prompted you to once again use a summary route. You will find by configuring a summary route to 0/0 on R1 S0/0 that a default route will be propagated into EIGRP AS30. If you have configured this correctly as shown in Example 2-17 with the resulting 0/0 route on R2, you have scored 2 points.

**Example 2-17**  *R1 EIGRP Summary 0/0 Configuration and R2 Route Output*

```
interface Serial0/0
 ip address 10.90.90.2 255.255.255.240
 ip summary-address eigrp 30 0.0.0.0 0.0.0.0

R2#sh ip route

C    172.16.0.0/16 is directly connected, FastEthernet0/0
     10.0.0.0/8 is variably subnetted, 2 subnets, 2 masks
D       10.0.0.0/8 [90/2172416] via 10.90.90.2, 00:16:43, Serial0/0
C       10.90.90.0/28 is directly connected, Serial0/0
D*   0.0.0.0/0 [90/2172416] via 10.90.90.2, 00:16:43, Serial0/0
```

- *Ensure that no host routes are propagated throughout the network at this point of the lab.*

You will find that R8 interface Lo0 has a /32 mask and, hence, will be advertised as a host route. You will need to perform further EIGRP summarization to expand the network range. You can expand the range using a sensible mask of your choice. If you have configured this correctly as shown in Example 2-18, you have scored 1 point.

**Example 2-18**  *R8 EIGRP Summary Lo0 Configuration*

```
interface FastEthernet0/0
 ip address 10.80.80.3 255.255.255.0
 ip summary-address eigrp 20 10.8.8.0 255.255.255.240
```

- *Encrypt all EIGRP routing updates using a method that will be difficult to detect the password.*

This is not a difficult question, but it is one of those that will eat into your time so ensure you accurately configure your routers; otherwise, you will end up wasting time trouble-shooting your own errors. You will need to configure MD5 authentication, which is in fact the only type available across all your EIGRP enabled interfaces as shown in Example 2-19 through Example 2-23. Bear in mind that even on networks with no neighbors at this point in time, you should still have the authentication statement. The obvious exception to this rule is loopback interfaces. If you have configured this correctly, you have scored 2 points.

---

**NOTE**    Consider creating a text file for repetitive configuration such as this and pasting to your
routers to save time.

---

**Example 2-19** *R1 EIGRP Authentication Configuration*

```
key chain EIGRP-MD5
 key 1
  key-string anna
 !
interface FastEthernet0/0
ip authentication mode eigrp 30 md5
ip authentication key-chain eigrp 30 EIGRP-MD5
 !
interface Serial0/0
ip authentication mode eigrp 30 md5
 ip authentication key-chain eigrp 30 EIGRP-MD5
```

**Example 2-20** *R2 EIGRP Authentication Configuration*

```
key chain EIGRP-MD5
 key 1
  key-string anna
 !
interface FastEthernet0/0
ip authentication mode eigrp 30 md5
ip authentication key-chain eigrp 30 EIGRP-MD5
 !
interface Serial0/0
ip authentication mode eigrp 30 md5
 ip authentication key-chain eigrp 30 EIGRP-MD5
```

**Example 2-21** *R3 EIGRP Authentication Configuration*

```
key chain EIGRP-MD5
 key 1
  key-string anna
 !
interface FastEthernet0/0
ip authentication mode eigrp 30 md5
ip authentication key-chain eigrp 30 EIGRP-MD5
```

**Example 2-22** *R6 EIGRP Authentication Configuration*

```
key chain EIGRP-MD5
 key 1
  key-string anna
 !
interface FastEthernet0/0
 ip authentication mode eigrp 20 md5
 ip authentication key-chain eigrp 20 EIGRP-MD5
```

**Example 2-23**  *R8 EIGRP Authentication Configuration*

```
key chain EIGRP-MD5
 key 1
  key-string anna
!
interface FastEthernet0/0
 ip authentication mode eigrp 20 md5
 ip authentication key-chain eigrp 20 EIGRP-MD5
```

# Section 2.2: OSPF (13 Points)

- *Configure OSPF as shown in Figure 2-13 with the process on each router as 30.*

- *Ensure that OSPF-only routers have their loopback interfaces advertised in the same area as that of the Ethernet interface.*

You will need to configure OSPF on R1, R4, R6, and R5 ensuring that the OSPF-only routers (R4 and R5) have their loopbacks advertised within their Ethernet assigned areas. R1 and R6 should have had their loopbacks advertised earlier within EIGRP. You will also need to configure a virtual link between R6 and R5 to extend area 0 out to R5 area 3 through area 4. Pay attention to your router IDs as you will add further loopback interfaces to your configuration, which will change the router ID, unless you manually configure your ID within OSPF as shown in the solution examples. If you have configured this correctly as shown in Example 2-24 through Example 2-27, you have scored 2 points.

**Example 2-24**  *R1 Initial OSPF Configuration*

```
router ospf 30
 network 10.10.10.0 0.0.0.15 area 0
 network 10.100.100.0 0.0.0.15 area 0
```

**Example 2-25**  *R4 Initial OSPF Configuration*

```
router ospf 30
 network 10.4.4.0 0.0.0.7 area 2
 network 10.10.10.0 0.0.0.15 area 0
 network 10.40.40.0 0.0.0.15 area 2
 network 10.100.100.0 0.0.0.15 area 0
 network 10.100.101.0 0.0.0.15 area 0
```

**Example 2-26**  *R5 Initial OSPF Configuration*

```
router ospf 30
 area 4 virtual-link 10.6.6.6 network 10.5.5.4 0.0.0.3 area 3
 network 10.50.50.0 0.0.0.7 area 3
 network 10.99.99.0 0.0.0.7 area 4
 router-id 10.5.5.5
```

**Example 2-27** *R6 Initial OSPF Configuration*

```
router ospf 30
 area 4 virtual-link 10.5.5.5 network 10.99.99.0 0.0.0.7 area 4
 network 10.100.101.0 0.0.0.15 area 0
 router-id 10.6.6.6
```

- *Do not use the interface command* **ip ospf network** *over the ATM network.*

The earlier ATM question ensured that the ATM network would be treated as NBMA. Even if you did configure an OSPF network type, you would still require broadcast capability, which you do not have, over the ATM to multicast OSPF between routers. The question calls for you to statically define a remote neighbor, which will then enable the routers to unicast OSPF to each other and form an adjacency. If you have configured **neighbor 10.99.99.1** and **neighbor 10.99.99.2** on R5 and R6, respectively, you have scored 1 point.

**NOTE**   The neighbor relationship will still form if only one neighbor statement is configured on either R5 or R6. If you have configured only one statement, this is still acceptable for a full score.

- *Add a loopback address of 10.200.200.1/29 onto R5 and ensure that this network is seen and reachable via the entire network. Do not add this network into existing R5 OSPF areas, redistribute as a connected network, or add further routing protocols on R5. Do not add any static routes pointing to R5 on any other routers. You may policy route in your solution.*

As you can not advertise the network from R5 and your network requires visibility of it, you must advertise it from another router. The problem lies in that you cannot use a static route and redistribute this. The only way to achieve this is to configure a similar network on R6 and add it into either EIGRP or OSPF. You can then summarize this network out to the original mask of that configured on R5 to ensure the entire network learns about the network that is actually configured on R5 but through R6. The next step is to ensure that when traffic destined for the network on R5 reaches R6 it is forced onward to R5 instead of terminating at R6. You will need to policy route to achieve this. Your policy routing should ensure that any traffic destined to 10.200.200.1 is forwarded to R5 and it will need to be placed on R6 Fast Ethernet and virtual-template interfaces where traffic would ingress for this destination from your entire network. If you have configured this correctly as shown in Example 2-28 and Example 2-29, which also shows the resulting ping verification from R1, you have scored 5 points.

**Example 2-28** *R5 Loopback Configuration*

```
interface Loopback1
 ip address 10.200.200.1 255.255.255.248
```

**Example 2-29**  *R6 Loopback Configuration, Policy Routing, and Ping Test from R1*

```
interface Loopback1
 ip address 10.200.200.5 255.255.255.252
 ip ospf network point-to-point
!
interface FastEthernet0/0
ip policy route-map 10.200.200.1-to-R5
!
interface Virtual-Template1
ip policy route-map 10.200.200.1-to-R5
!
router ospf 30
 area 4 range 10.200.200.0 255.255.255.248
 network 10.200.200.4 0.0.0.3 area 4
!
ip local policy route-map 10.200.200.1-to-R5
!
access-list 100 permit ip any host 10.200.200.1
!
route-map 10.200.200.1-to-R5 permit 10
 match ip address 100
 set ip next-hop 10.99.99.2

R5#debug ip icmp
ICMP packet debugging is on

R1#ping 10.200.200.1

Type escape sequence to abort.
Sending 5, 100-byte ICMP Echos to 10.200.200.1, timeout is 2 seconds:
!!!!!
Success rate is 100 percent (5/5), round-trip min/avg/max = 8/8/12 ms
R5#
00:45:46: ICMP: echo reply sent, src 10.200.200.1, dst 10.100.100.1
00:45:46: ICMP: echo reply sent, src 10.200.200.1, dst 10.100.100.1
00:45:46: ICMP: echo reply sent, src 10.200.200.1, dst 10.100.100.1
00:45:46: ICMP: echo reply sent, src 10.200.200.1, dst 10.100.100.1
00:45:46: ICMP: echo reply sent, src 10.200.200.1, dst 10.100.100.1
```

**NOTE**     R6 uses the command **ip ospf network point-to-point** under interface Loopack0 to ensure
the network is not advertised as a host route to the OSPF domain.

- *Ensure the only types of LSA propagated within OSPF area 2 are type 1, 2, and 3.*

You should recall that an OSPF stub area with the key word no-summary will restrict the
LSA types to 1 and 2 with the default route being advertised automatically with an LSA
type 3. R4 OSPF process should be configured with **area 2 stub no-summary**. If you have
configured this correctly, you have scored 2 points.

- *Encrypt all OSPF routing updates using a method that will be difficult to detect the password.*

This is another time-consuming question that will require OSPF updates to be authenticated on a per-interface basis using MD5 encryption. Remember to also add authentication to your virtual link. If you have configured this correctly as in Example 2-30 through Example 2-33, you have scored 2 points.

**Example 2-30** *R1 OSPF Authentication Configuration*

```
interface BRI0/0
ip ospf message-digest-key 1 md5 james
!
interface Virtual-Template1
ip ospf message-digest-key 1 md5 james
!
router ospf 30
area 0 authentication message-digest
```

**Example 2-31** *R4 OSPF Authentication Configuration*

```
interface FastEthernet0/0
 ip ospf message-digest-key 1 md5 james
!
interface BRI0/0
ip ospf message-digest-key 1 md5 james
!
interface Virtual-Template1
 ip ospf message-digest-key 1 md5 james
!
interface Virtual-Template2
 ip ospf message-digest-key 1 md5 james
!
router ospf 30
 log-adjacency-changes
 area 0 authentication message-digest
 area 2 authentication message-digest
```

**Example 2-32** *R5 OSPF Authentication Configuration*

```
interface FastEthernet0/0
 ip ospf message-digest-key 1 md5 james
!
interface ATM3/0
 ip address 10.99.99.2 255.255.255.248
 ip ospf message-digest-key 1 md5 james
!
router ospf 30
 log-adjacency-changes
 area 0 authentication message-digest
 area 3 authentication message-digest
 area 4 authentication message-digest

 area 4 virtual-link 10.6.6.6 message-digest-key 1 md5 james
```

**Example 2-33**  *R6 OSPF Authentication Configuration*

```
interface ATM1/0
 ip ospf message-digest-key 1 md5 james
!
interface Virtual-Template1
 ip ospf message-digest-key 1 md5 james
!
router ospf 30
 area 0 authentication message-digest
 area 4 authentication message-digest
 area 4 virtual-link 10.5.5.5 message-digest-key 1 md5 james
```

- *Ensure that no host routes are propagated throughout the network at this point of the lab.*

You will need to configure your loopback interfaces on R4, R5, and R6, which are adver-tised within OSPF with **ip ospf-network point-to-point** statements to ensure they are advertised with the correct mask as opposed to /32 host routes to your network. You will also need to configure your Virtual-Template interfaces on R1 and R4 with the command **no peer neighbor-route** to remove the /32 host routes that are added to the routing table when the PPP links becomes active. These would then be propagated into your OSPF domain. If you have configured this correctly, you have scored 1 point.

# Section 2.3: Redistribution (7 Points)

- *Redistribute EIGRP AS30 into OSPF, allow all routes found in AS30 into OSPF except for the 0/0 route, and do not use any distribute lists.*

You are not being requested to perform mutual redistribution here so you simply redis-tribute EIGRP into OSPF on R1. The default route will not be propagated by default as R1 would require the **default-information originate** command to achieve this. You need to remember that OSPF by default redistributes classfull networks so you will need the keyword **subnets** in your configuration along with your specified default metric. If you have configured this correctly as shown in Example 2-34, you have scored 2 points.

**Example 2-34**  *R1 EIGRP AS30 Initial Redistribution Configuration*

```
router ospf 30
 redistribute eigrp 30 subnets
 default-metric 4000
```

- *Redistribute only the EIGRP AS30 routes into EIGRP AS20; once again do not use any distribute lists and do not selectively redistribute by matching external OSPF routes to achieve this.*

Usually, you would selectively redistribute routes based on a distribute list or use a route matching the EIGRP routes from OSPF, which would appear as External routes; as you cannot do this, you must attach an identification to the EIGRP AS20 routes as they ingress the OSPF network. By tagging the EIGRP routes on R1 as they are redistributed into OSPF, you will be able to use a route map on R6 and match all the tagged routes searching for the value you entered on R1. You can then allow the tagged routes to be redistributed into EIGRP AS30. Example 2-35 shows how to tag the EIGRP AS30 routes on R1; Example 2-36 shows how the tagged routes are redistributed into EIGRP AS30 on R6 with the resulting topology shown with the redistributed tagged routes. If you have configured this correctly, you have scored 4 points.

**Example 2-35** *R1 EIGRP AS30 Redistribution with Tagging Configuration*

```
router ospf 30
 redistribute eigrp 30 subnets tag 7942
```

**Example 2-36** *R6 EIGRP AS30 Redistribution with Tagging Configuration and Confirmation*

```
router eigrp 20
 redistribute ospf 30 route-map ospf-7942-eigrp20
 default-metric 1000 10 255 1 1500
!
route-map ospf-7942-eigrp20 permit 10
 match tag 7942


R1#sh ip ospf database self-originate

            OSPF Router with ID (10.1.1.1) (Process ID 30)

            Router Link States (Area 0)

Link ID         ADV Router      Age       Seq#       Checksum Link count
10.1.1.1        10.1.1.1        243       0x80000005 0x002FD9 3

            Type-5 AS External Link States

Link ID         ADV Router      Age       Seq#       Checksum Tag
10.0.0.0        10.1.1.1        227       0x80000002 0x007651 7942
10.1.1.0        10.1.1.1        227       0x80000002 0x0005CF 7942
10.80.80.0      10.1.1.1        227       0x80000002 0x003FE7 7942
10.90.90.0      10.1.1.1        227       0x80000002 0x00FD24 7942
172.16.0.0      10.1.1.1        227       0x80000002 0x0073A1 7942

R6#sh ip eigrp topology
IP-EIGRP Topology Table for AS(20)/ID(10.6.6.6)

Codes: P - Passive, A - Active, U - Update, Q - Query, R - Reply,
       r - reply Status, s - sia Status

P 10.0.0.0/8, 1 successors, FD is 2562560, tag is 7942
        via Redistributed (2562560/0)
P 10.1.1.0/28, 1 successors, FD is 2562560, tag is 7942
        via Redistributed (2562560/0)
P 10.90.90.0/28, 1 successors, FD is 2562560, tag is 7942
```

**Example 2-36**  *R6 EIGRP AS30 Redistribution with Tagging Configuration and Confirmation (Continued)*

```
              via Redistributed (2562560/0)
P 10.8.8.0/28, 1 successors, FD is 156160
          via 10.80.80.3 (156160/128256), FastEthernet0/0
P 10.80.80.0/24, 1 successors, FD is 28160
          via Connected, FastEthernet0/0
P 10.6.6.0/29, 1 successors, FD is 128256
          via Connected, Loopback0
P 172.16.0.0/16, 1 successors, FD is 2562560, tag is 7942
          via Redistributed (2562560/0)
```

**NOTE**    R6 does not show network 10.80.80.0/24 as a tagged network learnt from OSPF via EIGRP AS30 because this is a connected interface.

- *Redistribute EIGRP AS20 into OSPF.*

Simply redistribute the EIGRP AS20 routes into OSPF on R6; this will ensure that the OSPF network learns about the networks advertised by R8. EIGRP AS20 does not require any tagging as R1 is not performing mutual redistribution. R1 will learn EIGRP AS20 routes via OSPF; R2 and R3 have a network 10/8 summary to R1 so they will have reach capability of EIGRP AS20 through R1. Remember to use the **subnets** keyword and **default-metric** as before or add the associated metrics to the **redistribute** statement. If you have configured this correctly as in Example 2-37, you have scored 1 point.

**Example 2-37**  *R6 EIGRP AS20 Redistribution Configuration*

```
router ospf 30
 redistribute eigrp 20 subnets
 default-metric 4000
```

# Section 3: ISDN (4 Points)

- *Ensure that the ISDN is used should the Frame Relay network fail; use a Layer 3 method of invoking the line. Make R1 initiate the call. Use CHAP for authentication.*

You have two methods of providing Layer 3 ISDN backup, Dialer Watch and an OSPF Demand circuit. As you have not been provided with which networks in particular require backing up, you have to configure the Demand circuit. When you configure an OSPF demand circuit, you should be aware that any topology change will cause your ISDN circuit to become active so you must ensure you have a stable network; otherwise, your line will constantly be connected. You configure only one end of the link with the **ip ospf demand-circuit** command and this should be placed on R1 as the question states that R1 should initiate the call. You can, therefore, configure R4 without a number to dial R1 so R4 never dials R1. Example 2-38 shows R1 with the ISDN line disconnected and still maintaining a full neighbor adjacency with R4 over the ISDN; Example 2-39 shows R4 in the same state.

**Example 2-38** *R1 OSPF Demand Status*

```
R1#sh isdn act
- - - - - - - - - - - - - - - - - - - - - - - - - - - - - - - - - - - - - - - - - - - - - - - - - - -
                                ISDN ACTIVE CALLS
- - - - - - - - - - - - - - - - - - - - - - - - - - - - - - - - - - - - - - - - - - - - - - - - - - -
Call    Calling     Called      Remote  Seconds Seconds Seconds Charges
Type    Number      Number      Name    Used    Left    Idle    Units/Currency
- - - - - - - - - - - - - - - - - - - - - - - - - - - - - - - - - - - - - - - - - - - - - - - - - - -
- - - - - - - - - - - - - - - - - - - - - - - - - - - - - - - - - - - - - - - - - - - - - - - - - - -

R1#sh ip ospf neigh

Neighbor ID     Pri   State         Dead Time   Address       Interface
10.4.4.4          1   FULL/ -       00:00:34    10.100.100.3  Virtual-Access1
10.4.4.4          1   FULL/ -           -       10.10.10.2    BRI0/0
```

**Example 2-39** *R4 OSPF Demand Status*

```
R4#sh isdn act
- - - - - - - - - - - - - - - - - - - - - - - - - - - - - - - - - - - - - - - - - - - - - - - - - - -
                                ISDN ACTIVE CALLS
- - - - - - - - - - - - - - - - - - - - - - - - - - - - - - - - - - - - - - - - - - - - - - - - - - -
Call    Calling     Called      Remote  Seconds Seconds Seconds Charges
Type    Number      Number      Name    Used    Left    Idle    Units/Currency
- - - - - - - - - - - - - - - - - - - - - - - - - - - - - - - - - - - - - - - - - - - - - - - - - - -
- - - - - - - - - - - - - - - - - - - - - - - - - - - - - - - - - - - - - - - - - - - - - - - - - - -

R4#sh ip ospf neigh

Neighbor ID     Pri   State         Dead Time   Address       Interface
10.1.1.1          1   FULL/ -       00:00:31    10.100.100.1  Virtual-Access1
10.200.200.5      1   FULL/ -       00:00:37    10.100.101.2  Virtual-Access2
10.1.1.1          1   FULL/ -           -       10.10.10.1    BRI0/0
```

It is good practice to configure PPP circuits with the command **no peer neighbor-route** to remove the /32 host route that is added to the routing table when a PPP link becomes active. You might find that when your ISDN line disconnects, this route will be removed from the routing table and cause an OPSF topology change; this will cause your ISDN line to re-establish. You should have already configured the peer route option on your virtual templates on R1 and R4 earlier within the OSPF section to remove the host routes. As requested in the question, you must use CHAP authentication; you should already have username and passwords configured for the PPP over Frame Relay section so simply enable **ppp authentication chap** on the ISDN interfaces of R1 and R4. Do not forget to add authentication to the ISDN network as itis part of OSPF area 0. If you have configured this correctly as shown in Example 2-40 and Example 2-41, you have scored 4 points.

**Example 2-40**  *R1 ISDN Configuration*

```
username R4 password 0 cisco
!
interface BRI0/0
 ip address 10.10.10.1 255.255.255.240
 encapsulation ppp
 ip ospf message-digest-key 1 md5 james
 ip ospf demand-circuit
 dialer map ip 10.10.10.2 name R4 broadcast 2222
 dialer-group 1
 isdn switch-type basic-net3
 no peer neighbor-route
 ppp authentication chap
!
dialer-list 1 protocol ip permit
```

**Example 2-41**  *R4 ISDN Configuration*

```
username R1 password 0 cisco
!
interface BRI0/0
 ip address 10.10.10.2 255.255.255.240
 encapsulation ppp
 ip ospf message-digest-key 1 md5 james
 dialer map ip 10.10.10.1 name R1 broadcast
 dialer-group 1
 isdn switch-type basic-net3
 no peer neighbor-route
 ppp authentication chap
!
dialer-list 1 protocol ip permit
```

# Section 4: EGP Protocols (16 Points)

- *Configure BGP as shown in Figure 2-14 with the following peering: R3–R2, R2–R1, R8–R1, R8–R6, R6–R1, R6–R4, R4–R1, R6–R5. Ensure loopback interfaces are used to peer where possible. Ensure minimal configuration on all BGP routers with multiple peers.*

You are required to configure the peering between the BGP autonomous systems as described. You should ensure that **no synchronization** is configured on IBGP routers R1, R2, R3, and R6, as per Lab 1; BGP is not synchronized with the underlying IGP. You should once again peer from your loopback interfaces where possible to maintain resiliency and because of the request to do so in the question; this is with the exception of R2 and R3. You will also need to configure peer groups on R4 and R8, which have multiple peers to the same remote autonomous system to minimize configuration. If you have configured this correctly as shown in Example 2-42 through Example 2-48, you have scored 3 points.

| NOTE | The peer statements will change on R1 and R6 in the following questions, so do not deduct any marks if your peer statements do not echo those in Example 2-42 and 2-47 at this point in time. |
|------|----------------------------------------------------------------------------------------------------------------------------------------------------------------------------------------------|

**Example 2-42** *R1 Initial BGP Configuration*

```
router bgp 61555
 no synchronization
 neighbor 10.4.4.4 remote-as 60555
 neighbor 10.4.4.4 ebgp-multihop 4
 neighbor 10.4.4.4 update-source Loopback0
 neighbor 10.6.6.6 remote-as 61555
neighbor 10.6.6.6 update-source Loopback0
 neighbor 10.8.8.8 remote-as 63555
 neighbor 10.8.8.8 ebgp-multihop 4
 neighbor 10.8.8.8 update-source Loopback0
 neighbor 10.90.90.1 remote-as 62555
neighbor 10.90.90.1 update-source Loopback0
```

**Example 2-43** *R2 Initial BGP Configuration*

```
router bgp 62555
 no synchronization
 neighbor 10.1.1.1 remote-as 61555
 neighbor 10.1.1.1 ebgp-multihop 2
 neighbor 172.16.0.2 remote-as 62555
```

**Example 2-44** *R3 Initial BGP Configuration*

```
router bgp 62555
 no synchronization
 neighbor 172.16.0.1 remote-as 62555
```

**Example 2-45** *R4 Initial BGP Configuration*

```
router bgp 60555
neighbor 61555 peer-group
 neighbor 61555 remote-as 61555
 neighbor 61555 ebgp-multihop 4
 neighbor 61555 update-source Loopback0
 neighbor 10.1.1.1 peer-group 61555
 neighbor 10.6.6.6 peer-group 61555
```

**Example 2-46** *R5 Initial BGP Configuration*

```
router bgp 64555
neighbor 10.6.6.6 remote-as 61555
 neighbor 10.6.6.6 ebgp-multihop 4
 neighbor 10.6.6.6 update-source Loopback0
```

**Example 2-47**  *R6 Initial BGP Configuration*

```
router bgp 61555
 no synchronization
 neighbor 10.1.1.1 remote-as 61555
 neighbor 10.1.1.1 update-source Loopback0
 neighbor 10.4.4.4 remote-as 60555
 neighbor 10.4.4.4 ebgp-multihop 255
 neighbor 10.4.4.4 update-source Loopback0
 neighbor 10.5.5.5 remote-as 64555
 neighbor 10.5.5.5 ebgp-multihop 4
 neighbor 10.5.5.5 update-source Loopback0
 neighbor 10.8.8.8 remote-as 63555
 neighbor 10.8.8.8 ebgp-multihop 4
 neighbor 10.8.8.8 update-source Loopback0
```

**Example 2-48**  *R8 Initial BGP Configuration*

```
router bgp 63555
 neighbor 61555 peer-group
 neighbor 61555 remote-as 61555
 neighbor 61555 ebgp-multihop 4
 neighbor 61555 update-source Loopback0
 neighbor 10.1.1.1 peer-group 61555
 neighbor 10.6.6.6 peer-group 61555
```

- *Inject the following networks into BGP via new loopback interfaces:*

  *R2: 2.2.2.2/29*

  *R4: 4.4.4.4/24*

  *R5: 5.5.5.5/27*

  *R8: 8.8.8.8/28*

Configure the loopback interfaces as shown and advertise them via the **network** command under the BGP process; ensure you use the relevant mask per network. If you have configured this correctly as shown in Example 2-49 through Example 2-52 you have scored 1 point.

**Example 2-49**  *R2 Loopback and BGP Advertisement Configuration*

```
interface Loopback0
 ip address 2.2.2.2 255.255.255.248
!
router bgp 62555
network 2.2.2.0 mask 255.255.255.248
```

**Example 2-50**  *R4 Loopback and BGP Advertisement Configuration*

```
interface Loopback1
 ip address 4.4.4.4 255.255.255.0
!
router bgp 60555
 network 4.4.4.0 mask 255.255.255.0
```

**Example 2-51** *R5 Loopback and BGP Advertisement Configuration*

```
interface Loopback2
 ip address 5.5.5.5 255.255.255.224
!
router bgp 64555
 network 5.5.5.0 mask 255.255.255.224
```

**Example 2-52** *R8 Loopback and BGP Advertisement Configuration*

```
interface Loopback1
 ip address 8.8.8.8 255.255.255.240
!
router bgp 63555
 network 8.8.8.0 mask 255.255.255.240
```

- *Configure your network so that when network 5.5.5.0/27 is advertised to AS62555 it appears as if the network originated from AS61555; do not perform any configuration on R5.*

Usually, you would configure AS Path prepending to alter the autonomous system path attribute, but you are not permitted to do so. You need to actually make the advertisement for network 5.5.5.0/27 appear as if it came from AS61555 and not from AS64555. As you cannot configure R5, you are left with only one method of achieving this; you should notice that AS64555 is actually the only autonomous system within your network that is a private autonomous system number (private autonomous system numbers range from 64512 to 65535). Private autonomous system numbers can be removed when advertised from one autonomous system to another about when the keyword **remove-private-AS** is configured on your peer statement. In this instance, R1 must be configured to remove the private autonomous system numbers; this ensures that when it advertises network 5.5.5.0/27 to AS62555, it appears to come directly from AS61555. Example 2-53 shows the BGP routing table on R2 pre-configuration and Example 2-54 shows the BGP routing table post-configuration.

**Example 2-53** *R2 BGP Routing Table Pre-Configuration*

```
R2#sh ip bgp
BGP table version is 63, local router ID is 172.16.0.1
Status codes: s suppressed, d damped, h history, * valid, > best, i - internal
Origin codes: i - IGP, e - EGP, ? - incomplete

   Network          Next Hop            Metric LocPrf Weight Path
*> 2.2.2.0/29       0.0.0.0                  0         32768 i
*> 4.4.4.0/24       10.1.1.1                               0 61555 60555 i
*> 5.5.5.0/27       10.1.1.1                               0 61555 64555 i
*> 8.8.8.0/28       10.1.1.1                               0 61555 63555 i
```

**Example 2-54**  *R2 BGP Routing Table Post-Configuration*

```
R2#sh ip bgp
BGP table version is 69, local router ID is 172.16.0.1
Status codes: s suppressed, d damped, h history, * valid, > best, i - internal
Origin codes: i - IGP, e - EGP, ? - incomplete

   Network          Next Hop           Metric LocPrf Weight Path
*> 2.2.2.0/29       0.0.0.0                 0         32768 i
*> 4.4.4.0/24       10.1.1.1                              0 61555 60555 i
*> 5.5.5.0/27       10.1.1.1                              0 61555 i
*> 8.8.8.0/28       10.1.1.1                              0 61555 63555 i
```

If you have configured this correctly as shown in Example 2-55, you have scored 5 points.

**Example 2-55**  *R1 BGP Private Autonomous System Configuration*

```
router bgp 61555
neighbor 10.90.90.1 remove-private-AS
```

- *Make the route 8.8.8.0/28 from AS63555 into R6 and R1 appear as if the previous autonomous system path was from AS60000. Do not use any autonomous system prepending and make sure that R8 is running router BGP 63555 as its BGP process.*

You cannot use autonomous system path prepending, and AS63555 is unfortunately not a private autonomous system number; this could be achieved by changing the BGP process number on R8 and repointing R1 and R6 peer statements to AS60000 but this is not permitted. BGP has a feature called local autonomous system, which is very useful for when an ISP merges with another ISP; it enables the routers to maintain their original autonomous system number but peer to other routers using a pseudo autonomous system number. The question states that you must run BGP 63555 on R8, but it does not state that R1 and R6 cannot attempt to peer with AS60000; by using the **local-as** command on R8 you will be able to establish a BGP session from R1 and R6 pointing to AS60000 while in fact the process on R8 is 63555. The resulting BGP route tables for R1 and R6 as shown in Example 2-56 show that R8 advertised network 8.8.8.0/28 now looks like it originated from AS60000 and then passed through AS63555. If you read the paper through and understood this question before configuration, you could have saved time by creating your initial peer statements to reflect this question.

**Example 2-56**  *R1 and R6 BGP Routing Tables After* **local-as** *Configuration*

```
R1#sh ip bgp
BGP table version is 5, local router ID is 10.1.1.1
Status codes: s suppressed, d damped, h history, * valid, > best, i - internal
Origin codes: i - IGP, e - EGP, ? - incomplete

   Network          Next Hop           Metric LocPrf Weight Path
*> 2.2.2.0/29       10.90.90.1              0             0 62555 i
*  i4.4.4.0/24      10.4.4.4                0    100      0 60555 i
*>                  10.4.4.4                0             0 60555 i
```

*continues*

**Example 2-56** *R1 and R6 BGP Routing Tables After* **local-as** *Configuration (Continued)*

```
*>i5.5.5.0/27      10.5.5.5              0    100     0 64555 i
* i8.8.8.0/28      10.8.8.8              0    100     0 60000 63555 i
*>                 10.8.8.8              0            0 60000 63555 i
R6#sh ip bgp
BGP table version is 7, local router ID is 10.200.200.5
Status codes: s suppressed, d damped, h history, * valid, > best, i - internal
Origin codes: i - IGP, e - EGP, ? - incomplete

   Network          Next Hop          Metric LocPrf Weight Path
*>i2.2.2.0/29       10.90.90.1            0    100     0 62555 i
* i4.4.4.0/24       10.4.4.4             0    100     0 60555 i
*>                  10.4.4.4             0            0 60555 i
*> 5.5.5.0/27       10.5.5.5             0            0 64555 i
* i8.8.8.0/28       10.8.8.8             0    100     0 60000 63555 i
*>                  10.8.8.8             0            0 60000 63555 i
```

- If you have configured this correctly as in Example 2-57 through 2-59 you have scored 4 points.

**Example 2-57** *R1* **local-as** *Configuration*

```
router bgp 61555
 neighbor 10.8.8.8 remote-as 60000
```

**Example 2-58** *R6* **local-as** *Configuration*

```
router bgp 61555
 neighbor 10.8.8.8 remote-as 60000
```

**Example 2-59** *R8* **local-as** *Configuration*

```
router bgp 63555
 neighbor 61555 local-as 60000
```

- *You will find that R4 prefers the BGP route to network 5.5.5.0/27 via next-hop R1 10.1.1.1. Ensure that R4 prefers this network via the next-hop of R5 10.5.5.5. You are only permitted to perform configuration on R1 within BGP and not by manipulating the underlying IGP. You must also not use any form of route map, autonomous system path manipulation, metric, or filter-related configuration.*

As you can see in Example 2-60, R4 has two routes to network 5.5.5.0/27 via both R1 next-hop 10.1.1.1 and R6 next-hop 10.6.6.6, but R1 is preferred. The ping test to 5.5.5.5 from R4 as shown in the example fails as traffic will be bounced between R1 and R4; R4 will send the ICMP traffic toward R1; and R1 will return it to R4 because R1 has a next-hop of 10.5.5.5, which must pass through R4 for network 5.5.5.0/27. You are instructed to use a feature within BGP on R1 but are very restricted. You will find the only method of achieving this within the constraints is by using the command **neighbor 10.4.4.4 next-hop-**

**unchanged** under the BGP process on R1. This command instructs R1 to send the next-hop to network 5.5.5.0/27 unchanged as it passes over the EBGP connection to R4 and as R1 itself sees the route from R6 over its IBGP connection with the next-hop of 10.5.5.5. If you have configured this correctly as shown in Example 2-61, you have scored 2 points.

**Example 2-60**  *R4 BGP Routes and Ping Test*

```
R4#sh ip bgp
BGP table version is 5, local router ID is 10.4.4.4
Status codes: s suppressed, d damped, h history, * valid, > best, i - internal
Origin codes: i - IGP, e - EGP, ? - incomplete

   Network          Next Hop            Metric LocPrf Weight Path
*  2.2.2.0/29       10.6.6.6                             0 61555 62555 i
*>                  10.1.1.1                             0 61555 62555 i
*> 4.4.4.0/24       0.0.0.0                  0       32768 i
*  5.5.5.0/27       10.6.6.6                             0 61555 64555 i
*>                  10.1.1.1                             0 61555 64555 i
*  8.8.8.0/28       10.6.6.6                             0 61555 60000 63555 i
*>                  10.1.1.1                             0 61555 60000 63555 i
R4#ping 5.5.5.5

Type escape sequence to abort.
Sending 5, 100-byte ICMP Echos to 5.5.5.5, timeout is 2 seconds:
.....
Success rate is 0 percent (0/5)
```

**Example 2-61**  *R1 BGP Configuration and Verification*

```
R1#conf t
R1(config)#router bgp 61555
R1(config-router)#neighbor 10.4.4.4 next-hop-unchanged


R4#sh ip bgp
BGP table version is 5, local router ID is 10.4.4.4
Status codes: s suppressed, d damped, h history, * valid, > best, i - internal
Origin codes: i - IGP, e - EGP, ? - incomplete

   Network          Next Hop            Metric LocPrf Weight Path
*  2.2.2.0/29       10.6.6.6                             0 61555 62555 i
*>                  10.1.1.1                             0 61555 62555 i
*> 4.4.4.0/24       0.0.0.0                  0       32768 i
*  5.5.5.0/27       10.6.6.6                             0 61555 64555 i
*>                  10.5.5.5                             0 61555 64555 i
*  8.8.8.0/28       10.6.6.6                             0 61555 60000 63555 i
*>                  10.1.1.1                             0 61555 60000 63555 i

R4#ping 5.5.5.5

Type escape sequence to abort.
Sending 5, 100-byte ICMP Echos to 5.5.5.5, timeout is 2 seconds:
!!!!!
```

*continues*

**Example 2-61** *R1 BGP Configuration and Verification (Continued)*

```
Success rate is 100 percent (5/5), round-trip min/avg/max = 4/6/8 ms

R4#trace 5.5.5.5

Type escape sequence to abort.
Tracing the route to 5.5.5.5

  1 10.100.101.2 4 msec 0 msec 0 msec
  2 10.99.99.2 8 msec 4 msec *
```

- *You will find that R4 prefers the BGP route to network 8.8.8.0/28 via next-hop R1 10.1.1.1. Ensure that R4 prefers this network via the next-hop of R6 10.6.6.6. You are only permitted to perform configuration on R1 and should use a Multi Exit Disriminator (MED) technique to ensure that this and only this route from R1 is effectively penalized.*

As you can see in Example 2-62, R4 has a next-hop of 10.1.1.1 to network 8.8.8.0/24. The example also shows that a ping test to this network fails for the same reasons described in the previous question with traffic bouncing between R1 and R4. This is, however, a very straightforward question where you are told exactly what to do in the text by setting up a MED metric attribute to the route 8.8.8.0/28 as it leaves R1 AS61555 to R4 AS60555. R4 will compare the routes for network 8.8.8.0/28 and find that the route received by R1 will now have the MED value set and that the route received by R6 will not, as a lower MED is preferred over a higher MED; R4 will select the route from R6 as this does not have a MED value explicitly set and as such is treated as 0. You should remember to clear your BGP connections each time you make a change like this. R4 will now have a next-hop to network 8.8.8.0/28 set as R6 10.6.6.6, and the ping test will now function correctly. If you have configured this correctly as shown in Example 2-63, you have scored 1 point.

**Example 2-62** *R4 BGP Routes and Ping Test*

```
R4#sh ip bgp
BGP table version is 5, local router ID is 10.4.4.4
Status codes: s suppressed, d damped, h history, * valid, > best, i - internal
Origin codes: i - IGP, e - EGP, ? - incomplete

   Network          Next Hop          Metric LocPrf Weight Path
*  2.2.2.0/29       10.6.6.6                          0 61555 62555 i
*>                  10.1.1.1                          0 61555 62555 i
*> 4.4.4.0/24       0.0.0.0                0     32768 i
*  5.5.5.0/27       10.6.6.6                          0 61555 64555 i
*>                  10.5.5.5                          0 61555 64555 i
*  8.8.8.0/28       10.6.6.6                          0 61555 60000 63555 i
*>                  10.1.1.1                          0 61555 60000 63555 i

R4#ping 8.8.8.8

Type escape sequence to abort.
Sending 5, 100-byte ICMP Echos to 8.8.8.8, timeout is 2 seconds:
.....
Success rate is 100 percent (5/5), round-trip min/avg/max = 4/4/8 ms
```

**Example 2-63**  *R1 BGP Configuration and Verification*

```
router bgp 61555
 neighbor 10.4.4.4 route-map metric out
!
access-list 1 permit 8.8.8.0 0.0.0.15
!
route-map metric permit 10
 match ip address 1
 set metric 50
!
route-map metric permit 20


R4#sh ip bgp
BGP table version is 5, local router ID is 10.4.4.4
Status codes: s suppressed, d damped, h history, * valid, > best, i - internal
Origin codes: i - IGP, e - EGP, ? - incomplete

   Network          Next Hop         Metric LocPrf Weight Path
*  2.2.2.0/29       10.6.6.6                          0 61555 62555 i
*>                  10.1.1.1                          0 61555 62555 i
*> 4.4.4.0/24       0.0.0.0              0       32768 i
*  5.5.5.0/27       10.6.6.6                          0 61555 64555 i
*>                  10.5.5.5                          0 61555 64555 i
*> 8.8.8.0/28       10.6.6.6                          0 61555 60000 63555 i
*                   10.1.1.1            50            0 61555 60000 63555 i

R4#ping 8.8.8.8

Type escape sequence to abort.
Sending 5, 100-byte ICMP Echos to 8.8.8.8, timeout is 2 seconds:
!!!!!
Success rate is 100 percent (5/5), round-trip min/avg/max = 4/4/8 ms
```

# Section 5: Voice (8 Points)

- *Use a Hoot and Holler configuration on your voice network so that you do not have to dial the remote phone numbers to make a connection. Use any numbering plan you wish. Configure VoIP in such a way that numerous further phones can be added into the network and these additional phones can join in the conversation automatically as if on a conference call, but without the need to dial any numbers. If you need to add any further networks to achieve this, use an OSPF area of your choice.*

**NOTE**    Ensure you are using a 1700, 2600, 3600, or 3700 voice enabled router for this question.

You might begin thinking that you could use **connection plar** to make the phone ring without dialing it, but then further on in the question, you have to make additional phones connect as if on a conference call. As you will not have the facility available to set up conference calls with additional equipment, you need to explore how you can make all the phones connect to each other; hopefully, you will search the CD or online connection and find that it is possible to multicast your voice to multiple destinations. Cisco has a feature called Hoot and Holler, which basically emulates the voice technology employed in brokerage firms for traders to communicate with each other in a number of locations; this is available on 1700, 2600, 3600, and 3700 voice-enabled platforms. The configuration is complex with a virtual interface defined for multicast fast switching; routers joining the same session must have their virtual interfaces on different subnets; otherwise, packets are not switched to the IP network. You need to add your virtual interfaces into OSPF and configure your voice ports for trunking as this will be a permanent connection; voice peers are required to multicast your voice. If you have configured this correctly as shown in Examples 2-64 and 2-65, you have scored 8 points.

**Example 2-64** *R1 VoIP Configuration*

```
ip multicast-routing
!
voice class permanent 1
signal timing oos timeout disabled
signal keepalive 65535
!
interface Vif1
 ip address 10.1.1.17 255.255.255.240
 ip pim dense-mode
!
interface Virtual-Template1
 ip address 10.100.100.1 255.255.255.240
 ip pim dense-mode
!
router ospf 30
 network 10.1.1.16 0.0.0.15 area 0
!
voice-port 1/0/0
 voice-class permanent 1
 connection trunk 111
!
dial-peer voice 111 voip
 destination-pattern 111
 session protocol multicast
 session target ipv4:235.035.0.035:22222
```

**Example 2-65** *R4 VoIP Configuration*

```
ip multicast-routing
!
voice class permanent 2
signal timing oos timeout disabled
```

**Example 2-65**  *R4 VoIP Configuration (Continued)*

```
signal keepalive 65535
!
interface Vif1
 ip address 10.4.4.9 255.255.255.248
 ip pim dense-mode
!
interface Virtual-Template1
 ip address 10.100.100.3 255.255.255.240
 ip pim dense-mode
!
router ospf 30
network 10.4.4.8 0.0.0.7 area 2
!
voice-port 1/1/0
 voice-class permanent 2
 connection trunk 111
!
dial-peer voice 111 voip
 destination-pattern 111
 session protocol multicast
 session target ipv4:235.035.0.035:22222
```

# Section 6: DLSw (4 Points)

- *The network manager deems the Frame Relay service to be susceptible to packet loss and requires that only TCP is used for DLSw+ features such as address resolution packets and unnumbered information frames. With this in mind, configure DLSw between VLAN3 and VLAN2. Peer from R4-R1 and R4-R6. Use the most appropriate encapsulation and peering method.*

You should obviously use TCP as your encapsulation type here but the question gives you additional information about the address resolution packets and unnumbered information frames. From this additional information, you should research these features and find that these are in fact transmitted by default in UDP to avoid congestion if errors are encountered. To ensure these features are transmitted reliably in TCP, you should configure R1 and R4 with the command **dlsw udp-disable.** You should be peering from loopback interfaces and configure VLAN2 and VLAN3 as the DLSw bridge points on your routers. If you have configured this correctly as shown in Example 2-66 through Example 2-68, you have scored 2 points.

**Example 2-66**  *R1 Initial DLSw Configuration*

```
dlsw local-peer peer-id 10.1.1.1
dlsw remote-peer 0 tcp 10.4.4.4
dlsw bridge-group 1
dlsw udp-disable
!
interface FastEthernet0/0
```

*continues*

**Example 2-66**  *R1 Initial DLSw Configuration (Continued)*

```
bridge-group 1
!
bridge 1 protocol ieee
```

**Example 2-67**  *R4 Initial DLSw Configuration*

```
dlsw local-peer peer-id 10.4.4.4
dlsw remote-peer 0 tcp 10.6.6.6
dlsw remote-peer 0 tcp 10.1.1.1
dlsw bridge-group 1
dlsw udp-disable
!
interface FastEthernet0/0
bridge-group 1
!
bridge 1 protocol ieee
```

**Example 2-68**  *R6 Initial DLSw Configuration*

```
dlsw local-peer peer-id 10.6.6.6
dlsw remote-peer 0 tcp 10.4.4.4
dlsw bridge-group 1
dlsw udp-disable
!
interface FastEthernet0/0
bridge-group 1
!
bridge 1 protocol ieee
```

- *Ensure both Frame Relay PVCs are utilized alternatively for each new circuit from R4.*

Because you have duplicate paths to the end destination, you should configure DLSw round-robin load sharing with the command **dlsw load-balance round-robin** on R4. If you have configured this correctly, you have scored 1 point.

- *Your network administrator complains of unnecessary DLSw traffic being sent over the network; keep the traffic off the network unless valid user traffic exists that is required to be sent between VLAN2 and VLAN3.*

You need to configure dynamic peering, which will only initiate sessions when you have valid user traffic to transport. If you have configured this correctly as shown in Example 2-69 through Example 2-71, which also show the final DLSw configurations for R1, R4, and R6, you have scored 1 point.

**Example 2-69**  *R1 Final DLSw Configuration*

```
dlsw local-peer peer-id 10.1.1.1
dlsw remote-peer 0 tcp 10.4.4.4 keepalive 0 timeout 90 dynamic
dlsw bridge-group 1
```

**Example 2-69**  *R1 Final DLSw Configuration (Continued)*

```
dlsw udp-disable
!
interface FastEthernet0/0
bridge-group 1
!
bridge 1 protocol ieee
```

**Example 2-70**  *R4 Final DLSw Configuration*

```
dlsw local-peer peer-id 10.4.4.4
dlsw load-balance round-robin
dlsw remote-peer 0 tcp 10.6.6.6 keepalive 0 timeout 90 dynamic
dlsw remote-peer 0 tcp 10.1.1.1 keepalive 0 timeout 90 dynamic
dlsw bridge-group 1
dlsw udp-disable
!
interface FastEthernet0/0
bridge-group 1
!
bridge 1 protocol ieee
```

**Example 2-71**  *R6 Final DLSw Configuration*

```
dlsw local-peer peer-id 10.6.6.6
dlsw remote-peer 0 tcp 10.4.4.4 keepalive 0 timeout 90 dynamic
dlsw bridge-group 1
dlsw udp-disable
!
interface FastEthernet0/0
bridge-group 1
!
bridge 1 protocol ieee
```

**NOTE**    The keepalive and timeout figures shown are the defaults.

# Section 7: IOS and IP Features (14 Points)

- *Ensure that when pinging to destination 10.80.80.255 from R3 that R1, R6, R8, and Switch1 reply.*

By default, the broadcast ping will be terminated by R1 but it will itself respond to the ping. By configuring R1 with the command **ip directed-broadcast** on Fast Ethernet0/0, R1 will then forward the ping to the whole destination subnet, which will result in R6, R8, and Switch1 also replying to the ping.

Example 2-72 shows verification of a broadcast ping to 10.80.80.255 initiated from R3 with replies received from R1, R6, R8, and Switch1.

If you have configured this correctly, you have scored 3 points.

**Example 2-72** *R3 Broadcast Ping Verification*

```
R3#debug ip icmp
ICMP packet debugging is on
R3#ping 10.80.80.255

Type escape sequence to abort.
Sending 5, 100-byte ICMP Echos to 10.80.80.255, timeout is 2 seconds:
!!!!!
Success rate is 100 percent (5/5), round-trip min/avg/max = 4/4/8 ms
R3#
01:35:39: ICMP: echo reply rcvd, src 10.90.90.2, dst 172.16.0.2
01:35:39: ICMP: echo reply rcvd, src 10.90.90.2, dst 172.16.0.2
01:35:39: ICMP: echo reply rcvd, src 10.80.80.2, dst 172.16.0.2
01:35:39: ICMP: echo reply rcvd, src 10.80.80.3, dst 172.16.0.2
01:35:39: ICMP: echo reply rcvd, src 10.80.80.2, dst 172.16.0.2
01:35:39: ICMP: echo reply rcvd, src 10.80.80.8, dst 172.16.0.2
01:35:39: ICMP: echo reply rcvd, src 10.80.80.3, dst 172.16.0.2
01:35:39: ICMP: echo reply rcvd, src 10.90.90.2, dst 172.16.0.2
01:35:39: ICMP: echo reply rcvd, src 10.80.80.2, dst 172.16.0.2
01:35:39: ICMP: echo reply rcvd, src 10.80.80.8, dst 172.16.0.2
01:35:39: ICMP: echo reply rcvd, src 10.80.80.3, dst 172.16.0.2
01:35:39: ICMP: echo reply rcvd, src 10.90.90.2, dst 172.16.0.2
01:35:39: ICMP: echo reply rcvd, src 10.80.80.2, dst 172.16.0.2
01:35:39: ICMP: echo reply rcvd, src 10.80.80.8, dst 172.16.0.2
01:35:39: ICMP: echo reply rcvd, src 10.80.80.3, dst 172.16.0.2
01:35:39: ICMP: echo reply rcvd, src 10.90.90.2, dst 172.16.0.2
01:35:39: ICMP: echo reply rcvd, src 10.80.80.2, dst 172.16.0.2
01:35:39: ICMP: echo reply rcvd, src 10.80.80.8, dst 172.16.0.2
01:35:39: ICMP: echo reply rcvd, src 10.80.80.3, dst 172.16.0.2
```

- *R7 used to belong to VLAN4 but has been moved to VLAN5 and is now unreachable. Configure the network in such a way that communication can still exist between VLAN4 and just the Ethernet address of R7 without modifying the IP address of R7.*

You need to configure LAM on R6 with an access group that only permits host 10.50.50.2. You have to redistribute mobile into OSPF on R6 so your network learns where host 10.50.50.2 is by the more specific host route that R6 will generate. R7 will now be able to communicate only with its home subnet VLAN4. Remember that R7 does not have routing capability at this point. If you have configured this correctly as shown in Example 2-73, you have scored 4 points.

**Example 2-73** *R6 LAM Configuration and Verification*

```
interface FastEthernet4/0
 ip address 10.60.60.1 255.255.255.248
 ip mobile arp access-group 50
```

**Example 2-73**  *R6 LAM Configuration and Verification (Continued)*

```
!
router ospf 30
redistribute mobile subnets
default-metric 4000
!
access-list 50 permit 10.50.50.2

R7#ping 10.50.50.1

Type escape sequence to abort.
Sending 5, 100-byte ICMP Echos to 10.50.50.1, timeout is 2 seconds:
.!!!!
Success rate is 80 percent (4/5), round-trip min/avg/max = 1/3/4 ms
```

- *Allow R7 to ping the IP addresses assigned to Loopback0 on R1, R4, R5, R6, and R8; do not assign any static, dynamic, or policy routes to achieve this. Perform configuration only on R7.*

As mentioned in the previous question, R7 does not have routing capability so you will have to manipulate the router to perform this connectivity. As you cannot use any form of routing to achieve this, you must forward the traffic for the destinations to R6, which has full visibility of the entire network. If you look at the ARP cache of R7, you will find that it already has an ARP entry for 10.50.50.1, which is, in fact, that of R6. Setting up static ARP entries in R7 for the remote destinations pointing to the MAC address of R6 should do the trick; however, it actually requires one further piece of configuration to make this work. As the remote networks are all in different IP subnets to that of R7 Fast Ethernet0/0, the static mappings will not work. By adding a secondary address on R7, which covers all subnets (that is, 10.0.0.1/8), you will find you now have full connectivity to the remote destinations. If you have configured this correctly as shown in Example 2-74 you have scored 5 points. Example 2-75, shows R7 ARP table and ping test results.

**Example 2-74**  *R7 LAM Configuration*

```
interface FastEthernet0/0
ip address 10.0.0.1 255.0.0.0 secondary
ip address 10.50.50.2 255.255.255.248
speed 100
full-duplex
!
arp 10.8.8.8 0001.9799.9870 ARPA
arp 10.1.1.1 0001.9799.9870 ARPA
arp 10.6.6.6 0001.9799.9870 ARPA
arp 10.4.4.4 0001.9799.9870 ARPA
arp 10.5.5.5 0001.9799.9870 ARPA
```

**Example 2-75** *R7 LAM Testing*

```
R7#sh arp
Protocol  Address          Age (min)  Hardware Addr   Type  Interface
Internet  10.8.8.8             -      0001.9799.9870  ARPA
Internet  10.50.50.2           -      0008.a3d1.9c20  ARPA  FastEthernet0/0
Internet  10.50.50.1           0      0001.9799.9870  ARPA  FastEthernet0/0
Internet  10.0.0.1             -      0008.a3d1.9c20  ARPA  FastEthernet0/0
Internet  10.1.1.1             -      0001.9799.9870  ARPA
Internet  10.6.6.6             -      0001.9799.9870  ARPA
Internet  10.4.4.4             -      0001.9799.9870  ARPA
Internet  10.5.5.5             -      0001.9799.9870  ARPA
R7#
R7#ping 10.1.1.1

Type escape sequence to abort.
Sending 5, 100-byte ICMP Echos to 10.1.1.1, timeout is 2 seconds:
!!!!!
Success rate is 100 percent (5/5), round-trip min/avg/max = 8/8/8 ms
R7#ping 10.4.4.4

Type escape sequence to abort.
Sending 5, 100-byte ICMP Echos to 10.4.4.4, timeout is 2 seconds:
!!!!!
Success rate is 100 percent (5/5), round-trip min/avg/max = 4/4/8 ms
R7#ping 10.5.5.5

Type escape sequence to abort.
Sending 5, 100-byte ICMP Echos to 10.5.5.5, timeout is 2 seconds:
!!!!!
Success rate is 100 percent (5/5), round-trip min/avg/max = 4/4/4 ms
R7#ping 10.6.6.6

Type escape sequence to abort.
Sending 5, 100-byte ICMP Echos to 10.6.6.6, timeout is 2 seconds:
!!!!!
Success rate is 100 percent (5/5), round-trip min/avg/max = 1/1/4 ms
R7#ping 10.8.8.8

Type escape sequence to abort.
Sending 5, 100-byte ICMP Echos to 10.8.8.8, timeout is 2 seconds:
!!!!!
Success rate is 100 percent (5/5), round-trip min/avg/max = 1/2/4 ms
R7#ping 10.50.50.1

Type escape sequence to abort.
Sending 5, 100-byte ICMP Echos to 10.50.50.1, timeout is 2 seconds:
!!!!!
Success rate is 100 percent (5/5), round-trip min/avg/max = 1/3/4 ms
```

- *Configure R4 so that if R1 and R6 both advertised VLAN2 within OSPF in the future that R4 would be able to load share to this destination across both Frame Relay PVCs; do not change the bandwidth statements on your PVCs.*

Before R4 would be able to load share for this future advertisement, you must ensure that the metrics for the route are exactly the same. As the network is to be advertised within OSPF and not redistributed with a default-metric cost, the network will be assigned a metric according to the assigned bandwidth statements on the Frame Relay PVCs. As you cannot change the bandwidth statements, you simply adjust the costs on the R4 interfaces to the same value for each PVC. If you have configured this correctly as in Example 2-76, you have scored 2 points. You will not be deducted points if you have not disabled the route caching feature, which is enabled by default.

**Example 2-76**  *R4 Future Load Sharing Configuration*

```
interface Virtual-Template1
  bandwidth 256
  ip ospf cost 400
!
interface Virtual-Template2
  bandwidth 512
  ip ospf cost 400
```

# Section 8: QoS (8 Points)

- *Configure your switch to trust DSCP QoS from the Cisco IP phones.*

You first need to enable QoS for the 3550 with the command **mls qos** and then under the Cisco IP Phone interfaces (port 0/16 and 0/17), configure **mls qos trust dscp**. If you have configured this correctly, you have scored 2 points. Example 2-77 shows the Cisco IP phone port QoS summary.

**Example 2-77**  *Switch1 Port 0/16 and 0/17 QoS Summary*

```
Switch1#sh mls qos int fastEthernet 0/16
FastEthernet0/16
trust state: trust dscp
trust mode: trust dscp
COS override: dis
default COS: 0
DSCP Mutation Map: Default DSCP Mutation Map
trust device: none

Switch1#sh mls qos int fastEthernet 0/17
FastEthernet0/17
trust state: trust dscp
trust mode: trust dscp
COS override: dis
default COS: 0
DSCP Mutation Map: Default DSCP Mutation Map
trust device: none
```

- *Ensure your switch does not trust QoS from the OEM IP phone.*

By default, the switch will not trust the QoS values unless configured to do so as shown in Example 2-77. If you have not configured any option here, you have scored 1 point. Example 2-78 shows the QoS port summary for port 0/18.

**Example 2-78** *Switch1 Port 0/18 QoS Summary*

```
Switch1#sh mls qos int fastEthernet 0/18
FastEthernet0/18
trust state: not trusted
trust mode: not trusted
COS override: dis
default COS: 0
DSCP Mutation Map: Default DSCP Mutation Map
trust device: none
```

- *You have a requirement to connect a PC that will be used in your office reception in the future. You have not been told the speed requirements or which VLAN this should be assigned to. You have been told that the PC will connect to port 0/15 on your 3550 and that a policy will be required to ensure that an IP precedence of critical is assigned to web traffic to an intranet server on 172.16.0.9; configure your switch appropriately.*

You need to configure a policy that matches on http traffic to destination host 172.16.0.9 on port 0/15; this traffic should then be assigned an IP precedence value of 5. If you have configured this correctly as shown in Example 2-79 you have scored 4 points. Example 2-80 shows the associated QoS policy summary for port 0/15.

**Example 2-79** *Switch1 Port 0/15 Policy*

```
class-map match-all intranet
  match access-group 100
!
!
policy-map intranet
  class intranet
    set ip precedence 5
!
interface FastEthernet0/15
 no ip address
 service-policy input intranet
!
access-list 100 permit tcp any host 172.16.0.9 eq www
```

**Example 2-80** *Switch1 Port 0/15 QoS Summary*

```
Switch1#sh mls qos int fastEthernet 0/15
FastEthernet0/15
Attached policy-map for Ingress: intranet
trust state: not trusted
trust mode: not trusted
COS override: dis
```

**Example 2-80**  *Switch1 Port 0/15 QoS Summary (Continued)*

```
default COS: 0
DSCP Mutation Map: Default DSCP Mutation Map
trust device: none
```

**NOTE**    As you have not been told which VLAN this port should belong to, it will, by default, belong to VLAN1.

- *Configure your voice to be of IP precedence flash value.*

Simply configure **ip precedence 3** within R1 and R4 VoIP **dial-peer** statements. If you have configured this correctly, you have scored 1 point.

# Section 9: Multicast (2 Points)

- *Ensure that R6 responds to pings from R4 to multicast address of 224.0.0.9; do not use PIM, any static mappings.*

This is a simple multicast question as you should have already configured multicast in the voice section. You should recognize 224.0.0.9 as the multicast address used by RIP V2. You will find without the use of PIM that by enabling RIP V2 on R6 it will respond when pinging 224.0.0.9. You only need RIP on R6 as, by default, R4 will forward multicast pings becasue of the broadcast capability of the Frame Relay network. If you have configured this correctly as shown in Example 2-81, you have scored 3 points. Example 2-82 shows R6 responding to a ping for 224.0.0.9.

**Example 2-81**  *R6 RIP V2 Multicast Configuration*

```
router rip
 version 2
 passive-interface default
 network 10.0.0.0
```

**Example 2-82**  *R4 RIP V2 Ping Testing*

```
R4#ping 224.0.0.9
Type escape sequence to abort.
Sending 1, 100-byte ICMP Echos to 224.0.0.9, timeout is 2 seconds:
Reply to request 0 from 10.100.101.2, 8 ms
```

# How Did You Do?

With the aid of the debrief section and full configurations and routing tables on the CD you, should now have an accurate evaluation of your lab. If you scored more than 80 points within the time frame (8 hours), you should congratulate yourself as you are well on the way to becoming a CCIE. You have demonstrated the ability to think laterally and confirmed an impressive knowledge of your subject. If you scored less than 80, don't worry; this will improve as you progress throughout the book and learn how to analyze each question and improve your core skills.

There were no major landmines in the lab, just a huge array of very complex questions that would make you configure quickly and quite possibly make errors.

For each question that you did not answer correctly, take the time to research the subject thoroughly and turn your weaknesses into your strengths. Research and plenty of practice will ultimately lead you to gain a passing score.

# Further Reading/URLs

To better prepare yourself and follow up on the topics covered in this lab, you should consult the http://www.cisco.com/public/pubsearch.html website for more information on the following topics:

PPP over Frame Relay
3550 Voice VLAN
VOIP 7960 7905
DLSw+ Load Sharing
DLSw+ udp-disable
BGP private autonomous system
Hoot and Holler
IGP Load Sharing
3550 QoS

# CHAPTER 3

# Practice Lab 3

The lab has been designed to challenge you in areas that you will find in the real exam with each lab having a distinct theme to enhance your study plan with Lab 3's being Border Gateway Protocol (BGP).

You will, of course, find the old favorites such as IGPs, DLSw+, and Voice but a complete understanding of BGP will earn you extra points in this lab.

Aim to adhere to the eight-hour time limit on this lab on the initial run through. Then, either score yourself at this point or continue until you feel you have met all the objectives. Keep a note of your score to plot your progress throughout the book and remember you are aiming to improve your technical knowledge, speed, and examination technique. The sections that follow guide you through the equipment requirements and pre-lab tasks in preparation for taking Practice Lab 3.

## Equipment List

You will need the following hardware and software components to commence Lab 3.

- Eight routers are required loaded with Cisco IOS Software Release 12.2-16 Enterprise image and the minimum interface configuration as documented in Table 3-1.

**Table 3-1**    *Interfaces Required per Router*

| Router | Ethernet Interface | Serial Interface | BRI Interface | Voice | ATM Interface |
|--------|--------------------|------------------|---------------|-------|---------------|
| R1 | 1 | 2 | 1 | 1 X FXS | - |
| R2 | 1 | 1 | - | - | - |
| R3 | 1 | - | - | - | - |
| R4 | 1 | 1 | 1 | 1 X FXS | - |
| R5 | 1 | 3 | - | - | 1 |
| R6 | 2 | 1 | - | - | 1 |
| R7 | 1 | - | - | - | - |
| R8 | 1 | - | - | - | - |

NOTE    Lab 3 was produced with R1, R2, R3, R4, R7, and R8 using 2600s, and R5 and R6 using 7200s.

- One Switch 3550 with Cisco IOS Software Release 12.1(12c) enterprise: c3550-i5q3l2-mz.121-12c.EA1.bin

# Setting Up the Lab

Feel free to use any combination of routers as long as you fulfill the topology diagram as shown in Figure 3-1. It is not compulsory to use the same model of routers but this will make life easier should you like to load configurations directly from the CD-ROM into your own devices.

NOTE    For each lab in the book you will have a set of initial configuration files that can be different from each other. Notice that some interfaces will not have IP address preconfigured; this is because you will either not be using that interface on that specific lab or because you will need to work on this interface through the exercise. The initial configurations can be found on the CD-ROM and should be used to pre-configure your routers and switch before the lab starts.

If you use the same equipment as used to produce the lab, you can simply paste the configurations into your own equipment; if not just configure your own equipment accordingly using the information supplied within the initial configurations.

Labs 1 through 3 in this book have been completed using 100-Mbps Fast Ethernet interfaces so if you have a mix of 10- and 100-Mbps Ethernet interfaces, adjust the bandwidth statements on the relevant interfaces to keep all interface speeds common. This will ensure that you do not get unwanted behavior because of differing IGP metrics.

## Lab Topology

Practice Lab 3 will use the topology as outlined in Figure 3-1, which you will need to create using the switch, Frame Relay, ATM, and ISDN information that follows.

**Figure 3-1**    *Lab 3 Topology Diagram*

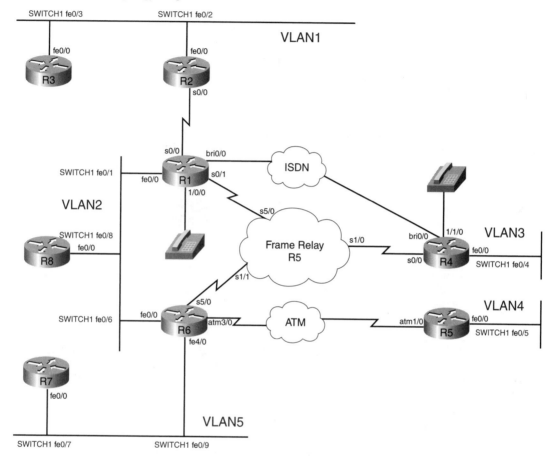

## Cabling Instructions

Follow the cabling requirements as outlined in Figure 3-2 and Table 3-2 to connect your routers to the switch.

**Figure 3-2** *3550 Cabling Diagram*

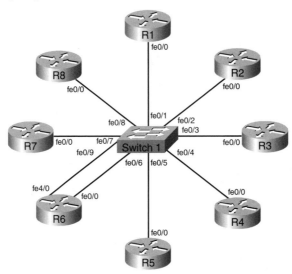

**Table 3-2** *3550 Cabling Guide*

| Ethernet Cabling | Switch1 Port Number |
| --- | --- |
| R1-Fast Ethernet0/0 | Port 0/1 |
| R2-Fast Ethernet0/0 | Port 0/2 |
| R3-Fast Ethernet0/0 | Port 0/3 |
| R4-Fast Ethernet0/0 | Port 0/4 |
| R5-Fast Ethernet0/0 | Port 0/5 |
| R6-Fast Ethernet0/0 | Port 0/6 |
| R7-Fast Ethernet0/0 | Port 0/7 |
| R8-Fast Ethernet0/0 | Port 0/8 |
| R6-Fast Ethernet4/0 | Port 0/9 |

# Frame Relay Switch Instructions

The Frame Relay portion of the lab is achieved by following the physical connectivity using R5 as a Frame Relay switch as shown in Figure 3-3.

**Figure 3-3**    *Frame Relay Switch Physical Connectivity*

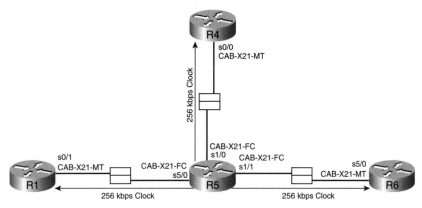

The physical Frame Relay connectivity (after configuration) will represent the logical Frame Relay network as shown in Figure 3-4.

**Figure 3-4**    *Frame Relay Switch Logical Connectivity*

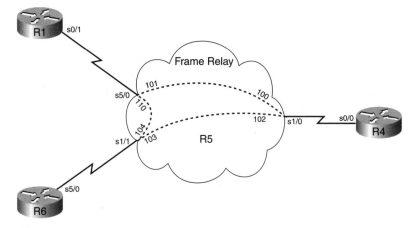

Configure one of your routers as a Frame Relay switch or have a dedicated router purely for this task. The first three lab scenarios use R5 to form the Frame Relay switch, and a fully meshed environment is configured between R1-R4-R6; pay attention in the lab to which PVCs are actually required. Keep the encapsulation and Local Management Interface (LMI) settings to default for this exercise but experiment with the settings outside the labs.

Keep your DCE cables at the Frame Relay switch end for simplicity and provide a clock rate of 256 kbps to all links. Should you require detailed information on how to configure one of your routers as a Frame Relay switch, this information can be found in Appendix A, "Frame Relay Switch Configuration."

---

**NOTE** The Frame Relay switch configuration for R5 is supplied on the CD-ROM, if required.

---

## ATM Switch Instructions

The ATM portion of the lab is achieved by following the physical connectivity between R5 and R6 as shown in Figure 3-5.

**Figure 3-5** *ATM Physical Connectivity*

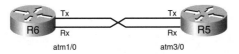

The physical ATM connectivity will represent the logical ATM network after configuration, as shown in Figure 3-6.

**Figure 3-6** *ATM Logical Connectivity*

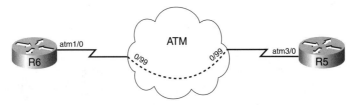

The ATM connectivity in Labs 1 through 3 will be provided by back-to-back connections between R6 and R5 over E3 ATM interfaces; you could also use a LightStream if available. Configure the PVCs as requested during the Lab exercise. If you are using a LightStream to provide your ATM connectivity and require information on how to set this up, this information can be found in Appendix B, "LS1010 ATM Switch Configuration."

## Serial Back-to-Back Instructions

R1 and R2 are connected back to back with serial cables as shown in Figure 3-7; ensure that the DCE cable is connected to R1 and generate a 2-Mbps clock from this point if using X21 cables as shown or reduce this to suit your own serial interfaces such as 1.5 Mbps for T1 connectivity.

**Figure 3-7**    *Serial Connectivity*

## ISDN Instructions

Connect R1 and R4 into either ISDN lines or an ISDN simulator. It is preferable that the ISDN supports CLI. Reconfigure the numbers as required if you are using live ISDN lines.

The lab has been produced using BRI S/T interfaces on R1 and R4 as shown in Figure 3-8.

**Figure 3-8**    *ISDN Connectivity*

## IP Address Instructions

Configure the IP addresses as shown in Figure 3-9 or load the initial router configurations for Lab 3 that can be found on the CD-ROM. If manually configuring, ensure you include the following loopback addresses:

R1 lo0 10.1.1.1/28
R2 lo0 10.2.2.2/28
R3 lo0 10.3.3.3/28
R4 lo0 10.4.4.4/28
R5 lo0 10.5.5.5/28
R6 lo0 10.6.6.6/28
R7 lo0 10.7.7.7/28
R8 lo0 10.8.8.8/28

**Figure 3-9** *IP Addressing Diagram*

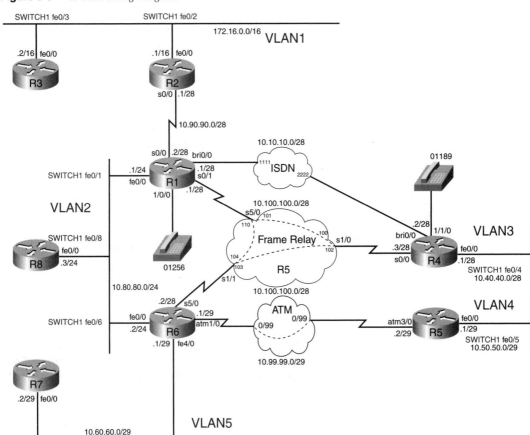

## Pre-Lab Tasks

- Build the lab topology as per Figure 3-1 and Figure 3-2.

- Configure your chosen Frame Relay switch router to provide the necessary Data Link Control Identifiers (DLCIs) as per Figure 3-4 or load the Frame Relay switch configuration from the CD-ROM.

- Configure the IP addresses on each router as shown in Figure 3-9 and add the loopback addresses (do not configure the Frame Relay or ATM IP addresses yet as you will need to select interface types within the lab beforehand); alternatively, you can load the initial configuration files from the CD-ROM.

- Configure passwords on all devices for console and vty access to "cisco" if not loading the initial configuration files.
- If you find yourself running out of time, choose questions that you are confident you can answer correctly. Failing this approach, choose questions with a higher point rating to maximize your potential score.
- Get into a comfortable and quiet environment where you can focus for the next eight hours.

# General Guidelines

- Please read the whole lab before you start.
- Do not configure any static/default or policy routes unless otherwise specified.
- Use only the DLCIs and ATM PVCs provided in the appropriate figures.
- Ensure full IP visibility between routers for ping testing/Telnet access to your devices with exception to **VLAN1 172.16.0.0/16** and R2 **Loopback0 10.2.2.0/28** as these will not be visible to the majority of your network.
- Take a 30-minute break midway through the exercise.
- Have available a Cisco Documentation CD-ROM or access online the latest documentation from the following URL:

  http://www.cisco.com/univercd/home/home.htm

| | |
|---|---|
| **NOTE** | Consider accessing only the preceding URL, not the entire Cisco.com website. If you will be allowed to use documentation during your CCIE lab exam, it will be restricted. |

# Practice Lab 3

You will now be answering questions in relation to the network topology as shown in Figure 3-10.

**Figure 3-10** *Lab 3 Topology Diagram*

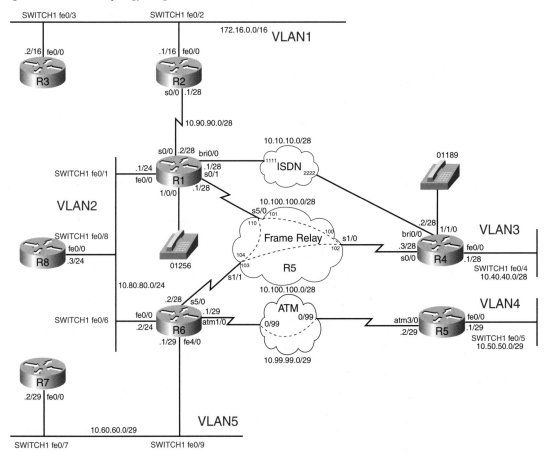

# Section 1: Bridging and Switching (18 Points)

## Section 1.1: Frame Relay Configuration (5 Points)

- Configure the Frame Relay portion of the network as shown in Figure 3-11 and ensure that DLCIs 110 and 104 between R1 and R6 are not used. Do not configure any subinterfaces, nor rely on inverse ARP, nor use the command **broadcast** in your configuration. Assume a CIR of 128 kbps per PVC for IGP reference.

- Configure the MTU on R1 and R6 to be 950 and leave the MTU on R4 as default.

**Figure 3-11**   *Frame Relay Diagram*

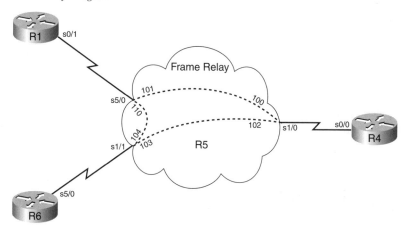

## Section 1.2: 3550 LAN Switch Configuration (10 Points)

- Configure VLAN numbers, VLAN names, and port assignment as per the topology diagram.

- The switch should be configured to log all debug information locally in a method so that it will not be lost in the event of a reset, it should also contain a timestamp.

- Configure your switch not to allow R1 to Telnet into R6. Use VLAN2 addresses for your configuration. Your solution should be applied to the whole VLAN as opposed to individual ports.

- Do not allow all ports on VLAN3 to multicast above 3 Mbps.

- Ensure the switch is reachable via the IP address of 10.80.80.8/24.

## Section 1.3: ATM Configuration (3 Points)

- Configure the ATM PVCs as shown in Figure 3-12. Use point-to-point subinterfaces and use the new format **PVC** *vpi/vci* when configuring the PVCs. Ensure that the ATM subinterfaces contain purely Layer 2 information, configure virtual Layer 3 addresses elsewhere for the ATM connectivity, and make this connectivity as secure as possible. This configuration does not require any form of bridging.

**Figure 3-12** *ATM Diagram*

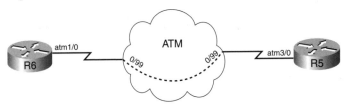

# Section 2: IP IGP Protocols (16 Points)

Configure the IP routing as in Figure 3-13 as directed.

## Section 2.1: EIGRP (7 Points)

- Configure EIGRP AS1 as shown in Figure 3-13. Initial loopback interfaces should be advertised within EIGRP for every router running EIGRP.
- Authenticate routing updates.
- Allow R3 to only receive routing updates from R2 even if a further EIGRP router is added to VLAN1.

## Section 2.2: OSPF (5 Points)

- Configure OSPF as shown in Figure 3-13 with the process on each router as 1. Ensure that all OSPF routers have their loopback interfaces advertised in the same area as that of the Ethernet interface.
- Do not use the **ip ospf network** command over the Frame Relay network.
- Ensure that no host routes are propagated throughout the network.

## Section 2.3: Redistribution (4 Points)

- Redistribute OSPF into EIGRP on R2; do not perform mutual redistribution and only allow OPSF routes with a mask greater than 255.255.0.0 into EIGRP.

**Figure 3-13**  *IP IGP Diagram*

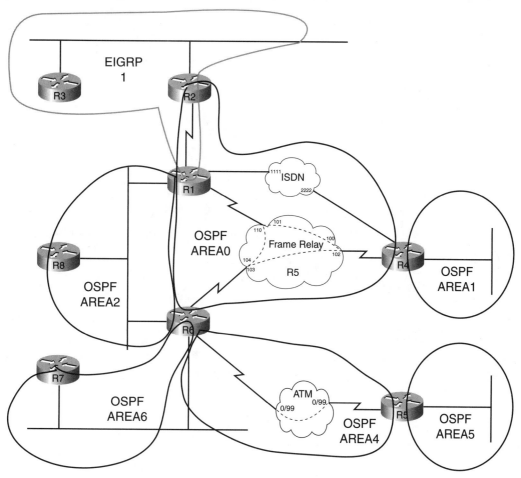

## Section 3: ISDN (4 Points)

- If your Frame Relay network fails, allow R4 to dial into R1. Use passwords that are difficult to detect. Ensure R4 dials out after 5 seconds of Frame Relay failure. If the Frame Relay network restores, keep the call connected for a further 45 seconds before disconnecting. OSPF is required over the ISDN network when a call is established. Do not configure any Layer 3 addressing on the physical ISDN interfaces.

# Section 4: EGP Protocols (25 Points)

- Configure BGP as shown in Figure 3-14 with the following peering:

  R2 172.16.0.1 – R3 172.16.0.2

  R2 172.16.0.1 – R1 10.80.80.1

  R1 10.80.80.1 – R8 10.8.8.8

  R1 10.80.80.1 – R6 10.6.6.6

  R6 10.6.6.6 – R4 10.4.4.4

  R6 10.6.6.6 – R5 10.5.5.5

  R6 10.6.6.6 – R7 10.7.7.7

  Where possible, minimize the configuration required.

- Inject the following networks into BGP, configure new loopback interfaces where required, do not use the **network** command, and ensure that all routes have a metric of 100 assigned to them:

  R1 – 10.1.1.1/28

  R2 – 2.2.2.2/28

  R3 – 3.3.3.3/28

  R4 – 10.4.4.4/28

  R5 – 10.5.5.5/28

  R6 – 10.6.6.6/28

  R7 – 10.7.7.7/28

  R8 – 10.8.8.8/28

- Configure R6 to extend the range of network 2.2.2.0/28 into 2.2.2.0/24 when advertised into AS12. Ensure that the original attributes of this network are visible from AS12.

- Users in AS11 are complaining that network 3.3.3.0 is unstable; configure R6 to control the instability of this route. Use the following values:

  Reuse-value 30

  Half-life 20

  Suppress-value 1000

  Maximum-suppress-time 130

- On R2, set up a new loopback 22.22.22.22/24, advertise this within BGP using the **network** command. Similarly, set up 11.11.11.11/24 on R1. If the BGP route 22.22.22.0 is present on R1's BGP table, do not advertise network 11.11.11.0/24 to R8. If network 22.22.22.0/24 disappears, do advertise network 11.11.11.0/24 to R8.

- On R5, set up a new loopback 5.5.5.5/28 and advertise this into AS11 using the **network** command, but do not allow this to be advertised into AS10 or AS12. Only configure R5 to achieve this.

- R2 is due to have external directly connected BGP neighbors added to it on VLAN1. This VLAN has a tendency to flap because of a faulty switch; configure R2 so that if the VLAN should fail, the BGP sessions are not immediately reset.

- Ensure that all BGP speakers within AS1 do not respond to hostile TCP resets or untrusted routing updates.

- All BGP peers are to be able to communicate with all advertised BGP networks.

**Figure 3-14**  *IP EGP Diagram*

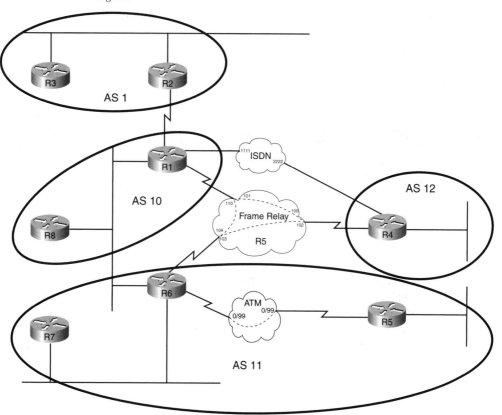

# Section 5: Voice (7 Points)

- Configure VoIP between R1 and R4 using the numbers supplied in Figure 3-10; ensure your VoIP is operational if the Frame Relay network fails.

- Set up a hunt group on R4 so that if the number 01189 is dialed and voice port 1/1/0 is in use, port 1/1/1 answers the call. Port 1/1/0 should always answer the call if the phone connected to this port is not in use first.

- Define an order of preference for selecting a codec when R1 initiates a call to R4. R1 should first negotiate to use a g728 codec and then fall back to a g729r8 with a 20-byte payload. Leave the R4 codec as default.

# Section 6: DLSw+ (6 Points)

- Configure DLSw+ with TCP encapsulation between R6-R4 and R6-R5. R4 should only be able to connect to R6 VLAN2 and R5 to VLAN5.

- If the DLSw+ connection from R4-R6 fails, allow R4 to connect to VLAN2 via R1. If the primary connection to R6 is restored, only keep the new connection to VLAN2 active for 60 seconds.

- R4 and R5 should show reachability of NetBIOS name **ccie** advertised from R6. This is the only NetBIOS name of which R6 should have visibility.

# Section 7: IOS and IP Features (10 Points)

- Configure R8 so that when R6 FastEthernet4/0 (10.60.60.1) connects to virtual IP address 10.80.80.12, that traffic is actually sent to R2 Serial 0/0 (10.90.90.1). When R1 receives the traffic from R6, it should see the source address of 10.8.8.2 for this operation. Do not perform any policy routing in your solution.

- Manipulate the EIGRP authentication to change the keys as follows: The first key should remain active from the time you started this lab today and remain active for two days after that; the second key should then become active permanently. Allow an overlap of 20 minutes but ensure that all EIGRP routers have a common synchronized time source provided by one of your routers to ensure reliable operation.

- Configure R7 not to send each character of a Telnet session as a separate CPU interrupt to your network devices. Characters should be buffered until an acknowledgment is received to reduce CPU interrupts and improve on bandwidth limitations.

- Prevent the configuration prompt from being displayed on R5 when in config mode.

# Section 8: QoS (5 Points)

- Configure a QoS policy on R2 for traffic flowing from VLAN1 toward the rest of your network. Traffic found to have an IP precedence of 7, 5, and 1 should be limited to a maximum of 2 Mbps. Traffic above this figure with the stated precedence should be discarded. Use only one ACL to accomplish this requirement. Assume normal and excess burst sizes to both be 40000.

- A future FXS module will be installed into R6 and VoIP traffic will flow between R1 and R6. Configure RSVP on R1 so that the RSVP setup must be complete before the destination phone rings. Each RSVP flow should be set to 100 kbps and allow for a maximum of 2 flows; allow a maximum of 15 seconds for this setup. You should also allow for 64 discard messages and 64 dynamic queues in your QoS configuration. You are not required to perform any configuration on R6 but can assume that the phone number on R6 will be 01962 when configuring the dial plan on R1.

# Section 9: Multicast (5 Points)

- Configure a new loopback interface on R1 of 10.9.9.1/24; advertise this out of FastEthernet0/0 (VLAN2) interface using RIP V1.

- Configure R5 to receive the RIP advertisement from R1. Use a multicast solution to achieve this and do not create any tunnel interfaces. You are not required to be able to ping 10.9.9.9 from R5.

# Section 10: Security (5 Points)

- Configure R3 to be managed by http with password access of **cisco** for username and **cisco** for the password.

- It is suspected that your network is being threatened by a W32.Blaster virus. You have been told that the virus is manipulating port 135, 139, and 445 and that it is attempting to enter your network from VLAN1. Configure R2 to block the virus entering the rest of your network and to provide as much detail at Layer 2 and 3 as to which devices might be initiating the attack. The worm will also attempt to send packets to random IP addresses, which do not exist. When this happens, the router will reply with an ICMP message. Configure R2 not to send this ICMP message.

# Practice Lab 3: "Ask the Proctor"

This section should only be used if you require clues to complete the questions. In the real CCIE lab, the proctor will not enter into any discussions regarding the questions or answers. He or she will be present to ensure you do not have problems with the lab environment and to maintain the timing element of the exam.

## Section 1.1: Frame Relay Configuration

Q: How do I know if the PVCs are all on the same subnet?
A: Look at Figure 3-10, which contains all relevant IP address information.

Q: If I do not use **broadcast** on my map statements, will this stop my routing protocols from functioning correctly?
A: If it does, you will need to resolve this within your routing protocol configuration.

Q: If I change the MTU values, will this stop my Frame Relay network from functioning?
A: Run a ping test between routers to confirm that your network is operating correctly.

## Section 1.2: 3550 LAN Switch Configuration

Q: Can I configure logging to a server to save the information permanently?
A: You are requested to log the information locally on the switch.

Q: So is **logging buffered** sufficient?
A: You might find that using this feature will result in the information being lost after a reset or power failure to the switch.

Q: Can I save the log information in flash?
A: Yes.

Q: Can I configure an access list to block Telnet as I would within a router?
A: No, your switch is not running IP routing.

Q: Do you want me to rate limit my multicast?
A: You do not have sufficient information to perform rate limiting and would have to block the entire multicast address range; a simple solution is available to you.

Q: Can I use R1 or R6 as my default gateway?
A: Yes, use whichever you choose but ensure full visibility from your network.

# Section 1.3: ATM Configuration

Q: If I cannot include Layer 3 information on my subinterfaces, can I use virtual templates as you can with Frame Relay?

A: Yes.

Q: If I use virtual templates with PPP do you require PAP or CHAP authentication?

A: You are requested to make this connection as secure as possible, so choose the best method available to you.

# Section 2.1: EIGRP

Q: If I configure authentication, will R3 receive updates only from R2 anyway?

A: An additional router could be installed on the same VLAN; if this was configured with the same authentication parameters, it could also send updates to R3.

Q: I do not have the neighbor feature available in this version of code, should I be using this?

A: No, you have a similar feature available to you, which is configurable in a different manner.

# Section 2.2: OSPF

Q: I have already advertised R1 loopback within EIGRP; do you still want me to do this in OSPF?

A: You should advertise this within both.

Q: I can't get an adjacency across my ATM as this is NBMA; if I cannot adjust what network it is under OSPF, how can I form a neighbor?

A: This is a back-to-basics type question; what mechanisms are available to you for NBMA network types?

Q: I have configured neighbor statements on my Frame Relay routers; is this sufficient?

A: This will help, but if you still cannot form an adjacency you need to investigate why. Try some of the OSPF debugs that are available to you.

Q: I can see there is an MTU issue when I debug OSPF; can I change the MTU back to default on the Frame Relay network?

A: No, you will need to find an OSPF workaround.

Q: My loopback interfaces have come out as host routes, is this acceptable?

A: No, use an OSPF feature to ensure they are advertised with the correct mask.

# Section 2.3: Redistribution

Q: If I only redistribute OSPF into EIGRP, my OSPF network will not have visibility of network 172.16.0.0/16 and network 10.2.2.0/24. Will this be a problem?

A: This is true, potentially it will be a problem. You are told in the lab instructions that VLAN1 and network 10.2.2.0/24 are exempt from the IP connectivity testing but if you find certain connectivity is required, you will need to find a workaround.

Q: Can I use a distribute list to allow specific masks?

A: No, but you are on the right track.

# Section 3: ISDN

Q: Because you want OSPF over the ISDN, can I use a demand circuit?

A: No, you are given sufficient information in the question to determine which method to use.

Q: Can I use the backup interface command?

A: Yes.

Q: If R4 is required to dial into R1, can I just configure a dial statement on R4 only?

A: Yes.

Q: If I cannot configure Layer 3 on the ISDN, can I just create a dialer interface?

A: Yes.

# Section 4: EGP Protocols

Q: For minimal configuration, are you looking for route reflectors or peer groups?

A: Where appropriate, both; certain peering might only be possible with route reflectors anyway.

Q: If I cannot use the network command, can I redistribute my IGP selectively?

A: No.

Q: Can I just set up an aggregate address to extend the network 2.2.2.0/28?

A: If this maintains the original attributes, yes, but you might care to check that it does.

Q: As soon as I set up the new interfaces and advertise them within BGP on R2 and R1, will R8 see both of these automatically?

A: Yes, it will unless you configure a specific BGP feature on R1.

Q: Do you want network 5.5.5.0 to be advertised into AS1 but not AS10 or AS12?

A: No, the question does not request this.

Q: I can stop network 5.5.5.0 from entering AS10 and AS12 by using a filter-list outbound on R6; will I score half marks by doing this?

A: No, the question specifically states you must only configure R5. You have a method available to you that will effectively inform R6 not to advertise this particular network.

Q: If the VLAN flaps, will the session be maintained for a small amount of time anyway?

A: No, two external neighbors peering on a connected interface will drop the session immediately.

Q: Do you want me to set up an access list between each BGP peer to only allow TCP port 179 between them so only the correct peers communicate?

A: No, use a BGP feature to make peering secure.

Q: Is it sufficient to use password authentication between BGP peers?

A: Yes.

Q: I seem to have a connectivity problem in AS10 from R8 to networks originated within AS1; should I be able to reach these networks from R8?

A: Yes, you should be able to communicate between all BGP networks from all routers.

Q: I have performed some debugging and found that R8 is attempting to send my ICMP test traffic to 172.16.0.1 for networks in AS1. I understood this network was not to be redistributed; is this correct?

A: Yes, network 172.16.0.0/16 should not be redistributed; use a BGP feature within AS10 to manipulate the BGP routing table on R8.

# Section 5: Voice

Q: Do you require any specific configuration to ensure the Voice functions should the Frame Relay fail?

A: If you have configured your session target IP addresses effectively and have your ISDN back up working, you will not need any specific configuration.

Q: I have found that I can configure POTS dial peers with the same number on R4; is this sufficient?

A: You must ensure that a specific port will always answer the call first.

Q: Can I set up two VoIP dial peers with different codecs so if the first fails, the second should work?

A: No, a more efficient method is available to you.

# Section 6: DLSw+

Q: If I use two Bridge Lists on R6, is this sufficient to separate the DLSw+?
A: Yes.

Q: I cannot enter a "?" within my configuration, is it acceptable to enter a wildcard or similar?
A: No, find a method of entering the "?" without it bringing up the help function.

# Section 7: IOS and IP Features

Q: Can I set up a secondary address on R8 for 10.80.80.12?
A: No, you do not need to.

Q: Can I use NAT on a Stick to answer the question?
A: You might find that this requires policy routing to function, which you are not permitted to use.

Q: Do you want the EIGRP routers to use NTP?
A: Yes.

Q: Can I configure the NTP master on any of the EIGRP routers?
A: You should carefully choose which router is configured as the Master.

# Section 8: QoS

Q: I have configured rate limiting on R2 but have used three access lists; do I score any points?
A: No, a method exists of matching all three different IP precedence values within the same ACL.

Q: Is standard RSVP sufficient to answer the question as long as the bandwidth requirements are met?
A: No, RSVP setup must be complete before the destination phone rings.

# Section 9: Multicast

Q: RIP V1 uses a broadcast address; would a multicast address such as that used by RIP V2 be required to be transported across a multicast network?
A: No, it is possible to send a broadcast over a multicast network; use your CD if you are not familiar with this solution.

Q: I have managed to configure my network for Multicast Helper but I still do not receive the RIP route in my routing table on R5; is this acceptable?

A: No, you need to have the route installed in the routing table to score any points; debug your routing updates to ensure you are receiving the route at R5 and if it is being accepted as a valid route.

# Section 10: Security (2 Points)

Q: Do you require the http authentication to be set up for a remote server somewhere?

A: No, keep all your configuration on R3.

Q: For the virus, I have not been told if it is using TCP or UDP?

A: Correct, the decision is yours.

Q: Can I just use the log feature within my ACL?

A: You need to provide details at both Layer 2 and Layer 3.

Q: Do you require the http authentication to be set up for a remote server somewhere?

A: No, keep all your configuration on R3.

Q: Do you require that the ICMP message be blocked by the same ACL?

A: No, this would not stop R2 from sending it but stop other devices from receiving it.

# Practice Lab 3 Debrief

The lab debrief section will now analyze each question showing you what was required and how to achieve the desired results. You should use this section to produce an overall score for your test.

# Section 1: Bridging and Switching (16 Points)

## Section 1.1: Frame Relay Configuration (5 Points)

- *Configure the Frame Relay portion of the network as shown in Figure 3-11 and ensure that DLCIs 110 and 104 between R1 and R6 are not used. Do not configure any subinterfaces, nor rely on inverse ARP, nor use the command **broadcast** in your configuration. Assume a CIR of 128 kbps per PVC for IGP reference.*

The question clearly states that DLCIs 110 and 104 are not to be used and that you should not use subinterfaces; you must, therefore, configure your physical serial interfaces and disable **inverse-arp** on R1, R4, and R6. Your map statements under the physical interfaces must be configured without broadcast capability; hence, you will need to configure OSPF to unicast further on in the lab. You should configure a bandwidth statement of 128 kbps on each router to ensure that OSPF can assign an accurate cost to the Frame Relay connectivity. If you have configured these items correctly as shown in Example 3-1 through Example 3-3, you have scored 2 points.

**Example 3-1**    *R1 Frame Relay Solution Configuration*

```
interface Serial0/1
 bandwidth 128
 ip address 10.100.100.1 255.255.255.240
 encapsulation frame-relay
 frame-relay map ip 10.100.100.2 101
 frame-relay map ip 10.100.100.3 101
 no frame-relay inverse-arp
```

**Example 3-2**    *R4 Frame Relay Solution Configuration*

```
interface Serial0/0
 bandwidth 128
 ip address 10.100.100.3 255.255.255.240
 encapsulation frame-relay
 frame-relay map ip 10.100.100.1 100
 frame-relay map ip 10.100.100.2 102
 no frame-relay inverse-arp
```

**Example 3-3**   *R6 Frame Relay Solution Configuration*

```
interface Serial5/0
 bandwidth 128
 ip address 10.100.100.2 255.255.255.240
 encapsulation frame-relay
 frame-relay map ip 10.100.100.1 103
 frame-relay map ip 10.100.100.3 103
 no frame-relay inverse-arp
```

- *Configure the MTU on R1 and R6 to be 950 and leave the MTU on R4 as default.*

Simply configure **ip mtu 950** on R1 s0/1 and R6 s5/0; this will cause you issues with OSPF as forming an adjacency OSPF requires neighbors to have the same MTU configured. This is in addition to having the same OSPF area, the same type of area such as stub or NSSA, the same subnet and subnet mask, and the same OSPF Hello and Dead timer values. Example 3-4 shows the OSPF initialization state of R4 as it attempts to form an adjacency later on when OSPF is configured; without rectification, it will not progress past this point.

**Example 3-4**   *R4 OSPF Adjacency Problems*

```
R4#sh ip ospf neigh
Neighbor ID     Pri   State           Dead Time   Address        Interface
10.6.6.6         1    EXCHANGE/DR     00:01:14    10.100.100.2   Serial0/0
N/A              1    ATTEMPT/DROTHER    -         10.100.100.1   Serial0/0
```

Example 3-5 shows an OSPF adjacency debug from R1. It can be seen that R1 is aware that R4 has a larger MTU than itself and the adjacency cannot complete.

**Example 3-5**   *R1 Debug OSPF Adjacency*

```
R1#debug ip ospf adj
OSPF adjacency events debugging is on
R1#
01:14:17: OSPF: Rcv DBD from 10.4.4.4 on Serial0/1 seq 0x581 opt 0x42 flag 0x7 len
32   mtu 1500 state EXSTART
01:14:17: OSPF: Nbr 10.4.4.4 has larger interface MTU
01:14:19: OSPF: Send DBD to 10.4.4.4 on Serial0/1 seq 0x1D9B opt 0x42 flag 0x7 len
32
01:14:19: OSPF: Retransmitting DBD to 10.4.4.4 on Serial0/1 [14]
01:14:22: OSPF: Rcv DBD from 10.4.4.4 on Serial0/1 seq 0x581 opt 0x42 flag 0x7 len
32   mtu 1500 state EXSTART
```

By configuring **ip ospf mtu-ignore** on R1 and R6 under the physical Frame Relay interfaces, you can successfully form a neighbor relationship. Although the OSPF issue comes later in the lab if you have configured this correctly, you have scored 3 points. If you have only configured the MTU without the OSPF fix, you have scored 1 point.

## Section 1.2: 3550 LAN Switch Configuration (10 Points)

- *Configure VLAN numbers, VLAN names, and port assignment as per the topology diagram.*

The switch in this instance is isolated again as in Chapter 1 and 2 so there is no need to configure it as a VTP server. From the VLAN database, add the required VLANs and name them accordingly. You should note that you can not change the VLAN name of VLAN1. You must ensure that the port speed and duplex is fixed to 100 Mbps and full duplex if your routers support this; leaving your ports in auto mode could cause connectivity problems. If you have configured these items correctly as in Example 3-6, you have scored 2 points.

**Example 3-6**  *3550 Switch1 Initial Configuration*

```
Switch1#vlan database
Switch1(vlan)#vlan 2 name VLAN2
VLAN 2 modified:
    Name: VLAN2
Switch1(vlan)#vlan 3 name VLAN3
VLAN 3 modified:
    Name: VLAN3
Switch1(vlan)#vlan 4 name VLAN4
VLAN 4 modified:
    Name: VLAN4
Switch1(vlan)#vlan 5 name VLAN5
VLAN 5 modified:
    Name: VLAN5
Switch1(vlan)#exit
APPLY completed.
Exiting....

hostname Switch1
!
enable password cisco
interface FastEthernet0/1
 switchport access vlan 2
 switchport mode access
 no ip address
 duplex full
 speed 100
!
interface FastEthernet0/2
 switchport mode access
 no ip address
 duplex full
 speed 100
!
interface FastEthernet0/3
 switchport mode access
 no ip address
 duplex full
 speed 100
!
```

**Example 3-6**    *3550 Switch1 Initial Configuration (Continued)*

```
interface FastEthernet0/4
 switchport access vlan 3
 switchport mode access
 no ip address
 duplex full
 speed 100
!
interface FastEthernet0/5
 switchport access vlan 4
 switchport mode access
 no ip address
 duplex full
 speed 100
!
interface FastEthernet0/6
 switchport access vlan 2
 switchport mode access
 no ip address
 duplex full
 speed 100
!
interface FastEthernet0/7
 switchport access vlan 5
 switchport mode access
 no ip address
 duplex full
 speed 100
!
interface FastEthernet0/8
 switchport access vlan 2
 switchport mode access
 no ip address
 duplex full
 speed 100
!
interface FastEthernet0/9
 switchport access vlan 5
 switchport mode access
 no ip address
 duplex full
 speed 100
```

**NOTE**    The VLAN configuration is completed under **Vlan database.**

- *The switch should be configured to log all debug information locally in a method so that it will not be lost in the event of a reset, it should also contain a timestamp.*

Information logged to the buffer would be lost in the event of a reset but you have the ability to log to Flash on the 3550. You will need to set the clock on the switch and configure timestamps for debugging. If you have configured this correctly as shown in Example 3-7, you have scored 2 points.

**Example 3-7**   *3550 Debug Logging Setup*

```
clock set 16:51:00 18 july 2004
Switch1#conf t
Enter configuration commands, one per line.  End with CNTL/Z.
Switch1(config)#service timestamps debug datetime
Switch1(config)#logging file flash:debug.text debugging
Switch1(config)#^Z
Switch1#debug ip packet
Switch1#sh flash
Directory of flash:/
    2  -rwx         316      Mar 01 1993 03:44:44  system_env_vars
    3  -rwx          72         Jul  18 2004 16:51:35  debug.text
    4  -rwx     3823261  Mar 01 1993 03:20:20  c3550-i5q3l2-mz.121-12c.EA1.bin
    5  -rwx        3298      Mar 01 1993 01:48:12  config.text
    6  -rwx         916      Mar 01 1993 00:00:35  vlan.dat
    7  drwx         192      Mar 01 1993 00:02:57  c3550-i9q3l2-mz.121-11.EA1
   22  -rwx           0      Mar 01 1993 03:44:44  env_vars
   23  -rwx           5      Mar 01 1993 01:48:12  private-config.text
```

**NOTE**   A **debug** command is issued to the switch to begin logging to flash for verification purposes.

- *Configure your switch not to allow R1 to Telnet into R6. Use VLAN2 addresses for your configuration. Your solution should be applied to the whole VLAN as opposed to individual ports.*

If IP routing was running on the switch, you could simply configure an IP access list to block Telnet between the routers and apply this to the relevant interface but you are requested to apply your solution to the entire VLAN. This requires a VACL (VLAN access control list) as shown in Example 3-8, with the verification testing from R1. If you have configured this correctly, you have scored 3 points.

**Example 3-8**   *3550 VACL Configuration and Testing*

```
ip access-list extended telnet
   permit tcp host 10.80.80.1 host 10.80.80.2 eq telnet
   Exit
ip access-list extended allowed
  permit ip any any
  exit
vlan access-map no-R1-R6 10
   match ip add telnet
```

**Example 3-8**    *3550 VACL Configuration and Testing (Continued)*

```
     action drop
     exit
vlan access-map no-R1-R6 20
     match ip add allowed
     action forward
     exit
vlan filter no-R1-R6 vlan 2

R1#ping 10.80.80.2
Type escape sequence to abort.
Sending 5, 100-byte ICMP Echos to 10.80.80.2, timeout is 2 seconds:
!!!!!
Success rate is 100 percent (5/5), round-trip min/avg/max = 1/1/4 ms
R1#telnet 10.80.80.2
Trying 10.80.80.2 ...
% Connection timed out; remote host not responding
```

- *Do not allow all ports on VLAN3 to multicast above 3 Mbps.*

You may have initially thought of configuring rate limiting and matching the entire multicast IP address range but a much simpler method is available. You are required to configure **storm control multicast level 3.00** under each interface on the switch that is connected to VLAN3, which is only port fe0/4 that connects to R4 fe0/0. If you are using routers with 10BASE-T interfaces, you should have configured the value to **30.00**. If you have configured this correctly, you have scored 2 points.

- *Ensure the switch is reachable via the IP address of 10.80.80.8/24.*

You will need to configure an **ip default-gateway 10.80.80.1** onto the 3550; this could also point to 10.80.80.2. You will also have to create an additional VLAN interface of VLAN2 on the 3550 and configure an IP address of 10.80.80.8/24 under this new interface. If you have configured this correctly, you have scored 1 point.

## Section 1.3: ATM Configuration (3 Points)

- *Configure the ATM PVCs as shown in Figure 3-12. Use point-to-point subinterfaces and use the new format **PVC** vpi/vci when configuring the PVCs. Ensure that the ATM subinterfaces contain purely Layer 2 information, configure virtual Layer 3 addresses elsewhere for the ATM connectivity, and make this connectivity as secure as possible. This configuration does not require any form of bridging.*

You are faced with a similar configuration to that of the Frame Relay in Lab 2. Usually, you would keep your Layer 3 information under the subinterface but it can be configured in another place. The clues to the question are not configuring Layer 3 and making it secure. Again, the only way of achieving this is using PPP. ATM is capable of running PPP but it requires the encapsulation type **aal5ciscoppp** and the reference to a **virtual-template** interface. The **virtual-template**, which is by default a PPP interface, can then contain the

Layer 3 address and CHAP statement required to make the PPP connection secure. You will also need a username and password as with ISDN CHAP. You should include the **broadcast** statement under your PVC configuration to ensure correct operation for your OSPF. If you have configured these items correctly as in Example 3-9 and Example 3-10, you have scored 3 points.

**Example 3-9**  *R5 ATM and PPP Configuration*

```
username R6 password 0 cisco
!
interface ATM3/0
 no ip address
 no atm ilmi-keepalive
!
interface ATM3/0.99 point-to-point

 pvc 0/99
  protocol ip 10.99.99.1 broadcast
  encapsulation aal5ciscoppp Virtual-Template1
!
interface Virtual-Template1
 ip address 10.99.99.2 255.255.255.248
 ppp authentication chap
```

**Example 3-10**  *R6 ATM and PPP Configuration*

```
username R5 password 0 cisco
!
interface ATM1/0
 no ip address
 no atm ilmi-keepalive
!
interface ATM1/0.99 point-to-point
 pvc 0/99
 protocol ip 10.99.99.2 broadcast
 encapsulation aal5ciscoppp Virtual-Template1
!
interface Virtual-Template1
 ip address 10.99.99.1 255.255.255.248
 ppp authentication chap
```

# Section 2: IP IGP Protocols (16 Points)

Configure the IP routing as in Figure 3-13 as directed.

## Section 2.1: EIGRP (7 Points)

- *Configure EIGRP AS1 as shown in Figure 3-13. Initial loopback interfaces should be advertised within EIGRP for every router running EIGRP.*

You should configure EIGRP AS1 on R1-R2-R3. You could just enable EIGRP with a **network 10.0.0.0** statement everywhere. But as you can see in Figure 3-13, R1 does not have all its network 10 interfaces included in EIGRP. You will need to configure an inverse mask for the networks you require advertised and included in EIGRP on R1; preferably, configure R2 and R3 in the same manner although you will not loose marks for this in this case. Do not forget to disable auto summarization on all your routers as a matter of good practice even though strictly speaking this is not required on R3. If you have configured this correctly as shown in Example 3-11 through Example 3-13, you have scored 2 points.

**Example 3-11** *R1 Initial EIGRP Configuration*

```
router eigrp 1
 network 10.1.1.0 0.0.0.15
 network 10.90.90.0 0.0.0.15
 no auto-summary
```

**Example 3-12** *R2 Initial EIGRP Configuration*

```
router eigrp 1
 network 10.2.2.0 0.0.0.15
 network 10.90.90.0 0.0.0.15
 network 172.16.0.0
 no auto-summary
```

**Example 3-13** *R3 Initial EIGRP Configuration*

```
router eigrp 1
 network 10.3.3.0 0.0.0.15
 network 172.16.0.0
 no auto-summary
```

- *Authenticate routing updates.*

As in Lab 2, a question, which will eat into your time, that is also in preparation for a task within the IOS section. To authenticate the EIGRP updates, you need to configure a key chain with appropriate key-string and enable it on the EIGRP interfaces (with exception to the loopbacks). If you configured this correctly as shown in Example 3-14 through Example 3-15, you have scored 2 points.

**Example 3-14** *R1 Initial EIGRP Authentication Configuration*

```
key chain Brussels
 key 1
  key-string Asterix
!
interface Serial0/0
 ip authentication mode eigrp 1 md5
 ip authentication key-chain eigrp 1 Brussels
```

**Example 3-15** *R2 Initial EIGRP Authentication Configuration*

```
key chain Brussels
 key 1
  key-string Asterix
 !
interface FastEthernet0/0
 ip authentication mode eigrp 1 md5
 ip authentication key-chain eigrp 1 Brussels
 !
interface Serial0/0
 ip authentication mode eigrp 1 md5
 ip authentication key-chain eigrp 1 Brussels
```

**Example 3-16** *R3 Initial EIGRP Authentication Configuration*

```
key chain Brussels
 key 1
  key-string Asterix
 !
interface FastEthernet0/0
 ip authentication mode eigrp 1 md5
 ip authentication key-chain eigrp 1 Brussels
```

- *Allow R3 to only receive routing updates from R2 even if a further EIGRP router is added to VLAN1.*

Versions of Cisco IOS Software prior to Release 12.2.16 had a **neighbor** command within EIGRP. Subsequent releases do not. Even though you are running authentication, further EIGRP speakers could be added to VLAN1 and configured with the correct authentication; if this happened, R3 would be able to receive routes from them. R3 can selectively receive routes by configuring a distribute-list with the gateway option enabled; this should contain purely R2's Ethernet address within a prefix-list. If you have configured this correctly as shown in Example 3-17, you have scored 3 points.

**Example 3-17** *R3 EIGRP Gateway Configuration*

```
router eigrp 1
 distribute-list gateway neighbor-R2 in FastEthernet 0/0
 !
ip prefix-list neighbor-R2 seq 5 permit 172.16.0.1/32
```

# Section 2.2: OSPF (5 Points)

- *Configure OSPF as shown in Figure 3-13 with the process on each router as 1. Ensure that all OSPF routers have their loopback interfaces advertised in the same area as that of the Ethernet interface.*

You will need to configure OSPF on R1, R2, R4, R5, R6, R7, and R8 ensuring that all OSPF-only routers have their loopback interfaces advertised within their Ethernet assigned areas. This means network 10.1.1.0/28 will be advertised within both EIGRP and OSPF. You will also need to configure a virtual link between R6 and R5 to extend area 0 out to R5 area 5 via area 4. You can manually configure your router ID within OSPF if you choose to even though it will not change within the lab. If you have configured this correctly as shown in Example 3-18 through Example 3-24, then you have scored 2 points.

**Example 3-18**  *R1 Initial OSPF Configuration*

```
router ospf 30
 network 10.1.1.0 0.0.0.15 area 0
 network 10.10.10.0 0.0.0.15 area 0
 network 10.100.100.0 0.0.0.15 area 0
 network 10.80.80.0 0.0.0.255 area 2
 network 10.90.90.0 0.0.0.15 area 0
```

**Example 3-19**  *R2 Initial OSPF Configuration*

```
router ospf 1
 network 10.90.90.0 0.0.0.15 area 0
```

**Example 3-20**  *R4 Initial OSPF Configuration*

```
router ospf 1
 network 10.4.4.0 0.0.0.15 area 1
 network 10.10.10.0 0.0.0.15 area 0
 network 10.40.40.0 0.0.0.15 area 1
 network 10.100.100.0 0.0.0.15 area 0
```

**Example 3-21**  *R5 OSPF Configuration*

```
router ospf 1
 router-id 10.5.5.5
 area 4 virtual-link 10.6.6.6
 network 10.5.5.0 0.0.0.15 area 5
 network 10.50.50.0 0.0.0.7 area 5
 network 10.99.99.0 0.0.0.7 area 4
```

**Example 3-22**  *R6 Initial OSPF Configuration*

```
router ospf 1
 router-id 10.6.6.6
 area 4 virtual-link 10.5.5.5
 network 10.6.6.0 0.0.0.15 area 6
 network 10.60.60.0 0.0.0.7 area 6
 network 10.80.80.0 0.0.0.255 area 2
 network 10.99.99.0 0.0.0.7 area 4
 network 10.100.100.0 0.0.0.15 area 0
```

**NOTE**     R6 loopback network 10.6.6.0/28 can be advertised within either area 2 or 6 because R6 has two Ethernet interfaces, one of which is in area 2 and the other in area 6.

**Example 3-23**  *R7 OSPF Configuration*

```
router ospf 1
 network 10.7.7.0 0.0.0.15 area 6
 network 10.60.60.0 0.0.0.7 area 6
```

**Example 3-24**  *R8 OSPF Configuration*

```
router ospf 1
 network 10.8.8.0 0.0.0.15 area 2
 network 10.80.80.0 0.0.0.255 area 2
```

• *Do not use the* **ip ospf network** *command over the Frame Relay network.*

The Frame Relay network is NBMA; without using the network command and without having broadcast capability within your Frame Relay maps, you will need to statically configure neighbors. You will need to configure **neighbor 10.100.100.1** and **neighbor 10.100.100.2** under the OSPF process on R4; you could also configure R1 and R6 with neighbor statements pointing to R4 but this could be considered overconfiguration as it is not strictly required to ensure operability. This particular Frame Relay scenario will also introduce a DR (Designated Router), which should be R4 as it is the hub; in fact, because the Router ID being highest, R6 would become the DR if permitted to. The simplest method of ensuring R4 becomes the DR is by not allowing R1 and R6 to enter into the DR negotiations by configuring **ip ospf priority 0** under the Frame Relay interfaces of R1 and R6. If you have configured these items correctly as shown in Example 3-25 through Example 3-27, you have scored 2 points.

**NOTE**     Example 3-25 through Example 3-27 also show the required configuration for the MTU issue, which has previously been discussed in the initial Frame Relay section of the debrief. Without configuring the command **ip ospf mtu-ignore** under the physical Frame Relay interfaces on R1 and R6, you will find that your OSPF network will fail over the Frame Relay.

**Example 3-25**  *R1 OSPF Frame Relay and Neighbor Configuration*

```
interface Serial0/1
 ip mtu 950
 encapsulation frame-relay
 ip ospf priority 0
 ip ospf mtu-ignore
```

**Example 3-26**  *R4 OSPF Neighbor Configuration*

```
router ospf 1
 neighbor 10.100.100.1
 neighbor 10.100.100.2
```

**Example 3-27**  *R6 OSPF Frame Relay and Neighbor Configuration*

```
interface Serial5/0
 ip mtu 950
 encapsulation frame-relay
 ip ospf priority 0
 ip ospf mtu-ignore
```

- *Ensure that no host routes are propagated throughout the network.*

You will need to configure your loopback interfaces on R1, R4, R5, R6, R7, and R8, which are advertised within OSPF with **ip ospf-network point-to-point** statements to ensure they are advertised with the correct mask as opposed to /32 host routes to your network. You will also need to configure your virtual-template interfaces on R5 and R6 with the command **no peer neighbor-route** to remove the /32 host routes that are added to the routing table when the PPP links become active over the ATM and on the serial interface connection between R1 and R2.

If you have configured this correctly, you have scored 1 point.

# Section 2.3: Redistribution (4 Points)

- *Redistribute OSPF into EIGRP on R2; do not perform mutual redistribution and only allow OPSF routes with a mask greater than 255.255.0.0 into EIGRP.*

You are not being requested to perform mutual redistribution here so you are required to redistribute OSPF into EIGRP on R2. To allow only OSPF routes with masks greater than /16, you need to configure a route map and prefix-list accordingly along with a default metric.

You should realize that the majority of your OSPF network will not have visibility of VLAN1 172.16.0.0/16 and R2 loopback0 10.2.2.0/28 as EIGRP has not been redistributed into OSPF. The lab guidelines do state that these networks are exempt from the full IP visibility required between routers and this will become apparent in the BGP section. If you have configured this correctly as shown in Example 3-28, you have scored 4 points.

**Example 3-28** *R2 OSPF Redistribution Configuration*

```
router eigrp 1
 redistribute ospf 1 route-map eigrp-ospf
 default-metric 1000 10 255 1 1500
!
!
ip prefix-list /16 seq 5 permit 0.0.0.0/0 ge 16
!
route-map eigrp-ospf permit 10
 match ip address prefix-list /16
```

# Section 3: ISDN (4 Points)

- *If your Frame Relay network fails, allow R4 to dial into R1. Use passwords that are difficult to detect. Ensure R4 dials out after 5 seconds of Frame Relay failure. If the Frame Relay network restores, keep the call connected for a further 45 seconds before disconnecting. OSPF is required over the ISDN network when a call is established. Do not configure any Layer 3 addressing on the physical ISDN interfaces.*

You only have one option here and you are given plenty of clues; you need to use the backup interface solution with the delay configured to meet the timing requirements. You only need to configure a backup interface on R4 as R1 is not required to dial into R4; therefore you can simply omit a dialer string on R1. Because OSPF is required over the link, it will need to be enabled on the ISDN network; it will not establish the link until the Frame Relay network fails. The Layer 3 addressing and PPP CHAP can simply be configured on a dialer interface as opposed to the physical BRI; they are joined by **dialer pool** statements. The command **no peer neighbor-route** is configured on the dialer interfaces to remove the /32 host route that would otherwise be present when the ISDN network is established. If you have configured this correctly as shown in Example 3-29 and Example 3-30, you have scored 4 points.

**Example 3-29** *R1 ISDN Backup Configuration*

```
username R4 password 0 cisco
!
interface BRI0/0
 no ip address
 encapsulation ppp
 dialer pool-member 1
 isdn switch-type basic-net3
!
interface Dialer0
 ip address 10.10.10.1 255.255.255.240
 encapsulation ppp no peer neighbor-route
 dialer pool 1
 dialer-group 1
 ppp authentication chap
!
dialer-list 1 protocol ip permit
```

**Example 3-30**  *R4 ISDN Backup Configuration*

```
username R1 password 0 cisco
!
interface BRI0/0
 no ip address
 encapsulation ppp
 dialer pool-member 1
 isdn switch-type basic-net3
!
interface Serial0/0
 backup delay 5 45
 backup interface Dialer0
!
interface Dialer0
 ip address 10.10.10.2 255.255.255.240
 encapsulation ppp
 no peer neighbor-route
 dialer pool 1
 dialer string 1111
 dialer-group 1
 ppp authentication chap
!
dialer-list 1 protocol ip permit
```

**NOTE**    The backup commands are entered under the Frame Relay interface s0/0 on R4. To test the backup disconnect, simply shut down the corresponding interface on the Frame Relay switch from R4 instead of shutting down the interface on R4, because this will not work.

Example 3-31 shows the backup process when the Frame Relay switch is disconnected from R4 using the **debug dialer** command.

**Example 3-31**  *R4 Backup Process*

```
R4#debug dialer
Dial on demand events debugging is on
R4#
R4#
01:16:19: %LINEPROTO-5-UPDOWN: Line protocol on Interface Serial0/0, changed state
to down
01:16:19: %LINK-3-UPDOWN: Interface Serial0/0, changed state to down
01:16:19: %OSPF-5-ADJCHG: Process 1, Nbr 10.1.1.1 on Serial0/0 from 2WAY to DOWN
, Neighbor Down: Interface down or detached
01:16:19: %OSPF-5-ADJCHG: Process 1, Nbr 10.6.6.6 on Serial0/0 from 2WAY to DOWN, N
eighbor Down: Interface down or detached
01:16:20: %LINEPROTO-5-UPDOWN: Line protocol on Interface Serial0/0, changed state
to down
01:16:24: Di0 DDR is shutdown, could not clear interface.
01:16:24: BR0/0 DDR: rotor dialout [best]
```

*continues*

**Example 3-31**  *R4 Backup Process (Continued)*

```
01:16:24: BR0/0 DDR: Dialing cause ip (s=10.10.10.2, d=224.0.0.5)
01:16:24: BR0/0 DDR: Attempting to dial 1111
01:16:24: BR0/0:2: interface must be fifo queue, force fifo
01:16:24: %LINK-3-UPDOWN: Interface BRI0/0:1, changed state to up
01:16:24: BR0/0:1: interface must be fifo queue, force fifo
01:16:24: %DIALER-6-BIND: Interface BR0/0:1 bound to profile Di0
01:16:24: BR0/0:1 DDR: dialer protocol up
01:16:24: %LINEPROTO-5-UPDOWN: Line protocol on Interface BRI0/0:1, changed state
to up
01:16:29: %ISDN-6-CONNECT: Interface BRI0/0:1 is now connected to 1111 R1
01:16:31: %OSPF-5-ADJCHG: Process 1, Nbr 10.1.1.1 on Dialer0 from LOADING to FULL,
Loading Done
```

Example 3-32 shows the backup process restoring to Frame Relay after the Frame Relay switch has been reconnected to R4—note the timing intervals.

**Example 3-32**  *R4 Backup Restoration*

```
R4#
01:18:01: %LINK-3-UPDOWN: Interface Serial0/0, changed state to up
01:18:02: %LINEPROTO-5-UPDOWN: Line protocol on Interface Serial0/0, changed
   state to up
01:18:46: BR0/0:1 DDR: disconnecting call
01:18:46: Di0 DDR: dialer shutdown complete
01:18:46: Di0 DDR: No bundle in dialer_fsm_up
01:18:197568495616: %ISDN-6-DISCONNECT: Interface BRI0/0:1
   disconnected from 1111 R1, call lasted 143 seconds
01:18:46: %OSPF-5-ADJCHG: Process 1, Nbr 10.1.1.1 on Dialer0 from FULL to DOWN,
Neighbor Down: Interface down or detached
01:18:46: %LINK-3-UPDOWN: Interface BRI0/0:1, changed state to down
01:18:46: BR0/0 DDR: has total 0 call(s), dial_out 0, dial_in 0
01:18:46: BR0/0:1 DDR: disconnecting call
01:18:46: %DIALER-6-UNBIND: Interface BR0/0:1 unbound from profile Di0
01:18:47: %LINEPROTO-5-UPDOWN: Line protocol on Interface BRI0/0:1,
   changed state to down
01:18:48: %LINK-5-CHANGED: Interface Dialer0, changed state to standby mode
```

# Section 4: EGP Protocols (24 Points)

- *Configure BGP as shown in Figure 3-14 with the following peering:*

  *R2 172.16.0.1 – R3 172.16.0.2*

  *R2 172.16.0.1 – R1 10.80.80.1*

  *R1 10.80.80.1 – R8 10.8.8.8*

  *R1 10.80.80.1 – R6 10.6.6.6*

  *R6 10.6.6.6 – R4 10.4.4.4*

*R6 10.6.6.6 – R5 10.5.5.5*

*R6 10.6.6.6 – R7 10.7.7.7*

*Where possible, minimize the configuration required.*

You are required to configure the peering between the BGP autonomous systems as described; pay particular attention to the update source of each router. You should ensure that **no synchronization** is configured on all IBGP routers R1, R2, R3, R5, R6, R7, and R8 because BGP will not be fully synchronized with the underlying IGP.

The next question prompts you to redistribute your connected loopback interfaces so you will need to disable auto summarization on all routers with the command **no auto-summary**; otherwise, only the entire classfull network will be advertised.

You will also need to configure a peer group on R6, which has multiple peers to the same remote AS to minimize configuration; as can be seen R4, R5, and R7 only peer to R6 so you will have to configure R6 as a route reflector. If you have configured this correctly as shown in Example 3-33 through Example 3-40, you have scored 3 points.

**Example 3-33**  *R1 Initial BGP Configuration*

```
router bgp 10
 no synchronization
 neighbor 10.6.6.6 remote-as 11
 neighbor 10.6.6.6 ebgp-multihop 3
 neighbor 10.6.6.6 update-source FastEthernet0/0
 neighbor 10.8.8.8 remote-as 10
 neighbor 10.8.8.8 update-source FastEthernet0/0
 neighbor 172.16.0.1 remote-as 1
 neighbor 172.16.0.1 ebgp-multihop 2
 neighbor 172.16.0.1 update-source FastEthernet0/0
 no auto-summary
```

**Example 3-34**  *R2 Initial BGP Configuration*

```
router bgp 1
 no synchronization
 neighbor 10.80.80.1 remote-as 10 neighbor 10.80.80.1 ebgp-multihop 2
 neighbor 10.80.80.1 update-source FastEthernet0/0
 neighbor 172.16.0.2 remote-as 1
 no auto-summary
```

**Example 3-35**  *R3 Initial BGP Configuration*

```
router bgp 1
 no synchronization
 neighbor 172.16.0.1 remote-as 1
 no auto-summary
```

**Example 3-36** *R4 Initial BGP Configuration*

```
router bgp 12
 neighbor 10.6.6.6 remote-as 11
 neighbor 10.6.6.6 ebgp-multihop 3
 neighbor 10.6.6.6 update-source Loopback0
 no auto-summary
```

**Example 3-37** *R5 Initial BGP Configuration*

```
router bgp 11
 no synchronization
 neighbor 10.6.6.6 remote-as 11
 neighbor 10.6.6.6 update-source Loopback0
 no auto-summary
```

**Example 3-38** *R6 Initial BGP Configuration*

```
router bgp 11
 no synchronization
 neighbor internal peer-group
 neighbor internal remote-as 11
 neighbor internal update-source Loopback0
 neighbor internal route-reflector-client
 neighbor 10.4.4.4 remote-as 12
 neighbor 10.4.4.4 ebgp-multihop 3
 neighbor 10.4.4.4 update-source Loopback0
 neighbor 10.5.5.5 peer-group internal
 neighbor 10.7.7.7 peer-group internal
 neighbor 10.80.80.1 remote-as 10
 neighbor 10.80.80.1 ebgp-multihop 3
 neighbor 10.80.80.1 update-source Loopback0
 no auto-summary
```

**Example 3-39** *R7 Initial BGP Configuration*

```
router bgp 11
 no synchronization
 neighbor 10.6.6.6 remote-as 11
 neighbor 10.6.6.6 update-source Loopback0
 no auto-summary
```

**Example 3-40**  *R8 Initial BGP Configuration*

```
router bgp 10
 no synchronization
 neighbor 10.80.80.1 remote-as 10
 neighbor 10.80.80.1 update-source Loopback0
 no auto-summary
```

- *Inject the following networks into BGP, configure new loopback interfaces where required, do not use the **network** command, and ensure that all routes have a metric of 100 assigned to them:*

  *R1 – 10.1.1.1/28*

  *R2 – 2.2.2.2/28*

  *R3 – 3.3.3.3/28*

  *R4 – 10.4.4.4/28*

  *R5 – 10.5.5.5/28*

  *R6 – 10.6.6.6/28*

  *R7 – 10.7.7.7/28*

  *R8 – 10.8.8.8/28*

To begin with, you need to configure new loopback interfaces on R2 and R3. Because you cannot use the **network** command, you will have to redistribute your connected interfaces with a route-map that just includes the loopback with a metric of 100. This is not a difficult question but it will sap your time with repetitive configuration; consider cutting and pasting the common parts for each router as shown in Example 3-41.

**Example 3-41**  *Loopback Advertisement Cut and Paste*

```
redistribute connected metric 100 route-map Loopback
exit
route-map Loopback permit 10
match ip address 10
exit
access-list 10 permit
```

| | |
|---|---|
| **NOTE** | Create the preceding configuration within notepad and paste it into each router under the appropriate BGP process; simply type in your loopback IP address after the **access-list 10 permit** statement. This is a good time-saving technique but be careful with the small changes that will be required for each router. |

If you have configured this correctly, regardless of if you used the shortcut method or not, you have scored 2 points. After you have successfully injected the networks into BGP, you should notice that you now have introduced a problem (if you are debugging the IP routing table or if you have spotted that the majority of your routers are peering to loopback networks advertised within the IGP, which are then also advertised within BGP). If you had not spotted an issue at this point, it would become apparent later as you view your BGP tables throughout the lab; they will be constantly changing. Example 3-42 shows the console output from R6.

**Example 3-42** *R6 Console Output*

```
R6#debug ip routing
00:37:38: RT: recursion error routing 10.4.4.4 - probable routing loop
00:37:39: RT: recursion error routing 10.4.4.4 - probable routing loop
00:37:48: RT: recursion error routing 10.4.4.4 - probable routing loop
00:37:49: RT: recursion error routing 10.4.4.4 - probable routing loop
00:37:56: RT: del 10.4.4.0/28 via 10.4.4.4, bgp metric [20/100]
00:37:56: RT: delete subnet route to 10.4.4.0/28
00:37:56: RT: add 10.4.4.0/28 via 10.100.100.3, ospf metric [110/782]
```

**TIP**     Consider using the **debug ip routing** command on all your routers during your lab, it is a very useful command that will tell you immediately of changes to the IP routing table on a router and could save you valuable points.

R6 is reporting a recursive routing loop to 10.4.4.0/28. This is because of the fact that it is actually peering to 10.4.4.4, which it previously learnt through OSPF; as soon as network 10.4.4.0/28 is learnt through BGP; it replaces the OSPF route in the routing table because of the more preferable AD that external BGP offers. This is then replaced by the original OSPF route, which leads to the reported loop. This problem is common to each router that peers to a loopback network also advertised within BGP so a fix is required for R1, R4, R5, R6, R7, and R8. By configuring a **backdoor** route to the loopback networks, the OSPF routes will be chosen over the external BGP routes and recursive issue is resolved.

It is, however, good practice to ensure that the IGP routes are always chosen over the BGP routes regardless of whether the networks are used for peering or not, so every BGP router should be configured with the relevant **backdoor** routes.

If you have configured this correctly as shown in Example 3-43 through Example 3-50 over and above the original peering, you have scored an additional 3 points.

If you have only applied the **backdoor** peering fix to R1, R4, R5, R6, R7, and R8, you have only scored 2 points.

**Example 3-43**  *R1 Backdoor Routes*

```
router bgp 10
 network 10.4.4.0 mask 255.255.255.240 backdoor
 network 10.5.5.0 mask 255.255.255.240 backdoor
 network 10.6.6.0 mask 255.255.255.240 backdoor
 network 10.7.7.0 mask 255.255.255.240 backdoor
 network 10.8.8.0 mask 255.255.255.240 backdoor
```

**Example 3-44**  *R2 Backdoor Routes*

```
router bgp 1
 network 10.1.1.0 mask 255.255.255.240 backdoor
 network 10.4.4.0 mask 255.255.255.240 backdoor
 network 10.5.5.0 mask 255.255.255.240 backdoor
 network 10.6.6.0 mask 255.255.255.240 backdoor
 network 10.7.7.0 mask 255.255.255.240 backdoor
 network 10.8.8.0 mask 255.255.255.240 backdoor
```

**Example 3-45**  *R3 Backdoor Routes*

```
router bgp 1
 network 10.1.1.0 mask 255.255.255.240 backdoor
 network 10.4.4.0 mask 255.255.255.240 backdoor
 network 10.5.5.0 mask 255.255.255.240 backdoor
 network 10.6.6.0 mask 255.255.255.240 backdoor
 network 10.7.7.0 mask 255.255.255.240 backdoor
 network 10.8.8.0 mask 255.255.255.240 backdoor
```

**Example 3-46**  *R4 Backdoor Routes*

```
router bgp 12
 network 10.1.1.0 mask 255.255.255.240 backdoor
 network 10.5.5.0 mask 255.255.255.240 backdoor
 network 10.6.6.0 mask 255.255.255.240 backdoor
 network 10.7.7.0 mask 255.255.255.240 backdoor
 network 10.8.8.0 mask 255.255.255.240 backdoor
```

**Example 3-47**  *R5 Backdoor Routes*

```
router bgp 11
 network 10.1.1.0 mask 255.255.255.240 backdoor
 network 10.4.4.0 mask 255.255.255.240 backdoor
 network 10.6.6.0 mask 255.255.255.240 backdoor
 network 10.7.7.0 mask 255.255.255.240 backdoor
 network 10.8.8.0 mask 255.255.255.240 backdoor
```

**Example 3-48**  *R6 Backdoor Routes*

```
router bgp 11
 network 10.1.1.0 mask 255.255.255.240 backdoor
 network 10.4.4.0 mask 255.255.255.240 backdoor
 network 10.5.5.0 mask 255.255.255.240 backdoor
 network 10.7.7.0 mask 255.255.255.240 backdoor
 network 10.8.8.0 mask 255.255.255.240 backdoor
```

**Example 3-49**  *R7 Backdoor Routes*

```
router bgp 11
 network 10.1.1.0 mask 255.255.255.240 backdoor
 network 10.4.4.0 mask 255.255.255.240 backdoor
 network 10.5.5.0 mask 255.255.255.240 backdoor
 network 10.6.6.0 mask 255.255.255.240 backdoor
 network 10.8.8.0 mask 255.255.255.240 backdoor
```

**Example 3-50**  *R8 Backdoor Routes*

```
router bgp 10
 network 10.1.1.0 mask 255.255.255.240 backdoor
 network 10.4.4.0 mask 255.255.255.240 backdoor
 network 10.5.5.0 mask 255.255.255.240 backdoor
 network 10.6.6.0 mask 255.255.255.240 backdoor
 network 10.7.7.0 mask 255.255.255.240 backdoor
```

- *Configure R6 to extend the range of network 2.2.2.0/28 into 2.2.2.0/24 when advertised into AS12. Ensure that the original attributes of this network are visible from AS12.*

This is a simple aggregation configuration on R6. Example 3-51 shows the BGP routing table on R4 AS12 pre-configuration on R6 detailing the original attributes in the form of AS path; network 2.2.2.0/28 is shown to originate from AS1 and passes through AS10 and AS11 before reaching AS12.

**Example 3-51**  *R4 Network 2.2.2.0/28 Original Attributes*

```
R4#sh ip bgp
BGP table version is 211, local router ID is 10.4.4.4
Status codes: s suppressed, d damped, h history, * valid, > best, i - intern
Origin codes: i - IGP, e - EGP, ? - incomplete
   Network          Next Hop          Metric  LocPrf Weight Path
*> 2.2.2.0/28       10.6.6.6                          0 11 10 1 ?
*> 3.3.3.0/28       10.6.6.6                          0 11 10 1 ?
*> 10.1.1.0/28      10.6.6.6                          0 11 10 ?
*> 10.4.4.0/28      0.0.0.0           100          32768 ?
*> 10.5.5.0/28      10.6.6.6                          0 11 ?
*> 10.6.6.0/28      10.6.6.6          100              0 11 ?
*> 10.7.7.0/28      10.6.6.6                          0 11 ?
*> 10.8.8.0/28      10.6.6.6                          0 11 10 ?
```

If R6 is configured with **aggregate-address 2.2.2.0 255.255.255.0 summary-only** to extend the range of this network to a /24, the original attributes are lost in the form of AS path as shown in Example 3-52; the network now appears to originate from AS11.

**Example 3-52**  *R4 Network 2.2.2.0/24 Post Summarization*

```
R4#sh ip bgp
BGP table version is 213, local router ID is 10.4.4.4
Status codes: s suppressed, d damped, h history, * valid, > best, i - internal
Origin codes: i - IGP, e - EGP, ? - incomplete
   Network          Next Hop          Metric LocPrf Weight Path
*> 2.2.2.0/24       10.6.6.6                            0 11 i
*> 3.3.3.0/28       10.6.6.6                            0 11 10 1 ?
*> 10.1.1.0/28      10.6.6.6                            0 11 10 ?
*> 10.4.4.0/28      0.0.0.0              100         32768 ?
*> 10.5.5.0/28      10.6.6.6                            0 11 ?
*> 10.6.6.0/28      10.6.6.6            100             0 11 ?
*> 10.7.7.0/28      10.6.6.6                            0 11 ?
*> 10.8.8.0/28      10.6.6.6                            0 11 10 ?
```

R6 requires the **as-set** option enabled within the summarization command to maintain the original AS path attributes. If you have configured R6 with **aggregate-address 2.2.2.0 255.255.255.0 summary-only as-set**, you have scored 2 points. Example 3-53 shows network 2.2.2.0 with the original attributes as seen by R4; the network is now seen to originate from AS1.

**Example 3-53**  *R4 Network 2.2.2.0/24 Post Summarization*

```
R4#sh ip bgp
BGP table version is 213, local router ID is 10.4.4.4
Status codes: s suppressed, d damped, h history, * valid, > best, i - internal
Origin codes: i - IGP, e - EGP, ? - incomplete
   Network          Next Hop          Metric LocPrf Weight Path
*> 2.2.2.0/24       10.6.6.6                            0 11 10 1 ?
*> 3.3.3.0/28       10.6.6.6                            0 11 10 1 ?
*> 10.1.1.0/28      10.6.6.6                            0 11 10 ?
*> 10.4.4.0/28      0.0.0.0              100         32768 ?
*> 10.5.5.0/28      10.6.6.6                            0 11 ?
*> 10.6.6.0/28      10.6.6.6            100             0 11 ?
*> 10.7.7.0/28      10.6.6.6                            0 11 ?
*> 10.8.8.0/28      10.6.6.6                            0 11 10 ?
```

- *Users in AS11 are complaining that network 3.3.3.0 is unstable; configure R6 to control the instability of this route. Use the following values:*

  *Reuse-value 30*

  *Half-life 20*

  *Suppress-value 1000*

  *Maximum-suppress-time 130*

A route-dampening question that is very straightforward, you are given all the information that you require and it is just a case of typing it in correctly. The question does lead you into configuring the values presented in order but beware as the order on the router is Half-life first then Reuse-value. If you typed the values in the wrong order, don't worry but do learn from it as it is an easy mistake to make when you are low on time. If you have configured this correctly as shown in Example 3-54, you have scored 2 points.

**Example 3-54** *Route Dampening Configuration*

```
router bgp 11
 bgp dampening route-map 3.3.3.0
!
access-list 11 permit 3.3.3.0 0.0.0.15
!
route-map 3.3.3.0 permit 10
 match ip address 11
 set dampening 20 30 1000 130
!
route-map 3.3.3.0 permit 20
```

- *On R2, set up a new loopback 22.22.22.22/24, advertise this within BGP using the* **network** *command. Similarly, set up 11.11.11.11/24 on R1. If the BGP route 22.22.22.0 is present on R1's BGP table, do not advertise network 11.11.11.0/24 to R8. If network 22.22.22.0/24 disappears, do advertise network 11.11.11.0/24 to R8.*

The question is asking you to configure BGP conditional advertisements; you have the ability to advertise selective networks to neighbors depending on which networks are present within your own AS. The configuration for R1 and R2 is shown in Example 3-55 and Example 3-56.

**Example 3-55** *R1 Conditional Advertisement Configuration*

```
interface Loopback1
 ip address 11.11.11.11 255.255.255.0
!
router bgp 10
network 11.11.11.0 mask 255.255.255.0
neighbor 10.8.8.8 advertise-map SEND non-exist-map MISSING
!
access-list 12 permit 11.11.11.0 0.0.0.255
access-list 13 permit 22.22.22.0 0.0.0.255
!
route-map SEND permit 10
 match ip address 12
!
route-map MISSING permit 10
 match ip address 13
```

**Example 3-56**  *R2 BGP Network 22.22.22.0/24 Setup*

```
interface Loopback2
 ip address 22.22.22.22 255.255.255.0
router bgp 1
 network 22.22.22.0 mask 255.255.255.0
```

Example 3-57 shows the BGP table on R1; because network 22.22.22.0/24 is present on R1 it will not advertise network 11.11.11.0/24 to R8 as shown in Example 3-58.

**Example 3-57**  *R1 BGP Table*

```
R1#sh ip bgp
BGP table version is 15, local router ID is 11.11.11.11
Status codes: s suppressed, d damped, h history, * valid, > best, i - internal
Origin codes: i - IGP, e - EGP, ? - incomplete
   Network          Next Hop          Metric LocPrf Weight Path
*> 2.2.2.0/28       172.16.0.1          100             0 1 ?
*> 3.3.3.0/28       172.16.0.1          100             0 1 ?
*> 10.1.1.0/28      0.0.0.0             100         32768 ?
*> 10.4.4.0/28      10.6.6.6                            0 11 12 ?
*> 10.5.5.0/28      10.6.6.6                            0 11 ?
*> 10.6.6.0/28      10.6.6.6            100             0 11 ?
*> 10.7.7.0/28      10.6.6.6                            0 11 ?
*>i10.8.8.0/28      10.8.8.8            100    100      0 ?
*> 11.11.11.0/24    0.0.0.0            100          32768 i
*> 22.22.22.0/24    172.16.0.1         100              0 1 i
```

**Example 3-58**  *R8 BGP Table*

```
R8#sh ip bgp
BGP table version is 10, local router ID is 10.8.8.8
Status codes: s suppressed, d damped, h history, * valid, > best, i - internal
Origin codes: i - IGP, e - EGP, ? - incomplete
   Network          Next Hop          Metric LocPrf Weight Path
*  i2.2.2.0/28      172.16.0.1          100    100      0 1 ?
*  i3.3.3.0/28      172.16.0.1                 100      0 1 ?
*>i10.1.1.0/28      10.80.80.1          100    100      0 ?
*>i10.4.4.0/28      10.80.80.1                 100      0 11 12 ?
*>i10.5.5.0/28      10.80.80.1                 100      0 11 ?
*>i10.6.6.0/28      10.80.80.1          100    100      0 11 ?
*>i10.7.7.0/28      10.80.80.1                 100      0 11 ?
*> 10.8.8.0/28      0.0.0.0             100         32768 ?
*>i22.22.22.0/24    10.80.80.1          100    100      0 1 i
```

When the loopback 1 on R2 is removed, R1 loses visibility of network 22.22.22.0/24 and then begins to advertise network 11.11.11.0/24 to R8 as shown in Example 3-59.

**Example 3-59** *Removal of Network 22.22.22.0/24 and Advertisement of Network 11.11.11.0/24*

```
R2#debug ip routing
R2#conf t
Enter configuration commands, one per line.  End with CNTL/Z.
R2(config)#no int lo2
R2(config)#
00:31:09: RT: delete route to 22.22.22.0 via 0.0.0.0, Loopback2
00:31:09: RT: no routes to 22.22.22.0, flushing
00:31:09: RT: delete network route to 22.0.0.0^Z
R1#debug ip routing
00:31:09: RT: del 22.22.22.0/24 via 172.16.0.1, bgp metric [20/100]
00:31:09: RT: delete subnet route to 22.22.22.0/24
00:31:09: RT: delete network route to 22.0.0.0
R8#debug ip routing
00:31:09: RT: del 22.22.22.0/24 via 10.80.80.1, bgp metric [200/100]
00:31:09: RT: delete subnet route to 22.22.22.0/24
00:31:09: RT: delete network route to 22.0.0.0
00:32:03: RT: add 11.11.11.0/24 via 10.80.80.1, bgp metric [200/100]
R8#sh ip bgp
BGP table version is 12, local router ID is 10.8.8.8
Status codes: s suppressed, d damped, h history, * valid, > best, i - interna
Origin codes: i - IGP, e - EGP, ? - incomplete

   Network          Next Hop            Metric LocPrf Weight Path
*>i10.1.1.0/28      10.80.80.1             100    100      0 ?
*>i10.4.4.0/28      10.80.80.1                    100      0 11 12 ?
*>i10.5.5.0/28      10.80.80.1                    100      0 11 ?
*>i10.6.6.0/28      10.80.80.1             100    100      0 11 ?
*>i10.7.7.0/28      10.80.80.1                    100      0 11 ?
*> 10.8.8.0/28      0.0.0.0                100         32768 ?
*>i11.11.11.0/24    10.80.80.1             100    100      0 i
```

If you have configured this correctly as shown in Example 3-54 and 3-55 you have scored 4 points.

- *On R5, set up a new loopback 5.5.5.5/28 and advertise this into AS11 using the* **network** *command, but do not allow this to be advertised into AS10 or AS12. Only configure R5 to achieve this.*

Because you can only configure R5, you only have two options to stop R6 advertising network 5.5.5.0/28; this is by tagging the network with a community of **no-export** or **local-AS**. By doing this, the route will stay locally within AS11 but will not be permitted to be advertised to external BGP peers. If you have configured this correctly as shown in Example 3-60, you have scored 2 points.

**Example 3-60**   *R5 Network 5.5.5.0/28 no-export Configuration*

```
interface Loopback1
 ip address 5.5.5.5 255.255.255.240
router bgp 11
 network 5.5.5.0 mask 255.255.255.240
 neighbor 10.6.6.6 send-community
 neighbor 10.6.6.6 route-map community out
access-list 11 permit 5.5.5.0 0.0.0.15
!
route-map community permit 10
 match ip address 11
 set community no-export
route-map community permit 20
```

Example 3-61 shows the BGP entry for network 5.5.5.0/28 after configuration on R5; it will now only propagate this network internally.

**Example 3-61**   *R6 Network 5.5.5.0/28 Entry*

```
R6#sh ip bgp 5.5.5.5
BGP routing table entry for 5.5.5.0/28, version 61
Paths: (1 available, best #1, table Default-IP-Routing-Table, not advertised to EBG
P peer)
Flag: 0x208
  Advertised to peer-groups:
     internal
  Local, (Received from a RR-client)
    10.5.5.5 (metric 2) from 10.5.5.5 (10.5.5.5)
      Origin IGP, metric 100, localpref 100, valid, internal, best
      Community: no-export
```

- *R2 is due to have external directly connected BGP neighbors added to it on VLAN1. This VLAN has a tendency to flap because of a faulty switch; configure R2 so that if the VLAN should fail, the BGP sessions are not immediately reset.*

BGP has a feature called Fast External Fallover, which immediately resets the BGP sessions of directly adjacent external peers when the link between them fails; this is enabled by default. By configuring R2 with the command **no bgp fast-external-fallover** under the BGP process, you can maintain the sessions to future peers configured in the same manner if the VLAN fails but is quickly restored. If you have configured this correctly, you have scored 2 points.

- *Ensure that all BGP speakers within AS1 do not respond to hostile TCP resets or untrusted routing updates.*

To achieve this, you are required to configure password authentication between peers R2 and R3 within AS1. This MD5 encrypted password will stop hackers from sending spoofed routing updates or hostile TCP resets. The BGP **neighbor** statement must be configured with a password as shown in Example 3-62 for R2 and Example 3-63 for R3. If you have configured this correctly on each router, you have scored 2 points.

**Example 3-62**   *R2 MD5 Authentication*

```
router bgp 1
 neighbor 172.16.0.2 password valencia
```

**Example 3-63**   *R3 MD5 Authentication*

```
router bgp 1
 neighbor 172.16.0.1 password valencia
```

- *All BGP peers are to be able to communicate with all advertised BGP networks.*

The only router that should have a connectivity issue is R8. Example 3-64 shows that networks 2.2.2.0/28 and 3.3.3.0/28 show a next hop of 172.16.0.1. You should remember that within the redistribution section you were not requested to perform mutual redistribution and, hence, network 172.16.0.0/16 is not visible to your OSPF network with the exception of R1; this is why the ping testing fails.

**Example 3-64**   *R8 BGP Reach Ability Testing*

```
R8#sh ip bgp
BGP table version is 113, local router ID is 10.8.8.8
Status codes: s suppressed, d damped, h history, * valid, > best, i - internal
Origin codes: i - IGP, e - EGP, ? - incomplete
   Network          Next Hop        Metric LocPrf Weight Path
 * i2.2.2.0/28      172.16.0.1         100    100      0 1 ?
 * i3.3.3.0/28      172.16.0.1                100      0 1 ?
 *>i10.1.1.0/28     10.80.80.1         100    100      0 ?
 *>i10.4.4.0/28     10.6.6.6                  100      0 11 12 ?
 *>i10.5.5.0/28     10.6.6.6                  100      0 11 ?
 *>i10.6.6.0/28     10.6.6.6           100    100      0 11 ?
 *>i10.7.7.0/28     10.6.6.6                  100      0 11 ?
 *> 10.8.8.0/28     0.0.0.0            100         32768 ?
 * i22.22.22.0/24   172.16.0.1         100    100      0 1 i
R8#ping 2.2.2.2
Type escape sequence to abort.
Sending 5, 100-byte ICMP Echos to 2.2.2.2, timeout is 2 seconds:
.....
Success rate is 0 percent (0/5)
R8#ping 3.3.3.3
Type escape sequence to abort.
Sending 5, 100-byte ICMP Echos to 3.3.3.3, timeout is 2 seconds:
.....
Success rate is 0 percent (0/5)
```

The next hop field for networks 2.2.2.0/28 and 3.3.3.0/28 needs to be set to that of R1, which is reachable via R8. By configuring R1 with the command **neighbor 10.8.8.8 next-hop-self** as shown in Example 3-65 and with the resulting change on R8's BGP table, the networks are now reachable. If you configured this correctly, you have scored 1 point.

**Example 3-65** *R8 BGP Reach Ability Testing*

```
R1(config)#router bgp 10
R1(config-router)#neighbor 10.8.8.8 next-hop-self
R8#sh ip bgp
BGP table version is 50, local router ID is 10.8.8.8
Status codes: s suppressed, d damped, h history, * valid, > best, i -
Origin codes: i - IGP, e - EGP, ? - incomplete

   Network          Next Hop         Metric LocPrf Weight Path
*>i2.2.2.0/28       10.80.80.1          100    100      0 1 ?
*>i3.3.3.0/28       10.80.80.1                 100      0 1 ?
*>i10.1.1.0/28      10.80.80.1          100    100      0 ?
*>i10.4.4.0/28      10.80.80.1                 100      0 11 12 ?
*>i10.5.5.0/28      10.80.80.1                 100      0 11 ?
*>i10.6.6.0/28      10.80.80.1          100    100      0 11 ?
*>i10.7.7.0/28      10.80.80.1                 100      0 11 ?
*> 10.8.8.0/28      0.0.0.0             100          32768 ?
*>i22.22.22.0/24    10.80.80.1          100    100      0 1 i

R8#ping 2.2.2.2
Type escape sequence to abort.
Sending 5, 100-byte ICMP Echos to 2.2.2.2, timeout is 2 seconds:
!!!!!
Success rate is 100 percent (5/5), round-trip min/avg/max = 1/2/4 ms
R8#ping 3.3.3.3
Type escape sequence to abort.
Sending 5, 100-byte ICMP Echos to 3.3.3.3, timeout is 2 seconds:
!!!!!
Success rate is 100 percent (5/5), round-trip min/avg/max = 1/1/4 ms
```

# Section 5: Voice (7 Points)

- *Configure VoIP between R1 and R4 using the numbers supplied in Figure 3-10; ensure your VoIP is operational if the Frame Relay network fails.*

A basic VoIP scenario, to ensure VoIP is operational in the event of Frame Relay failure, you simply need to point your session target IP addresses to the loopback interfaces on R1 and R4, which will still be reachable in the event of a failure over the ISDN. If you have configured this correctly as shown in Example 3-66 and Example 3-67, you have scored 2 points.

**Example 3-66** *R1 VoIP Configuration*

```
dial-peer voice 1 pots
 destination-pattern 01256
 port 1/0/0
```

*continues*

**Example 3-66**  *R1 VoIP Configuration (Continued)*

```
!
dial-peer voice 01189 voip
 destination-pattern 01189
 session target ipv4:10.4.4.4
```

**Example 3-67**  *R4 VoIP Configuration*

```
dial-peer voice 1 pots
 destination-pattern 01189
 port 1/1/0
!
dial-peer voice 1256 voip
 destination-pattern 01256
 session target ipv4:10.1.1.1
```

- *Set up a hunt group on R4 so that if the number 01189 is dialed and voice port 1/1/0 is in use, port 1/1/1 answers the call. Port 1/1/0 should always answer the call if the phone connected to this port is not in use first.*

To create a hunt group, you need to configure an additional **pots dial-peer** statement on R4 for the same number of 01189; by assigning preference values to each dial-peer you can manipulate which port answers the call first and that the secondary answers when the primary is in use. The lower the preference value is the higher the priority will be. If you have configured this as shown in Example 3-68, you have scored 2 points.

**Example 3-68**  *R4 Hunt Group Configuration*

```
dial-peer voice 1 pots
 preference 1
 destination-pattern 01189
 port 1/1/0
!
dial-peer voice 2 pots
 preference 2
 destination-pattern 01189
 port 1/1/1
```

- *Define an order of preference for selecting a codec when R1 initiates a call to R4. R1 should first negotiate to use a g728 codec and then fall back to a g729r8 with a 20-byte payload. Leave the R4 codec as default.*

By assigning a **voice-class codec** on R4's VoIP dial-peer, you can define which codec is used. If the first codec fails, you can define what the fallback codec is by assigning preferences. If you have configured this correctly as shown in Example 3-69, you have scored 3 points.

**Example 3-69** *R4 Hunt Group Configuration*

```
voice class codec 1
 codec preference 1 g728
 codec preference 2 g729r8
!
dial-peer voice 1189 voip
 destination-pattern 01189
 voice-class codec 1
 session target ipv4:10.4.4.4
```

# Section 6: DLSw+ (6 Points)

- *Configure DLSw+ with TCP encapsulation between R6-R4 and R6-R5. R4 should only be able to connect to R6 VLAN2 and R5 to VLAN5.*

If you configured straightforward peering between each of the routers, they would have full connectivity to each VLAN on R6. This question requires bridge-lists to separate the DLSw connectivity for the two peers to each VLAN connected to R6. If you have configured this correctly as shown in Example 3-70 through Example 3-72, you have scored 2 points.

**Example 3-70** *R4 Initial DLSw+ Configuration*

```
dlsw local-peer peer-id 10.4.4.4
dlsw remote-peer 0 tcp 10.6.6.6
dlsw bridge-group 1
!
interface FastEthernet0/0
 bridge-group 1
!
bridge 1 protocol ieee
```

**Example 3-71** *R5 Initial DLSw+ Configuration*

```
dlsw local-peer peer-id 10.5.5.5
dlsw remote-peer 0 tcp 10.6.6.6
dlsw bridge-group 1
!
interface FastEthernet0/0
 bridge-group 1
!
bridge 1 protocol ieee
```

**Example 3-72** *R6 Initial DLSw+ Configuration*

```
dlsw local-peer peer-id 10.6.6.6
dlsw bgroup-list 1 bgroups 1
dlsw bgroup-list 2 bgroups 2
```

*continues*

**Example 3-72** *R6 Initial DLSw+ Configuration (Continued)*

```
dlsw remote-peer 2 tcp 10.5.5.5
dlsw remote-peer 1 tcp 10.4.4.4
dlsw bridge-group 1
dlsw bridge-group 2
!
interface FastEthernet0/0
 bridge-group 1
!
interface FastEthernet4/0
 bridge-group 2
!
bridge 1 protocol ieee
bridge 2 protocol ieee
```

- *If the DLSw+ connection from R4-R6 fails, allow R4 to connect to VLAN2 via R1. If the primary connection to R6 is restored, only keep the new connection to VLAN2 active for 60 seconds.*

You are now required to configure a backup peer from R4 to R1. If the primary peer to R6 fails on R4, the backup peer will be used. To keep the backup peer active when the primary peering to R6 is re-established, you will need to use the **linger** option. Remember that **linger** is expressed in minutes and not seconds and that R1 will require a **promiscuous** statement to peer with R4 in addition to the basic DLSw+ configuration. If you have configured this correctly as shown in Example 3-73 and Example 3-74, you have scored 2 points.

**Example 3-73** *R4 DLSw+ Backup Configuration*

```
dlsw remote-peer 0 tcp 10.1.1.1 backup-peer 10.6.6.6 linger 1
```

**Example 3-74** *R1 DLSw+ Backup Configuration*

```
dlsw local-peer peer-id 10.1.1.1 promiscuous
dlsw bridge-group 1
!
interface FastEthernet0/0
 bridge-group 1
!
bridge 1 protocol ieee
```

- *R4 and R5 should show reachability of NetBIOS name **ccie** advertised from R6. This is the only NetBIOS name of which R6 should have visibility.*

You need to configure DLSw+ NetBIOS reachability in the form of an **icanreach** statement on R6. Because this is the only NetBIOS name that R6 can reach, you should include the **dlsw icanreach netbios-exclusive** command. If you have configured this correctly as shown in Example 3-75, you have scored 2 points. Example 3-76 shows the DLSw+ capabilities on R4 and R5 with the cached NetBIOS name.

**Example 3-75**  *R6 NetBIOS Configuration*

```
dlsw icanreach netbios-exclusive
dlsw icanreach netbios-name ccie????
```

---

**NOTE**    To enter a **?** within the command line without bringing up the help function, you need to enter **^v** (**Shift+6, then v**) first.

---

**Example 3-76**  *R4 and R5 DLSw+ Capabilities*

```
R4#sh dlsw capabilities
DLSw: Capabilities for peer 10.6.6.6(2065)
  vendor id (OUI)          : '00C' (cisco)
  version number           : 2
  release number           : 0
  init pacing window       : 20
  unsupported saps         : none
  num of tcp sessions      : 1
  loop prevent support     : no
  icanreach mac-exclusive  : no
  icanreach netbios-excl.  : yes
  reachable mac addresses  : none
  reachable netbios names  : ccie????
  V2 multicast capable     : yes
  DLSw multicast address   : none
  cisco version number     : 1
  peer group number        : 0
  peer cluster support     : no
  border peer capable      : no
  peer cost                : 3
  biu-segment configured   : no
  UDP Unicast support      : yes
  Fast-switched HPR supp.  : no
  NetBIOS Namecache length : 15
  local-ack configured     : yes
  priority configured      : no
  cisco RSVP support       : no
  configured ip address    : 10.6.6.6
  peer type                : conf
  version string           :
Cisco Internetwork Operating System Software
IOS (tm) 7200 Software (C7200-JS-M), Version 12.2(16), RELEASE SOFTWARE (fc3)
Copyright  1986-2003 by cisco Systems, Inc.
Compiled Thu 06-Mar-03 21:37 by pwade
R5#sh dlsw capabilities
DLSw: Capabilities for peer 10.6.6.6(2065)
  vendor id (OUI)          : '00C' (cisco)
```

*continues*

**Example 3-76** *R4 and R5 DLSw+ Capabilities (Continued)*

```
      version number        : 2
      release number        : 0
      init pacing window    : 20
      unsupported saps      : none
      num of tcp sessions   : 1
      loop prevent support  : no
      icanreach mac-exclusive : no
      icanreach netbios-excl. : yes
      reachable mac addresses : none
      reachable netbios names : ccie????
      V2 multicast capable  : yes
      DLSw multicast address : none
      cisco version number  : 1
      peer group number     : 0
      peer cluster support  : no
      border peer capable   : no
      peer cost             : 3
      biu-segment configured : no
      UDP Unicast support   : yes
      Fast-switched HPR supp. : no
      NetBIOS Namecache length : 15
      local-ack configured  : yes
      priority configured   : no
      cisco RSVP support    : no
      configured ip address : 10.6.6.6
      peer type             : conf
      version string        :
Cisco Internetwork Operating System Software
IOS (tm) 7200 Software (C7200-JS-M), Version 12.2(16), RELEASE SOFTWARE (fc3)
Copyright  1986-2003 by cisco Systems, Inc.
Compiled Thu 06-Mar-03 21:37 by pwade
```

# Section 7: IOS and IP Features (10 Points)

- *Configure R8 so that when R6 FastEthernet4/0 (10.60.60.1) connects to virtual IP address 10.80.80.12, that traffic is actually sent to R2 Serial 0/0 (10.90.90.1). When R1 receives the traffic from R6, it should see the source address of 10.8.8.2 for this operation. Do not perform any policy routing in your solution.*

This is an advanced NAT question. At first glance, you might have felt that this could be achieved by using "NAT on a Stick" where you would use a combination of NAT statements in conjunction with policy routing to achieve the desired result; however, policy routing is not permitted. In this scenario, a static NAT statement is required on R8 to proxy-arp for 10.80.80.12 (as this IP address does not exist) and to change the destination to 10.90.90.1. A further NAT statement is required to change return traffic destined for 10.8.8.2 to 10.60.60.1. Finally, a NAT pool changes the source IP address of traffic flowing toward

10.90.90.1. If you have configured this correctly as shown in Example 3-77, you have scored 5 points.

**Example 3-77**  *R8 NAT Configuration*

```
interface FastEthernet0/0
 ip address 10.80.80.3 255.255.255.0
 no ip redirects
 ip nat outside
!
ip nat pool test 10.8.8.2 10.8.8.2 netmask 255.255.255.240
ip nat inside source static 10.90.90.1 10.80.80.12
ip nat inside source static 10.60.60.1 10.8.8.2
ip nat outside source list 199 pool test
access-list 199 permit ip host 10.60.60.1 host 10.80.80.12
```

**NOTE**      This will not work correctly unless you disable **ip redirects** on R8 FastEthernet0/0. Remember to test with extended pings from R6 to ensure your source address is 10.60.60.1.

Example 3-78 shows the testing procedure, using an extended ping from R6 to the virtual IP address of 10.80.80.12; NAT debugs on R8, and an ICMP debug on R2 shows the entire process.

**Example 3-78**  *NAT Testing and Verification*

```
R6#ping
Protocol [ip]:
Target IP address: 10.80.80.12
Repeat count [5]:
Datagram size [100]:
Timeout in seconds [2]:
Extended commands [n]: y
Source address or interface: 10.60.60.1
Type of service [0]:
Set DF bit in IP header? [no]:
Validate reply data? [no]:
Data pattern [0xABCD]:
Loose, Strict, Record, Timestamp, Verbose[none]:
Sweep range of sizes [n]:
Type escape sequence to abort.
Sending 5, 100-byte ICMP Echos to 10.80.80.12, timeout is 2 seconds:
Packet sent with a source address of 10.60.60.1
.!!!!
Success rate is 80 percent (4/5), round-trip min/avg/max = 4/6/8 ms
R8#debug ip nat
01:25:30: NAT*: s=10.60.60.1->10.8.8.2, d=10.80.80.12 [195]
01:25:30: NAT*: s=10.8.8.2, d=10.80.80.12->10.90.90.1 [195]
01:25:30: NAT*: s=10.90.90.1, d=10.8.8.2->10.60.60.1 [195]
01:25:30: NAT*: s=10.60.60.1->10.8.8.2, d=10.80.80.12 [196]
```

*continues*

**Example 3-78** *NAT Testing and Verification (Continued)*

```
01:25:30: NAT*: s=10.8.8.2, d=10.80.80.12->10.90.90.1 [196]
01:25:30: NAT*: s=10.90.90.1, d=10.8.8.2->10.60.60.1 [196]
01:25:30: NAT*: s=10.60.60.1->10.8.8.2, d=10.80.80.12 [197]
01:25:30: NAT*: s=10.8.8.2, d=10.80.80.12->10.90.90.1 [197]
01:25:30: NAT*: s=10.90.90.1, d=10.8.8.2->10.60.60.1 [197]
01:25:30: NAT*: s=10.60.60.1->10.8.8.2, d=10.80.80.12 [198]
01:25:30: NAT*: s=10.8.8.2, d=10.80.80.12->10.90.90.1 [198]
01:25:30: NAT*: s=10.90.90.1, d=10.8.8.2->10.60.60.1 [198]
01:25:30: NAT*: s=10.60.60.1->10.8.8.2, d=10.80.80.12 [199]
01:25:30: NAT*: s=10.8.8.2, d=10.80.80.12->10.90.90.1 [199]
01:25:30: NAT*: s=10.90.90.1, d=10.8.8.2->10.60.60.1 [199]
R2#debug ip icmp
01:25:30: ICMP: echo reply sent, src 10.90.90.1, dst 10.8.8.2
01:25:30: ICMP: echo reply sent, src 10.90.90.1, dst 10.8.8.2
01:25:30: ICMP: echo reply sent, src 10.90.90.1, dst 10.8.8.2
01:25:30: ICMP: echo reply sent, src 10.90.90.1, dst 10.8.8.2
01:25:30: ICMP: echo reply sent, src 10.90.90.1, dst 10.8.8.2
```

- *Manipulate the EIGRP authentication to change the keys as follows: The first key should remain active from the time you started this lab today and remain active for two days after that; the second key should then become active permanently. Allow an overlap of 20 minutes but ensure that all EIGRP routers have a common synchronized time source provided by one of your routers to ensure reliable operation.*

You are required to configure an additional Key Chain and appropriate Key Management. Your original Key Chain should include an **accept-lifetime** and **send-lifetime** with a **duration** of 172800 seconds (2 days); the additional key should begin 1 day, 23 hours, and 40 minutes later to allow for the 20-minute overlap, this key should then have a lifetime, which is **infinite**. A synchronized time source can only be Network Time Protocol (NTP) to ensure that each EIGRP router has a synchronized clock and manages its keys effectively. If you do not configure R2 as the NTP master, you could run into problems as this is the only router that has direct connections to the other EIGRP routers; if, for example, you configured R1 as the master, R3 can only access the NTP server via an EIGRP route. This might not appear to be a problem on the surface but just see what happens when you reset your routers. If you configured this correctly as shown in Example 3-79 through Example 3-82, you have scored 3 points.

**Example 3-79** *EIGRP Key Chain Configuration for R1, R2, and R3*

```
key chain Brussels
 key 1
  key-string Asterix
  accept-lifetime 09:00:00 Jul 18 2004 duration 172800
  send-lifetime 09:00:00 Jul 18 2004 duration 172800
 key 2
  key-string Obelix
  accept-lifetime 08:40:00 Jul 20 2004 infinite
  send-lifetime 08:40:00 Jul 20 2004 infinite
```

| NOTE | An alternate solution to configuring duration can be to configure the end time. |
|------|---------------------------------------------------------------------------------|

**Example 3-80**  *R2 NTP Configuration*

```
R2# clock set 15:01:00 18 july 2004
R2#conf t
R2(config)#ntp master
R2(config)#^Z
```

**Example 3-81**  *R1 NTP Configuration*

```
ntp server 10.90.90.1
```

**Example 3-82**  *R3 NTP Configuration*

```
ntp server 172.16.0.1
```

- *Configure R7 not to send each character of a Telnet session as a separate CPU interrupt to your network devices. Characters should be buffered until an acknowledgment is received to reduce CPU interrupts and improve on bandwidth limitations.*

By default, each Telnet character actually causes a CPU interrupt. To enable the buffering feature, you need to configure R7 with the **service nagle** command. If you have configured this correctly, you have scored 1 point.

- *Prevent the configuration prompt from being displayed on R5 when in config mode.*

The command **no service prompt** prevents the configuration prompt from being displayed; the usual prompt is still displayed in EXEC mode. If you have configured this correctly as shown in Example 3-83, you have scored 1 point.

**Example 3-83**  *R5 Service Prompt Configuration*

```
R5(config)#no service prompt config

R5#conf t
00:24:14: %SYS-5-CONFIG_I: Configured from console by console
Enter configuration commands, one per line.  End with CNTL/Z.
int fast 0/0
no shut
exit
exit
R5#
```

# Section 8: QoS (5 Points)

- *Configure a QoS policy on R2 for traffic flowing from VLAN1 toward the rest of your network. Traffic found to have an IP precedence of 7, 5, and 1 should be limited to a maximum of 2 Mbps. Traffic above this figure with the stated precedence should be discarded. Use only one ACL to accomplish this requirement. Assume normal and excess burst sizes to both be 40000.*

You are required to configure rate limiting inbound on R2 FastEthernet0/0. As you can only use one ACL to match on the precedence value, you must use a precedence mask. To match on precedence values, you must first convert these values in an 8-bit format where 00000001 is for precedence 0, 00000010 is for precedence 1, 00000100 for 2, 00001000 for 3, 00010000 for 4, 00100000 for 5, 01000000 for 6, and 10000000 for 7. 10100010 matches precedence values 7, 5, and 1 as the mask is an add operation of the individual values. This value is then converted into Hex giving the mask value of A2, which is used in the access-list. If you have configured this correctly as shown in Example 3-84, you have scored 2 points.

**Example 3-84** *R2 Rate Limiting Configuration*

```
interface FastEthernet0/0
 rate-limit input access-group rate-limit 20 2000000 40000 40000
   conform-action transmit exceed-action drop
!
access-list rate-limit 20 mask A2
```

- *A future FXS module will be installed into R6 and VoIP traffic will flow between R1 and R6. Configure RSVP on R1 so that the RSVP setup must be complete before the destination phone rings. Each RSVP flow should be set to 100 kbps and allow for a maximum of 2 flows; allow a maximum of 15 seconds for this setup. You should also allow for 64 discard messages and 64 dynamic queues in your QoS configuration. You are not required to perform any configuration on R6 but can assume that the phone number on R6 will be 01962 when configuring the dial plan on R1.*

A vast amount of information is supplied to you within this question; you just need to make sense of it all and put it into a valid configuration. Your flows are to be 100 kbps with a maximum of two flows, so your RSVP statement will be **ip rsvp bandwidth 200 100**. Fifteen seconds for this setup is enabled by the command **call rsvp-sync resv-timer 15** and your fair-queue configuration should include the 64 discard messages, 64 dynamic queues, and, finally, the 2 RSVP flows using the command **fair-queue 64 64 2**. If you have configured this correctly as shown in Example 3-85, you have scored 3 points.

**Example 3-85** *R1 RSVP Voice QoS Configuration*

```
call rsvp-sync
call rsvp-sync resv-timer 15
!
interface FastEthernet0/0
fair-queue 64 64 2
```

**Example 3-85**  *R1 RSVP Voice QoS Configuration (Continued)*

```
ip rsvp bandwidth 200 100
!
voice-port 1/0/0
!
dial-peer voice 01962 voip
 destination-pattern 01962
 session target ipv4:10.80.80.2
 req-qos controlled-load
 acc-qos controlled-load
```

# Section 9: Multicast (5 Points)

- *Configure a new loopback interface on R1 of 10.9.9.1/24; advertise this out of FastEthernet0/0 (VLAN2) interface using RIP V1.*

This is required for the multicast question to follow; you should ensure that FastEthernet0/0 is the only interface that is enabled for RIP. If you have configured this correctly as shown in Example 3-86, you have scored 1 point.

**Example 3-86**  *R1 RIP V1 Configuration*

```
interface Loopback2
 ip address 10.9.9.9 255.255.255.0
!
router rip
 passive-interface default
 no passive-interface FastEthernet0/0
 network 10.0.0.0
 version 1
```

- *Configure R5 to receive the RIP advertisement from R1. Use a multicast solution to achieve this and do not create any tunnel interfaces. You are not required to be able to ping 10.9.9.9 from R5.*

This is where it begins to get interesting. You now have to transport the RIP advertisements across your network to R5. A number of ways are normally available to accomplish this including enabling RIP all the way along the path at each interface, creating a tunnel interface between routers and enable RIP through this tunnel, or by bridging within the switch; however, you must use a multicast method. An IOS feature exists called IP Multicast Helper, which is similar to an IP Helper Address; however, this takes a defined broadcast and converts this into a multicast. You should remember that RIP V1 broadcasts its routing updates. R6 will receive the RIP broadcast on its VLAN2 interface and can be considered the first hop router for the multicast scenario. R6 converts the broadcast stream arriving at incoming interface FastEthernet0/0 destined for UDP port 520 (RIP) to a multicast stream. Access-list 130 allows only RIP to be forwarded into the multicast cloud. The traffic is sent to multicast address 224.9.9.9 using PIM Dense Mode. The command

**ip forward-protocol udp rip** is required to ensure the proper process level is used to perform the conversion. The second configuration on the last hop router R5 converts the multicast stream at incoming interface virtual-template1 (not ATM3/0) back to a broadcast. Only traffic destined for UDP port 520 should be converted back to broadcast. After configuration, Example 3-87 shows the RIP traffic arriving at R6.

**Example 3-87** *R6 Multicast Helper Testing*

```
R6(config)#access-list 130 permit udp any any eq rip
R6#debug ip packet 130 det
IP packet debugging is on (detailed) for access list 130
R6#
00:03:46: IP: s=10.80.80.1 (FastEthernet0/0), d=255.255.255.255, len 52, rcvd 2
00:03:46:     UDP src=520, dst=520
00:03:56: IP: s=10.80.80.1 (FastEthernet0/0), d=255.255.255.255, len 52, rcvd 2
00:03:56:     UDP src=520, dst=520
00:03:56: IP: s=10.80.80.1 (FastEthernet0/0), d=255.255.255.255, len 52, rcvd 2
00:03:56:     UDP src=520, dst=520
```

Example 3-88 shows the multicast traffic being converted into RIP on R5. Notice how RIP ignored the update as it assumes a bad source. This is rectified by configuring RIP with the command **no validate-update-source** on R5. Example 3-89 shows the valid RIP update after the source is ignored. You should also notice that the route has come through as a /29 and not a /24. The route has taken the attributes of the interface on which it was effectively received on which is also a /29. If you have configured this correctly as shown in Example 3-90 and Example 3-91, you have scored 4 points.

**Example 3-88** *R5 Multicast Helper Testing*

```
R5(config)#access-list 130 permit udp any any eq rip
R5#debug ip pack 130 det
IP packet debugging is on (detailed) for access list 130
R5#
00:03:54: IP: s=10.80.80.1 (Virtual-Access1), d=224.9.9.9, len 52, rcvd 0
00:03:54:     UDP src=520, dst=520
00:04:03: IP: s=10.80.80.1 (Virtual-Access1), d=224.9.9.9, len 52, rcvd 0
00:04:03:     UDP src=520, dst=520
00:04:03: IP: s=10.80.80.1 (Virtual-Access1), d=224.9.9.9, len 52, rcvd 0
00:04:03:     UDP src=520, dst=520
00:04:05: IP: s=10.80.80.1 (Virtual-Access1), d=224.9.9.9, len 52, rcvd 0
00:04:05:     UDP src=520, dst=520
00:04:22: IP: s=10.80.80.1 (Virtual-Access1), d=224.9.9.9, len 52, rcvd 0
00:04:22:     UDP src=520, dst=520
00:04:48: IP: s=10.80.80.1 (Virtual-Access1), d=224.9.9.9, len 52, rcvd 0
00:04:48:     UDP src=520, dst=520
00:05:17: IP: s=10.80.80.1 (Virtual-Access1), d=224.9.9.9, len 52, rcvd 0
00:05:17:     UDP src=520, dst=520
R5#debug ip rip
RIP protocol debugging is on
R5#
00:05:48: RIP: ignored v1 update from bad source 10.80.80.1 on Virtual-Access1
```

**Example 3-89**  *R5 Multicast Helper Testing*

```
R5#debug ip rip
01:41:46: RIP: received v1 update from 10.80.80.1 on Virtual-Access1
01:41:46:      10.9.9.0 in 1 hops
R5#sh ip route rip
     10.0.0.0/8 is variably subnetted, 16 subnets, 4 masks
R        10.9.9.0/29 [120/1] via 10.80.80.1, 00:00:05
```

**Example 3-90**  *R6 Multicast Helper Configuration*

```
ip multicast-routing
!
interface FastEthernet0/0
 ip address 10.80.80.2 255.255.255.0
 ip directed-broadcast
 ip pim dense-mode
 ip multicast helper-map broadcast 224.9.9.9 130
!
interface Virtual-Template1
 ip pim dense-mode
!
ip forward-protocol udp rip
!
access-list 130 permit udp any any eq rip
```

**Example 3-91**  *R5 Multicast Helper Configuration*

```
ip multicast-routing
!
interface FastEthernet0/0
 ip address 10.50.50.1 255.255.255.248

!
interface Virtual-Template1
 ip pim dense-mode
 ip directed-broadcast
 ip multicast helper-map 224.9.9.9 10.50.50.7 130
!
router rip
 no validate-update-source
 passive-interface default
 network 10.0.0.0
!
ip forward-protocol udp rip
!
access-list 130 permit udp any any eq rip
```

**NOTE**    This configuration will actually also allow the broadcast to be propagated out onto VLAN4
network 10.50.50.0/29. As well as answering the question, this would be the normal
practice for this feature for transporting broadcast traffic end-to-end over a multicast-
enabled network.

# Section 10: Security (10 Points)

- *Configure R3 to be managed by http with password access of **cisco** for username and
  **cisco** for the password.*

You can manage a router via http as the command **ip http server** is enabled by default; to
add local password access, use the command **ip http authentication local**, and then
configure a username and password on the router both to **cisco**. Figure 3-15 shows the
Password screen when attempting to access R3 by HTTP. If you configured this correctly
as shown in Example 3-92, you have scored 2 points.

**Figure 3-15**   *R3 HTTP Access*

**Example 3-92**   *1R3 HTTP Access*

```
username cisco password 0 cisco
!
ip http authentication local
```

- *It is suspected that your network is being threatened by a W32.Blaster virus. You have
  been told that the virus is manipulating port 135, 139, and 445 and that it is
  attempting to enter your network from VLAN1. Configure R2 to block the virus
  entering the rest of your network and to provide as much detail at Layer 2 and 3 as to
  which devices might be initiating the attack. The worm will also attempt to send
  packets to random IP addresses, which do not exist. When this happens, the router will
  reply with an ICMP message. Configure R2 not to send this ICMP message.*

You need to configure an access list to block port 135, 139, and 445 on R2 FastEthernet0/0. Because you have not been told if this is TCP or UDP, you must block both. To provide the detailed information, you are required to enable logging and use the **log-input** command at the end of your access list. Doing so will provide both MAC and IP address details of any device that matches the list on VLAN2. If an IP address is targeted that does not exist, the router will send an ICMP unreachable message, which will increase CPU resource activity. To stop this, you are required to configure **no ip unreachables** under interface FastEthernet0/0.

Although you have only been requested to block the virus from entering your network, it is good practice to also stop it from leaving your network so you are not responsible for spreading the virus if your network does become infected. If you have configured this correctly as shown in Example 3-93, you have scored 3 points. If you have only configured the ACL inbound on R2 and not also outbound, you have only scored 2 points.

**Example 3-93**  *R2 Virus Protection Configuration*

```
logging buffered
!
interface FastEthernet0/0
  ip address 172.16.0.1 255.255.0.0
  ip access-group 115 in
  ip access-group 115 out
  no ip unreachables
!
access-list 115 deny tcp any any eq 135 log-input
access-list 115 deny udp any any eq 135 log-input
access-list 115 deny tcp any any eq 139 log-input
access-list 115 deny udp any any eq 139 log-input
access-list 115 deny tcp any any eq 145 log-input
access-list 115 deny udp any any eq 145 log-inputaccess-list 115 permit ip any any
```

# How Did You Do?

With the aid of the debrief section and full configurations and routing tables on the CD, you should now have an accurate evaluation of your lab. If you scored more than 80 points within the time frame (8 hours) you should congratulate yourself, you are well on the way to becoming a CCIE. You have demonstrated the ability to think laterally and shown an impressive knowledge of your subject. If you scored less than 80 don't worry, this will improve as you progress throughout the book and learn how to analyze each question and improve your core skills.

There was one landmine in the lab: the changing of the MTU, which would not let OSPF form an adjacency over the Frame Relay. If you got stuck at that point, you have failed the lab. If you find you have an issue in your real lab or during your study, just get back to basics; remove things in turn that could be causing you a problem; if you cannot figure out a work-around to an obvious landmine, sacrifice one or two points to safeguard many more later on in the lab.

For each question that you did not answer correctly, take the time to research the subject thoroughly and turn your weaknesses into your strengths. This with plenty of practice is how ultimately you will gain your number.

## Further Reading/URLs

To better prepare yourself and follow up on the topics covered in this lab, you should consult the http://www.cisco.com/public/pubsearch.html website for more information on the following topics:

> 3550 VACLs
> PPP over ATM
> OSPF adjacency issues
> BGP Conditional Advertisements, Authentication, Backdoor Routes, Aggregation
> VoIP Codec Preference, Hunt Groups
> DLSw Backup Peers, Bridge-lists
> QoS Rate Limiting, IP Precedence Mask
> Virus Control

# Topology 2, the Brace of Switches Labs

# CHAPTER 4

# Practice Lab 4

You will now be starting Practice Lab 4. The topology and equipment are identical for Lab 4 through Lab 6 and differ from Lab 1 through Lab 3, although these labs will maintain the same challenges that you have seen so far. The main objective of the change is to ensure you practice on a variety of subjects and scenarios that covers the potential CCIE Lab Exam content. The main changes you will encounter are a fully meshed Frame Relay network for all serial connections and an additional Cisco Catalyst 3550 switch. If your equipment does not exactly match that used to produce the lab, it does not matter as long as you have the required interfaces. Having the exact equipment, however, will aid you in pasting in configuration files.

Quite often, the questions will be straightforward, so try to keep your solutions simple and avoid complicating the matter for yourself. Sometimes, you will need to pay attention to the wording because although the question might look quite simple, it could involve a "hidden" concept regarding a specific area or section in the exercise. Keep in mind that the main objective of these lab exercises is to give you challenges that will drive you through the areas you must explore to be well prepared to take the CCIE Lab Exam with successful results. The challenges are designed to thoroughly prepare you to better apply your skills in the real world.

The router and switch initial configurations, Frame Relay switch configuration, and now backbone router configurations are provided to help you in this lab. Solutions for the entire lab including configurations and common **show** command outputs from all the devices in the topology can be found on the accompanying CD-ROM. The "Ask the Proctor" section which will give you clues is included at the end of the lab. This section is followed by the lab debrief, which will analyze each question showing you what was required and how to achieve the desired results. Finally, you will find a list of handy references at the end of the chapter should you require additional study information.

Practice Lab 4 introduces you the new topology and it will guide you through the basic network setup, and then to challenge you on the next labs. As part of any exam preparation, the more you practice (even on the tasks you might think are basic tasks), the more comfortable you will be taking the exam.

You will now be guided through the equipment requirements and pre-lab tasks in preparation for taking Practice Lab 4.

# Equipment List

- 2 Catalyst 3550 switches (3550 X 24 Fast Ethernet ports with Cisco IOS Software Release 12.1 Enhanced Multilayer Software image [EMI])
- 6 Cisco routers (2600, 3600, and 3725)
- A backbone router (Cisco 7200)
- A Frame Relay switch router (Cisco 4000)

The routers are loaded with Cisco IOS Software Release 12.2 Enterprise Mainline image (all Cisco equipment). The exception is the 3725 router that is loaded with 12.2(T) image.

Follow the router interface specifications included in Table 4-1.

**Table 4-1** *Interfaces Required per Router*

| Router | Ethernet Interface | Serial Interface | BRI Interface | Voice | ATM Interface |
|---|---|---|---|---|---|
| R1 (2611) | 2 | 2 | - | - | - |
| R2 (3725) | 2 | 2 | - | - | - |
| R3 (2621) | 2 | 2 | 1 | 2 FXS | - |
| R4 (3640) | 1 | 2 | - | 2 FXS | - |
| R5 (2621) | 2 | 2 | 1 | - | - |
| R6 (3640) | 2 | 2 | - | | 1 |
| BB_Router (7200) | 2 | - | - | - | 1 |
| FR_SWITCH (4000) | - | 12 | - | - | - |

**NOTE**     Although you will be provided with fully meshed physical connectivity (LAN and WAN), you may not use all routers or interfaces in all lab exercises. This is to optimize your setup for the next two labs.

# Setting Up the Lab

Feel free to use any combination of routers as long as you fulfill the topology diagram as shown in Figure 4-1. It is not compulsory to use the same model of routers, but this will make life easier should you like to load configurations directly from the CD-ROM into your own devices.

NOTE   If you have a mix of 10- and 100-Mbps Ethernet interfaces, adjust the **bandwidth** statements on the relevant interfaces to keep all interface speeds common. This will ensure that you do not get unwanted behavior because of differing IGP metrics.

From now on, you will find some routers using a mix of 10- and 100-Mbps Ethernet interfaces.

## Lab Topology

Practice Lab 4 will use the topology as outlined in Figure 4-1, which you will need to create using the switch, Frame Relay, ATM, and ISDN information that follows.

**Figure 4-1**   *Lab 4 Topology Diagram*

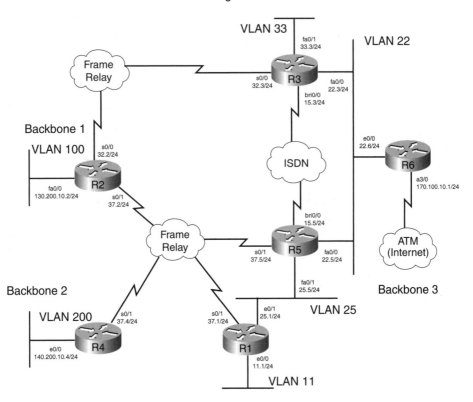

## Cabling Instructions

You will have all the router interfaces precabled, although you will not be using all interfaces for the Lab 4 exercises. Table 4-2 documents the cabling instructions.

**Table 4-2**  *3550 Cabling Diagram*

| Interface | Switch-1 | Switch-2 |
|---|---|---|
| R1 e0/0 (2611) | fa0/1 | - |
| R1 e0/1(2611) | - | fa0/1 |
| R2 fa0/0 (3725) | fa0/2 | - |
| R2 fa0/1 (3725) | - | fa0/2 |
| R3 fa0/0 (2621) | fa0/3 | - |
| R3 fa0/1(2621) | - | fa0/3 |
| R4 e0/0 (3640) | fa0/4 | - |
| R5 fa0/0 (2621) | fa0/5 | - |
| R5 fa0/1(2621) | - | fa0/5 |
| R6 e0/0 (3640) | fa0/6 | - |
| R6 fa1/0 (3640) | - | fa0/6 |
| Backbone 1 | fa0/13 | - |
| Backbone 2 | - | fa0/13 |
| Trunk | fa0/15 | fa0/15 |
| Trunk | fa0/17 | fa0/17 |

## Frame Relay Switch Instructions

The Frame Relay switch is a 4000 router with 12 interfaces connecting all 6 core routers (as you see in Table 4-3) in a full mesh environment. Refer also to Figure 4-2 for the Frame Relay logical assignment and to the Frame Relay sample configuration from the CD-ROM.

**Table 4-3**  *Frame Relay Switch Physical Connectivity*

| Router/Interface | FR_Switch Interface |
|---|---|
| R1 s0/0 | Serial 0 |
| R1 s0/1 | Serial 1 |
| R2 s0/0 | Serial 2 |
| R2 s0/1 | Serial 3 |
| R3 s0/0 | Serial 4 |
| R3 s0/1 | Serial 5 |

**Table 4-3**   *Frame Relay Switch Physical Connectivity (Continued)*

| Router/Interface | FR_Switch Interface |
|---|---|
| R4 s0/0 | Serial 6 |
| R4 s0/1 | Serial 7 |
| R5 s0/0 | Serial 8 |
| R5 s0/1 | Serial 9 |
| R6 s0/0 | Serial 10 |
| R6 s0/1 | Serial 11 |

**Figure 4-2**   *Frame Relay Switch Logical Connectivity*

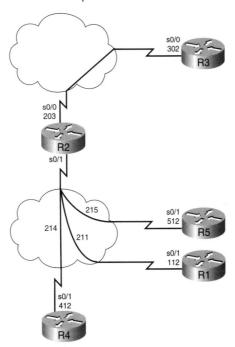

Configure a 4000 router as a Frame Relay switch or equivalent that can provide the connectivity for this lab. The next two lab scenarios will use this topology as a reference.

Keep your DCE cables at the frame switch end for simplicity and provide a clock rate of 2 Mbps to all links. Should you require detailed information on how to configure one of your routers as a Frame Relay switch this information can be found in Appendix A, "Frame Relay Switch Configuration" (and/or from the CD-ROM).

## ATM Switch Instructions

You will have a back-to-back connection between R6 and the backbone router using OC-3 Multimode connection, as shown in Figure 4-3.

**Figure 4-3**   *ATM Physical Connectivity*

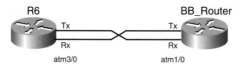

Figure 4-4 shows the logical setup for the ATM connection. You should always pay attention to the PVCs you are going to use because the PVC numbers might change in other Lab exercises.

**Figure 4-4**   *ATM Logical Connectivity*

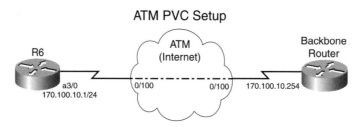

The ATM connectivity in Labs 4 through 6 will be provided by a back-to-back connection between R6 and BB_Router over E3 ATM interfaces. You could also use a Cisco Light-Stream (LS1010 Switch) if available. Configure the PVCs as requested during the lab exercise. If you are using a LightStream to provide your ATM connectivity and require information on how to set this up, this information can be found in Appendix B, "LS1010 ATM Switch Configuration."

## ISDN Instructions

Connect R3 and R5 into either ISDN lines or an ISDN simulator as shown on Figure 4-5. R3 and R5 use BRI S/T interfaces. It is preferable that the ISDN supports command-line interface (CLI). Reconfigure the numbers as required if you are using live ISDN lines.

**Figure 4-5**   *ISDN Connectivity*

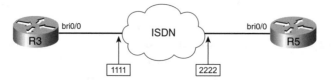

## IP Address Instructions

Configure the IP addresses as shown in Figure 4-6.

**Figure 4-6**  *IP Addressing Diagram*

Network 160.10.0.0 - IP Addressing

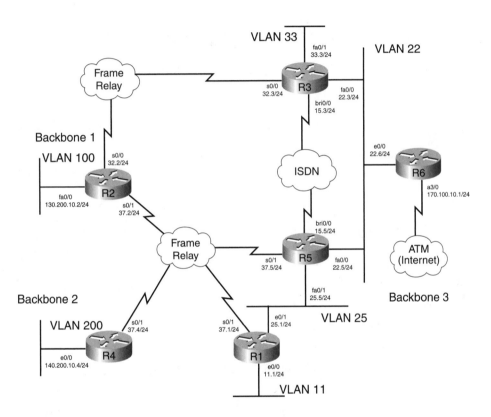

The CD-ROM includes initial configuration files for all routers and switches that include the basic IP addressing as shown in Figure 4-6. The initial configuration also includes the loop-back interfaces.

# Pre-Lab Tasks

- Build the lab topology as per Figure 4-1 through Figure 4-6.
- Configure your chosen Frame Relay switch router to provide the necessary DLCIs as per Figure 4-2 and from the Frame Relay switch sample configuration file found on the CD-ROM.

- Load the initial configuration files for this lab. The files will contain the basic IP addressing as referred to in Figure 4-6; hostnames have been configured and the line console and line vty pre-configured with the password **cisco**.

- Get into a comfortable and quiet environment where you can focus for the next eight hours.

- Start your lab in the morning and work straight through the eight-hour timeframe. Do not panic or give up if you feel you will not be able to complete the whole exercise. If it happens, use the remaining time as a "practice" to focus on the parts where you got into difficulty.

- Have available a Cisco Documentation CD-ROM or access online the latest documentation from the following URL: http://www.cisco.com/univercd/home/home.htm.

---

**NOTE**     Consider accessing only the preceding URL, not the whole Cisco.com website. If you will be allowed to use documentation during your CCIE lab exam, it will be restricted.

---

- Go for a walk to relax before you get started.

## General Guidelines

- Please read the whole lab before you start.
- Do not configure any static/default routes unless otherwise specified/required.
- Use only the DLCIs and ATM PVCs provided in the appropriate figures.
- Follow the question instructions and requirements.
- Take a 30-minute break midway through the exercise.
- If you find yourself running out of time, choose questions that you are confident you can answer. Failing this approach, choose questions with a higher point rating to maximize your potential score.

# Practice Lab 4

You will now be answering questions in relation to the network topology as shown in Figure 4-7.

**Figure 4-7**    *Lab 4 Topology and IP Addressing Diagram*

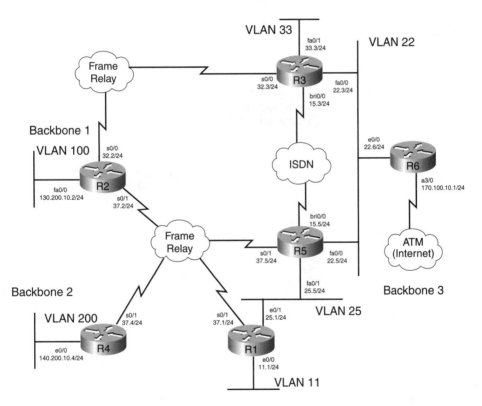

Network Topology and Addressing -
160.0.0.0/24

# Section 1: Bridging and Switching (18 Points)

## Section 1.1: Frame Relay Configuration (3 Points)

- Configure the Frame Relay portion of the network as shown in Figure 4-8 and ensure that only the PVCs shown in Figure 4-8 will be used. Use of dynamic PVCs is not permitted.

- You are permitted to use subinterfaces on R2 interface s0/1.

- Do NOT configure subinterfaces on any other routers.

- You must be able to **ping** across the Frame Relay cloud.

**Figure 4-8**   *Frame Relay Diagram*

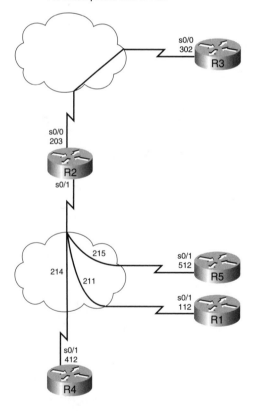

# Section 1.2: 3550 LAN Switch Configuration (12 Points)

- Sw1 and Sw2 are connected via a crossover cable using ports fa0/15. Configure an ISL trunk between Sw1 and Sw2.

- All Ethernet ports are pre-cabled as per Table 4-4. Note that not all ports will be used on this lab.

**Table 4-4**    *3550 Cabling Guide*

| Interface | Switch-1 | Switch-2 |
|-----------|----------|----------|
| R1 e0/0 (2611) | fa0/1 | - |
| R1 e0/1(2611) | - | fa0/1 |
| R2 fa0/0 (3725) | fa0/2 | - |
| R2 fa0/1 (3725) | - | fa0/2 |
| R3 fa0/0 (2621) | fa0/3 | - |
| R3 fa0/1(2621) | - | fa0/3 |
| R4 e0/0 (3640) | fa0/4 | - |
| R5 fa0/0 (2621) | fa0/5 | - |
| R5 fa0/1(2621) | - | fa0/5 |
| R6 e0/0 (3640) | fa0/6 | - |
| R6 fa1/0 (3640) | - | fa0/6 |
| Backbone 1 | fa0/13 | - |
| Backbone 2 | - | fa0/13 |
| Trunk | fa0/15 | fa0/15 |
| Trunk | fa0/17 | fa0/17 |

- Configure the VLANs as follows:

    VLAN_11: Connected to R1-e0/0 (VLAN_11)

    VLAN_22: Connected to R3-fa0/0, R5-fa0/0, and R6-E0/0 (VLAN_22)

    VLAN_25: Connected to R1-e0/1 and R5-fa0/1 (VLAN_25)

    VLAN_33: Connected to R3-fa0/1 (VLAN_33)

    VLAN_100: Connected to R2-fa0/0 and Sw1-fa0/13 (VLAN_100)

    VLAN_200: Connected to R4-Ee0/0 and Sw2-fa0/13 (VLAN_200)

- Configure Sw1 to be the VTP server for the domain. Sw2 is a VTP client. Be sure that Sw2 can see the VLAN configuration from Sw1.

- Configure Sw1, using VLAN_11 with the IP address 160.10.11.10/24. After you have finished your routing section, all routers should be able to ping this interface.

- Configure VLAN_11 on Sw1 to be the secondary root switch.

- Configure Sw1 to permit any SNMP manager to access all objects with read-only permission using the community string *public*. The switch also sends VTP traps to the hosts 160.10.11.111 and 160.10.11.33 using SNMPv1 and to the host 160.10.11.27 using SNMPv2C. The community string *public* is sent with the traps.

## Section 1.3: ATM Configuration (3 Points)

- Configure the ATM as shown in Figure 4-9.

- There is a PVC configured between R6 and the backbone router. Do not configure subinterfaces.

- Use explicit address mapping. Do not depend on the remoter backbone router for inverse ARP.

- You must be able to ping the backbone router address 170.100.10.254/24.

**Figure 4-9**    *ATM Diagram*

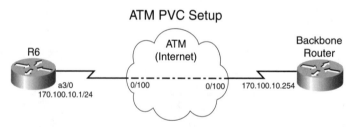

## Section 2: IP IGP Protocols (30 Points)

Configure the IP routing as shown in Figure 4-10, following the directions.

**Figure 4-10**  *IP IGP Diagram*

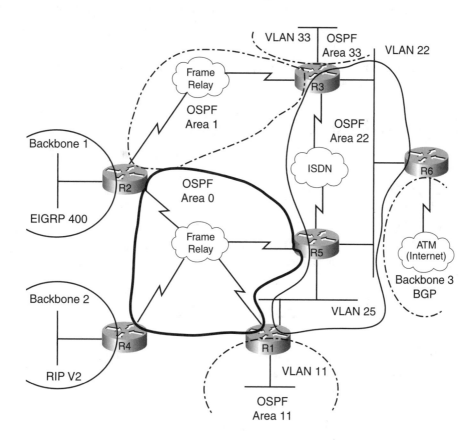

IP Routing

## Section 2.1: OSPF (11 Points)

- Configure OSPF according to the diagram in Figure 4-10. R1-s0/1, R2-s0/1, R4-S0/1, and R5-s0/1 are to be part of the OSPF area 0.

- R2-s0/0 and R3-s0/0 are to be configured as OSPF area 1.

- R1-e0/0 is to be configured as OSPF area 11.

- R1-e0/1, R3-fa0/0, R3-bri0/0, R5-fa0/0, R5 fa0/1, R5-bri0/0, and R6-e0/0 are to be configured as OSPF area 22.

- R3-fa0/1 is to be configured as OSPF area 33.

- Configure the loopback addresses to be part of the OSPF process.

- Make sure you are able to ping any OSPF interface from any router.

## Section 2.2: EIGRP (10 Points)

- Configure EIGRP between R2 and BB1. R2-fa0/0 must be the only interface configured for EIGRP on R2. R2 routing table should be populated with EIGRP routes from BB1.

- Configure the routing waiting time for EIGRP on R2 to remain active indefinitely.

- Redistribute EIGRP into OSPF. Make sure all routers have the EIGRP routes in their routing tables.

## Section 2.3: RIP (9 Points)

- Configure RIP between R4 and BB2. R4-e0/0 must be the only interface configured for RIP on R4. You should receive updates and R4 routing table will be populated with some RIP routes from BB2.

- Configure a filter that will allow only networks 20.0.0.0/8 to be accepted on R4 from BB2.

- Redistribute between RIP and OSPF. Make sure all others routers have network 20.0.0.0 in their routing tables.

# Section 3: BGP Protocol (12 points)

- Configure the EBGP and IBGP as shown in Figure 4-11.

- Configure EBGP between R6 and BB3. R6 will be AS 100 and the BB3 router AS is 300. R6 will receive updates for networks 200.20.X.0 and 198.18.X.0. X is any number. See to Figure 4-11.

- Configure a fully meshed IBGP between R2, R4, and R6; use AS 100. R2 and R4 should be able to see all BGP BB3 routes in their routing tables. Use the loopback interfaces as your peers. See Figure 4-11.

- Configure R2 to accept the maximum of 100 prefixes from R6. If the prefixes received reaches 75 percent of this value, configure appropriately to generate a warning.

# Section 4: ISDN (6 Points)

- Configure ISDN on R3 and R5 using PPP. R3 and R5 should be able to ping each other across the ISDN link.

- Make sure that only when the ISDN link is up that it will pass routing protocol across the link.

- The ISDN link should pass routing protocol only when R5-s0/1 and/or R5-fa0/0 and/or R5-fa0/1 is down. Consider that the routing protocol can pass through the ISDN link when topology changes happen.

**Figure 4-11** *Boundaries Between the Autonomous Systems*

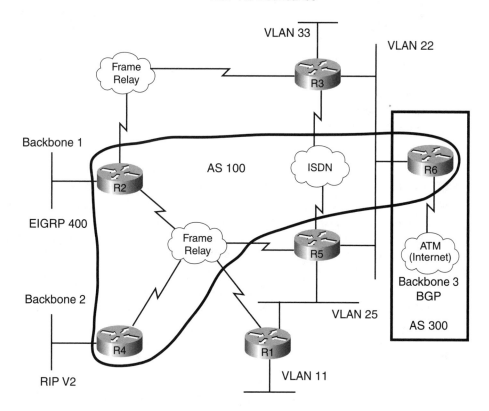

BGP AS Boundaries

# Section 5: IP and IOS Features (10 Points)

- Configure R6 to provide DHCP service to clients located on VLAN 22. Consider the following information:

  — Bindings are stored on Host 160.10.22.253; the file transfer protocol is FTP and the server should wait 4 minutes before writing database changes.

  — Username: user

  — Password: password

  — Filename: router-dhcp

  — DNS servers: 160.10.22.100 and 160.10.22.101

  — Default routers: 160.10.22.3 and 160.10.22.5

  — Domain name: mycompany.com

  — Hosts most retain the DHCP assignment for one week.

- You have some users on VLAN_25 that must have R1 configured as their default gateway; other users must have R5 as their default gateway. Configure R1 and R5 not to send redirect messages to the originator PC.

- The BB2 router is reporting some problems and it is not stable. Configure R4 to save a core dump via FTP in case BB2 fails or crashes. Consider the FTP username CISCO, password CCIE, FTP server IP address 140.200.10.200, and filename dumpfile. Use passive mode also.

- You have some security concerns regarding the use of BOOTP services on R2. Disable the BOOTP services on this router.

# Section 6: DLSw (4 Points)

- Configure DLSw between VLAN_11 and VLAN_33. Use TCP encapsulation.

- You have some users exchanging data through your DLSw connection, but you no not want to compromise the IP traffic, because the DLSw is not your high priority. Configure your DLSw peers to reserve bandwidth and so that they do not use more than 60 kbps as an average bit rate and maximum burst rate of 30 kbps.

- The SNA servers exchanging data between VLAN_11 and VLAN_33 have a high CPU utilization and, therefore, cause unexpected longer timeouts. To adjust the situation, configure a timeout of 10 minutes to accommodate an explorer response before marking a resource unreachable.

# Section 7: QoS (6 Points)

- Configure R1 to give high priority to IP traffic and medium priority to DLSw going out through s0/1. Use a congestion management approach.

- Configure R3 so that any incoming traffic on fa0/1 has medium priority.

- Configure R2 s0/0–Frame Relay so that real-time traffic should never reserve more than 256 kbps and no more than 50 kbps for a specific session.

# Section 8: Multicast (6 Points)

- Configure Multicast PIM Sparse-mode on VLAN_22 to allow multicast traffic between R3, R5, and R6. Make R6 the rendezvous point.

- To better control the interval of PIM query messages, change the frequency of sending these messages to 1 minute.

# Section 9: Security (8 Points)

- The users on VLAN_33 belong to a development department and they are under strict supervision. They are not permitted to access e-mail (where the server is outside VLAN_33) between 08:00 AM to 08:00 PM, Monday through Friday. Configure an access list to accomplish this.

- Configure R2 fa0/0 to prioritize security options on packets coming to this interface. Leave the level and authority as the default values.

- Configure Sw1-fa0/17 to allow only the host MAC address 0010.DE48.2223 to access the switch through this interface. If a security violation occurs, make the interface go to "shutdown" mode.

# Practice Lab 4: "Ask the Proctor"

This section should only be used if you require clues to complete the questions. In the real CCIE lab, the proctor will not enter into any discussions regarding the questions or answers. He or she will be present to ensure you do not have problems with lab environment, help you to clarify the questions, and maintain the timing element of the exam.

## Section 1.1: Frame Relay Configuration

Q: Do I need to configure subinterfaces on R2?
A: The question says you are "permitted" to configure a subinterface. This is up to you.

Q: I disable the inverse ARP but I still have other PVCs on my map.
A: There are some other procedures you might need to perform to have on your Frame Relay map only the PVCs you want.

## Section 1.2: 3550 LAN Switch Configuration

Q: Can I leave my switch ports in auto mode?
A: The questions do not specifically ask you to configure speed and duplex but you should do this to avoid any mismatches that could cause you problems.

Q: Should I name the VLANs as VLAN_11, and so on?
A: If the question named the VLANs, you should configure them as you see in the question.

Q: Should I be able to ping the switches loopback?
A: You are not required to accomplish this.

## Section 1.3: ATM Configuration

Q: What kind of subinterface do you want on R6?
A: Please, read and double-check the question again. The question states to not configure subinterfaces.

Q: What ATM encapsulation should I use?
A: This is a back-to-back configuration and the backbone is using the default encapsulation.

Q: Do you want me to configure "broadcast" under my ATM interfaces?
A: You need to determine what type of traffic/protocols will use the ATM network.

# Section 2.1: OSPF

Q: Can I use any OSPF process ID?
A: Yes.

Q: Can I configure **ip ospf network point-to-point**?
A: There is no specific requirement for what to use.

Q: In which OSPF area should I configure my loopback interfaces?
A: It is your choice.

Q: Do I need to able to ping all routers interfaces?
A: You should be able to ping all OSPF routers interfaces.

# Section 2.2: EIGRP

Q: Can I configure any process ID for EIGRP?
A: Please refer to your IP routing diagram.

Q: Do I need to configure mutual redistribution between EIGRP and OSPF?
A: Please refer to your lab text. A mutual redistribution is not required.

# Section 2.3: RIP

Q: Can I use the **passive-interface** command to make sure only R4-e0/0 will advertise
   RIP?
A: You have a better way to solve this. Just follow the instructions and you may
   discover it. Also, you have some tools to help you make sure it is working.

Q: Do I need to filter the network 20.0.0.0 in or going out from R4?
A: Please refer to your text. The requirement is clear on the text.

# Section 3: BGP Protocol

Q: Do I need to configure AS 100 on R6?
A: I suggest that you follow the lab text instructions. If it says AS 100, you should
   follow it.

Q: Should I use BGP Confederation or any other method?
A: All you are requested to configure is a fully meshed environment. It is your choice
   how to configure and, hence, accomplish this.

Q: I have some IGP problems and not all of my routers can see all loopback interfaces,
   but my BGP is configured acceptable. Will this be acceptable?
A: No, you must have a TCP connection between your BGP peers to receive full
   credit.

# Section 4: ISDN

Q: Are you asking me to configure "dialer-watch"?

A: To accomplish the requirement and make it stable you need to decide what to configure.

Q: I cannot have any traffic at all passing through the ISDN link?

A: No. Traffic can only go through the ISDN link if R5 loses all others interface connectivity.

Q: Should I configure any kind of authentication?

A: You are not required to do that. Sometimes you need a minimum configuration to have your basic ISDN working.

# Section 5: IP and IOS Features

Q: Can I configure an ACL to deny the IP redirects?

A: No, you can find a specific feature to accomplish this.

Q: Also to avoid the BOOTP small server, is it done with an ACL?

A: No, to disable this function you should find a specific command.

# Section 6: DLSw

Q: Can I configure my local peer as "Promiscuous"?

A: Well, you have basically only two peers.

Q: I still have my IGP problem. I think I configured the DLSw acceptable. Will I still receive some credit?

A: Yes, you might receive some credits from those questions that do not require IGP connectivity.

# Section 7: QoS

Q: Along with IP traffic, should I consider other traffic when configuring the queue?

A: Basically you don't have any other kind of traffic above DLSw and IP.

Q: Are you asking that all incoming traffic on R3-fa0/1 will have medium priority?

A: This is exactly what the question says.

# Section 8: Multicast

Q: Do you want me to configure multicast on R3-Fa0/1?

A: The question states only VLAN_22 be configured.

# Section 9: Security

Q: Do you want me to configure an ACL to prioritize packets with security options?

A: Look for other ways or features to accomplish this.

Q: Are you talking about a MAC ACL to be configured and applied on Sw1-fa0/17?

A: No, you have a better way to accomplish this.

# Practice Lab 4 Debrief

## Section 1: Bridging and Switching (18 Points)

### Section 1.1: Frame Relay Configuration (3 Points)

- *Configure the Frame Relay portion of the network as shown in Figure 4-8 and ensure that only the PVCs shown in Figure 4-8 will be used. Use of dynamic PVCs is not permitted.*

The question clearly states that you must use only the PVCs as shown in Figure 4-8. You must therefore disable inverse-arp on the routers. It is good practice to ensure that all routers do not rely on inverse-arp, so you should have configured **no frame-relay inverse-arp** under R1, R2, R3, R4, and R5 on their serial interfaces.

- *You are permitted to use subinterfaces on R2 interface S0/1.*

- *Do not configure subinterfaces on any other routers.*

- *You must be able to* **ping** *across the Frame Relay cloud.*

R2 will be connecting to R1, R4, and R5. Because they are in the same subnet you do not need to configure subinterfaces, even though the question says *"you are permitted to* use *subinterfaces on R2 interface S0/1.* (Notice that you are permitted, so you can use one if you want to.) You should be able to ping across the Frame Relay cloud.

If you configured this correctly as shown in Example 4-1 through Example 4-10, you will get 3 points.

---

**NOTE**     When configuring the Frame Relay serial interfaces it is a very good idea for you to shut down the interfaces while you are configuring. This procedure will ensure you do not have unexpected behavior because of dynamic maps, etc., although you have configured the "no frame-relay inverse-arp." Another useful command is "clear frame-relay inarp interface" to clear your inverse ARP entries from the map table. Also, reloading the router may fix it. The following examples show the initial Frame Relay configuration on R1, R2, R3, R4, and R5.

---

**Example 4-1**     *R1 Initial Frame Relay Solution Configuration*

```
R1#show run int s0/1
Building configuration...
Current configuration : 285 bytes
!
interface Serial0/1
 ip address 160.10.37.1 255.255.255.0
```

**Example 4-1**    *R1 Initial Frame Relay Solution Configuration (Continued)*

```
 encapsulation frame-relay
 frame-relay map ip 160.10.37.2 112 broadcast
 frame-relay map ip 160.10.37.4 112 broadcast
 frame-relay map ip 160.10.37.5 112 broadcast
 no frame-relay inverse-arp
 frame-relay lmi-type ansi
end
R1#
```

**Example 4-2**    *R2 Initial Frame Relay Solution Configuration*

```
R2#show run int s0/0
Building configuration...
Current configuration : 193 bytes
!
interface Serial0/0
 ip address 160.10.32.2 255.255.255.0
 encapsulation frame-relay
 frame-relay map ip 160.10.32.3 203 broadcast
 no frame-relay inverse-arp
 frame-relay lmi-type ansi
end
R2#
R2#show run int s0/1
Building configuration...
Current configuration : 285 bytes
!
interface Serial0/1
 ip address 160.10.37.2 255.255.255.0
 encapsulation frame-relay
 frame-relay map ip 160.10.37.1 211 broadcast
 frame-relay map ip 160.10.37.4 214 broadcast
 frame-relay map ip 160.10.37.5 215 broadcast
 no frame-relay inverse-arp
 frame-relay lmi-type ansi
end
R2#
```

**Example 4-3**    *R3 Initial Frame Relay Solution Configuration*

```
R3#show run int s0/0
Building configuration...
Current configuration : 193 bytes
!
interface Serial0/0
 ip address 160.10.32.3 255.255.255.0
 encapsulation frame-relay
 frame-relay map ip 160.10.32.2 302 broadcast
 no frame-relay inverse-arp
 frame-relay lmi-type ansi
end
R3#
```

**Example 4-4** *R4 Initial Frame Relay Solution Configuration*

```
R4#show run int s0/1
Building configuration...
Current configuration : 285 bytes
!
interface Serial0/1
 ip address 160.10.37.4 255.255.255.0
 encapsulation frame-relay
 frame-relay map ip 160.10.37.1 412 broadcast
 frame-relay map ip 160.10.37.2 412 broadcast
 frame-relay map ip 160.10.37.5 412 broadcast
 no frame-relay inverse-arp
 frame-relay lmi-type ansi
end
R4#
```

**Example 4-5** *R5 Initial Frame Relay Solution Configuration*

```
R5#show run int s0/1
Building configuration...
Current configuration : 285 bytes
!
interface Serial0/1
 ip address 160.10.37.5 255.255.255.0
 encapsulation frame-relay
 frame-relay map ip 160.10.37.1 512 broadcast
 frame-relay map ip 160.10.37.2 512 broadcast
 frame-relay map ip 160.10.37.4 512 broadcast
 no frame-relay inverse-arp
 frame-relay lmi-type ansi
end
R5#
```

The commands in Example 4-6 through Example 4-10 verify the connectivity and the
Frame Relay maps. These commands are useful to double check if you have connectivity,
and if not, to help you to find mistakes such as mismatching IP address, mapping to the
wrong peer, and so on.

**Example 4-6** *R1 show Commands and Pings to Verify Functionality*

```
R1#show fram map
Serial0/1 (up): ip 160.10.37.2 dlci 112(0x70,0x1C00), static,
               broadcast,
               CISCO, status defined, active
Serial0/1 (up): ip 160.10.37.4 dlci 112(0x70,0x1C00), static,
               broadcast,
               CISCO, status defined, active
Serial0/1 (up): ip 160.10.37.5 dlci 112(0x70,0x1C00), static,
               broadcast,
               CISCO, status defined, active
R1#
R1#ping 160.10.37.2
Type escape sequence to abort.
Sending 5, 100-byte ICMP Echos to 160.10.37.2, timeout is 2 seconds:
```

**Example 4-6**   *R1* **show** *Commands and Pings to Verify Functionality (Continued)*

```
!!!!!
Success rate is 100 percent (5/5), round-trip min/avg/max = 1/2/4 ms
R1#ping 160.10.37.4
Type escape sequence to abort.
Sending 5, 100-byte ICMP Echos to 160.10.37.4, timeout is 2 seconds:
!!!!!
Success rate is 100 percent (5/5), round-trip min/avg/max = 4/6/8 ms
R1#ping 160.10.37.5
Type escape sequence to abort.
Sending 5, 100-byte ICMP Echos to 160.10.37.5, timeout is 2 seconds:
!!!!!
Success rate is 100 percent (5/5), round-trip min/avg/max = 4/5/8 ms
R1#
```

**Example 4-7**   *R2* **show** *Commands and Pings to Verify Functionality*

```
R2#show fram map
Serial0/0 (up): ip 160.10.32.3 dlci 203(0xCB,0x30B0), static,
             broadcast,
             CISCO, status defined, active
Serial0/1 (up): ip 160.10.37.1 dlci 211(0xD3,0x3430), static,
             broadcast,
             CISCO, status defined, active
Serial0/1 (up): ip 160.10.37.4 dlci 214(0xD6,0x3460), static,
             broadcast,
             CISCO, status defined, active
Serial0/1 (up): ip 160.10.37.5 dlci 215(0xD7,0x3470), static,
             broadcast,
             CISCO, status defined, active
R2#
R2#
R2#ping 160.10.32.3
Type escape sequence to abort.
Sending 5, 100-byte ICMP Echos to 160.10.32.3, timeout is 2 seconds:
!!!!!
Success rate is 100 percent (5/5), round-trip min/avg/max = 1/3/4 ms
R2#ping 160.10.37.1
Type escape sequence to abort.
Sending 5, 100-byte ICMP Echos to 160.10.37.1, timeout is 2 seconds:
!!!!!
Success rate is 100 percent (5/5), round-trip min/avg/max = 1/3/4 ms
R2#ping 160.10.37.4
Type escape sequence to abort.
Sending 5, 100-byte ICMP Echos to 160.10.37.4, timeout is 2 seconds:
!!!!!
Success rate is 100 percent (5/5), round-trip min/avg/max = 1/3/4 ms
R2#ping 160.10.37.5
Type escape sequence to abort.
Sending 5, 100-byte ICMP Echos to 160.10.37.5, timeout is 2 seconds:
!!!!!
Success rate is 100 percent (5/5), round-trip min/avg/max = 1/2/4 ms
R2#
```

**Example 4-8** *R3* **show** *Commands and Pings to Verify Functionality*

```
R3#show fram map
Serial0/0 (up): ip 160.10.32.2 dlci 302(0x12E,0x48E0), static,
               broadcast,
               CISCO, status defined, active
R3#ping 160.10.32.2
Type escape sequence to abort.
Sending 5, 100-byte ICMP Echos to 160.10.32.2, timeout is 2 seconds:
!!!!!
Success rate is 100 percent (5/5), round-trip min/avg/max = 1/3/4 ms
R3#
```

**Example 4-9** *R4* **show** *Commands and Pings to Verify Functionality*

```
R4#show fram map
Serial0/1 (up): ip 160.10.37.1 dlci 412(0x19C,0x64C0), static,
               broadcast,
               CISCO, status defined, active
Serial0/1 (up): ip 160.10.37.2 dlci 412(0x19C,0x64C0), static,
               broadcast,
               CISCO, status defined, active
Serial0/1 (up): ip 160.10.37.5 dlci 412(0x19C,0x64C0), static,
               broadcast,
               CISCO, status defined, active
R4#
R4#ping 160.10.37.1
Type escape sequence to abort.
Sending 5, 100-byte ICMP Echos to 160.10.37.1, timeout is 2 seconds:
!!!!!
Success rate is 100 percent (5/5), round-trip min/avg/max = 4/6/8 ms
R4#ping 160.10.37.2
Type escape sequence to abort.
Sending 5, 100-byte ICMP Echos to 160.10.37.2, timeout is 2 seconds:
!!!!!
Success rate is 100 percent (5/5), round-trip min/avg/max = 1/2/4 ms
R4#ping 160.10.37.5
Type escape sequence to abort.
Sending 5, 100-byte ICMP Echos to 160.10.37.5, timeout is 2 seconds:
!!!!!
Success rate is 100 percent (5/5), round-trip min/avg/max = 4/6/8 ms
R4#
```

**Example 4-10** *R5* **show** *Commands and Pings to Verify Functionality*

```
R5#show fram map
Serial0/1 (up): ip 160.10.37.1 dlci 512(0x200,0x8000), static,
               broadcast,
               CISCO, status defined, active
Serial0/1 (up): ip 160.10.37.2 dlci 512(0x200,0x8000), static,
               broadcast,
               CISCO, status defined, active
Serial0/1 (up): ip 160.10.37.4 dlci 512(0x200,0x8000), static,
               broadcast,
```

**Example 4-10**  *R5* **show** *Commands and Pings to Verify Functionality (Continued)*

```
                       CISCO, status defined, active
R5#
R5#ping 160.10.37.1
Type escape sequence to abort.
Sending 5, 100-byte ICMP Echos to 160.10.37.1, timeout is 2 seconds:
!!!!!
Success rate is 100 percent (5/5), round-trip min/avg/max = 4/6/8 ms
R5#ping 160.10.37.2
Type escape sequence to abort.
Sending 5, 100-byte ICMP Echos to 160.10.37.2, timeout is 2 seconds:
!!!!!
Success rate is 100 percent (5/5), round-trip min/avg/max = 1/3/4 ms
R5#ping 160.10.37.4
Type escape sequence to abort.
Sending 5, 100-byte ICMP Echos to 160.10.37.4, timeout is 2 seconds:
!!!!!
Success rate is 100 percent (5/5), round-trip min/avg/max = 4/5/8 ms
R5#
```

# Section 1.2: 3550 LAN Switch Configuration (12 Points)

- *Sw1 and Sw2 are connected via a crossover cable using ports fa0/15. Configure an ISL trunk between Sw1 and Sw2.*

If you configured this correctly as shown in Example 4-11 through Example 4-13, you have scored 2 points.

**Example 4-11**  *3550 Sw1 Initial Trunk Configuration*

```
Sw1#show run int fa0/15
Building configuration...
Current configuration : 108 bytes
!
interface FastEthernet0/15
 switchport trunk encapsulation isl
 switchport mode trunk
 no ip address
end
Sw1#
```

**Example 4-12**  *3550 Sw2 Initial Trunk Configuration*

```
Sw2#show run int fa0/15
Building configuration...
Current configuration : 108 bytes
!
interface FastEthernet0/15
 switchport trunk encapsulation isl
 switchport mode trunk
 no ip address
end
Sw2
```

**Example 4-13** *3550 Sw1 and Sw2 **show** Commands Output to Verify Configuration and Functionality*

```
Sw1#show int trunk
Port        Mode         Encapsulation  Status       Native vlan
Fa0/15      on           isl            trunking     1
Port        Vlans allowed on trunk
Fa0/15      1-4094
Port        Vlans allowed and active in management domain
Fa0/15      1
Port        Vlans in spanning tree forwarding state and not pruned
Fa0/15      1
Sw1#
Sw2#show int trunk
Port        Mode         Encapsulation  Status       Native vlan
Fa0/15      on           isl            trunking     1
Port        Vlans allowed on trunk
Fa0/15      1-4094
Port        Vlans allowed and active in management domain
Fa0/15      1
Port        Vlans in spanning tree forwarding state and not pruned
Fa0/15      1
Sw2#
```

- *All Ethernet ports are pre-cabled as per Table 4-4. Note that not all ports will be used on this lab.*

- *Configure the VLANs as follows:*

  *VLAN_11: Connected to R1-e0/0 (VLAN_11)*

  *VLAN_22: Connected to R3-fa0/0, R5-fa0/0, and R6-e0/0 (VLAN_22)*

  *VLAN_25: Connected to R1-e0/1 and R5-fa0/1 (VLAN_25)*

  *VLAN_33: Connected to R3-fa0/1 (VLAN_33)*

  *VLAN_100: Connected to R2-fa0/0 and Sw1-fa0/13 (VLAN_100)*

  *VLAN_200: Connected to R4-e0/0 and Sw2-fa0/13 (VLAN_200)*

- *Configure Sw1 to be the VTP server for the domain. Sw2 is a VTP client. Be sure that Sw2 can see the VLAN configuration from Sw1.*

If you configured this correctly as shown in Example 4-14, you have scored 3 points.

An important thing to notice here is that creating the VLANs 25 and 33 on Sw2 will be possible if the VTP mode is still server on Sw2. When you configure Sw1 as VTP mode server and Sw2 as client as the question requires, you will be able to create the VLANs only on Sw1 (the VTP mode server), and Sw2 will learn all VLANs from Sw1 via trunk. Also, the VTP domain name must be the same.

The commands in Example 4-14 can help you not only to verify if you have configured correctly, but also can help you to identify problems and mistakes. In other words, these commands will help you to troubleshoot why a router cannot ping another router or why a router is not able to ping and receive routes from the backbone, and even identify why a VTP mode client switch is not seeing the VLANs.

---

**NOTE**    The VLAN configuration is completed under **Vlan database**.

---

**Example 4-14**  *3550 Sw1 and Sw2 VLAN and VTP Configuration*

```
Sw1#show vlan brief
VLAN Name                             Status    Ports
---- -------------------------------- --------- ------------------------------
1    default                          active    Fa0/7, Fa0/8, Fa0/9, Fa0/10
                                                Fa0/11, Fa0/12, Fa0/14, Fa0/16
                                                Fa0/17, Fa0/18, Fa0/19, Fa0/20
                                                Fa0/21, Fa0/22, Fa0/23, Fa0/24
                                                Gi0/1, Gi0/2
11   VLAN_11                          active    Fa0/1
22   VLAN_22                          active    Fa0/3, Fa0/5, Fa0/6
25   VLAN_25                          active
33   VLAN_33                          active
100  VLAN_100                         active    Fa0/2, Fa0/13
200  VLAN_200                         active    Fa0/4
1002 fddi-default                     active
1003 token-ring-default               active
1004 fddinet-default                  active
1005 trnet-default                    active
Sw1#
Sw2#show vlan brief
VLAN Name                             Status    Ports
---- -------------------------------- --------- ------------------------------
1    default                          active    Fa0/2, Fa0/4, Fa0/6, Fa0/7
                                                Fa0/8, Fa0/9, Fa0/10, Fa0/11
                                                Fa0/12, Fa0/14, Fa0/16, Fa0/17
                                                Fa0/18, Fa0/19, Fa0/20, Fa0/21
                                                Fa0/22, Fa0/23, Fa0/24, Gi0/1
                                                Gi0/2
11   VLAN_11                          active
22   VLAN_22                          active
25   VLAN_25                          active    Fa0/1, Fa0/5
33   VLAN_33                          active    Fa0/3
100  VLAN_100                         active
200  VLAN_200                         active    Fa0/13
1002 fddi-default                     active
1003 token-ring-default               active
1004 fddinet-default                  active
1005 trnet-default                    active
Sw2#
Sw1#
Sw1#show vtp stat
```

*continues*

**Example 4-14** *3550 Sw1 and Sw2 VLAN and VTP Configuration (Continued)*

```
VTP Version                          : 2
Configuration Revision               : 1
Maximum VLANs supported locally      : 1005
Number of existing VLANs             : 11
VTP Operating Mode                   : Server
VTP Domain Name                      : CCIE
VTP Pruning Mode                     : Disabled
VTP V2 Mode                          : Disabled
VTP Traps Generation                 : Disabled
MD5 digest                           : 0x36 0xC9 0xB9 0x93 0x5C 0xE6 0x7B 0x1D
Configuration last modified by 160.10.7.7 at 3-19-93 04:55:23
Local updater ID is 160.10.11.10 on interface Vl11 (lowest numbered VLAN interface
found)
Sw1#
Sw2#show vtp stat
VTP Version                          : 2
Configuration Revision               : 1
Maximum VLANs supported locally      : 1005
Number of existing VLANs             : 11
VTP Operating Mode                   : Client
VTP Domain Name                      : CCIE
VTP Pruning Mode                     : Disabled
VTP V2 Mode                          : Disabled
VTP Traps Generation                 : Disabled
MD5 digest                           : 0x36 0xC9 0xB9 0x93 0x5C 0xE6 0x7B 0x1D
Configuration last modified by 160.10.7.7 at 3-19-93 04:55:23
Sw2#
```

**NOTE**     The VTP domain name is arbitrarily called CCIE. It could be any name because it was not
requested to configure any specific name.

- *Configure Sw1, using VLAN_11 with the IP address 160.10.11.10/24. After you have
  finished your routing section, all routers should be able to ping this interface.*

If you configured this correctly as shown in Example 4-15, you have scored 1 point.

**Example 4-15** *3550 Sw1 Management Interface Configuration*

```
Sw1#
Sw1#show run int vlan 11
Building configuration...
Current configuration : 63 bytes
!
interface Vlan11
 ip address 160.10.11.10 255.255.255.0
!
!
ip route 0.0.0.0 0.0.0.0 160.10.11.1
```

**NOTE**    In this moment, Sw1 will be able to ping only R1-e0/0. With the static route highlighted in Example 4-15, you will be able to ping the Sw1-VLAN_11 interface from any router after completion of your IP IGP routing.

Example 4-16 first shows a basic test using a ping from the Sw1 to R1-0/0. This is basic because they are in the same VLAN_11. The second test is to be done after you have your routing section finished, and then you can have Sw1 able to ping, for example R6-lo0.

**Example 4-16**  *3550 Sw1 Management Interface Output Verification*

```
Sw1#ping 160.10.11.1
! R1-E0/0
Type escape sequence to abort.
Sending 5, 100-byte ICMP Echos to 160.10.11.1, timeout is 2 seconds:
!!!!!
Success rate is 100 percent (5/5), round-trip min/avg/max = 1/2/4 ms
Sw1#
Sw1#ping 160.10.6.6
! Sw1 able to ping R6-Lo0 (After all IGP routing is finished)

Type escape sequence to abort.
Sending 5, 100-byte ICMP Echos to 160.10.6.6, timeout is 2 seconds:
!!!!!
Success rate is 100 percent (5/5), round-trip min/avg/max = 4/5/8 ms
Sw1#
```

- *Configure VLAN_11 on Sw1 to be the secondary root switch.*

If you configured this correctly as shown in Example 4-17, you have scored 2 points.

This questions has a little trick. It tells you to make the configuration on Sw1. The use of the **spanning-tree vlan 11 root secondary** command on Sw1 alone will not make Sw1 the "secondary" root. The effect will be changing the VLAN_11 root priority on Sw1 to 2872, which is still "lesser" than Sw2, so Sw1 is still the spanning-tree root.

In this case, you need to configure on Sw2 the **spanning-tree vlan 11 root primary** command that will change the spanning-tree root priority on Sw2 to 24576 (lesser than Sw1), so now Sw1 is the secondary spanning-tree root.

**Example 4-17**  *3550 Sw1 and Sw2 Secondary Root Configuration and Verification*

```
Sw1#
Sw1#conf t
Enter configuration commands, one per line.  End with CNTL/Z.
Sw1(config)#spanning-tree vlan 11 root secondary
Sw1(config)#
!
Sw2#conf t
Enter configuration commands, one per line.  End with CNTL/Z.
Sw2(config)#spanning-tree vlan 11 root primary
```

*continues*

**Example 4-17** *3550 Sw1 and Sw2 Secondary Root Configuration and Verification (Continued)*

```
!
Sw1#sh spanning-tree detail active

VLAN0011 is executing the ieee compatible Spanning Tree protocol
  Bridge Identifier has priority 28672, sysid 11, address 0009.e8ef.1800
  Configured hello time 2, max age 20, forward delay 15
  Current root has priority 24587, address 0009.e8ee.f200
  Root port is 15 (FastEthernet0/15), cost of root path is 19
  Topology change flag not set, detected flag not set
  Number of topology changes 3 last change occurred 00:50:41 ago
          from FastEthernet0/15
  Times:  hold 1, topology change 35, notification 2
          hello 2, max age 20, forward delay 15
  Timers: hello 0, topology change 0, notification 0, aging 300

 Port 1 (FastEthernet0/1) of VLAN0011 is forwarding
   Port path cost 100, Port priority 128, Port Identifier 128.1.
   Designated root has priority 24587, address 0009.e8ee.f200
   Designated bridge has priority 28683, address 0009.e8ef.1800
   Designated port id is 128.1, designated path cost 19
   Timers: message age 0, forward delay 0, hold 0
   Number of transitions to forwarding state: 1
   Link type is shared by default
   BPDU: sent 547165, received 40
!
Sw2#sh spanning-tree detail

VLAN0011 is executing the ieee compatible Spanning Tree protocol
  Bridge Identifier has priority 24576, sysid 11, address 0009.e8ee.f200
  Configured hello time 2, max age 20, forward delay 15
  We are the root of the spanning tree
  Topology change flag not set, detected flag not set
  Number of topology changes 4 last change occurred 00:51:38 ago
  Times:  hold 1, topology change 35, notification 2
          hello 2, max age 20, forward delay 15
  Timers: hello 0, topology change 0, notification 0, aging 300

 Port 15 (FastEthernet0/15) of VLAN0011 is forwarding
   Port path cost 19, Port priority 128, Port Identifier 128.15.
   Designated root has priority 24587, address 0009.e8ee.f200
   Designated bridge has priority 24587, address 0009.e8ee.f200
   Designated port id is 128.15, designated path cost 0
   Timers: message age 0, forward delay 0, hold 0
   Number of transitions to forwarding state: 1
   Link type is point-to-point by default
   BPDU: sent 1565, received 545717
```

- *Configure Sw1 to permit any SNMP manager to access all objects with read-only permission using the community string public. The switch also sends VTP traps to the hosts 160.10.11.111 and 160.10.11.33 using SNMPv1 and to the host 160.10.11.27 using SNMPv2C. The community string public is sent with the traps.*

If you configured this correctly as shown in Example 4-18, you have scored 2 points.

Example 4-18 shows the SNMP configuration to accomplish the question requirement. Notice that to allow "read-only" permission you do not need extra configuration because it is the default permission. The SNMP version 1 is also the default.

**Example 4-18**  *3550 Sw1 SNMP Configuration and Verification*

```
Sw1#sh run | include snmp
snmp-server community public RO
snmp-server enable traps vtp
snmp-server host 160.10.11.111 public
snmp-server host 160.10.11.27 version 2c public
snmp-server host 160.10.11.33 public
Sw1#
!
Sw1#sh snmp
!
SNMP logging: enabled
    Logging to 160.10.11.111.162, 0/10, 0 sent, 0 dropped.
    Logging to 160.10.11.33.162, 0/10, 0 sent, 0 dropped.
    Logging to 160.10.11.27.162, 0/10, 0 sent, 0 dropped.
SNMP agent enabled
Sw1#
```

# Section 1.3: ATM Configuration (3 Points)

- *Configure the ATM as shown in Figure 4-9.*
- *There is a PVC configured between R6 and the backbone router. Do not configure subinterfaces.*
- *Use explicit address mapping. Do not depend on the remoter backbone router for inverse ARP.*
- *You must be able to ping the backbone router address 170.100.10.254/24.*

Example 4-19 provides a basic ATM PVC configuration where an important note here is to not forget to configure the **broadcast** keyword. If you fail to do so, you will not be able to exchange routing protocol between R6 and the backbone router. The commands in Example 4-19 show the configuration, the ping test, and whether your ATM PVC is up and running.

**Example 4-19**  *R6 ATM Configuration, Map Verification, and Access to Backbone Router*

```
R6#show run int a3/0
Building configuration...
Current configuration : 140 bytes
```

*continues*

**Example 4-19**  *R6 ATM Configuration, Map Verification, and Access to Backbone Router (Continued)*

```
!
interface ATM3/0
 ip address 170.100.10.1 255.255.255.0
 no atm ilmi-keepalive
 pvc 0/100
  protocol ip 170.100.10.254 broadcast
 !
end
R6#ping 170.100.10.254
Type escape sequence to abort.
Sending 5, 100-byte ICMP Echos to 170.100.10.254, timeout is 2 seconds:
!!!!!
Success rate is 100 percent (5/5), round-trip min/avg/max = 1/2/4 ms
R6#sh atm vc
          VCD /                                      Peak  Avg/Min Burst
Interface Name          VPI  VCI Type  Encaps  SC   Kbps   Kbps   Cells  Sts
3/0       3               0  100 PVC   SNAP    UBR  155000                UP
R6#
```

# Section 2: IP IGP Protocols (30 Points)

## Section 2.1: OSPF (11 Points)

- *Configure OSPF according to the diagram in Figure 4-10. R1-s0/1, R2-s0/1, R4-s0/1, and R5-s0/1 are to be part of the OSPF area 0.*

- *R2-s0/0 and R3-S0/0 are to be configured as OSPF area 1.*

- *R1-e0/0 is to be configured as OSPF area 11.*

- *R1-e0/1, R3-fa0/0, R3-bri0/0, R5-fa0/0, R5 fa0/1, R5-bri0/0, and R6-e0/0 are to be configured as OSPF area 22.*

- *R3-fa0/1 is to be configured as OSPF area 33.*

If you configured this correctly as shown in Example 4-20 through Example 4-25 you have scored 6 points:

- *Configure the loopback addresses to be part of the OSPF process.*

If you configured this correctly as shown in Example 4-20 through Example 4-25 you have scored 2 points:

- *Make sure you are able to ping any OSPF interface from any router.*

If you configured this correctly as shown in Example 4-20 through Example 4-25 you have scored 3 points.

This is a basic OSPF configuration. You might think the IGP topology looks unusual, but the idea is to make you start from the basic configuration to more complex environments in the following lab exercises.

An important thing to observe is that although we have five OSPF areas, we will need only one virtual link to be configured. This is because the ABR routers R1 are connected to area 0 and area 11, and R5 is connected to area 0 and area 22.

Example 4-20 through Example 4-25 show the basic OSPF configuration and the output from the routing table. It is important to observe the right interfaces or subnets configured to the right area.

**Example 4-20**  *OSPF Configuration: R1 Output*

```
R1#show run
interface Loopback0
 ip address 160.10.1.1 255.255.255.0
 ip ospf network point-to-point
!
interface Ethernet0/0
 ip address 160.10.11.1 255.255.255.0
 half-duplex

!
interface Ethernet0/1
 ip address 160.10.25.1 255.255.255.0
 no ip redirects
 half-duplex
!
interface Serial0/1
 ip address 160.10.37.1 255.255.255.0
 encapsulation frame-relay
 ip ospf network point-to-multipoint
 !
router ospf 1
 log-adjacency-changes
 network 160.10.1.0 0.0.0.255 area 0
 network 160.10.11.0 0.0.0.255 area 11
 network 160.10.25.0 0.0.0.255 area 22
 network 160.10.37.0 0.0.0.255 area 0
!
!
R1#show ip route ospf
     160.10.0.0/16 is variably subnetted, 16 subnets, 2 masks
O IA    160.10.32.0/24 [110/112] via 160.10.37.2, 00:00:04, Serial0/1
O       160.10.37.5/32 [110/112] via 160.10.37.2, 00:00:04, Serial0/1
O IA    160.10.33.0/24 [110/113] via 160.10.37.2, 00:00:04, Serial0/1
O       160.10.37.4/32 [110/112] via 160.10.37.2, 00:00:04, Serial0/1
O       160.10.37.2/32 [110/64] via 160.10.37.2, 00:00:04, Serial0/1
O       160.10.15.0/24 [110/1572] via 160.10.25.5, 00:02:18, Ethernet0/1
O       160.10.2.0/24 [110/65] via 160.10.37.2, 00:00:04, Serial0/1
O IA    160.10.3.0/24 [110/113] via 160.10.37.2, 00:00:04, Serial0/1
O       160.10.6.0/24 [110/12] via 160.10.25.5, 00:02:18, Ethernet0/1
O       160.10.4.0/24 [110/113] via 160.10.37.2, 00:00:04, Serial0/1
O       160.10.5.0/24 [110/113] via 160.10.37.2, 00:00:04, Serial0/1
O       160.10.22.0/24 [110/11] via 160.10.25.5, 00:02:19, Ethernet0/1
R1#
```

**Example 4-21**  *OSPF Configuration: R2 Output*

```
R2#show run
interface Loopback0
 ip address 160.10.2.2 255.255.255.0
 ip ospf network point-to-point
!
interface Serial0/0
 ip address 160.10.32.2 255.255.255.0
 encapsulation frame-relay
 ip ospf network point-to-point
 !
interface Serial0/1
 ip address 160.10.37.2 255.255.255.0
 encapsulation frame-relay
 ip ospf network point-to-multipoint
 !
router ospf 1
 log-adjacency-changes
 area 1 virtual-link 160.10.3.3
 redistribute eigrp 400 metric 100 subnets
 network 160.10.2.0 0.0.0.255 area 0
 network 160.10.32.0 0.0.0.255 area 1
 network 160.10.37.0 0.0.0.255 area 0
!
!
R2#sh ip route ospf
     160.10.0.0/16 is variably subnetted, 16 subnets, 2 masks
O       160.10.37.5/32 [110/48] via 160.10.37.5, 00:00:34, Serial0/1
O IA    160.10.33.0/24 [110/49] via 160.10.32.3, 00:00:34, Serial0/0
O       160.10.37.4/32 [110/48] via 160.10.37.4, 00:00:34, Serial0/1
O       160.10.37.1/32 [110/48] via 160.10.37.1, 00:00:34, Serial0/1
O IA    160.10.11.0/24 [110/58] via 160.10.37.1, 00:00:34, Serial0/1
O IA    160.10.15.0/24 [110/1610] via 160.10.32.3, 00:00:34, Serial0/0
                       [110/1610] via 160.10.37.5, 00:00:34, Serial0/1
O       160.10.3.0/24 [110/49] via 160.10.32.3, 00:00:34, Serial0/0
O       160.10.1.0/24 [110/49] via 160.10.37.1, 00:00:34, Serial0/1
O IA    160.10.6.0/24 [110/50] via 160.10.32.3, 00:00:34, Serial0/0
                      [110/50] via 160.10.37.5, 00:00:34, Serial0/1
O       160.10.4.0/24 [110/49] via 160.10.37.4, 00:00:34, Serial0/1
O       160.10.5.0/24 [110/49] via 160.10.37.5, 00:00:34, Serial0/1
O IA    160.10.25.0/24 [110/49] via 160.10.37.5, 00:00:35, Serial0/1
O IA    160.10.22.0/24 [110/49] via 160.10.32.3, 00:00:35, Serial0/0
                       [110/49] via 160.10.37.5, 00:00:35, Serial0/1
R2#
```

**Example 4-22**  *OSPF Configuration: R3 Output*

```
R3#show run
interface Loopback0
 ip address 160.10.3.3 255.255.255.0
 ip ospf network point-to-point
 !
```

**Example 4-22**  *OSPF Configuration: R3 Output (Continued)*

```
interface FastEthernet0/0
 ip address 160.10.22.3 255.255.255.0
 duplex auto
 speed auto
!
interface Serial0/0
 ip address 160.10.32.3 255.255.255.0
 encapsulation frame-relay
 ip ospf network point-to-point
 !
interface BRI0/0
 ip address 160.10.15.3 255.255.255.0
 ip ospf demand-circuit
 no peer neighbor-route
 no cdp enable
!
interface FastEthernet0/1
 ip address 160.10.33.3 255.255.255.0
 !
router ospf 1
 log-adjacency-changes
 area 1 virtual-link 160.10.2.2
 network 160.10.3.0 0.0.0.255 area 1
 network 160.10.15.0 0.0.0.255 area 22
 network 160.10.22.0 0.0.0.255 area 22
 network 160.10.32.0 0.0.0.255 area 1
 network 160.10.33.0 0.0.0.255 area 33
!
!
R3#show ip route ospf
      160.10.0.0/16 is variably subnetted, 16 subnets, 2 masks
O        160.10.37.5/32 [110/112] via 160.10.32.2, 00:02:10, Serial0/0
O        160.10.37.4/32 [110/112] via 160.10.32.2, 00:02:10, Serial0/0
O        160.10.37.2/32 [110/64] via 160.10.32.2, 00:02:10, Serial0/0
O        160.10.37.1/32 [110/112] via 160.10.32.2, 00:02:10, Serial0/0
O IA     160.10.11.0/24 [110/122] via 160.10.32.2, 00:02:10, Serial0/0
O        160.10.2.0/24 [110/65] via 160.10.32.2, 00:02:10, Serial0/0
O        160.10.1.0/24 [110/113] via 160.10.32.2, 00:02:10, Serial0/0
O        160.10.6.0/24 [110/2] via 160.10.22.6, 18:45:16, FastEthernet0/0
O        160.10.4.0/24 [110/113] via 160.10.32.2, 00:02:10, Serial0/0
O        160.10.5.0/24 [110/113] via 160.10.32.2, 00:02:10, Serial0/0
O        160.10.25.0/24 [110/2] via 160.10.22.5, 18:45:16, FastEthernet0/0
R3#
```

**Example 4-23**  *OSPF Configuration: R4 Output*

```
R4#show run
interface Loopback0
 ip address 160.10.4.4 255.255.255.0
 ip ospf network point-to-point
 !
```

*continues*

**Example 4-23**  *OSPF Configuration: R4 Output (Continued)*

```
interface Serial0/1
 ip address 160.10.37.4 255.255.255.0
 encapsulation frame-relay
 ip ospf network point-to-multipoint
 !
router ospf 1
 log-adjacency-changes

 network 160.10.4.0 0.0.0.255 area 0
 network 160.10.37.0 0.0.0.255 area 0
 !
 !
R4#show ip route ospf
     160.10.0.0/16 is variably subnetted, 16 subnets, 2 masks
O       160.10.37.5/32 [110/112] via 160.10.37.2, 00:03:19, Serial0/1
O IA    160.10.32.0/24 [110/112] via 160.10.37.2, 00:03:19, Serial0/1
O IA    160.10.33.0/24 [110/113] via 160.10.37.2, 00:03:19, Serial0/1
O       160.10.37.2/32 [110/64] via 160.10.37.2, 00:03:19, Serial0/1
O       160.10.37.1/32 [110/112] via 160.10.37.2, 00:03:19, Serial0/1
O IA    160.10.11.0/24 [110/122] via 160.10.37.2, 00:03:19, Serial0/1
O IA    160.10.15.0/24 [110/1674] via 160.10.37.2, 00:03:19, Serial0/1
O       160.10.2.0/24 [110/65] via 160.10.37.2, 00:03:19, Serial0/1
O IA    160.10.3.0/24 [110/113] via 160.10.37.2, 00:03:19, Serial0/1
O       160.10.1.0/24 [110/113] via 160.10.37.2, 00:03:19, Serial0/1
O IA    160.10.6.0/24 [110/114] via 160.10.37.2, 00:03:19, Serial0/1
O       160.10.5.0/24 [110/113] via 160.10.37.2, 00:03:19, Serial0/1
O IA    160.10.25.0/24 [110/113] via 160.10.37.2, 00:03:19, Serial0/1
O IA    160.10.22.0/24 [110/113] via 160.10.37.2, 00:03:20, Serial0/1
R4#
```

**Example 4-24**  *OSPF Configuration: R5 Output*

```
R5#show run
interface Loopback0
 ip address 160.10.5.5 255.255.255.0
 ip ospf network point-to-point
 !
interface FastEthernet0/0
 ip address 160.10.22.5 255.255.255.0
 duplex auto
 speed auto
 !
interface BRI0/0
 ip address 160.10.15.5 255.255.255.0
 encapsulation ppp
 ip ospf demand-circuit
 no peer neighbor-route
 no cdp enable
 ppp authentication chap
 !
interface FastEthernet0/1
```

**Example 4-24** *OSPF Configuration: R5 Output (Continued)*

```
 ip address 160.10.25.5 255.255.255.0
 duplex auto
 speed auto
!
interface Serial0/1
 ip address 160.10.37.5 255.255.255.0
 encapsulation frame-relay
 ip ospf network point-to-multipoint
 !
router ospf 1
 log-adjacency-changes
 network 160.10.5.0 0.0.0.255 area 22
 network 160.10.15.0 0.0.0.255 area 22
 network 160.10.22.0 0.0.0.255 area 22
 network 160.10.25.0 0.0.0.255 area 22
 network 160.10.37.0 0.0.0.255 area 0
 !
 !
R5#show ip route ospf
      160.10.0.0/16 is variably subnetted, 16 subnets, 2 masks
O IA    160.10.32.0/24 [110/112] via 160.10.37.2, 00:04:11, Serial0/1
O IA    160.10.33.0/24 [110/113] via 160.10.37.2, 00:04:11, Serial0/1
O       160.10.37.4/32 [110/112] via 160.10.37.2, 00:04:11, Serial0/1
O       160.10.37.2/32 [110/64] via 160.10.37.2, 00:04:11, Serial0/1
O       160.10.37.1/32 [110/112] via 160.10.37.2, 00:04:11, Serial0/1
O IA    160.10.11.0/24 [110/122] via 160.10.37.2, 00:04:11, Serial0/1
O       160.10.2.0/24 [110/65] via 160.10.37.2, 00:04:11, Serial0/1
O IA    160.10.3.0/24 [110/113] via 160.10.37.2, 00:04:11, Serial0/1
O       160.10.1.0/24 [110/113] via 160.10.37.2, 00:04:11, Serial0/1
O       160.10.6.0/24 [110/2] via 160.10.22.6, 18:47:14, FastEthernet0/0
O       160.10.4.0/24 [110/113] via 160.10.37.2, 00:04:11, Serial0/1
R5
```

**Example 4-25** *OSPF Configuration: R6 Output*

```
R6#show run
interface Loopback0
 ip address 160.10.6.6 255.255.255.0
 ip ospf network point-to-point
 !
interface Ethernet0/0
 ip address 160.10.22.6 255.255.255.0
 half-duplex
 !
router ospf 1
 log-adjacency-changes
 network 160.10.6.0 0.0.0.255 area 22
 network 160.10.22.0 0.0.0.255 area 22
 !
 !
R6#show ip route ospf
```

**Example 4-25** *OSPF Configuration: R6 Output (Continued)*

```
        160.10.0.0/16 is variably subnetted, 16 subnets, 2 masks
O IA     160.10.37.5/32 [110/10] via 160.10.22.5, 18:48:33, Ethernet0/0
O IA     160.10.32.0/24 [110/74] via 160.10.22.3, 18:48:33, Ethernet0/0
O IA     160.10.37.4/32 [110/122] via 160.10.22.3, 18:48:33, Ethernet0/0
                        [110/122] via 160.10.22.5, 18:48:33, Ethernet0/0
O IA     160.10.33.0/24 [110/11] via 160.10.22.3, 18:48:33, Ethernet0/0
O IA     160.10.37.2/32 [110/74] via 160.10.22.3, 18:48:33, Ethernet0/0
                        [110/74] via 160.10.22.5, 18:48:33, Ethernet0/0
O IA     160.10.37.1/32 [110/11] via 160.10.22.5, 18:48:33, Ethernet0/0
O IA     160.10.11.0/24 [110/21] via 160.10.22.5, 18:48:33, Ethernet0/0
O        160.10.15.0/24 [110/1572] via 160.10.22.3, 18:48:53, Ethernet0/0
                        [110/1572] via 160.10.22.5, 18:48:53, Ethernet0/0
O IA     160.10.2.0/24 [110/75] via 160.10.22.3, 18:48:35, Ethernet0/0
                        [110/75] via 160.10.22.5, 18:48:35, Ethernet0/0
O IA     160.10.3.0/24 [110/11] via 160.10.22.3, 18:48:35, Ethernet0/0
O IA     160.10.1.0/24 [110/12] via 160.10.22.5, 18:48:35, Ethernet0/0
O IA     160.10.4.0/24 [110/123] via 160.10.22.3, 18:48:35, Ethernet0/0
                        [110/123] via 160.10.22.5, 18:48:35, Ethernet0/0
O IA     160.10.5.0/24 [110/11] via 160.10.22.5, 18:48:34, Ethernet0/0
O        160.10.25.0/24 [110/11] via 160.10.22.5, 18:48:55, Ethernet0/0
R6#
```

# Section 2.2: EIGRP (10 Points)

- *Configure EIGRP between R2 and BB1. R2-fa0/0 must be the only interface configured for EIGRP on R2. R2 routing table should be populated with EIGRP routes from BB1.*

If you configured this correctly as shown in Example 4-26, you have scored 4 points.

- *Configure the routing waiting time for EIGRP on R2 to remain active indefinitely.*

If you configured this correctly as shown in Example 4-26, you have scored 3 points.

- *Redistribute EIGRP into OSPF. Make sure all routers have the EIGRP routes in their routing tables.*

If you configured this correctly as shown in Example 4-26, you have scored 3 points.

This is a basic setup to have R2 receiving EIGRP routes from BB1. We begin here the concept of using features that are very important areas you need to explore. The redistribution into OSPF will be done only in one way. It is important to notice during the redistribution into OSPF that you use the **subnets** command to allow networks that are "subnetted" to be redistributed into OSPF.

The **timers active-time disable** command accommodates the requirement of the waiting time be set up to "indefinitely."

**Example 4-26**  *EIGRP Configuration: R2 Output and R6 OSPF Routing Table Verification*

```
R2#sh run | b router eigrp
router eigrp 400
 timers active-time disabled
 passive-interface default
 no passive-interface FastEthernet0/0
 network 130.200.10.0 0.0.0.255
 no auto-summary
 no eigrp log-neighbor-changes
!
!
router ospf 1
 redistribute eigrp 400 metric 100 subnets
!
R2#show ip route eigrp
     50.0.0.0/24 is subnetted, 1 subnets
D       50.5.5.0 [90/156160] via 130.200.10.200, 00:12:53, FastEthernet0/0
D    193.118.9.0/24 [90/156160] via 130.200.10.200, 00:12:53, FastEthernet0/0
D    193.118.8.0/24 [90/156160] via 130.200.10.200, 00:12:53, FastEthernet0/0
D    193.118.10.0/24 [90/156160] via 130.200.10.200, 00:12:53, FastEthernet0/0
D    193.118.5.0/24 [90/156160] via 130.200.10.200, 00:12:53, FastEthernet0/0
D    193.118.4.0/24 [90/156160] via 130.200.10.200, 00:12:53, FastEthernet0/0
D    193.118.7.0/24 [90/156160] via 130.200.10.200, 00:12:53, FastEthernet0/0
     40.0.0.0/24 is subnetted, 1 subnets
D       40.4.4.0 [90/156160] via 130.200.10.200, 00:12:53, FastEthernet0/0
D    193.118.6.0/24 [90/156160] via 130.200.10.200, 00:12:53, FastEthernet0/0
D    193.118.1.0/24 [90/156160] via 130.200.10.200, 00:12:53, FastEthernet0/0
D    193.118.3.0/24 [90/156160] via 130.200.10.200, 00:12:53, FastEthernet0/0
D    193.118.2.0/24 [90/156160] via 130.200.10.200, 00:12:53, FastEthernet0/0
R2#
!
!
! R6 routing table has the EIGRP routes showing as OSPF external. Notice the "E2"
that means OSPF external routes.
R6#show ip route ospf | include E2
O E2    50.5.5.0 [110/100] via 160.10.22.3, 23:30:52, Ethernet0/0
O E2    140.200.10.0 [110/1] via 160.10.22.3, 23:30:52, Ethernet0/0
O E2 193.118.9.0/24 [110/100] via 160.10.22.3, 23:30:52, Ethernet0/0
O E2 20.0.0.0/8 [110/1] via 160.10.22.3, 23:30:52, Ethernet0/0
O E2 193.118.8.0/24 [110/100] via 160.10.22.3, 23:30:52, Ethernet0/0
O E2 193.118.10.0/24 [110/100] via 160.10.22.3, 23:30:52, Ethernet0/0
O E2 193.118.5.0/24 [110/100] via 160.10.22.3, 23:30:52, Ethernet0/0
O E2 193.118.4.0/24 [110/100] via 160.10.22.3, 23:30:52, Ethernet0/0
O E2 193.118.7.0/24 [110/100] via 160.10.22.3, 23:30:52, Ethernet0/0
O E2    40.4.4.0 [110/100] via 160.10.22.3, 23:30:52, Ethernet0/0
O E2    130.200.10.0 [110/100] via 160.10.22.3, 23:30:52, Ethernet0/0
O E2 193.118.6.0/24 [110/100] via 160.10.22.3, 23:30:52, Ethernet0/0
O E2 193.118.1.0/24 [110/100] via 160.10.22.3, 23:30:52, Ethernet0/0
O E2 193.118.3.0/24 [110/100] via 160.10.22.3, 23:30:52, Ethernet0/0
O E2 193.118.2.0/24 [110/100] via 160.10.22.3, 23:30:52, Ethernet0/0
```

*continues*

**Example 4-26** *EIGRP Configuration: R2 Output and R6 OSPF Routing Table Verification (Continued)*

```
R6#show ip route ospf
      50.0.0.0/24 is subnetted, 1 subnets
O E2    50.5.5.0 [110/100] via 160.10.22.3, 00:00:42, Ethernet0/0
                 [110/100] via 160.10.22.5, 00:00:42, Ethernet0/0
O E2 193.118.9.0/24 [110/100] via 160.10.22.3, 00:00:42, Ethernet0/0
                    [110/100] via 160.10.22.5, 00:00:42, Ethernet0/0
O E2 193.118.8.0/24 [110/100] via 160.10.22.3, 00:00:42, Ethernet0/0
                    [110/100] via 160.10.22.5, 00:00:42, Ethernet0/0
O E2 193.118.10.0/24 [110/100] via 160.10.22.3, 00:00:42, Ethernet0/0
                     [110/100] via 160.10.22.5, 00:00:42, Ethernet0/0
O E2 193.118.5.0/24 [110/100] via 160.10.22.3, 00:00:42, Ethernet0/0
                    [110/100] via 160.10.22.5, 00:00:42, Ethernet0/0
O E2 193.118.4.0/24 [110/100] via 160.10.22.3, 00:00:42, Ethernet0/0
                    [110/100] via 160.10.22.5, 00:00:42, Ethernet0/0
      160.10.0.0/16 is variably subnetted, 16 subnets, 2 masks
O IA    160.10.37.5/32 [110/10] via 160.10.22.5, 18:54:46, Ethernet0/0
O IA    160.10.32.0/24 [110/74] via 160.10.22.3, 18:54:47, Ethernet0/0
O IA    160.10.37.4/32 [110/122] via 160.10.22.3, 18:54:47, Ethernet0/0
                       [110/122] via 160.10.22.5, 18:54:47, Ethernet0/0
O IA    160.10.33.0/24 [110/11] via 160.10.22.3, 18:54:47, Ethernet0/0
O IA    160.10.37.2/32 [110/74] via 160.10.22.3, 18:54:47, Ethernet0/0
                       [110/74] via 160.10.22.5, 18:54:47, Ethernet0/0
O IA    160.10.37.1/32 [110/11] via 160.10.22.5, 18:54:47, Ethernet0/0
O IA    160.10.11.0/24 [110/21] via 160.10.22.5, 18:54:47, Ethernet0/0
O       160.10.15.0/24 [110/1572] via 160.10.22.3, 18:55:08, Ethernet0/0
                       [110/1572] via 160.10.22.5, 18:55:08, Ethernet0/0
O IA    160.10.2.0/24 [110/75] via 160.10.22.3, 18:54:48, Ethernet0/0
                      [110/75] via 160.10.22.5, 18:54:48, Ethernet0/0
O IA    160.10.3.0/24 [110/11] via 160.10.22.3, 18:54:48, Ethernet0/0
O IA    160.10.1.0/24 [110/12] via 160.10.22.5, 18:54:48, Ethernet0/0
O IA    160.10.4.0/24 [110/123] via 160.10.22.3, 18:54:48, Ethernet0/0
                      [110/123] via 160.10.22.5, 18:54:48, Ethernet0/0
O IA    160.10.5.0/24 [110/11] via 160.10.22.5, 18:54:48, Ethernet0/0
O       160.10.25.0/24 [110/11] via 160.10.22.5, 18:55:08, Ethernet0/0
O E2 193.118.7.0/24 [110/100] via 160.10.22.3, 00:00:44, Ethernet0/0
                    [110/100] via 160.10.22.5, 00:00:44, Ethernet0/0
      40.0.0.0/24 is subnetted, 1 subnets
O E2    40.4.4.0 [110/100] via 160.10.22.3, 00:00:44, Ethernet0/0
                 [110/100] via 160.10.22.5, 00:00:44, Ethernet0/0
      130.200.0.0/24 is subnetted, 1 subnets
O E2    130.200.10.0 [110/100] via 160.10.22.3, 00:00:46, Ethernet0/0
                     [110/100] via 160.10.22.5, 00:00:46, Ethernet0/0
O E2 193.118.6.0/24 [110/100] via 160.10.22.3, 00:00:46, Ethernet0/0
                    [110/100] via 160.10.22.5, 00:00:46, Ethernet0/0
O E2 193.118.1.0/24 [110/100] via 160.10.22.3, 00:00:46, Ethernet0/0
                    [110/100] via 160.10.22.5, 00:00:46, Ethernet0/0
O E2 193.118.3.0/24 [110/100] via 160.10.22.3, 00:00:46, Ethernet0/0
                    [110/100] via 160.10.22.5, 00:00:46, Ethernet0/0
O E2 193.118.2.0/24 [110/100] via 160.10.22.3, 00:00:48, Ethernet0/0
                    [110/100] via 160.10.22.5, 00:00:48, Ethernet0/0
R6#
```

## Section 2.3: RIP (9 Points)

- *Configure RIP between R4 and BB2. R4-e0/0 must be the only interface configured for RIP on R4. You should receive updates and R4 routing table will be populated with some RIP routes from BB2.*

If you configured this correctly as shown in Example 4-27, you have scored 4 points.

- *Configure a filter that will allow only networks 20.0.0.0/8 to be accepted on R4 from BB2.*

If you configured this correctly as shown in Example 4-27, you have scored 2 points.

- *Redistribute between RIP and OSPF. Make sure all others routers have network 20.0.0.0 in their routing tables.*

If you configured this correctly as shown in Example 4-27, you have scored 3 points.

RIP V.2 is running on BB2 and advertising routes to R4. A basic filter and redistribution into OSPF is used to accomplish this task. Note the RIP configuration in Example 4-27 that and what is relevant to look at.

**Example 4-27**  *R4 Output RIP Configuration and R6 Routing Table Verification*

```
R4#sh run | b router rip
router rip
 version 2
 network 140.200.0.0
 distribute-list 1 in Ethernet0/0
 no auto-summary
!
!
R4#sh run | b router ospf
router ospf 1
 log-adjacency-changes
 redistribute rip metric 1 subnets
!
R4#sh ip access-lists 1
Standard IP access list 1
    permit 20.0.0.0, wildcard bits 0.0.0.255 (39660 matches)
R4#
!
! R4 RIP Routing table before filter:
R4#show ip route rip
R    196.1.8.0/24 [120/1] via 140.200.10.200, 00:00:00, Ethernet0/0
R    196.1.9.0/24 [120/1] via 140.200.10.200, 00:00:00, Ethernet0/0
R    196.1.10.0/24 [120/1] via 140.200.10.200, 00:00:00, Ethernet0/0
R    20.0.0.0/8 [120/1] via 140.200.10.200, 00:00:00, Ethernet0/0
R    196.1.1.0/24 [120/1] via 140.200.10.200, 00:00:00, Ethernet0/0
R    196.1.2.0/24 [120/1] via 140.200.10.200, 00:00:00, Ethernet0/0
R    196.1.3.0/24 [120/1] via 140.200.10.200, 00:00:00, Ethernet0/0
R    196.1.4.0/24 [120/1] via 140.200.10.200, 00:00:00, Ethernet0/0
R    196.1.5.0/24 [120/1] via 140.200.10.200, 00:00:00, Ethernet0/0
R    196.1.6.0/24 [120/1] via 140.200.10.200, 00:00:00, Ethernet0/0
```

*continues*

**Example 4-27** *R4 Output RIP Configuration and R6 Routing Table Verification (Continued)*

```
R      196.1.7.0/24 [120/1] via 140.200.10.200, 00:00:00, Ethernet0/0
R      30.0.0.0/8 [120/1] via 140.200.10.200, 00:00:00, Ethernet0/0
R4#
!
! R6 has not the 20.0.0.0 network on its Routing table:
R6#show ip route ¦ include 20.0.0
! No output here
R6#
!
! R4 RIP Routing table after filter be comfigured:
R4#
R4#show ip route rip
R      20.0.0.0/8 [120/1] via 140.200.10.200, 00:00:22, Ethernet0/0
R4#
!
!
! R6 OSPF Routing table has also RIP network 20.0.0.0/24:
R6#show ip route ¦ include 20.0.0
O E2 20.0.0.0/8 [110/1] via 160.10.22.3, 23:47:18, Ethernet0/0
```

# Section 3: BGP (12 Points)

- *Configure EBGP between R6 and BB3. R6 will be AS 100 and the BB3 router AS is 300. R6 will receive updates for networks 200.20.X.0 and 198.18.X.0. X is any number. See Figure 4-11.*

If you configured this correctly as shown in Example 4-28, you have scored 6 points.

The EBGP configuration on R6 is a simple task. Again, you will need the basic BGP concepts to accomplish this, as shown in Example 4-28. You will also see on R4 BGP routing table that R4 is receiving all BGP routes from Backbone 3.

**Example 4-28** *R6 EBGP Configuration*

```
R6#show run ¦ b router bgp
router bgp 100
 no synchronization
 neighbor 170.100.10.254 remote-as 300
 no auto-summary
!
!
R6#show ip bgp
BGP table version is 141, local router ID is 170.100.10.1
Status codes: s suppressed, d damped, h history, * valid, > best, i - internal
Origin codes: i - IGP, e - EGP, ? - incomplete
   Network          Next Hop            Metric LocPrf Weight Path
*> 198.18.1.0       170.100.10.254           0             0 300 i
*> 198.18.2.0       170.100.10.254           0             0 300 i
*> 198.18.3.0       170.100.10.254           0             0 300 i
*> 198.18.4.0       170.100.10.254           0             0 300 i
```

**Example 4-28**  *R6 EBGP Configuration (Continued)*

```
*> 198.18.5.0       170.100.10.254      0        0 300 i
*> 198.18.6.0       170.100.10.254      0        0 300 i
*> 198.18.7.0       170.100.10.254      0        0 300 i
*> 198.18.8.0       170.100.10.254      0        0 300 i
*> 198.18.9.0       170.100.10.254      0        0 300 i
*> 198.18.10.0      170.100.10.254      0        0 300 i
*> 200.20.1.0       170.100.10.254      0        0 300 i
*> 200.20.2.0       170.100.10.254      0        0 300 i
*> 200.20.3.0       170.100.10.254      0        0 300 i
*> 200.20.4.0       170.100.10.254      0        0 300 i
*> 200.20.5.0       170.100.10.254      0        0 300 i
*> 200.20.6.0       170.100.10.254      0        0 300 i
*> 200.20.7.0       170.100.10.254      0        0 300 i
*> 200.20.8.0       170.100.10.254      0        0 300 i
*> 200.20.9.0       170.100.10.254      0        0 300 i
*> 200.20.10.0      170.100.10.254      0        0 300 i
R6#
```

- *Configure a fully meshed IBGP between R2, R4, and R6; Use AS 100. R2 and R4 should be able to see all BGP BB3 routes in their routing tables. Use the loopback interfaces as your peers. See Figure 4-11.*

If you configured this correctly as shown in Example 4-29, you have scored 3 points.

You will need to make a fully meshed BGP configuration and make sure R2 and R4 routing tables will be populated with BGP BB3 routes and show the routers as ">" best via R6 Loopback0. As the question requires, make sure to use the loopback interface address to make up your peers. Disabling the **synchronization** and the **next-hop-self** statements are keys to making this happen.

**Example 4-29**  *R2, R4, and R6 IBGP Configuration*

```
R2#show run | b router bgp
router bgp 100
 no synchronization
 bgp log-neighbor-changes
 neighbor 160.10.4.4 remote-as 100
 neighbor 160.10.4.4 update-source Loopback0
 neighbor 160.10.6.6 remote-as 100
 neighbor 160.10.6.6 update-source Loopback0
 no auto-summary
!
R2#show ip bgp sum
BGP router identifier 160.10.2.2, local AS number 100
BGP table version is 1, main routing table version 1
20 network entries and 20 paths using 2740 bytes of memory
1 BGP path attribute entries using 60 bytes of memory
1 BGP AS-PATH entries using 24 bytes of memory
0 BGP route-map cache entries using 0 bytes of memory
0 BGP filter-list cache entries using 0 bytes of memory
BGP activity 20/80 prefixes, 20/0 paths, scan interval 60 secs
```

*continues*

**Example 4-29** *R2, R4, and R6 IBGP Configuration (Continued)*

```
Neighbor        V     AS MsgRcvd MsgSent  TblVer  InQ OutQ Up/Down  State/PfxRcd
160.10.4.4      4    100     103     103       1    0    0 01:39:29           0
160.10.6.6      4    100     105     104       1    0    0 01:40:38          20
R2#
!
R2#show ip bgp
BGP table version is 21, local router ID is 160.10.2.2
Status codes: s suppressed, d damped, h history, * valid, > best, i - internal,
              r RIB-failure, S Stale
Origin codes: i - IGP, e - EGP, ? - incomplete

   Network          Next Hop          Metric LocPrf Weight Path
*>i198.18.1.0       160.10.6.6             0    100      0 300 i
*>i198.18.2.0       160.10.6.6             0    100      0 300 i
*>i198.18.3.0       160.10.6.6             0    100      0 300 i
*>i198.18.4.0       160.10.6.6             0    100      0 300 i
*>i198.18.5.0       160.10.6.6             0    100      0 300 i
*>i198.18.6.0       160.10.6.6             0    100      0 300 i
*>i198.18.7.0       160.10.6.6             0    100      0 300 i
*>i198.18.8.0       160.10.6.6             0    100      0 300 i
*>i198.18.9.0       160.10.6.6             0    100      0 300 i
*>i198.18.10.0      160.10.6.6             0    100      0 300 i
*>i200.20.1.0       160.10.6.6             0    100      0 300 i
*>i200.20.2.0       160.10.6.6             0    100      0 300 i
*>i200.20.3.0       160.10.6.6             0    100      0 300 i
*>i200.20.4.0       160.10.6.6             0    100      0 300 i
*>i200.20.5.0       160.10.6.6             0    100      0 300 i
*>i200.20.6.0       160.10.6.6             0    100      0 300 i
*>i200.20.7.0       160.10.6.6             0    100      0 300 i
   Network          Next Hop          Metric LocPrf Weight Path
*>i200.20.8.0       160.10.6.6             0    100      0 300 i
*>i200.20.9.0       160.10.6.6             0    100      0 300 i
*>i200.20.10.0      160.10.6.6             0    100      0 300 i
R2#
!
R4#show run | b router bgp
router bgp 100
 bgp log-neighbor-changes
 neighbor 160.10.2.2 remote-as 100
 neighbor 160.10.2.2 update-source Loopback0
 neighbor 160.10.6.6 remote-as 100
 neighbor 160.10.6.6 update-source Loopback0
!
!
R4#show ip bgp sum
BGP router identifier 160.10.4.4, local AS number 100
BGP table version is 1, main routing table version 1
20 network entries using 1940 bytes of memory
20 path entries using 720 bytes of memory
1 BGP path attribute entries using 60 bytes of memory
1 BGP AS-PATH entries using 24 bytes of memory
0 BGP route-map cache entries using 0 bytes of memory
```

**Example 4-29**  *R2, R4, and R6 IBGP Configuration (Continued)*

```
0 BGP filter-list cache entries using 0 bytes of memory
BGP using 2744 total bytes of memory
BGP activity 20/0 prefixes, 20/0 paths, scan interval 60 secs
Neighbor        V    AS MsgRcvd MsgSent   TblVer  InQ OutQ Up/Down  State/PfxRcd
160.10.2.2      4   100     104     104        1    0    0 01:40:02           0
160.10.6.6      4   100     105     104        1    0    0 01:40:10          20
R4#
!
R4#show ip bgp
BGP table version is 21, local router ID is 160.10.4.4
Status codes: s suppressed, d damped, h history, * valid, > best, i - internal
Origin codes: i - IGP, e - EGP, ? - incomplete

   Network          Next Hop          Metric LocPrf Weight Path
*>i198.18.1.0       160.10.6.6             0    100      0 300 i
*>i198.18.2.0       160.10.6.6             0    100      0 300 i
*>i198.18.3.0       160.10.6.6             0    100      0 300 i
*>i198.18.4.0       160.10.6.6             0    100      0 300 i
*>i198.18.5.0       160.10.6.6             0    100      0 300 i
*>i198.18.6.0       160.10.6.6             0    100      0 300 i
*>i198.18.7.0       160.10.6.6             0    100      0 300 i
*>i198.18.8.0       160.10.6.6             0    100      0 300 i
*>i198.18.9.0       160.10.6.6             0    100      0 300 i
*>i198.18.10.0      160.10.6.6             0    100      0 300 i
*>i200.20.1.0       160.10.6.6             0    100      0 300 i
*>i200.20.2.0       160.10.6.6             0    100      0 300 i
*>i200.20.3.0       160.10.6.6             0    100      0 300 i
*>i200.20.4.0       160.10.6.6             0    100      0 300 i
*>i200.20.5.0       160.10.6.6             0    100      0 300 i
*>i200.20.6.0       160.10.6.6             0    100      0 300 i
*>i200.20.7.0       160.10.6.6             0    100      0 300 i
*>i200.20.8.0       160.10.6.6             0    100      0 300 i
   Network          Next Hop          Metric LocPrf Weight Path
*>i200.20.9.0       160.10.6.6             0    100      0 300 i
*>i200.20.10.0      160.10.6.6             0    100      0 300 i
R4#
!
R6#show run | b router bgp
router bgp 100
 no synchronization
 bgp log-neighbor-changes
 neighbor 160.10.2.2 remote-as 100
 neighbor 160.10.2.2 update-source Loopback0
 neighbor 160.10.2.2 next-hop-self
 neighbor 160.10.4.4 remote-as 100
 neighbor 160.10.4.4 update-source Loopback0
 neighbor 160.10.4.4 next-hop-self
 neighbor 170.100.10.254 remote-as 300
 !
 !
R6#show ip bgp sum
BGP router identifier 170.100.10.1, local AS number 100
```

*continues*

**Example 4-29** *R2, R4, and R6 IBGP Configuration (Continued)*

```
BGP table version is 141, main routing table version 141
20 network entries using 1940 bytes of memory
20 path entries using 720 bytes of memory
1 BGP path attribute entries using 60 bytes of memory
1 BGP AS-PATH entries using 24 bytes of memory
0 BGP route-map cache entries using 0 bytes of memory
0 BGP filter-list cache entries using 0 bytes of memory
BGP using 2744 total bytes of memory
BGP activity 80/60 prefixes, 80/60 paths, scan interval 60 secs
Neighbor        V    AS MsgRcvd MsgSent   TblVer  InQ OutQ Up/Down  State/PfxRcd
160.10.2.2      4   100     105     106      141    0    0 01:41:37            0
160.10.4.4      4   100     104     105      141    0    0 01:40:36            0
170.100.10.254  4   300   19073   19069      141    0    0 1w2d               20
R6#
!
R6#show ip bgp
BGP table version is 21, local router ID is 160.10.6.6
Status codes: s suppressed, d damped, h history, * valid, > best, i - internal
Origin codes: i - IGP, e - EGP, ? - incomplete

   Network          Next Hop         Metric LocPrf Weight Path
*> 198.18.1.0       170.100.10.254        0          0 300 i
*> 198.18.2.0       170.100.10.254        0          0 300 i
*> 198.18.3.0       170.100.10.254        0          0 300 i
*> 198.18.4.0       170.100.10.254        0          0 300 i
*> 198.18.5.0       170.100.10.254        0          0 300 i
*> 198.18.6.0       170.100.10.254        0          0 300 i
*> 198.18.7.0       170.100.10.254        0          0 300 i
*> 198.18.8.0       170.100.10.254        0          0 300 i
*> 198.18.9.0       170.100.10.254        0          0 300 i
*> 198.18.10.0      170.100.10.254        0          0 300 i
*> 200.20.1.0       170.100.10.254        0          0 300 i
*> 200.20.2.0       170.100.10.254        0          0 300 i
*> 200.20.3.0       170.100.10.254        0          0 300 i
*> 200.20.4.0       170.100.10.254        0          0 300 i
*> 200.20.5.0       170.100.10.254        0          0 300 i
*> 200.20.6.0       170.100.10.254        0          0 300 i
*> 200.20.7.0       170.100.10.254        0          0 300 i
*> 200.20.8.0       170.100.10.254        0          0 300 i
   Network          Next Hop         Metric LocPrf Weight Path
*> 200.20.9.0       170.100.10.254        0          0 300 i
*> 200.20.10.0      170.100.10.254        0          0 300 i
R6#
!
*> 200.20.9.0       170.100.10.254        0          0 300 i
*> 200.20.10.0      170.100.10.254        0          0 300 i
R6#
```

● *Configure R2 to accept the maximum of 100 prefixes from R6. If the prefixes received reaches 75 percent of this value, configure appropriately to generate a warning.*

If you configured this correctly as shown in Example 4-30, you have scored 3 points.

It is interesting to observe here that the use of the **neighbor maximum-prefix** command is simple, but you must pay attention to accomplish the requirement to generate a warning when 75 percent is reached, because you do not actually need to configure any threshold.

---

NOTE     Seventy-five percent is the default to generate a warning. Verify and study the commands and features noting defaults to avoid you falling into a trap of overconfiguration.

---

Example 4-30  *R2 maximum-prefix Command*

```
R2#
R2#show run | b router bgp
router bgp 100
 no synchronization
 bgp log-neighbor-changes
 neighbor 160.10.4.4 remote-as 100
 neighbor 160.10.4.4 update-source Loopback0
 neighbor 160.10.6.6 remote-as 100
 neighbor 160.10.6.6 update-source Loopback0
 neighbor 160.10.6.6 maximum-prefix 100
 no auto-summary
!
!
R2#sh ip bgp neighbors 160.10.6.6
BGP neighbor is 160.10.6.6,  remote AS 100, internal link
  BGP version 4, remote router ID 170.100.10.1
  BGP state = Established, up for 21:30:03
  Last read 00:00:06, hold time is 180, keepalive interval is 60 seconds
  Neighbor capabilities:
    Route refresh: advertised and received(old & new)
    Address family IPv4 Unicast: advertised and received
  Received 1295 messages, 0 notifications, 0 in queue
  Sent 1294 messages, 0 notifications, 0 in queue
  Default minimum time between advertisement runs is 5 seconds
 For address family: IPv4 Unicast
  BGP table version 1, neighbor version 1
  Index 2, Offset 0, Mask 0x4
  Route refresh request: received 0, sent 0
  20 accepted prefixes consume 800 bytes
  Prefix advertised 0, suppressed 0, withdrawn 0, maximum limit 100
  Threshold for warning message 75%
  Connections established 1; dropped 0
  Last reset never
Connection state is ESTAB, I/O status: 1, unread input bytes: 0
Local host: 160.10.2.2, Local port: 11001
Foreign host: 160.10.6.6, Foreign port: 179
Total option bytes= 4, padded length=4
 Basic security: Class: unclassified  Auth: genser
```

*continues*

**Example 4-30** *R2* **maximum-prefix** *Command (Continued)*

```
Enqueued packets for retransmit: 0, input: 0  mis-ordered: 0 (0 bytes)
Event Timers (current time is 0x5C88C52C):
Timer          Starts   Wakeups         Next
Retrans        1296        1            0x0
TimeWait          0        0            0x0
AckHold        1293     1115            0x0
SendWnd           0        0            0x0
KeepAlive         0        0            0x0
GiveUp            0        0            0x0
PmtuAger          0        0            0x0
DeadWait          0        0            0x0
iss: 1084218813  snduna: 1084243426  sndnxt: 1084243426     sndwnd:  16251
irs: 2068401015  rcvnxt: 2068425763  rcvwnd:        16118  delrcvwnd:  266
SRTT: 300 ms, RTTO: 303 ms, RTV: 3 ms, KRTT: 0 ms
minRTT: 4 ms, maxRTT: 300 ms, ACK hold: 200 ms
Flags: higher precedence, nagle
Datagrams (max data segment is 532 bytes):
Rcvd: 2566 (out of order: 0), with data: 1293, total data bytes: 24747
Sent: 2458 (retransmit: 1, fastretransmit: 0), with data: 1294, total data bytes:
24612
R2#
```

# Section 4: ISDN (6 Points)

- *Configure ISDN on R3 and R5 using PPP. R3 and R5 should be able to ping each other across the ISDN link.*

If you configured this correctly as shown in Example 4-31, you have scored 3 points.

- *Make sure that only when the ISDN link is up that it will pass routing protocol across the link.*

- *The ISDN link should pass routing protocol only when R5-s0/1 and/or R5-fa0/0 and/ or R5-fa0/1 is down. Consider that the routing protocol can pass through the ISDN link when topology changes happen.*

If you configured this correctly as shown in Example 4-31 and Example 4-32, you have scored 3 points.

The key to configuring as requested is to avoid the ISDN to advertise or pass traffic through the link when the other physical interfaces on R5 are up. Notice in the **show** command output what is basic to accomplish these requirements. Commands such as **no cdp enable** and **no peer neighbor-route** help to prevent unnecessary protocols' packets from exchanging information through the IDN link. The **ip ospf demand-circuit** command helps to avoid OSPF Hellos from being sent through the ISDN link; however, when a topology change occurs, R5 will send information through the ISDN link.

**Example 4-31**  *R3 and R5 ISDN Configuration*

```
R3#
!
username R5 password 0 cisco

R3#sh run int bri0/0
Building configuration...
Current configuration : 265 bytes
!
interface BRI0/0
 ip address 160.10.15.3 255.255.255.0
 encapsulation ppp
 ip ospf demand-circuit
 dialer map ip 160.10.15.5 name R5 broadcast 2222
 dialer-group 1
 isdn switch-type basic-5ess
 no peer neighbor-route
 no cdp enable
 ppp authentication chap
end
!
dialer-list 1 protocol ip permit
!
R3#
!
R5#
!
username R5 password 0 cisco
!
R5#sh run int bri0/0
Building configuration...
Current configuration : 265 bytes
!
interface BRI0/0
 ip address 160.10.15.5 255.255.255.0
 encapsulation ppp
 ip ospf demand-circuit
 dialer map ip 160.10.15.3 name R3 broadcast 1111
 dialer-group 1
 isdn switch-type basic-5ess
 no peer neighbor-route
 no cdp enable
 ppp authentication chap
end
R5#
R5#ping 160.10.15.3
Type escape sequence to abort.
Sending 5, 100-byte ICMP Echos to 160.10.15.3, timeout is 2 seconds:
2w3d: %LINK-3-UPDOWN: Interface BRI0/0:1, changed state to up..!!!
Success rate is 60 percent (3/5), round-trip min/avg/max = 32/33/36 ms
R5#
2w3d: %LINEPROTO-5-UPDOWN: Line protocol on Interface BRI0/0:1, changed state to up
2w3d: %ISDN-6-CONNECT: Interface BRI0/0:1 is now connected to 1111 R3
```

The output in Example 4-32 shows the behavior of a backup environment using ISDN. Example 4-32 also shows the steps that were used to test it. Notice the highlighted notes and marks.

**Example 4-32**  *R5 Routing Backup Output*

```
! Notice on R5 the routes comig from the Serial S0/1

R5#show ip route
Codes: C - connected, S - static, I - IGRP, R - RIP, M - mobile, B - BGP
       D - EIGRP, EX - EIGRP external, O - OSPF, IA - OSPF inter area
       N1 - OSPF NSSA external type 1, N2 - OSPF NSSA external type 2
       E1 - OSPF external type 1, E2 - OSPF external type 2, E - EGP
       i - IS-IS, L1 - IS-IS level-1, L2 - IS-IS level-2, ia - IS-IS inter area
       * - candidate default, U - per-user static route, o - ODR
       P - periodic downloaded static route
Gateway of last resort is not set
     50.0.0.0/24 is subnetted, 1 subnets
O E2    50.5.5.0 [110/100] via 160.10.37.2, 02:39:35, Serial0/1
     140.200.0.0/24 is subnetted, 1 subnets
O E2    140.200.10.0 [110/1] via 160.10.37.2, 02:35:48, Serial0/1
O E2 193.118.9.0/24 [110/100] via 160.10.37.2, 02:39:35, Serial0/1
O E2 20.0.0.0/8 [110/1] via 160.10.37.2, 02:29:08, Serial0/1
O E2 193.118.8.0/24 [110/100] via 160.10.37.2, 02:39:35, Serial0/1
O E2 193.118.10.0/24 [110/100] via 160.10.37.2, 02:39:35, Serial0/1
O E2 193.118.5.0/24 [110/100] via 160.10.37.2, 02:39:36, Serial0/1
O E2 193.118.4.0/24 [110/100] via 160.10.37.2, 02:39:36, Serial0/1
     160.10.0.0/16 is variably subnetted, 16 subnets, 2 masks
O IA    160.10.32.0/24 [110/112] via 160.10.37.2, 02:39:46, Serial0/1
O IA    160.10.33.0/24 [110/113] via 160.10.37.2, 02:39:46, Serial0/1
O       160.10.37.4/32 [110/112] via 160.10.37.2, 02:39:47, Serial0/1
O       160.10.37.2/32 [110/64] via 160.10.37.2, 02:39:47, Serial0/1
O       160.10.37.1/32 [110/112] via 160.10.37.2, 02:39:47, Serial0/1
C       160.10.37.0/24 is directly connected, Serial0/1
O IA    160.10.11.0/24 [110/122] via 160.10.37.2, 02:39:47, Serial0/1
C       160.10.15.0/24 is directly connected, BRI0/0
O       160.10.2.0/24 [110/65] via 160.10.37.2, 02:39:47, Serial0/1
O IA    160.10.3.0/24 [110/113] via 160.10.37.2, 02:39:47, Serial0/1
O       160.10.1.0/24 [110/113] via 160.10.37.2, 02:39:47, Serial0/1
O       160.10.6.0/24 [110/2] via 160.10.22.6, 2d00h, FastEthernet0/0
O       160.10.4.0/24 [110/113] via 160.10.37.2, 02:39:47, Serial0/1
C       160.10.5.0/24 is directly connected, Loopback0
C       160.10.25.0/24 is directly connected, FastEthernet0/1
C       160.10.22.0/24 is directly connected, FastEthernet0/0
O E2 193.118.7.0/24 [110/100] via 160.10.37.2, 02:39:37, Serial0/1
     40.0.0.0/24 is subnetted, 1 subnets
O E2    40.4.4.0 [110/100] via 160.10.37.2, 02:39:39, Serial0/1
     130.200.0.0/24 is subnetted, 1 subnets
O E2    130.200.10.0 [110/100] via 160.10.37.2, 02:39:39, Serial0/1
O E2 193.118.6.0/24 [110/100] via 160.10.37.2, 02:39:39, Serial0/1
O E2 193.118.1.0/24 [110/100] via 160.10.37.2, 02:39:39, Serial0/1
O E2 193.118.3.0/24 [110/100] via 160.10.37.2, 02:39:39, Serial0/1
O E2 193.118.2.0/24 [110/100] via 160.10.37.2, 02:39:39, Serial0/1
R5#
```

**Example 4-32**  *R5 Routing Backup Output (Continued)*

```
R5#
! Here we are shuting down R5-Fa0/0 to test the contingency
R5#
R5#conf t
Enter configuration commands, one per line.  End with CNTL/Z.
R5(config)#int fa0/0
R5(config-if)#shut
R5(config-if)#
2w3d: %OSPF-5-ADJCHG: Process 1, Nbr 160.10.6.6 on FastEthernet0/0 from FULL to
  DOWN, Neighbor Down: Interface down or detached
2w3d: %OSPF-5-ADJCHG: Process 1, Nbr 160.10.3.3 on FastEthernet0/0 from FULL to
  DOWN, Neighbor Down: Interface down or detached
2w3d: %LINK-3-UPDOWN: Interface BRI0/0:1, changed state to up
2w3d: %LINEPROTO-5-UPDOWN: Line protocol on Interface BRI0/0:1, changed state to up
2w3d: %LINK-5-CHANGED: Interface FastEthernet0/0, changed state to
  administratively down
2w3d: %LINEPROTO-5-UPDOWN: Line protocol on Interface FastEthernet0/0, changed
  state to down
R5(config-if)#
R5(config-if)#
R5(config-if)#int fa0/0
2w3d: %ISDN-6-CONNECT: Interface BRI0/0:1 is now connected to 1111 R5
R5(config-if)#int fa0/1
R5(config-if)#shut
R5(config-if)#
2w3d: %OSPF-5-ADJCHG: Process 1, Nbr 160.10.1.1 on FastEthernet0/1 from FULL
  to DOWN, Neighbor Down: Interface down or detached
2w3d: %LINK-5-CHANGED: Interface FastEthernet0/1, changed state to
  administratively down
2w3d: %LINEPROTO-5-UPDOWN: Line protocol on Interface FastEthernet0/1, changed
  state to down
R5(config-if)#
R5(config-if)#int s0/1
R5(config-if)#shut
R5(config-if)#
2w3d: %OSPF-5-ADJCHG: Process 1, Nbr 160.10.2.2 on Serial0/1 from FULL to DOWN,
  Neighbor Down: Interface down or detached
R5(config-if)#
2w3d: %LINK-5-CHANGED: Interface Serial0/1, changed state to administratively down
2w3d: %LINEPROTO-5-UPDOWN: Line protocol on Interface Serial0/1, changed state
  to down
R5(config-if)#
R5#
2w3d: %SYS-5-CONFIG_I: Configured from console by console
R5#
R5#
! Notice that all routes are learned through the BRI0/0:
! Now we see the routes coming through interface BRI 0/0

R5#show ip route
Codes: C - connected, S - static, I - IGRP, R - RIP, M - mobile, B - BGP
       D - EIGRP, EX - EIGRP external, O - OSPF, IA - OSPF inter area
```

*continues*

**Example 4-32** *R5 Routing Backup Output (Continued)*

```
                 N1 - OSPF NSSA external type 1, N2 - OSPF NSSA external type 2
                 E1 - OSPF external type 1, E2 - OSPF external type 2, E - EGP
                 i - IS-IS, L1 - IS-IS level-1, L2 - IS-IS level-2, ia - IS-IS inter area
                 * - candidate default, U - per-user static route, o - ODR
                 P - periodic downloaded static route
Gateway of last resort is not set
     50.0.0.0/24 is subnetted, 1 subnets
O E2    50.5.5.0 [110/100] via 160.10.15.3, 00:00:08, BRI0/0
     140.200.0.0/24 is subnetted, 1 subnets
O E2    140.200.10.0 [110/1] via 160.10.15.3, 00:00:08, BRI0/0
O E2 193.118.9.0/24 [110/100] via 160.10.15.3, 00:00:08, BRI0/0
O E2 20.0.0.0/8 [110/1] via 160.10.15.3, 00:00:08, BRI0/0
O E2 193.118.8.0/24 [110/100] via 160.10.15.3, 00:00:08, BRI0/0
O E2 193.118.10.0/24 [110/100] via 160.10.15.3, 00:00:08, BRI0/0
O E2 193.118.5.0/24 [110/100] via 160.10.15.3, 00:00:09, BRI0/0
O E2 193.118.4.0/24 [110/100] via 160.10.15.3, 00:00:09, BRI0/0
     160.10.0.0/16 is variably subnetted, 16 subnets, 2 masks
O IA    160.10.37.5/32 [110/1674] via 160.10.15.3, 00:00:09, BRI0/0
O IA    160.10.32.0/24 [110/1626] via 160.10.15.3, 00:00:09, BRI0/0
O IA    160.10.37.4/32 [110/1674] via 160.10.15.3, 00:00:10, BRI0/0
O IA    160.10.33.0/24 [110/1563] via 160.10.15.3, 00:00:10, BRI0/0
O IA    160.10.37.2/32 [110/1626] via 160.10.15.3, 00:00:10, BRI0/0
O IA    160.10.37.1/32 [110/1674] via 160.10.15.3, 00:00:10, BRI0/0
O IA    160.10.11.0/24 [110/1684] via 160.10.15.3, 00:00:10, BRI0/0
C       160.10.15.0/24 is directly connected, BRI0/0
O IA    160.10.2.0/24 [110/1627] via 160.10.15.3, 00:00:10, BRI0/0
O IA    160.10.3.0/24 [110/1563] via 160.10.15.3, 00:00:10, BRI0/0
O IA    160.10.1.0/24 [110/1675] via 160.10.15.3, 00:00:10, BRI0/0
O       160.10.6.0/24 [110/1564] via 160.10.15.3, 00:00:20, BRI0/0
O IA    160.10.4.0/24 [110/1675] via 160.10.15.3, 00:00:10, BRI0/0
C       160.10.5.0/24 is directly connected, Loopback0
O IA    160.10.25.0/24 [110/1684] via 160.10.15.3, 00:00:10, BRI0/0
O       160.10.22.0/24 [110/1563] via 160.10.15.3, 00:00:20, BRI0/0
O E2 193.118.7.0/24 [110/100] via 160.10.15.3, 00:00:10, BRI0/0
     40.0.0.0/24 is subnetted, 1 subnets
O E2    40.4.4.0 [110/100] via 160.10.15.3, 00:00:01, BRI0/0
     130.200.0.0/24 is subnetted, 1 subnets
O E2    130.200.10.0 [110/100] via 160.10.15.3, 00:00:01, BRI0/0
O E2 193.118.6.0/24 [110/100] via 160.10.15.3, 00:00:01, BRI0/0
O E2 193.118.1.0/24 [110/100] via 160.10.15.3, 00:00:01, BRI0/0
O E2 193.118.3.0/24 [110/100] via 160.10.15.3, 00:00:01, BRI0/0
O E2 193.118.2.0/24 [110/100] via 160.10.15.3, 00:00:01, BRI0/0
R5#
```

# Section 5: IP and IOS Features (10 Points)

- *Configure R6 to provide DHCP service to clients located on VLAN 22. Consider the following information:*

— *Bindings are stored on Host 160.10.22.253, the file transfer protocol is FTP and the server should wait 4 minutes before writing database changes.*

— *Username: user*

— *Password: password*

— *Filename: router-dhcp*

— *DNS servers: 160.10.22.100 and 160.10.22.101*

— *Default routers: 160.10.22.3 and 160.10.22.5*

— *Domain name: mycompany.com*

— *Hosts most retain the DHCP assignment for one week.*

If you configured this correctly as shown in Example 4-33, you have scored 4 points.

The DHCP feature is very useful and many companies use it. Here you have a concept of a host that stores the DHCP bindings. Notice which commands in Example 4-33 are relevant to accomplish this task.

**Example 4-33**  *R6 DHCP Configuration*

```
R6#show run | b dhcp
ip dhcp database ftp://user:password@160.10.22.253/router-dhcp write-delay 240
ip dhcp excluded-address 160.10.22.3 160.10.22.6
!
ip dhcp pool VLAN_22
   network 160.10.22.0 255.255.255.0
   dns-server 160.10.22.100 160.10.22.101
   default-router 160.10.22.3 160.10.22.5
   domain-name mycompany.com
   lease 7
```

● *You have some users on VLAN_25 that must have R1 configured as their default gateway; other users must have R5 as their default gateway. Configure R1 and R5 not to send redirect messages to the originator PC.*

If you configured this correctly as shown in Example 4-34, you have scored 2 points.

The **ip redirects** command allows the interface to redirect incoming packets to a better path. Disabling the feature with **no ip redirects** forces the interfaces to accept the packet and to not redirect it.

**Example 4-34**  *R5 Disabling the ICMP Redirect Feature*

```
R1#show run int e0/1
Building configuration...
Current configuration : 97 bytes
!
interface Ethernet0/1
 ip address 160.10.25.1 255.255.255.0
 no ip redirects
 half-duplex
```

*continues*

**Example 4-34** *R5 Disabling the ICMP Redirect Feature (Continued)*

```
end
R1#
!
!
R5#show run int fa0/1
Building configuration...
Current configuration : 113 bytes
!
interface FastEthernet0/1
 ip address 160.10.25.5 255.255.255.0
 no ip redirects
 duplex auto
 speed auto
end
R5#
```

- *The BB2 router is reporting some problems and it is not stable. Configure R4 to save a core dump via FTP in case BB2 fails or crashes. Consider the FTP username CISCO, password CCIE, FTP server IP address 140.200.10.200, and filename dumpfile. Use passive mode also.*

If you configured this correctly as shown in Example 4-35, you have scored 2 points.

In Example 4-35, you have the necessary configuration to accomplish this task. Notice that the requirement to use "passive mode" will not require any configuration, because it is the default mode and will not show in your configuration.

**Example 4-35** *R4 Configuration to Get via FTP a Core Dump*

```
R4#show run
Building configuration...
Current configuration : 97 bytes
!
!
ip ftp source-interface Ethernet0/0
ip ftp username CISCO
ip ftp password CCIE
!
!
exception protocol ftp
exception dump 140.200.10.200
exception core-file dumpfile
!
R4#
```

- *You have some security concerns regarding the use of BOOTP services on R2. Disable the BOOTP services on this router.*

If you configured this correctly as shown in Example 4-36, you have scored 2 points.

**Example 4-36**  *R2 Disabling BOOTP Services Configuration*

```
R2#show run | i bootp
no ip bootp server
R2#
```

# Section 6: DLSw (4 Points)

- *Configure DLSw between VLAN_11 and VLAN_33. Use TCP encapsulation.*

If you configured this correctly as shown in Example 4-37, you have scored 2 points.

Example 4-37 shows the basic configuration to configure the DLSw. Because it is a "bridge" environment, you need to enable Spanning Tree Protocol, which you accomplish using the **bridge** protocol command. Also, the **show** commands tell you if the DLSw peers are up and running. Look for the state field from **show dlsw peers** and if it is "CONNECT" it is acceptable; otherwise, double check your configuration for mistakes in IP addressing or missing configuration. Double check on both sides, R1 and R3.

**Example 4-37**  *R1 and R3 Basic DLSw Configuration*

```
R1#show run
!
dlsw local-peer peer-id 160.10.1.1
dlsw remote-peer 0 tcp 160.10.3.3
dlsw bridge-group 1
!
interface Ethernet0/0
 ip address 160.10.11.1 255.255.255.0

 bridge-group 1
!
!
!
bridge 1 protocol ieee
!
!
R3#show run
!
!
dlsw local-peer peer-id 160.10.3.3
dlsw remote-peer 0 tcp 160.10.1.1
dlsw bridge-group 1
!
!
!
interface FastEthernet0/1
 ip address 160.10.33.3 255.255.255.0
 bridge-group 1
!
```

*continues*

**Example 4-37** *R1 and R3 Basic DLSw Configuration (Continued)*

```
!
bridge 1 protocol ieee
!
!
R1#show dlsw peers
Peers:              state     pkts_rx   pkts_tx  type  drops ckts TCP   uptime
  TCP 160.10.3.3    CONNECT      3298      3298  conf      0    0   0   1d03h
Total number of connected peers: 1
Total number of connections:     1
R1#
!
!
R3#show dlsw peers
Peers:              state     pkts_rx   pkts_tx  type  drops ckts TCP   uptime
  TCP 160.10.1.1    CONNECT      3299      3299  conf      0    0   0   1d03h
Total number of connected peers: 1
Total number of connections:     1
R3#
```

- *You have some users exchanging data through your DLSw connection, but you don't want to compromise the IP traffic, because the DLSw is not your high priority. Configure your DLSw peers to reserve bandwidth and so that they do not use more than 60 kbps as an average bit rate and maximum burst rate of 30 kbps.*

If you configured this correctly as shown in Example 4-38, you have scored 1 point.

Example 4-38 shows the configuration for RSVP or Bandwidth Reservation to DLSw sessions. Another useful command is **show ip rsvp reservation**, which shows if the bandwidth is reserved; however, you must have a DLSw session exchange traffic to see any output.

**Example 4-38** *R1 and R3 RSVP Configuration*

```
R1#show run
!
dlsw rsvp 60 30
!
R3#sh run
!
!
dlsw rsvp 60 30
!
```

- *The SNA servers exchanging data between VLAN_11 and VLAN_33 have a high CPU utilization and, therefore, cause unexpected longer timeouts. To adjust the situation, configure a timeout of 10 minutes to accommodate an explorer response before marking a resource unreachable.*

If you configured this correctly as shown in Example 4-39, you have scored 1 point.

Example 4-39 shows the configuration that adjusts the "timer" for the explorer packets from the default of 6 seconds to 600 seconds or 10 minutes.

**Example 4-39**  *R1 and R3 RSVP Configuration*

```
R1#show run
!
dlsw timer sna-explorer-timeout 600
!
!
!
R3#show run
!
!
dlsw timer sna-explorer-timeout 600
!
!
```

# Section 7: QoS (6 Points)

- *Configure R1 to give high priority to IP traffic and medium priority to DLSw going out through s0/1. Use a congestion management approach.*

If you configured this correctly as shown in Example 4-40, you have scored 2 points.

You need to create a priority queue to accommodate the high and medium priorities.

**Example 4-40**  *R1 Priority Queue Configuration*

```
R1#show run int s0/1

 priority-group 1

!
priority-list 1 protocol dlsw medium
priority-list 1 protocol ip high
```

- *Configure R3 so that any incoming traffic on fa0/1 has medium priority.*

If you configured this correctly as shown in Example 4-41, you have scored 2 points.

**Example 4-41**  *R3 Priority Queue Configuration*

```
R3#show run int fa0/1
Building configuration...
Current configuration : 158 bytes
!
interface FastEthernet0/1
priority-group 2

!
priority-list 2 interface FastEthernet0/1 medium
```

- *Configure R2 s0/0–Frame Relay so that real-time traffic should never reserve more than 256 kbps and no more than 50 kbps for a specific session.*

If you configured this correctly as shown in Example 4-42 ,you have scored 2 points.

Example 4-42 shows a basic use of the RSVP configuration to reserve the bandwidth requested.

**Example 4-42**   *R2 RSVP Configuration*

```
R2#sh run int s0/0
interface Serial0/0
 ip address 160.10.32.2 255.255.255.0
 encapsulation frame-relay
 !
 ip rsvp bandwidth 256 50
end
```

# Section 8: Multicast (6 Points)

- *Configure Multicast PIM Sparse-mode on VLAN_22 to allow Multicast traffic between R3, R5, and R6. Make R6 the rendezvous point.*

If you configured this correctly as shown in Example 4-43, you have scored 3 points.

- *To better control the interval of PIM query messages, change the frequency of sending these messages to 1 minute.*

If you configured this correctly as shown in Example 4-43, you have scored 3 points.

Example 4-43 shows the multicast configuration according to the question requirement regarding the PIM mode and the rendezvous point. The **show** commands tell you if the RP is found and if the neighborhood is made.

**Example 4-43**   *R3, R5, and R6 Multicast Configuration*

```
R3#show run
Building configuration...
!
!
ip multicast-routing
!
!
interface FastEthernet0/0
 ip address 160.10.22.3 255.255.255.0
 ip pim query-interval 60
 ip pim sparse-mode
!
ip pim rp-address 160.10.22.6
 !
```

**Example 4-43**  *R3, R5, and R6 Multicast Configuration (Continued)*

```
!
R5#show run
Building configuration...
!
!
ip multicast-routing
!
!
interface FastEthernet0/0
 ip address 160.10.22.5 255.255.255.0
 ip pim query-interval 60
 ip pim sparse-mode
!
!
ip pim rp-address 160.10.22.6
!
!
R6#show run
Building configuration...
!
!
ip multicast-routing
!
!
interface Ethernet0/0
 ip address 160.10.22.6 255.255.255.0
 ip pim query-interval 60
 ip pim sparse-mode
!
!
!
R3#show ip pim rp
Group: 224.0.1.40, RP: 160.10.22.6, uptime 1d01h, expires never
!
!
R5#show ip pim rp
Group: 224.0.1.40, RP: 160.10.22.6, uptime 1d01h, expires never
R5#
!
R6#sh ip pim neighbor
PIM Neighbor Table
Neighbor          Interface            Uptime/Expires    Ver   DR
Address                                                        Prio/Mode
160.10.22.5       Ethernet0/0          1d04h/00:03:14    v2    1 / S
160.10.22.3       Ethernet0/0          1d04h/00:03:26    v2    1 / S
R6#
```

# Section 9: Security (8 Points)

- *The users on VLAN_33 belong to a development department and they are under strict supervision. They are not permitted to access e-mail (where the server is outside VLAN_33) between 08:00AM to 08:00PM, Monday through Friday. Configure an access list to accomplish this.*

If you configured this correctly as shown in Example 4-44, you have scored 3 points.

---

**NOTE**   When configuring the **time-range** feature, do not forget to configure the clock on the router; otherwise, it will not work (the **time-range** will remain inactive). Use the **clock set** command from the router enable mode prompt.

The **time-range** feature shown on Example 4-44 is used to limit certain access or sessions to specific protocols in a certain period of time.

---

**Example 4-44**   *R3 Access List and* **time-range** *Configuration*

```
R3#show run
!
!
interface FastEthernet0/1
 ip address 160.10.33.3 255.255.255.0
 ip access-group NO-SMTP in
!
!
ip access-list extended NO-SMTP
 deny   tcp any any eq smtp time-range no-SMTP
 permit ip any any
!
time-range no-SMTP
 periodic weekdays 8:00 to 20:00
!
R3#sh time-range
time-range entry: no-SMTP (inactive)
   periodic weekdays 8:00 to 20:00
   used in: IP ACL entry
R3#
```

- *Configure R2 fa0/0 to prioritize security options on packets coming to this interface. Leave the level and authority as the default values.*

If you configured this correctly as shown in Example 4-45, you have scored 2 points.

Example 4-45 show the configuration to accomplish the question's requirements. To enable the IP security options, use the command **ip security dedicated**. Level "unclassified," and authority "genser" are the default values. To prioritize the packets, configure the **ip security first** command.

**Example 4-45**  *R2 IP Security Option (IPSO) Configuration*

```
R2#show run int fa0/0
Building configuration...
Current configuration : 160 bytes
!
interface FastEthernet0/0
 ip address 130.200.10.2 255.255.255.0
 ip security dedicated unclassified genser
 ip security first
R2#
```

- *Configure Sw1 fa0/17 to allow only the host MAC address 0010.DE48.2223 to access the switch through this interface. If a security violation occurs, make the interface go to shutdown mode.*

If you configured this correctly as shown in Example 4-46, you have scored 3 points.

The configuration in Example 4-46 is the minimum configuration needed to enable the port-security feature. Observe that to configure the shutdown option you do not need to configure any extra command as it is the default.

**Example 4-46**  *Sw1 Port-Security Configuration*

```
Sw1#show run int fa0/17
Building configuration...
Current configuration : 152 bytes
!
interface FastEthernet0/17
 switchport mode access
 switchport port-security
 switchport port-security mac-address 0010.de48.2223
 no ip address
end
Sw1#
!
!
Sw1#show port-security int fa0/17
Port Security : Enabled
Port status : SecureUp
Violation mode : Shutdown
Maximum MAC Addresses : 1
Total MAC Addresses : 1
Configured MAC Addresses : 1
Sticky MAC Addresses : 0
Aging time : 0 mins
Aging type : Absolute
SecureStatic address aging : Disabled
Security Violation count : 0
Sw1#
```

# How Did You Do?

With the aid of the answers section and full configurations and routing tables on the CD, you should now have an accurate evaluation of your lab. If you scored more than 80 points within the timeframe, you should congratulate yourself; you are well on the way to becoming a CCIE. You have demonstrated the ability to think linearly and shown an impressive knowledge of your subject. If you scored less than 80, do not worry; this will improve as you progress throughout the book and learn how to analyze each question and improve your core skills.

Did you spot the landmines in the lab? The classics in Lab 4 were to give you, under a new topology, the basic setup for OSPF, RIP V2, EIGRP, and BGP that are big "candidates" to being in the real lab exam. Also an important thing to keep in mind is the feature each area has. You need to explore these going through Cisco documentation.

In Lab 5 and Lab 6, you will be required to demonstrate your knowledge in more complex tasks, environment, and behaviors and be able to solve the issues. The real one-day lab exam does not have the troubleshooting section anymore, but, on the other hand, during the exam you can find yourself in a "troubleshooting" situation if you do not have a solid knowledge of what you are configuring. Keep in mind that you will need to perform some "basic" troubleshooting during the exam. The hands-on experience will give you the confidence that you need.

You might feel that some questions were too vague or did not have sufficient time to complete the lab, but this is intentionally made to force you to study and research. You will find on the real CCIE lab exam similar challenges, and your ability to spot landmines, ask the right questions, and increase your configuration speed will improve as you tackle each practice lab.

For each question that you did not answer correctly, take the time to research the subject thoroughly and turn your weaknesses into your strengths. Research and plenty of practice will ultimately lead you to gain a passing score.

# Further Reading/URLs

To better prepare yourself and follow up on the topics covered in this lab, you should consult the http://www.cisco.com/public/pubsearch.html website for more information on the following topics:

Configuring Frame Relay
Configuring 3550
Configuring ATM
Configuring Routing Protocols
Configuring ISDN
Configuring IP Features
Configuring IOS Features

Configuring DLSw
Configuring QoS
Configuring Multicast
Configuring Security

All topics, concepts and question used in this chapter came from the following sources:

All Routing, Features, BGP, etc. (Cisco Documentation for 12.2 mainline under:
http://www.cisco.com/univercd/home/home.html)
http://www.cisco.com/univercd/cc/td/doc/product/software/ios122/index.htm
For the Catalyst 3550 (the 12.1 EMI image documentation): http://www.cisco.com/
univercd/cc/td/doc/product/lan/c3550/1219ea1/3550scg/index.htm

# CHAPTER 5

# Practice Lab 5

You will now be starting Practice Lab 5. We will be adding IS-IS routing protocol for this lab, and then you will find some interesting behaviors and situations involving IS-IS configuration itself and redistribution aspects between routing protocols. We will be practicing other features and methods to configure, you will also notice small changes on addressing more specifically on network masks. You might think you are going through the same tasks you tackled before, but the more you practice the more you become familiar with the equipment and commands that will make you comfortable to perform the tasks during the CCIE Lab Exam as well in your professional duties. The main objective still remains the same: to ensure you practice on a variety of subjects and scenarios that covers the potential CCIE Lab Exam content. As before, if your equipment does not exactly match that used to produce the lab it does not matter, as long as you have the required interfaces. Having the exact equipment, however, will aid you in pasting in configuration files.

Quite often the questions will be straightforward, so try to keep your solutions simple and avoid complicating the matter and yourself. Sometimes, you will need to pay attention to the wording and although the question looks like quite simple, it could involve a "hidden" concept knowledge regarding a specific area or section in the exercise. Keep in mind that the main objective of these lab exercises is to give you challenges that will drive you through the areas you must explore to be well prepared to take the CCIE Lab Exam with success, and, therefore, be thoroughly prepared to better apply your skills in the real world.

As in the previous labs you will find to assist you; the routers and switches initial configurations, Frame Relay switch configuration and now backbone router configurations. Solutions for the entire lab including configurations and common show command outputs from all the devices in the topology can be found on the accompanying CD. An "Ask the Proctor" section is included at the end of the lab which will give you clues if required followed by the lab debrief, which will analyze each question showing you what was required and how to achieve the desired results. Finally, you will find handy references should you require additional study information.

You will now be guided through the equipment requirements and pre-lab tasks in preparation for taking Practice Lab 5.

# Equipment List

- 2 Catalyst 3550 switches (3550 X 24 Fast Ethernet ports with Cisco IOS Software Release 12.1 Enhanced Multilayer Software image [EMI])
- 6 Cisco routers (2600, 3600, and 3725)
- A backbone router (Cisco 7200)
- A Frame Relay switch router (Cisco 4000)

The routers are loaded with Cisco IOS Software Release 12.2 Enterprise Mainline image (all Cisco equipment). The exception is the 3725 router that is loaded with 12.2(T) image.

- Follow the routers interface specification as shown in Table 5-1.

**Table 5-1**   *Interfaces Required per Router*

| Router | Ethernet Interface | Serial Interface | BRI Interface | Voice | ATM Interface |
|---|---|---|---|---|---|
| R1 (2611) | 2 | 2 | - | - | - |
| R2 (3725) | 2 | 2 | - | - | - |
| R3 (2621) | 2 | 2 | 1 | 2 FXS | - |
| R4 (3640) | 1 | 2 | - | 2 FXS | - |
| R5 (2621) | 2 | 2 | 1 | - | - |
| R6 (3640) | 2 | 2 | - | | 1 |
| BB_Router (7200) | 2 | - | - | - | 1 |
| FR_SWITCH (4000) | - | 12 | - | - | - |

**NOTE**   Although you will be provided with fully meshed physical connectivity (LAN and WAN), you may not use all Routers or interfaces in all lab exercises. This is to optimize your setup for the next lab.

# Setting Up the Lab

Feel free to use any combination of routers as long as you fulfill the topology diagram as shown in Figure 5-1. It is not compulsory to use the same model of routers but this will make life easier should you like to load configurations directly from the CD-ROM into your own devices.

NOTE    If you have a mix of 10- and 100-Mbps Ethernet interfaces, adjust the bandwidth statements on the relevant interfaces to keep all interface speeds common. This will ensure that you do not get unwanted behavior because of differing IGP metrics.

You will find some routers using a mix of 10- and 100-Mbps Ethernet interfaces.

## Lab Topology

Practice Lab 5 will use the topology as outlined in Figure 5-1, which you will need to create using the switch, Frame Relay, ATM, and ISDN information that follows.

**Figure 5-1**    *Lab 5 Topology Diagram*

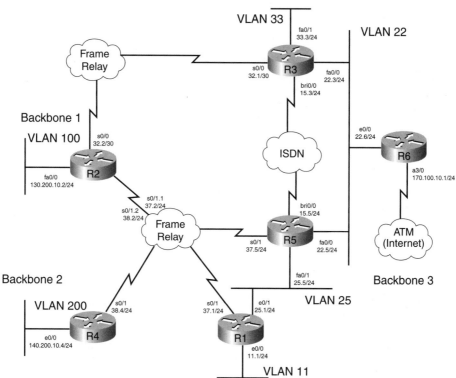

Network Topology
160.10.0.0

# Cabling Instructions

You will have all the router interfaces pre-cabled, although you will not be using all interfaces for the Lab 5 exercises. Table 5-2 documents the cabling instructions.

**Table 5-2**   *3550 Cabling Diagram*

| Interface | Switch-1 | Switch-2 |
|---|---|---|
| R1 e0/0 (2611) | fa0/1 | - |
| R1 e0/1(2611) | - | fa0/1 |
| R2 fa0/0 (3725) | fa0/2 | - |
| R2 fa0/1 (3725) | - | fa0/2 |
| R3 fa0/0 (2621) | fa0/3 | - |
| R3 fa0/1(2621) | - | fa0/3 |
| R4 e0/0 (3640) | fa0/4 | - |
| R5 fa0/0 (2621) | fa0/5 | - |
| R5 fa0/1(2621) | - | fa0/5 |
| R6 e0/0 (3640) | fa0/6 | - |
| R6 fa1/0 (3640) | - | fa0/6 |
| Backbone 1 | fa0/13 | - |
| Backbone 2 | - | fa0/13 |
| Trunk | fa0/15 | fa0/15 |
| Trunk | fa0/17 | fa0/17 |

# Frame Relay Switch Instructions

The Frame Relay switch is a 4000 router with 12 interfaces connecting all 6 core routers in a full mesh as shown in Table 5-3. Refer also to Figure 5-2 for the Frame Relay logical assignment and to the Frame Relay sample configuration from the CD-ROM.

**Table 5-3**   *Frame Relay Switch Physical Connectivity*

| Router/Interface | FR_Switch Interface |
|---|---|
| R1 s0/0 | Serial 0 |
| R1 s0/1 | Serial 1 |
| R2 s0/0 | Serial 2 |
| R2 s0/1 | Serial 3 |
| R3 s0/0 | Serial 4 |
| R3 s0/1 | Serial 5 |

**Table 5-3**    *Frame Relay Switch Physical Connectivity (Continued)*

| Router/Interface | FR_Switch Interface |
| --- | --- |
| R4 s0/0 | Serial 6 |
| R4 s0/1 | Serial 7 |
| R5 s0/0 | Serial 8 |
| R5 s0/1 | Serial 9 |
| R6 s0/0 | Serial 10 |
| R6 s0/1 | Serial 11 |

**Figure 5-2**    *Frame Relay Switch Logical Connectivity*

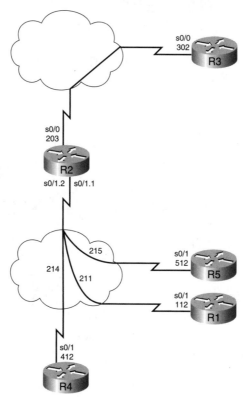

Frame Relay Setup
Frame Relay switch ports are DCE.
Routers ports are DTE.

Configure a 4000 router as a Frame Relay switch or equivalent that can provide the connectivity for this lab. The next five lab scenarios will use this topology as a reference.

Keep your DCE cables at the frame switch end for simplicity and provide a clock rate of 2 Mbps to all links. Should you require detailed information on how to configure one of your routers as a Frame Relay switch, this information can be found in Appendix A, "Frame Relay Switch Configuration" (and/or from the CD-ROM).

## ATM Switch Instructions

You will have a back-to-back connection between R6 and the backbone router using OC-3 Multimode connection, as shown in Figure 5-3.

**Figure 5-3** *ATM Physical Connectivity*

Figure 5-4 shows the logical setup for the ATM connection. You should always pay attention to the PVCs you are going to use because the PVC numbers might change in other lab exercises.

**Figure 5-4** *ATM Logical Connectivity*

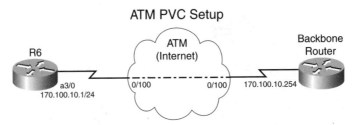

The ATM connectivity in Labs 5 and 6 will be provided by a back-to-back connection between R6 and BB_Router over E3 ATM interfaces. You could also use a Cisco Light-Stream (LS1010 Switch) if available. Configure the PVCs as requested during the lab exercise. If you are using a LightStream to provide your ATM connectivity and require information on how to set this up, this information can be found in Appendix B, "LS1010 ATM Switch Configuration."

## ISDN Instructions

Connect R3 and R5 into either ISDN lines or an ISDN simulator. It is preferable that the ISDN supports command-line interface (CLI). Reconfigure the numbers as required if you are using live ISDN lines (see Figure 5-5).

**Figure 5-5** *ISDN Connectivity*

## IP Address Instructions

Configure the IP addresses as shown in Figure 5-6.

**Figure 5-6** *IP Addressing Diagram*

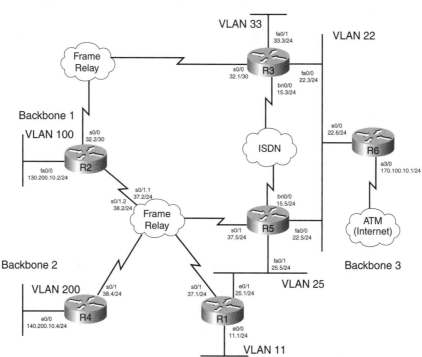

The CD-ROM includes initial configuration files for all routers and switches that include the basic IP addressing as shown in Figure 5-6. The initial configuration also includes the loopback interfaces.

# Pre-Lab Tasks

- Build the lab topology as per Figure 5-1 and Figure 5-2.

- Configure your chosen Frame Relay switch router to provide the necessary DLCIs as per Figure 5-2 and from the Frame Relay switch sample configuration file from the CD-ROM.

- Load the initial configuration files for this lab. The files will contain the basic IP addressing as referred to on Figure 5-6, hostnames have been configured and the line console and line vty pre-configured with the password **cisco**. These configurations are also on the CD-ROM.

- Get into a comfortable and quiet environment where you can focus for the next eight hours.

- Start you lab in the morning and be straight with the eight hour timeframe. Do not panic or give up if you feel you will not be able to complete the whole exercise. If it happens, use the remaining time as a "practice" to focus on the parts where you got into difficulty.

- Have available a Cisco Documentation CD-ROM or access online the latest documentation from the following URL: http//:www.cisco.com/univercd/home/home.htm.

---

**NOTE**     Consider accessing only the preceding URL, not the whole Cisco.com website. If you will be allowed to use documentation during your CCIE Lab Exam, it will be restricted.

---

- Go for a walk to relax before you get started.

# General Guidelines

- Please read the whole lab before you start.
- Do not configure any static/default routes unless otherwise specified/required.
- Use only the DLCIs and ATM PVCs provided in the appropriate figures.
- Follow the question instructions and requirements.
- Take a 30-minute break midway through the exercise.
- If you find yourself running out of time, choose questions that you are confident you can answer; failing this, choose questions with a higher point rating to maximize your potential score.

# Practice Lab 5

You will now be answering questions in relation to the network topology as shown in Figure 5-7.

**Figure 5-7**   *Lab 5 Topology and IP Addressing Diagram*

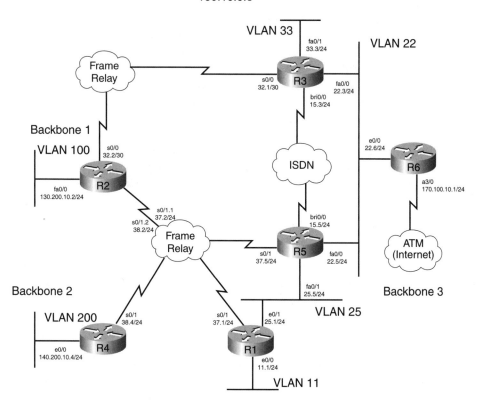

Network Topology
160.10.0.0

# Section 1: Bridging and Switching (18 Points)

## Section 1.1: Frame Relay Configuration (3 Points)

- Configure the Frame Relay portion of the network as shown in Figure 5-8 and ensure that only the PVCs illustrated in Figure 5-8 will be used. Use of dynamic PVCs is not permitted.
- You must use subinterfaces on R2 interface s0/1.
- Do not configure subinterfaces on any other routers.
- You must be able to ping across the Frame Relay cloud.

**Figure 5-8** *Frame Relay Diagram*

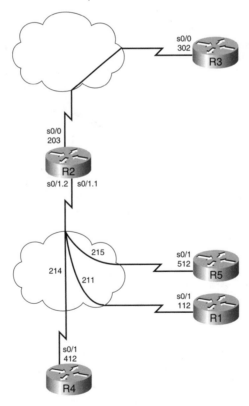

Frame Relay Setup
Frame Relay switch ports are DCE.
Routers ports are DTE.

# Section 1.2: 3550 LAN Switch Configuration (12 Points)

- Sw1 and Sw2 are connected via a crossover cable using ports fa0/15. Configure a Dot1q (801.1Q) trunk between Sw1 and Sw2.

- All Ethernet ports are pre-cabled as per Table 5-4. Note that not all ports will be used on this lab.

**Table 5-4**   *3550 Cabling Guide*

| Interface | Switch-1 | Switch-2 |
|-----------|----------|----------|
| R1 e0/0 (2611) | fa0/1 | - |
| R1 e0/1(2611) | - | fa0/1 |
| R2 fa0/0 (3725) | Fa0/2 | - |
| R2 fa0/1 (3725) | - | fa0/2 |
| R3 fa0/0 (2621) | fa0/3 | - |
| R3 fa0/1(2621) | - | fa0/3 |
| R4 e0/0 (3640) | fa0/4 | - |
| R5 fa0/0 (2621) | fa0/5 | - |
| R5 fa0/1(2621) | - | fa0/5 |
| R6 e0/0 (3640) | fa0/6 | - |
| R6 fa1/0 (3640) | - | fa0/6 |
| Backbone 1 | fa0/13 | - |
| Backbone 2 | - | fa0/13 |
| Trunk | fa0/15 | fa0/15 |
| Trunk | fa0/17 | fa0/17 |

- Configure the VLANs as follows:
    - VLAN_11: Connected to R1-e0/0 (VLAN_11)
    - VLAN_22: Connected to R3-fa0/0, R5-fa0/0, and R6-e0/0 (VLAN_22)
    - VLAN_25: Connected to R1-e0/1 and R5-fa0/1 (VLAN_25)
    - VLAN_33: Connected to R3-fa0/1 (VLAN_33)
    - VLAN_100: Connected to R2-fa0/0 and BB1_Router-e2/0 (VLAN_100)
    - VLAN_200: Connected to R4-e0/0 and BB2_Router-e2/4 (VLAN_200)
- Configure Sw1 to be the VTP server for the domain. Sw2 is a VTP client. Be sure that Sw2 can see the VLAN configuration from Sw1. The VTP domain name is "CCIE."

- Configure Sw1, using VLAN_11 with the IP address 160.10.11.10/24. After you have finished all tasks related to the IGP section, all routers on your topology should be able to ping Sw1 VLAN_11 interface. R1 should also be able to ping this interface. Sw1 will not participate on the IP routing.

- You are planning to connect your Sw2 to an external network and you are concerned about sending some of your network information through this port. Configure Sw2-fa0/18 to not send CDP advertisements to the remote side.

## Section 1.3: ATM Configuration (3 Points)

- Configure the ATM connection as shown in Figure 5-9.

- A PVC is configured between R6 and the backbone router. Do not configure subinterfaces.

- Use explicit address mapping. Do not depend on the remoter backbone router for inverse ARP.

- You must be able to ping the backbone router address 170.100.10.254.

**Figure 5-9** *ATM Diagram*

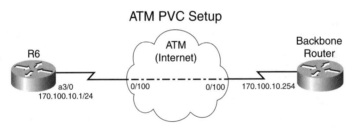

## Section 2: IP IGP Protocols (30 Points)

Configure the IP routing as illustrated in Figure 5-10, following the directions.

**Figure 5-10**  *IP IGP Diagram*

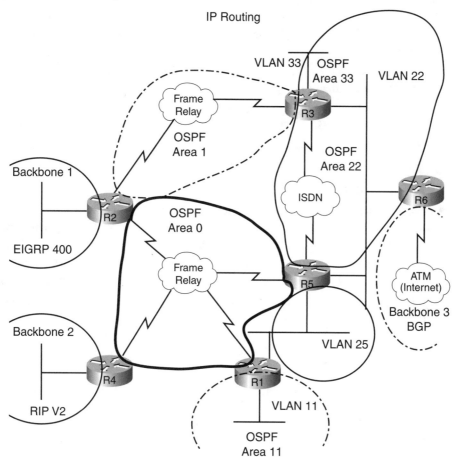

## Section 2.1: OSPF (10 Points)

- Configure OSPF according to Figure 5-10. R1-s0/1, R2-s0/1, R4-s0/1, and R5-s0/1 are to be part of the OSPF area 0.

- R2-s0/0 and R3-S0/0 are to be configured as OSPF area 1.

- R1-e0/0 is to be configured as OSPF area 11.

- R1-e0/1 and R5 fa0/1 are to be configured as OSPF area 25.

- Configure the loopback addresses to be part of the OSPF process.

- Make sure you are able to ping any OSPF interface from any router.

## Section 2.2: EIGRP (8 Points)

- Configure EIGRP between R2 and the BB1. R2-fa0/0 must be the only interface configured for EIGRP on R2. The R2 routing table should be populated with EIGRP routes from BB1.

- On R2, redistribute EIGRP into OSPF mutually. Make sure all routers have the EIGRP routes in their routing tables.

- Configure R2 to receive only advertisements from BB1 for networks 193.118.1.0, 193.118.2.0, and 193.118.3.0. Use a minimum number of commands to accomplish this task.

## Section 2.3: RIP (7 Points)

- Configure RIP between R4 and BB2. R4-e0/0 must be the only interface configured for RIP on R4. You should receive updates and R4 routing table will be populated with some RIP routes from BB2.

- Configure on R4 a filter that will allow only networks 196.1.2.0, 196.1.8.0, and 196.1.10.0 on R2 from BB2. Use an ACL with a minimal number of lines.

- Redistribute RIP into OSPF. Make sure all other routers have those three networks in their routing tables.

## Section 2.4: IS-IS (5 Points)

- Configure IS-IS according to Figure 5-10. R3-fa0/0, R3-fa0/1, R5-fa0/1, R6-e0/0, and the ISDN cloud are part of the IS-IS domain. Use area 49.0004 and only level 2 adjacencies.

- You should have the RT of all IS-IS routers populated with the IS-IS networks.

- You should be able to ping all interfaces of all routers under the IS-IS network.

- Redistribute IS-IS into OSPF on R5. In its routing table, R6 should see all routes from your topology.

# Section 3: BGP Protocol (12 Points)

- Configure EBGP between R6 and BB3. R6 will be AS 100 and the BB3 router AS is 300. R6 will receive updates for networks 200.20.X.0 and 198.18.X.0, where X is any number.

  See Figure 5-11.

**Figure 5-11**  *BGP Boundaries Between the Autonomous Systems*

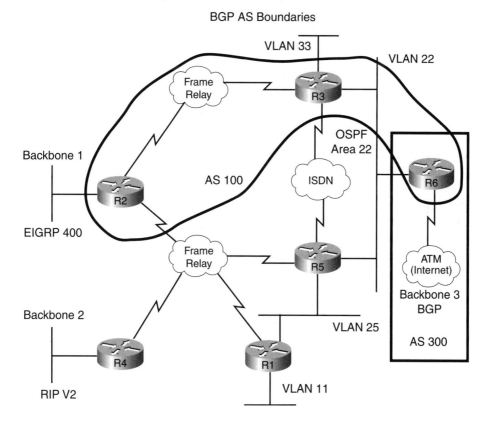

BGP AS Boundaries

- Configure IBGP between R2, R3, and R6; use AS 100. R2 should not peer direct to R6. R2 and R3 should be able to see all BGP BB3 routes in their routing tables. Refer to Figure 5-11. Use the loopbacks to make up your peers.
- Configure R2 such that all BGP routes learned from R3 will have weight 40000.

# Section 4: ISDN (6 Points)

- Configure ISDN on R3 and R5 using PPP. R3 and R5 should be able to ping each other across the ISDN link.
- Make sure that routing protocols will pass through the ISDN link only when it is up.
- The ISDN link should pass routing protocols when R5-fa0/0 goes down.

# Section 5: IP and IOS Features (10 Points)

- Configure R4 to reach (ping and Telnet) all other routers and Sw1 by using their hostnames.

- You have installed on VLAN_33 HP users that use HP Probe Proxy services. Configure R3 to provide this service to users on VLAN_33. Consider the server name HP_Probe and its IP address as 160.10.33.254.

- Configure R1 to be the TFTP server if you need to download IOS for R3 and R5, but only for requests coming from R3 and R5.

- Configure R3 such that if it fails to load the system file from Flash memory; R3 will load a system image from the network instead.

# Section 6: DLSw (4 Points)

- Configure DLSw between VLAN_11 and VLAN_33. Use FST encapsulation.

- You have some users exchanging data through your DLSw connection, but you do not want to compromise the IP traffic of others because DLSw is not your high priority. Configure your DLSw peers so they do not use more than 60 kbps as an average bit rate and set the maximum burst rate of 30 kbps.

- Configure R1 and R3 to not send UDP Unicast and to have the peers sending the resolution address via the existing FST connection.

# Section 7: QoS (6 Points)

- Configure a Traffic Class and apply it on incoming direction R6-E0/0, which will classify all BGP traffic and set IP precedence to immediate.

- Configure Committed Access Rate on R6-a3/0, so that web traffic will be sent but using IP precedence 5 for the web traffic that conforms to the first rate policy, and so that nonconforming web traffic will use the IP precedence 0 (best effort). Any remaining traffic is limited to 8 Mbps, with a normal burst size of 16,000 bytes and an Excess Burst size of 24,000 bytes. Traffic that conforms is sent with an IP precedence of 5. Traffic that does not conform should be dropped.

- Configure policy-based routing on R1 such that all packets with a source of 160.10.11.10 prefer a next-hop 160.10.5.5 address.

# Section 8: Multicast (6 Points)

- Configure Multicast PIM Sparse-mode on VLAN_22 to allow multicast traffic between R3, R5, and R6. Make R6 the rendezvous point.

- Configure Multicast Routing Monitor between R3, R5, and R6 with R6 as the Manager. Make R3 the "test sender" and R5 the "test receiver."

# Section 9: Security (8 Points)

- Configure a reflexive access list on R6 and apply it to the R6-a3/0 internal interface, allowing BGP and any other interesting traffic.

- Consider having a server with an IP address of 160.10.33.1 on VLAN_33 and configure R3 to intercept all TCP traffic to this server. Also, configure R3 to drop random connections.

- Configure Sw1-fa0/17 to allow only the host MAC address 0010.DE48.2223 to access the switch through this interface. If a security violation occurs, force the interface to go into restrict mode.

# Practice Lab 5: "Ask the Proctor"

This section should only be used if you require clues to complete the questions. In the real CCIE Lab, the proctor will not enter into any discussions regarding the questions or answers. He or she will be present to ensure you do not have problems with the lab environment, help you to clarify the questions, and to maintain the timing element of the exam.

## Section 1.1: Frame Relay Configuration

Q: Do I need to configure subinterfaces on R2?
A: Yes. The question says you must use subinterfaces on R2.

Q: I disable the inverse ARP but I still have other PVCs on my map.
A: There are some other procedures you may need to perform to have on your Frame Relay map only the PVCs you want.

Q: Do I need to be able to ping my own router interface?
A: No. We expect you to able to ping across the Frame Relay cloud.

## Section 1.2: 3550 LAN Switch Configuration

Q: Can I leave my switch ports in auto mode?
A: The questions do not specifically ask you to configure speed and duplex but you should do this to avoid any mismatches that could cause you problems.

Q: Should I name the VLANs as VLAN_11, and so on?
A: If the question named the VLANs, you should configure them as you see in the question.

Q: Should I be able to ping the switches loopback?
A: Unless you find a specific requirement on any question you are not required to accomplish this.

## Section 1.3: ATM Configuration

Q: What kind of subinterface do you want on R6?
A: The question states to not configure subinterfaces.

Q: What ATM encapsulation should I use?
A: This is a back-to-back configuration and the backbone is using the default encapsulation.

Q: Do you want me to configure "broadcast" under my ATM interfaces?
A: You need to determine what type of traffic/protocols will use the ATM network.

# Section 2.1: OSPF

Q: Can I use any OSPF process ID?
A: Yes.

Q: Can I configure "ip ospf network point-to-point"?
A: There is no specific requirement for what to use.

Q: In which OSPF area should I configure my loopback interfaces?
A: It is your choice.

Q: Do I need to able to ping all routers interfaces?
A: You should be able to ping all OSPF routers interfaces at that point.

# Section 2.2: EIGRP

Q: Can I configure any process ID for EIGRP?
A: Please refer to your IP routing diagram.

Q: Do I need to configure mutual redistribution between EIGRP and OSPF?
A: Please refer to your lab text. A mutual redistribution is not required.

# Section 2.3: RIP

Q: What RIP version do I need to configure, version 1 or 2?
A: Please refer to your IP IGP diagram. It is also part of your information. It is RIP version 2.

Q: Can I use the "passive-interface" command to make sure only R4-e0/0 will advertise RIP?
A: The exercise does not say you cannot use it, although you have a better way to solve this.

Q: I can configure three different solutions to achieve the filter part. Do you have a preference?
A: I do not have a preference. You can configure any solution because the criteria is matched.

# Section 2.4: IS-IS

Q: Can I configure any area for IS-IS?
A: No. You must refer to your text and your diagram for directions.

Q: Should I need to have connectivity to others routers from R6?
A: Yes. R6 routing table should have all networks. Also, consider R6 might need to be reachable by other later tasks on this exercises.

# Section 3: BGP Protocol

Q: Do I need to configure AS 100 on R6?

A: I suggest that you follow the lab text instructions. If it says AS 100, you should follow it.

Q: Should I use BGP Confederation or any other method?

A: You are requested to configure such, as R2 does not peer directly to R6. Confederations or another method will be acceptable.

Q: I have some IGP problems and not all of my routers can see all loopback interfaces, but my BGP is configured correctly. Will this be acceptable?

A: No, you must have an established TCP connection between your BGP peers in to receive full credit.

# Section 4: ISDN

Q: Are you asking me to configure "dialer-watch"?

A: To accomplish the requirement and make it stable, you need to decide what to configure.

Q: I cannot have any traffic at all passing through the ISDN link?

A: No. Traffic can only go through the ISDN link if R5 loses Fa0/0 interface connectivity.

Q: Should I configure any kind of authentication?

A: You are not required to do that. Sometimes you need a minimum configuration to have your basic ISDN working.

# Section 5: IP and IOS Features

Q: Should I configure the exactly hostnames to map?

A: Yes, you should use the exactly hostnames as your routers and switches have.

Q: Do I need to configure ARP proxy for the HP services?

A: You should configure everything to allow the services to work properly.

# Section 6: DLSw

Q: Can I configure my local peer as "Promiscuous"?
A: Well, you have basically only two peers.

Q: I still have my IGP problem. I think I configured the DLSW correctly. Will I still receive some credit?
A: Yes, you may receive some credit from those questions that do not require IGP connectivity.

# Section 7: QoS

Q: Along with IP traffic should I consider other traffic when configuring the queue?
A: Basically, you do not have any other kind of traffic above DLSw and IP.

Q: Are you asking that all incoming traffic on R1 must have as next-hop R5-Lo0?
A: Please refer to the question. It explicitly is saying a specific source address.

# Section 8: Multicast

Q: Do you want me to configure multicast on R3-fa0/1?
A: The question states only VLAN_22 be configured.

Q: Can I configure R3 as sender and R5 as receiver?
A: Yes, either way is fine because R6 is still the Manager.

# Section 9: Security

Q: Do you want me to configure a filter or allow specific traffic in?
A: You need to think and figure out what needs to be filtered and what traffic needs to be allowed.

Q: Are you talking about a MAC ACL to be configured and applied on Sw1-fa0/17?
A: No, you have a better way to accomplish this.

# Practice Lab 5 Debrief

The lab debrief section will now analyze each question showing you what was required and how to achieve the desired results. You should use this section to produce an overall score for your test.

# Section 1: Bridging and Switching (18 Points)

## Section 1.1: Frame Relay Configuration (3 Points)

- *Configure the Frame Relay portion of the network as shown in Figure 5-8 and ensure that only the PVCs illustrated in Figure 5-8 will be used. Use of dynamic PVCs is not permitted.*

The question clearly states that you must use only the PVCs as shown in Figure 5-8. You must, therefore, disable inverse ARP on the routers. It is good practice to ensure that all routers do not rely on inverse ARP so you should have configured **no frame-relay inverse-arp** under routers R1, R2, R3, R4, and R5 on their serial interfaces.

If you configured this correctly as shown in Example 5-1 through Example 5-5, you have scored 2 points.

- *You must use subinterfaces on R2 interface S0/1.*
- *Do NOT configure subinterfaces on any other routers.*
- *You must be able to ping across the Frame Relay cloud.*

R2 will be connecting to R1, R4, and R5. Notice that the subnet addresses between R2 and R4 are different. You should be able to ping across the Frame Relay cloud.

Example 5-1 through Example 5-10 show the Frame Relay configuration and Example 5-6 to Example 5-10, show the connectivity tests.

If you configured this correctly as shown in Example 5-6 through Example 5-10, you have scored 1 point

**NOTE**     When configuring the Frame Relay serial interfaces, it is a very good idea for you to shut down the interfaces while you are configuring. This procedure will ensure you do not have unexpected behavior because of dynamic maps, etc., although you have configured the **no frame-relay inverse-arp**. Another useful command is **clear frame-relay inarp interface,** which clears your inverse ARP entries from the map table.

**Example 5-1**   *R1 Initial Frame Relay Solution Configuration*

```
R1#show run int s0/1
Building configuration...
Current configuration : 285 bytes
!
interface Serial0/1
 ip address 160.10.37.1 255.255.255.0
 encapsulation frame-relay
 frame-relay map ip 160.10.37.2 112 broadcast
 frame-relay map ip 160.10.37.5 112 broadcast
 no frame-relay inverse-arp
 frame-relay lmi-type ansi
end
R1#
```

**Example 5-2**   *R2 Initial Frame Relay Solution Configuration*

```
R2#show run int s0/0
Building configuration...
Current configuration : 193 bytes
!
interface Serial0/0
 ip address 160.10.32.2 255.255.255.252
 encapsulation frame-relay
 frame-relay map ip 160.10.32.1 203 broadcast
 no frame-relay inverse-arp
 frame-relay lmi-type ansi
end
R2#
R2#show run int s0/1
Building configuration...
Current configuration : 285 bytes
!
interface Serial0/1
 no ip address
 encapsulation frame-relay
 no frame-relay inverse-arp
 frame-relay lmi-type ansi
end
!
interface Serial0/1.1 multipoint
 ip address 160.10.37.2 255.255.255.0
```

*continues*

**Example 5-2** *R2 Initial Frame Relay Solution Configuration*

```
 frame-relay map ip 160.10.37.1 211 broadcast
 frame-relay map ip 160.10.37.5 215 broadcast
 end
!
R2#sh run int s0/1.2
Building configuration...
Current configuration : 117 bytes
!
interface Serial0/1.2 point-to-point
 ip address 160.10.38.2 255.255.255.0
 frame-relay interface-dlci 214
end
R2#
```

**Example 5-3** *R3 Initial Frame Relay Solution Configuration*

```
R3#show run int s0/0
Building configuration...
Current configuration : 193 bytes
!
interface Serial0/0
 ip address 160.10.32.1 255.255.255.252
 encapsulation frame-relay
 frame-relay map ip 160.10.32.2 302 broadcast
 no frame-relay inverse-arp
 frame-relay lmi-type ansi
end
R3#
```

**Example 5-4** *R4 Initial Frame Relay Solution Configuration*

```
R4#show run int s0/1
Building configuration...
Current configuration : 285 bytes
!
interface Serial0/1
 ip address 160.10.38.4 255.255.255.0
 encapsulation frame-relay
 frame-relay map ip 160.10.38.2 412 broadcast
 no frame-relay inverse-arp
 frame-relay lmi-type ansi
end
R4#
```

**Example 5-5** *R5 Initial Frame Relay Solution Configuration*

```
R5#show run int s0/1
Building configuration...
Current configuration : 285 bytes
```

**Example 5-5**    *R5 Initial Frame Relay Solution Configuration (Continued)*

```
!
interface Serial0/1
 ip address 160.10.37.5 255.255.255.0
 encapsulation frame-relay
 frame-relay map ip 160.10.37.1 512 broadcast
 frame-relay map ip 160.10.37.2 512 broadcast
 no frame-relay inverse-arp
 frame-relay lmi-type ansi
end
R5#
```

**Example 5-6**    *R1 show Commands and Pings to Verify Functionality*

```
R1#show fram map
Serial0/1 (up): ip 160.10.37.2 dlci 112(0x70,0x1C00), static,
                broadcast,
                CISCO, status defined, active
Serial0/1 (up): ip 160.10.37.5 dlci 112(0x70,0x1C00), static,
                broadcast,
                CISCO, status defined, active
R1#
R1#ping 160.10.37.2
Type escape sequence to abort.
Sending 5, 100-byte ICMP Echos to 160.10.37.2, timeout is 2 seconds:
!!!!!
Success rate is 100 percent (5/5), round-trip min/avg/max = 1/2/4 ms
R1#ping 160.10.37.5
Type escape sequence to abort.
Sending 5, 100-byte ICMP Echos to 160.10.37.5, timeout is 2 seconds:
!!!!!
Success rate is 100 percent (5/5), round-trip min/avg/max = 4/5/8 ms
R1#
```

**Example 5-7**    *R2 show Commands and Pings to Verify Functionality*

```
R2#show fram map
Serial0/0 (up): ip 160.10.32.1 dlci 203(0xCB,0x30B0), static,
                broadcast,
                CISCO, status defined, active
Serial0/1.1 (up): ip 160.10.37.1 dlci 211(0xD3,0x3430), static,
                broadcast,
                CISCO, status defined, active
Serial0/1.1 (up): ip 160.10.37.5 dlci 215(0xD7,0x3470), static,
                broadcast,
                CISCO, status defined, active
Serial0/1.2 (up): point-to-point dlci, dlci 214(0xD6,0x3460), broadcast
            status defined, active
R2#
R2#
R2#ping 160.10.32.1
Type escape sequence to abort.
```

*continues*

**Example 5-7** *R2* **show** *Commands and Pings to Verify Functionality (Continued)*

```
Sending 5, 100-byte ICMP Echos to 160.10.32.1, timeout is 2 seconds:
!!!!!
Success rate is 100 percent (5/5), round-trip min/avg/max = 1/3/4 ms
R2#ping 160.10.37.1
Type escape sequence to abort.
Sending 5, 100-byte ICMP Echos to 160.10.37.1, timeout is 2 seconds:
!!!!!
Success rate is 100 percent (5/5), round-trip min/avg/max = 1/3/4 ms
R2#ping 160.10.37.5
Type escape sequence to abort.
Sending 5, 100-byte ICMP Echos to 160.10.37.5, timeout is 2 seconds:
!!!!!
Success rate is 100 percent (5/5), round-trip min/avg/max = 1/2/4 ms
R2#
R2#ping 160.10.38.4
Type escape sequence to abort.
Sending 5, 100-byte ICMP Echos to 160.10.38.4, timeout is 2 seconds:
!!!!!
Success rate is 100 percent (5/5), round-trip min/avg/max = 1/3/4 ms
```

**Example 5-8** *R3* **show** *Commands and Pings to Verify Functionality*

```
R3#show fram map
Serial0/0 (up): ip 160.10.32.2 dlci 302(0x12E,0x48E0), static,
                broadcast,
                CISCO, status defined, active
R3#ping 160.10.32.2
Type escape sequence to abort.
Sending 5, 100-byte ICMP Echos to 160.10.32.2, timeout is 2 seconds:
!!!!!
Success rate is 100 percent (5/5), round-trip min/avg/max = 1/3/4 ms
R3#
```

**Example 5-9** *R4* **show** *Commands and Pings to Verify Functionality*

```
R4#show fram map
Serial0/1 (up): ip 160.10.38.2 dlci 412(0x19C,0x64C0), static,
                broadcast,
                CISCO, status defined, active
R4#
R4#ping 160.10.38.2
Type escape sequence to abort.
Sending 5, 100-byte ICMP Echos to 160.10.38.2, timeout is 2 seconds:
!!!!!
Success rate is 100 percent (5/5), round-trip min/avg/max = 4/6/8 ms
R4#
```

**Example 5-10**  *R5* **show** *Commands and Pings to Verify Functionality*

```
R5#show fram map
R5#sh fram map
Serial0/1 (up): ip 160.10.37.1 dlci 512(0x200,0x8000), static,
              broadcast,
              CISCO, status defined, active
Serial0/1 (up): ip 160.10.37.2 dlci 512(0x200,0x8000), static,
              broadcast,
              CISCO, status defined, active R5#
R5#ping 160.10.37.1
Type escape sequence to abort.
Sending 5, 100-byte ICMP Echos to 160.10.37.1, timeout is 2 seconds:
!!!!!
Success rate is 100 percent (5/5), round-trip min/avg/max = 4/6/8 ms
R5#ping 160.10.37.2
Type escape sequence to abort.
Sending 5, 100-byte ICMP Echos to 160.10.37.2, timeout is 2 seconds:
!!!!!
Success rate is 100 percent (5/5), round-trip min/avg/max = 1/3/4 ms
R5#
```

# Section 1.2: 3550 LAN Switch Configuration (12 Points)

- *Sw1 and Sw2 are connected via a crossover cable using ports fa0/15. Configured a Dot1q (801.1Q) trunk between Sw1 and Sw2.*

This is a basic trunk configuration. Example 5-11 and Example 5-13, show the trunk configuration. Example 5-13 tells you through the show commands the verification. If you configured this correctly as shown in Example 5-11 through Example 5-13, you have scored 2 points.

**Example 5-11**  *3550 Sw1 Initial Trunk Configuration*

```
Sw1#show run int fa0/15
Building configuration...
Current configuration : 108 bytes
!
interface FastEthernet0/15
 switchport trunk encapsulation dot1q
 switchport mode trunk
 no ip address
end
Sw1#
```

**Example 5-12**  *3550 Sw2 Initial Trunk Configuration*

```
Sw2#show run int fa0/15
Building configuration...
Current configuration : 108 bytes
!
interface FastEthernet0/15
 switchport trunk encapsulation dot1q
```

*continues*

**Example 5-12** *3550 Sw2 Initial Trunk Configuration (Continued)*

```
 switchport mode trunk
 no ip address
end
Sw2
```

**Example 5-13** *3550 Sw1 and Sw2 **show** Command Output to Verify Configuration and Functionality*

```
Sw1#show int trunk
Port      Mode        Encapsulation  Status       Native vlan
Fa0/15    on          802.1q         trunking     1
Port      Vlans allowed on trunk
Fa0/15    1-4094
Port      Vlans allowed and active in management domain
Fa0/15    1
Port      Vlans in spanning tree forwarding state and not pruned
Fa0/15    1
Sw1#
Sw2#show int trunk
Port      Mode        Encapsulation  Status       Native vlan
Fa0/15    on          802.1q         trunking     1
Port      Vlans allowed on trunk
Fa0/15    1-4094
Port      Vlans allowed and active in management domain
Fa0/15    1
Port      Vlans in spanning tree forwarding state and not pruned
Fa0/15    1
Sw2#
```

- *All Ethernet ports are precabled as per Table 5-4. Note that not all ports will be used on this lab.*

- *Configure the VLANs as follows:*

    — *VLAN_11: Connected to R1-e0/0 (VLAN_11)*

    — *VLAN_22: Connected to R3-fa0/0, R5-fa0/0, and R6-e0/0 (VLAN_22)*

    — *VLAN_25: Connected to R1-e0/1 and R5-fa0/1 (VLAN_25)*

    — *VLAN_33: Connected to R3-fa0/1 (VLAN_33)*

    — *VLAN_100: Connected to R2-fa0/0 and BB1_Router-e2/0 (VLAN_100)*

    — *VLAN_200: Connected to R4-e0/0 and BB2_Router-e2/4 (VLAN_200)*

If you configured this correctly as shown in Example 5-14, you have scored 3 points.

- *Configure Sw1 to be the VTP server for the domain. Sw2 is a VTP client. Be sure that Sw2 can see the VLAN configuration from Sw1. The VTP domain name is "CCIE."*

If you configured this correctly as shown in Example 5-14, you have scored 3 points.

**NOTE**    The VLAN configuration is completed under **Vlan database.**

**Example 5-14**  *3550 Sw1 and Sw2 VLAN and VTP Configuration*

```
Sw1#show vlan brief
VLAN Name                             Status     Ports
---- ------------------------------   --------   ------------------------------
1    default                          active     Fa0/7, Fa0/8, Fa0/9, Fa0/10
                                                 Fa0/11, Fa0/12, Fa0/14, Fa0/16
                                                 Fa0/17, Fa0/18, Fa0/19, Fa0/20
                                                 Fa0/21, Fa0/22, Fa0/23, Fa0/24
                                                 Gi0/1, Gi0/2
11   VLAN_11                          active     Fa0/1
22   VLAN_22                          active     Fa0/3, Fa0/5, Fa0/6
25   VLAN_25                          active
33   VLAN_33                          active
100  VLAN_100                         active     Fa0/2, Fa0/13
200  VLAN_200                         active     Fa0/4
1002 fddi-default                     active
1003 token-ring-default               active
1004 fddinet-default                  active
1005 trnet-default                    active
Sw1#
```

```
Sw2#show vlan brief
VLAN Name                             Status     Ports
---- ------------------------------   --------   ------------------------------
1    default                          active     Fa0/2, Fa0/4, Fa0/6, Fa0/7
                                                 Fa0/8, Fa0/9, Fa0/10, Fa0/11
                                                 Fa0/12, Fa0/14, Fa0/16, Fa0/17
                                                 Fa0/18, Fa0/19, Fa0/20, Fa0/21
                                                 Fa0/22, Fa0/23, Fa0/24, Gi0/1
                                                 Gi0/2
11   VLAN_11                          active
22   VLAN_22                          active
25   VLAN_25                          active     Fa0/1, Fa0/5
33   VLAN_33                          active     Fa0/3
100  VLAN_100                         active
200  VLAN_200                         active     Fa0/13
1002 fddi-default                     active
1003 token-ring-default               active
1004 fddinet-default                  active
1005 trnet-default                    active
Sw2#
```

```
Sw1#
Sw1#show vtp stat
VTP Version                     : 2
Configuration Revision          : 1
Maximum VLANs supported locally : 1005
Number of existing VLANs        : 11
VTP Operating Mode              : Server
```

*continues*

**Example 5-14** *3550 Sw1 and Sw2 VLAN and VTP Configuration (Continued)*

```
VTP Domain Name              : CCIE
VTP Pruning Mode             : Disabled
VTP V2 Mode                  : Disabled
VTP Traps Generation         : Disabled
MD5 digest                   : 0x36 0xC9 0xB9 0x93 0x5C 0xE6 0x7B 0x1D
Configuration last modified by 160.10.7.7 at 3-19-93 04:55:23
Local updater ID is 160.10.11.10 on interface Vl11 (lowest numbered VLAN interface
found)
Sw1#
```
```
Sw2#show vtp stat
VTP Version                  : 2
Configuration Revision       : 1
Maximum VLANs supported locally : 1005
Number of existing VLANs     : 11
VTP Operating Mode           : Client
VTP Domain Name              : CCIE
VTP Pruning Mode             : Disabled
VTP V2 Mode                  : Disabled
VTP Traps Generation         : Disabled
MD5 digest                   : 0x36 0xC9 0xB9 0x93 0x5C 0xE6 0x7B 0x1D
Configuration last modified by 160.10.7.7 at 3-19-93 04:55:23
Sw2#
```

**NOTE**    The VTP domain name must be called CCIE. It needs to be exactly as the question is asking
for.

- *Configure Sw1, using VLAN_11 with the IP address 160.10.11.10/24. After you have
  finished all tasks related to the IGP section, all routers on your topology should be
  able to ping Sw1 VLAN_11 interface. R1 should also be able to ping this interface.
  Sw1 will not participate on the IP routing.*

If you configured this correctly as shown in Example 5-15, you have scored 2 points.

Example 5-15 shows the Sw1 virtual interface configuration and Example 5-16 shows the
connectivity test.

**Example 5-15** *3550 Sw1 Management Interface Configuration*

```
Sw1#
Sw1#show run int vlan 11
Building configuration...
Current configuration : 63 bytes
!
interface Vlan11
 ip address 160.10.11.10 255.255.255.0
!
!
ip default-gateway 160.10.11.1
```

NOTE    In this moment, Sw1 will be able to ping only the directly connected interfaces on R1 (R1-e0/0, R1-s0/1 and R1-lo0). In fact, you are not required to reach the switches from other routers.

**Example 5-16**  *3550 Sw1 Management Interface Output Verification*

```
Sw1#ping 160.10.11.1
! R1-E0/0
Type escape sequence to abort.
Sending 5, 100-byte ICMP Echos to 160.10.11.1, timeout is 2 seconds:
!!!!!
Success rate is 100 percent (5/5), round-trip min/avg/max = 1/2/4 ms
Sw1#
Sw1#ping 160.10.1.1
! R1-Loopback 0

Type escape sequence to abort.
Sending 5, 100-byte ICMP Echos to 160.10.1.1, timeout is 2 seconds:
!!!!!
Success rate is 100 percent (5/5), round-trip min/avg/max = 1/2/4 ms

Sw1#
Sw1#ping 160.10.37.1
! R1-S0/0
Type escape sequence to abort.
Sending 5, 100-byte ICMP Echos to 160.10.1.1, timeout is 2 seconds:
!!!!!
Success rate is 100 percent (5/5), round-trip min/avg/max = 1/2/4 ms
Sw1#
```

- *You are planning to connect your Sw2 to an external network and you are concerned about sending some of your network information through this port. Configure Sw2-fa0/18 to not send CDP advertisements to the remote side.*

If you configured this correctly as shown in Example 5-17, you have scored 2 points.

Example 5-17 shows the necessary configuration to disable the CDP protocol.

**Example 5-17**  *3550 Sw1 Secondary Root Configuration and Verification*

```
Sw1#sh cdp interface fa0/18
! Before to disable CDP
FastEthernet0/18 is down, line protocol is down
  Encapsulation ARPA
  Sending CDP packets every 60 seconds
  Holdtime is 180 seconds
!
Sw1# sh run int fa0/18
Building configuration...
```

*continues*

**Example 5-17** *3550 Sw1 Secondary Root Configuration and Verification (Continued)*

```
Current configuration : 64 bytes
!
interface FastEthernet0/18
 no ip address
 no cdp enable
end
Sw1#sh cdp interface fa0/18
! After to disable CDP
! No output
Sw1#
```

# Section 1.3: ATM Configuration (3 Points)

- *Configure the ATM connection as shown in Figure 5-9.*

- *A PVC is configured between R6 and the backbone router. Do not configure subinterfaces.*

- *Use explicit address mapping. Do not depend on the remoter backbone router for inverse ARP.*

- *You must be able to ping the backbone router address 170.100.10.254.*

If you configured this correctly as shown in Example 5-18 you have scored 3 points.

Example 5-18 shows the ATM PVC configuration as well as the connectivity test to the backbone router.

**Example 5-18** *R6 ATM Configuration, Map Verification, and Access to Backbone Router*

```
R6#show run int a3/0
Building configuration...
Current configuration : 140 bytes
!
interface ATM3/0
 ip address 170.100.10.1 255.255.255.0
 no atm ilmi-keepalive
 pvc 0/100
  protocol ip 170.100.10.254 broadcast
 !
end
R6#ping 170.100.10.254
Type escape sequence to abort.
Sending 5, 100-byte ICMP Echos to 170.100.10.254, timeout is 2 seconds:
!!!!!
Success rate is 100 percent (5/5), round-trip min/avg/max = 1/2/4 ms
R6#sh atm vc
            VCD /                              Peak  Avg/Min Burst
Interface   Name     VPI  VCI  Type  Encaps  SC  Kbps  Kbps    Cells  Sts
3/0         3         0   100  PVC   SNAP    UBR 155000               UP
R6#
```

# Section 2: IP IGP Protocols (30 Points)

Configure the IP routing as illustrated in Figure 5-10, following the directions.

## Section 2.1: OSPF (10 Points)

- *Configure OSPF according to Figure 5-10. R1-s0/1, R2-s0/1, R4-s0/1, and R5-s0/1 are to be part of the OSPF area 0.*
- *R2-s0/0 and R3-s0/0 are to be configured as OSPF area 1.*
- *R1-e0/0 is to be configured as OSPF area 11.*
- *R1-e0/1 and R5 fa0/1 are to be configured as OSPF area 25.*

If you configured this correctly as shown in Example 5-19 through Example 5-23, you have scored 5 points.

- *Configure the loopback addresses to be part of the OSPF process*

If you configured this correctly as shown in Example 5-19 through Example 5-23, you have scored 3 points.

- *Make sure you are able to ping any OSPF interface from any router.*

If you configured this correctly as shown in Example 5-19 through Example 5-23, you have scored 2 points.

This is a basic OSPF configuration. The idea is to make you more familiar with the OSPF configuration to go to a more complex environment in the next Lab exercise Chapter 6 "Practice Lab 6."

Although the question did not specify how the Loopback masks should appear up on the OSPF routing tables, the following examples show the Loopback address configured with **ip ospf network point-to-point** so the address mask will shown up as /24. Without this, commands the address will show up as /32.

Also, an important thing to observe is that you do not need any virtual link because all ABR routers are connected to area 0.

**Example 5-19**  *OSPF Configuration: R1 Output*

```
R1#show run
interface Loopback0
 ip address 160.10.1.1 255.255.255.0
 ip ospf network point-to-point
!
interface Ethernet0/0
 ip address 160.10.11.1 255.255.255.0
 half-duplex
!
interface Ethernet0/1
 ip address 160.10.25.1 255.255.255.0
!
```

*continues*

**Example 5-19** *OSPF Configuration: R1 Output (Continued)*

```
interface Serial0/1
 ip address 160.10.37.1 255.255.255.0
 encapsulation frame-relay
 ip ospf network point-to-multipoint
 !
router ospf 1
 log-adjacency-changes
 network 160.10.1.0 0.0.0.255 area 0
 network 160.10.11.0 0.0.0.255 area 11
 network 160.10.25.0 0.0.0.255 area 25
 network 160.10.37.0 0.0.0.255 area 0
 !
 !
R1#show ip route ospf
     160.10.0.0/16 is variably subnetted, 12 subnets, 3 masks
O        160.10.37.5/32 [110/128] via 160.10.37.2, 00:06:04, Serial0/1
O IA     160.10.32.0/30 [110/128] via 160.10.37.2, 00:06:04, Serial0/1
O        160.10.38.0/24 [110/128] via 160.10.37.2, 00:06:04, Serial0/1
O        160.10.37.2/32 [110/64] via 160.10.37.2, 00:06:04, Serial0/1
O        160.10.2.0/24 [110/65] via 160.10.37.2, 00:06:04, Serial0/1
O IA     160.10.3.0/24 [110/129] via 160.10.37.2, 00:06:04, Serial0/1
O        160.10.4.0/24 [110/129] via 160.10.37.2, 00:06:04, Serial0/1
O        160.10.5.0/24 [110/129] via 160.10.37.2, 00:06:04, Serial0/1
R1#
```

**Example 5-20** *OSPF Configuration: R2 Output*

```
R2#show run
interface Loopback0
 ip address 160.10.2.2 255.255.255.0
 ip ospf network point-to-point
 !
interface Serial0/0
 ip address 160.10.32.2 255.255.255.252
 encapsulation frame-relay
 ip ospf network point-to-point
 !
interface Serial0/1
  no ip address
 encapsulation frame-relay
 no frame-relay inverse-arp
 frame-relay lmi-type ansi
 !
interface Serial0/1.1 multipoint
 ip address 160.10.37.2 255.255.255.0
 ip ospf network point-to-multipoint
 !
interface Serial0/1.2 point-to-point
 ip address 160.10.38.2 255.255.255.0
 ip ospf network point-to-point
 !
```

**Example 5-20**  *OSPF Configuration: R2 Output (Continued)*

```
router ospf 1
 log-adjacency-changes
network 160.10.2.0 0.0.0.255 area 0
network 160.10.32.0 0.0.0.3 area 1
network 160.10.37.0 0.0.0.255 area 0
network 160.10.38.0 0.0.0.255 area 0
!
R2#sh ip route ospf
     160.10.0.0/16 is variably subnetted, 12 subnets, 3 masks
O        160.10.37.5/32 [110/64] via 160.10.37.5, 00:10:50, Serial0/1.1
O        160.10.37.1/32 [110/64] via 160.10.37.1, 00:10:50, Serial0/1.1
O IA     160.10.11.0/24 [110/74] via 160.10.37.1, 00:10:50, Serial0/1.1
O        160.10.3.0/24 [110/65] via 160.10.32.1, 00:26:12, Serial0/0
O        160.10.1.0/24 [110/65] via 160.10.37.1, 00:10:50, Serial0/1.1
O        160.10.4.0/24 [110/65] via 160.10.38.4, 00:10:50, Serial0/1.2
O        160.10.5.0/24 [110/65] via 160.10.37.5, 00:10:50, Serial0/1.1
O IA     160.10.25.0/24 [110/65] via 160.10.37.5, 00:10:50, Serial0/1.1
R2#
```

**Example 5-21**  *OSPF Configuration: R3 Output*

```
R3#show run
interface Loopback0
 ip address 160.10.3.3 255.255.255.0
 ip ospf network point-to-point
!
interface Serial0/0
 ip address 160.10.32.1 255.255.255.252
 encapsulation frame-relay
 ip ospf network point-to-point
 !

router ospf 1
 log-adjacency-changes

network 160.10.3.0 0.0.0.255 area 1
  network 160.10.32.0 0.0.0.3 area 1
!
R3#show ip route ospf
     160.10.0.0/16 is variably subnetted, 14 subnets, 3 masks
O IA     160.10.37.5/32 [110/128] via 160.10.32.2, 00:14:22, Serial0/0
O IA     160.10.38.0/24 [110/128] via 160.10.32.2, 00:29:43, Serial0/0
O IA     160.10.37.2/32 [110/64] via 160.10.32.2, 00:29:43, Serial0/0
O IA     160.10.37.1/32 [110/128] via 160.10.32.2, 00:29:43, Serial0/0
O IA     160.10.11.0/24 [110/138] via 160.10.32.2, 00:29:43, Serial0/0
O IA     160.10.2.0/24 [110/65] via 160.10.32.2, 00:29:43, Serial0/0
O IA     160.10.1.0/24 [110/129] via 160.10.32.2, 00:29:43, Serial0/0
O IA     160.10.4.0/24 [110/129] via 160.10.32.2, 00:26:13, Serial0/0
O IA     160.10.5.0/24 [110/129] via 160.10.32.2, 00:14:22, Serial0/0
O IA     160.10.25.0/24 [110/129] via 160.10.32.2, 00:14:22, Serial0/0
R3#
```

**Example 5-22** *OSPF Configuration: R4 Output*

```
R4#show run
interface Loopback0
 ip address 160.10.4.4 255.255.255.0
 ip ospf network point-to-point
!
interface Serial0/1
 ip address 160.10.38.4 255.255.255.0
 encapsulation frame-relay
 ip ospf network point-to-point
 !
router ospf 1
 log-adjacency-changes
 network 160.10.4.0 0.0.0.255 area 0
 network 160.10.37.0 0.0.0.255 area 0
!

R4#show ip route ospf
     160.10.0.0/16 is variably subnetted, 12 subnets, 3 masks
O       160.10.37.5/32 [110/128] via 160.10.38.2, 00:16:34, Serial0/1
O IA    160.10.32.0/30 [110/128] via 160.10.38.2, 00:16:34, Serial0/1
O       160.10.37.2/32 [110/64] via 160.10.38.2, 00:16:34, Serial0/1
O       160.10.37.1/32 [110/128] via 160.10.38.2, 00:16:34, Serial0/1
O IA    160.10.11.0/24 [110/138] via 160.10.38.2, 00:16:34, Serial0/1
O       160.10.2.0/24 [110/65] via 160.10.38.2, 00:16:34, Serial0/1
O IA    160.10.3.0/24 [110/129] via 160.10.38.2, 00:16:34, Serial0/1
O       160.10.1.0/24 [110/129] via 160.10.38.2, 00:16:34, Serial0/1
O       160.10.5.0/24 [110/129] via 160.10.38.2, 00:16:34, Serial0/1
O IA    160.10.25.0/24 [110/129] via 160.10.38.2, 00:16:34, Serial0/1
R4#
```

**Example 5-23** *OSPF Configuration: R5 Output*

```
R5#show run
interface Loopback0
 ip address 160.10.5.5 255.255.255.0
 ip ospf network point-to-point
!
!
interface Serial0/1
 ip address 160.10.37.5 255.255.255.0
 encapsulation frame-relay
 ip ospf network point-to-multipoint
 !
router ospf 1
 log-adjacency-changes

 network 160.10.5.0 0.0.0.255 area 0
  network 160.10.37.0 0.0.0.255 area 0
!
R5#show ip route ospf
     160.10.0.0/16 is variably subnetted, 13 subnets, 3 masks
```

**Example 5-23**  *OSPF Configuration: R5 Output (Continued)*

```
O IA    160.10.32.0/30 [110/128] via 160.10.37.2, 00:19:24, Serial0/1
O       160.10.38.0/24 [110/128] via 160.10.37.2, 00:19:24, Serial0/1
O       160.10.37.2/32 [110/64] via 160.10.37.2, 00:19:24, Serial0/1
O       160.10.37.1/32 [110/128] via 160.10.37.2, 00:19:24, Serial0/1
O IA    160.10.11.0/24 [110/138] via 160.10.37.2, 00:19:24, Serial0/1
O       160.10.2.0/24 [110/65] via 160.10.37.2, 00:19:24, Serial0/1
O IA    160.10.3.0/24 [110/129] via 160.10.37.2, 00:19:24, Serial0/1
O       160.10.1.0/24 [110/129] via 160.10.37.2, 00:19:24, Serial0/1
O       160.10.4.0/24 [110/129] via 160.10.37.2, 00:19:24, Serial0/1
R5
```

# Section 2.2: EIGRP (8 Points)

- *Configure EIGRP between R2 and the BB1. R2-fa0/0 must be the only interface configured for EIGRP on R2. The R2 routing table should be populated with EIGRP routes from BB1.*

If you configured this correctly as shown in Example 5-24, you have scored 3 points.

- *On R2, redistribute EIGRP into OSPF mutually. Make sure all routers have the EIGRP routes in their routing tables.*

If you configured this correctly as shown in Example 5-24, you have scored 3 points.

This is a basic setup to have R2 receiving EIGRP routes from BB1. An important thing is to observe the EIGRP AS number is given in the IP IGP diagram in Figure 5-10. You must follow it. Pay attention when configuring the redistribution to explore the **redistribute** command to make sure no networks will be missing.

Example 5-24 shows the necessary commands to configure the question's requirement as well as the output from the R2 and BB_Router routing tables.

**NOTE**    To have R2 to advertise the OSPF networks to BB1, you need to configure under the EIGRP process the network 160.10.0.0 or the redistribution of OSPF into EIGRP.

**Example 5-24**  *R2 Output: EIGRP Configuration*

```
R2#sh run | b router eigrp
router eigrp 400
 redistribute ospf 1 metric 100 10 255 255 1500

 network 130.200.10.0 0.0.0.255
no auto-summary
 no eigrp log-neighbor-changes
!
!
```

*continues*

**Example 5-24** *R2 Output: EIGRP Configuration (Continued)*

```
router ospf 1
 redistribute eigrp 400 metric 100 subnets
!
R2#show ip route eigrp
     50.0.0.0/24 is subnetted, 1 subnets
D       50.5.5.0 [90/156160] via 130.200.10.200, 00:12:53, FastEthernet0/0
D    193.118.9.0/24 [90/156160] via 130.200.10.200, 00:12:53, FastEthernet0/0
D    193.118.8.0/24 [90/156160] via 130.200.10.200, 00:12:53, FastEthernet0/0
D    193.118.10.0/24 [90/156160] via 130.200.10.200, 00:12:53, FastEthernet0/0
D    193.118.5.0/24 [90/156160] via 130.200.10.200, 00:12:53, FastEthernet0/0
D    193.118.4.0/24 [90/156160] via 130.200.10.200, 00:12:53, FastEthernet0/0
D    193.118.7.0/24 [90/156160] via 130.200.10.200, 00:12:53, FastEthernet0/0
     40.0.0.0/24 is subnetted, 1 subnets
D       40.4.4.0 [90/156160] via 130.200.10.200, 00:12:53, FastEthernet0/0
D    193.118.6.0/24 [90/156160] via 130.200.10.200, 00:12:53, FastEthernet0/0
D    193.118.1.0/24 [90/156160] via 130.200.10.200, 00:12:53, FastEthernet0/0
D    193.118.3.0/24 [90/156160] via 130.200.10.200, 00:12:53, FastEthernet0/0
D    193.118.2.0/24 [90/156160] via 130.200.10.200, 00:12:53, FastEthernet0/0
R2#
!
!
! R5 Routing table has the backbone EIGRP routes
R5#show ip route ospf | I E2
! R5 has the EIGRP Backbone routes as External "E2"
50.0.0.0/24 is subnetted, 1 subnets
O E2    50.5.5.0 [110/100] via 160.10.37.2, 00:27:34, Serial0/1
O E2 193.118.9.0/24 [110/100] via 160.10.37.2, 00:27:34, Serial0/1
O E2 193.118.8.0/24 [110/100] via 160.10.37.2, 00:27:34, Serial0/1
O E2 193.118.10.0/24 [110/100] via 160.10.37.2, 00:27:34, Serial0/1
O E2 193.118.5.0/24 [110/100] via 160.10.37.2, 00:27:34, Serial0/1
O E2 193.118.4.0/24 [110/100] via 160.10.37.2, 00:27:34, Serial0/1

O E2 193.118.7.0/24 [110/100] via 160.10.37.2, 00:27:36, Serial0/1
     40.0.0.0/24 is subnetted, 1 subnets
O E2    40.4.4.0 [110/100] via 160.10.37.2, 00:27:36, Serial0/1
     130.200.0.0/24 is subnetted, 1 subnets
O E2    130.200.10.0 [110/100] via 160.10.37.2, 00:27:36, Serial0/1
O E2 193.118.6.0/24 [110/100] via 160.10.37.2, 00:27:36, Serial0/1
O E2 193.118.1.0/24 [110/100] via 160.10.37.2, 00:27:37, Serial0/1
O E2 193.118.3.0/24 [110/100] via 160.10.37.2, 00:27:37, Serial0/1
O E2 193.118.2.0/24 [110/100] via 160.10.37.2, 00:27:37, Serial0/1
R5#
!
! BB_ROUTER Routing table has the OSPF routes or 160.10.0.0 subnets
BB_ROUTER#sh ip ro eigrp
     160.10.0.0/16 is variably subnetted, 12 subnets, 3 masks
D EX    160.10.37.5/32 [170/25628160] via 130.200.10.2, 00:00:06, Ethernet2/0
D       160.10.32.0/30 [90/2195456] via 130.200.10.2, 00:10:10, Ethernet2/0
D       160.10.38.0/24 [90/2195456] via 130.200.10.2, 00:10:10, Ethernet2/0
D EX    160.10.37.1/32 [170/25628160] via 130.200.10.2, 00:00:06, Ethernet2/0
D       160.10.37.0/24 [90/2195456] via 130.200.10.2, 00:10:10, Ethernet2/0
D EX    160.10.11.0/24 [170/25628160] via 130.200.10.2, 00:00:06, Ethernet2/0
```

**Example 5-24**  *R2 Output: EIGRP Configuration (Continued)*

```
D        160.10.2.0/24 [90/409600] via 130.200.10.2, 00:10:10, Ethernet2/0
D EX     160.10.3.0/24 [170/25628160] via 130.200.10.2, 00:00:06, Ethernet2/0
D EX     160.10.1.0/24 [170/25628160] via 130.200.10.2, 00:00:06, Ethernet2/0
D EX     160.10.4.0/24 [170/25628160] via 130.200.10.2, 00:00:06, Ethernet2/0
D EX     160.10.5.0/24 [170/25628160] via 130.200.10.2, 00:00:06, Ethernet2/0
D EX     160.10.25.0/24 [170/25628160] via 130.200.10.2, 00:00:06, Ethernet2/0
BB_ROUTER#
```

- *Configure R2 to receive only advertisements from BB1 for networks 193.118.1.0, 193.118.2.0, and 193.118.3.0. Use a minimum number of commands to accomplish this task.*

If you configured this correctly as shown in Example 5-25, you have scored 2 points.

You can accomplish this using a minimum number of commands by using a one-line access list manipulating the wildcard bits and applying with a distribute list.

Example 5-25 shows the access list and the distribute list configurations and the updated routing table after the commands have been applied.

**Example 5-25**  *EIGRP Filter Configuration on R2*

```
R2#sh run | b router eigrp
router eigrp 400
 distribute-list 1 in FastEthernet0/0
 no auto-summary
 no eigrp log-neighbor-changes!
!
access-list 1 permit 193.118.0.0 0.0.3.255
!
! R2 EIGRP Routing table has only the 3 networks
R2#sh ip ro eigrp
D    193.118.1.0/24 [90/156160] via 130.200.10.200, 00:10:29, FastEthernet0/0
D    193.118.3.0/24 [90/156160] via 130.200.10.200, 00:10:29, FastEthernet0/0
D    193.118.2.0/24 [90/156160] via 130.200.10.200, 00:10:29, FastEthernet0/0
R2#
```

# Section 2.3: RIP (7 Points)

- *Configure RIP between R4 and BB2. R4-e0/0 must be the only interface configured for RIP on R4. You should receive updates and R4 routing table will be populated with some RIP routes from BB2.*

If you configured this correctly as shown in Example 5-26, you have scored 3 points.

- *Configure on R4 a filter that will allow only networks 196.1.2.0, 196.1.8.0, and 196.1.10.0 on R2 from BB2. Use an ACL with a minimal number of lines.*

If you configured this correctly as shown in Example 5-26, you have scored 2 points.

- *Redistribute RIP into OSPF. Make sure all other routers have those three networks in their routing tables.*

If you configured this correctly as shown in Example 5-26, you have scored 2 points.

RIP V.2 is running on BB2 and advertising routes to R4. A filter and redistribution into OSPF is used to accomplish this task. Here we are also exercising the possibilities of wildcard mask.

**Example 5-26** *R4 Output: RIP Configuration*

```
R4#sh run ¦ b router rip
router rip
 version 2
 network 140.200.0.0
 distribute-list 1 in Ethernet0/0
 no auto-summary
!
access-list 1 permit 196.1.0.0 0.0.10.255
!
!
R4#sh run ¦ b router
router ospf 1
 log-adjacency-changes
 redistribute rip metric 1 subnets
!
! R4 RIP Routing table before filter. All RIP routes from the Backbone
R4#show ip route rip
R     196.1.8.0/24 [120/1] via 140.200.10.200, 00:00:00, Ethernet0/0
R     196.1.9.0/24 [120/1] via 140.200.10.200, 00:00:00, Ethernet0/0
R     196.1.10.0/24 [120/1] via 140.200.10.200, 00:00:00, Ethernet0/0
R     20.0.0.0/8 [120/1] via 140.200.10.200, 00:00:00, Ethernet0/0
R     196.1.1.0/24 [120/1] via 140.200.10.200, 00:00:00, Ethernet0/0
R     196.1.2.0/24 [120/1] via 140.200.10.200, 00:00:00, Ethernet0/0
R     196.1.3.0/24 [120/1] via 140.200.10.200, 00:00:00, Ethernet0/0
R     196.1.4.0/24 [120/1] via 140.200.10.200, 00:00:00, Ethernet0/0
R     196.1.5.0/24 [120/1] via 140.200.10.200, 00:00:00, Ethernet0/0
R     196.1.6.0/24 [120/1] via 140.200.10.200, 00:00:00, Ethernet0/0
R     196.1.7.0/24 [120/1] via 140.200.10.200, 00:00:00, Ethernet0/0
R     30.0.0.0/8 [120/1] via 140.200.10.200, 00:00:00, Ethernet0/0
R4#
!
! R4 RIP Routing table after filter be configured
R4#
R4#show ip route rip
R     196.1.8.0/24 [120/1] via 140.200.10.200, 00:00:27, Ethernet0/0
R     196.1.10.0/24 [120/1] via 140.200.10.200, 00:00:27, Ethernet0/0
R     196.1.2.0/24 [120/1] via 140.200.10.200, 00:00:27, Ethernet0/0
R4#
!
!
! R5 OSPF Routing table has also the 3 RIP networks
```

**Example 5-26**  *R4 Output: RIP Configuration (Continued)*

```
R5# sh ip ro ospf | incl 196
O E2 196.1.8.0/24 [110/1] via 160.10.37.2, 00:00:47, Serial0/1
O E2 196.1.10.0/24 [110/1] via 160.10.37.2, 00:00:47, Serial0/1
O E2 196.1.2.0/24 [110/1] via 160.10.37.2, 00:00:47, Serial0/1
R5#
```

# Section 2.4: IS-IS (5 Points)

- *Configure IS-IS according to Figure 5-10. R3-fa0/0, R3-fa0/1, R5-fa0/1, R6-e0/0 and the ISDN cloud are part of the IS-IS domain. Use area 49.0004 and only level 2 adjacencies.*

- *You should have the RT of all IS-IS routers populated with the IS-IS networks.*

- *You should be able to ping all interfaces of all routers under the IS-IS network.*

If you configured this correctly as shown in Example 5-27, you have scored 3 points.

- *Redistribute IS-IS into OSPF on R5. In its routing table, R6 should see all routes from your topology.*

If you configured this correctly as shown in Example 5-27, you have scored 2 points.

This is a basic IS-IS configuration into a single area. It is a good idea to configure your R6-loopback address under IS-IS because R6 is running only IS-IS, and you might need later to have R6-lo0 be reachable.

Example 5-27 shows the IS-IS configuration, and the important commands to enable the IS-IS are also highlighted. Notice you need to add the **ip router isis** command to the router interfaces and the **isis circuit-type** command also to the interfaces that are participating on the IS-IS process. The **clns routing** command is not necessary if you do not have CLNS traffic. You are configuring here to show the behavior under the ISDN scenario later. Also, an alternative solution to configure the circuit-type desired is on the IS-IS routing process instead of to the interface. To redistribute IS-IS into OSPF on R5, use the **redistribute connected** command within the OSPF process to force advertisement of the 160.10.22.0/24 network into OSPF.

**Example 5-27**  *IS-IS Configuration and Output from R3, R5, and R6*

```
R3#sh run
Building configuration...
Current configuration : 1614 bytes
!
hostname R3
!


!
interface FastEthernet0/0
 ip address 160.10.22.3 255.255.255.0
 ip router isis
```

*continues*

**Example 5-27** *IS-IS Configuration and Output from R3, R5, and R6 (Continued)*

```
 isis circuit-type level-2-only
 !
 !
interface BRI0/0
 ip address 160.10.15.3 255.255.255.0
 ip router isis
 isis circuit-type level-2-only
 !
interface FastEthernet0/1
 ip address 160.10.33.3 255.255.255.0
 ip router isis
 isis circuit-type level-2-only
 !
router isis
 net 49.0004.0000.0000.0003.00
 !
 !
end
R3#
R3#sh isis topology
IS-IS paths to level-1 routers
System Id          Metric  Next-Hop          Interface  SNPA
R3                 --  ➔No Level-1 routers ←
IS-IS paths to level-2 routers
System Id          Metric  Next-Hop          Interface  SNPA
R3                 --
R5                 10      R5                Fa0/0      0009.43a7.34c0
R6                 10      R6                Fa0/0      0004.9a67.3f41
R3#
```
```
R5#sh run
Building configuration...
Current configuration : 1751 bytes
!
hostname R5
!
no ip domain-lookup
!
!
interface FastEthernet0/0
 ip address 160.10.22.5 255.255.255.0
 ip router isis
 isis circuit-type level-2-only
 !
interface BRI0/0
 ip address 160.10.15.5 255.255.255.0
 ip router isis
 isis circuit-type level-2-only
 !
 !
router ospf 1
 log-adjacency-changes
```

**Example 5-27**  *IS-IS Configuration and Output from R3, R5, and R6 (Continued)*

```
 redistribute connected metric 100 subnets
 redistribute isis level-2 metric 100 subnets
!
router isis
 net 49.0004.0000.0000.0005.00
 redistribute ospf 1 metric 10
!
R5#
R5#sh isis topology
IS-IS paths to level-1 routers
System Id                 Metric  Next-Hop          Interface   SNPA
R5                          - -
! No level-1 routers
IS-IS paths to level-2 routers
System Id                 Metric  Next-Hop          Interface   SNPA
R3                          10      R3                Fa0/0       0009.43a7.3520
R5                          - -
R6                          10      R6                Fa0/0       0004.9a67.3f41
R5#
R6#sh run
Building configuration...
Current configuration : 1372 bytes
!
!
hostname R6
!
interface Loopback0
 ip address 160.10.6.6 255.255.255.0
 ip router isis
 isis circuit-type level-2-only
!
interface Ethernet0/0
 ip address 160.10.22.6 255.255.255.0
 ip router isis
 isis circuit-type level-2-only
!
!
router isis
 net 49.0004.0000.0000.0006.00
!
R6#sh isis topology
IS-IS paths to level-1 routers
System Id                 Metric  Next-Hop          Interface   SNPA
R6                          - -
! No level-1 routers
IS-IS paths to level-2 routers
System Id                 Metric  Next-Hop          Interface   SNPA
R3                          10      R3                Et0/0       0009.43a7.3520
R5                          10      R5                Et0/0       0009.43a7.34c0
R6                          - -
R6#
R6#sh ip route
```

*continues*

**Example 5-27** *IS-IS Configuration and Output from R3, R5, and R6 (Continued)*

```
! R6 has all OSPF networks within its routing table
Codes: C - connected, S - static, I - IGRP, R - RIP, M - mobile, B - BGP
       D - EIGRP, EX - EIGRP external, O - OSPF, IA - OSPF inter area
       N1 - OSPF NSSA external type 1, N2 - OSPF NSSA external type 2
       E1 - OSPF external type 1, E2 - OSPF external type 2, E - EGP
       i - IS-IS, L1 - IS-IS level-1, L2 - IS-IS level-2, ia - IS-IS inter area
       * - candidate default, U - per-user static route, o - ODR
       P - periodic downloaded static route
Gateway of last resort is not set
i L2 196.1.8.0/24 [115/20] via 160.10.22.5, Ethernet0/0
     170.100.0.0/24 is subnetted, 1 subnets
C       170.100.10.0 is directly connected, ATM3/0
i L2 196.1.10.0/24 [115/20] via 160.10.22.5, Ethernet0/0
     140.200.0.0/24 is subnetted, 1 subnets
i L2    140.200.10.0 [115/20] via 160.10.22.5, Ethernet0/0
     160.10.0.0/16 is variably subnetted, 15 subnets, 3 masks
i L2    160.10.32.0/30 [115/20] via 160.10.22.5, Ethernet0/0
i L2    160.10.33.0/24 [115/20] via 160.10.22.3, Ethernet0/0
i L2    160.10.38.0/24 [115/20] via 160.10.22.5, Ethernet0/0
i L2    160.10.37.2/32 [115/20] via 160.10.22.5, Ethernet0/0
i L2    160.10.37.1/32 [115/20] via 160.10.22.5, Ethernet0/0
i L2    160.10.37.0/24 [115/20] via 160.10.22.5, Ethernet0/0
i L2    160.10.11.0/24 [115/20] via 160.10.22.5, Ethernet0/0
i L2    160.10.2.0/24 [115/20] via 160.10.22.5, Ethernet0/0
i L2    160.10.3.0/24 [115/20] via 160.10.22.5, Ethernet0/0
i L2    160.10.1.0/24 [115/20] via 160.10.22.5, Ethernet0/0
C       160.10.6.0/24 is directly connected, Loopback0
i L2    160.10.4.0/24 [115/20] via 160.10.22.5, Ethernet0/0
i L2    160.10.5.0/24 [115/20] via 160.10.22.5, Ethernet0/0
i L2    160.10.25.0/24 [115/20] via 160.10.22.5, Ethernet0/0
C       160.10.22.0/24 is directly connected, Ethernet0/0
i L2 196.1.2.0/24 [115/20] via 160.10.22.5, Ethernet0/0
     130.200.0.0/24 is subnetted, 1 subnets
i L2    130.200.10.0 [115/20] via 160.10.22.5, Ethernet0/0
i L2 193.118.1.0/24 [115/20] via 160.10.22.5, Ethernet0/0
i L2 193.118.3.0/24 [115/20] via 160.10.22.5, Ethernet0/0
i L2 193.118.2.0/24 [115/20] via 160.10.22.5, Ethernet0/0
R6#
R6#ping 160.10.5.5
Type escape sequence to abort.
Sending 5, 100-byte ICMP Echos to 160.10.5.5, timeout is 2 seconds:
!!!!!
Success rate is 100 percent (5/5), round-trip min/avg/max = 1/2/4 ms
R6#
R6#
R6#ping 160.10.2.2

Type escape sequence to abort.
Sending 5, 100-byte ICMP Echos to 160.10.2.2, timeout is 2 seconds:
!!!!!
Success rate is 100 percent (5/5), round-trip min/avg/max = 4/4/4 ms
R6#
```

# Section 3: BGP (12 Points)

- *Configure EBGP between R6 and BB3. R6 will be AS 100 and the BB3 router AS is
  300. R6 will receive updates for networks 200.20.X.0 and 198.18.X.0, where X is any
  number.*

If you configured this correctly as shown in Example 5-28, you have scored 6 points.

The EBGP configuration on R6 is a simple task. Again, you will need the basic BGP
concepts to accomplish this.

Example 5-28 shows the BGP configuration on R6. The **no synchronization** command that
you might see referred to a lot of times makes routes not synchronized between BGP and
IGP protocols. This way, the IGP will carry fewer routes and allow BGP to converge
quickly.

**Example 5-28**  *R6 EBGP Configuration*

```
R6#show run | b router bgp
router bgp 100
 no synchronization
 neighbor 170.100.10.254 remote-as 300
!
!
R6#show ip bgp
BGP table version is 141, local router ID is 170.100.10.1
Status codes: s suppressed, d damped, h history, * valid, > best, i - internal
Origin codes: i - IGP, e - EGP, ? - incomplete
   Network          Next Hop            Metric LocPrf Weight Path
*> 198.18.1.0       170.100.10.254           0             0 300 i
*> 198.18.2.0       170.100.10.254           0             0 300 i
*> 198.18.3.0       170.100.10.254           0             0 300 i
*> 198.18.4.0       170.100.10.254           0             0 300 i
*> 198.18.5.0       170.100.10.254           0             0 300 i
*> 198.18.6.0       170.100.10.254           0             0 300 i
*> 198.18.7.0       170.100.10.254           0             0 300 i
*> 198.18.8.0       170.100.10.254           0             0 300 i
*> 198.18.9.0       170.100.10.254           0             0 300 i
*> 198.18.10.0      170.100.10.254           0             0 300 i
*> 200.20.1.0       170.100.10.254           0             0 300 i
*> 200.20.2.0       170.100.10.254           0             0 300 i
*> 200.20.3.0       170.100.10.254           0             0 300 i
*> 200.20.4.0       170.100.10.254           0             0 300 i
*> 200.20.5.0       170.100.10.254           0             0 300 i
*> 200.20.6.0       170.100.10.254           0             0 300 i
*> 200.20.7.0       170.100.10.254           0             0 300 i
*> 200.20.8.0       170.100.10.254           0             0 300 i
*> 200.20.9.0       170.100.10.254           0             0 300 i
*> 200.20.10.0      170.100.10.254           0             0 300 i
R6#
```

- *Configure IBGP between R2, R3, and R6; use AS 100. R2 should not peer direct to R6. R2 and R3 should be able to see all BGP BB3 routes in their routing tables. Refer to Figure 5-11. Use the loopbacks to make up your peers.*

If you configured this correctly as shown in Example 5-29, you have scored 3 points.

You can choose either Confederations or Router-Reflectors to accomplish this task. The solution demonstrated here shows a solution using Router-Reflectors.

**Example 5-29** *R2, R3, and R6 IBGP Configuration*

```
R2#show run ¦ b router bgp

router bgp 100
 no synchronization
 bgp log-neighbor-changes
 neighbor 160.10.3.3 remote-as 100
 neighbor 160.10.3.3 update-source Loopback0
 no auto-summary
!
R2#show ip bgp sum
! R2 peer only with R3

BGP router identifier 160.10.2.2, local AS number 100
BGP table version is 21, main routing table version 21
20 network entries using 2020 bytes of memory
20 path entries using 960 bytes of memory
1 BGP path attribute entries using 60 bytes of memory
1 BGP rrinfo entries using 24 bytes of memory
1 BGP AS-PATH entries using 24 bytes of memory
0 BGP route-map cache entries using 0 bytes of memory
0 BGP filter-list cache entries using 0 bytes of memory
BGP using 3088 total bytes of memory
BGP activity 20/0 prefixes, 20/0 paths, scan interval 60 secs
Neighbor        V    AS MsgRcvd MsgSent   TblVer  InQ OutQ Up/Down  State/PfxRcd
160.10.3.3      4   100      30      29       21    0    0 00:12:14        20
R2#
!
R2#sh ip bgp
BGP table version is 21, local router ID is 160.10.2.2
Status codes: s suppressed, d damped, h history, * valid, > best, i - internal,
              r RIB-failure, S Stale
Origin codes: i - IGP, e - EGP, ? - incomplete
   Network          Next Hop            Metric LocPrf Weight Path
*>i198.18.1.0       160.10.6.6               0    100      0 300 i
*>i198.18.2.0       160.10.6.6               0    100      0 300 i
*>i198.18.3.0       160.10.6.6               0    100      0 300 i
*>i198.18.4.0       160.10.6.6               0    100      0 300 i
*>i198.18.5.0       160.10.6.6               0    100      0 300 i
*>i198.18.6.0       160.10.6.6               0    100      0 300 i
*>i198.18.7.0       160.10.6.6               0    100      0 300 i
*>i198.18.8.0       160.10.6.6               0    100      0 300 i
*>i198.18.9.0       160.10.6.6               0    100      0 300 i
*>i198.18.10.0      160.10.6.6               0    100      0 300 i
```

**Example 5-29**  *R2, R3, and R6 IBGP Configuration (Continued)*

```
*>i200.20.1.0      160.10.6.6            0    100    0 300 i
*>i200.20.2.0      160.10.6.6            0    100    0 300 i
*>i200.20.3.0      160.10.6.6            0    100    0 300 i
*>i200.20.4.0      160.10.6.6            0    100    0 300 i
*>i200.20.5.0      160.10.6.6            0    100    0 300 i
*>i200.20.6.0      160.10.6.6            0    100    0 300 i
*>i200.20.7.0      160.10.6.6            0    100    0 300 i
   Network         Next Hop        Metric LocPrf Weight Path
*>i200.20.8.0      160.10.6.6            0    100    0 300 i
*>i200.20.9.0      160.10.6.6            0    100    0 300 i
*>i200.20.10.0     160.10.6.6            0    100    0 300 i
R2#
!
R3#show run | b router bgp
router bgp 100
 no synchronization
 bgp log-neighbor-changes
 neighbor 160.10.2.2 remote-as 100
 neighbor 160.10.2.2 update-source Loopback0
 neighbor 160.10.2.2 route-reflector-client
neighbor 160.10.6.6 remote-as 100
 neighbor 160.10.6.6 update-source Loopback0!
 !
R3#show ip bgp sum

BGP router identifier 160.10.3.3, local AS number 100
BGP table version is 21, main routing table version 21
20 network entries using 1940 bytes of memory
20 path entries using 720 bytes of memory
1 BGP path attribute entries using 60 bytes of memory
1 BGP AS-PATH entries using 24 bytes of memory
0 BGP route-map cache entries using 0 bytes of memory
0 BGP filter-list cache entries using 0 bytes of memory
BGP using 2744 total bytes of memory
BGP activity 40/20 prefixes, 40/20 paths, scan interval 60 secs
Neighbor        V    AS MsgRcvd MsgSent   TblVer  InQ OutQ Up/Down  State/PfxRcd
160.10.2.2      4   100      31      32       21    0    0 00:14:54           0
160.10.6.6      4   100      33      30       21    0    0 00:13:55          20
R3#
!
R3#sh ip bgp
BGP table version is 21, local router ID is 160.10.3.3
Status codes: s suppressed, d damped, h history, * valid, > best, i - internal
Origin codes: i - IGP, e - EGP, ? - incomplete
   Network         Next Hop        Metric LocPrf Weight Path
*>i198.18.1.0      160.10.6.6            0    100    0 300 i
*>i198.18.2.0      160.10.6.6            0    100    0 300 i
*>i198.18.3.0      160.10.6.6            0    100    0 300 i
*>i198.18.4.0      160.10.6.6            0    100    0 300 i
*>i198.18.5.0      160.10.6.6            0    100    0 300 i
*>i198.18.6.0      160.10.6.6            0    100    0 300 i
*>i198.18.7.0      160.10.6.6            0    100    0 300 i
```

*continues*

**Example 5-29** *R2, R3, and R6 IBGP Configuration (Continued)*

```
 *>i198.18.8.0      160.10.6.6             0    100      0 300 i
 *>i198.18.9.0      160.10.6.6             0    100      0 300 i
 *>i198.18.10.0     160.10.6.6             0    100      0 300 i
 *>i200.20.1.0      160.10.6.6             0    100      0 300 i
 *>i200.20.2.0      160.10.6.6             0    100      0 300 i
 *>i200.20.3.0      160.10.6.6             0    100      0 300 i
 *>i200.20.4.0      160.10.6.6             0    100      0 300 i
 *>i200.20.5.0      160.10.6.6             0    100      0 300 i
 *>i200.20.6.0      160.10.6.6             0    100      0 300 i
 *>i200.20.7.0      160.10.6.6             0    100      0 300 i
 *>i200.20.8.0      160.10.6.6             0    100      0 300 i
    Network         Next Hop            Metric LocPrf Weight Path
 *>i200.20.9.0      160.10.6.6             0    100      0 300 i
 *>i200.20.10.0     160.10.6.6             0    100      0 300 i
R3#
!
R6#show run | b router bgp
router bgp 100
 no synchronization
 bgp log-neighbor-changes
 neighbor 160.10.3.3 remote-as 100
 neighbor 160.10.3.3 update-source Loopback0

 neighbor 160.10.3.3 next-hop-self
 neighbor 170.100.10.254 remote-as 300
!
R6#show ip bgp sum

R6#
BGP router identifier 160.10.6.6, local AS number 100
BGP table version is 21, main routing table version 21
20 network entries using 1940 bytes of memory
20 path entries using 720 bytes of memory
1 BGP path attribute entries using 60 bytes of memory
1 BGP AS-PATH entries using 24 bytes of memory
0 BGP route-map cache entries using 0 bytes of memory
0 BGP filter-list cache entries using 0 bytes of memory
BGP using 2744 total bytes of memory
BGP activity 20/0 prefixes, 20/0 paths, scan interval 60 secs
Neighbor        V    AS MsgRcvd MsgSent   TblVer  InQ OutQ Up/Down  State/PfxRcd
160.10.3.3      4   100      33      36       21    0    0 00:16:01        0
170.100.10.254  4   300      38      37       21    0    0 00:33:36       20
R6#
R6#
!
R6#sh ip bgp
BGP table version is 21, local router ID is 160.10.6.6
Status codes: s suppressed, d damped, h history, * valid, > best, i - internal
Origin codes: i - IGP, e - EGP, ? - incomplete
    Network         Next Hop            Metric LocPrf Weight Path
 *> 198.18.1.0      170.100.10.254         0              0 300 i
 *> 198.18.2.0      170.100.10.254         0              0 300 i
```

**Example 5-29**  *R2, R3, and R6 IBGP Configuration (Continued)*

```
*> 198.18.3.0      170.100.10.254          0        0 300 i
*> 198.18.4.0      170.100.10.254          0        0 300 i
*> 198.18.5.0      170.100.10.254          0        0 300 i
*> 198.18.6.0      170.100.10.254          0        0 300 i
*> 198.18.7.0      170.100.10.254          0        0 300 i
*> 198.18.8.0      170.100.10.254          0        0 300 i
*> 198.18.9.0      170.100.10.254          0        0 300 i
*> 198.18.10.0     170.100.10.254          0        0 300 i
*> 200.20.1.0      170.100.10.254          0        0 300 i
*> 200.20.2.0      170.100.10.254          0        0 300 i
*> 200.20.3.0      170.100.10.254          0        0 300 i
*> 200.20.4.0      170.100.10.254          0        0 300 i
*> 200.20.5.0      170.100.10.254          0        0 300 i
*> 200.20.6.0      170.100.10.254          0        0 300 i
*> 200.20.7.0      170.100.10.254          0        0 300 i
*> 200.20.8.0      170.100.10.254          0        0 300 i
   Network          Next Hop           Metric LocPrf Weight Path
*> 200.20.9.0      170.100.10.254          0        0 300 i
*> 200.20.10.0     170.100.10.254          0        0 300 i
R6#
```

- *Configure R2 such that all BGP routes learned from R3 will have weight 40000.*

If you configured this correctly as shown in Example 5-30, you have scored 3 points.

This can be accomplished configuring the **neighbor weight** command or you can also use a route map.

**Example 5-30**  *R2 Weight Configuration*

```
R2#
R2#show run ¦ b router bgp

router bgp 100
 no synchronization
 bgp log-neighbor-changes
 neighbor 160.10.3.3 remote-as 100
 neighbor 160.10.3.3 update-source Loopback0
 neighbor 160.10.3.3 weight 40000
 no auto-summary!
!

R2#sh ip bgp
BGP table version is 21, local router ID is 160.10.2.2
Status codes: s suppressed, d damped, h history, * valid, > best, i - internal,
              r RIB-failure, S Stale
Origin codes: i - IGP, e - EGP, ? - incomplete
   Network          Next Hop           Metric LocPrf Weight Path
*>i198.18.1.0       160.10.6.6              0     100  40000 300 i
*>i198.18.2.0       160.10.6.6              0     100  40000 300 i
*>i198.18.3.0       160.10.6.6              0     100  40000 300 i
*>i198.18.4.0       160.10.6.6              0     100  40000 300 i
```

*continues*

**Example 5-30** *R2 Weight Configuration (Continued)*

```
*>i198.18.5.0      160.10.6.6            0   100   40000 300 i
*>i198.18.6.0      160.10.6.6            0   100   40000 300 i
*>i198.18.7.0      160.10.6.6            0   100   40000 300 i
*>i198.18.8.0      160.10.6.6            0   100   40000 300 i
*>i198.18.9.0      160.10.6.6            0   100   40000 300 i
*>i198.18.10.0     160.10.6.6            0   100   40000 300 i
*>i200.20.1.0      160.10.6.6            0   100   40000 300 i
*>i200.20.2.0      160.10.6.6            0   100   40000 300 i
*>i200.20.3.0      160.10.6.6            0   100   40000 300 i
*>i200.20.4.0      160.10.6.6            0   100   40000 300 i
*>i200.20.5.0      160.10.6.6            0   100   40000 300 i
*>i200.20.6.0      160.10.6.6            0   100   40000 300 i
*>i200.20.7.0      160.10.6.6            0   100   40000 300 i
   Network         Next Hop        Metric LocPrf Weight Path
*>i200.20.8.0      160.10.6.6            0   100   40000 300 i
*>i200.20.9.0      160.10.6.6            0   100   40000 300 i
*>i200.20.10.0     160.10.6.6            0   100   40000 300 i
R2#
```

# Section 4: ISDN (6 Points)

- *Configure ISDN on R3 and R5 using PPP. R3 and R5 should be able to ping each other across the ISDN link.*

If you configured this correctly as shown in Example 5-31, you have scored 2 points.

- *Make sure that routing protocols will pass through the ISDN link only when it is up.*

If you configured this correctly as shown in Example 5-31, you have scored 2 points.

The key to configuring as requested is to avoid the ISDN to advertise or pass traffic through the link when R5-fa0/0 is up. R3 and R5 are running CLNS, which makes the scenario even more interesting. Remember that your ISDN or BRI interfaces are running IS-IS.

Example 5-31 shows the comfiguration to accomplish the ISDN requirements. To make your ISDN work in some IOS versions, you need to configure the authentication "CHAP" or "PAP"; in other IOS versions, you do not need to configure the authentication to have your ISDN link work (for example, 12.2). IOS Release 12.2 is the assumed version here used to configure an authentication method.

**Example 5-31** *R3 and R5 ISDN Configuration*

```
R3#sh run int bri0/0
Building configuration...
Current configuration : 340 bytes
!
username R5 password 0 cisco
!
interface BRI0/0
 ip address 160.10.15.3 255.255.255.0
```

**Example 5-31**  *R3 and R5 ISDN Configuration (Continued)*

```
 ip router isis
 encapsulation ppp
 dialer map clns 49.0004.0000.0000.0005.00 name R5 broadcast 2222
 dialer map ip 160.10.15.5 name R5 broadcast 2222
 dialer-group 1
 isdn switch-type basic-ni
 isdn spid1 1111
 ppp authentication chap
 isis circuit-type level-2-only
!
!
dialer-list 1 protocol ip permit
dialer-list 1 protocol clns permitR3#
R5#sh run int bri0/0
Building configuration...
Current configuration : 340 bytes
!
username R3 password 0 cisco
!
interface BRI0/0
 ip address 160.10.15.5 255.255.255.0
 ip router isis
 encapsulation ppp
 dialer map clns 49.0004.0000.0000.0003.00 name R3 broadcast 1111
 dialer map ip 160.10.15.3 name R3 broadcast 1111
 dialer-group 1
 isdn switch-type basic-ni
 isdn spid1 2222
 ppp authentication chap
 isis circuit-type level-2-only
end
R5#
R5#ping 160.10.15.3
Type escape sequence to abort.
Sending 5, 100-byte ICMP Echos to 160.10.15.3, timeout is 2 seconds:
5w1d: %LINK-3-UPDOWN: Interface BRI0/0:1, changed state to up..!!!
Success rate is 60 percent (3/5), round-trip min/avg/max = 32/33/36 ms
R5#
5w1d: %LINEPROTO-5-UPDOWN: Line protocol on Interface BRI0/0:1, changed state to up
5w1d: %ISDN-6-CONNECT: Interface BRI0/0:1 is now connected to 1111 R3
```

- *The ISDN link should pass routing protocols should R5-fa0/0 goes down.*

If you configured this correctly as shown in Example 5-32 you have scored 2 points.

**Example 5-32**  *R5 Routing Backup Output*

```
R5#show ip route
Codes: C - connected, S - static, I - IGRP, R - RIP, M - mobile, B - BGP
       D - EIGRP, EX - EIGRP external, O - OSPF, IA - OSPF inter area
       N1 - OSPF NSSA external type 1, N2 - OSPF NSSA external type 2
       E1 - OSPF external type 1, E2 - OSPF external type 2, E - EGP
```

*continues*

**Example 5-32** *R5 Routing Backup Output (Continued)*

```
              i - IS-IS, L1 - IS-IS level-1, L2 - IS-IS level-2, ia - IS-IS inter area
              * - candidate default, U - per-user static route, o - ODR
              P - periodic downloaded static route
Gateway of last resort is not set
O E2 196.1.8.0/24 [110/1] via 160.10.37.2, 03:14:25, Serial0/1
O E2 196.1.10.0/24 [110/1] via 160.10.37.2, 03:14:25, Serial0/1
     140.200.0.0/24 is subnetted, 1 subnets
O E2    140.200.10.0 [110/1] via 160.10.37.2, 03:14:25, Serial0/1
     160.10.0.0/16 is variably subnetted, 16 subnets, 3 masks
O IA    160.10.32.0/30 [110/128] via 160.10.37.2, 03:14:35, Serial0/1
i L2    160.10.33.0/24 [115/20] via 160.10.22.3, FastEthernet0/0
O       160.10.38.0/24 [110/128] via 160.10.37.2, 03:14:35, Serial0/1
O       160.10.37.2/32 [110/64] via 160.10.37.2, 03:14:36, Serial0/1
O       160.10.37.1/32 [110/128] via 160.10.37.2, 03:14:36, Serial0/1
C       160.10.37.0/24 is directly connected, Serial0/1
O IA    160.10.11.0/24 [110/138] via 160.10.37.2, 03:14:36, Serial0/1
C       160.10.15.0/24 is directly connected, BRI0/0
O       160.10.2.0/24 [110/65] via 160.10.37.2, 03:14:36, Serial0/1
O IA    160.10.3.0/24 [110/129] via 160.10.37.2, 03:14:36, Serial0/1
O       160.10.1.0/24 [110/129] via 160.10.37.2, 03:14:36, Serial0/1
i L2    160.10.6.0/24 [115/20] via 160.10.22.6, FastEthernet0/0
O       160.10.4.0/24 [110/129] via 160.10.37.2, 03:14:36, Serial0/1
C       160.10.5.0/24 is directly connected, Loopback0
C       160.10.25.0/24 is directly connected, FastEthernet0/1
C       160.10.22.0/24 is directly connected, FastEthernet0/0
O E2 196.1.2.0/24 [110/1] via 160.10.37.2, 03:14:26, Serial0/1
     130.200.0.0/24 is subnetted, 1 subnets
O E2    130.200.10.0 [110/100] via 160.10.37.2, 03:14:26, Serial0/1
O E2 193.118.1.0/24 [110/100] via 160.10.37.2, 03:14:26, Serial0/1
O E2 193.118.3.0/24 [110/100] via 160.10.37.2, 03:14:26, Serial0/1
O E2 193.118.2.0/24 [110/100] via 160.10.37.2, 03:14:26, Serial0/ R5#
R5#
R5#
R5#
! R5-Fa0/0 goes down
5w1d: %LINEPROTO-5-UPDOWN: Line protocol on Interface FastEthernet0/0, changed state
to down
! CLNS ping fails
R5#ping clns 49.0004.0000.0000.0003.00
Type escape sequence to abort.
Sending 5, 100-byte CLNS Echos with timeout 2 seconds
CLNS: cannot send ECHO.
CLNS: cannot send ECHO.
CLNS: cannot send ECHO.
CLNS: cannot send ECHO.
CLNS: cannot send ECHO.
Success rate is 0 percent (0/5)
R5#
R5#ping 160.10.15.3
Type escape sequence to abort.
Sending 5, 100-byte ICMP Echos to 160.10.15.3, timeout is 2 seconds:
5w1d: %LINK-3-UPDOWN: Interface BRI0/0:1, changed state to up..!!!
```

**Example 5-32**  *R5 Routing Backup Output (Continued)*

```
Success rate is 60 percent (3/5), round-trip min/avg/max = 32/33/36 ms
R5#
5w1d: %LINEPROTO-5-UPDOWN: Line protocol on Interface BRI0/0:1, changed state to up
5w1d: %ISDN-6-CONNECT: Interface BRI0/0:1 is now connected to 1111 R3
R5#
! Now ISDN link is up
R5#
R5#
R5#ping clns 49.0004.0000.0000.0003.00
Type escape sequence to abort.
Sending 5, 100-byte CLNS Echos with timeout 2 seconds
!!!!!
Success rate is 100 percent (5/5), round-trip min/avg/max = 36/38/40 ms
R5#sh ip ro
Codes: C - connected, S - static, I - IGRP, R - RIP, M - mobile, B - BGP
       D - EIGRP, EX - EIGRP external, O - OSPF, IA - OSPF inter area
       N1 - OSPF NSSA external type 1, N2 - OSPF NSSA external type 2
       E1 - OSPF external type 1, E2 - OSPF external type 2, E - EGP
       i - IS-IS, L1 - IS-IS level-1, L2 - IS-IS level-2, ia - IS-IS inter area
       * - candidate default, U - per-user static route, o - ODR
       P - periodic downloaded static route
Gateway of last resort is not set
O E2 196.1.8.0/24 [110/1] via 160.10.37.2, 03:20:03, Serial0/1
O E2 196.1.10.0/24 [110/1] via 160.10.37.2, 03:20:03, Serial0/1
     140.200.0.0/24 is subnetted, 1 subnets
O E2    140.200.10.0 [110/1] via 160.10.37.2, 03:20:03, Serial0/1
     160.10.0.0/16 is variably subnetted, 17 subnets, 3 masks
O IA    160.10.32.0/30 [110/128] via 160.10.37.2, 03:20:13, Serial0/1
i L2    160.10.33.0/24 [115/20] via 160.10.15.3, BRI0/0
O       160.10.38.0/24 [110/128] via 160.10.37.2, 03:20:13, Serial0/1
O       160.10.37.2/32 [110/64] via 160.10.37.2, 03:20:14, Serial0/1
O       160.10.37.1/32 [110/128] via 160.10.37.2, 03:20:14, Serial0/1
C       160.10.37.0/24 is directly connected, Serial0/1
O IA    160.10.11.0/24 [110/138] via 160.10.37.2, 03:20:14, Serial0/1
C       160.10.15.0/24 is directly connected, BRI0/0
C       160.10.15.3/32 is directly connected, BRI0/0
O       160.10.2.0/24 [110/65] via 160.10.37.2, 03:20:18, Serial0/1
O IA    160.10.3.0/24 [110/129] via 160.10.37.2, 03:20:18, Serial0/1
O       160.10.1.0/24 [110/129] via 160.10.37.2, 03:20:18, Serial0/1
i L2    160.10.6.0/24 [115/30] via 160.10.15.3, BRI0/0
O       160.10.4.0/24 [110/129] via 160.10.37.2, 03:20:18, Serial0/1
C       160.10.5.0/24 is directly connected, Loopback0
C       160.10.25.0/24 is directly connected, FastEthernet0/1
i L2    160.10.22.0/24 [115/20] via 160.10.15.3, BRI0/0
O E2 196.1.2.0/24 [110/1] via 160.10.37.2, 03:20:08, Serial0/1
     130.200.0.0/24 is subnetted, 1 subnets
O E2    130.200.10.0 [110/100] via 160.10.37.2, 03:20:08, Serial0/1
O E2 193.118.1.0/24 [110/100] via 160.10.37.2, 03:20:08, Serial0/1
O E2 193.118.3.0/24 [110/100] via 160.10.37.2, 03:20:08, Serial0/1
O E2 193.118.2.0/24 [110/100] via 160.10.37.2, 03:20:08, Serial0/1
```

# Section 5: IP and IOS Features (10 Points)

- *Configure R4 to reach (ping and Telnet) all other routers and Sw1 by using their hostnames.*

If you configured this correctly as shown in Example 5-33, you have scored 3 points.

This task is accomplished by mapping the IP addresses to the respective hostnames. Example 5-33 shows the necessary commands to accomplish this task and the verification.

**Example 5-33** *R4 IP Hostnames Configuration*

```
R4#sh run
Building configuration...
Current configuration : 1561 bytes
!
version 12.2
!
hostname R4
!
!
no ip domain-lookup
ip host Sw1 160.10.11.10
ip host R6 160.10.6.6
ip host R5 160.10.5.5
ip host R4 160.10.4.4
ip host R3 160.10.3.3
ip host R2 160.10.2.2
ip host R1 160.10.1.1
!
R4#
R4#ping r6
Type escape sequence to abort.
Sending 5, 100-byte ICMP Echos to 160.10.6.6, timeout is 2 seconds:
!!!!!
Success rate is 100 percent (5/5), round-trip min/avg/max = 4/5/8 ms
R4#
R4#telnet sw1
Trying Sw1 (160.10.11.10)... Open
User Access Verification
Password:
Sw1>en
Password:
Sw1#exit
[Connection to sw1 closed by foreign host]
R4#
```

- *You have installed on VLAN_33 HP users that use HP Probe Proxy services. Configure R3 to provide this service to users on VLAN_33. Consider the server name HP_Probe and its IP address as 160.10.33.254.*

If you configured this correctly as shown in Example 5-34, you have scored 2 points.

Example 5-34 shows the necessary command to accomplish this task. HP Probe Proxy support allows the Cisco IOS software to respond to HP Probe Proxy name requests. These requests are typically used at sites that have HP equipment and are already using HP Probe Proxy. The **ip probe proxy** command allows Cisco IOS to respond to HP Probe Proxy name requests. The **ip hp-host** command maps the HP Probe host.

**Example 5-34**  *R3 Configuring HP Probe Proxy (IP Addressing and Services Configuration)*

```
R3#sh run ¦ incl hp
ip hp-host HP_Probe 160.10.33.254
R3#
R3#
R3#sh run int fa0/1
Building configuration...
Current configuration : 172 bytes
!
interface FastEthernet0/1
 ip address 160.10.33.3 255.255.255.0
 ip probe proxy

end
R3#
```

- *Configure R1 to be the TFTP server if you need to download IOS for R3 and R5, but only for requests coming from R3 and R5.*

If you configured this correctly as shown in Example 5-35, you have scored 3 points.

Example 5-35 shows the configuration needed to be applied on R1. The IP addresses used on ACL 2 in R1 came from a traceroute from R3 and R5 to verify which path is used for each router to reach R1.

**Example 5-35**  *R1 Configuration as TFTP Server with Access List to Permit Access Only from R3 and R5*

```
R1#sh run ¦ b access-list 2
access-list 2 permit 160.10.32.2
access-list 2 permit 160.10.37.2
!
tftp-server flash:c2600-jk8o3s-mz.122-16.bin 2
!
```

- *Configure R3 such that if it fails to load the system file from Flash memory; R3 will load a system image from the network instead.*

If you configured this correctly as shown in Example 5-36, you have scored 2 points.

Example 5-36 shows the configuration need on R3. As in the previous question, if R3 fails to get the IOS image from Flash memory, R3 will try to get it from R1.

NOTE     You should also to change the configuration register to 0x010F to complete the task. You do not need to configure. This is to give you an idea, you need to go through the IOS features to understand what is available and how to configure them.

**Example 5-36** *R3 Configuration to Load a System File from a Remote Location*

```
R3#sh run | b boot
boot system flash c2600-jk8o3s-mz.122-16.bin
boot system tftp c2600-jk8o3s-mz.122-16.bin 160.10.1.1
```

# Section 6: DLSw (4 Points)

- *Configure DLSw between VLAN_11 and VLAN_33. Use FST encapsulation.*

If you configured this correctly as shown in Example 5-37, you have scored 2 points.

Example 5-37 has the DLSw configuration between R1 and R3 using FST encapsulation. Example 5-37 shows how to set up the peers and how to verify if the DLSw configuration up and running. Notice the state "CONNECT," which means the DLSw tunnel is up, running, and connected. If the state shows something different, you need to doublecheck your configurations and make sure your IGP is also running fine.

Because it is a "bridge" environment, you need to have the Spanning Tree Protocol enabled. You enable Spanning Tree Protocol using the **bridge** protocol command.

**Example 5-37** *R1 and R3 Basic DLSw Configuration*

```
R1#show run
!
dlsw local-peer peer-id 160.10.1.1
dlsw remote-peer 0 fst 160.10.3.3
dlsw bridge-group 1
!
interface Ethernet0/0
 ip address 160.10.11.1 255.255.255.0
 bridge-group 1
!
bridge 1 protocol ieee
!
!
R3#show run
!
!
dlsw local-peer peer-id 160.10.3.3
dlsw remote-peer 0 fst 160.10.1.1
dlsw bridge-group 1
!
interface FastEthernet0/1
 ip address 160.10.33.3 255.255.255.0
```

**Example 5-37**  *R1 and R3 Basic DLSw Configuration  (Continued)*

```
  bridge-group 1
  !
  !
  bridge 1 protocol ieee
  !
  !
R1#show dlsw pee
Peers:                  state      pkts_rx    pkts_tx   type   drops ckts TCP     uptime
  FST 160.10.3.3        CONNECT       3298       3298   conf       0    0   0      1d03h
Total number of connected peers: 1
Total number of connections:     1
R1#
  !
  !
R3#show dlsw pee
Peers:                  state      pkts_rx    pkts_tx   type   drops ckts TCP     uptime
  FST 160.10.1.1        CONNECT       3299       3299   conf       0    0   0      1d03h
Total number of connected peers: 1
Total number of connections:     1
R3#
```

- *You have some users exchanging data through your DLSw connection, but you do not want to compromise the IP traffic of others because DLSw is not your high priority. Configure your DLSw peers so they do not use more than 60 kbps as an average bit rate and set the maximum burst rate of 30 kbps.*

If you configured this correctly as shown in Example 5-38, you have scored 1 point.

Example 5-38 shows the necessary configuration to accomplish the task. It is a basic RSVP implementation to reserve bandwidth to the DLSw sessions.

**Example 5-38**  *R1 and R3 RSVP Configuration*

```
R1#show run
  !
  dlsw rsvp 60 30
  !
  !
  !
R3#sh run
  !
  !
  dlsw rsvp 60 30
  !
  !
```

- *Configure R1 and R3 to not send UDP Unicast and to have the peers sending the resolution address via the existing FST connection.*

If you configured this correctly as shown in Example 5-39, you have scored 1 point.

Example 5-39 shows the necessary command to disable the UDP unicast packets to being sent by R1 and R3.

**Example 5-39** *R1 and R3 RSVP Configuration*

```
R1#sh run | incl dlsw
!
dlsw udp-disable
!
!
R3#sh run | incl dlsw
!
dlsw udp-disable
!
!
```

# Section 7: QoS (6 Points)

- *Configure a Traffic Class and apply it on incoming direction R6-e0/0, which will classify all BGP traffic and set IP precedence to immediate.*

If you configured this correctly as shown in Example 5-40, you have scored 2 points.

Example 5-40 shows a configuration of Traffic Classification based on the concept of Modular QoS CLI configuration. You are going to create a Traffic Class and ACL to match the traffic you want to classify and then create a policy map to apply the class map and set the BGP traffic to precedence "immediate," to enable CEF and to apply to R6-E0/0. Also, the **show** commands verify if the Traffic Class is working properly.

**Example 5-40** *R6 Policy Classification Configuration and Verification*

```
R6#sh run
Building configuration...

Current configuration : 2609 bytes
!
ip cef
!
class-map match-all class1
  match access-group 103
!
!
policy-map BGP_Policy
  class class1
    set ip precedence 2
!
interface Ethernet0/0
  ip address 160.10.22.6 255.255.255.0
  !
  service-policy input BGP_Policy
```

**Example 5-40**   *R6 Policy Classification Configuration and Verification (Continued)*

```
!
R6#sh ip access-lists 103
Extended IP access list 103
    permit tcp any any eq bgp (33 matches)
R6#
!
R6#sh policy-map interface e0/0 Ethernet0/0
  Service-policy input: BGP_Policy
    Class-map: class1 (match-all)
      35 packets, 2360 bytes
      5 minute offered rate 0 bps, drop rate 0 bps
      Match: access-group 103
      QoS Set
        ip precedence 2
          Packets marked 35

    Class-map: class-default (match-any)
      2 packets, 146 bytes
      5 minute offered rate 0 bps, drop rate 0 bps
      Match: any
R6#
!
!
```

- *Configure Committed Access Rate on R6-a3/0, so that web traffic will be sent but using IP precedence 5 for the web traffic that conforms to the first rate policy, nonconforming web traffic, and so that will use the IP precedence 0 (best effort). Any remaining traffic is limited to 8 Mbps, with a normal burst size of 16,000 bytes and an Excess Burst size of 24,000 bytes. Traffic that conforms is sent with an IP precedence of 5. Traffic that does not conform should be dropped.*

If you configured this correctly as shown in Example 5-41, you have scored 2 points.

Example 5-41 has the configuration for CAR and the ACL necessary for that. The output from the **show** command verifies if the interface is correctly configured and using the desired criteria.

**Example 5-41**   *R6 CAR Configuration and Verification*

```
R6#sh run int a3/0
Building configuration...
Current configuration : 359 bytes
!
interface ATM3/0
 ip address 170.100.10.1 255.255.255.0
 rate-limit output access-group 101 20000000 24000 32000 conform-action set-prec-
transmit 5 exceed-action set-prec-transmit 0
 rate-limit output 8000000 16000 24000 conform-action set-prec-transmit 5 exceed-
action drop
!
end
```

*continues*

**Example 5-41** *R6 CAR Configuration and Verification (Continued)*

```
R6#sh ip access
Extended IP access list 101
    permit tcp any any eq www
R6#

R6#sh interfaces a3/0 rate-limit

ATM3/0
  Output
    matches: access-group 101
      params:  20000000 bps, 24000 limit, 32000 extended limit
      conformed 0 packets, 0 bytes; action: set-prec-transmit 5
      exceeded 0 packets, 0 bytes; action: set-prec-transmit 0
      last packet: 11004728ms ago, current burst: 0 bytes
      last cleared 03:03:11 ago, conformed 0 bps, exceeded 0 bps
    matches: all traffic
      params:  8000000 bps, 16000 limit, 24000 extended limit
      conformed 290 packets, 18644 bytes; action: set-prec-transmit 5
      exceeded 0 packets, 0 bytes; action: drop
      last packet: 21060ms ago, current burst: 0 bytes
      last cleared 03:03:11 ago, conformed 0 bps, exceeded 0 bps
R6#
```

- *Configure policy-based routing on R1 such that all packets with a source of 160.10.11.10 prefer a next-hop 160.10.5.5 address.*

If you configured this correctly as shown in Example 5-42, you have scored 2 points.

Example 5-42 shows the policy-based routing configuration that will set R5 as the next-hop for packets that the source is the address 160.10.11.10 or the Sw1.

**Example 5-42** *R1 Policy-Based Routing Configuration*

```
R1#sh run
Building configuration...
Current configuration : 126 bytes
!
interface Ethernet0/0
 ip address 160.10.11.1 255.255.255.0
 ip policy route-map FROM_SW1

R1#
!
access-list 1 permit 160.10.11.10
route-map FROM_SW1 permit 10
 match ip address 1
 set ip next-hop 160.10.5.5
end
```

# Section 8: Multicast (6 Points)

- *Configure Multicast PIM Sparse-mode on VLAN_22 to allow multicast traffic between R3, R5, and R6. Make R6 the rendezvous point.*

If you configured this correctly as shown in Example 5-43, you have scored 3 points.

Example 5-43 shows the configuration to set up the Multicast between R3, R5, and R6 with R6 as the RP of the group.

**Example 5-43**  *R3, R5, and R6 Multicast Configuration*

```
R3#show run
Building configuration...
!
!
ip multicast-routing
!
!
interface FastEthernet0/0
 ip address 160.10.22.3 255.255.255.0
 ip pim sparse-mode
!
!
ip pim rp-address 160.10.22.6
!
!
R5#show run
Building configuration...
!
!
ip multicast-routing
!
!
interface FastEthernet0/0
 ip address 160.10.22.5 255.255.255.0
 ip pim sparse-mode
!
!
ip pim rp-address 160.10.22.6
!
!
!
R6#show run
Building configuration...
!
!
ip multicast-routing
!
!
interface Ethernet0/0
 ip address 160.10.22.6 255.255.255.0
  ip pim sparse-mode
!
```

*continues*

**Example 5-43** *R3, R5, and R6 Multicast Configuration (Continued)*

```
R3#show ip pim rp
Group: 224.0.1.40, RP: 160.10.22.6, uptime 1d01h, expires never
!
!
```
```
R5#show ip pim rp
Group: 224.0.1.40, RP: 160.10.22.6, uptime 1d01h, expires never
R5#
```

- *Configure Multicast Routing Monitor between R3, R5, and R6 with R6 as the Manager. Make R3 the "test sender" and R5 the "test receiver."*

If you configured this correctly as shown in Example 5-44, you have scored 3 points.

Example 5-44 has the configuration for Multicast Routing Monitor (MRM) on R3 and R5. The MRM feature is a management diagnostic tool that provides network fault detection and isolation in a multicast routing infrastructure. It is designed to notify a network administrator of multicast routing problems in near real time. If the Test Receiver detects an error (such as packet loss or duplicate packets), it sends an error report to the router configured as the Manager. The Manager immediately displays the error report. (Also, by issuing a certain **show** EXEC command, you can see the error reports, if any.) You then troubleshoot your multicast environment as normal, perhaps using the **mtrace** command from the source to the Test Receiver.

**Example 5-44** *R3, R5, and R6 MRM Configuration*

```
R3#sh run int fa0/0
Building configuration...
Current configuration : 185 bytes
!
interface FastEthernet0/0
 ip address 160.10.22.3 255.255.255.0
 ip pim sparse-mode
 ip mrm test-sender
!
```
```
R5#sh run int fa0/0
Building configuration...
Current configuration : 187 bytes
!
interface FastEthernet0/0
 ip address 160.10.22.5 255.255.255.0
 ip pim sparse-mode
 ip mrm test-receiver
 end
!
```
```
R6#sh run | b TEST1
ip mrm manager TEST1
 manager Ethernet0/0 group 239.1.1.1
 senders 1
 receivers 2 sender-list 1
!
```

**Example 5-44**  *R3, R5, and R6 MRM Configuration (Continued)*

```
!
access-list 1 permit 160.10.22.3
access-list 2 permit 160.10.22.5
!
R6#
!
```

```
R3#sh ip mrm interface
Interface               Address          Mode              Status
FastEthernet0/0         160.10.22.3      Test-Sender       Up
R3#
!
```

```
R5#sh ip mrm interface
Interface               Address          Mode              Status
FastEthernet0/0         160.10.22.5      Test-Receiver     Up
R5#
!
```

```
R6#sh ip mrm manager
Manager:TEST1/160.10.22.6 is not running
  Beacon interval/holdtime/ttl:60/86400/32
  Group:239.1.1.1, UDP port test-packet/status-report:16384/65535
  Test senders:
    160.10.22.3
  Test receivers:
    160.10.22.5
```

# Section 9: Security (8 Points)

- *Configure a reflexive access list on R6 and apply it to the R6-a3/0 internal interface, allowing BGP and any other interesting traffic.*

If you configured this correctly as shown in Example 5-45, you have scored 3 points.

Example 5-45 has the output configuration for the reflexive access list that accomplishes the question requirements. Reflexive access list s allow IP packets to be filtered based on upper-layer session information and the requirements implies to look at BGP packets on R6 and the relevant traffic is ICMP.

**Example 5-45**  *R6 Reflexive Access List Configuration*

```
R6#sh run int a3/0
Building configuration...
Current configuration : 147 bytes
!
interface ATM3/0
ip access-group in_filters in
 ip access-group out_filters out
 R6#
R6#sh run
Building configuration...
Current configuration : 2604 bytes
```

*continues*

**Example 5-45** *R6 Reflexive Access List Configuration (Continued)*

```
!
ip access-list extended in_filters
 permit tcp any any reflect TCP_Traffic

ip access-list extended out_filters
 permit tcp any any eq bgp
 permit pim any any
 permit icmp any any

 deny ip any any
 evaluate TCP_Traffic
!
R6#sh access-lists
!
Reflexive IP access list TCP_Traffic
     permit tcp host 160.10.6.6 eq bgp host 160.10.3.3 eq 11003 (70 matches) (time
left 91)
     permit tcp host 170.100.10.1 eq 11000 host 170.100.10.254 eq bgp (24 matches)
(time left 61)
Extended IP access list in_filters
     permit tcp any any reflect TCP_Traffic
Extended IP access list out_filters
     permit tcp any any eq bgp
     permit pim any any
     permit icmp any any
     deny ip any any
     evaluate TCP_Traffic
R6#
```

- *Consider having a server with an IP address of 160.10.33.1 on VLAN_33 and configure R3 to intercept all TCP traffic to this server. Also, configure R3 to drop random connections.*

If you configured this correctly as shown in Example 5-46, you have scored 2 points.

Example 5-46 shows the configuration for IP Intercept to monitor all traffic going to the server 160.10.33.1.

**Example 5-46** *R3 TCP Intercept Configuration*

```
R3#sh run
Building configuration...
Current configuration : 2729 bytes
!
hostname R3
!
ip tcp intercept list 101
ip tcp intercept drop-mode random
R3#
access-list 101 permit tcp any any
```

- *Configure Sw1-fa0/17 to allow only the host MAC address 0010.DE48.2223 to access the switch through this interface. If a security violation occurs, force the interface to go into restrict mode.*

If you configured this correctly as shown in Example 5-47 you have scored 3 points.

The configuration in Example 5-47, is the minimum configuration needed to enable the port-security feature applying another violation mode: restrict.

**Example 5-47** *Sw1 Port-Security Configuration*

```
Sw1#show run int fa0/17
Building configuration...
Current configuration : 152 bytes
!
interface FastEthernet0/17
 switchport mode access
 switchport port-security
switchport port-security violation restrict
 switchport port-security mac-address 0010.de48.2223
 no ip address
end
Sw1#
!
!
Sw1#show port-security int fa0/17
Port Security : Enabled
Port status : SecureUp
Violation mode : Restrict
Maximum MAC Addresses : 1
Total MAC Addresses : 1
Configured MAC Addresses : 1
Sticky MAC Addresses : 0
Aging time : 0 mins
Aging type : Absolute
SecureStatic address aging : Disabled
Security Violation count : 0
Sw1#
```

# How Did You Do?

With the aid of the answers section and full configurations and routing tables on the CD, you should now have an accurate evaluation of your lab. If you scored more than 80 points within the time-frame you should congratulate yourself. You are well on the way to becoming a CCIE, you have demonstrated the ability to think laterally and shown an impressive knowledge of your subject. If you scored less than 80 do not worry; this will improve as you progress throughout the book and learn how to analyze each question and improve your core skills.

Did you spot the landmines in the lab? The classics in Lab 5 were to give you, under a new IP IGP topology, the basic setup for OSPF, RIP V2, EIGRP, BGP, as well as IS-IS. These are the big "candidates" for the real lab exam. Also, an important thing to keep in mind is the feature each area has. You need to explore these going through Cisco Documentation. You need to explore on each section of the documentation especially the features that are available.

In Practice Lab 6, you'll be required to demonstrate your knowledge in more complex tasks, environments, and behaviors, and be able to resolve these more complex issues. The real one-day lab exam does not have the Troubleshooting section anymore, but, on the other hand during the exam you can find yourself in a "troubleshooting" situation if you do not have a solid knowledge of what you are configuring. Keep in mind that you will need to perform some "basic" troubleshooting during the exam. The hands-on experience will give you the confidence that you need. Always be careful when configuring network masks and pay attention as to which router you are working on.

You might feel that the some questions were too vague or you did not have sufficient time to complete the lab. Your ability to spot landmines, ask the right questions, and increase your configuration speed will improve as you tackle each practice lab.

For each question that you did not answer correctly, take the time to research the subject thoroughly and turn your weaknesses into your strengths. Research and plenty of practice will ultimately lead you to gain a passing score.

# Further Reading/URLs

To better prepare yourself and follow up on the topics covered in this lab, you should consult the http://www.cisco.com/public/pubsearch.html website for more information on the following topics:

Configuring Frame Relay
Configuring 3550
Configuring ATM
Configuring Routing Protocols
Configuring ISDN
Configuring IP Features
Configuring IOS Features
Configuring DLSw
Configuring QoS
Configuring Multicast
Configuring Security

All topics, concepts, and question used in this chapter came also from the following resources:

All Routing, Features, BGP, etc (Cisco Documentation for 12.2 mainline under "www.cisco.com/univercd/home/home.html"): http://www.cisco.com/univercd/cc/td/doc/product/software/ios122/index.htm
For the Catalyst 3550 (the 12.1 EMI image documentation): http://www.cisco.com/univercd/cc/td/doc/product/lan/c3550/1219ea1/3550scg/index.htm
Book: *IS-IS Network Design Solutions*—Abe Martey—Cisco Press

# CHAPTER 6

# Practice Lab 6

You will now be starting Practice Lab 6. This lab adds some voice over IP (VoIP), security involving authentication of routing protocols, and some routing on the Catalyst 3550s.

You will notice that the Lab 6 topology is basically the same as Lab 5. This is intentional and shows you how you can obtain the maximum from your topology in different ways. You might feel you are performing the same tasks you tackled previously, but the more you practice the more you become familiar with the equipment and commands that will make you comfortable to perform the tasks during the CCIE Lab Exam as well in your professional duties. You will also be practicing additional features within Lab 6.

The main objective still remains the same: to ensure you practice on a variety of subjects and scenarios that covers the potential CCIE Lab Exam content. As before, if your equipment does not exactly match that used to produce the lab it does not matter, as long as you have the required interfaces. Having the exact equipment, however, will aid you in pasting in configuration files.

Quite often the questions will be straightforward, so try to keep your solutions simple and avoid complicating the matter and yourself. Sometimes, you will need to pay attention to the wording and although the question looks like quite simple, it could involve a "hidden" concept knowledge regarding a specific area or section in the exercise.

Keep in mind that the main objective of these lab exercises is to give you challenges that will drive you through the areas you must explore to be well prepared to take the CCIE Lab Exam with success, and, therefore, be thoroughly prepared to better apply your skills in the real world.

As in the previous labs you will find to assist you, the router and switch initial configurations, Frame Relay switch configuration, and backbone router configurations. Solutions for the entire lab including configurations and common **show** command outputs from all the devices in the topology can be found on the accompanying CD. An "Ask the Proctor" section, which will give you clues if required, is included at the end of the lab followed by the lab debrief, which will analyze each question showing you what was required and how to achieve the desired results. Finally, you will find handy references should you require additional study information.

You will now be guided through the equipment requirements and pre-lab tasks in preparation for taking Practice Lab 6.

# Equipment List

- 2 Catalyst 3550 Switches using two 3550 X 24 Fast Ethernet ports with IOS 12.1 Enhanced Multilayer Software image (EMI).

- 6 Cisco Routers including 2600, 3600, and 3725, plus a backbone router (Cisco 7200) and a Frame Relay switch router (Cisco 4000) are required. Also, a 2500 or 2600 to be your communication server. The routers are loaded with Cisco IOS Software Release 12.2 Enterprise Mainline image. The exception is the Cisco Router 3725 that uses an IOS Release 12.2(T) image and the Catalyst 3550 series that uses an IOS Release 12.1 image.

  Follow the router interface specification outlined in Table 6-1.

**Table 6-1**  *Interfaces Required per Router*

| Router | Ethernet Interface | Serial Interface | BRI Interface | Voice | ATM Interface |
|--------|--------------------|------------------|---------------|-------|---------------|
| R1 (2611) | 2 | 2 | - | - | - |
| R2 (3725) | 2 | 2 | - | - | - |
| R3 (2621) | 2 | 2 | 1 | 2 FXS | - |
| R4 (3640) | 1 | 2 | - | 2 FXS | - |
| R5 (2621) | 2 | 2 | 1 | - | - |
| R6 (3640) | 2 | 2 | - | - | 1 |
| BB_Router (7200) | 2 | - | - | - | 1 |
| FR_SWITCH (4000) | - | 12 | - | - | - |

**NOTE**    Although you will be provided with fully meshed physical connectivity (LAN and WAN), you might not use all routers or interfaces in all lab exercises. This is to optimize your setup for the next labs.

# Setting Up the Lab

Feel free to use any combination of routers as long as you fulfill the topology diagram as shown in Figure 6-1. It is not compulsory to use the same model of routers, but this will make life easier should you like to load configurations directly from the CD-ROM into your own devices.

**NOTE**    If you have a mix of 10- and 100-Mbps Ethernet interfaces, adjust the bandwidth statements on the relevant interfaces to keep all interface speeds common. This will ensure that you do not get unwanted behavior because of differing IGP metrics.

You will find some routers using a mix of 10- and 100-Mbps Ethernet interfaces.

## Lab Topology

Practice Lab 6 will use the topology as outlined in Figure 6-1, which you will need to create using the switch, Frame Relay, ATM, and ISDN information that follows.

**Figure 6-1**    *Lab 6 Topology Diagram*

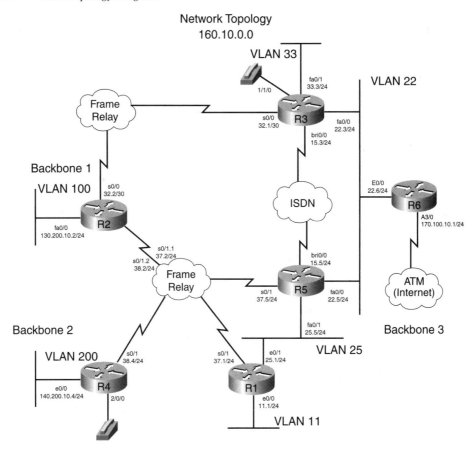

# Cabling Instructions

You will have all the router interfaces precabled, although you will not be using all interfaces for the Lab 6 exercises. Table 6-2 documents the cabling instructions.

**Table 6-2** *3550 Cabling*

| Interface | Switch-1 | Switch-2 |
|-----------|----------|----------|
| R1 e0/0 (2611) | fa0/1 | - |
| R1 e0/1(2611) | - | fa0/1 |
| R2 fa0/0 (3725) | fa0/2 | - |
| R2 fa0/1 (3725) | - | fa0/2 |
| R3 fa0/0 (2621) | fa0/3 | - |
| R3 fa0/1(2621) | - | fa0/3 |
| R4 e0/0 (3640) | fa0/4 | - |
| R5 fa0/0 (2621) | fa0/5 | - |
| R5 fa0/1(2621) | - | fa0/5 |
| R6 e0/0 (3640) | fa0/6 | - |
| R6 fa1/0 (3640) | - | fa0/6 |
| Backbone 1 | fa0/13 | - |
| Backbone 2 | - | fa0/13 |
| Trunk | fa0/15 | fa0/15 |
| Trunk | fa0/17 | fa0/17 |

# Frame Relay Switch Instructions

The Frame Relay switch is a 4000 router with 12 interfaces connecting all 6 core routers in a full mesh as shown in Table 6-3. Refer also to Figure 6-2 for the Frame Relay logical assignment and refer to the Frame Relay sample configuration from the CD-ROM.

**Table 6-3** *Frame Relay Switch Physical Connectivity*

| Router/Interface | FR_Switch Interface |
|------------------|---------------------|
| R1 s0/0 | Serial 0 |
| R1 s0/1 | Serial 1 |
| R2 s0/0 | Serial 2 |
| R2 s0/1 | Serial 3 |
| R3 s0/0 | Serial 4 |
| R3 s0/1 | Serial 5 |

**Table 6-3**   *Frame Relay Switch Physical Connectivity (Continued)*

| Router/Interface | FR_Switch Interface |
| --- | --- |
| R4 s0/0 | Serial 6 |
| R4 s0/1 | Serial 7 |
| R5 s0/0 | Serial 8 |
| R5 s0/1 | Serial 9 |
| R6 s0/0 | Serial 10 |
| R6 s0/1 | Serial 11 |

**Figure 6-2**   *Frame Relay Switch Logical Connectivity*

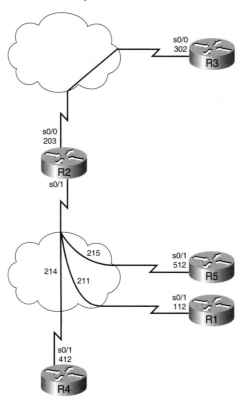

Frame Relay Setup
Frame Relay switch ports are DCE.
Routers ports are DTE.

Configure a 4000 router as a Frame Relay switch or equivalent that can provide the connectivity for this lab.

Keep your DCE cables at the frame switch end for simplicity and provide a clock rate of 2 Mbps to all links. Should you require detailed information on how to configure one of your routers as a Frame Relay switch, this information can be found in Appendix A, "Frame Relay Switch Configuration" (and/or from the CD-ROM).

---

**NOTE**     If you do not have a spare router to make up as your Frame Relay switch with 12 serial interfaces, you certainly can accommodate your needs with a smaller router for each specific lab exercise or even make back-to-back connections in some situations.

---

## ATM Switch Instructions

You will have a back-to-back connection between R6 and the backbone router using fibers, as shown in Figure 6-3.

**Figure 6-3**     *ATM Physical Connectivity*

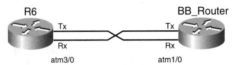

Figure 6-4 shows the logical setup for the ATM connectivity. You should always pay attention to the PVCs that you are going to use.

**Figure 6-4**     *ATM Logical Connectivity*

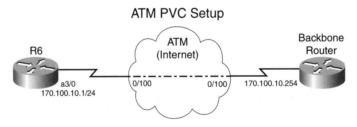

The ATM connectivity in Lab 6 will be provided by a back-to-back connection between R6 and (the) BB_Router over E3 ATM interfaces. You could also use a Cisco LightStream (LS1010 Switch) if available. Configure the PVCs as requested during the lab exercise. If you are using a LightStream to provide your ATM connectivity and require information on how to set this up, this information can be found in Appendix B, "LS1010 ATM Switch Configuration."

| | |
|---|---|
| **NOTE** | Although you are working with a back-to-back PVC environment as opposed to using an ATM switch such as a LS1010, you should consider studying other possible ATM configurations such as ATM SVC, PPPoATM, and so forth. |

## ISDN Instructions

Connect R3 and R5 into either ISDN lines or an ISDN simulator. It is preferable that the ISDN supports command-line interface (CLI). Reconfigure the numbers as required if you are using live ISDN lines. Figure 6-5 illustrates the ISDN connectivity.

**Figure 6-5**    *ISDN Connectivity*

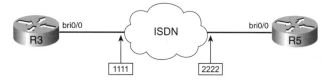

## IP Address Instructions

Configure the IP addresses as shown in Figure 6-6.

**Figure 6-6**  *IP Addressing Diagram*

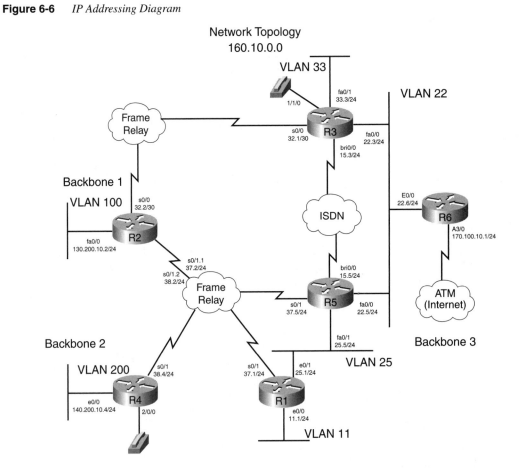

The CD-ROM includes initial configuration files for all routers and switches that include the basic IP addressing as shown in Figure 6-6.

# Pre-Lab Tasks

- Build the lab topology as per Figure 6-1 and Figure 6-2.
- Configure your chosen Frame Relay switch router to provide the necessary DLCIs as per Figure 6-2 and from the Frame Relay switch sample configuration file.
- Load the configuration for the BB_Router from your CD-ROM.

- Load the initial configuration files for this lab. The files will contain the basic IP addressing as referred to on Figure 6-6. Hostnames have been configured and the line console and line vty are preconfigured with the password **cisco**.

- Get into a comfortable and quiet environment where you can focus for the next eight hours.

- Start your lab in the morning and adhere to the eight hour timeframe. Do not panic or give up if you feel you will not be able to complete the whole exercise. If it happens, use the remaining time as a "practice" to focus on the parts where you encountered difficulty.

- Have available a Cisco Documentation CD-ROM or access online the latest documentation from the following URL:

  http://www.cisco.com/univercd/home/home.htm

---

**NOTE**    Consider accessing only the preceding URL, not the entire Cisco.com website. If you will be allowed to use documentation during your CCIE lab exam, it will be restricted.

---

- Go for a walk to relax before you get started.

# General Guidelines

- Please read the whole lab before you start.
- Do not configure any static/default routes unless otherwise specified/required.
- Use only the DLCIs and ATM PVCs provided in the appropriate figures.
- Follow the question instructions and requirements.
- Take a 30-minute break midway through the exercise.
- If you find yourself running out of time, choose questions that you are confident you can answer; failing this, choose questions with a higher point rating to maximize your potential score.

# Practice Lab 6 Exercise

You will now be answering questions in relation to the network topology and IP addressing as shown in Figure 6-7.

**Figure 6-7** *Lab 6 Topology and IP Addressing Diagram*

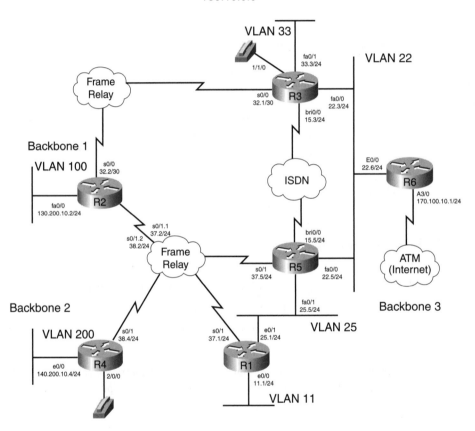

# Section 1: Bridging and Switching (18 Points)

## Section 1.1: Frame Relay Configuration (2 Points)

- Configure the Frame Relay portion of the network as shown in Figure 6-8 and ensure that only the PVCs illustrated in Figure 6-8 will be used. Use of dynamic PVCs is not permitted.

- You must use subinterfaces on R2 interface s0/1.

- Do not configure subinterfaces on any other routers.

- You must be able to ping across the Frame Relay cloud.

**Figure 6-8**    *Frame Relay Diagram*

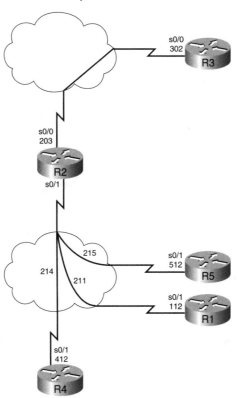

# Section 1.2: 3550 LAN Switch Configuration (12 Points)

- Sw1 and Sw2 are connected via a crossover cable using ports Fa0/15 and Fa0/17. Configure a Dot1q (801.1Q) trunk between Sw1 and Sw2.

- All Ethernet ports are pre-cabled as per Table 6-4. Note that not all ports will be used on this lab.

**Table 6-4**  *3550 Cabling*

| Interface | Switch-1 | Switch-2 |
|-----------|----------|----------|
| R1 e0/0 (2611) | fa0/1 | - |
| R1 e0/1(2611) | - | fa0/1 |
| R2 fa0/0 (3725) | fa0/2 | - |
| R2 fa0/1 (3725) | - | fa0/2 |
| R3 fa0/0 (2621) | fa0/3 | - |
| R3 fa0/1(2621) | - | fa0/3 |
| R4 e0/0 (3640) | fa0/4 | - |
| R5 fa0/0 (2621) | fa0/5 | - |
| R5 fa0/1(2621) | - | fa0/5 |
| R6 e0/0 (3640) | fa0/6 | - |
| R6 fa1/0 (3640) | - | fa0/6 |
| Backbone 1 | fa0/13 | - |
| Backbone 2 | - | fa0/13 |
| Trunk | fa0/15 | fa0/15 |
| Trunk | fa0/17 | fa0/17 |

- Configure the VLANs as follows:
    - VLAN_11: Connected to R1-e0/0 (VLAN_11)
    - VLAN_22: Connected to R3-fa0/0, R5-fa0/0, and R6-e0/0 (VLAN_22)
    - VLAN_25: Connected to R1-e0/1 and R5-fa0/1 (VLAN_25)
    - VLAN_33: Connected to R3-fa0/1 (VLAN_33)
    - VLAN_100: Connected to R2-fa0/0 and BB1_Router-e2/0 (VLAN_100)
    - VLAN_200: Connected to R4-e0/0 and BB2_Router-e2/4 (VLAN_200)
- Configure Sw1 to be the VTP server for the domain. Sw2 is a VTP client. Be sure that Sw2 can see the VLAN configuration from Sw1. The VTP domain name is "CISCO."

- Configure Sw1, using VLAN_11 with the IP address 160.10.11.10/24. After you have finished all tasks related to the IGP section, all routers on your topology should be able to ping Sw1 VLAN_11 interface.

- Configure Sw2, using VLAN_33 with the IP address 160.10.33.10/24. After you have finished all tasks related to the IGP section, all routers on your topology should be able to ping Sw2 VLAN_33 interface. R3 also should be able to ping this interface.

- Configure Sw1 and Sw2 such that you will have the traffic related to VLAN_100 pass primarily through fa0/15 trunk port and the traffic related to VLAN_200 pass primarily through fa0/17 trunk port. If one of the trunks should fail, the remaining trunk must carry all traffic.

- You have high-priority traffic running on VLAN_22 between routers R3, R5, and R6. Configure Sw1 such that the ports connected to these routers will wait eight seconds before changing from learning state to forwarding state.

## Section 1.3: ATM Configuration (4 Points)

- Configure the ATM connection as shown in Figure 6-9.

- A PVC is configured between R6 and the backbone router. Configure your router to communicate with the BB router. Do not configure subinterfaces.

- Use explicit address mapping. Do not depend on the remoter backbone router for inverse ARP.

- You must be able to ping the backbone router address 170.100.10.254.

- You have users on Backbone 3 using an application that requires a 512-kbps Input Peak Cell Rate. Configure your ATM interface to guarantee this requirement.

**Figure 6-9**   *ATM Diagram*

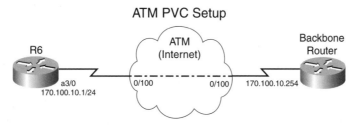

## Section 2: IP IGP Protocols (30 Points)

Configure the IP routing as illustrated in Figure 6-10, following the directions.

**Figure 6-10** *IP IGP Diagram*

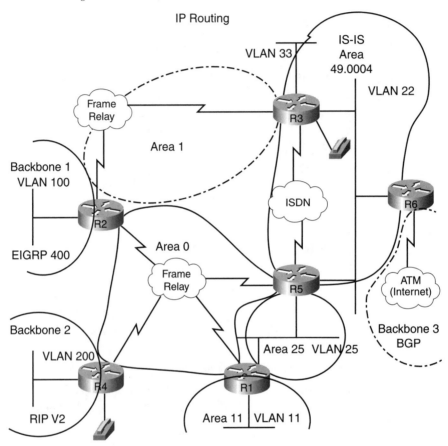

## Section 2.1: OSPF (10 Points)

- Configure OSPF according to Figure 6-10. R1-s0/1, R2-s0/1, R4-s0/1, and R5-s0/1 are to be part of the OSPF area 0.

- R2-s0/0 and R3-s0/0 are to be configured as OSPF area 1.

- R1-e0/0 and Sw1-interface VLAN 11 are to be configured as OSPF area 11.

- R1-e0/1 and R5 fa0/1 are to be configured as OSPF area 25.

- Configure the loopback addresses to be part of the OSPF process. These interfaces should appear in the OSPF routing table with their original /24 mask.

- Make sure you are able to ping any OSPF interface from any router.

- Configure R1 such that the interface on VLAN_25 will have a cost of 20.

## Section 2.2: EIGRP (8 Points)

- Configure EIGRP between R2 and BB1. Configure EIGRP as AS 400. R2-fa0/0 must be the only interface configured for EIGRP on R2. The R2 routing table should be populated with EIGRP routes from BB1.

- Redistribute mutually between EIGRP and OSPF. Make sure all routers have the EIGRP routes in their routing tables.

- Configure R2 to allow only the networks 50.5.5.0/24 and 40.4.4.0/24 from BB1.

- You want to guarantee a minimum of 70 percent of the bandwidth for the EIGRP traffic. Configure R2 to accommodate this.

## Section 2.3: RIP (7 Points)

- Configure RIPv2 between R4 and BB2. R4-e0/0 must be the only interface configured for RIP on R4. You should receive updates and the R4 routing table will be populated with some RIP routes from BB2.

- Redistribute RIP into OSPF such that networks 20.0.0.0/8 and 30.0.0.0/8 will have a metric of 128 kbps and network 196.1.0.0/16 will have a metric of 56 kbps.

- Configure R4 to adjust RIP timers so the time that a route is declared invalid will be set to 200 seconds.

## Section 2.4: IS-IS (5 Points)

- Configure IS-IS according to Figure 6-10. R3-fa0/0, R3-fa0/1, R5-fa0/0, R6-e0/0, and the ISDN cloud are part of the IS-IS domain. Use area 49.0004 and level 1 and 2 adjacencies.

- You should have the routing table of all IS-IS routers populated with the IS-IS networks.

- You should be able to ping all interfaces of all routers within the IS-IS network.

- Redistribute IS-IS into OSPF on R5. R6 should see in its routing table all routes from your topology and R6 must be able to ping all other router loopback0 address.

- To avoid overloading the CPU of the IS-IS routers on VLAN_22 during LSP transmission and reception, configure the routers to reduce the LSP transmission rate to 100 ms.

# Section 3: BGP (12 points)

- Configure IBGP and EBGP as shown in Figure 6-11.

**Figure 6-11** *IBGP and EBGP Configuration*

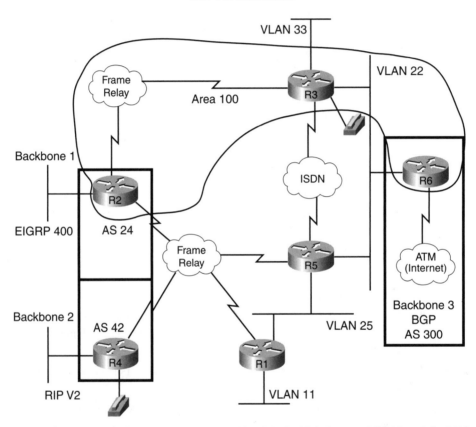

BGP AS Boundaries

- Configure EBGP between R6 and BB3. R6 will belong to AS 100 and the BB3 router AS is 300. R6 will receive updates for networks 200.20.X.0 and 198.18.X.0, where X is any number.

- Configure IBGP between R2, R3, and R6. Use AS 100. R2 should not peer directly with R6. R2 and R3 should be able to see all BGP BB3 routes in their BGP routing tables.

- Configure an EBGP peering between R2 to AS 24 and R4 to AS 42. R4 should have all BB3 backbone routes within its BGP routing table. Do not change the R2 affiliation with AS 100 as accomplished in the preceding task and do not use a Confederation to accomplish this.

# Section 4: ISDN (6 Points)

- Configure ISDN on R3 and R5 using PPP. R3 and R5 should be able to ping each other across the ISDN link.

- Make sure that your routing protocol is passed across the ISDN link only when the connectivity is established.

- The ISDN link should only pass a routing protocol if R5-fa0/0 is down.

- Configure R3 to override specific cause codes that are sent to the switch in case of a disconnection. Should this event occur, ensure that R3 uses "Channel-Not-Available" code message.

# Section 5: IP and IOS Features (7 Points)

- Configure R4 to have a list of the following default domain names: **ccie.com**, **rip.com**, and **isis.com**.

- Assume you have on the LAN segment of BB1 a DNS server with an IP address of 130.200.10.200. Configure R3 so any host on VLAN 33 that needs to resolve a name server can reach the DNS server.

- Configure on R1 an incoming banner to welcome the users connecting to use R1 via Telnet. Use the following messages:

    — *Banner message:* This is a lab exercise to help you in preparation for the CCIE Routing and Switching Lab Exam. Unauthorized access prohibited.

    — *Message of the day:* The router will go down at 6:00 PM today for a software upgrade.

- Configure R2 such that all attempts to reach or connect the Backbone 1 address 130.200.10.200 with source address of 160.10.32.0/24 will be seen as 130.200.10.15-20/24.

# Section 6: DLSw (4 Points)

- Configure DLSw between VLAN_11 and VLAN_33. Use FST encapsulation.

- Configure R3 to accommodate the NetBIOS users on VLAN_33 when a cache entry is requested and mark it as stable for six minutes.

# Section 7: QoS (4 Points)

- Configure the Frame Relay connection between R2 and R3 such that the connection can adapt to congestion when a BECN is received from the network. Assume a 1544 kbps access rate and a CIR of 64 kbps.

- Consider VoIP to be a "critical" application. Configure Priority-Queing-Class-Based Weight Fair Queing (PQ-CBWFQ) on R3 and R4 to guarantee a bandwidth of 256 kbps on VoIP traffic and Fair-Queue with a queue size of 32 for all other traffic types.

# Section 8: Multicast (6 Points)

- Configure Multicast PIM Sparse-mode on VLAN_22 to allow Multicast traffic between R3, R5, and R6. Make R6 the rendezvous point. Make this a static configuration.
- Configure R3, R5, and R6 to prune their groups in eight seconds.

# Section 9: Security (7 Points)

- You are concerned that you cannot trust some users on VLAN_25. Configure the interfaces for R1 and R5 to authenticate the routing protocol updates through the LAN with the best authentication method.
- Configure R3, R5, and R6 to authenticate any routing updates on the IS-IS running on VLAN_22. Make this configuration on the interface level.
- Configure Sw2 to permit only Telnet access from R3 with source address of 160.10.3.3. Also make sure that both successful and failed Telnet connections are logged.

# Section 10: VoIP (6 Points)

- Configure a basic VoIP connection between R3 and R4. Consider the R3 local number to be "33" and R4 local number to be "44."
- Configure your dial peers to provide silence when the remote party is not speaking. You can assume that Voice Activity Detection (VAD) is enabled.

# Practice Lab 6 "Ask the Proctor"

This section should only be used if you require clues to complete the questions. In the real CCIE Lab, the proctor will not enter into any discussions regarding the questions or answers. He or she will be present to ensure you do not have problems with the lab environment, help you to clarify the questions, and to maintain the timing element of the exam.

## Section 1.1: Frame Relay Configuration

Q: If I want to, can I configure R2 without subinterfaces?

A: No. The question says you must use subinterfaces on R2.

Q: Can I disable inverse ARP but still have other PVCs on my map?

A: You might need to perform some other procedures to have only the PVCs you want on your Frame Relay map.

Q: Do I need to be able to ping my own router interface?

A: No. You are expected to ping across the Frame Relay cloud.

Q: I think I am having a problem on my Frame Relay switch. I have my configuration right and I am still not able to ping between R2 and R1, but between R2 and R5 is just fine. Could you please take a look in my Frame Relay switch?

A: Sure, I will verify the switch, but please double-check your configuration and make sure you are not missing anything or you are not mismatching anything.

## Section 1.2: 3550 LAN Switch Configurations

Q: Can I leave my switch ports in auto mode?

A: The questions do not specifically ask you to configure speed and duplex but you should do this to avoid any mismatches that could cause you problems. It might cause your switch to enter in a loop and stop your entire network.

Q: Should I name the VLANs as VLAN_11, and so on?

A: If the question named the VLANs, you should configure them as you see in the question.

Q: Should I be able to ping the switch's loopback?

A: Unless you find a specific requirement on any question, you are not required to accomplish this.

Q: I think after I have configured the vtp connection, I should be able to see all VLANs in both switches, but I do not. Why?

A: Yes, you are right. Please double-check your configuration. You could be missing something in your configuration.

# Section 1.3: ATM Configuration

Q: What kind of sub-interface do you want on R6?

A: Please read and double-check the question again. The question states to not configure subinterfaces.

Q: What ATM encapsulation should I use?

A: This is a back-to-back configuration and the backbone is using the default encapsulation.

Q: Do you want me to configure "broadcast" under my ATM interfaces?

A: You need to determine what type of traffic/protocols will use the ATM network.

Q: I have my ATM configured and the map statement too, but I still am not receiving any routes from the backbone. Can I verify if the backbone is acceptable?

A: Yes, I can verify. But also please double-check your configuration to ensure that nothing is missing.

# Section 2.1: OSPF

Q: Can I use any OSPF process ID?

A: Yes.

Q: Can I configure **ip ospf network point-to-point**?

A: There is no specific requirement for what to use.

Q: In which OSPF area should I configure my loopback interfaces?

A: It is your choice. An important thing to do is to examine the question for restrictions such as "do not use this or that." If you see no restriction, you are free to configure what you think will be the best solution.

Q: Do I need to able to ping all router interfaces?

A: You should be able to ping all OSPF router interfaces at that point.

# Section 2.2: EIGRP

Q: Can I configure any process ID for EIGRP?

A: Please refer to the IP routing diagram in Figure 6-10. It is important to follow the documentation available and the diagram has relevant information.

Q: Do I need to configure mutual redistribution between EIGRP and OSPF?

A: Please refer to your lab text. A mutual redistribution is not required; however, keep in mind that sometimes you will be required to be able to see all networks in the routing tables of all routers.

# Section 2.3: RIP

Q: What RIP version do I need to configure, version 1 or 2?

A: Please refer to your IP IGP diagram. It is also part of your lab documentation.

Q: Can I use the **passive-interface** command to make sure only R4-e0/0 will advertise RIP?

A: The exercise does not say you cannot use it, so there is no restriction barring you from using it.

Q: I can configure three different solutions to achieve the filter part. Is there a preferential approach?

A: You can configure any solution because the criteria is matched.

Q: I am not receiving any routes from BB2. Can you verify if the BB2 is up?

A: Yes, I will verify. Can you ping the BB2 RIP address? If not, please go back to your Layer 2 configurations, the VLAN setup, and make sure you did not miss anything. If you can ping and you are still not seeing any routes from BB2, I will definitely double-check the BB2.

Q: I configured the filter on R4, but I am still seeing all routes from BB2. Can you verify that I do not have an IOS bug?

A: No, we do not have an IOS bug. I have been running this lab exercise and it works just fine. Please double-check your configuration.

# Section 2.4: IS-IS

Q: Can I configure any area for IS-IS?

A: No. You must refer to your text and diagram for directions.

Q: Should I need to have connectivity to other routers from R6?

A: Yes. The R6 routing table should have all networks. Also, consider that R6 might need to be reachable during later tasks in this exercise.

Q: I am typing the **isis circuit-type** command, but the routers do not take it. Can you verify if there is an IOS problem or bug?

A: Yes, I can verify, but we do not have any IOS issues. Please double-check your configuration to ensure that it is done properly.

# Section 3: BGP

Q: Do I need to configure AS 100 on R6?

A: I suggest that you follow the lab text instructions. If it says AS 100, you should follow it.

Q: Should I use BGP Confederation or any other method?

A: You are requested to configure as such, because R2 does not peer directly to R6. Confederations or another method will be acceptable.

Q: I have some IGP problems and not all of my routers can see all loopback interfaces, but BGP is configured correctly. Will this be acceptable?

A: No, you must have a TCP connection between your BGP peers to receive full credit.

# Section 4: ISDN

Q: Are you asking me to configure **dialer-watch**?

A: To accomplish the requirement and make it stable, you need to decide what to configure.

Q: Can I have any traffic at all passing through the ISDN link?

A: No. Traffic can only go through the ISDN link if R5 loses fa0/0 interface connectivity.

Q: Should I configure any kind of authentication?

A: You are not required to do so. Sometimes you need a minimum configuration to have your basic ISDN working.

# Section 5: IP and IOS Features

Q: Do you want me to configure any special phrase on the banner?

A: No, the main issue is to provide the correct configuration in terms of commands. No special requirements regarding phrases or words exist.

Q: I cannot ping the DNS server address (130.200.10.200). Is this acceptable?

A: Yes, this is acceptable. The question says to "assume" you have a server and, in fact, the server does not exist. The main issue is to provide the correct configuration.

# Section 6: DLSw

Q: Can I configure my local peer as *promiscuous*?

A: Well, you have basically only two peers. But no restrictions exist regarding that.

Q: I still have an IGP problem. I think I configured the DLSw correctly. Will I receive some credit?

A: Yes, you will receive some credit from those questions that do not require IGP connectivity such as DLSw+ features. But if your IGP is not working properly and your DLSw+ peers are not connected, no credit will be given.

# Section 7: QoS

Q: What do you want here, to configure congestion avoidance?

A: I cannot answer yes or no, otherwise I will be giving the answer, but I can tell you that you need to think about a mechanism to guarantee adaptability to congestion.

Q: Can you tell me what precedence I need to configure?

A: I'm sorry, but I cannot answer that. Please refer to the Cisco.com/univercd documentation to research.

# Section 8: Multicast

Q: Do you want me to configure multicast on R3-fa0/1?

A: The question states only VLAN_22 be configured.

Q: Are you asking me to configure some kind of delay to accomplish the "prune" question?

A: You need to configure your routers to have them prune faster, but I cannot discuss with you what kind of solution to provide for that.

# Section 9: Security

Q: Do you want me to configure authentication to the entire OSPF network?

A: Refer to your text. The question is concerned about a specific part of your OSPF network. Configure the way you think will be best to accomplish it.

Q: I am thinking I have different ways to accomplish the Telnet restriction on Sw2. Is there a preference for which approach to take?

A: Any approach is fine as long as you configure a solution that meets the criteria.

# Section 10: VoIP

Q: Can I use any IP address to configure my VoIP peers?

A: Yes, it is your choice.

Q: I have some different ways to improve the quality. What direction do you want me to take?

A: I do not have any preference. Think about configuring the best way that meets the question criteria.

# Practice Lab 6 Debrief

The lab debrief section will now analyze each question showing you what was required and how to achieve the desired results. You should use this section to produce an overall score for your test.

# Section 1: Bridging and Switching (18 Points)

## Section 1.1: Frame Relay Configuration (2 Points)

- *Configure the Frame Relay portion of the network as shown in Figure 6-8 and ensure that only the PVCs illustrated in Figure 6-8 will be used. Use of dynamic PVCs is not permitted.*

The question clearly states that you must use only the PVCs as shown in Figure 6-8. You must, therefore, disable inverse ARP on the routers. It is good practice to ensure that all routers do not rely on inverse ARP, so you should have configured **no frame-relay inverse-arp** under R1, R2, R3, R4, and R5 on their serial interfaces.

If you configured this correctly in Example 6-1, you have scored 2 points.

- *You must use subinterfaces on R2 interface s0/1.*
- *Do not configure subinterfaces on any other routers.*
- *You must be able to ping across the Frame Relay cloud.*

R2 will be connecting to R1, R4, and R5. Notice that a different subnet address exists on either side of the connection between R2 and R4. You should be able to ping across the Frame Relay cloud. Also notice that you "must" configure subinterfaces on R2.

If you configured this correctly as shown in Example 6-1 through Example 6-5, you have scored 3 points.

Example 6-6 through Example 6-10 show how to verify if your configuration is working properly.

| NOTE | When configuring the Frame Relay serial interfaces, it is a very good idea for you to shut down the interfaces while you are configuring. This procedure will ensure you do not have unexpected behavior because of dynamic maps, and so on. Although you have configured **no frame-relay inverse-arp**, another useful command to use is **clear frame-relay inarp interface**, which clears your inverse ARP entries from the map table. Sometimes, you might also need to reload the router to remove dynamic maps. |

**Example 6-1**  *R1 Initial Frame Relay Solution Configuration*

```
R1#show run int s0/1
Building configuration...

Current configuration : 285 bytes
!
interface Serial0/1
 ip address 160.10.37.1 255.255.255.0
 encapsulation frame-relay
 frame-relay map ip 160.10.37.2 112 broadcast
 frame-relay map ip 160.10.37.5 112 broadcast
 no frame-relay inverse-arp
 frame-relay lmi-type ansi
end
R1#
```

**Example 6-2**  *R2 Initial Frame Relay Solution Configuration*

```
R2#show run int s0/0
Building configuration...

Current configuration : 193 bytes
!
interface Serial0/0
 ip address 160.10.32.2 255.255.255.252
 encapsulation frame-relay
 frame-relay map ip 160.10.32.1 203 broadcast
 no frame-relay inverse-arp
 frame-relay lmi-type ansi
end
R2#
R2#show run int s0/1
Building configuration...

Current configuration : 285 bytes
!
interface Serial0/1
 no ip address
 encapsulation frame-relay
 no frame-relay inverse-arp
 frame-relay lmi-type ansi
end
!
interface Serial0/1.1 multipoint
 ip address 160.10.37.2 255.255.255.0
 frame-relay map ip 160.10.37.1 211 broadcast
 frame-relay map ip 160.10.37.5 215 broadcast
 end
!
R2#sh run int s0/1.2
Building configuration...
```

*continues*

**Example 6-2**   *R2 Initial Frame Relay Solution Configuration (Continued)*

```
Current configuration : 117 bytes
!
interface Serial0/1.2 point-to-point
 ip address 160.10.38.2 255.255.255.0
 frame-relay interface-dlci 214
end
R2#
```

**Example 6-3**   *R3 Initial Frame Relay Solution Configuration*

```
R3#show run int s0/0
Building configuration...

Current configuration : 193 bytes
!
interface Serial0/0
 ip address 160.10.32.1 255.255.255.252
 encapsulation frame-relay
 frame-relay map ip 160.10.32.2 302 broadcast
 no frame-relay inverse-arp
 frame-relay lmi-type ansi
end
R3#
```

**Example 6-4**   *R4 Initial Frame Relay Solution Configuration*

```
R4#show run int s0/1
Building configuration...

Current configuration : 285 bytes
!
interface Serial0/1
 ip address 160.10.38.4 255.255.255.0
 encapsulation frame-relay
 frame-relay map ip 160.10.38.2 412 broadcast
 no frame-relay inverse-arp
 frame-relay lmi-type ansi
end

R4#
```

**Example 6-5**   *R5 Initial Frame Relay Solution Configuration*

```
R5#show run int s0/1
Building configuration...

Current configuration : 285 bytes
!
interface Serial0/1
 ip address 160.10.37.5 255.255.255.0
 encapsulation frame-relay
```

**Example 6-5**  *R5 Initial Frame Relay Solution Configuration (Continued)*

```
 frame-relay map ip 160.10.37.1 512 broadcast
 frame-relay map ip 160.10.37.2 512 broadcast
 no frame-relay inverse-arp
 frame-relay lmi-type ansi
end

R5#
```

**Example 6-6**  *R1* **show** *Commands and Pings to Verify Functionality*

```
R1#show fram map
Serial0/1 (up): ip 160.10.37.2 dlci 112(0x70,0x1C00), static,
               broadcast,
               CISCO, status defined, active
Serial0/1 (up): ip 160.10.37.5 dlci 112(0x70,0x1C00), static,
               broadcast,
               CISCO, status defined, active
R1#
R1#ping 160.10.37.2

Type escape sequence to abort.
Sending 5, 100-byte ICMP Echos to 160.10.37.2, timeout is 2 seconds:
!!!!!
Success rate is 100 percent (5/5), round-trip min/avg/max = 1/2/4 ms

R1#ping 160.10.37.5

Type escape sequence to abort.
Sending 5, 100-byte ICMP Echos to 160.10.37.5, timeout is 2 seconds:
!!!!!
Success rate is 100 percent (5/5), round-trip min/avg/max = 4/5/8 ms
R1#
```

**Example 6-7**  *R2* **show** *Commands and Pings to Verify Functionality*

```
R2#show fram map
Serial0/0 (up): ip 160.10.32.1 dlci 203(0xCB,0x30B0), static,
               broadcast,
               CISCO, status defined, active
Serial0/1.1 (up): ip 160.10.37.1 dlci 211(0xD3,0x3430), static,
               broadcast,
               CISCO, status defined, active
Serial0/1.1 (up): ip 160.10.37.5 dlci 215(0xD7,0x3470), static,
               broadcast,
               CISCO, status defined, active
Serial0/1.2 (up): point-to-point dlci, dlci 214(0xD6,0x3460), broadcast
          status defined, active
R2#
R2#
R2#ping 160.10.32.1

Type escape sequence to abort.
Sending 5, 100-byte ICMP Echos to 160.10.32.1, timeout is 2 seconds:
```

*continues*

**Example 6-7** *R2* **show** *Commands and Pings to Verify Functionality (Continued)*

```
!!!!!
Success rate is 100 percent (5/5), round-trip min/avg/max = 1/3/4 ms
R2#ping 160.10.37.1

Type escape sequence to abort.
Sending 5, 100-byte ICMP Echos to 160.10.37.1, timeout is 2 seconds:
!!!!!
Success rate is 100 percent (5/5), round-trip min/avg/max = 1/3/4 ms

R2#ping 160.10.37.5

Type escape sequence to abort.
Sending 5, 100-byte ICMP Echos to 160.10.37.5, timeout is 2 seconds:
!!!!!
Success rate is 100 percent (5/5), round-trip min/avg/max = 1/2/4 ms
R2#
R2#ping 160.10.38.4

Type escape sequence to abort.
Sending 5, 100-byte ICMP Echos to 160.10.38.4, timeout is 2 seconds:
!!!!!
Success rate is 100 percent (5/5), round-trip min/avg/max = 1/3/4 ms
```

**Example 6-8** *R3* **show** *Commands and Pings to Verify Functionality*

```
R3#show fram map
Serial0/0 (up): ip 160.10.32.2 dlci 302(0x12E,0x48E0), static,
              broadcast,
              CISCO, status defined, active
R3#ping 160.10.32.2

Type escape sequence to abort.
Sending 5, 100-byte ICMP Echos to 160.10.32.2, timeout is 2 seconds:
!!!!!
Success rate is 100 percent (5/5), round-trip min/avg/max = 1/3/4 ms
R3#
```

**Example 6-9** *R4* **show** *Commands and Pings to Verify Functionality*

```
R4#show fram map
Serial0/1 (up): ip 160.10.38.2 dlci 412(0x19C,0x64C0), static,
              broadcast,
              CISCO, status defined, active
R4#
R4#ping 160.10.38.2

Type escape sequence to abort.
Sending 5, 100-byte ICMP Echos to 160.10.38.2, timeout is 2 seconds:
!!!!!
Success rate is 100 percent (5/5), round-trip min/avg/max = 4/6/8 ms
R4#
```

**Example 6-10**  *R5* **show** *Commands and Pings to Verify Functionality*

```
R5#show fram map
R5#sh fram map
Serial0/1 (up): ip 160.10.37.1 dlci 512(0x200,0x8000), static,
              broadcast,
              CISCO, status defined, active
Serial0/1 (up): ip 160.10.37.2 dlci 512(0x200,0x8000), static,
              broadcast,
              CISCO, status defined, active R5#
R5#ping 160.10.37.1

Type escape sequence to abort.
Sending 5, 100-byte ICMP Echos to 160.10.37.1, timeout is 2 seconds:
!!!!!
Success rate is 100 percent (5/5), round-trip min/avg/max = 4/6/8 ms
R5#ping 160.10.37.2

Type escape sequence to abort.
Sending 5, 100-byte ICMP Echos to 160.10.37.2, timeout is 2 seconds:
!!!!!
Success rate is 100 percent (5/5), round-trip min/avg/max = 1/3/4 ms
R5#
```

# Section 1.2: 3550 LAN Switch Configuration (12 Points)

- *Sw1 and Sw2 are connected via a crossover cable using ports fa0/15 and fa0/17. Configure a Dot1q (801.1Q) trunk between Sw1 and Sw2.*

If you configured this correctly as shown in Example 6-11 and Example 6-12, you have scored 1 point. Both show a basic trunk configuration. Example 6-13 verifies the configuration for both switches.

**Example 6-11**  *3550 Sw1 Initial Trunk Configuration*

```
Sw1#show run int fa0/15
Building configuration...

Current configuration : 108 bytes
!
interface FastEthernet0/15
 switchport trunk encapsulation dot1q
 switchport mode trunk
 no ip address
end

Sw1#
Sw1#show run int fa0/17
Building configuration...

Current configuration : 108 bytes
```

*continues*

**Example 6-11** *3550 Sw1 Initial Trunk Configuration (Continued)*

```
!
interface FastEthernet0/17
 switchport trunk encapsulation dot1q
 switchport mode trunk
 no ip address
end

Sw1#
```

**Example 6-12** *3550 Sw2 Initial Trunk Configuration*

```
Sw2#show run int fa0/15
Building configuration...

Current configuration : 108 bytes
!
interface FastEthernet0/15
 switchport trunk encapsulation dot1q
 switchport mode trunk
 no ip address
end
Sw2#
Sw2#show run int fa0/17
Building configuration...

Current configuration : 108 bytes
!
interface FastEthernet0/17
 switchport trunk encapsulation dot1q
 switchport mode trunk
 no ip address
end

Sw2#
```

**Example 6-13** *3550 Sw1 and Sw2* **show** *Command Output to Verify Configuration and Functionality*

```
Sw1#show int trunk

Port        Mode        Encapsulation   Status      Native vlan
Fa0/15      on          802.1q          trunking    1
Fa0/17      on          802.1q          trunking    1

Port        Vlans allowed on trunk
Fa0/15      1-4094
Fa0/17      1-4094

Port        Vlans allowed and active in management domain
Fa0/15      1
Fa0/17      1
```

**Example 6-13**  *3550 Sw1 and Sw2* **show** *Command Output to Verify Configuration and Functionality (Continued)*

```
Port          Vlans in spanning tree forwarding state and not pruned
Fa0/15        1
Fa0/17        1
Sw1#
Sw2#show int trunk

Port          Mode            Encapsulation  Status        Native vlan
Fa0/15        on              802.1q         trunking      1
Fa0/17        on              802.1q         trunking      1

Port          Vlans allowed on trunk
Fa0/15        1-4094
Fa0/17        1-4094

Port          Vlans allowed and active in management domain
Fa0/15        1
Fa0/17        1

Port          Vlans in spanning tree forwarding state and not pruned
Fa0/15        1
Fa0/17        none
Sw2#
```

- *All Ethernet ports are pre-cabled as per Table 6-4. Note that not all ports will be used on this lab.*
- *Configure the VLANs as follows:*
    - *VLAN_11: Connected to R1-e0/0 (VLAN_11)*
    - *VLAN_22: Connected to R3-fa0/0, R5-fa0/0, and R6-e0/0 (VLAN_22)*
    - *VLAN_25: Connected to R1-e0/1 and R5-fa0/1 (VLAN_25)*
    - *VLAN_33: Connected to R3-fa0/1 (VLAN_33)*
    - *VLAN_100: Connected to R2-fa0/0 and BB1_Router-e2/0 (VLAN_100)*
    - *VLAN_200: Connected to R4-e0/0 and BB2_Router-e2/4 (VLAN_200)*

If you configured this correctly as shown in Example 6-14, you have scored 2 points.

- *Configure Sw1 to be the VTP server for the domain. Sw2 is a VTP client. Be sure that Sw2 can see the VLAN configuration from Sw1. The VTP domain name is "CISCO."*

It is important to notice how VTP domains work. All VLAN configuration must be done on the VTP Server switch (Sw1) and then all information will be propagated to the VTP Client switch (Sw2), even though you do have some VLANs that will be only connected on Sw2. Notice the VTP domain name "CISCO" is a requirement and is case sensitive, so "CISCO" will be different than "CiSCO" and it will not work.

If you configured this correctly as shown in Example 6-14, you have scored 2 points.

---

**NOTE**     The VLAN configuration is completed under **Vlan database**.

---

**Example 6-14**  *3550 Sw1 and Sw2 VLAN and VTP Configuration*

```
Sw1#show vlan brief

VLAN Name                             Status    Ports
---- -------------------------------- --------- -------------------------------
1    default                          active    Fa0/7, Fa0/8, Fa0/9, Fa0/10
                                                Fa0/11, Fa0/12, Fa0/14, Fa0/16
                                                Fa0/17, Fa0/18, Fa0/19, Fa0/20
                                                Fa0/21, Fa0/22, Fa0/23, Fa0/24
                                                Gi0/1, Gi0/2
11   VLAN_11                          active    Fa0/1
22   VLAN_22                          active    Fa0/3, Fa0/5, Fa0/6
25   VLAN_25                          active
33   VLAN_33                          active
100  VLAN_100                         active    Fa0/2, Fa0/13
200  VLAN_200                         active    Fa0/4
1002 fddi-default                     active
1003 token-ring-default               active
1004 fddinet-default                  active
1005 trnet-default                    active
Sw1#
Sw2#show vlan brief

VLAN Name                             Status    Ports
---- -------------------------------- --------- -------------------------------
1    default                          active    Fa0/2, Fa0/4, Fa0/6, Fa0/7
                                                Fa0/8, Fa0/9, Fa0/10, Fa0/11
                                                Fa0/12, Fa0/14, Fa0/16, Fa0/17
                                                Fa0/18, Fa0/19, Fa0/20, Fa0/21
                                                Fa0/22, Fa0/23, Fa0/24, Gi0/1
                                                Gi0/2
11   VLAN_11                          active
22   VLAN_22                          active
25   VLAN_25                          active    Fa0/1, Fa0/5
33   VLAN_33                          active    Fa0/3
100  VLAN_100                         active
200  VLAN_200                         active    Fa0/13
1002 fddi-default                     active
1003 token-ring-default               active
1004 fddinet-default                  active
1005 trnet-default                    active
Sw2#
Sw1#
Sw1#show vtp stat
```

**Example 6-14**  *3550 Sw1 and Sw2 VLAN and VTP Configuration (Continued) (Continued)*

```
VTP Version                         : 2
Configuration Revision              : 1
Maximum VLANs supported locally : 1005
Number of existing VLANs            : 11
VTP Operating Mode                  : Server
VTP Domain Name                     : CISCO
VTP Pruning Mode                    : Disabled
VTP V2 Mode                         : Disabled
VTP Traps Generation                : Disabled
MD5 digest                          : 0x36 0xC9 0xB9 0x93 0x5C 0xE6 0x7B 0x1D
Configuration last modified by 160.10.7.7 at 3-19-93 04:55:23
Local updater ID is 160.10.11.10 on interface Vl11 (lowest numbered VLAN interface
found)
Sw1#
Sw2#show vtp stat
VTP Version                         : 2
Configuration Revision              : 1
Maximum VLANs supported locally : 1005
Number of existing VLANs            : 11
VTP Operating Mode                  : Client
VTP Domain Name                     : CISCO
VTP Pruning Mode                    : Disabled
VTP V2 Mode                         : Disabled
VTP Traps Generation                : Disabled
MD5 digest                          : 0x36 0xC9 0xB9 0x93 0x5C 0xE6 0x7B 0x1D
Configuration last modified by 160.10.7.7 at 3-19-93 04:55:23
Sw2#
```

**NOTE**      The VTP domain name must be called CISCO. It needs to be exactly as the question is
asking for.

- *Configure Sw1, using VLAN_11 with the IP address 160.10.11.10/24. After you have
  finished all tasks related to the IGP section, all routers on your topology should be
  able to ping Sw1 VLAN_11 interface.*

If you configured this correctly as shown in Example 6-15, you have scored 2 points.

**Example 6-15**  *3550 Sw1 Management Interface Configuration*

```
Sw1#
Sw1#show run int vlan 11
Building configuration...

Current configuration : 63 bytes
!
interface Vlan11
 ip address 160.10.11.10 255.255.255.0
!
!
```

**NOTE**   You are expected to have Sw1 reachable after you have your IGP routing section done. For example, R6 should be able to ping Sw1 interface VLAN_11.

- *Configure Sw2, using VLAN_33 with the IP address 160.10.33.10/24. After you have finished all tasks related to the IGP section, all routers on your topology should be able to ping Sw2 VLAN_33 interface. R3 also should be able to ping this interface.*

If you configured this correctly as shown in Example 6-16, you have scored 2 points. Example 6-17 verifies the configuration.

**NOTE**   At this moment, Sw2 will be able to ping only R3-fa0/1, which is its default-gateway and is in the same VLAN_33. In fact, you are not required to reach the switches from other routers.

**Example 6-16**  *3550 Sw2 Management Interface Configuration*

```
Sw2#
Sw2#sh run int vlan 33
Building configuration...

Current configuration : 63 bytes
!
interface Vlan33
 ip address 160.10.33.10 255.255.255.0
end
!
!
ip default-gateway 160.10.33.3
Sw2#
!
```

**Example 6-17**  *3550 Sw2 Management Interface Output Verification (Sw2 Pinging R3-fa0/1)*

```
Sw2#ping 160.10.33.3

Type escape sequence to abort.
Sending 5, 100-byte ICMP Echos to 160.10.33.3, timeout is 2 seconds:
!!!!!
Success rate is 100 percent (5/5), round-trip min/avg/max = 1/2/4 ms
Sw2
```

- *Configure Sw1 and Sw2 such that you will have the traffic related to VLAN_100 pass primarily through fa0/15 trunk port and the traffic related to VLAN_200 pass primarily through fa0/17 trunk port. If one of the trunks should fail, the remaining trunk must carry all traffic.*

The question is looking for a loading balance between the port trunks on Sw1 and Sw2 for VLAN_100 and VLAN_200. One possible solution is the use of **spanning-tree vlan port-priority** command, where you need to configure a smaller value on both sides (both trunks). You can also achieve the solution using the **spanning-tree vlan cost** command, where, in this case, the **cost** is to be changed to a smaller value on the "root" only. Pay attention to what is highlighted in the following example.

If you configured this correctly as shown in Example 6-18, you have scored 2 points.

**Example 6-18**  *Sw1 and Sw2* **spanning-tree vlan port-priority** *Configuration*

```
Sw1#sh run int fa0/15
Building configuration...

Current configuration : 136 bytes
!
interface FastEthernet0/15
 switchport trunk encapsulation dot1q
 switchport mode trunk
 spanning-tree vlan 100 port-priority 16
end

Sw1#
Sw1#sh run int fa0/17
Building configuration...

Current configuration : 136 bytes
!
interface FastEthernet0/17
 switchport trunk encapsulation dot1q
 switchport mode trunk
 spanning-tree vlan 200 port-priority 16
end
!
Sw1#sh spanning-tree vlan 100

VLAN0100
  Spanning tree enabled protocol ieee
  Root ID    Priority    32868
             Address     0009.e8ee.f200
             Cost        19
             Port        15 (FastEthernet0/15)
             Hello Time   2 sec  Max Age 20 sec  Forward Delay 15 sec

  Bridge ID  Priority    32868  (priority 32768 sys-id-ext 100)
             Address     0009.e8ef.1800
             Hello Time   2 sec  Max Age 20 sec  Forward Delay 15 sec
             Aging Time 300
```

*continues*

**Example 6-18** *Sw1 and Sw2* **spanning-tree vlan port-priority** *Configuration (Continued)*

```
Interface        Role Sts Cost      Prio.Nbr Type
---------------- ---- --- ---------- -------- --------------------------------
Fa0/2            Desg FWD 19         128.2    Shr
Fa0/13           Desg FWD 100        128.13   Shr
Fa0/15           Root FWD 19          16.15   P2p
Fa0/17           Altn BLK 19         128.17   P2p

Sw1#
Sw1#sh spanning-tree vlan 200

VLAN0200
  Spanning tree enabled protocol ieee
  Root ID    Priority    32968
             Address     0009.e8ee.f200
             Cost        19
             Port        17 (FastEthernet0/17)
             Hello Time   2 sec  Max Age 20 sec  Forward Delay 15 sec

  Bridge ID  Priority    32968   (priority 32768 sys-id-ext 200)
             Address     0009.e8ef.1800
             Hello Time   2 sec  Max Age 20 sec  Forward Delay 15 sec
             Aging Time 300

Interface        Role Sts Cost      Prio.Nbr Type
---------------- ---- --- ---------- -------- --------------------------------
Fa0/4            Desg FWD 100        128.4    Shr
Fa0/15           Altn BLK 19         128.15   P2p
Fa0/17           Root FWD 19          16.17   P2p

Sw1#
!
!
Sw2#
Sw2#sh run int fa0/15
Building configuration...

Current configuration : 136 bytes
!
interface FastEthernet0/15
 switchport trunk encapsulation dot1q
 switchport mode trunk
 spanning-tree vlan 100 port-priority 16
end

Sw2#
Sw2#sh run int fa0/17
Building configuration...

Current configuration : 136 bytes
!
interface FastEthernet0/17
```

**Example 6-18**  *Sw1 and Sw2* **spanning-tree vlan port-priority** *Configuration (Continued)*

```
 switchport trunk encapsulation dot1q
 switchport mode trunk
 spanning-tree vlan 200 port-priority 16
end

Sw2#
Sw2#sh spanning-tree vlan 100

VLAN0100
  Spanning tree enabled protocol ieee
  Root ID    Priority    32868
             Address     0009.e8ee.f200
             This bridge is the root
             Hello Time   2 sec  Max Age 20 sec  Forward Delay 15 sec

  Bridge ID  Priority    32868  (priority 32768 sys-id-ext 100)
             Address     0009.e8ee.f200
             Hello Time   2 sec  Max Age 20 sec  Forward Delay 15 sec
             Aging Time 300

Interface        Role Sts Cost      Prio.Nbr Type
---------------- ---- --- --------- -------- --------------------------------
Fa0/15           Desg FWD 19          16.15  P2p
Fa0/17           Desg FWD 19         128.17  P2p

Sw2#
Sw2#sh spanning-tree vlan 200

VLAN0200
  Spanning tree enabled protocol ieee
  Root ID    Priority    32968
             Address     0009.e8ee.f200
             This bridge is the root
             Hello Time   2 sec  Max Age 20 sec  Forward Delay 15 sec

  Bridge ID  Priority    32968  (priority 32768 sys-id-ext 200)
             Address     0009.e8ee.f200
             Hello Time   2 sec  Max Age 20 sec  Forward Delay 15 sec
             Aging Time 300

Interface        Role Sts Cost      Prio.Nbr Type
---------------- ---- --- --------- -------- --------------------------------
Fa0/13           Desg FWD 100        128.13  Shr
Fa0/15           Desg FWD 19         128.15  P2p
Fa0/17           Desg FWD 19          16.17  P2p

Sw2#
```

- *You have high-priority traffic running on VLAN_22 between routers R3, R5, and R6. Configure Sw1 such that the ports connected to these routers will wait eight seconds before changing from learning state to forwarding state.*

Configure the **forward-delay** feature so that you can change the wait delay time from learning to forward state. The default delay is 15 seconds. The use of the **portfast** feature does not apply here because you are still having the ports going through all states. The **portfast** feature will make a port go from blocking state to the forward state immediately, bypassing the listening and the learning states.

If you configured this correctly as shown in Example 6-19, you have scored 2 points.

**Example 6-19** *3550 Sw1* **forward-delay** *Configuration*

```
Sw1#sh run
Building configuration...

Current configuration : 2944 bytes
!
version 12.1
no service pad
!
hostname Sw1
!
spanning-tree vlan 22 forward-time 8
!
```

# Section 1.3: ATM Configuration (4 Points)

- *Configure the ATM connection as shown in Figure 6-9.*

- *A PVC is configured between R6 and the backbone router. Configure your router to communicate with the BB router. Do not configure subinterfaces.*

- *Use explicit address mapping. Do not depend on the remoter backbone router for inverse ARP.*

- *You must be able to ping the backbone router address 170.100.10.254.*

If you configured this correctly as shown in Example 6-20, you have scored 2 points.

**Example 6-20** *R6 ATM Configuration, Map Verification, and Access to Backbone Router*

```
R6#show run int a3/0
Building configuration...

Current configuration : 140 bytes
!
interface ATM3/0
 ip address 170.100.10.1 255.255.255.0
 no atm ilmi-keepalive
 pvc 0/100
  protocol ip 170.100.10.254 broadcast
```

**Example 6-20**  *R6 ATM Configuration, Map Verification, and Access to Backbone Router (Continued)*

```
 !
end

R6#ping 170.100.10.254

Type escape sequence to abort.
Sending 5, 100-byte ICMP Echos to 170.100.10.254, timeout is 2 seconds:
!!!!!
Success rate is 100 percent (5/5), round-trip min/avg/max = 1/2/4 ms

R6#show atm vc
             VCD /                                     Peak  Avg/Min Burst
Interface   Name          VPI  VCI  Type   Encaps   SC   Kbps   Kbps  Cells  Sts
3/0          3             0   100  PVC    SNAP    UBR  155000              UP
R6#
```

- *You have users on Backbone 3 using an application that requires a 512-kbps Input Peak Cell Rate. Configure your ATM interface to guarantee this requirement.*

You have a UBR service on the ATM interface and you will need to create an ATM class to apply the PCR required. You need to define a VC Class and apply within the interface using the command **class-int**.

If you configured this correctly as shown in Example 6-21, you have scored 2 points.

**Example 6-21**  *ATM Class for UBR Configuration*

```
R6#sh run
!
!
hostname R6
!
!
vc-class atm UBR
  ubr 155000 512
!
R6#sh run int a3/0
Building configuration...

Current configuration : 155 bytes
!
interface ATM3/0
 ip address 170.100.10.1 255.255.255.0
 class-int UBR
 no atm ilmi-keepalive
 pvc 0/100
  protocol ip 170.100.10.254 broadcast
 !
end

R6#
```

# Section 2: IP IGP Protocols (30 Points)

## Section 2.1 OSPF (10 Points)

- *Configure OSPF according to Figure 6-10. R1-s0/1, R2-s0/1, R4-s0/1, and R5-s0/1 are to be part of the OSPF area 0.*
- *R2-s0/0 and R3-s0/0 are to be configured as OSPF area 1.*
- *R1-e0/0 and Sw1-interface VLAN_11 are to be configured as OSPF area 11.*
- *R1-e0/1 and R5 fa0/1 are to be configured as OSPF area 25.*

If you configured this correctly as shown in Example 6-21 through Example 6-26, you have scored 4 points.

- *Configure the loopback addresses to be part of the OSPF process. These interfaces should appear in the OSPF routing table with their original /24 mask.*

If you configured this correctly as shown in Example 6-22 through Example 6-27, you have scored 2 points.

- *Make sure you are able to ping any OSPF interface from any router.*

If you configured this correctly as shown in Example 6-22 through Example 6-27, you have scored 2 points.

This is a basic OSPF configuration. The idea is to make you more familiar with the OSPF configuration especially adding routing on the Catalyst 3550.

**Example 6-22** *OSPF Configuration: R1 Output*

```
R1#show run
interface Loopback0
 ip address 160.10.1.1 255.255.255.0
 ip ospf network point-to-point
!
interface Ethernet0/0
 ip address 160.10.11.1 255.255.255.0

!
interface Ethernet0/1
 ip address 160.10.25.1 255.255.255.0

!
interface Serial0/1
 ip address 160.10.37.1 255.255.255.0
 encapsulation frame-relay
 ip ospf network point-to-multipoint
 !
router ospf 1
 log-adjacency-changes
 network 160.10.1.0 0.0.0.255 area 0
```

**Example 6-22**  *OSPF Configuration: R1 Output (Continued)*

```
   network 160.10.11.0 0.0.0.255 area 11
   network 160.10.25.0 0.0.0.255 area 25
   network 160.10.37.0 0.0.0.255 area 0
 !
 !
R1#show ip route ospf
    160.10.0.0/16 is variably subnetted, 13 subnets, 3 masks
O        160.10.37.5/32 [110/128] via 160.10.37.2, 01:24:17, Serial0/1
O IA     160.10.32.0/30 [110/128] via 160.10.37.2, 01:09:08, Serial0/1
O        160.10.38.0/24 [110/128] via 160.10.37.2, 01:24:17, Serial0/1
O        160.10.37.2/32 [110/64] via 160.10.37.2, 01:24:17, Serial0/1
O        160.10.7.0/24 [110/11] via 160.10.11.10, 01:09:08, Ethernet0/0
O        160.10.5.0/24 [110/129] via 160.10.37.2, 01:24:17, Serial0/1
O        160.10.4.0/24 [110/129] via 160.10.37.2, 01:24:17, Serial0/1
O IA     160.10.3.0/24 [110/129] via 160.10.37.2, 01:09:08, Serial0/1
O        160.10.2.0/24 [110/65] via 160.10.37.2, 01:24:17, Serial0/1
R1#
```

**Example 6-23**  *OSPF Configuration: R2 Output*

```
R2#show run
interface Loopback0
 ip address 160.10.2.2 255.255.255.0
 ip ospf network point-to-point
 !
interface Serial0/0
 ip address 160.10.32.2 255.255.255.252
 encapsulation frame-relay
 ip ospf network point-to-point
 !
interface Serial0/1
  no ip address
 encapsulation frame-relay
 no frame-relay inverse-arp
 frame-relay lmi-type ansi
 !
interface Serial0/1.1 multipoint
 ip address 160.10.37.2 255.255.255.0
 ip ospf network point-to-multipoint
 !
interface Serial0/1.2 point-to-point
 ip address 160.10.38.2 255.255.255.0
 ip ospf network point-to-point
 !
router ospf 1
 log-adjacency-changes

 network 160.10.2.0 0.0.0.255 area 0
 network 160.10.32.0 0.0.0.3 area 1
 network 160.10.37.0 0.0.0.255 area 0
 network 160.10.38.0 0.0.0.255 area 0
```

*continues*

**Example 6-23**  *OSPF Configuration: R2 Output (Continued)*

```
!

R2#sh ip route ospf
      160.10.0.0/16 is variably subnetted, 13 subnets, 3 masks
O        160.10.37.5/32 [110/64] via 160.10.37.5, 00:01:13, Serial0/1.1
O        160.10.37.1/32 [110/64] via 160.10.37.1, 00:01:13, Serial0/1.1
O IA     160.10.11.0/24 [110/74] via 160.10.37.1, 00:01:13, Serial0/1.1
O IA     160.10.7.0/24 [110/75] via 160.10.37.1, 00:01:13, Serial0/1.1
O        160.10.5.0/24 [110/65] via 160.10.37.5, 00:01:13, Serial0/1.1
O        160.10.4.0/24 [110/65] via 160.10.38.4, 00:01:13, Serial0/1.2
O        160.10.3.0/24 [110/65] via 160.10.32.1, 01:38:58, Serial0/0
O        160.10.1.0/24 [110/65] via 160.10.37.1, 00:01:13, Serial0/1.1
O IA     160.10.25.0/24 [110/65] via 160.10.37.5, 00:01:13, Serial0/1.1
  R2#
```

**Example 6-24**  *OSPF Configuration: R3 Output*

```
R3#show run
interface Loopback0
 ip address 160.10.3.3 255.255.255.0
 ip ospf network point-to-point
!
interface Serial0/0
 ip address 160.10.32.1 255.255.255.252
 encapsulation frame-relay
 ip ospf network point-to-point
 !

router ospf 1
 log-adjacency-changes

 network 160.10.3.0 0.0.0.255 area 1
  network 160.10.32.0 0.0.0.3 area 1
!
R3#show ip route ospf
      160.10.0.0/16 is variably subnetted, 15 subnets, 3 masks
O IA     160.10.37.5/32 [110/128] via 160.10.32.2, 00:01:00, Serial0/0
O IA     160.10.38.0/24 [110/128] via 160.10.32.2, 00:01:00, Serial0/0
O IA     160.10.37.2/32 [110/64] via 160.10.32.2, 00:01:00, Serial0/0
O IA     160.10.37.1/32 [110/128] via 160.10.32.2, 00:01:00, Serial0/0
O IA     160.10.11.0/24 [110/138] via 160.10.32.2, 00:01:00, Serial0/0
O IA     160.10.2.0/24 [110/65] via 160.10.32.2, 00:01:00, Serial0/0
O IA     160.10.7.0/24 [110/139] via 160.10.32.2, 00:01:00, Serial0/0
O IA     160.10.5.0/24 [110/129] via 160.10.32.2, 00:01:00, Serial0/0
O IA     160.10.4.0/24 [110/129] via 160.10.32.2, 00:01:00, Serial0/0
O IA     160.10.1.0/24 [110/129] via 160.10.32.2, 00:01:00, Serial0/0
O IA     160.10.25.0/24 [110/129] via 160.10.32.2, 00:01:00, Serial0/0
R3#
```

**Example 6-25**  *OSPF Configuration: R4 Output*

```
R4#show run
interface Loopback0
 ip address 160.10.4.4 255.255.255.0
 ip ospf network point-to-point
 !

interface Serial0/1
 ip address 160.10.38.4 255.255.255.0
 encapsulation frame-relay
 ip ospf network point-to-point
 !
router ospf 1
 log-adjacency-changes
 network 160.10.4.0 0.0.0.255 area 0
 network 160.10.38.0 0.0.0.255 area 0
 !
 !
R4#show ip route ospf
     160.10.0.0/16 is variably subnetted, 13 subnets, 3 masks
O       160.10.37.5/32 [110/128] via 160.10.38.2, 00:02:34, Serial0/1
O IA    160.10.32.0/30 [110/128] via 160.10.38.2, 00:02:34, Serial0/1
O       160.10.37.2/32 [110/64] via 160.10.38.2, 00:02:34, Serial0/1
O       160.10.37.1/32 [110/128] via 160.10.38.2, 00:02:34, Serial0/1
O IA    160.10.11.0/24 [110/138] via 160.10.38.2, 00:02:34, Serial0/1
O       160.10.2.0/24 [110/65] via 160.10.38.2, 00:02:34, Serial0/1
O IA    160.10.3.0/24 [110/129] via 160.10.38.2, 00:02:34, Serial0/1
O IA    160.10.7.0/24 [110/139] via 160.10.38.2, 00:02:34, Serial0/1
O       160.10.5.0/24 [110/129] via 160.10.38.2, 00:02:34, Serial0/1
O       160.10.1.0/24 [110/129] via 160.10.38.2, 00:02:34, Serial0/1
O IA    160.10.25.0/24 [110/129] via 160.10.38.2, 00:02:34, Serial0/1
R4#
```

**Example 6-26**  *OSPF Configuration: R5 Output*

```
R5#show run
interface Loopback0
 ip address 160.10.5.5 255.255.255.0
 ip ospf network point-to-point
 !
interface FastEthernet0/1
 ip address 160.10.25.5 255.255.255.0
 duplex auto
 speed auto
 !
interface Serial0/1
 ip address 160.10.37.5 255.255.255.0
 encapsulation frame-relay
 ip ospf network point-to-multipoint
 !
router ospf 1
 log-adjacency-changes
```

*continues*

**Example 6-26** *OSPF Configuration: R5 Output (Continued)*

```
network 160.10.5.0 0.0.0.255 area 0
network 160.10.25.0 0.0.0.255 area 25
network 160.10.37.0 0.0.0.255 area 0
!
!
R5#show ip route ospf
     160.10.0.0/16 is variably subnetted, 14 subnets, 3 masks
O IA    160.10.32.0/30 [110/128] via 160.10.37.2, 00:02:52, Serial0/1
O       160.10.38.0/24 [110/128] via 160.10.37.2, 00:02:52, Serial0/1
O       160.10.37.2/32 [110/64] via 160.10.37.2, 00:02:52, Serial0/1
O       160.10.37.1/32 [110/128] via 160.10.37.2, 00:02:52, Serial0/1
O IA    160.10.11.0/24 [110/138] via 160.10.37.2, 00:02:52, Serial0/1
O       160.10.2.0/24 [110/65] via 160.10.37.2, 00:02:52, Serial0/1
O IA    160.10.3.0/24 [110/129] via 160.10.37.2, 00:02:52, Serial0/1
O IA    160.10.7.0/24 [110/139] via 160.10.37.2, 00:02:52, Serial0/1
O       160.10.1.0/24 [110/129] via 160.10.37.2, 00:02:52, Serial0/1
O       160.10.4.0/24 [110/129] via 160.10.37.2, 00:02:52, Serial0/1
R5#
```

**Example 6-27** *OSPF Configuration: Sw1 Output*

```
Sw1#sh run
!
!
ip subnet-zero
ip routing
!
no ip domain-lookup
!
!
interface Loopback0
 ip address 160.10.7.7 255.255.255.0
 ip ospf network point-to-point
!
!
interface Vlan11
 ip address 160.10.11.10 255.255.255.0
!
router ospf 1
 log-adjacency-changes
 network 160.10.7.0 0.0.0.255 area 11
 network 160.10.11.0 0.0.0.255 area 11
!
!
Sw1#sh ip ro ospf
     160.10.0.0/16 is variably subnetted, 13 subnets, 3 masks
O IA    160.10.37.5/32 [110/129] via 160.10.11.1, 00:00:00, Vlan11
O IA    160.10.32.0/30 [110/129] via 160.10.11.1, 00:00:00, Vlan11
O IA    160.10.38.0/24 [110/129] via 160.10.11.1, 00:00:00, Vlan11
O IA    160.10.37.2/32 [110/65] via 160.10.11.1, 00:00:00, Vlan11
O IA    160.10.37.1/32 [110/1] via 160.10.11.1, 00:00:00, Vlan11
```

**Example 6-27**  *OSPF Configuration: Sw1 Output (Continued)*

```
O IA     160.10.2.0/24 [110/66] via 160.10.11.1, 00:00:00, Vlan11
O IA     160.10.3.0/24 [110/130] via 160.10.11.1, 00:00:00, Vlan11
O IA     160.10.1.0/24 [110/2] via 160.10.11.1, 00:00:00, Vlan11
O IA     160.10.4.0/24 [110/130] via 160.10.11.1, 00:00:00, Vlan11
O IA     160.10.5.0/24 [110/130] via 160.10.11.1, 00:00:00, Vlan11
O IA     160.10.25.0/24 [110/11] via 160.10.11.1, 00:00:00, Vlan11
Sw1#
```

- *Configure R1 such that the interface on VLAN_25 will have a cost of 20.*

To change the cost on the interface, you need to work with the command **ip ospf cost** command under the interface level.

If you configured this correctly as shown in Example 6-28, you have scored 2 points.

**Example 6-28**  *OSPF Configuration to Block LSA Flooding*

```
R1#sh run int e0/1
Building configuration...

Current configuration : 136 bytes
!
interface Ethernet0/1
 ip address 160.10.25.1 255.255.255.0
 ip ospf cost 20
 half-duplex
end

R1#
! Below the output showing the interface cost before change. Notice the cost = 10
(default)
R1#show ip ospf interface e0/1
Ethernet0/1 is up, line protocol is up
  Internet Address 160.10.25.1/24, Area 25
  Process ID 1, Router ID 160.10.1.1, Network Type BROADCAST, Cost: 10
  Transmit Delay is 1 sec, State BDR, Priority 1
!
<>
!
R1#

! Below the output showing the interface cost after change. Notice the cost = 20.

R1#show ip ospf interface e0/1
Ethernet0/1 is up, line protocol is up
  Internet Address 160.10.25.1/24, Area 25
  Process ID 1, Router ID 160.10.1.1, Network Type BROADCAST, Cost: 20
  Transmit Delay is 1 sec, State BDR, Priority 1
!
<>
!
R1#
```

## Section 2.2: EIGRP (8 Points)

- *Configure EIGRP between R2 and BB1. Configure EIGRP as AS 400. R2-fa0/0 must be the only interface configured for EIGRP on R2. The R2 routing table should be populated with EIGRP routes from BB1.*

If you configured this correctly as shown in Example 6-29, you have scored 2 points.

- *Redistribute mutually between EIGRP and OSPF. Make sure all routers have the EIGRP routes in their routing tables.*

If you configured this correctly as shown in Example 6-29, you have scored 2 points.

This is a basic setup to have R2 receiving EIGRP routes from BB1. An important thing is to observe and follow the EIGRP AS number given on the IP IGP diagram. Pay attention when configuring redistribution to explore the **redistribute** command to ensure that no networks will be missing.

**NOTE**  To have R2 to advertise the OSPF networks to BB1, we need to configure under the EIGRP process the network 160.10.0.0.

**Example 6-29**  *R2, R5, and Sw1 Output: EIGRP Configuration and Verification*

```
R2#sh run | b router eigrp
router eigrp 400
 redistribute ospf 1 metric 100 10 255 255 1500

 network 130.200.10.0 0.0.0.255
 network 160.10.0.0
 no auto-summary
 no eigrp log-neighbor-changes
!
!
router ospf 1
 redistribute eigrp 400 metric 100 subnets
!
R2# show ip route eigrp
     50.0.0.0/24 is subnetted, 1 subnets
D       50.5.5.0 [90/156160] via 130.200.10.200, 00:01:54, FastEthernet0/0
D    193.118.9.0/24 [90/156160] via 130.200.10.200, 00:01:54, FastEthernet0/0
D    193.118.8.0/24 [90/156160] via 130.200.10.200, 00:01:54, FastEthernet0/0
D    193.118.10.0/24 [90/156160] via 130.200.10.200, 00:01:54, FastEthernet0/0
D    193.118.5.0/24 [90/156160] via 130.200.10.200, 00:01:54, FastEthernet0/0
D    193.118.4.0/24 [90/156160] via 130.200.10.200, 00:01:54, FastEthernet0/0
D    193.118.7.0/24 [90/156160] via 130.200.10.200, 00:01:54, FastEthernet0/0
     40.0.0.0/24 is subnetted, 1 subnets
D       40.4.4.0 [90/156160] via 130.200.10.200, 00:01:54, FastEthernet0/0
D    193.118.6.0/24 [90/156160] via 130.200.10.200, 00:01:54, FastEthernet0/0
D    193.118.1.0/24 [90/156160] via 130.200.10.200, 00:01:54, FastEthernet0/0
```

**Example 6-29**  *R2, R5, and Sw1 Output: EIGRP Configuration and Verification (Continued)*

```
D      193.118.3.0/24 [90/156160] via 130.200.10.200, 00:01:54, FastEthernet0/0
D      193.118.2.0/24 [90/156160] via 130.200.10.200, 00:01:54, FastEthernet0/0
R2#
!
! R5 Routing table has the EIGRP routes as external OSPF routes
R5# sh ip ro ospf
       50.0.0.0/24 is subnetted, 1 subnets
O E2    50.5.5.0 [110/100] via 160.10.37.2, 00:01:02, Serial0/1
O E2 193.118.9.0/24 [110/100] via 160.10.37.2, 00:01:02, Serial0/1
O E2 193.118.8.0/24 [110/100] via 160.10.37.2, 00:01:02, Serial0/1
O E2 193.118.10.0/24 [110/100] via 160.10.37.2, 00:01:02, Serial0/1
O E2 193.118.5.0/24 [110/100] via 160.10.37.2, 00:01:02, Serial0/1
O E2 193.118.4.0/24 [110/100] via 160.10.37.2, 00:01:02, Serial0/1
       160.10.0.0/16 is variably subnetted, 14 subnets, 3 masks
O IA    160.10.32.0/30 [110/128] via 160.10.37.2, 00:01:12, Serial0/1
O       160.10.38.0/24 [110/128] via 160.10.37.2, 00:01:12, Serial0/1
O       160.10.37.2/32 [110/64] via 160.10.37.2, 00:01:12, Serial0/1
O       160.10.37.1/32 [110/128] via 160.10.37.2, 00:01:12, Serial0/1
O IA    160.10.11.0/24 [110/138] via 160.10.37.2, 00:01:12, Serial0/1
O       160.10.2.0/24 [110/65] via 160.10.37.2, 00:01:12, Serial0/1
O IA    160.10.3.0/24 [110/129] via 160.10.37.2, 00:01:12, Serial0/1
O       160.10.1.0/24 [110/129] via 160.10.37.2, 00:01:13, Serial0/1
O IA    160.10.7.0/24 [110/139] via 160.10.37.2, 00:01:13, Serial0/1
O       160.10.4.0/24 [110/129] via 160.10.37.2, 00:01:13, Serial0/1
O E2 193.118.7.0/24 [110/100] via 160.10.37.2, 00:01:03, Serial0/1
       40.0.0.0/24 is subnetted, 1 subnets
O E2    40.4.4.0 [110/100] via 160.10.37.2, 00:01:03, Serial0/1
       130.200.0.0/24 is subnetted, 1 subnets
O E2    130.200.10.0 [110/100] via 160.10.37.2, 00:01:03, Serial0/1
O E2 193.118.6.0/24 [110/100] via 160.10.37.2, 00:01:04, Serial0/1
O E2 193.118.1.0/24 [110/100] via 160.10.37.2, 00:01:04, Serial0/1
O E2 193.118.3.0/24 [110/100] via 160.10.37.2, 00:01:04, Serial0/1
O E2 193.118.2.0/24 [110/100] via 160.10.37.2, 00:01:04, Serial0/1
R5#
! Sw1 Routing table has the EIGRP routes as OSPF external
Sw1#sh ip ro ospf
       50.0.0.0/24 is subnetted, 1 subnets
O E2    50.5.5.0 [110/100] via 160.10.11.1, 00:03:17, Vlan11
O E2 193.118.9.0/24 [110/100] via 160.10.11.1, 00:03:17, Vlan11
O E2 193.118.8.0/24 [110/100] via 160.10.11.1, 00:03:17, Vlan11
O E2 193.118.10.0/24 [110/100] via 160.10.11.1, 00:03:17, Vlan11
O E2 193.118.5.0/24 [110/100] via 160.10.11.1, 00:03:17, Vlan11
O E2 193.118.4.0/24 [110/100] via 160.10.11.1, 00:03:17, Vlan11
       160.10.0.0/16 is variably subnetted, 13 subnets, 3 masks
O IA    160.10.37.5/32 [110/129] via 160.10.11.1, 00:14:52, Vlan11
O IA    160.10.32.0/30 [110/129] via 160.10.11.1, 00:14:52, Vlan11
O IA    160.10.38.0/24 [110/129] via 160.10.11.1, 00:14:52, Vlan11
O IA    160.10.37.2/32 [110/65] via 160.10.11.1, 00:14:52, Vlan11
O IA    160.10.37.1/32 [110/1] via 160.10.11.1, 00:14:52, Vlan11
O IA    160.10.2.0/24 [110/66] via 160.10.11.1, 00:14:52, Vlan11
O IA    160.10.3.0/24 [110/130] via 160.10.11.1, 00:14:52, Vlan11
O IA    160.10.1.0/24 [110/2] via 160.10.11.1, 00:14:52, Vlan11
```

*continues*

**Example 6-29** *R2, R5, and Sw1 Output: EIGRP Configuration and Verification (Continued)*

```
O IA    160.10.4.0/24 [110/130] via 160.10.11.1, 00:14:52, Vlan11
O IA    160.10.5.0/24 [110/130] via 160.10.11.1, 00:14:52, Vlan11
O IA    160.10.25.0/24 [110/11] via 160.10.11.1, 00:14:52, Vlan11
O E2 193.118.7.0/24 [110/100] via 160.10.11.1, 00:03:18, Vlan11
        40.0.0.0/24 is subnetted, 1 subnets
O E2    40.4.4.0 [110/100] via 160.10.11.1, 00:03:18, Vlan11
        130.200.0.0/24 is subnetted, 1 subnets
O E2    130.200.10.0 [110/100] via 160.10.11.1, 00:03:20, Vlan11
O E2 193.118.6.0/24 [110/100] via 160.10.11.1, 00:03:20, Vlan11
O E2 193.118.1.0/24 [110/100] via 160.10.11.1, 00:03:20, Vlan11
O E2 193.118.3.0/24 [110/100] via 160.10.11.1, 00:03:20, Vlan11
O E2 193.118.2.0/24 [110/100] via 160.10.11.1, 00:03:20, Vlan11
Sw1#
! BB_ROUTER Routing table has the OSPF routes
BB_ROUTER# sh ip ro eigrp
        160.10.0.0/16 is variably subnetted, 13 subnets, 3 masks
D       160.10.32.0/30 [90/2195456] via 130.200.10.2, 00:03:50, Ethernet2/0
D EX    160.10.37.5/32 [170/25628160] via 130.200.10.2, 00:03:50, Ethernet2/0
D       160.10.38.0/24 [90/2195456] via 130.200.10.2, 00:03:50, Ethernet2/0
D EX    160.10.37.1/32 [170/25628160] via 130.200.10.2, 00:03:50, Ethernet2/0
D       160.10.37.0/24 [90/2195456] via 130.200.10.2, 00:03:50, Ethernet2/0
D EX    160.10.11.0/24 [170/25628160] via 130.200.10.2, 00:03:50, Ethernet2/0
D       160.10.2.0/24 [90/409600] via 130.200.10.2, 00:03:50, Ethernet2/0
D EX    160.10.3.0/24 [170/25628160] via 130.200.10.2, 00:03:50, Ethernet2/0
D EX    160.10.1.0/24 [170/25628160] via 130.200.10.2, 00:03:50, Ethernet2/0
D EX    160.10.7.0/24 [170/25628160] via 130.200.10.2, 00:03:50, Ethernet2/0
D EX    160.10.4.0/24 [170/25628160] via 130.200.10.2, 00:03:50, Ethernet2/0
D EX    160.10.5.0/24 [170/25628160] via 130.200.10.2, 00:03:50, Ethernet2/0
D EX    160.10.25.0/24 [170/25628160] via 130.200.10.2, 00:03:51, Ethernet2/0
BB_ROUTER#
```

- *Configure R2 to allow only the networks 50.5.5.0/24 and 40.4.4.0/24 from BB1.*

If you configured this correctly as shown in Example 6-30, you have scored 2 points.

An access list permiting only those two networks and applying under the EIGRP process with a distribute list accomplishes the requirement. It is important to notice that at this point you might need to clear all the routing tables within all routers to have a fast convergence to see only the two networks, considering you have already updated the routing tables with all EIGRP backbone routes.

**Example 6-30** *EIGRP Filter Configuration on R2 and Verification on R5*

```
R2#sh run ¦ b router eigrp
router eigrp 400
 distribute-list 2 in FastEthernet0/0
 no auto-summary
 no eigrp log-neighbor-changes
!

access-list 2 permit 50.5.5.0 0.0.0.255
```

**Example 6-30**  *EIGRP Filter Configuration on R2 and Verification on R5 (Continued)*

```
access-list 2 permit 40.4.4.0 0.0.0.255
!
! R2 EIGRP Routing table has only the 2 EIGRP networks
R2#sh ip ro eigrp
50.0.0.0/24 is subnetted, 1 subnets
D       50.5.5.0 [90/156160] via 130.200.10.200, 00:09:21, FastEthernet0/0
     40.0.0.0/24 is subnetted, 1 subnets
D       40.4.4.0 [90/156160] via 130.200.10.200, 00:09:21, FastEthernet0/0R2#
!
! R5 OSPF Routing table has only the 2 networks
R5#sh ip ro ospf
 50.0.0.0/24 is subnetted, 1 subnets
O E2    50.5.5.0 [110/100] via 160.10.37.2, 00:00:03, Serial0/1
     160.10.0.0/16 is variably subnetted, 14 subnets, 3 masks
O IA    160.10.32.0/30 [110/128] via 160.10.37.2, 00:07:59, Serial0/1
O       160.10.38.0/24 [110/128] via 160.10.37.2, 00:07:59, Serial0/1
O       160.10.37.2/32 [110/64] via 160.10.37.2, 00:07:59, Serial0/1
O       160.10.37.1/32 [110/128] via 160.10.37.2, 00:07:59, Serial0/1
O IA    160.10.11.0/24 [110/138] via 160.10.37.2, 00:07:59, Serial0/1
O       160.10.2.0/24 [110/65] via 160.10.37.2, 00:07:59, Serial0/1
O IA    160.10.3.0/24 [110/129] via 160.10.37.2, 00:07:59, Serial0/1
O       160.10.1.0/24 [110/129] via 160.10.37.2, 00:07:59, Serial0/1
O IA    160.10.7.0/24 [110/139] via 160.10.37.2, 00:07:59, Serial0/1
O       160.10.4.0/24 [110/129] via 160.10.37.2, 00:07:59, Serial0/1
     130.200.0.0/24 is subnetted, 1 subnets
O E2    130.200.10.0 [110/100] via 160.10.37.2, 00:07:49, Serial0/1
     40.0.0.0/24 is subnetted, 1 subnets
O E2    40.4.4.0 [110/100] via 160.10.37.2, 00:00:07, Serial0/1R5#
!
!
```

- *You want to guarantee a minimum of 70 percent of the bandwidth for the EIGRP traffic. Configure R2 to accommodate this.*

To adjust the bandwidth for EIGRP on R2 from the default of 50 percent you need to use the **ip bandwidth-percent eigrp** command.

If you configured this correctly as shown in Example 6-31, you have scored 2 points.

**Example 6-31**  *EIGRP Bandwidth Command Configuration*

```
R2#sh run int fa0/0
Building configuration...

Current configuration : 132 bytes
!
interface FastEthernet0/0
 ip address 130.200.10.2 255.255.255.0
 ip bandwidth-percent eigrp 400 70

R2#
```

*continues*

## Section 2.3: RIP (7 Points)

- *Configure RIPv2 between R4 and BB2. R4-e0/0 must be the only interface configured for RIP on R4. You should receive updates and the R4 routing table will be populated with some RIP routes from BB2.*

If you configured this correctly as shown in Example 6-32, you have scored 2 points.

- *Redistribute RIP into OSPF such that networks 20.0.0.0/8 and 30.0.0.0/8 will have a metric of 128 kbps and network 196.1.0.0/16 will have metric of 56 kbps.*

If you configured this correctly as shown in Example 6-32, you have scored 2 points.

RIPv2 is running on BB2 and advertising routes to R4. A combination of filter, route map, and redistribution into OSPF is used to accomplish this task.

**Example 6-32**  *R4 and R1 Output: RIP Configuration and Verification*

```
R4#sh run | b router rip
router rip
 version 2
 network 140.200.0.0
 no auto-summary
!
!
R4#sh run | b router
router ospf 1
 log-adjacency-changes
 redistribute rip subnets route-map RIP_METRIC!
access-list 1 permit 196.1.0.0 0.0.255.255
access-list 2 permit 30.0.0.0 0.255.255.255
access-list 2 permit 20.0.0.0 0.255.255.255
route-map RIP_METRIC permit 10
 match ip address 1
 set metric 56
!
route-map RIP_METRIC permit 20
 match ip address 2
 set metric 128
!
! R1 OSPF Routing table before filter and route-map. Observe the RIP routes metrics
values
R1#show ip route ospf
O E2 196.1.8.0/24 [110/20] via 160.10.37.2, 00:00:56, Serial0/1
O E2 196.1.9.0/24 [110/20] via 160.10.37.2, 00:00:56, Serial0/1
O E2 196.1.10.0/24 [110/20] via 160.10.37.2, 00:00:56, Serial0/1
O E2 20.0.0.0/8 [110/20] via 160.10.37.2, 00:00:56, Serial0/1
O E2 196.1.1.0/24 [110/20] via 160.10.37.2, 00:00:56, Serial0/1
       160.10.0.0/16 is variably subnetted, 17 subnets, 3 masks
O IA    160.10.32.0/30 [110/128] via 160.10.37.2, 00:44:16, Serial0/1
O       160.10.37.5/32 [110/128] via 160.10.37.2, 00:44:16, Serial0/1
O E2    160.10.33.0/24 [110/100] via 160.10.25.5, 00:43:45, Ethernet0/1
O       160.10.38.0/24 [110/128] via 160.10.37.2, 00:44:16, Serial0/1
O       160.10.37.2/32 [110/64] via 160.10.37.2, 00:44:16, Serial0/1
```

**Example 6-32**  *R4 and R1 Output: RIP Configuration and Verification (Continued)*

```
O E2    160.10.15.0/24 [110/100] via 160.10.25.5, 00:44:16, Ethernet0/1
O       160.10.2.0/24 [110/65] via 160.10.37.2, 00:44:16, Serial0/1
O IA    160.10.3.0/24 [110/129] via 160.10.37.2, 00:44:17, Serial0/1
O E2    160.10.6.0/24 [110/100] via 160.10.25.5, 00:44:17, Ethernet0/1
O       160.10.7.0/24 [110/11] via 160.10.11.10, 00:44:17, Ethernet0/0
O       160.10.4.0/24 [110/129] via 160.10.37.2, 00:44:17, Serial0/1
O       160.10.5.0/24 [110/129] via 160.10.37.2, 00:44:17, Serial0/1
O E2    160.10.22.0/24 [110/100] via 160.10.25.5, 00:44:17, Ethernet0/1
O E2 196.1.2.0/24 [110/20] via 160.10.37.2, 00:00:57, Serial0/1

     130.200.0.0/24 is subnetted, 1 subnets
O E2    130.200.10.0 [110/100] via 160.10.37.2, 00:44:18, Serial0/1
O E2 196.1.3.0/24 [110/20] via 160.10.37.2, 00:00:58, Serial0/1
O E2 196.1.4.0/24 [110/20] via 160.10.37.2, 00:00:58, Serial0/1
O E2 196.1.5.0/24 [110/20] via 160.10.37.2, 00:00:58, Serial0/1
O E2 196.1.6.0/24 [110/20] via 160.10.37.2, 00:00:58, Serial0/1
O E2 196.1.7.0/24 [110/20] via 160.10.37.2, 00:00:58, Serial0/1
O E2 30.0.0.0/8 [110/20] via 160.10.37.2, 00:00:58, Serial0/1
R1#!
! R1 OSPF Routing table after filter and route-map being configured. Observe that
RIP routes metrics have changed
R1#show ip route ospf
O E2 196.1.8.0/24 [110/56] via 160.10.37.2, 00:00:16, Serial0/1
O E2 196.1.9.0/24 [110/56] via 160.10.37.2, 00:00:16, Serial0/1
O E2 196.1.10.0/24 [110/56] via 160.10.37.2, 00:00:16, Serial0/1
O E2 20.0.0.0/8 [110/128] via 160.10.37.2, 00:00:16, Serial0/1
O E2 196.1.1.0/24 [110/56] via 160.10.37.2, 00:00:16, Serial0/1
     160.10.0.0/16 is variably subnetted, 17 subnets, 3 masks
O IA    160.10.32.0/30 [110/128] via 160.10.37.2, 00:48:10, Serial0/1
O       160.10.37.5/32 [110/128] via 160.10.37.2, 00:48:10, Serial0/1
O E2    160.10.33.0/24 [110/100] via 160.10.25.5, 00:47:40, Ethernet0/1
O       160.10.38.0/24 [110/128] via 160.10.37.2, 00:48:10, Serial0/1
O       160.10.37.2/32 [110/64] via 160.10.37.2, 00:48:10, Serial0/1
O E2    160.10.15.0/24 [110/100] via 160.10.25.5, 00:48:10, Ethernet0/1
O       160.10.2.0/24 [110/65] via 160.10.37.2, 00:48:10, Serial0/1
O IA    160.10.3.0/24 [110/129] via 160.10.37.2, 00:48:11, Serial0/1
O E2    160.10.6.0/24 [110/100] via 160.10.25.5, 00:48:11, Ethernet0/1
O       160.10.7.0/24 [110/11] via 160.10.11.10, 00:48:11, Ethernet0/0
O       160.10.4.0/24 [110/129] via 160.10.37.2, 00:48:11, Serial0/1
O       160.10.5.0/24 [110/129] via 160.10.37.2, 00:48:11, Serial0/1
O E2    160.10.22.0/24 [110/100] via 160.10.25.5, 00:48:11, Ethernet0/1
O E2 196.1.2.0/24 [110/56] via 160.10.37.2, 00:00:17, Serial0/1
         130.200.0.0/24 is subnetted, 1 subnets
O E2    130.200.10.0 [110/100] via 160.10.37.2, 00:48:12, Serial0/1
O E2 196.1.3.0/24 [110/56] via 160.10.37.2, 00:00:18, Serial0/1
O E2 196.1.4.0/24 [110/56] via 160.10.37.2, 00:00:18, Serial0/1
O E2 196.1.5.0/24 [110/56] via 160.10.37.2, 00:00:18, Serial0/1
O E2 196.1.6.0/24 [110/56] via 160.10.37.2, 00:00:18, Serial0/1
O E2 196.1.7.0/24 [110/56] via 160.10.37.2, 00:00:18, Serial0/1
O E2 30.0.0.0/8 [110/128] via 160.10.37.2, 00:00:18, Serial0/1
R1#
```

- *Configure R4 to adjust RIP timers so the time that a route is declared invalid will be set to 200 seconds.*

To adjust the invalid timer, you need to use the **timers basic** *update invalid holdown flush* command and configure 200 seconds to the *invalid* portion of the command. You can leave the other values as the default values.

If you configured this correctly as shown in Example 6-33, you have scored 3 points.

**Example 6-33** *R4 Output: RIP Timer Configuration*

```
R4#sh run | b router rip
router rip
 version 2
 timers basic 30 200 180 240
 network 140.200.0.0
 !
```

# Section 2.4: IS-IS (5 Points)

- *Configure IS-IS according to Figure 6-10. R3-fa0/0, R3-fa0/1, R5-fa0/0, R6-e0/0, and the ISDN cloud are part of the IS-IS domain. Use area 49.0004 and level 1 and 2 adjacencies.*

- *You should have the routing table of all IS-IS routers populated with the IS-IS networks.*

- *You should be able to ping all interfaces of all routers within the IS-IS network.*

Notice that to establish level 1 and 2 adjacencies you do not need to configure the **isis circuit-type** interface command or **is-type** router process command because this is the default.

If you configured this correctly as shown in Example 6-34, you have scored 2 points.

- *Redistribute IS-IS into OSPF on R5. R6 should see in its routing table all routes from your topology and R6 must be able to ping all other router loopback0 address.*

If you configured this correctly as shown in Example 6-34, you have scored 2 points.

This is a basic IS-IS configuration into a single area. It is a good idea to configure your R6-loopback address under IS-IS because R6 is running only IS-IS and you might need to have R6-lo0 be reachable later in the lab.

**Example 6-34** *IS-IS Configuration and Output from R3, R5, and R6*

```
R3#sh run
!
clns routing
!
interface FastEthernet0/0
 ip address 160.10.22.3 255.255.255.0
 ip router isis
```

**Example 6-34** *IS-IS Configuration and Output from R3, R5, and R6 (Continued)*

```
!
!
interface BRI0/0
 ip address 160.10.15.3 255.255.255.0
 ip router isis
 encapsulation ppp

!
interface FastEthernet0/1
 ip address 160.10.33.3 255.255.255.0
 ip router isis
!
!
router isis
 net 49.0004.0000.0000.0003.00
!
R5#sh run
!
clns routing
!
!
interface FastEthernet0/0
 ip address 160.10.22.5 255.255.255.0
 ip router isis
!
!
interface BRI0/0
 ip address 160.10.15.5 255.255.255.0
 ip router isis
 encapsulation ppp

!
!
!
router ospf 1
 log-adjacency-changes

 redistribute connected metric 100 subnets
 redistribute isis level-1-2 metric 100 subnets
!
router isis
 net 49.0004.0000.0000.0005.00
 redistribute ospf 1 metric 10 level-1-2
R5#
!
R6#sh run
!
!
!
interface Loopback0
 ip address 160.10.6.6 255.255.255.0
 ip router isis
```

*continues*

**Example 6-34**  *IS-IS Configuration and Output from R3, R5, and R6 (Continued)*

```
!
interface Ethernet0/0
 ip address 160.10.22.6 255.255.255.0
 ip router isis
!
router isis
 net 49.0004.0000.0000.0006.00
!
R6#
!
R6#sh ip ro

i L1 196.1.8.0/24 [115/20] via 160.10.22.5, Ethernet0/0
        170.100.0.0/24 is subnetted, 1 subnets
C       170.100.10.0 is directly connected, ATM3/0
        50.0.0.0/24 is subnetted, 1 subnets
i L1    50.5.5.0 [115/20] via 160.10.22.5, Ethernet0/0
i L1 196.1.9.0/24 [115/20] via 160.10.22.5, Ethernet0/0
i L1 196.1.10.0/24 [115/20] via 160.10.22.5, Ethernet0/0
i L1 20.0.0.0/8 [115/20] via 160.10.22.5, Ethernet0/0
i L1 196.1.1.0/24 [115/20] via 160.10.22.5, Ethernet0/0
        160.10.0.0/16 is variably subnetted, 17 subnets, 3 masks
i L1    160.10.32.0/30 [115/20] via 160.10.22.5, Ethernet0/0
i L1    160.10.33.0/24 [115/20] via 160.10.22.3, Ethernet0/0
i L1    160.10.38.0/24 [115/20] via 160.10.22.5, Ethernet0/0
i L1    160.10.37.2/32 [115/20] via 160.10.22.5, Ethernet0/0
i L1    160.10.37.1/32 [115/20] via 160.10.22.5, Ethernet0/0
i L1    160.10.37.0/24 [115/20] via 160.10.22.5, Ethernet0/0
i L1    160.10.11.0/24 [115/20] via 160.10.22.5, Ethernet0/0
i L1    160.10.15.0/24 [115/20] via 160.10.22.5, Ethernet0/0
                       [115/20] via 160.10.22.3, Ethernet0/0
i L1    160.10.2.0/24 [115/20] via 160.10.22.5, Ethernet0/0
i L1    160.10.3.0/24 [115/20] via 160.10.22.5, Ethernet0/0
                       [115/20] via 160.10.22.3, Ethernet0/0
i L1    160.10.1.0/24 [115/20] via 160.10.22.5, Ethernet0/0
C       160.10.6.0/24 is directly connected, Loopback0
i L1    160.10.7.0/24 [115/20] via 160.10.22.5, Ethernet0/0
i L1    160.10.4.0/24 [115/20] via 160.10.22.5, Ethernet0/0
i L1    160.10.5.0/24 [115/20] via 160.10.22.5, Ethernet0/0
i L1    160.10.25.0/24 [115/20] via 160.10.22.5, Ethernet0/0
C       160.10.22.0/24 is directly connected, Ethernet0/0
i L1 196.1.2.0/24 [115/20] via 160.10.22.5, Ethernet0/0
        40.0.0.0/24 is subnetted, 1 subnets
i L1    40.4.4.0 [115/20] via 160.10.22.5, Ethernet0/0
        130.200.0.0/24 is subnetted, 1 subnets
i L1    130.200.10.0 [115/20] via 160.10.22.5, Ethernet0/0
B       198.18.1.0/24 [20/0] via 170.100.10.254, 01:25:08
i L1 196.1.3.0/24 [115/20] via 160.10.22.5, Ethernet0/0
i L1 196.1.4.0/24 [115/20] via 160.10.22.5, Ethernet0/0
i L1 196.1.5.0/24 [115/20] via 160.10.22.5, Ethernet0/0
i L1 196.1.6.0/24 [115/20] via 160.10.22.5, Ethernet0/0
```

**Example 6-34**  *IS-IS Configuration and Output from R3, R5, and R6 (Continued)*

```
 i L1 196.1.7.0/24 [115/20] via 160.10.22.5, Ethernet0/0
 i L1 30.0.0.0/8 [115/20] via 160.10.22.5, Ethernet0/0
 R6#
 R6#ping 160.10.5.5

 Type escape sequence to abort.
 Sending 5, 100-byte ICMP Echos to 160.10.5.5, timeout is 2 seconds:
 !!!!!
 Success rate is 100 percent (5/5), round-trip min/avg/max = 1/2/4 ms
 R6#

 R6#ping 160.10.2.2

 Type escape sequence to abort.
 Sending 5, 100-byte ICMP Echos to 160.10.2.2, timeout is 2 seconds:
 !!!!!
 Success rate is 100 percent (5/5), round-trip min/avg/max = 4/4/4 ms
 R6#
 !
 !
 R2#sh ip ro
 Codes: C - connected, S - static, R - RIP, M - mobile, B - BGP
        D - EIGRP, EX - EIGRP external, O - OSPF, IA - OSPF inter area
        N1 - OSPF NSSA external type 1, N2 - OSPF NSSA external type 2
        E1 - OSPF external type 1, E2 - OSPF external type 2
        i - IS-IS, L1 - IS-IS level-1, L2 - IS-IS level-2, ia - IS-IS inter area
        * - candidate default, U - per-user static route, o - ODR
        P - periodic downloaded static route

 Gateway of last resort is not set

 O E2 196.1.8.0/24 [110/1] via 160.10.38.4, 06:26:27, Serial0/1.2
 B    198.18.10.0/24 [200/0] via 160.10.6.6, 06:26:37
 B    200.20.4.0/24 [200/0] via 160.10.6.6, 06:26:37
 B    200.20.5.0/24 [200/0] via 160.10.6.6, 06:26:37
 O E2 196.1.10.0/24 [110/1] via 160.10.38.4, 06:26:27, Serial0/1.2
 B    198.18.8.0/24 [200/0] via 160.10.6.6, 06:26:37
 B    200.20.6.0/24 [200/0] via 160.10.6.6, 06:26:37
 B    198.18.9.0/24 [200/0] via 160.10.6.6, 06:26:37
 B    200.20.7.0/24 [200/0] via 160.10.6.6, 06:26:37
      140.200.0.0/24 is subnetted, 1 subnets
 O E2    140.200.10.0 [110/1] via 160.10.38.4, 06:26:28, Serial0/1.2
 B    200.20.1.0/24 [200/0] via 160.10.6.6, 06:26:38
 B    200.20.2.0/24 [200/0] via 160.10.6.6, 06:26:38
 B    200.20.3.0/24 [200/0] via 160.10.6.6, 06:26:39
 B    198.18.2.0/24 [200/0] via 160.10.6.6, 06:26:39
 B    198.18.3.0/24 [200/0] via 160.10.6.6, 06:26:39
      160.10.0.0/16 is variably subnetted, 17 subnets, 3 masks
 O        160.10.37.5/32 [110/64] via 160.10.37.5, 06:27:01, Serial0/1.1
 C        160.10.32.0/30 is directly connected, Serial0/0
 O E2     160.10.33.0/24 [110/100] via 160.10.37.5, 06:26:29, Serial0/1.1
 C        160.10.38.0/24 is directly connected, Serial0/1.2
```

*continues*

**Example 6-34** *IS-IS Configuration and Output from R3, R5, and R6 (Continued)*

```
O          160.10.37.1/32 [110/64] via 160.10.37.1, 06:27:01, Serial0/1.1
C          160.10.37.0/24 is directly connected, Serial0/1.1
O IA       160.10.11.0/24 [110/74] via 160.10.37.1, 06:26:51, Serial0/1.1
O E2       160.10.15.0/24 [110/100] via 160.10.37.5, 04:33:49, Serial0/1.1
C          160.10.2.0/24 is directly connected, Loopback0
O          160.10.3.0/24 [110/65] via 160.10.32.1, 06:26:51, Serial0/0
O          160.10.1.0/24 [110/65] via 160.10.37.1, 06:27:01, Serial0/1.1
O E2       160.10.6.0/24 [110/100] via 160.10.37.5, 06:26:30, Serial0/1.1
O IA       160.10.7.0/24 [110/75] via 160.10.37.1, 06:26:53, Serial0/1.1
O          160.10.4.0/24 [110/65] via 160.10.38.4, 06:27:03, Serial0/1.2
O          160.10.5.0/24 [110/65] via 160.10.37.5, 06:27:03, Serial0/1.1
O IA       160.10.25.0/24 [110/65] via 160.10.37.5, 06:26:39, Serial0/1.1
O E2       160.10.22.0/24 [110/100] via 160.10.37.5, 04:33:51, Serial0/1.1
O E2 196.1.2.0/24 [110/1] via 160.10.38.4, 06:26:30, Serial0/1.2
     130.200.0.0/24 is subnetted, 1 subnets
C       130.200.10.0 is directly connected, FastEthernet0/0
B    198.18.1.0/24 [200/0] via 160.10.6.6, 06:26:41
B    198.18.6.0/24 [200/0] via 160.10.6.6, 06:26:41
B    200.20.8.0/24 [200/0] via 160.10.6.6, 06:26:41
D    193.118.1.0/24 [90/156160] via 130.200.10.200, 1d18h, FastEthernet0/0
B    198.18.7.0/24 [200/0] via 160.10.6.6, 06:26:41
B    200.20.9.0/24 [200/0] via 160.10.6.6, 06:26:41
B    198.18.4.0/24 [200/0] via 160.10.6.6, 06:26:41
B    200.20.10.0/24 [200/0] via 160.10.6.6, 06:26:41
D    193.118.3.0/24 [90/156160] via 130.200.10.200, 1d18h, FastEthernet0/0
B    198.18.5.0/24 [200/0] via 160.10.6.6, 06:26:41
D    193.118.2.0/24 [90/156160] via 130.200.10.200, 1d18h, FastEthernet0/0
R2#
!
!
R2#ping 160.10.6.6

Type escape sequence to abort.
Sending 5, 100-byte ICMP Echos to 160.10.6.6, timeout is 2 seconds:
!!!!!
Success rate is 100 percent (5/5), round-trip min/avg/max = 1/3/4 ms
R2#
```

- *To avoid overloading the CPU of the IS-IS routers on VLAN_22 during LSP transmission and reception, configure the routers to reduce the LSP transmission rate to 100 ms.*

To adjust the LSP transmission rate, use the **isis lsp-interval** command set to 100 ms.

If you configured this correctly as shown in Example 6-35, you have scored 1 point.

**Example 6-35** *IS-IS LSP Transmission Timer Configuration*

```
R3#sh run int fa0/0
!
interface FastEthernet0/0
 ip address 160.10.22.3 255.255.255.0
```

**Example 6-35**  *IS-IS LSP Transmission Timer Configuration*

```
  ip router isis

  isis lsp-interval 100
 !
R5# sh run int fa0/0
 !
interface FastEthernet0/0
 ip address 160.10.22.5 255.255.255.0
 ip router isis

 isis lsp-interval 100

 !
R6#sh run int e0/0
 !
interface Ethernet0/0
 ip address 160.10.22.6 255.255.255.0
 ip router isis

 isis lsp-interval 100

R6#
```

# Section 3: BGP (12 Points)

- *Configure EBGP between R6 and BB3. R6 will belong to AS 100 and the BB3 router AS is 300. R6 will receive updates for networks 200.20.X.0 and 198.18.X.0, where X is any number.*

If you configured this correctly as shown in Example 6-36, you have scored 6 points.

The EBGP configuration on R6 is a simple task. Again, you will need the basic BGP concepts to accomplish this.

**Example 6-36**  *R6 EBGP Configuration*

```
R6#show run | b router bgp
router bgp 100
 no synchronization
 neighbor 170.100.10.254 remote-as 300
 no auto-summary
 !
 !
R6# sh ip bgp
BGP table version is 21, local router ID is 160.10.6.6
Status codes: s suppressed, d damped, h history, * valid, > best, i - internal
Origin codes: i - IGP, e - EGP, ? - incomplete

   Network          Next Hop            Metric LocPrf Weight Path
*> 198.18.1.0       170.100.10.254           0             0 300 i
*> 198.18.2.0       170.100.10.254           0             0 300 i
```

*continues*

**Example 6-36** *R6 EBGP Configuration (Continued)*

```
 *> 198.18.3.0       170.100.10.254             0             0 300 i
 *> 198.18.4.0       170.100.10.254             0             0 300 i
 *> 198.18.5.0       170.100.10.254             0             0 300 i
 *> 198.18.6.0       170.100.10.254             0             0 300 i
 *> 198.18.7.0       170.100.10.254             0             0 300 i
 *> 198.18.8.0       170.100.10.254             0             0 300 i
 *> 198.18.9.0       170.100.10.254             0             0 300 i
 *> 198.18.10.0      170.100.10.254             0             0 300 i
 *> 200.20.1.0       170.100.10.254             0             0 300 i
 *> 200.20.2.0       170.100.10.254             0             0 300 i
 *> 200.20.3.0       170.100.10.254             0             0 300 i
 *> 200.20.4.0       170.100.10.254             0             0 300 i
 *> 200.20.5.0       170.100.10.254             0             0 300 i
 *> 200.20.6.0       170.100.10.254             0             0 300 i
 *> 200.20.7.0       170.100.10.254             0             0 300 i
 *> 200.20.8.0       170.100.10.254             0             0 300 i
    Network          Next Hop           Metric LocPrf Weight Path
 *> 200.20.9.0       170.100.10.254             0             0 300 i
 *> 200.20.10.0      170.100.10.254             0             0 300 i
R6#
```

- *Configure IBGP between R2, R3, and R6. Use AS 100. R2 should not peer directly with R6. R2 and R3 should be able to see all BGP BB3 routes in their BGP routing tables.*

If you configured this correctly as shown in Example 6-37, you have scored 3 points.

You can choose either Confederations or Router-Reflectors to accomplish this task. Example 6-37 shows a solution using Router-Reflectors.

**Example 6-37** *R2, R3, and R6 IBGP Configuration*

```
R2#show run | b router bgp

router bgp 100
 no synchronization
 bgp log-neighbor-changes
 neighbor 160.10.3.3 remote-as 100
 neighbor 160.10.3.3 update-source Loopback0
 no auto-summary
!
R2#show ip bgp sum

BGP router identifier 160.10.2.2, local AS number 100
BGP table version is 21, main routing table version 21
20 network entries using 2020 bytes of memory
20 path entries using 960 bytes of memory
1 BGP path attribute entries using 60 bytes of memory
1 BGP rrinfo entries using 24 bytes of memory
1 BGP AS-PATH entries using 24 bytes of memory
0 BGP route-map cache entries using 0 bytes of memory
0 BGP filter-list cache entries using 0 bytes of memory
BGP using 3088 total bytes of memory
```

**Example 6-37**  *R2, R3, and R6 IBGP Configuration (Continued)*

```
BGP activity 20/0 prefixes, 20/0 paths, scan interval 60 secs

Neighbor        V    AS MsgRcvd MsgSent   TblVer  InQ OutQ Up/Down  State/PfxRcd
160.10.3.3      4   100     30      29       21    0    0 00:12:14       20
R2#
!
R2#sh ip bgp
BGP table version is 21, local router ID is 160.10.2.2
Status codes: s suppressed, d damped, h history, * valid, > best, i - internal,
              r RIB-failure, S Stale
Origin codes: i - IGP, e - EGP, ? - incomplete

   Network          Next Hop          Metric LocPrf Weight Path
*>i198.18.1.0       160.10.6.6             0    100      0 300 i
*>i198.18.2.0       160.10.6.6             0    100      0 300 i
*>i198.18.3.0       160.10.6.6             0    100      0 300 i
*>i198.18.4.0       160.10.6.6             0    100      0 300 i
*>i198.18.5.0       160.10.6.6             0    100      0 300 i
*>i198.18.6.0       160.10.6.6             0    100      0 300 i
*>i198.18.7.0       160.10.6.6             0    100      0 300 i
*>i198.18.8.0       160.10.6.6             0    100      0 300 i
*>i198.18.9.0       160.10.6.6             0    100      0 300 i
*>i198.18.10.0      160.10.6.6             0    100      0 300 i
*>i200.20.1.0       160.10.6.6             0    100      0 300 i
*>i200.20.2.0       160.10.6.6             0    100      0 300 i
*>i200.20.3.0       160.10.6.6             0    100      0 300 i
*>i200.20.4.0       160.10.6.6             0    100      0 300 i
*>i200.20.5.0       160.10.6.6             0    100      0 300 i
*>i200.20.6.0       160.10.6.6             0    100      0 300 i
*>i200.20.7.0       160.10.6.6             0    100      0 300 i
   Network          Next Hop          Metric LocPrf Weight Path
*>i200.20.8.0       160.10.6.6             0    100      0 300 i
*>i200.20.9.0       160.10.6.6             0    100      0 300 i
*>i200.20.10.0      160.10.6.6             0    100      0 300 i
R2#
!
R3#show run | b router bgp

router bgp 100
 no synchronization
 bgp log-neighbor-changes
 neighbor 160.10.2.2 remote-as 100
 neighbor 160.10.2.2 update-source Loopback0
 neighbor 160.10.2.2 route-reflector-client
 neighbor 160.10.6.6 remote-as 100
 neighbor 160.10.6.6 update-source Loopback0
neighbor 160.10.6.6 route-reflector-client

 !
 !
R3#show ip bgp sum
```

*continues*

**Example 6-37** *R2, R3, and R6 IBGP Configuration (Continued)*

```
BGP router identifier 160.10.3.3, local AS number 100
BGP table version is 21, main routing table version 21
20 network entries using 1940 bytes of memory
20 path entries using 720 bytes of memory
1 BGP path attribute entries using 60 bytes of memory
1 BGP AS-PATH entries using 24 bytes of memory
0 BGP route-map cache entries using 0 bytes of memory
0 BGP filter-list cache entries using 0 bytes of memory
BGP using 2744 total bytes of memory
BGP activity 40/20 prefixes, 40/20 paths, scan interval 60 secs

Neighbor        V    AS MsgRcvd MsgSent   TblVer  InQ OutQ Up/Down  State/PfxRcd
160.10.2.2      4   100      31      32       21    0    0 00:14:54        0
160.10.6.6      4   100      33      30       21    0    0 00:13:55       20
R3#
!
R3#sh ip bgp
BGP table version is 21, local router ID is 160.10.3.3
Status codes: s suppressed, d damped, h history, * valid, > best, i - internal
Origin codes: i - IGP, e - EGP, ? - incomplete

   Network          Next Hop          Metric LocPrf Weight Path
*>i198.18.1.0       160.10.6.6             0    100      0 300 i
*>i198.18.2.0       160.10.6.6             0    100      0 300 i
*>i198.18.3.0       160.10.6.6             0    100      0 300 i
*>i198.18.4.0       160.10.6.6             0    100      0 300 i
*>i198.18.5.0       160.10.6.6             0    100      0 300 i
*>i198.18.6.0       160.10.6.6             0    100      0 300 i
*>i198.18.7.0       160.10.6.6             0    100      0 300 i
*>i198.18.8.0       160.10.6.6             0    100      0 300 i
*>i198.18.9.0       160.10.6.6             0    100      0 300 i
*>i198.18.10.0      160.10.6.6             0    100      0 300 i
*>i200.20.1.0       160.10.6.6             0    100      0 300 i
*>i200.20.2.0       160.10.6.6             0    100      0 300 i
*>i200.20.3.0       160.10.6.6             0    100      0 300 i
*>i200.20.4.0       160.10.6.6             0    100      0 300 i
*>i200.20.5.0       160.10.6.6             0    100      0 300 i
*>i200.20.6.0       160.10.6.6             0    100      0 300 i
*>i200.20.7.0       160.10.6.6             0    100      0 300 i
*>i200.20.8.0       160.10.6.6             0    100      0 300 i
   Network          Next Hop          Metric LocPrf Weight Path
*>i200.20.9.0       160.10.6.6             0    100      0 300 i
*>i200.20.10.0      160.10.6.6             0    100      0 300 i
R3#
!
R6#show run | b router bgp
router bgp 100
 no synchronization
 bgp log-neighbor-changes
 neighbor 160.10.3.3 remote-as 100
 neighbor 160.10.3.3 update-source Loopback0
```

**Example 6-37**  *R2, R3, and R6 IBGP Configuration (Continued)*

```
 neighbor 160.10.3.3 next-hop-self
 neighbor 170.100.10.254 remote-as 300
!
R6#show ip bgp sum

BGP router identifier 160.10.6.6, local AS number 100
BGP table version is 21, main routing table version 21
20 network entries using 1940 bytes of memory
20 path entries using 720 bytes of memory
1 BGP path attribute entries using 60 bytes of memory
1 BGP AS-PATH entries using 24 bytes of memory
0 BGP route-map cache entries using 0 bytes of memory
0 BGP filter-list cache entries using 0 bytes of memory
BGP using 2744 total bytes of memory
BGP activity 20/0 prefixes, 20/0 paths, scan interval 60 secs

Neighbor        V    AS MsgRcvd MsgSent   TblVer  InQ OutQ Up/Down   State/PfxRcd
160.10.3.3      4   100      33      36       21    0    0 00:16:01         0
170.100.10.254  4   300      38      37       21    0    0 00:33:36        20
R6#
```

- *Configure an EBGP peering between R2 to AS 24 and R4 to AS 42. R4 should have all BB3 backbone routes within its BGP routing table. Do not change the R2 affiliation with AS 100 as accomplished in the preceding task and do not use a Confederation to accomplish this.*

R2 is peering with R3 using AS100 (IBGP) and you cannot change it. To make an EBGP peering between R2 and R4 using AS24 you can configure it using "Confederations," which was a restriction to use or the "local-as," which is a BGP feature.

If you configured this correctly as shown in Example 6-38, you have scored 3 points.

**Example 6-38**  *R2 and R4 Output Configuration417*

```
R2#sh run | begin router bgp
router bgp 100
 no synchronization
 bgp log-neighbor-changes
 neighbor 160.10.3.3 remote-as 100
 neighbor 160.10.3.3 update-source Loopback0
 neighbor 160.10.38.4 remote-as 42
 neighbor 160.10.38.4 local-as 24
 no auto-summaryR4#sh run | b router bgp
router bgp 42
 bgp log-neighbor-changes
 neighbor 160.10.38.2 remote-as 24
!
R4#sh ip bgp sum
BGP router identifier 160.10.4.4, local AS number 42
BGP table version is 21, main routing table version 21
20 network entries using 1940 bytes of memory
```

*continues*

**Example 6-38**  *R2 and R4 Output Configuration417*

```
20 path entries using 720 bytes of memory
1 BGP path attribute entries using 60 bytes of memory
1 BGP AS-PATH entries using 24 bytes of memory
0 BGP route-map cache entries using 0 bytes of memory
0 BGP filter-list cache entries using 0 bytes of memory
BGP using 2744 total bytes of memory
BGP activity 20/0 prefixes, 20/0 paths, scan interval 60 secs


Neighbor        V    AS MsgRcvd MsgSent   TblVer  InQ OutQ Up/Down  State/PfxRcd
160.10.38.2     4    24     32      31       21    0    0 00:27:24          20
R4#
R4#show ip bgp
BGP table version is 21, local router ID is 160.10.4.4
Status codes: s suppressed, d damped, h history, * valid, > best, i - internal
Origin codes: i - IGP, e - EGP, ? - incomplete

   Network          Next Hop          Metric LocPrf Weight Path
*> 198.18.1.0       160.10.38.2                        0 24 100 300 i
*> 198.18.2.0       160.10.38.2                        0 24 100 300 i
*> 198.18.3.0       160.10.38.2                        0 24 100 300 i
*> 198.18.4.0       160.10.38.2                        0 24 100 300 i
*> 198.18.5.0       160.10.38.2                        0 24 100 300 i
*> 198.18.6.0       160.10.38.2                        0 24 100 300 i
*> 198.18.7.0       160.10.38.2                        0 24 100 300 i
*> 198.18.8.0       160.10.38.2                        0 24 100 300 i
*> 198.18.9.0       160.10.38.2                        0 24 100 300 i
*> 198.18.10.0      160.10.38.2                        0 24 100 300 i
*> 200.20.1.0       160.10.38.2                        0 24 100 300 i
*> 200.20.2.0       160.10.38.2                        0 24 100 300 i
*> 200.20.3.0       160.10.38.2                        0 24 100 300 i
*> 200.20.4.0       160.10.38.2                        0 24 100 300 i
*> 200.20.5.0       160.10.38.2                        0 24 100 300 i
*> 200.20.6.0       160.10.38.2                        0 24 100 300 i
*> 200.20.7.0       160.10.38.2                        0 24 100 300 i
*> 200.20.8.0       160.10.38.2                        0 24 100 300 i
   Network          Next Hop          Metric LocPrf Weight Path
*> 200.20.9.0       160.10.38.2                        0 24 100 300 i
*> 200.20.10.0      160.10.38.2                        0 24 100 300 i
R4#
```

# Section 4: ISDN (6 Points)

- *Configure ISDN on R3 and R5 using PPP. R3 and R5 should be able to ping each other across the ISDN link.*

If you configured this correctly as shown in Example 6-39, you have scored 2 points.

- *Make sure that your routing protocol is passed across the ISDN link only when the connectivity is established.*

If you configured this correctly as shown in Example 6-39, you have scored 2 points.

The key to configuring as requested is to avoid having ISDN advertise or pass traffic through the link when R5-fa0/0 is up. R3 and R5 are running CLNS, which makes the scenario even more interesting.

**Example 6-39**  *R3 and R5 ISDN Configuration*

```
R3#sh run int bri0/0
Building configuration...

Current configuration : 340 bytes
!
interface BRI0/0
 ip address 160.10.15.3 255.255.255.0
 ip router isis
 encapsulation ppp
 dialer map clns 49.0004.0000.0000.0005.00 name R5 broadcast 2222
 dialer map ip 160.10.15.5 name R5 broadcast 2222
 dialer-group 1
 isdn switch-type basic-ni
 isdn spid1 1111
 ppp authentication chap
end

R3#
!
!
```

```
R5#sh run int bri0/0
Building configuration...

Current configuration : 340 bytes
!
interface BRI0/0
 ip address 160.10.15.5 255.255.255.0
 ip router isis
 encapsulation ppp
 dialer map clns 49.0004.0000.0000.0003.00 name R3 broadcast 1111
 dialer map ip 160.10.15.3 name R3 broadcast 1111
 dialer-group 1
 isdn switch-type basic-ni
 isdn spid1 2222
 ppp authentication chap
end

R5#
R5#ping 160.10.15.3

Type escape sequence to abort.
Sending 5, 100-byte ICMP Echos to 160.10.15.3, timeout is 2 seconds:

5w1d: %LINK-3-UPDOWN: Interface BRI0/0:1, changed state to up..!!!
Success rate is 60 percent (3/5), round-trip min/avg/max = 32/33/36 ms
R5#
5w1d: %LINEPROTO-5-UPDOWN: Line protocol on Interface BRI0/0:1, changed state to up
5w1d: %ISDN-6-CONNECT: Interface BRI0/0:1 is now connected to 1111 R3
```

- *The ISDN link should only pass a routing protocol if R5-fa0/0 is down.*

If you configured this correctly as shown in Example 6-40, you have scored 2 points.

**Example 6-40** *R5 Routing Backup Output and R2 Output Routing Table Verification*

```
R5#sh ip ro
Codes: C - connected, S - static, I - IGRP, R - RIP, M - mobile, B - BGP
       D - EIGRP, EX - EIGRP external, O - OSPF, IA - OSPF inter area
       N1 - OSPF NSSA external type 1, N2 - OSPF NSSA external type 2
       E1 - OSPF external type 1, E2 - OSPF external type 2, E - EGP
       i - IS-IS, L1 - IS-IS level-1, L2 - IS-IS level-2, ia - IS-IS inter area
       * - candidate default, U - per-user static route, o - ODR
       P - periodic downloaded static route

Gateway of last resort is not set

O E2 196.1.8.0/24 [110/1] via 160.10.37.2, 02:01:59, Serial0/1
O E2 196.1.10.0/24 [110/1] via 160.10.37.2, 02:01:59, Serial0/1
     140.200.0.0/24 is subnetted, 1 subnets
O E2    140.200.10.0 [110/1] via 160.10.37.2, 02:01:59, Serial0/1
     160.10.0.0/16 is variably subnetted, 18 subnets, 3 masks
O IA    160.10.32.0/30 [110/128] via 160.10.37.2, 02:02:09, Serial0/1
i L1    160.10.33.0/24 [115/20] via 160.10.15.3, BRI0/0
O       160.10.38.0/24 [110/128] via 160.10.37.2, 02:02:09, Serial0/1
O       160.10.37.2/32 [110/64] via 160.10.37.2, 02:02:10, Serial0/1
O       160.10.37.1/32 [110/128] via 160.10.37.2, 02:02:10, Serial0/1
C       160.10.37.0/24 is directly connected, Serial0/1
O IA    160.10.11.0/24 [110/138] via 160.10.37.2, 02:02:10, Serial0/1
C       160.10.15.0/24 is directly connected, BRI0/0
C       160.10.15.3/32 is directly connected, BRI0/0
O       160.10.2.0/24 [110/65] via 160.10.37.2, 02:02:12, Serial0/1
O IA    160.10.3.0/24 [110/129] via 160.10.37.2, 02:02:12, Serial0/1
O       160.10.1.0/24 [110/129] via 160.10.37.2, 02:02:12, Serial0/1
i L1    160.10.6.0/24 [115/30] via 160.10.15.3, BRI0/0
O IA    160.10.7.0/24 [110/139] via 160.10.37.2, 02:02:12, Serial0/1
O       160.10.4.0/24 [110/129] via 160.10.37.2, 02:02:12, Serial0/1
C       160.10.5.0/24 is directly connected, Loopback0
C       160.10.25.0/24 is directly connected, FastEthernet0/1
i L1    160.10.22.0/24 [115/20] via 160.10.15.3, BRI0/0
O E2 196.1.2.0/24 [110/1] via 160.10.37.2, 02:02:02, Serial0/1
     130.200.0.0/24 is subnetted, 1 subnets
O E2    130.200.10.0 [110/100] via 160.10.37.2, 02:02:02, Serial0/1
O E2 193.118.1.0/24 [110/100] via 160.10.37.2, 02:02:02, Serial0/1
O E2 193.118.3.0/24 [110/100] via 160.10.37.2, 02:02:02, Serial0/1
O E2 193.118.2.0/24 [110/100] via 160.10.37.2, 02:02:02, Serial0/1
!
! Routes from IS-IS domain are still coming via OSPF although R5-Fa0/0 is down.
R2#show ip route
     160.10.0.0/16 is variably subnetted, 18 subnets, 3 masks
O       160.10.37.5/32 [110/64] via 160.10.37.5, 00:00:28, Serial0/1.1
C       160.10.32.0/30 is directly connected, Serial0/0
O E2    160.10.33.0/24 [110/100] via 160.10.37.5, 00:00:28, Serial0/1.1
C       160.10.38.0/24 is directly connected, Serial0/1.2
```

**Example 6-40**  *R5 Routing Backup Output and R2 Output Routing Table Verification (Continued)*

```
O          160.10.37.1/32 [110/64] via 160.10.37.1, 00:00:28, Serial0/1.1
C          160.10.37.0/24 is directly connected, Serial0/1.1
O IA       160.10.11.0/24 [110/74] via 160.10.37.1, 00:00:29, Serial0/1.1
O E2       160.10.15.0/24 [110/100] via 160.10.37.5, 00:00:29, Serial0/1.1
O E2       160.10.15.3/32 [110/100] via 160.10.37.5, 00:00:15, Serial0/1.1
C          160.10.2.0/24 is directly connected, Loopback0
O          160.10.3.0/24 [110/65] via 160.10.32.1, 00:03:32, Serial0/0
O          160.10.1.0/24 [110/65] via 160.10.37.1, 00:00:29, Serial0/1.1
O E2       160.10.6.0/24 [110/100] via 160.10.37.5, 00:00:29, Serial0/1.1
O IA       160.10.7.0/24 [110/75] via 160.10.37.1, 00:00:29, Serial0/1.1
O          160.10.4.0/24 [110/65] via 160.10.38.4, 00:00:29, Serial0/1.2
O          160.10.5.0/24 [110/65] via 160.10.37.5, 00:00:29, Serial0/1.1
O IA       160.10.25.0/24 [110/65] via 160.10.37.5, 00:00:29, Serial0/1.1
O E2       160.10.22.0/24 [110/100] via 160.10.37.5, 00:00:29, Serial0/1.1

R2#
```

- *Configure R3 to override specific cause codes that are sent to the switch in case of a disconnection. Should this event occur, ensure that R3 uses "Channel-Not-Available" code message.*

To accommodate this and override the disconnect codes, use the **isdn disconnect-cause** command.

If you configured this correctly as shown in Example 6-41, you have scored 1 point.

**Example 6-41**  *R5 Routing Backup Output*

```
R3#sh run int bri0/0
Building configuration...

Current configuration : 345 bytes
!
interface BRI0/0
 ip address 160.10.15.3 255.255.255.0
 ip router isis
 encapsulation ppp
 dialer map clns 49.0004.0000.0000.0005.00 name R5 broadcast 2222
 dialer map ip 160.10.15.5 name R5 broadcast 2222
 dialer-group 1
 isdn switch-type basic-ni
 isdn spid1 1111
 isdn disconnect-cause not-available
 ppp authentication chap
end

R3#
```

# Section 5: IP and IOS Features (7 Points)

- *Configure R4 to have a list of the following default domain names: **ccie.com**, **rip.com**, and **isis.com**.*

If you configured this correctly as shown in Example 6-42, you have scored 1 point.

This task is accomplished configuring the **ip domain-list** command where you can define a list of default domain-names.

**Example 6-42** *R4 Domain Name and Domain List Configuration*

```
R4#sh run
!
ip domain-list ccie.com
ip domain-list rip.com
ip domain-list isis.com
!
```

- *Assume you have on the LAN segment of BB1 a DNS server with an IP address of 130.200.10.200. Configure R3 so any host on VLAN_33 that needs to resolve a name server can reach the DNS server.*

Here you will configure the IP help-address feature on R3-fa0/1 for clients on VLAN_33. Notice that the **ip forward** command enables the forwarding of UDP traffic port 53.

If you configured this correctly as shown in Example 6-43, you have scored 2 points.

**Example 6-43** *R3 IP Help Address Configuration*

```
R3#show run int fa0/1
!
interface FastEthernet0/1
 ip address 160.10.33.3 255.255.255.0
 ip helper-address 130.200.10.200

R3#
```

- *Configure on R1 an incoming banner to welcome the users connecting to use R1 via Telnet. Use the following messages:*
  - *Banner message: This is a lab exercise to help you in preparation for the CCIE Routing and Switching Lab Exam. Unauthorized access prohibited.*
  - *Message of the day: The router will go down at 6:00 PM today for a software upgrade*

If you configured this correctly as shown in Example 6-44, you have scored 2 points.

**Example 6-44**  *R1 Incoming Banner Configuration*

```
R1#sh run
banner exec ^C
 This is a Lab exercise to help you in preparation for the CCIE R&S lab exam.

 Unauthorized access prohibited.
 ^C
banner motd ^C
 The router will go down at 6pm today for a software upgrade

^C
!
line vty 0 4

 exec-timeout 0 0
 password cisco
 login
 transport input telnet
!
R1#
```

- *Configure R2 such that all attempts to reach or connect the Backbone 1 address 130.200.10.200 with source address of 160.10.32.0/24 will be seen as 130.200.10.15-20/24.*

To achieve this task requires a configuration of a Dynamic Inside Source Translation. It is an application of NAT.

If you configured this correctly as shown in Example 6-45, you have scored 2 points.

**Example 6-45**  *R2 Dynamic NAT Configuration*

```
R2#sh run | i ip nat
!
ip nat pool BB1 130.200.10.15 130.200.10.20 netmask 255.255.255.0
ip nat inside source list 20 pool BB1
R2#
!
R2#sh run int fa0/0
Building configuration...

Current configuration : 148 bytes
!
interface FastEthernet0/0
 ip address 130.200.10.2 255.255.255.0
 ip nat outside
 speed auto
 half-duplex
end

R2#
!
```

*continues*

**Example 6-45** *R2 Dynamic NAT Configuration (Continued)*

```
R2#sh run int s0/0
Building configuration...

Current configuration : 377 bytes
!
interface Serial0/0
 ip address 160.10.32.2 255.255.255.252
 !
 ip nat inside
 !
access-list 20 permit 160.10.32.0 0.0.0.255
 !

R2#
! R2#
R2#show ip nat tra
R2#sh ip nat translations
Pro Inside global    Inside local     Outside local    Outside global
--- 130.200.10.15     160.10.32.2      ---              ---
R2#
!
R2#show ip nat statistics
Total active translations: 1 (0 static, 1 dynamic; 0 extended)
Outside interfaces:
  FastEthernet0/0
Inside interfaces:
  Serial0/0
Hits: 90  Misses: 1
Expired translations: 0
Dynamic mappings:
-- Inside Source
[Id: 1] access-list 20 pool BB1 refcount 1
 pool BB1: netmask 255.255.255.0
        start 130.200.10.15 end 130.200.10.20
        type generic, total addresses 6, allocated 1 (16%), misses 0
R2#
```

# Section 6: DLSw (4 Points)

- *Configure DLSw between VLAN_11 and VLAN_33. Use FST encapsulation.*

If you configured this correctly as shown in Example 6-46, you have scored 2 points.

**Example 6-46** *R1 and R3 Basic DLSw Configuration*

```
R1#show run
!
dlsw local-peer peer-id 160.10.1.1
```

**Example 6-46**  *R1 and R3 Basic DLSw Configuration*

```
dlsw remote-peer 0 fst 160.10.3.3
dlsw bridge-group 1
!
interface Ethernet0/0
 ip address 160.10.11.1 255.255.255.0
bridge-group 1

!
bridge 1 protocol ieee
!
!
R3#show run
!
dlsw local-peer peer-id 160.10.3.3
dlsw remote-peer 0 fst 160.10.1.1
dlsw bridge-group 1
!
!
!
interface FastEthernet0/1
 ip address 160.10.33.3 255.255.255.0
 bridge-group 1
!
!
bridge 1 protocol ieee
!
!
R1#show dlsw peer
Peers:                 state      pkts_rx   pkts_tx  type  drops ckts TCP   uptime
 FST 160.10.3.3       CONNECT      3298       3298  conf     0    0   0    1d03h
Total number of connected peers: 1
Total number of connections:     1

R1#
!
!
R3#show dlsw peer
Peers:                 state      pkts_rx   pkts_tx  type  drops ckts TCP   uptime
 FST 160.10.1.1       CONNECT      3299       3299  conf     0    0   0    1d03h
Total number of connected peers: 1
Total number of connections:     1

R3#
```

- *Configure R3 to accommodate the NetBIOS users on VLAN_33 when a cache entry is requested and mark it as stable for six minutes.*

If you configured this correctly as shown in Example 6-47, you have scored 2 points.

Notice that the **dlsw timer netbios-verify-interval** is in seconds.

**Example 6-47**  *R3 DLSw Timer Configuration*

```
R3#sh run
!
dlsw timer netbios-verify-interval 360
!
```

# Section 7: QoS (4 Points)

- *Configure the Frame Relay connection between R2 and R3 such that the connection can adapt to congestion when a BECN is received from the network. Assume a 1544 kbps access rate and a CIR of 64 kbps.*

If you configured this correctly as shown in Example 6-48, you have scored 2 points.

This is an application of Traffic Shaping to accommodate congestion. Notice the configuration of the **traffic-shape fecn-adapt** on both ends of the link. The far end will reflect received FECNs as BECNs in the Q.922 TEST RESPONSE messages.

**Example 6-48**  *R2 and R3* **traffic-shape** *Adaptability Configuration*

```
R2#sh run int s0/0
Building configuration...

Current configuration : 362 bytes
!
interface Serial0/0
 ip address 160.10.32.2 255.255.255.252
 ip helper-address 130.200.10.200
 encapsulation frame-relay
 ip ospf network point-to-point
 traffic-shape rate 1544000 38600 38600 1000
 traffic-shape adaptive 64000
 traffic-shape fecn-adapt
 frame-relay map ip 160.10.32.1 203 broadcast
 no frame-relay inverse-arp
 frame-relay lmi-type ansi
end

R2#
```
```
R3#sh run int s0/0
Building configuration...

Current configuration : 328 bytes
!
interface Serial0/0
 ip address 160.10.32.1 255.255.255.252
 encapsulation frame-relay
 ip ospf network point-to-point
 traffic-shape rate 1544000 38600 38600 1000
 traffic-shape adaptive 64000
```

**Example 6-48**  *R2 and R3* **traffic-shape** *Adaptability Configuration (Continued)*

```
traffic-shape fecn-adapt
frame-relay map ip 160.10.32.2 302 broadcast
no frame-relay inverse-arp
frame-relay lmi-type ansi
end

R3#
```

- *Consider VoIP to be a "critical" application. Configure PQ-CBWFQ (Priority Queueing-Class-Based Weight Fair Queueing) on R3 and R4 to guarantee a bandwidth of 256 kbps on VoIP traffic and Fair-Queue with a queue size of 32 for all other traffic types.*

Class Based Weight Fair Queue (CBWFQ) with Low Latency Queue (LLQ) is used to guarantee quality to VoIP applications. This technique is what is recommended for VoIP.

If you configured this correctly as shown in Example 6-49, you have scored 2 points.

**Example 6-49**  *R3 and R4 LLQ-CBWFQ Configuration*

```
R4#sh run
!
class-map match-all VOICE
  match input-interface Serial0/0
!
!
policy-map Class1
  class VOICE
    priority 256
  class class-default
    fair-queue 32
R4#show policy-map interface s0/1

 Serial0/1

  Service-policy output: Class1

    Class-map: VOICE (match-all)
      35 packets, 1260 bytes
      5 minute offered rate 0 bps, drop rate 0 bps
      Match: input-interface Serial0/0
      Queueing
        Strict Priority
        Output Queue: Conversation 40
        Bandwidth 256 (kbps) Burst 6400 (Bytes)
        (pkts matched/bytes matched) 35/1260
        (total drops/bytes drops) 0/0

    Class-map: class-default (match-any)
      410 packets, 28471 bytes
      5 minute offered rate 0 bps, drop rate 0 bps
```

*continues*

**Example 6-49** *R3 and R4 LLQ-CBWFQ Configuration (Continued)*

```
              Match: any
              Queueing
                Flow Based Fair Queueing
                Maximum Number of Hashed Queues 32
                (total queued/total drops/no-buffer drops) 0/0/0

!
!
R3#sh run
              (total queued/total drops/no-buffer drops) 0/0/0
!
class-map match-all VOICE
   match input-interface Serial0/0
!
!
policy-map Class1
   class VOICE
      priority 256
   class class-default
     fair-queue 32
!
!
R3#sh run int s0/0
Building configuration...

Current configuration : 358 bytes
!
interface Serial0/0
  ip address 160.10.32.1 255.255.255.252
  service-policy output Class1
  encapsulation frame-relay
  end

R3#sh policy-map interface s0/0

  Serial0/0

   Service-policy output: Class1

     Class-map: VOICE (match-all)
        36 packets, 1296 bytes
        5 minute offered rate 0 bps, drop rate 0 bps
        Match: input-interface Serial0/0
        Queueing
          Strict Priority
          Output Queue: Conversation 40
          Bandwidth 256 (kbps) Burst 6400 (Bytes)
          (pkts matched/bytes matched) 36/1296
          (total drops/bytes drops) 0/0

     Class-map: class-default (match-any)
        734 packets, 50212 bytes
```

**Example 6-49**  *R3 and R4 LLQ-CBWFQ Configuration (Continued)*

```
        5 minute offered rate 4000 bps, drop rate 0 bps
      Match: any
      Queueing
        Flow Based Fair Queueing
        Maximum Number of Hashed Queues 32
        (total queued/total drops/no-buffer drops) 0/0
```

# Section 8: Multicast (6 Points)

- *Configure Multicast PIM Sparse-mode on VLAN_22 to allow Multicast traffic between R3, R5, and R6. Make R6 the rendezvous point. Make this a static configuration.*

If you configured this correctly as shown in Example 6-50, you have scored 3 points.

**Example 6-50**  *R3, R5, and R6 Multicast Configuration*

```
R3#show run
Building configuration...
!

ip multicast-routing
!

interface FastEthernet0/0
 ip address 160.10.22.3 255.255.255.0
 ip pim sparse-mode
!

ip pim rp-address 160.10.22.6
!
R3#
!

R5#show run
Building configuration...
!

ip multicast-routing
!

interface FastEthernet0/0
 ip address 160.10.22.5 255.255.255.0
 ip pim sparse-mode

!
ip pim rp-address 160.10.22.6
!
R5#
!
!

R6#show run
```

*continues*

**Example 6-50** *R3, R5, and R6 Multicast Configuration (Continued)*

```
Building configuration...
!
ip multicast-routing
!
!
interface Ethernet0/0
 ip address 160.10.22.6 255.255.255.0
  ip pim sparse-mode
!
R6#
!
!
```

```
R3#show ip pim rp
Group: 224.0.1.40, RP: 160.10.22.6, uptime 1d01h, expires never
R3#
!
!
```

```
R5#show ip pim rp
Group: 224.0.1.40, RP: 160.10.22.6, uptime 1d01h, expires never
R5#
```

- *Configure R3, R5, and R6 to prune their groups in eight seconds.*

The idea is to have the responder router to respond quickly to an IGMP query message before the router deletes the group. The default is 10 seconds, so you need to configure a value a little less than 10 seconds.

If you configured this correctly as shown in Example 6-51, you have scored 3 points.

**Example 6-51** *R3, R5, and R6 Maximum Query Response Time Change Configuration*

```
R3#sh run int fa0/0
Building configuration...

Current configuration : 185 bytes
!
interface FastEthernet0/0
 ip address 160.10.22.3 255.255.255.0
 ip igmp query-max-response-time 8
!
R3#
!
```

```
R5#sh run int fa0/0
Building configuration...

Current configuration : 187 bytes
!
interface FastEthernet0/0
 ip address 160.10.22.5 255.255.255.0
 ip igmp query-max-response-time 8
```

**Example 6-51**  *R3, R5, and R6 Maximum Query Response Time Change Configuration (Continued)*

```
  end
!
R5#
!
R6#sh run int e0/0
Building configuration...

Current configuration : 152 bytes
!
interface Ethernet0/0
 ip address 160.10.22.6 255.255.255.0
 ip igmp query-max-response-time 8
end

R6#
```

# Section 9: Security (7 Points)

- *You are concerned that you cannot trust some users on VLAN_25. Configure the interfaces for R1 and R5 to authenticate the routing protocol updates through the LAN with the best authentication method.*

If you configured this correctly as shown in Example 6-52, you have scored 2 points.

Here we have an OSPF interface authentication configuration. The authentication is starting here intentionally to exercise with something that can break your network. This requirement could be found also under the specific IGP section but has been left to this stage within the lab.

**Example 6-52**  *R1 and R5 OSPF Interface Authentication*

```
R1#sh run int e0/1
Building configuration...

Current configuration : 119 bytes
!
interface Ethernet0/1
 ip address 160.10.25.1 255.255.255.0
 ip ospf message-digest-key 1 md5 ccie
 half-duplex
end
R1#
R1#
R1#sh run ¦ b router ospf
router ospf 1
 log-adjacency-changes
 area 25 authentication message-digest
!
R1#
!
```

*continues*

**Example 6-52** *R1 and R5 OSPF Interface Authentication (Continued)*

```
R5#sh run int fa0/1
Building configuration...

Current configuration : 135 bytes
!
interface FastEthernet0/1
 ip address 160.10.25.5 255.255.255.0
 ip ospf message-digest-key 1 md5 ccie
 duplex auto
 speed auto
end
R5#
R5#sh run ¦ b router ospf
router ospf 1
 log-adjacency-changes
 area 25 authentication message-digest
!
R5#
!
```

- *Configure R3, R5, and R6 to authenticate any routing updates on the IS-IS running on VLAN_22. Make this configuration on the interface level.*

If you configured this correctly as shown in Example 6-53, you have scored 2 points.

**Example 6-53** *R3, R5, and R6 IS-IS Interface Authentication*

```
R3#sh run int fa0/0
Building configuration...

Current configuration : 188 bytes
!
interface FastEthernet0/0
 ip address 160.10.22.3 255.255.255.0
 ip router isis
 isis password ccie
end

R3#
!
```

```
R5#sh run int fa0/0
Building configuration...

Current configuration : 188 bytes
!
interface FastEthernet0/0
 ip address 160.10.22.5 255.255.255.0
 ip router isis
 isis password ccie
end
```

**Example 6-53**  *R3, R5, and R6 IS-IS Interface Authentication (Continued)*

```
R5#
!
R6#sh run int e0/0
Building configuration...

Current configuration : 172 bytes
!
interface Ethernet0/0
 ip address 160.10.22.6 255.255.255.0
 ip router isis
 isis password ccie
end

R6#
```

- *Configure Sw2 to permit only Telnet access from R3 with source address of 160.10.3.3. Also make sure that both successful and failed Telnet connections are logged.*

This is basically an access list configuration on Sw2.

If you configured this correctly as shown in Example 6-54, you have scored 2 points.

**Example 6-54**  *Sw2 Access List Configuration to Permit R3-lo0 Address*

```
Sw2#sh run ! b line vty 0 4
Building configuration...

Current configuration : 2633 bytes
!
!

!
ip access-list standard ccie

 permit 160.10.3.3 log
deny any log
!
!
line vty 0 4
 access-class ccie in
 exec-timeout 0 0
 password cisco
end

Sw2#
R3#telnet 160.10.33.10 /source-interface fastEthernet 0/0
Trying 160.10.33.10 ...
% Connection refused by remote host

R3#
!
Sw2#
```

*continues*

**Example 6-54** *Sw2 Access List Configuration to Permit R3-lo0 Address (Continued)*

```
 5d05h: %SEC-6-IPACCESSLOGS: list ccie denied 160.10.22.3
!
Sw2#
!
!
R3#telnet 160.10.33.10 /source-interface loopback 0
Trying 160.10.33.10 ... Open


User Access Verification

Password:
Sw2>
!
!
Sw2#
5d05h: %SEC-6-IPACCESSLOGS: list ccie permitted 160.10.3.3 1 packet
```

# Section 10: VoIP (6 Points)

- *Configure a basic VoIP connection between R3 and R4. Consider the R3 local number to be "33" and R4 local number to be "44."*

If you configured this correctly as shown in Example 6-55, you have scored 3 points.

- *Configure your dial peers to provide silence when the remote party is not speaking. You can assume that Voice Activity Detection (VAD) is enabled.*

You have a VoIP peer configuration and you need to disable VAD in order to have a better voice quality.

If you configured this correctly as shown in Example 6-55, you have scored 3 points.

**Example 6-55** *VoIP Configuration and Disabling the Background Noise*

```
R4#sh run | b dial-peer
dial-peer cor custom
!
!
voice-port 2/0/0
 no comfort-noise
!
!
dial-peer voice 4 pots
 destination-pattern 44
 port 2/0/0
!
dial-peer voice 40 voip
 destination-pattern 33
 session target ipv4:160.10.3.3
```

**Example 6-55**  *VoIP Configuration and Disabling the Background Noise (Continued)*

```
R4#
!
R3#sh run | b dial-peer
dial-peer cor custom
!
voice-port 1/1/0
 no comfort-noise
!

dial-peer voice 30 voip
 destination-pattern 44
 session target ipv4:160.10.4.4

 !
dial-peer voice 3 pots
 destination-pattern 33
 port 1/1/0
 !
R3#
```

# How Did You Do?

With the aid of the answers section and full configurations and routing tables on the CD, you should now have an accurate evaluation of your lab. If you scored more than 80 points within the timeframe, you should congratulate yourself. You are well on the way to becoming a CCIE; you have demonstrated the ability to think laterally and shown an impressive knowledge of your subject. If you scored less than 80, do not worry, take the lab again when you can to improve your score.

Did you spot the landmines in the lab? The classics in Lab 6 were to give you, under this IP IGP topology, the basic setup for OSPF, RIPv2, EIGRP, and BGP, as well as QoS, IOS features, and IP features. These subjects are possible candidates to be found in the real lab exam.

This lab added some routing authentication and some VoIP, too. Section 9 provided coverage of routing authentication to intentionally give you an idea about one more variable that can break your topology. This part could be found directly on the IGP section. Also, an important thing to keep in mind is the feature each area has. You need to explore these going through Cisco Documentation. You need to explore on each section of the documentation specially the features that are available.

On each of the labs throughout the book, you were required to demonstrate your knowledge in more complex tasks, environments, and behaviors, and prove yourself to be capable of solving the issues. The real one-day lab exam does not have the Troubleshooting section anymore, but, on the other hand, during the exam you can find yourself in a "troubleshooting" situation if you do not have a solid knowledge of what you are configuring. Keep in mind that you will need to perform some "basic" troubleshooting during the exam. The hands-on experience will give you the confidence that you need. Always be careful when configuring network masks and pay attention to which router you are working on.

Your ability to spot landmines, ask the right questions, and increase your configuration speed will improve as you tackle each practice lab.

For each question that you did not answer correctly, take the time to research the subject thoroughly and turn your weaknesses into your strengths. Research and plenty of practice will ultimately lead you to gain a passing score.

# Further Reading/URLs

To better prepare yourself and follow up on the topics covered in this lab, you should consult the http://www.cisco.com/public/pubsearch.html website for more information on the following topics:

Configuring Frame Relay
Configuring 3550
Configuring ATM
Configuring Routing Protocols
Configuring ISDN
Configuring IP Features
Configuring IOS Features
Configuring DLSw
Configuring QoS
Configuring Multicast
Configuring Security
Configuring VoIP

All topics, concepts, and question used in this chapter came from the following resources:

All Routing, Features, BGP, and so on (Cisco documentation for 12.2 mainline): http://www.cisco.com/univercd/home/home.html
For the Catalyst 3550 (the 12.1 EMI image documentation): http://www.cisco.com/univercd/home/home.html
Book: *IS-IS Network Design Solutions*—Abe Martey—Cisco Press
Book: *IP Quality of Service*—Srinivas Vegesma—Cisco Press
Book: *CCIE Practical Studies: Security*—Dmitry Bokotey, Andrew Mason, Raymond Morrow—Cisco Press

# PART III

# Appendixes

# Frame Relay Switch Configuration

Unless you have a dedicated Frame Relay switch at your disposal, you will need to configure one of your routers to simulate a Frame Relay switch.

NOTE Your chosen router can be one, that you use within the lab scenarios or a dedicated router such as a 4000 with sufficient serial interfaces for this task.

Once configured appropriately, your router will provide the necessary mesh of permanent virtual circuits (PVCs) to meet the requirements stipulated in the lab scenarios.

Figure A-1 shows connectivity from R1 to R4 with R5 acting as the Frame Relay switch. In this example, R5 connects to both R1 and R4 using X21 female data communications equipment (DCE) cables; these will provide a clock signal to the X21 male data terminal equipment (DTE) cables attached to R1 and R4.

**Figure A-1**  *Frame Relay Switch Physical Connectivity*

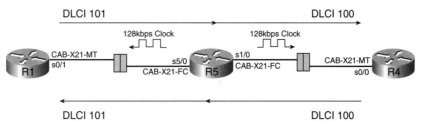

R5 will be configured to supply Data Link Control Identifier (DLCI) 101 on interface Serial 5/0 toward R1 and DLCI 100 on interface Serial 1/0 toward R4. It will send data from R1 PVC associated to DLCI 101 to DLCI 100 and data from R4 PVC associated to DLCI 100 to DLCI 101 by using Frame Relay routing commands. The final configuration will result in the logical connectivity as shown in Figure A-2.

**Figure A-2**   *Frame Relay Switch Logical Connectivity*

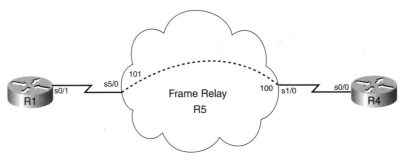

Example A-1 shows the configuration for R5.

**Example A-1**   *R5 Frame Relay Switching Configuration*

```
frame-relay switching
!
interface Serial1/0
 no ip address
 encapsulation frame-relay
 no shutdown
 clockrate 128000
 frame-relay intf-type dce
 frame-relay route 100 interface Serial5/0 101
!
interface Serial5/0
 no ip address
 no shutdown
 encapsulation frame-relay
 clockrate 128000
 frame-relay intf-type dce
 frame-relay route 101 interface Serial1/0 100
```

By default, the Frame Relay Local Management Interface (LMI), which is used for the signalling between the Frame Relay switch and router, will be set to **cisco**. You should experiment with the other settings of **ansi** and **q933a**; however, be aware that the router will attempt to auto negotiate this parameter.

To verify your configuration, use the command **show frame-relay pvc** as demonstrated in Example A-2. The output displays DLCI status information, and a successful configuration will result in PVC status **Active** for each DLCI.

**Example A-2**  show frame-relay pvc *Command Output*

```
R5#show frame-relay pvc

PVC Statistics for interface Serial1/0 (Frame Relay DCE)


DLCI = 100, DLCI USAGE = SWITCHED, PVC STATUS = ACTIVE, INTERFACE = Serial1/0

   input pkts 0            output pkts 0          in bytes 0
   out bytes 0             dropped pkts 6         in FECN pkts 0
   in BECN pkts 0          out FECN pkts 0        out BECN pkts 0
   in DE pkts 0            out DE pkts 0
   out bcast pkts 0        out bcast bytes 0
   pvc create time 09:25:16, last time pvc status changed 08:09:30
   Num Pkts Switched 0

PVC Statistics for interface Serial5/0 (Frame Relay DCE)


DLCI = 101, DLCI USAGE = SWITCHED, PVC STATUS = ACTIVE, INTERFACE = Serial5/0

   input pkts 0            output pkts 0          in bytes 0
   out bytes 0             dropped pkts 6         in FECN pkts 0
   in BECN pkts 0          out FECN pkts 0        out BECN pkts 0
   in DE pkts 0            out DE pkts 0
   out bcast pkts 0        out bcast bytes 0
   pvc create time 09:25:16, last time pvc status changed 08:15:03
   Num Pkts Switched 0
```

You can also verify your Frame Relay routing configuration and ensure that each PVC is active in a more concise manner by issuing the command **show frame-relay route** as shown in Example A-3.

**Example A-3**  show frame-relay route *Command Output*

```
R5#show frame-relay route
Input Intf     Input Dlci     Output Intf     Output Dlci     Status
Serial1/0      100            Serial5/0       101             active
Serial5/0      101            Serial1/0       100             active
```

# LS1010 ATM Switch Configuration

Throughout the lab exercises, ATM connectivity was achieved by a back-to-back connection between two routers. This scenario limits configurations to permanent virtual circuits (PVCs) only; however, you should be familiar with a Cisco LightStream 1010 to provide both PVC and SVC configurations.

The LightStream 1010 or LS1010 is a Cisco workgroup ATM switch that is used to connect power users and create departmental LANs within a single building or a small campus. You might also find a LS1010 in most of the practice labs that training companies offer.

The following example shows the LS1010 configuration to have Router_A and Router_B to communicate using PVCs.

Figure B-1 shows the physical connectivity from Router_A to Router_B with a LS1010 as the ATM switch.

**Figure B-1**  *LS1010 Physical Connectivity*

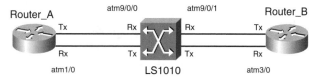

The LS1010 switch will provide the signaling to both routers to deliver data from PVC 100 coming from Router_A to PVC 100 toward Router_B and vice versa.

The final configuration will result in the logical connectivity as shown in Figure B-2.

**Figure B-2**  *LS1010 Switch Logical Connectivity*

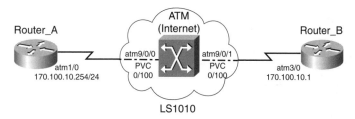

Example B-1 shows the configuration for LS1010 switch, Router_A, and Router_B.

**Example B-1** *LS1010 Switch, Router_A, and Router_B Configuration*

```
Router_A#show run interface atm1/0
Building configuration...
Current configuration : 101 bytes
!
interface ATM1/0
ip address 170.100.10.254 255.255.255.0
 no ip address

 no atm ilmi-keepalive

!
 pvc 0/100
  protocol ip 170.100.10.1 broadcast
 !
end
```

```
Router_B#show run interface atm3/0
Building configuration...
Current configuration : 140 bytes
!
interface ATM3/0
 ip address 170.100.10.1 255.255.255.0
 no atm ilmi-keepalive
!
 pvc 0/100
  protocol ip 170.100.10.254 broadcast
 !
end
!
```

```
! The Following is an alternative configuration on Router_B, in an older fashion,
! that works as well. You need to configure map-list and map-group commands
! in order to achieve the same result:
Router_B#show run interface atm3/0
Building configuration...
Current configuration : 140 bytes
!
interface ATM3/0
 ip address 170.100.10.1 255.255.255.0
map-group PVC
atm pvc 1 0 101 aal5snap
 no atm ilmi-keepalive
!
map-list PVC
 ip 170.100.10.254 atm-vc 1 broadcast
 !
end
```

```
ls1010#show running-config
Building configuration...
Current configuration:
!
version 12.0
!
!
```

**Example B-1**   *LS1010 Switch, Router_A, and Router_B Configuration (Continued)*

```
hostname ls1010
!
enable password cisco
!

interface ATM9/0/0
 description Router_A-ATM1/0
 no ip address
 no ip directed-broadcast
 logging event subif-link-status
 no atm ilmi-keepalive
 atm pvc 0 100  interface  ATM9/0/1 0 100
!
interface ATM9/0/1
 description Router_B-ATM3/0
 no ip address
 no ip directed-broadcast
 logging event subif-link-status
 no atm ilmi-keepalive
!
interface Ethernet13/0/0
shutdown
!
ip classless
!
line con 0
 transport input none
line aux 0
line vty 0 4
 password cisco
 login
!
end
```

By default, the encapsulation on the routers is **AAL5**. The configuration for PVC is very simple on the LS1010 and, contrary to the configuration on a Frame Relay switch, you need only "map" the PVC in one interface, as you can see for interface ATM9/0/0 in Example B-1.

To verify your configuration, use the command **show atm pvc**, which will display the active PVCs and status as demonstrated in Example B-2.

**Example B-2** **show atm vc and show atm svc** *Output*

```
Router_A#show atm vc
              VCD /                    Peak  Avg/Min Burst
  Interface  Name  VPI  VCI  Type  Encaps  SC  Kbps   Kbps Cells  Sts
  1/0         1     0    100  PVC   SNAP    UBR 155000_              UP
Router_A#
Router_B#
Router_B#show atm vc
              VCD /                    Peak  Avg/Min Burst
  Interface  Name  VPI  VCI  Type  Encaps  SC  Kbps   Kbps Cells  Sts
  3/0         1     0   100  PVC   SNAP    UBR 155000               UP
Router_B#
ls1010#show atm vc
  Interface  VPI  VCI  Type   X-Interface    X-VPI X-VCI Encap  Status
  ATM9/0/0    0   100  PVC    ATM9/0/1         0    100          UP
  ATM9/0/1    0   100  PVC    ATM9/0/0         0    100          UP
  ls1010#
```

The following example shows the required configuration for an SVC environment. Figure B-3 shows the physical connectivity from Router_A to Router_B with a LS1010 as the ATM switch.

**Figure B-3** *LS1010 Physical Connectivity*

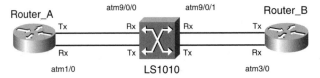

The LS1010 switch will provide the signaling to both routers and deliver data from Router_A toward Router_B and vice versa.

The final configuration will result in the logical connectivity as shown in Figure B-4.

**Figure B-4** *LS1010 Switch Logical Connectivity*

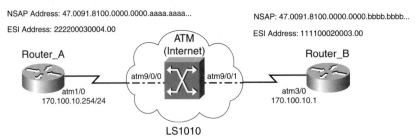

Example B-3 shows the configuration for the LS1010 switch, Router_A, and Router_B.

**Example B-3** *LS1010 Switch, Router_A, and Router_B Configuration*

```
Router_A#show run interface atm1/0
Building configuration...
Current configuration : 293 bytes
!
interface ATM1/0
 ip address 170.100.10.254 255.255.255.0
 no ip route-cache
 no ip mroute-cache
 atm esi-address 222200030004.00
 no atm ilmi-keepalive
 pvc 0/5 qsaal
 !
 pvc 0/16 ilmi
 !
 !
 svc nsap 47.0091810000000000BBBBBBBB.111100020003.00
  protocol ip 170.100.10.1 broadcast
 !
end
Router_A#show atm svc
              VCD /                                Peak   Avg/Min Burst
Interface Name VPI   VCI  Type  Encaps   SC      Kbps    Kbps   Cells Sts
1/0       211   0    51   SVC   SNAP    UBR     155000                 UP
Router_A#
Router_A#show atm vc
              VCD /                                Peak   Avg/Min Burst
Interface Name VPI   VCI  Type  Encaps   SC      Kbps  Kbps Cells  Sts
1/0        1    0    5    PVC   SAAL    UBR     155000                UP
1/0        2    0    16   PVC   ILMI    UBR     155000                UP
1/0       211   0    51   SVC   SNAP    UBR     155000                UP
Router_A#
Router_A#ping 170.100.10.1
Type escape sequence to abort.
Sending 5, 100-byte ICMP Echos to 170.100.10.1, timeout is 2 seconds:
!!!!!
Success rate is 100 percent (5/5), round-trip min/avg/max = 1/2/4 ms
Router_A#
Router_B#show run interface atm3/0
Building configuration...
Current configuration : 171 bytes
!
interface ATM3/0
 ip address 170.100.10.1 255.255.255.0
 map-group AAAA
 atm esi-address 111100020003.00
 no atm ilmi-keepalive
 pvc 0/5 qsaal
 !
 pvc 0/16 ilmi
 !
end
!
```

*continues*

**Example B-3** *LS1010 Switch, Router_A, and Router_B Configuration (Continued)*

```
!
map-list AAAA
 ip 170.100.10.254 atm-nsap 47.0091810000000000AAAAAAAA.222200030004.00 broadcast
!

Router_B#show atm svc
            VCD /                                 Peak   Avg/Min Burst
Interface Name VPI   VCI  Type   Encaps   SC      Kbps   Kbps    Cells  Sts
3/0        1011  0    36   SVC    SNAP     UBR     155000                 UP
Router_B#Router_B#
Router_B#sh atm vc
            VCD /                                 Peak   Avg/Min  Burst
Interface Name   VPI   VCI  Type  Encaps  SC      Kbps   Kbps     Cells  Sts
3/0       1     0    5    PVC   SAAL    UBR     155000                   UP
3/0       2     0    16   PVC   ILMI    UBR     155000                   UP
3/0       1011  0    36   SVC   SNAP    UBR     155000                   UP
Router_B#
Router_B#ping 170.100.10.254
Type escape sequence to abort.
Sending 5, 100-byte ICMP Echos to 170.100.10.254, timeout is 2 seconds:
!!!!!
Success rate is 100 percent (5/5), round-trip min/avg/max = 1/2/4 ms
ls1010#show running-config
Building configuration...
Current configuration:
!
interface ATM9/0/0
 description Router_A
 no ip address
 no ip directed-broadcast
 logging event subif-link-status
 no atm ilmi-keepalive
 atm prefix 47.0091.8100.0000.0000.aaaa.aaaa...
!
interface ATM9/0/1
 description Router_B
 no ip address
 no ip directed-broadcast
 logging event subif-link-status
 no atm ilmi-keepalive
 atm prefix 47.0091.8100.0000.0000.bbbb.bbbb...
end

ls1010#show atm vc

Interface   VPI  VCI  Type   X-Interface   X-VPI X-VCI  Encap Status
ATM9/0/0    0    5    PVC    ATM13/0/0     0     60     QSAAL UP
ATM9/0/0    0    16   PVC    ATM13/0/0     0     36     ILMI  UP
ATM9/0/0    0    36   SVC    ATM9/0/1      0     51           UP
ATM9/0/1    0    5    PVC    ATM13/0/0     0     73     QSAAL UP
ATM9/0/1    0    16   PVC    ATM13/0/0     0     49     ILMI  UP
ATM9/0/1    0    51   SVC    ATM9/0/0      0     36           UP
```

Configuring SVCs is simple on the LS1010. Contrasted with PVCs, for SVCs the "map" is completed on the routers, not on the LS1010.

An important thing to consider is that you need to configure the PVC 0/5 for ATM Adapter Layer (AAL) signaling and PVC 0/16 for Integrated Local Management Interface (ILMI). The ATM switch will use the Public-Network Node Interface (PNNI) protocol to route through the ATM network.

Notice that two different techniques are used to configure the maps between Router_A and Router_B. On Router_A, the **svc nsap** command was configured to map the remote ATM Network Service Access Point (NSAP) address and the IP address. On Router_B, the **map-list** and **map-group** commands were configured to also map the remotely ATM NSAP and IP address.

If you do not configure the **atm prefix** command within LS1010, it is still working, because the ILMI on the routers will learn the ATM Prefix address (NSAP) from the switch (LS1010) and add the End System Identifier (ESI) address or local address, to make up the entire NSAP address. You just need to use the **show interface atm** command on the routers to see the ATM address to use on the **map** or **svc nsap** commands. Example B-4 shows the output from a **show interface atm** command on Router_A to capture the ATM NSAP address.

**Example B-4**  **show interface** *on Router_A*

```
Router_A#show interface atm 1/0
ATM1/0 is up, line protocol is up
  Hardware is TI1570 ATM
  Internet address is 170.100.10.254/24
  MTU 4470 bytes, sub MTU 4470, BW 155520 Kbit, DLY 80 usec,
    reliability 255/255, txload 1/255, rxload 1/255
  NSAP address: 47.0091810000000090B14C9C01.222200030004.00
  Encapsulation ATM, loopback not set
  Encapsulation(s): AAL5, PVC mode
  2047 maximum active VCs, 1024 VCs per VP, 3 current VCCs
  VC idle disconnect time: 300 seconds
  Signalling vc = 1, vpi = 0, vci = 5
        UNI Version = 4.0, Link Side = user
  Last input 00:00:07, output 00:00:07, output hang never
  Last clearing of "show interface" counters never
  Input queue: 0/75/0/0 (size/max/drops/flushes); Total output drops: 0
  Queueing strategy: fifo
  Output queue: 0/40 (size/max)
  5 minute input rate 0 bits/sec, 0 packets/sec
  5 minute output rate 0 bits/sec, 0 packets/sec
     19136 packets input, 238100 bytes, 0 no buffer
     Received 0 broadcasts, 0 runts, 0 giants, 0 throttles
     0 input errors, 0 CRC, 0 frame, 1 overrun, 0 ignored, 0 abort
     19299 packets output, 245785 bytes, 0 underruns
     7 output errors, 0 collisions, 3 interface resets
     0 output buffer failures, 0 output buffers swapped out
Router_A#
```

# Troubleshooting Tips

The original two-day CCIE lab had a "Troubleshooting" section where a host of faults were introduced into your network and you had two hours to rectify them. This final section of the exam was where most candidates failed and missed out on their number—it was extremely tough. The new one-day format, as you should be aware, does not have this "Troubleshooting" section. You might think this is excellent news, but you have to realize that you only have eight hours to perform your configuration. You cannot afford to spend any time *troubleshooting* problems you cause yourself through invalid configuration or by a landmine question breaking earlier configuration.

This appendix provides some tips you can use to verify what probably caused your network to stop receiving routing updates, why you are not able to ping a specific router, or even why everything was working before and suddenly not anymore.

As stated in earlier chapters, the proctors will make sure there are no problems with the backbone, ISDN switch, or physical problems on the routers and switches in your rack, but any problem concerning your configuration is your own responsibility to rectify. So, that is the intention of this appendix. It is not a troubleshooting course; instead, it is quick reference about the most common problems you may find during your lab exam.

The best approach is to avoid getting trapped in problems by reading the session questions to get the big picture and identify landmines before you begin typing commands. One of the most common error-introducing problems are typos.

## Basic Troubleshooting Approach: What Has Changed?

Figure C-1 shows a basic troubleshooting model.

**Figure C-1**  *Troubleshooting Model*

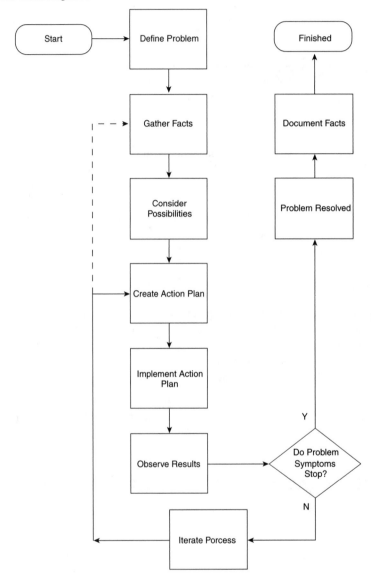

| | |
|---|---|
| **NOTE** | Remember that during the CCIE Lab Exam that any notes or documentation you make cannot be taken with you when you leave the lab. This model is to help you to create a standard method to troubleshoot problems that will help you to quickly identify problems during your exam. |

When analyzing a problem you should consider the flowchart in Figure C-1 and the following facts:

- Make sure you have a clear definition of the problem.

- Gather all the relevant facts and consider the likely possibilities.

- Create and implement an action plan and then observe the results. Before beginning to troubleshoot a problem, ensure that you save a backup copy of the configuration that you can use to fall back to if your action plan does not resolve the problem.

- If the symptoms do not stop, try another action plan and gather additional facts. If you try one thing and it does not work, you should take that configuration or feature off. In case you make the situation worse, always keep it basic and get back to a known position.

- If the symptoms do stop, document how you fixed the problem.

This model can help you to identify and fix network problems, especially network implementation problems. Every fact (or question) that you gather is very important and most of the time will lead you to the primary reason for a failed implementation. When implementing or solving a real problem or during your CCIE Lab Exam, ask yourself the following questions:

- What has changed?

- What was the last change or configuration made?

These questions can quickly identify what is causing or caused your network to stop receiving routes updates or stopped a previously successful ping to a router's interface, and so on.

Because you are implementing a network following a set of sequential requirements, the potential number of ways you have to "break" something during the exam is high. Because of this, you need to have complete control of what is happening and in what you are configuring. Documentation is the key to tracking your progress and identifying problems.

# Some Useful Tips and Commands to Help Identify Problems During the CCIE Lab

When taking your CCIE Lab Exam, time matters. Consider the following steps and advice during your lab exam:

**Step 1**   Read the entire exam before beginning.

**Step 2**   Begin with simple or basic questions (basic Layer 2 setup, basic routing protocols and BGP setup, and so on).

**Step 3** Leave the more complex questions or features for later—keep the layered approach.

**Step 4** Pay attention when configuring maps, network statements, IP addresses, and so on. Typos are the most common cause of problems found during the lab exam.

**Step 5** Verify each question to ensure it is working before moving on to other questions. This will assure you that you can move on without any problem left behind. If everything was working and after you have configured a new section or question you notice a failure on your exam, you will know exactly what is the cause of the failure.

**Step 6** Keep saving your configurations before moving on to another question. If all else fails, you can always reload a device and work on something else while it comes back up in a known state.

These approaches will help you keep your work under strict control.

The sections that follow list and demonstrate some useful commands to help troubleshoot some of the areas covered in Practice Labs 1–6.

## Frame Relay

Troubleshooting commands for Frame Relay configuration include the following:

- **show interfaces serial**
- **show frame-relay map**
- **show frame-relay lmi**
- **show frame-relay pvc**
- **clear frame-relay inarp**
- **clear interface**
- **debug serial interface**
- **debug frame-relay lmi**
- **debug frame-delay events**
- **debug frame-relay packets**

Example C-1 provides commented output from these key commands.

**Example C-1**  *Some Frame Relay Troubleshooting Commands*

```
R2#show frame-relay map
! It is important here to notice if the right remote IP address is mapped
! to the right DLCI.

Serial0/0 (up): ip 160.10.32.1 dlci 203(0xCB,0x30B0), static, broadcast,
            CISCO, status defined, active
Serial0/1.1 (up): ip 160.10.37.1 dlci 211(0xD3,0x3430), static,
            broadcast,
            CISCO, status defined, active
Serial0/1.1 (up): ip 160.10.37.5 dlci 215(0xD7,0x3470), static,
            broadcast,
            CISCO, status defined, active
Serial0/1.2 (up): point-to-point dlci, dlci 214(0xD6,0x3460), broadcast
            status defined, active
R2#
R2#
R2#show frame-relay lmi
! Look for the LMI TYPE to make sure it is in accordance with the
! Frame Relay switch

LMI Statistics for interface Serial0/0 (Frame Relay DTE) LMI TYPE = ANSI
  Invalid Unnumbered info 0        Invalid Prot Disc 0
  Invalid dummy Call Ref 0         Invalid Msg Type 0
  Invalid Status Message 0         Invalid Lock Shift 0
  Invalid Information ID 0         Invalid Report IE Len 0
  Invalid Report Request 0         Invalid Keep IE Len 0
  Num Status Enq. Sent 252696      Num Status msgs Rcvd 252697
  Num Update Status Rcvd 0         Num Status Timeouts 0

LMI Statistics for interface Serial0/1 (Frame Relay DTE) LMI TYPE = ANSI
  Invalid Unnumbered info 0        Invalid Prot Disc 0
  Invalid dummy Call Ref 0         Invalid Msg Type 0
  Invalid Status Message 0         Invalid Lock Shift 0
  Invalid Information ID 0         Invalid Report IE Len 0
  Invalid Report Request 0         Invalid Keep IE Len 0
  Num Status Enq. Sent 250259      Num Status msgs Rcvd 250259
  Num Update Status Rcvd 0         Num Status Timeouts 0
R2#
R2#
R2#show frame-relay pvc

!Look for the interfaces you need to be up and verify their DLCI and PVC STATUS.
! Also look the input packets and output packets to verify if packets
! are being exchanged.

PVC Statistics for interface Serial0/0 (Frame Relay DTE)
                Active      Inactive      Deleted       Static
  Local           1            4             0             0
  Switched        0            0             0             0
  Unused          0            0             0             0
DLCI = 201, DLCI USAGE = LOCAL, PVC STATUS = INACTIVE, INTERFACE = Serial0/0
  input pkts 23            output pkts 17             in bytes 7636
```

*continues*

**Example C-1** *Some Frame Relay Troubleshooting Commands (Continued)*

```
  out bytes 5644            dropped pkts 0         in pkts dropped 0
  out pkts dropped 0              out bytes dropped 0
  in FECN pkts 0          in BECN pkts 0        out FECN pkts 0
  out BECN pkts 0         in DE pkts 0          out DE pkts 0
  out bcast pkts 17       out bcast bytes 5644
  5 minute input rate 0 bits/sec, 0 packets/sec
  5 minute output rate 0 bits/sec, 0 packets/sec
  pvc create time 4w1d, last time pvc status changed 4w1d

DLCI = 203, DLCI USAGE = LOCAL, PVC STATUS = ACTIVE, INTERFACE = Serial0/0
  input pkts 505707       output pkts 509709     in bytes 30978546
  out bytes 34593695      dropped pkts 0         in pkts dropped 0
  out pkts dropped 0             out bytes dropped 0
  in FECN pkts 0          in BECN pkts 0        out FECN pkts 0
  out BECN pkts 0         in DE pkts 0          out DE pkts 0
  out bcast pkts 265708   out bcast bytes 22984244
  5 minute input rate 0 bits/sec, 0 packets/sec
  5 minute output rate 0 bits/sec, 0 packets/sec
  pvc create time 4w1d, last time pvc status changed 4w0d



PVC Statistics for interface Serial0/1 (Frame Relay DTE)
               Active      Inactive      Deleted       Static
  Local         3            0             0             0
  Switched      0            0             0             0
  Unused        0            2             0             0
DLCI = 211, DLCI USAGE = LOCAL, PVC STATUS = ACTIVE, INTERFACE = Serial0/1.1
  input pkts 259401       output pkts 185410     in bytes 16210516
  out bytes 12698272      dropped pkts 0         in pkts dropped 0
  out pkts dropped 0             out bytes dropped 0
  in FECN pkts 0          in BECN pkts 0        out FECN pkts 0
  out BECN pkts 0         in DE pkts 0          out DE pkts 0
  out bcast pkts 83421    out bcast bytes 7341032
  5 minute input rate 0 bits/sec, 0 packets/sec
  5 minute output rate 0 bits/sec, 0 packets/sec
  pvc create time 4w1d, last time pvc status changed 4w0d

DLCI = 214, DLCI USAGE = LOCAL, PVC STATUS = ACTIVE, INTERFACE = Serial0/1.2
  input pkts 257970       output pkts 304963     in bytes 19103988
  out bytes 36371224      dropped pkts 0         in pkts dropped 0
  out pkts dropped 0             out bytes dropped 0
  in FECN pkts 0          in BECN pkts 0        out FECN pkts 0
  out BECN pkts 0         in DE pkts 0          out DE pkts 0
  out bcast pkts 304928   out bcast bytes 36367584
  5 minute input rate 0 bits/sec, 0 packets/sec
  5 minute output rate 0 bits/sec, 0 packets/sec
  pvc create time 4w1d, last time pvc status changed 4w0d

DLCI = 215, DLCI USAGE = LOCAL, PVC STATUS = ACTIVE, INTERFACE = Serial0/1.1
  input pkts 251325       output pkts 179623     in bytes 17224383
  out bytes 13859561      dropped pkts 0         in pkts dropped 0
```

**Example C-1**  *Some Frame Relay Troubleshooting Commands (Continued)*

```
 out pkts dropped 0                      out bytes dropped 0
 in FECN pkts 0          in BECN pkts 0              out FECN pkts 0
 out BECN pkts 0         in DE pkts 0                out DE pkts 0
 out bcast pkts 83416     out bcast bytes 7340596
 5 minute input rate 0 bits/sec, 0 packets/sec
 5 minute output rate 0 bits/sec, 0 packets/sec
 pvc create time 4w1d, last time pvc status changed 4w0d
R2#show interfaces serial 0/0
!Look the Interface encapsulation, if the packets are being sent and received.
! If the LMI TYPE, if the LMI is up and exchanging messages

Serial0/0 is up, line protocol is up
  Hardware is GT96K Serial
  Internet address is 160.10.32.2/30
  MTU 1500 bytes, BW 1544 Kbit, DLY 20000 usec,
     reliability 255/255, txload 1/255, rxload 1/255
  Encapsulation FRAME-RELAY, loopback not set
  Keepalive set (10 sec)
  LMI enq sent  252702, LMI stat recvd 252703, LMI upd recvd 0, DTE LMI up
  LMI enq recvd 0, LMI stat sent  0, LMI upd sent  0
  LMI DLCI 0  LMI type is ANSI Annex D  frame relay DTE
  FR SVC disabled, LAPF state down
  Broadcast queue 0/64, broadcasts sent/dropped 265783/0, interface broadcasts
265771
  Last input 00:00:01, output 00:00:08, output hang never
  Last clearing of "show interface" counters 4w1d
  Input queue: 0/75/0/0 (size/max/drops/flushes); Total output drops: 0
  Queueing strategy: weighted fair
  Output queue: 0/1000/64/0 (size/max total/threshold/drops)
     Conversations  0/1/256 (active/max active/max total)
     Reserved Conversations 0/0 (allocated/max allocated)
     Available Bandwidth 1158 kilobits/sec
  5 minute input rate 0 bits/sec, 0 packets/sec
  5 minute output rate 0 bits/sec, 0 packets/sec
     758622 packets input, 35638551 bytes, 0 no buffer
     Received 0 broadcasts, 0 runts, 0 giants, 0 throttles
     0 input errors, 0 CRC, 0 frame, 0 overrun, 0 ignored, 0 abort
     762500 packets output, 38155977 bytes, 0 underruns
     0 output errors, 0 collisions, 3 interface resets
     0 output buffer failures, 0 output buffers swapped out
     2 carrier transitions
     DCD=up  DSR=up  DTR=up  RTS=up  CTS=up

R2#show interfaces serial 0/1
Serial0/1 is up, line protocol is up
  Hardware is GT96K Serial
  MTU 1500 bytes, BW 1544 Kbit, DLY 20000 usec,
     reliability 255/255, txload 1/255, rxload 1/255
  Encapsulation FRAME-RELAY, loopback not set
  Keepalive set (10 sec)
  LMI enq sent  250266, LMI stat recvd 250266, LMI upd recvd 0, DTE LMI up
  LMI enq recvd 0, LMI stat sent  0, LMI upd sent  0
```

*continues*

**Example C-1** *Some Frame Relay Troubleshooting Commands (Continued)*

```
 LMI DLCI 0   LMI type is ANSI Annex D   frame relay DTE
  FR SVC disabled, LAPF state down
  Broadcast queue 0/64, broadcasts sent/dropped 471772/0, interface broadcasts
346645
  Last input 00:00:01, output 00:00:01, output hang never
  Last clearing of "show interface" counters 4w1d
  Input queue: 0/75/0/0 (size/max/drops/flushes); Total output drops: 0
  Queueing strategy: weighted fair
  Output queue: 0/1000/64/0 (size/max total/threshold/drops)
     Conversations  0/2/256 (active/max active/max total)
     Reserved Conversations 0/0 (allocated/max allocated)
     Available Bandwidth 1158 kilobits/sec
  5 minute input rate 0 bits/sec, 0 packets/sec
  5 minute output rate 0 bits/sec, 0 packets/sec
     1018973 packets input, 57086147 bytes, 0 no buffer
     Received 0 broadcasts, 0 runts, 0 giants, 0 throttles
     0 input errors, 0 CRC, 0 frame, 0 overrun, 0 ignored, 0 abort
     920273 packets output, 66433800 bytes, 0 underruns
     0 output errors, 0 collisions, 1 interface resets
     0 output buffer failures, 0 output buffers swapped out
     0 carrier transitions
     DCD=up  DSR=up  DTR=up  RTS=up  CTS=up
R2#
R2#debug frame-relay lmi
Frame Relay LMI debugging is on
Displaying all Frame Relay LMI data

! If you are experiencing problems to have your Frame relay Link to come up
! look on the debug output if LMI messages are being sent and received on the
! router interface. Observe the "message sequence" on Interfaces S0/0 and S0/1.
*Mar 30 06:53:48.841: Serial0/0(out): StEnq, myseq 43, yourseen 42, DTE up
*Mar 30 06:53:48.841: datagramstart = 0x6001C54, datagramsize = 14
*Mar 30 06:53:48.841: FR encap = 0x00010308
*Mar 30 06:53:48.841: 00 75 95 01 01 00 03 02 2B 2A
*Mar 30 06:53:48.841:
*Mar 30 06:53:48.841: Serial0/0(in): Status, myseq 43
*Mar 30 06:53:48.841: RT IE 1, length 1, type 0
*Mar 30 06:53:48.841: KA IE 3, length 2, yourseq 43, myseq 43
*Mar 30 06:53:48.841: PVC IE 0x7 , length 0x3 , dlci 201, status 0x0
*Mar 30 06:53:48.841: PVC IE 0x7 , length 0x3 , dlci 203, status 0x2
*Mar 30 06:53:48.841: PVC IE 0x7 , length 0x3 , dlci 204, status 0x0
*Mar 30 06:53:48.841: PVC IE 0x7 , length 0x3 , dlci 205, status 0x0
*Mar 30 06:53:48.841: PVC IE 0x7 , length 0x3 , dlci 206, status 0x0
*Mar 30 06:53:52.229: Serial0/1(out): StEnq, myseq 187, yourseen 186, DTE up
*Mar 30 06:53:52.229: datagramstart = 0x63F5234, datagramsize = 14
*Mar 30 06:53:52.229: FR encap = 0x00010308
*Mar 30 06:53:52.229: 00 75 95 01 01 01 03 02 BB BA
*Mar 30 06:53:52.229:
*Mar 30 06:53:52.229: Serial0/1(in): Status, myseq 187
*Mar 30 06:53:52.229: RT IE 1, length 1, type 1
*Mar 30 06:53:52.229: KA IE 3, length 2, yourseq 187, myseq 187
*Mar 30 06:53:58.841: Serial0/0(out): StEnq, myseq 44, yourseen 43, DTE up
```

**Example C-1**  *Some Frame Relay Troubleshooting Commands (Continued)*

```
*Mar 30 06:53:58.841: datagramstart = 0x6001394, datagramsize = 14
*Mar 30 06:53:58.841: FR encap = 0x00010308
*Mar 30 06:53:58.841: 00 75 95 01 01 01 03 02 2C 2B
*Mar 30 06:53:58.841:
*Mar 30 06:53:58.841: Serial0/0(in): Status, myseq 44
*Mar 30 06:53:58.841: RT IE 1, length 1, type 1
*Mar 30 06:53:58.841: KA IE 3, length 2, yourseq 44, myseq 44
*Mar 30 06:54:02.229: Serial0/1(out): StEnq, myseq 188, yourseen 187, DTE up
*Mar 30 06:54:02.229: datagramstart = 0x6000AD4, datagramsize = 14
*Mar 30 06:54:02.229: FR encap = 0x00010308
*Mar 30 06:54:02.229: 00 75 95 01 01 00 03 02 BC BB
*Mar 30 06:54:02.229:
*Mar 30 06:54:02.229: Serial0/1(in): Status, myseq 188
*Mar 30 06:54:02.229: RT IE 1, length 1, type 0
*Mar 30 06:54:02.229: KA IE 3, length 2, yourseq 188, myseq 188
*Mar 30 06:54:02.229: PVC IE 0x7 , length 0x3 , dlci 211, status 0x2
*Mar 30 06:54:02.229: PVC IE 0x7 , length 0x3 , dlci 213, status 0x0
*Mar 30 06:54:02.229: PVC IE 0x7 , length 0x3 , dlci 214, status 0x2
*Mar 30 06:54:02.229: PVC IE 0x7 , length 0x3 , dlci 215, status 0x2
*Mar 30 06:54:02.229: PVC IE 0x7 , length 0x3 , dlci 216, status 0x0
R2#
R2#debug frame-relay packet
Frame Relay packet debugging is on
! Observe the "packet type" and the "packet size" as well the DCLI number to
! verify if traffic is being exchanged. You will notice that IP packets and
! CDP packets are being exchanged.

*Mar 30 06:58:57.377: Serial0/0(i): dlci 203(0x30B1), pkt type 0x800, datagramsize 72
*Mar 30 06:58:57.881: Serial0/0: broadcast search
*Mar 30 06:58:57.881: Serial0/0(o): dlci 203(0x30B1), pkt type 0x800(IP),
datagramsize 84
*Mar 30 06:58:57.949: broadcast dequeue
*Mar 30 06:58:57.949: Serial0/0(o):Pkt sent on dlci 203(0x30B1), pkt type
0x800(IP), datagramsize 84
*Mar 30 06:58:58.781: Serial0/1.2: broadcast search
*Mar 30 06:58:58.781: Serial0/1.2(o): dlci 214(0x3461), pkt type 0x800(IP),
datagramsize 84
*Mar 30 06:58:58.849: broadcast dequeue
*Mar 30 06:58:58.849: Serial0/1.2(o):Pkt sent on dlci 214(0x3461), pkt type
0x800(IP), datagramsize 84
*Mar 30 06:58:59.457: Serial0/1(i): dlci 214(0x3461), pkt type 0x800, datagramsize 72
*Mar 30 06:59:01.817: Serial0/1(i): dlci 215(0x3471), pkt type 0x800, datagramsize 72
*Mar 30 06:59:01.817: Serial0/1(i): dlci 215(0x3471), pkt type 0x800, datagramsize 72
*Mar 30 06:59:07.389: Serial0/0(i): dlci 203(0x30B1), pkt type 0x800, datagramsize 72
*Mar 30 06:59:07.881: Serial0/0: broadcast search
*Mar 30 06:59:07.881: Serial0/0(o): dlci 203(0x30B1), pkt type 0x800(IP),
datagramsize 84
*Mar 30 06:59:07.949: broadcast dequeue
```

*continues*

**Example C-1** *Some Frame Relay Troubleshooting Commands (Continued)*

```
*Mar 30 06:59:07.949: Serial0/0(o):Pkt sent on dlci 203(0x30B1), pkt type
0x800(IP), datagramsize 84
*Mar 30 06:59:08.781: Serial0/1.2: broadcast search
*Mar 30 06:59:08.781: Serial0/1.2(o): dlci 214(0x3461), pkt type 0x800(IP),
datagramsize 84
*Mar 30 06:59:08.845: Serial0/1.2: Broadcast on DLCI 214 link 65(CDP)
*Mar 30 06:59:08.845: Serial0/1.2(o): dlci 214(0x3461), pkt type 0x2000(CDP),
datagramsize 328
*Mar 30 06:59:08.849: broadcast dequeue
*Mar 30 06:59:08.849: Serial0/1.2(o):Pkt sent on dlci 214(0x3461), pkt type
0x800(IP), datagramsize 84
*Mar 30 06:59:08.849: broadcast dequeue
*Mar 30 06:59:08.849: Serial0/1.2(o):Pkt sent on dlci 214(0x3461), pkt type
0x2000(CDP), datagramsize 328
```

# 3550 Switches

Troubleshooting commands for 3550 switch configuration include the following:

- **show interfaces**
- **show interfaces trunk**
- **show vlan brief**
- **show vtp status**
- **clear interface**

Example C-2 provides commented output from these key commands.

**Example C-2** *Some Catalyst 3550 Troubleshooting Commands*

```
Sw1#
Sw1#show interfaces ?
! Here we explore the possibilities of the "show" command on the Catalyst 3550.

  Async             Async interface
  BVI               Bridge-Group Virtual Interface
  Dialer            Dialer interface
  FastEthernet      FastEthernet IEEE 802.3
  GigabitEthernet   GigabitEthernet IEEE 802.3z
  Loopback          Loopback interface
  Multilink         Multilink-group interface
  Null              Null interface
  Port-channel      Ethernet Channel of interfaces
  Tunnel            Tunnel interface
  Virtual-Template  Virtual Template interface
  Virtual-TokenRing Virtual TokenRing
  Vlan              Catalyst Vlans
  accounting        Show interface accounting
  capabilities      Show interface capabilities information
  counters          Show interface counters
```

**Example C-2**  *Some Catalyst 3550 Troubleshooting Commands (Continued)*

```
  crb              Show interface routing/bridging info
  debounce         Show interface debounce time info
  description      Show interface description
  etherchannel     Show interface etherchannel information
  fair-queue       Show interface Weighted Fair Queueing (WFQ) info
  fcpa             Fiber Channel
  flowcontrol      Show interface flowcontrol information
  irb              Show interface routing/bridging info
  mac-accounting   Show interface MAC accounting info
  media            Show interface media info
  precedence       Show interface precedence accounting info
  private-vlan     Show interface private vlan information
  pruning          Show interface trunk VTP pruning information
  random-detect    Show interface Weighted Random Early Detection (WRED) info
  rate-limit       Show interface rate-limit info
  stats            Show interface packets & octets, in & out, by switching
                   path
  status           Show interface line status
  switchport       Show interface switchport information
  trunk            Show interface trunk information
  |                Output modifiers
  <cr>
Sw1#show interfaces fastEthernet 0/15
! The "show interfaces" command has similar output as you see on the routers.
! Look for the interface status  (is it is up and connected) and if packets
! are being sent and received on the interface.

FastEthernet0/15 is up, line protocol is up (connected)
  Hardware is Fast Ethernet, address is 0009.e8ef.180f (bia 0009.e8ef.180f)
  MTU 1500 bytes, BW 100000 Kbit, DLY 100 usec,
     reliability 255/255, txload 1/255, rxload 1/255
  Encapsulation ARPA, loopback not set
  Keepalive set (10 sec)
  Full-duplex, 100Mb/s
  input flow-control is off, output flow-control is off
  ARP type: ARPA, ARP Timeout 04:00:00
  Last input 00:00:00, output 00:00:00, output hang never
  Last clearing of "show interface" counters never
  Input queue: 0/75/0/0 (size/max/drops/flushes); Total output drops: 0
  Queueing strategy: fifo
  Output queue: 0/40 (size/max)
  5 minute input rate 5000 bits/sec, 3 packets/sec
  5 minute output rate 15000 bits/sec, 4 packets/sec
     7927602 packets input, 1463727947 bytes, 0 no buffer
     Received 7673767 broadcasts (0 multicast)
     0 runts, 0 giants, 0 throttles
     0 input errors, 0 CRC, 0 frame, 0 overrun, 0 ignored
     0 watchdog, 7672375 multicast, 0 pause input
     0 input packets with dribble condition detected
     11153955 packets output, 742431432 bytes, 0 underruns
     0 output errors, 0 collisions, 1 interface resets
     0 babbles, 0 late collision, 0 deferred
```

*continues*

**Example C-2**  *Some Catalyst 3550 Troubleshooting Commands (Continued)*

```
        0 lost carrier, 0 no carrier, 0 PAUSE output
        0 output buffer failures, 0 output buffers swapped out
Sw1#
Sw1#show interfaces trunk
! Here you can verify the trunk encapsulation and if the VLANs are allowed on
! the trunk. Notice that interfaces Fa0/15 and Fa0/17 are trunk between Sw1 and
! Sw2 but not using "FastEtherChannel". Also notice that all VLANs are allowed
! to pass through the trunk.

Port          Mode          Encapsulation  Status      Native vlan
Fa0/15        on            802.1q         trunking    1
Fa0/17        on            802.1q         trunking    1
Port          Vlans allowed on trunk
Fa0/15        1-4094
Fa0/17        1-4094
Port          Vlans allowed and active in management domain
Fa0/15        1,11,22,25,33,100,200
Fa0/17        1,11,22,25,33,100,200
Port          Vlans in spanning tree forwarding state and not pruned
Fa0/15        1,11,22,25,33,100
Fa0/17        1,11,200
Sw1#
Sw1#
Sw1#show vlan brief
! Very useful command that shows us if the VLANs are created as requested
! (or how you would like to) and if the right ports or interfaces are assigned
! to the correct VLAN.

VLAN Name                             Status     Ports
---- -------------------------------- ---------  -------------------------------
1    default                          active     Fa0/7, Fa0/8, Fa0/9, Fa0/10
                                                 Fa0/11, Fa0/12, Fa0/14, Fa0/16
                                                 Fa0/18, Fa0/19, Fa0/20, Fa0/21
                                                 Fa0/22, Fa0/23, Fa0/24, Gi0/1
                                                 Gi0/2
11   VLAN_11                          active     Fa0/1
22   VLAN_22                          active     Fa0/3, Fa0/5, Fa0/6
25   VLAN_25                          active
33   VLAN_33                          active
100  VLAN_100                         active     Fa0/2, Fa0/13
200  VLAN_200                         active     Fa0/4
1002 fddi-default                     act/unsup
1003 token-ring-default               act/unsup
1004 fddinet-default                  act/unsup
1005 trnet-default                    act/unsup
Sw1#
Sw1#
Sw1#show vtp status
! The "show vtp status' command will help you to identify why for example the
! VLANs are not showing on the VLAN table. Look the VTP Mode, VTP Domain Name and
! it is important to notice VTP Domain Name is case sensitive.
```

**Example C-2**   *Some Catalyst 3550 Troubleshooting Commands (Continued)*

```
VTP Version                        : 2
Configuration Revision             : 6
Maximum VLANs supported locally : 1005
Number of existing VLANs           : 11
VTP Operating Mode                 : Server
VTP Domain Name                    : CISCO
VTP Pruning Mode                   : Disabled
VTP V2 Mode                        : Disabled
VTP Traps Generation               : Disabled
MD5 digest                         : 0xAE 0x02 0xC5 0x62 0xBA 0xC3 0xE7 0x3C
Configuration last modified by 160.10.11.10 at 3-1-93 02:47:28
Local updater ID is 160.10.11.10 on interface Vl11 (lowest numbered VLAN interface
found)
```

# ATM

Troubleshooting commands for ATM configuration include the following:

- **show interfaces**
- **show atm pvc**
- **show atm svc**
- **show atm map**
- **show atm traffic**

Example C-3 provides commented output from these key commands.

**Example C-3**   *Some ATM Troubleshooting Commands*

```
R6#
R6#show interfaces atm 3/0
! Look to see if the interface is up and line protocol is up. Verify the
! encapsulation and if the interface is sending and receiving packets.

ATM3/0 is up, line protocol is up
  Hardware is RS8234 ATMOC3
  Internet address is 170.100.10.1/24
  MTU 4470 bytes, sub MTU 4470, BW 155000 Kbit, DLY 80 usec,
     reliability 255/255, txload 1/255, rxload 1/255
  Encapsulation ATM, loopback not set
  Encapsulation(s): AAL5
  1023 maximum active VCs, 1 current VCCs
  VC idle disconnect time: 300 seconds
  Last input 00:00:42, output 00:00:42, output hang never
  Last clearing of "show interface" counters never
  Input queue: 0/75/0/0 (size/max/drops/flushes); Total output drops: 0
  Queueing strategy: Per VC Queueing
  5 minute input rate 0 bits/sec, 0 packets/sec
  5 minute output rate 0 bits/sec, 0 packets/sec
     9425 packets input, 583958 bytes, 0 no buffer
```

*continues*

**Example C-3** *Some ATM Troubleshooting Commands (Continued)*

```
        Received 0 broadcasts, 0 runts, 0 giants, 0 throttles
        0 input errors, 0 CRC, 0 frame, 0 overrun, 0 ignored, 0 abort
        8905 packets output, 556790 bytes, 0 underruns
        0 output errors, 0 collisions, 1 interface resets
        0 output buffer failures, 0 output buffers swapped out

R6#show atm pvc
! Here you can verify the PVC status and encapsulation.

             VCD /                              Peak  Avg/Min Burst
Interface    Name        VPI  VCI  Type  Encaps  SC   Kbps  Kbps   Cells  Sts
3/0          1           0    100  PVC   SNAP    UBR  155000               UP
R6#
R6#show atm map
! From this output observe the remote IP address mapping and make sure no
! mistakes were made, like typos.

Map list ATM3/0pvc1 : PERMANENT
ip 170.100.10.254 maps to VC 1, VPI 0, VCI 100, ATM3/0 , broadcast
R6#
R6#show atm traffic
! It is important to observe here if the "Input packets" and "Output packets"
! queues are increasing, so you know that traffic is being sent and received.

9431 Input packets
8911 Output packets
0 Broadcast packets
0 Packets received on non-existent VC
0 Packets attempted to send on non-existent VC
0 OAM cells received
F5 InEndloop: 0, F5 InSegloop: 0, F5 InAIS: 0, F5 InRDI: 0
F4 InEndloop: 0, F4 InSegloop: 0, F4 InAIS: 0, F4 InRDI: 0
0 OAM cells sent
F5 OutEndloop: 0, F5 OutSegloop: 0,    F5 OutRDI: 0
F4 OutEndloop: 0, F4 OutSegloop: 0,    F4 OutRDI: 0
0 OAM cell drops
R6#
```

# OSPF

Troubleshooting commands for OSPF configuration include the following:

- **show ip ospf**
- **show ip ospf interfaces**
- **show ip ospf neighbor**
- **show ip ospf database**
- **show ip ospf virtual-links**

- **debug ip ospf events**
- **debug ip ospf hello**
- **debug ip ospf packet**

Example C-4 provides commented output from these key commands.

**Example C-4**  *Some OSPF Troubleshooting Commands*

```
R2#show ip ospf
! This command shows key information that will help in troubleshooting.
! Look at the "router process" and "router ID", the OSPF areas
! (that is, Area 0, NSSA, stub, etc) and number of interfaces on each area,
! which others IGP routing protocols are being redistributed into OSPF,
! if the OSPF has authentication and area ranges (summarization) is being injected.
! It is important to notice that the OSPF area 0 may expand its interfaces
! if for example you have OSPF Virtual Link configured.

 Routing Process "ospf 1" with ID 160.10.2.2
 Supports only single TOS(TOS0) routes
 Supports opaque LSA
 Supports Link-local Signaling (LLS)
 It is an area border and autonomous system boundary router
 Redistributing External Routes from,
    eigrp 400 with metric mapped to 100, includes subnets in redistribution
 Initial SPF schedule delay 5000 msecs
 Minimum hold time between two consecutive SPFs 10000 msecs
 Maximum wait time between two consecutive SPFs 10000 msecs
 Minimum LSA interval 5 secs. Minimum LSA arrival 1 secs
 LSA group pacing timer 240 secs
 Interface flood pacing timer 33 msecs
 Retransmission pacing timer 66 msecs
 Number of external LSA 12. Checksum Sum 0x058931
 Number of opaque AS LSA 0. Checksum Sum 0x000000
 Number of DCbitless external and opaque AS LSA 0
 Number of DoNotAge external and opaque AS LSA 0
 Number of areas in this router is 2. 2 normal 0 stub 0 nssa
 External flood list length 0
    Area BACKBONE(0)
        Number of interfaces in this area is 3
        Area has no authentication
        SPF algorithm last executed 02:32:07.344 ago
        SPF algorithm executed 31 times
        Area ranges are
        Number of LSA 11. Checksum Sum 0x05BF7D
        Number of opaque link LSA 0. Checksum Sum 0x000000
        Number of DCbitless LSA 0
        Number of indication LSA 0
        Number of DoNotAge LSA 0
        Flood list length 0
    Area 1
        Number of interfaces in this area is 1
        Area has no authentication
        SPF algorithm last executed 02:31:47.344 ago
```

*continues*

**Example C-4** *Some OSPF Troubleshooting Commands (Continued)*

```
              SPF algorithm executed 17 times
              Area ranges are
              Number of LSA 15. Checksum Sum 0x08A42F
              Number of opaque link LSA 0. Checksum Sum 0x000000
              Number of DCbitless LSA 0
              Number of indication LSA 0
              Number of DoNotAge LSA 0
              Flood list length 0
R2#
R2#show ip ospf interface
! Important to observe here is if the interface is configured into the right area.
! Look the process ID and router id. The "network type" is crucial that it
! "matches" to the peer or remote side. Otherwise it won't work. Timers and
! adjacencies are import to verify in case of troubleshooting an OSPF problem.

Serial0/1.2 is up, line protocol is up
  Internet Address 160.10.38.2/24, Area 0
  Process ID 1, Router ID 160.10.2.2, Network Type POINT_TO_POINT, Cost: 64
  Transmit Delay is 1 sec, State POINT_TO_POINT,
  Timer intervals configured, Hello 10, Dead 40, Wait 40, Retransmit 5
    oob-resync timeout 40
    Hello due in 00:00:08
  Index 3/4, flood queue length 0
  Next 0x0(0)/0x0(0)
  Last flood scan length is 2, maximum is 10
  Last flood scan time is 0 msec, maximum is 4 msec
  Neighbor Count is 1, Adjacent neighbor count is 1
    Adjacent with neighbor 160.10.4.4
  Suppress hello for 0 neighbor(s)
Serial0/1.1 is up, line protocol is up
  Internet Address 160.10.37.2/24, Area 0
  Process ID 1, Router ID 160.10.2.2, Network Type POINT_TO_MULTIPOINT, Cost: 64
  Transmit Delay is 1 sec, State POINT_TO_MULTIPOINT,
  Timer intervals configured, Hello 30, Dead 120, Wait 120, Retransmit 5
    oob-resync timeout 120
    Hello due in 00:00:13
  Index 2/3, flood queue length 0
  Next 0x0(0)/0x0(0)
  Last flood scan length is 1, maximum is 8
  Last flood scan time is 0 msec, maximum is 4 msec
  Neighbor Count is 2, Adjacent neighbor count is 2
    Adjacent with neighbor 160.10.5.5
    Adjacent with neighbor 160.10.1.1
  Suppress hello for 0 neighbor(s)
Loopback0 is up, line protocol is up
  Internet Address 160.10.2.2/24, Area 0
  Process ID 1, Router ID 160.10.2.2, Network Type POINT_TO_POINT, Cost: 1
  Transmit Delay is 1 sec, State POINT_TO_POINT,
  Timer intervals configured, Hello 10, Dead 40, Wait 40, Retransmit 5
    oob-resync timeout 40
  Index 1/1, flood queue length 0
  Next 0x0(0)/0x0(0)
```

**Example C-4**  *Some OSPF Troubleshooting Commands (Continued)*

```
        Last flood scan length is 0, maximum is 0
        Last flood scan time is 0 msec, maximum is 0 msec
        Neighbor Count is 0, Adjacent neighbor count is 0
        Suppress hello for 0 neighbor(s)
Serial0/0 is up, line protocol is up
   Internet Address 160.10.32.2/30, Area 1
   Process ID 1, Router ID 160.10.2.2, Network Type POINT_TO_POINT, Cost: 64
   Transmit Delay is 1 sec, State POINT_TO_POINT,
   Timer intervals configured, Hello 10, Dead 40, Wait 40, Retransmit 5
      oob-resync timeout 40
      Hello due in 00:00:03
   Index 1/2, flood queue length 0
   Next 0x0(0)/0x0(0)
   Last flood scan length is 1, maximum is 17
   Last flood scan time is 0 msec, maximum is 4 msec
   Neighbor Count is 1, Adjacent neighbor count is 1
      Adjacent with neighbor 160.10.3.3
   Suppress hello for 0 neighbor(s)
R2#
R2#show ip ospf neighbor
! Look for the neighbors and verify their state and addresses. This information
! will indicate if the adjacencies are made or not. The state "FULL" indicates
! routers a fully adjacent with each other.
Neighbor ID     Pri   State         Dead Time   Address         Interface
160.10.4.4        0   FULL/  -      00:00:35    160.10.38.4     Serial0/1.2
160.10.5.5        0   FULL/  -      00:01:58    160.10.37.5     Serial0/1.1
160.10.1.1        0   FULL/  -      00:01:50    160.10.37.1     Serial0/1.1
160.10.3.3        0   FULL/  -      00:00:34    160.10.32.1     Serial0/0
R2#
R2#show ip ospf database
! Observe the router ID and process ID. The OSPF areas into R2 process and
! the LSA packets types that indicates what kind of advertisement is being sent.
! OSPF has 7 types of LSA and the type depends on your topology and we can
! have different topologies per OSPF area. (look the last block of the
! output below).


            OSPF Router with ID (160.10.2.2) (Process ID 1)
               Router Link States (Area 0)
Link ID         ADV Router      Age      Seq#       Checksum Link count
160.10.1.1      160.10.1.1      914      0x800004F7 0x00A4DD 3
160.10.2.2      160.10.2.2      675      0x80000509 0x001D82 6
160.10.4.4      160.10.4.4      403      0x800004F9 0x005ECD 3
160.10.5.5      160.10.5.5      1440     0x800004D5 0x007B0B 3
               Summary Net Link States (Area 0)
Link ID         ADV Router      Age      Seq#       Checksum
160.10.3.0      160.10.2.2      675      0x80000006 0x003A60
160.10.7.0      160.10.1.1      914      0x800004EB 0x0025BF
160.10.11.0     160.10.1.1      914      0x800004F1 0x00E2F8
160.10.25.0     160.10.1.1      914      0x800004F7 0x00A01D
160.10.25.0     160.10.5.5      1440     0x800004F6 0x00AF1A
160.10.32.0     160.10.2.2      675      0x800004F2 0x00F798
               Summary ASB Link States (Area 0)
```

*continues*

**Example C-4** *Some OSPF Troubleshooting Commands (Continued)*

```
Link ID         ADV Router      Age       Seq#       Checksum
160.10.5.5      160.10.1.1      914       0x800004D4 0x00836B
                Router Link States (Area 1)
Link ID         ADV Router      Age       Seq#       Checksum Link count
160.10.2.2      160.10.2.2      677       0x800004F8 0x008C76 2
160.10.3.3      160.10.3.3      741       0x800004DA 0x005212 3
                Summary Net Link States (Area 1)
Link ID         ADV Router      Age       Seq#       Checksum
160.10.1.0      160.10.2.2      677       0x800004DA 0x009A29
160.10.2.0      160.10.2.2      677       0x800004F1 0x00DE0D
160.10.4.0      160.10.2.2      677       0x800004DB 0x007748
160.10.5.0      160.10.2.2      677       0x800004D6 0x00764D
160.10.7.0      160.10.2.2      677       0x800004DA 0x00BCF6
160.10.11.0     160.10.2.2      677       0x800004DA 0x00862A
160.10.25.0     160.10.2.2      677       0x800004DA 0x00911A
160.10.37.1     160.10.2.2      677       0x800004DA 0x00F8A6
160.10.37.2     160.10.2.2      678       0x800004E5 0x00567D
160.10.37.5     160.10.2.2      678       0x800004D6 0x00D8C6
160.10.38.0     160.10.2.2      678       0x800004E5 0x00E1B2

                Summary ASB Link States (Area 1)
Link ID         ADV Router      Age       Seq#       Checksum
160.10.4.4      160.10.2.2      678       0x800004DB 0x003784
160.10.5.5      160.10.2.2      679       0x800004D6 0x002C92
                Type-5 AS External Link States
! This indicates LSA type 5 that is "Autonomous System (AS)
! External Link Advertisements.
Link ID         ADV Router      Age       Seq#       Checksum Tag
130.200.10.0    160.10.2.2      1937      0x800004F0 0x0096C1 0
140.200.10.0    160.10.4.4      407       0x800004F0 0x001895 0
160.10.6.0      160.10.5.5      1192      0x80000094 0x00C98D 0
160.10.15.0     160.10.5.5      1444      0x800004D4 0x00D930 0
160.10.22.0     160.10.5.5      1444      0x800004D6 0x008878 0
160.10.33.0     160.10.5.5      1444      0x800004D8 0x000BE8 0
193.118.1.0     160.10.2.2      177       0x80000095 0x006271 0
193.118.2.0     160.10.2.2      177       0x80000095 0x00577B 0
193.118.3.0     160.10.2.2      177       0x80000095 0x004C85 0
196.1.2.0       160.10.4.4      148       0x80000095 0x00B5EE 0
196.1.8.0       160.10.4.4      149       0x80000095 0x00732B 0
196.1.10.0      160.10.4.4      149       0x80000095 0x005D3F 0
R2#
R2#debug ip ospf events
! Here you can see hello packets being received and sent on a specific
! interfaces, that means the OSPF is active on this link.

OSPF events debugging is on
*Mar 30 10:01:27.136: OSPF: Rcv hello from 160.10.3.3 area 1 from Serial0/0
160.10.32.1
*Mar 30 10:01:27.136: OSPF: End of hello processing
*Mar 30 10:01:27.880: OSPF: Send hello to 224.0.0.5 area 1 on Serial0/0 from
160.10.32.2
```

**Example C-4**    *Some OSPF Troubleshooting Commands (Continued)*

```
*Mar 30 10:01:37.176: OSPF: Rcv hello from 160.10.3.3 area 1 from Serial0/0
160.10.32.1
*Mar 30 10:01:37.176: OSPF: End of hello processing
*Mar 30 10:01:37.880: OSPF: Send hello to 224.0.0.5 area 1 on Serial0/0 from
160.10.32.2
*Mar 30 10:01:47.176: OSPF: Rcv hello from 160.10.3.3 area 1 from Serial0/0
160.10.32.1
*Mar 30 10:01:47.176: OSPF: End of hello processing
R2#debug ip ospf hello
! Here you have a similar information as the previous output
! where you see the hello packets being exchanged.

OSPF hello events debugging is on
R2#
*Mar 30 10:03:17.116: OSPF: Rcv hello from 160.10.3.3 area 1 from Serial0/0
160.10.32.1
*Mar 30 10:03:17.116: OSPF: End of hello processing
*Mar 30 10:03:17.880: OSPF: Send hello to 224.0.0.5 area 1 on Serial0/0 from
160.10.32.2
*Mar 30 10:03:27.116: OSPF: Rcv hello from 160.10.3.3 area 1 from Serial0/0
160.10.32.1
*Mar 30 10:03:27.116: OSPF: End of hello processing
*Mar 30 10:03:27.880: OSPF: Send hello to 224.0.0.5 area 1 on Serial0/0 from
160.10.32.2
*Mar 30 10:03:37.116: OSPF: Rcv hello from 160.10.3.3 area 1 from Serial0/0
160.10.32.1
*Mar 30 10:03:37.116: OSPF: End of hello processing
R2#debug ip ospf packet
! The command shows that packtes are being exchanged through the interface.
! Important to look at is: "rid" that is the router ID, "aid" is the
! area number and "aut" is the authentication method if there is any.

OSPF packet debugging is on
R2#
*Mar 30 10:04:58.884: OSPF: rcv. v:2 t:1 l:48 rid:160.10.4.4
      aid:0.0.0.0 chk:B67F aut:0 auk: from Serial0/1.2
*Mar 30 10:05:01.624: OSPF: rcv. v:2 t:1 l:48 rid:160.10.5.5
      aid:0.0.0.0 chk:B51A aut:0 auk: from Serial0/1.1
*Mar 30 10:05:01.624: OSPF: rcv. v:2 t:1 l:48 rid:160.10.5.5
      aid:0.0.0.0 chk:B51A aut:0 auk: from Serial0/1.1
*Mar 30 10:05:07.156: OSPF: rcv. v:2 t:1 l:48 rid:160.10.3.3
      aid:0.0.0.1 chk:B683 aut:0 auk: from Serial0/0
*Mar 30 10:05:08.880: OSPF: rcv. v:2 t:1 l:48 rid:160.10.4.4
      aid:0.0.0.0 chk:B67F aut:0 auk: from Serial0/1.2
```

# EIGRP

Troubleshooting commands for EIGRP configuration include the following:

- **show ip eigrp interfaces**
- **show ip eigrp neighbors**

- **show ip eigrp topology**
- **show ip eigrp traffic**
- **debug ip eigrp**

Example C-5 provides commented output from these key commands.

**Example C-5** *Some EIGRP Troubleshooting Commands*

```
R2#show ip eigrp interfaces
! The command shows the interfaces that are participating within
! EIGRP routing process.

IP-EIGRP interfaces for process 400
                      Xmit Queue   Mean   Pacing Time   Multicast    Pending
Interface      Peers  Un/Reliable  SRTT   Un/Reliable   Flow Timer   Routes
Fa0/0            1       0/0         1        0/10          50          0
R2#
R2#show ip eigrp neighbors
! This command revels the EIGRP neighbors. If no output is shown means
! some problem is happening, then you should double check your configuration
! or verify if the interface is up.

IP-EIGRP neighbors for process 400
H    Address             Interface     Hold Uptime   SRTT   RTO  Q  Seq Type
                                       (sec)         (ms)        Cnt Num
0    130.200.10.200      Fa0/0         14 3d10h       1    200  0  10
R2#
R2#show ip eigrp topology
! It shows the EIGRP AS number and I, who is the successor candidates
! and the interfaces participating on the routing process and if
! the interface is directed connected, if it was learned frm a neighbor or
! if it was learned via redistribution.

IP-EIGRP Topology Table for AS(400)/ID(160.10.2.2)
Codes: P - Passive, A - Active, U - Update, Q - Query, R - Reply,
       r - reply Status, s - sia Status
P 130.200.10.0/24, 1 successors, FD is 28160
        via Connected, FastEthernet0/0
P 140.200.10.0/24, 1 successors, FD is 25602560
        via Redistributed (25602560/0)
P 160.10.32.0/30, 1 successors, FD is 2169856
        via Connected, Serial0/0
Codes: P - Passive, A - Active, U - Update, Q - Query, R - Reply,
       r - reply Status, s - sia Status
P 160.10.15.0/24, 1 successors, FD is 25602560
        via Redistributed (25602560/0)
P 193.118.2.0/24, 1 successors, FD is 156160
        via 130.200.10.200 (156160/128256), FastEthernet0/0
R2#
R2#show ip eigrp traffic
! The output shows the traffic that was sent and received on the interface
! as well the EIGRP AS number.
```

**Example C-5**    *Some EIGRP Troubleshooting Commands (Continued)*

```
IP-EIGRP Traffic Statistics for AS 400
  Hellos sent/received: 549415/549363
  Updates sent/received: 52/46
  Queries sent/received: 31/1
  Replies sent/received: 1/31
  Acks sent/received: 74/76
  Input queue high water mark 1, 0 drops
  SIA-Queries sent/received: 0/0
  SIA-Replies sent/received: 0/0
  Hello Process ID: 108
  PDM Process ID: 145


R2#debug ip eigrp
! Notice the advertisements are sent out and received. Observe the
! IP address and interfaces as well the metric of sent and received routes.

IP-EIGRP Route Events debugging is on
R2#
*Mar 30 10:25:54.052: IP-EIGRP(Default-IP-Routing-Table:400): 140.200.10.0/24 - do
advertise out FastEthernet0/0
*Mar 30 10:25:54.052: IP-EIGRP(Default-IP-Routing-Table:400): Ext 140.200.10.0/24
metric 4294967295 - 25600000 4294967295
*Mar 30 10:25:54.052: IP-EIGRP(Default-IP-Routing-Table:400): 160.10.37.5/32 - do
advertise out FastEthernet0/0
* Mar 30 10:25:54.052: IP-EIGRP(Default-IP-Routing-Table:400): Processing incoming
REPLY packet

* Mar 30 10:25:54.052: IP-EIGRP(Default-IP-Routing-Table:400): ExtS 140.200.10.0/24
M 4294967295 - 0 4294967295 SM 4294967295 - 0 4294967295
```

# RIP

Troubleshooting commands for RIP configuration include the following:

- **show ip rip database**
- **debug ip rip**
- **debug ip rip database**
- **debug ip rip events**

Example C-6 provides commented output from these key commands.

**Example C-6**    *Some RIP Troubleshooting Commands*

```
R4#show ip rip database
! Here you can see the networks participating within RIP routing process
! and the interfaces participating.

140.200.0.0/16     auto-summary
140.200.10.0/24     directly connected, Ethernet0/0
196.1.2.0/24     auto-summary
```

*continues*

**Example C-6** *Some RIP Troubleshooting Commands (Continued)*

```
196.1.2.0/24
    [1] via 140.200.10.200, 00:00:26, Ethernet0/0
196.1.8.0/24    auto-summary
196.1.8.0/24
    [1] via 140.200.10.200, 00:00:26, Ethernet0/0
196.1.10.0/24    auto-summary
196.1.10.0/24
    [1] via 140.200.10.200, 00:00:26, Ethernet0/0
R4#
R4#debug ip rip
RIP protocol debugging is on
! The output from this command shows the RIP routes being exchanged.
! Observe the interfaces, routes and RIP version.

3d08h: RIP: sending request on Ethernet0/0 to 224.0.0.9
3d08h: RIP: sending request on Ethernet0/0 to 224.0.0.9
3d08h: RIP: received v2 update from 140.200.10.200 on Ethernet0/0
3d08h:     20.0.0.0/8 via 0.0.0.0 in 1 hops
3d08h:     30.0.0.0/8 via 0.0.0.0 in 1 hops
3d08h:     196.1.1.0/24 via 0.0.0.0 in 1 hops
3d08h:     196.1.2.0/24 via 0.0.0.0 in 1 hops
3d08h:     196.1.3.0/24 via 0.0.0.0 in 1 hops
3d08h:     196.1.4.0/24 via 0.0.0.0 in 1 hops
3d08h:     196.1.5.0/24 via 0.0.0.0 in 1 hops
3d08h:     196.1.6.0/24 via 0.0.0.0 in 1 hops
3d08h:     196.1.7.0/24 via 0.0.0.0 in 1 hops
3d08h:     196.1.8.0/24 via 0.0.0.0 in 1 hops
3d08h:     196.1.9.0/24 via 0.0.0.0 in 1 hops
3d08h:     196.1.10.0/24 via 0.0.0.0 in 1 hops
3d08h: RIP: sending v2 flash update to 224.0.0.9 via Ethernet0/0 (140.200.10.4)
3d08h: RIP: build flash update entries - suppressing null update
3d08h: RIP: received v2 update from 140.200.10.200 on Ethernet0/0

R4#debug ip rip database
RIP database events debugging is on
! You can see below the RIP routes being updated and installed into the
! routing table.

R4#
4w1d: RIP-DB: network_update with 196.1.2.0/24 succeeds
4w1d: RIP-DB: adding 196.1.2.0/24 (metric 1) via 140.200.10.200 on Ethernet0/0 to
RIP database
4w1d: RIP-DB: network_update with 196.1.8.0/24 succeeds
4w1d: RIP-DB: adding 196.1.8.0/24 (metric 1) via 140.200.10.200 on Ethernet0/0 to
RIP database
4w1d: RIP-DB: network_update with 196.1.10.0/24 succeeds
4w1d: RIP-DB: adding 196.1.10.0/24 (metric 1) via 140.200.10.200 on Ethernet0/0 to
RIP database
R4#debug ip rip events
RIP event debugging is on
! This output has some similarities with the output above. You can notice
! what is being sent and received through interface Etherneth0/0.
```

**Example C-6**  *Some RIP Troubleshooting Commands (Continued)*

```
! Also notice the updates are sent via the well-know Multicast Group
! address "224.0.0.9". The "suppressing null update means that 'no routes
! are being advertised.

R4#
4w1d: RIP: sending v2 update to 224.0.0.9 via Ethernet0/0 (140.200.10.4) -
suppressing null update
4w1d: RIP: received v2 update from 140.200.10.200 on Ethernet0/0
4w1d: RIP: Update contains 12 routes
4w1d: RIP: sending v2 update to 224.0.0.9 via Ethernet0/0 (140.200.10.4) -
suppressing null update
4w1d: RIP: received v2 update from 140.200.10.200 on Ethernet0/0
4w1d: RIP: Update contains 12 routes
4w1d: RIP: sending v2 update to 224.0.0.9 via Ethernet0/0 (140.200.10.4) -
suppressing null update
4w1d: RIP: received v2 update from 140.200.10.200 on Ethernet0/0
4w1d: RIP: Update contains 12 routes
4w1d: RIP: sending v2 update to 224.0.0.9 via Ethernet0/0 (140.200.10.4) -
suppressing null update
4w1d: RIP: received v2 update from 140.200.10.200 on Ethernet0/0
4w1d: RIP: Update contains 12 routes
4w1d: RIP: sending v2 update to 224.0.0.9 via Ethernet0/0 (140.200.10.4) -
suppressing null update
4w1d: RIP: received v2 update from 140.200.10.200 on Ethernet0/0
4w1d: RIP: Update contains 12 routes
4w1d: RIP: sending v2 update to 224.0.0.9 via Ethernet0/0 (140.200.10.4) -
suppressing null update
4w1d: RIP: received v2 update from 140.200.10.200 on Ethernet0/0
4w1d: RIP: Update contains 12 routes
4w1d: RIP: sending v2 update to 224.0.0.9 via Ethernet0/0 (140.200.10.4) -
suppressing null update
R4#
```

# IS-IS

Troubleshooting commands for IS-IS configuration include the following:

- **show isis database**
- **show isis topology**
- **show clns protocol**
- **show clns interface**
- **show clns neighbors**

Example C-7 provides commented output from these key commands.

**Example C-7**  *Some IS-IS Troubleshooting Commands*

```
R6#show isis database
! Here we have the IS-IS database that shows R6 having Level-1 and Level-2
! Circuit types. Important to notice are the LSPID
```

*continues*

**Example C-7** *Some IS-IS Troubleshooting Commands (Continued)*

```
! (The Link State Packet identifier). The first six octets form the
! system ID of the router that originated the LSP), and the fields ATT/P/OL,
! where ATT is the Attached bit that indicates that the router is a
! Level-2 router and can reach others areas. The P bit is the IS is
! area repair capable. Cisco routers do not support area repair capable.
! The OL bit indicates if IS is congested.

IS-IS Level-1 Link State Database:
LSPID                 LSP Seq Num  LSP Checksum  LSP Holdtime      ATT/P/OL
R3.00-00              0x00000CB1   0x51AE        889               0/0/0
R5.00-00              0x00000CCB   0xAE51        940               0/0/0
R6.00-00            * 0x0000070D   0x5EC9        748               0/0/0
R6.02-00            * 0x00000706   0x02A6        543               0/0/0
IS-IS Level-2 Link State Database:
LSPID                 LSP Seq Num  LSP Checksum  LSP Holdtime      ATT/P/OL
R3.00-00              0x00000CCB   0xBE67        758               0/0/0
R5.00-00              0x00000CDA   0x8223        911               0/0/0
R6.00-00            * 0x00000712   0x44EF        845               0/0/0
R6.02-00            * 0x00000708   0xAF7F        1167              0/0/0
R6#
R6#show isis topology
! This command shows a list of all routers in all areas. You can see the
! paths to Level-1 and to Level-2 routers. Also notice the Metric as
! "10" that is the default.


IS-IS paths to level-1 routers
System Id           Metric  Next-Hop            Interface   SNPA
R3                  10      R3                  Et0/0       0009.43a7.2c60
R5                  10      R5                  Et0/0       0009.43a7.2f60
R6                  --
IS-IS paths to level-2 routers
System Id           Metric  Next-Hop            Interface   SNPA
R3                  10      R3                  Et0/0       0009.43a7.2c60
R5                  10      R5                  Et0/0       0009.43a7.2f60
R6                  --
R6#
R6#show clns protocol
! This command shows you some specific information regarding the CLNS Protocol.
! Look at the System ID, IS-Type, Manual areas address and the interfaces
! supported by IS-IS.


IS-IS Router: <Null Tag>
  System Id: 0000.0000.0006.00  IS-Type: level-1-2
  Manual area address(es):
      49.0004
  Routing for area address(es):
      49.0004
  Interfaces supported by IS-IS:
      Ethernet0/0 - IP
      Loopback0 - IP
  Redistribute:
    static (on by default)
```

**Example C-7**   *Some IS-IS Troubleshooting Commands (Continued)*

```
    Distance for L2 CLNS routes: 110
    RRR level: none
    Generate narrow metrics: level-1-2
    Accept narrow metrics:   level-1-2
    Generate wide metrics:   none
    Accept wide metrics:     none
R6#
R6#show clns interface
! This command lists specific information about the CLNS interfaces.
! Observe the interface status, the IS-IS as the routing protocol running
! and the Circuit Type.

Ethernet0/0 is up, line protocol is up
  Checksums enabled, MTU 1497, Encapsulation SAP
  ERPDUs enabled, min. interval 10 msec.
  RDPDUs enabled, min. interval 100 msec., Addr Mask enabled
  Congestion Experienced bit set at 4 packets
  CLNS fast switching enabled
  CLNS SSE switching disabled
  DEC compatibility mode OFF for this interface
  Next ESH/ISH in 26 seconds
  Routing Protocol: IS-IS
    Circuit Type: level-1-2
    Interface number 0x1, local circuit ID 0x2
    Level-1 Metric: 10, Priority: 64, Circuit ID: R6.02
    Number of active level-1 adjacencies: 2
    Level-2 Metric: 10, Priority: 64, Circuit ID: R6.02
    Number of active level-2 adjacencies: 2
    Next IS-IS LAN Level-1 Hello in 2 seconds
    Next IS-IS LAN Level-2 Hello in 924 milliseconds
Serial0/0 is administratively down, line protocol is down
  CLNS protocol processing disabled
TokenRing0/0 is administratively down, line protocol is down
  CLNS protocol processing disabled
Serial0/1 is administratively down, line protocol is down
  CLNS protocol processing disabled
FastEthernet1/0 is administratively down, line protocol is down
  CLNS protocol processing disabled
ATM3/0 is up, line protocol is up
  CLNS protocol processing disabled
Loopback0 is up, line protocol is up
  Checksums enabled, MTU 1514, Encapsulation LOOPBACK
  ERPDUs enabled, min. interval 10 msec.
  RDPDUs enabled, min. interval 100 msec., Addr Mask enabled
  Congestion Experienced bit set at 4 packets
  CLNS fast switching disabled
  CLNS SSE switching disabled
  DEC compatibility mode OFF for this interface
  Next ESH/ISH in 32 seconds
  Routing Protocol: IS-IS
    Circuit Type: level-1-2
    Interface number 0x0, local circuit ID 0x1
```

*continues*

**Example C-7**   *Some IS-IS Troubleshooting Commands (Continued)*

```
      Level-1 Metric: 10, Priority: 64, Circuit ID: R6.01
      Number of active level-1 adjacencies: 0
      Level-2 Metric: 10, Priority: 64, Circuit ID: R6.01
      Number of active level-2 adjacencies: 0
      Next IS-IS LAN Level-1 Hello in 2 seconds
      Next IS-IS LAN Level-2 Hello in 6 seconds
R6#
R6#show clns neighbors
! This command shows you R6 neighbors establishments and the Type
! protocol or Circuit Type for each neighbor.

System Id      Interface   SNPA             State  Holdtime  Type Protocol
R3             Et0/0       0009.43a7.2c60   Up     25        L1L2 IS-IS
R5             Et0/0       0009.43a7.2f60   Up     27        L1L2 IS-IS
R6#
```

# BGP

Troubleshooting commands for BGP configuration include the following:

- **show ip bgp**
- **show ip bgp summary**
- **show ip route bgp**
- **show ip bgp neighbors**
- **show ip bgp neighbors** *neighbor-ip-address*
- **debug ip bgp**

Example C-8 provides commented output from these key commands.

**Example C-8**   *Some BGP Troubleshooting Commands*

```
R6#show ip bgp
! This command displays the entries in the BGP routing table.
! It is important to observe the BGP table version, that is incremented
! whenever the table changes and the router ID. The status code is important
! also because identify how the route will be treated. For example the "*"
! indicates a valid path and ">" indicates that the entry is the best entry to
! use for that network and indicates that the network will be installed on the
! IP table. The "Next Hop" is the next system used when forwarding a packet
! to the destination network. The "Path" is the Autonomous system paths
! to the destination network.

BGP table version is 21, local router ID is 160.10.6.6
Status codes: s suppressed, d damped, h history, * valid, > best, i - internal
Origin codes: i - IGP, e - EGP, ? - incomplete
   Network          Next Hop            Metric LocPrf Weight Path
*> 198.18.1.0       170.100.10.254           0           0 300 i
*> 198.18.2.0       170.100.10.254           0           0 300 i
*> 198.18.3.0       170.100.10.254           0           0 300 i
```

**Example C-8**  *Some BGP Troubleshooting Commands (Continued)*

```
    *> 198.18.4.0      170.100.10.254            0            0 300 i
    *> 198.18.5.0      170.100.10.254            0            0 300 i
    *> 198.18.6.0      170.100.10.254            0            0 300 i
    *> 198.18.7.0      170.100.10.254            0            0 300 i
    *> 198.18.8.0      170.100.10.254            0            0 300 i
    *> 198.18.9.0      170.100.10.254            0            0 300 i
    *> 198.18.10.0     170.100.10.254            0            0 300 i
    *> 200.20.1.0      170.100.10.254            0            0 300 i
    *> 200.20.2.0      170.100.10.254            0            0 300 i
    *> 200.20.3.0      170.100.10.254            0            0 300 i
    *> 200.20.4.0      170.100.10.254            0            0 300 i
    *> 200.20.5.0      170.100.10.254            0            0 300 i
    *> 200.20.6.0      170.100.10.254            0            0 300 i
    *> 200.20.7.0      170.100.10.254            0            0 300 i
    *> 200.20.8.0      170.100.10.254            0            0 300 i
       Network         Next Hop          Metric LocPrf Weight Path
    *> 200.20.9.0      170.100.10.254            0            0 300 i
    *> 200.20.10.0     170.100.10.254            0            0 300 i
    R6#
    R6#show ip bgp summary
    ! The output displays the Local AS number, the neighbors AS, how long the
    ! neighbors is up (UP/DOWN) and how many prefixes are being received
    ! form a specific neighbor.

    BGP router identifier 160.10.6.6, local AS number 100
    BGP table version is 21, main routing table version 21
    20 network entries using 1940 bytes of memory
    20 path entries using 720 bytes of memory
    1 BGP path attribute entries using 60 bytes of memory
    1 BGP AS-PATH entries using 24 bytes of memory
    0 BGP route-map cache entries using 0 bytes of memory
    0 BGP filter-list cache entries using 0 bytes of memory
    BGP using 2744 total bytes of memory
    BGP activity 20/0 prefixes, 20/0 paths, scan interval 60 secs
    Neighbor        V    AS MsgRcvd MsgSent    TblVer  InQ OutQ Up/Down  State/PfxRcd
    160.10.3.3      4   100    5039    5040        21    0    0 3d11h            0
    170.100.10.254  4   300    5041    5039        21    0    0 3d11h           20
    R6#
    R6#show ip route bgp
    ! The output below shows the best BGP routes the fed the IP routing table.

    B    198.18.10.0/24 [20/0] via 170.100.10.254, 3d11h
    B    200.20.4.0/24 [20/0] via 170.100.10.254, 3d11h
    B    200.20.5.0/24 [20/0] via 170.100.10.254, 3d11h
    B    198.18.8.0/24 [20/0] via 170.100.10.254, 3d11h
    B    200.20.6.0/24 [20/0] via 170.100.10.254, 3d11h
    B    198.18.9.0/24 [20/0] via 170.100.10.254, 3d11h
    B    200.20.7.0/24 [20/0] via 170.100.10.254, 3d11h
    B    200.20.1.0/24 [20/0] via 170.100.10.254, 3d11h
    B    200.20.2.0/24 [20/0] via 170.100.10.254, 3d11h
    B    200.20.3.0/24 [20/0] via 170.100.10.254, 3d11h
    B    198.18.2.0/24 [20/0] via 170.100.10.254, 3d11h
```

*continues*

**Example C-8** *Some BGP Troubleshooting Commands (Continued)*

```
B    198.18.3.0/24 [20/0] via 170.100.10.254, 3d11h
B    198.18.1.0/24 [20/0] via 170.100.10.254, 3d11h
B    198.18.6.0/24 [20/0] via 170.100.10.254, 3d11h
B    200.20.8.0/24 [20/0] via 170.100.10.254, 3d11h
B    198.18.7.0/24 [20/0] via 170.100.10.254, 3d11h
B    200.20.9.0/24 [20/0] via 170.100.10.254, 3d11h
B    198.18.4.0/24 [20/0] via 170.100.10.254, 3d11h
B    200.20.10.0/24 [20/0] via 170.100.10.254, 3d11h
B    198.18.5.0/24 [20/0] via 170.100.10.254, 3d11h
R6

R6#show ip bgp neighbors
! The output shows the TCP and BGP connections to neighbors.
! Notice the BGP neighbor IP address, the neighbor or remote AS and router ID.
! Also the "internal" link means iBGP and "external" link means EBGP
! (look below the output for neighbor 170.100.10.254).

BGP neighbor is 160.10.3.3,  remote AS 100, internal link
  BGP version 4, remote router ID 160.10.3.3
  BGP state = Established, up for 3d12h
  Last read 00:00:53, hold time is 180, keepalive interval is 60 seconds
  Neighbor capabilities:
    Route refresh: advertised and received(old & new)
    Address family IPv4 Unicast: advertised and received
  Message statistics:
    InQ depth is 0
    OutQ depth is 0
                         Sent       Rcvd
    Opens:                  1          1
    Notifications:          0          0
    Updates:                1          0
    Keepalives:          5047       5046
    Route Refresh:          0          0
    Total:               5049       5047
  Default minimum time between advertisement runs is 5 seconds
 For address family: IPv4 Unicast
  BGP table version 21, neighbor version 21
  Index 1, Offset 0, Mask 0x2
  Route-Reflector Client
  NEXT_HOP is always this router
                         Sent       Rcvd
  Prefix activity:       ----       ----
    Prefixes Current:      20          0
    Prefixes Total:        20          0
    Implicit Withdraw:      0          0
    Explicit Withdraw:      0          0
    Used as bestpath:     n/a          0
    Used as multipath:    n/a          0
                       Outbound    Inbound
  Local Policy Denied Prefixes:  --------   -------
    Total:                  0          0
  Number of NLRIs in the update sent: max 20, min 0
```

**Example C-8**   *Some BGP Troubleshooting Commands (Continued)*

```
   Connections established 1; dropped 0
   Last reset never
 ! Observe below the Connection State as "STABilished", the local host or
 ! source IP address and TCP Port = 1103 and the Foreign host or
 ! remote/destination TCP port = 179.

 Connection state is ESTAB, I/O status: 1, unread input bytes: 0
 Local host: 160.10.6.6, Local port: 179
 Foreign host: 160.10.3.3, Foreign port: 11003
 Enqueued packets for retransmit: 0, input: 0  mis-ordered: 0 (0 bytes)
 Event Timers (current time is 0x120AE458):
 Timer          Starts      Wakeups            Next
 Retrans         5050            0             0x0
 TimeWait           0            0             0x0
 AckHold         5047         4754             0x0
 SendWnd            0            0             0x0
 KeepAlive          0            0             0x0
 GiveUp             0            0             0x0
 PmtuAger           0            0             0x0
 DeadWait           0            0             0x0
 iss: 2690266982  snduna: 2690363056  sndnxt: 2690363056    sndwnd:  16175
 irs: 4088662438  rcvnxt: 4088758358  rcvwnd:      16327 delrcvwnd:     57
 SRTT: 300 ms, RTTO: 303 ms, RTV: 3 ms, KRTT: 0 ms
 minRTT: 4 ms, maxRTT: 300 ms, ACK hold: 200 ms
 Flags: passive open, nagle, gen tcbs

 Datagrams (max data segment is 536 bytes):
 Rcvd: 9883 (out of order: 0), with data: 5048, total data bytes: 95938
 Sent: 9979 (retransmit: 0, fastretransmit: 0), with data: 5049, total data bytes:
 96073

BGP neighbor is 170.100.10.254,  remote AS 300, external link
  BGP version 4, remote router ID 200.20.1.254
  BGP state = Established, up for 3d12h
  Last read 00:00:38, hold time is 180, keepalive interval is 60 seconds
  Neighbor capabilities:
    Route refresh: advertised and received(old & new)
    Address family IPv4 Unicast: advertised and received
  Message statistics:
    InQ depth is 0
    OutQ depth is 0
                        Sent       Rcvd
    Opens:                 1          1
    Notifications:         0          0
    Updates:               0          1
    Keepalives:         5047       5047
    Route Refresh:         0          0
    Total:              5048       5049
  Default minimum time between advertisement runs is 30 seconds
 For address family: IPv4 Unicast
  BGP table version 21, neighbor version 21
  Index 2, Offset 0, Mask 0x4
```

*continues*

**Example C-8** *Some BGP Troubleshooting Commands (Continued)*

```
                                    Sent        Rcvd
  Prefix activity:                  ----        ----
    Prefixes Current:               0           20 (Consumes 720 bytes)
    Prefixes Total:                 0           20
    Implicit Withdraw:              0           0
    Explicit Withdraw:              0           0
    Used as bestpath:               n/a         20
    Used as multipath:              n/a         0
                                    Outbound    Inbound
  Local Policy Denied Prefixes:     --------    -------
    Bestpath from this peer:        20          n/a
    Total:                          20          0
  Number of NLRIs in the update sent: max 0, min 0
  Connections established 1; dropped 0
  Last reset never

! Observe below the Connection State as "STABilished", the local host or
! source IP address and TCP Port = 1100 and the Foreign host or
! remote/destination TCP port = 179.

Connection state is ESTAB, I/O status: 1, unread input bytes: 0
Local host: 170.100.10.1, Local port: 11000
Foreign host: 170.100.10.254, Foreign port: 179
Enqueued packets for retransmit: 0, input: 0  mis-ordered: 0 (0 bytes)
Event Timers (current time is 0x120B4A90):
Timer          Starts    Wakeups          Next
Retrans        5049      0                0x0
TimeWait       0         0                0x0
AckHold        5048      4120             0x0
SendWnd        0         0                0x0
KeepAlive      0         0                0x0
GiveUp         0         0                0x0
PmtuAger       0         0                0x0
DeadWait       0         0                0x0
iss:  256698678  snduna:  256794617  sndnxt:  256794617     sndwnd:  13800
irs: 3486541483  rcvnxt: 3486637550  rcvwnd:        13686  delrcvwnd:  2698
SRTT: 300 ms, RTTO: 303 ms, RTV: 3 ms, KRTT: 0 ms
minRTT: 0 ms, maxRTT: 300 ms, ACK hold: 200 ms
Flags: higher precedence, nagle

Datagrams (max data segment is 4430 bytes):
Rcvd: 9711 (out of order: 0), with data: 5048, total data bytes: 96066
Sent: 9191 (retransmit: 0, fastretransmit: 0), with data: 5048, total data bytes:
95938

R6#show ip bgp neighbors 170.100.10.254
! The output displays a specific neighbor TCP and BGP connections to that neighbor.

BGP neighbor is 170.100.10.254,  remote AS 300, external link
  BGP version 4, remote router ID 200.20.1.254
  BGP state = Established, up for 3d12h
  Last read 00:00:21, hold time is 180, keepalive interval is 60 seconds
```

**Example C-8**  *Some BGP Troubleshooting Commands (Continued)*

```
  Neighbor capabilities:
    Route refresh: advertised and received(old & new)
    Address family IPv4 Unicast: advertised and received
  Message statistics:
    InQ depth is 0
    OutQ depth is 0
                        Sent       Rcvd
    Opens:                1          1
    Notifications:        0          0
    Updates:              0          1
    Keepalives:         5045       5045
    Route Refresh:        0          0
    Total:              5046       5047
  Default minimum time between advertisement runs is 30 seconds
 For address family: IPv4 Unicast
 BGP table version 21, neighbor version 21
 Index 2, Offset 0, Mask 0x4
                        Sent       Rcvd
 Prefix activity:       ----       ----
   Prefixes Current:      0         20 (Consumes 720 bytes)
   Prefixes Total:        0         20
   Implicit Withdraw:     0          0
   Explicit Withdraw:     0          0
   Used as bestpath:    n/a         20
   Used as multipath:   n/a          0
                       Outbound   Inbound
 Local Policy Denied Prefixes:    --------   -------
   Bestpath from this peer:          20        n/a
   Total:                            20         0
 Number of NLRIs in the update sent: max 0, min 0
 Connections established 1; dropped 0
 Last reset never
! Observe below the Connection State as "STABilished", the local host or
! source IP address and TCP Port = 1100 and the Foreign host or
! remote/destination TCP port = 179.

Connection state is ESTAB, I/O status: 1, unread input bytes: 0
Local host: 170.100.10.1, Local port: 11000
Foreign host: 170.100.10.254, Foreign port: 179
Enqueued packets for retransmit: 0, input: 0  mis-ordered: 0 (0 bytes)
Event Timers (current time is 0x12093888):
Timer          Starts      Wakeups          Next
Retrans         5047          0             0x0
TimeWait           0          0             0x0
AckHold         5046       4118             0x0
SendWnd            0          0             0x0
KeepAlive          0          0             0x0
GiveUp             0          0             0x0
PmtuAger           0          0             0x0
DeadWait           0          0             0x0
iss:  256698678 snduna:  256794579 sndnxt:  256794579     sndwnd:  13838
irs: 3486541483 rcvnxt: 3486637512 rcvwnd:      13724 delrcvwnd:   2660
```

*continues*

**Example C-8**    *Some BGP Troubleshooting Commands (Continued)*

```
SRTT: 300 ms, RTTO: 303 ms, RTV: 3 ms, KRTT: 0 ms
minRTT: 0 ms, maxRTT: 300 ms, ACK hold: 200 ms
Flags: higher precedence, nagle

Datagrams (max data segment is 4430 bytes):
Rcvd: 9707 (out of order: 0), with data: 5046, total data bytes: 96028
Sent: 9187 (retransmit: 0, fastretransmit: 0), with data: 5046, total data bytes:
95900

R6#clear ip bgp ?
! "clear ip bgp" will cause to reset a BGP connections oe all BGP connections.
  *                 Clear all peers
  <1-65535>         Clear peers with the AS number
  A.B.C.D           BGP neighbor address to clear
  dampening         Clear route flap dampening information
  external          Clear all external peers
  flap-statistics   Clear route flap statistics
  ipv4              Address family
  peer-group        Clear all members of peer-group
 vpnv4              Address family
R6#debug ip bgp ?
  A.B.C.D     BGP neighbor address
  dampening   BGP dampening
  events      BGP events
  in          BGP Inbound information
  keepalives  BGP keepalives
  out         BGP Outbound information
  updates     BGP updates
  vpnv4       VPNv4 NLRI information
  <cr>

R6#debug ip bgp events
BGP events debugging is on
! The debug ip bgp events command will trace the events that occur
! between the neighbors.

R6#
3d12h: BGP: Import timer expired. Walking from 1 to 1
3d12h: BGP: Import timer expired. Walking from 1 to 1
3d12h: BGP: Import timer expired. Walking from 1 to 1
R6#clear ip bgp *
R6#
3d12h: BGP: reset all neighbors due to User reset
3d12h: BGP: 160.10.3.3 reset due to User reset
3d12h: %BGP-5-ADJCHANGE: neighbor 160.10.3.3 Down User reset
3d12h: BGP: 170.100.10.254 reset due to User reset
3d12h: %BGP-5-ADJCHANGE: neighbor 170.100.10.254 Down User reset
3d12h: BGP: Performing BGP general scanning
3d12h: BGP(0): scanning IPv4 Unicast routing tables
3d12h: BGP(1): scanning VPNv4 Unicast routing tables
3d12h: BGP(2): scanning IPv4 Multicast routing tables
3d12h: BGP: Import timer expired. Walking from 1 to 1
```

**Example C-8**  *Some BGP Troubleshooting Commands (Continued)*

```
3d12h: %BGP-5-ADJCHANGE: neighbor 160.10.3.3 Up
3d12h: BGP: Delaying initial update for up to 120 seconds
3d12h: BGP: Import timer expired. Walking from 1 to 1
3d12h: BGP: Import timer expired. Walking from 1 to 1
3d12h: %BGP-5-ADJCHANGE: neighbor 170.100.10.254 Up
3d12h: BGP: compute bestpath
3d12h: BGP: Performing BGP general scanning
3d12h: BGP(0): scanning IPv4 Unicast routing tables
3d12h: BGP(IPv4 Unicast): Performing BGP Nexthop scanning for general scan
3d12h: BGP(1): scanning VPNv4 Unicast routing tables
3d12h: BGP(VPNv4 Unicast): Performing BGP Nexthop scanning for general scan
3d12h: BGP(2): scanning IPv4 Multicast routing tables
3d12h: BGP(IPv4 Multicast): Performing BGP Nexthop scanning for general scan
3d12h: BGP: Import timer expired. Walking from 1 to 1
```

# ISDN

Troubleshooting commands for ISDN configuration include the following:

- **show interfaces bri** *number*
- **show interfaces bri** *number* **1 2**
- **show isdn status**
- **show dialer interface bri** *number*
- **show ppp multilink**
- **debug isdn q931**
- **debug ppp negotiation**
- **debug ppp authentication**
- **debug dialer**

Example C-9 provides commented output from these key commands.

**Example C-9**  *Some ISDN Troubleshooting Commands*

```
R5#show interfaces bri 0/0
! The command shows the status of the BRI interface, its IP address,
! encapsulation, etc.

BRI0/0 is up, line protocol is up (spoofing)
  Hardware is PQUICC BRI
  Internet address is 160.10.15.5/24
  MTU 1500 bytes, BW 64 Kbit, DLY 20000 usec,
     reliability 255/255, txload 1/255, rxload 1/255
  Encapsulation PPP, loopback not set
  Last input 00:00:03, output never, output hang never
  Last clearing of "show interface" counters 4w0d
  Input queue: 0/75/0/0 (size/max/drops/flushes); Total output drops: 0
  Queueing strategy: weighted fair
```

*continues*

**Example C-9** *Some ISDN Troubleshooting Commands (Continued)*

```
        Output queue: 0/1000/64/0 (size/max total/threshold/drops)
           Conversations  0/1/16 (active/max active/max total)
           Reserved Conversations 0/0 (allocated/max allocated)
           Available Bandwidth 48 kilobits/sec
        5 minute input rate 0 bits/sec, 0 packets/sec
        5 minute output rate 0 bits/sec, 0 packets/sec
           496808 packets input, 1987304 bytes, 0 no buffer
           Received 0 broadcasts, 0 runts, 0 giants, 0 throttles
           0 input errors, 0 CRC, 0 frame, 0 overrun, 0 ignored, 0 abort
           496808 packets output, 1987347 bytes, 0 underruns
           0 output errors, 0 collisions, 0 interface resets
           0 output buffer failures, 0 output buffers swapped out
           1 carrier transitions
     R5#
     R5#show interfaces bri 0/0 1 2
     ! This command displays the interface BRI and its B channels, in this case
     ! channels 1 and 2. Also observe the protocols, that are closed in the
     ! output below, as LCP, OSICP (CLNS), IPCP (IP) and CDPCP (CDP).
     ! The input packets and output packets indicate traffic being exchanged.

     BRI0/0:1 is down, line protocol is down
        Hardware is PQUICC BRI
        MTU 1500 bytes, BW 64 Kbit, DLY 20000 usec,
           reliability 255/255, txload 1/255, rxload 1/255
        Encapsulation PPP, loopback not set
        Keepalive set (10 sec)
        LCP Closed
        Closed: OSICP, IPCP, CDPCP
        Last input 4w0d, output 4w0d, output hang never
        Last clearing of "show interface" counters never
        Input queue: 0/75/0/0 (size/max/drops/flushes); Total output drops: 0
        Queueing strategy: weighted fair
        Output queue: 0/1000/64/0 (size/max total/threshold/drops)
           Conversations  0/2/16 (active/max active/max total)
           Reserved Conversations 0/0 (allocated/max allocated)
           Available Bandwidth 48 kilobits/sec
        5 minute input rate 0 bits/sec, 0 packets/sec
        5 minute output rate 0 bits/sec, 0 packets/sec
           158 packets input, 84813 bytes, 0 no buffer
           Received 0 broadcasts, 0 runts, 0 giants, 0 throttles
           0 input errors, 0 CRC, 0 frame, 0 overrun, 0 ignored, 0 abort
           1353 packets output, 83976 bytes, 0 underruns
           0 output errors, 0 collisions, 0 interface resets
           0 output buffer failures, 0 output buffers swapped out
           7 carrier transitions
     BRI0/0:2 is down, line protocol is down
        Hardware is PQUICC BRI
        MTU 1500 bytes, BW 64 Kbit, DLY 20000 usec,
           reliability 255/255, txload 1/255, rxload 1/255
        Encapsulation PPP, loopback not set
        Keepalive set (10 sec)
        LCP Closed
```

**Example C-9** *Some ISDN Troubleshooting Commands (Continued)*

```
   Closed: OSICP, IPCP, CDPCP
   Last input never, output never, output hang never
   Last clearing of "show interface" counters never
   Input queue: 0/75/0/0 (size/max/drops/flushes); Total output drops: 0
   Queueing strategy: weighted fair
   Output queue: 0/1000/64/0 (size/max total/threshold/drops)
      Conversations  0/0/16 (active/max active/max total)
      Reserved Conversations 0/0 (allocated/max allocated)
      Available Bandwidth 48 kilobits/sec
   5 minute input rate 0 bits/sec, 0 packets/sec
   5 minute output rate 0 bits/sec, 0 packets/sec
      0 packets input, 0 bytes, 0 no buffer
      Received 0 broadcasts, 0 runts, 0 giants, 0 throttles
      0 input errors, 0 CRC, 0 frame, 0 overrun, 0 ignored, 0 abort
      0 packets output, 0 bytes, 0 underruns
      0 output errors, 0 collisions, 0 interface resets
      0 output buffer failures, 0 output buffers swapped out
      0 carrier transitions
R5#
R5#show isdn status
! Look at the Layer 2 status and in this case the "SPID" status.
! Notice that Layer 3 status is active but no calls established.

Global ISDN Switchtype = basic-ni
ISDN BRI0/0 interface
        dsl 0, interface ISDN Switchtype = basic-ni
    Layer 1 Status:
        ACTIVE
    Layer 2 Status:
        TEI = 64, Ces = 1, SAPI = 0, State = MULTIPLE_FRAME_ESTABLISHED
        TEI 64, ces = 1, state = 5(init)
            spid1 configured, no LDN, spid1 sent, spid1 valid
            Endpoint ID Info: epsf = 0, usid = 70, tid = 1
    Layer 3 Status:
        0 Active Layer 3 Call(s)
    Active dsl 0 CCBs = 0
    The Free Channel Mask:  0x80000003
    Total Allocated ISDN CCBs = 0
R5#
R5#show dialer interface bri 0/0
! This command display the ISDN connections if there is any.
! Observe the dial string and the last status.

BRI0/0 - dialer type = ISDN
Dial String      Successes      Failures     Last DNIS    Last status
1111                    3            0        4w0d         successful
0 incoming call(s) have been screened.
0 incoming call(s) rejected for callback.
BRI0/0:1 - dialer type = ISDN
Idle timer (120 secs), Fast idle timer (20 secs)
Wait for carrier (30 secs), Re-enable (15 secs)
Dialer state is idle
```

*continues*

**Example C-9**   *Some ISDN Troubleshooting Commands (Continued)*

```
BRI0/0:2 - dialer type = ISDN
Idle timer (120 secs), Fast idle timer (20 secs)
Wait for carrier (30 secs), Re-enable (15 secs)
Dialer state is idle
R5#
!
R5#show dialer interface bri0/0
! Here we have the same output command but now showing
! established connections. Notice that B channel 1  BRI/0:1 is
! being used and R5 is connected to R3 (1111).

BRI0/0 - dialer type = ISDN

Dial String      Successes    Failures    Last DNIS    Last status
1111                     2           0     00:00:21     successful
0 incoming call(s) have been screened.
0 incoming call(s) rejected for callback.

BRI0/0:1 - dialer type = ISDN
Idle timer (120 secs), Fast idle timer (20 secs)
Wait for carrier (30 secs), Re-enable (15 secs)
Dialer state is data link layer up
Dial reason: ip (s=160.10.15.5, d=160.10.15.3)
Time until disconnect 102 secs
Connected to 1111 (R3)

BRI0/0:2 - dialer type = ISDN
Idle timer (120 secs), Fast idle timer (20 secs)
Wait for carrier (30 secs), Re-enable (15 secs)
Dialer state is idle
R5#
R5#debug isdn q931
ISDN Q931 packets debugging is on
! The output from this debug shows you the sequence of commands used to
! establish and to release the connection

R5#ping 160.10.15.3

Type escape sequence to abort.
Sending 5, 100-byte ICMP Echos to 160.10.15.3, timeout is 2 seconds:

3d15h: ISDN BR0/0: TX -> SETUP pd = 8  callref = 0x03
3d15h:         Bearer Capability i = 0x8890
3d15h:         Channel ID i = 0x83
3d15h:         Keypad Facility i = '1111'
3d15h: ISDN BR0/0: RX <- CALL_PROC pd = 8  callref = 0x83
3d15h:         Channel ID i = 0x89
3d15h: ISDN BR0/0: RX <- CONNECT pd = 8  callref = 0x83
3d15h:         Channel ID i = 0x89
3d15h: %LINK-3-UPDOWN: Interface BRI0/0:1, changed state to up.!
3d15h: ISDN BR0/0: TX -> CONNECT_ACK pd = 8  callref = 0x03!!!
Success rate is 80 percent (4/5), round-trip min/avg/max = 32/34/36 ms
```

**Example C-9**  *Some ISDN Troubleshooting Commands (Continued)*

```
R5#
3d15h: %LINEPROTO-5-UPDOWN: Line protocol on Interface BRI0/0:1, changed state to up
3d15h: %ISDN-6-CONNECT: Interface BRI0/0:1 is now connected to 1111 R3
R5#
R5#
3d15h: %ISDN-6-DISCONNECT: Interface BRI0/0:1  disconnected from 1111 R3, call
lasted 121 seconds
3d15h: ISDN BR0/0: TX -> DISCONNECT pd = 8  callref = 0x03
3d15h:          Cause i = 0x8090 - Normal call clearing
3d15h: ISDN BR0/0: RX <- RELEASE pd = 8  callref = 0x83
3d15h: %LINK-3-UPDOWN: Interface BRI0/0:1, changed state to down
3d15h: ISDN BR0/0: TX -> RELEASE_COMP pd = 8  callref = 0x03
3d15h: %LINEPROTO-5-UPDOWN: Line protocol on Interface BRI0/0:1, changed state to
down
R5#R5#
R5#
R5#debug ppp negotiation
PPP protocol negotiation debugging is on
! The output shows the PPP negotiation in order to establish de connection. Observe
the LCP and CHAP protocols messages. Look below the IP, CDP and CLNS protocols being
established.
R5#
4w0d: %LINK-3-UPDOWN: Interface BRI0/0:1, changed state to up
4w0d: BR0/0:1 PPP: Using dialer call direction
4w0d: BR0/0:1 PPP: Treating connection as a callin
4w0d: BR0/0:1 PPP: Phase is ESTABLISHING, Passive Open [0 sess, 0 load]
4w0d: BR0/0:1 LCP: State is Listen
4w0d: BR0/0:1 LCP: TIMEout: State Listen
4w0d: BR0/0:1 LCP: O CONFREQ [Listen] id 8 len 15
4w0d: BR0/0:1 LCP:    AuthProto CHAP (0x0305C22305)
4w0d: BR0/0:1 LCP:    MagicNumber 0x9DFDE9CD (0x05069DFDE9CD)
4w0d: BR0/0:1 LCP: I CONFACK [REQsent] id 8 len 15
4w0d: BR0/0:1 LCP:    AuthProto CHAP (0x0305C22305)
4w0d: BR0/0:1 LCP:    MagicNumber 0x9DFDE9CD (0x05069DFDE9CD)
4w0d: BR0/0:1 LCP: I CONFREQ [ACKrcvd] id 9 len 15
4w0d: BR0/0:1 LCP:    AuthProto CHAP (0x0305C22305)
4w0d: BR0/0:1 LCP:    MagicNumber 0x9DFDF362 (0x05069DFDF362)
4w0d: BR0/0:1 LCP: O CONFACK [ACKrcvd] id 9 len 15
4w0d: BR0/0:1 LCP:    AuthProto CHAP (0x0305C22305)
4w0d: BR0/0:1 LCP:    MagicNumber 0x9DFDF362 (0x05069DFDF362)
4w0d: BR0/0:1 LCP: State is Open
4w0d: BR0/0:1 PPP: Phase is AUTHENTICATING, by both [0 sess, 0 load]
4w0d: BR0/0:1 CHAP: O CHALLENGE id 6 len 23 from "R5"
4w0d: BR0/0:1 CHAP: I CHALLENGE id 6 len 23 from "R3"
4w0d: BR0/0:1 CHAP: Waiting for peer to authenticate first
4w0d: BR0/0:1 CHAP: I RESPONSE id 6 len 23 from "R3"
4w0d: BR0/0:1 CHAP: O SUCCESS id 6 len 4
4w0d: BR0/0:1 CHAP: Processing saved Challenge, id 6
4w0d: BR0/0:1 CHAP: O RESPONSE id 6 len 23 from "R5"
4w0d: BR0/0:1 CHAP: I SUCCESS id 6 len 4
4w0d: BR0/0:1 PPP: Phase is UP [0 sess, 0 load]
4w0d: BR0/0:1 OSICP: O CONFREQ [Closed] id 6 len 4
```

*continues*

**Example C-9** *Some ISDN Troubleshooting Commands (Continued)*

```
4w0d: BR0/0:1 IPCP: O CONFREQ [Closed] id 6 len 10
4w0d: BR0/0:1 IPCP:    Address 160.10.15.5 (0x0306A00A0F05)
4w0d: BR0/0:1 CDPCP: O CONFREQ [Closed] id 6 len 4
4w0d: BR0/0:1 OSICP: I CONFREQ [REQsent] id 6 len 4
4w0d: BR0/0:1 OSICP: O CONFACK [REQsent] id 6 len 4
4w0d: BR0/0:1 IPCP: I CONFREQ [REQsent] id 6 len 10
4w0d: BR0/0:1 IPCP:    Address 160.10.15.3 (0x0306A00A0F03)
4w0d: BR0/0:1 IPCP: O CONFACK [REQsent] id 6 len 10
4w0d: BR0/0:1 IPCP:    Address 160.10.15.3 (0x0306A00A0F03)
4w0d: BR0/0:1 CDPCP: I CONFREQ [REQsent] id 6 len 4
4w0d: BR0/0:1 CDPCP: O CONFACK [REQsent] id 6 len 4
4w0d: BR0/0:1 OSICP: I CONFACK [ACKsent] id 6 len 4
4w0d: BR0/0:1 OSICP: State is Open
4w0d: BR0/0:1 IPCP: I CONFACK [ACKsent] id 6 len 10
4w0d: BR0/0:1 IPCP:    Address 160.10.15.5 (0x0306A00A0F05)
4w0d: BR0/0:1 IPCP: State is Open
4w0d: BR0/0:1 CDPCP: I CONFACK [ACKsent] id 6 len 4
4w0d: BR0/0:1 CDPCP: State is Open
4w0d: BR0/0 IPCP: Install route to 160.10.15.3
4w0d: %LINEPROTO-5-UPDOWN: Line protocol on Interface BRI0/0:1, changed state to up
4w0d: %ISDN-6-CONNECT: Interface BRI0/0:1 is now connected to 1111 R3
R5#
! Now observe a sample of the protocols connections being disconnected
! and released. Notice the route being removed.

3d16h: %ISDN-6-DISCONNECT: Interface BRI0/0:1  disconnected from 1111 R3, call
lasted 124 seconds
3d16h: %LINK-3-UPDOWN: Interface BRI0/0:1, changed state to down
3d16h: BR0/0:1 OSICP: State is Closed
3d16h: BR0/0:1 IPCP: State is Closed
3d16h: BR0/0:1 CDPCP: State is Closed
3d16h: BR0/0:1 PPP: Phase is TERMINATING [0 sess, 1 load]
3d16h: BR0/0:1 LCP: State is Closed
3d16h: BR0/0:1 PPP: Phase is DOWN [0 sess, 1 load]
3d16h: BR0/0 IPCP: Remove route to 160.10.15.3
3d16h: %LINEPROTO-5-UPDOWN: Line protocol on Interface BRI0/0:1, changed state to
down
R5#debug ppp authentication
PPP authentication debugging is on
! The output below shows the "ppp" negotiation with the CHAP messages
! being exchanged.
R5#
4w0d: %LINK-3-UPDOWN: Interface BRI0/0:1, changed state to up
4w0d: BR0/0:1 PPP: Using dialer call direction
4w0d: BR0/0:1 PPP: Treating connection as a callin
4w0d: BR0/0:1 CHAP: O CHALLENGE id 7 len 23 from "R5"
4w0d: BR0/0:1 CHAP: I CHALLENGE id 7 len 23 from "R3"
4w0d: BR0/0:1 CHAP: Waiting for peer to authenticate first
4w0d: BR0/0:1 CHAP: I RESPONSE id 7 len 23 from "R3"
4w0d: BR0/0:1 CHAP: O SUCCESS id 7 len 4
4w0d: BR0/0:1 CHAP: Processing saved Challenge, id 7
4w0d: BR0/0:1 CHAP: O RESPONSE id 7 len 23 from "R5"
```

**Example C-9**  *Some ISDN Troubleshooting Commands (Continued)*

```
4w0d: BR0/0:1 CHAP: I SUCCESS id 7 len 4
4w0d: %LINEPROTO-5-UPDOWN: Line protocol on Interface BRI0/0:1, changed state to up
4w0d: %ISDN-6-CONNECT: Interface BRI0/0:1 is now connected to 1111 R3
R5#
! It is important to observe that in some IOS images the authentication is
! no longer necessary in order to bring the ISDN link connected.

R5#debug dialer
Dial on demand events debugging is on
! This command shows DDR messages that establish the ISDN connection.
! Notice the dialer protocol messages.

R5#
R5#ping 160.10.15.3

Type escape sequence to abort.
Sending 5, 100-byte ICMP Echos to 160.10.15.3, timeout is 2 seconds:

3d17h: BR0/0 DDR: Dialing cause ip (s=160.10.15.5, d=160.10.15.3)
3d17h: BR0/0 DDR: Attempting to dial 1111
3d17h: %LINK-3-UPDOWN: Interface BRI0/0:1, changed state to up.
3d17h: BR0/0:1 DDR: dialer protocol up
3d17h: BR0/0:1 DDR: dialer protocol up.
3d17h: %LINEPROTO-5-UPDOWN: Line protocol on Interface BRI0/0:1, changed state to up
3d17h: %LINK-3-UPDOWN: Interface BRI0/0:2, changed state to up
3d17h: BR0/0:2 DDR: dialer protocol up
3d17h: BR0/0:2 DDR: dialer protocol up.!!
Success rate is 40 percent (2/5), round-trip min/avg/max = 32/34/36 ms
R5#
3d17h: %LINEPROTO-5-UPDOWN: Line protocol on Interface BRI0/0:2, changed state to up
3d17h: %ISDN-6-CONNECT: Interface BRI0/0:1 is now connected to 1111 R3
R5#
```

# DLSw

Troubleshooting commands for DLSw configuration include the following:

- **show dlsw peers**
- **show capabilities**
- **debug dlsw peers**

Example C-10 provides commented output from these key commands.

**Example C-10**  *Some DLSw Troubleshooting Commands*

```
R3#show dlsw ?
  capabilities    Display DLSw capabilities information
  circuits        Display DLSw circuit information
  fastcache       Display DLSw fast cache for FST and Direct
  local-circuit   Display DLSw local circuits
```

*continues*

**Example C-10** *Some DLSw Troubleshooting Commands (Continued)*

```
        peers         Display DLSw peer information
        reachability  Display DLSw reachability information
        statistics    Display DLSw statistical information
        transparent   Display MAC address mappings
R3#show dlsw peers
! Here the output shows R3 peering to R1 using FST. Important is to
! notice the State "CONNECT", the type "conf" meaning configured
! (not promiscuous).

Peers:                 state     pkts_rx   pkts_tx  type  drops ckts TCP    uptime
  FST 160.10.1.1       CONNECT    83387     83388   conf    0    -   -       4w0d
          Expected: 0  Next Send: 0  Seq errors: 0
Total number of connected peers: 1
Total number of connections:     1
R3#show dlsw capabilities
! The output shows all parameters that are being used on this DLSW connection.
DLSw: Capabilities for peer 160.10.1.1(0)
      vendor id (OUI)          : '00C' (cisco)
      version number           : 2
      release number           : 0
      init pacing window       : 20
      unsupported saps         : none
      num of tcp sessions      : 1
      loop prevent support     : no
      icanreach mac-exclusive  : no
      icanreach netbios-excl.  : no
      reachable mac addresses  : none
      reachable netbios names  : none
      V2 multicast capable     : yes
      DLSw multicast address   : none
      cisco version number     : 1
      peer group number        : 0
      peer cluster support     : no
      border peer capable      : no
      peer cost                : 3
      biu-segment configured   : no
      UDP Unicast support      : yes
      Fast-switched HPR supp.  : no
      NetBIOS Namecache length : 15
      local-ack configured     : yes
      priority configured      : no
      cisco RSVP support       : no
      configured ip address    : 160.10.1.1
      peer type                : conf
      version string           :
Cisco Internetwork Operating System Software
IOS (tm) C2600 Software (C2600-JK803S-M), Version 12.2(16), RELEASE SOFTWARE (fc3)
Copyright  1986-2003 by cisco Systems, Inc.
Compiled Fri 07-Mar-03 01:45 by pwade
R3#
R3#debug dlsw peers
! This "debug" shows the establishment of the DLSW connection.
```

**Example C-10** *Some DLSw Troubleshooting Commands (Continued)*

```
! Notice the messages that are being exchanged.
DLSw peer debugging is on
R3#
4w0d: DLSw: START-FSTPFSM (peer 160.10.1.1(0)): event:DLX-KEEPALIVE REQ
state:CONNECT
4w0d: DLSw: dfstp_action_g() keepalive request from peer 160.10.1.1(0)
4w0d: DLSw: Keepalive Response sent to peer 160.10.1.1(0))
4w0d: DLSw: END-FSTPFSM (peer 160.10.1.1(0)): state:CONNECT->CONNECT
4w0d: DLSw: START-FSTPFSM (peer 160.10.1.1(0)): event:DLX-KEEPALIVE REQ
state:CONNECT
4w0d: DLSw: dfstp_action_g() keepalive request from peer 160.10.1.1(0)
4w0d: DLSw: Keepalive Response sent to peer 160.10.1.1(0))
4w0d: DLSw: END-FSTPFSM (peer 160.10.1.1(0)): state:CONNECT->CONNEC

! Below observe below a example of a DLSW session disconnection. Observe the
messages.

1d01h: DLSw: Unknown run-time CV 81 with length 5 from peer 160.10.1.1(0)
1d01h: DLSw: END-FSTPFSM (peer 160.10.1.1(0)): state:CONNECT->CONNECT

1d01h: DLSw: Processing delayed event:ADMIN-CLOSE CONNECTION - prev state:CONNECT
1d01h: DLSw: START-FSTPFSM (peer 160.10.1.1(0)): event:ADMIN-CLOSE CONNECTION
state:CONNECT
1d01h: DLSw: dfstp_action_d() close connection for peer 160.10.1.1(0)
1d01h: DLSw: FST aborting connection for peer 160.10.1.1
1d01h: DLSw: END-FSTPFSM (peer 160.10.1.1(0)): state:CONNECT->DISCONN

R3#
1d01h: DLSw: START-FSTPFSM (peer 160.10.1.1(0)): event:ADMIN-OPEN CONNECTION
state:DISCONN
1d01h: DLSw: dfstp_action_a() attempting to connect peer 160.10.1.1(0)
1d01h: DLSw: Connection opened for peer 160.10.1.1(0)
1d01h: DLSw: CapExId Msg sent to peer 160.10.1.1(0)
1d01h: DLSw: END-FSTPFSM (peer 160.10.1.1(0)): state:DISCONN->WAIT_CAP

1d01h: DLSw: START-FSTPFSM (peer 160.10.1.1(0)): event:SSP-CAP MSG RCVD
state:WAIT_CAP
1d01h: DLSw: dfstp_action_e() cap msg rcvd for peer 160.10.1.1(0)
1d01h: DLSw: Recv CapExId Msg from peer 160.10.1.1(0)
1d01h: DLSw: received fhpr capex from peer 160.10.1.1(0): support: false, fst-prio:
false
1d01h: DLSw: Pos CapExResp sent to peer 160.10.1.1(0)
1d01h: DLSw: END-FSTPFSM (peer 160.10.1.1(0)): state:WAIT_CAP->WAIT_CAP

1d01h: DLSw: START-FSTPFSM (peer 160.10.1.1(0)): event:TIMER-TIMER EXPIRED
state:WAIT_CAP
1d01h: DLSw: dfstp_action_d() close connection for peer 160.10.1.1(0)
1d01h: DLSw: FST aborting connection for peer 160.10.1.1
1d01h: DLSw: END-FSTPFSM (peer 160.10.1.1(0)): state:WAIT_CAP->DISCONN
undebug all
```

# Additional Troubleshooting Sources

To better prepare yourself and follow up on the troubleshooting topics covered in this appendix, you should consult the http://www.cisco.com/public/pubsearch.html website for more information on the following topics:

Troubleshoot Frame Relay
Troubleshoot Frame Relay
Troubleshoot ATM
Troubleshoot Routing Protocols
Troubleshoot ISDN
Troubleshoot IP Features
Troubleshoot IOS Features
Troubleshoot DLSw
Troubleshoot QoS
Troubleshoot Multicast
Troubleshoot Security
Troubleshoot VoIP

For complete and additional resources for troubleshooting, please refer to

http://www.cisco.com/univercd/home/home.htm
*Cisco Internet Troubleshooting*—Cisco Press—Laura Chappell and Dan Farkas
*Cisco Troubleshooting IP Routing Protocols*—Cisco Press—Faraz Shamim, Zaheer Aziz, Johnson Liu, and Abe Martey
*Cisco BGP-4 Command and Configuration Handbook*—Cisco Press— William R. Parkhurst
*Cisco OSPF Command and Configuration Handbook*—Cisco Press— William R. Parkhurst

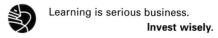